WINDOWS® 95
by PicTorial

PicTorial Series

Dennis P. Curtin, Series Editor

Titles Available for Windows® 95
Windows® 95 by PicTorial
Microsoft® Word for Windows® 95 (Version 7.0) by PicTorial
Microsoft® Excel for Windows® 95 (Version 7.0) by PicTorial
Microsoft Access® for Windows® 95 (Version 7.0) by PicTorial

Titles Available for Windows® 3.1
Microsoft® Word 6.0 for Windows® by PicTorial
WordPerfect® 6.0 for Windows® by PicTorial
Microsoft® Excel 5.0 by PicTorial
Microsoft Access® 2.0 by PicTorial
Windows® 3.1 by PicTorial
Essentials of Windows® 3.1 by PicTorial

WINDOWS® 95
by PicTorial

Dennis P. Curtin

Prentice Hall, Upper Saddle River, New Jersey 07458

Acquisitions editor: Carolyn Henderson
Marketing manager: Nancy Evans
Director of production and manufacturing: Joanne Jay
Managing editor: Nicholas Radhuber
Production manager: Lorraine Patsco
Illustrator: Warren Fischbach
Design director: Patricia Wosczyk
Interior designer: Kenny Beck
Cover designer: Suzanne Behnke
Manufacturing buyer: Paul Smolenski
Editorial assistant: Audrey Regan
Development editor and project manager: Cecil Yarbrough

Cover art by Marjory Dressler
Screen shots and electronic composition by Cathleen Morin
Additional design and electronic composition by Christy Mahon

© 1996 by Prentice-Hall, Inc.
A Division of Simon & Schuster
Upper Saddle River, NJ 07458

ISBN 0-13-456674-2

Prentice-Hall International (UK) Limited, *London*
Prentice-Hall of Australia Pty. Limited, *Sydney*
Prentice-Hall of Canada Inc., *Toronto*
Prentice-Hall Hispanoamericana, S.A., *Mexico*
Prentice-Hall of India Private Limited, *New Delhi*
Prentice-Hall of Japan, Inc., *Tokyo*
Simon & Schuster Asia Ptd. Ltd., *Singapore*
Editora Prentice-Hall do Brasil, Ltda., *Rio de Janeiro*

CONTENTS

QUICKSTEPS BOXES

PREFACE

Operating systems are what make it possible for computers to work, and Windows 95 is the latest version of the world's most popular operating system. Windows 95 has three immediately noticeable features. First, its screen is very graphic, with buttons you can click to execute commands. Second, it also lists commands on menus, giving you another way to choose an action. Finally, Windows lets you run more than one program at a time. This ability is especially useful when you want to transfer data from one program to another.

This text introduces you to Windows 95 without assuming that you have prior computing experience. Everything you need to know to become a proficient Windows 95 user is presented here. You needn't bring anything else to your learning experience except a willingness to explore a new and exciting way to compute.

CONTENTS AND APPROACH

As you'll soon see, you do useful work on a computer using application programs, not the operating system. One of the main functions of Windows is to make it easy to start and use these application programs. Typical application programs are those that you use for word processing, spreadsheet analysis, graphics preparation, and database management. Windows also has a number of built-in application programs. For example, My Computer and Windows Explorer help you manage your system; WordPad allows you to create, edit, and format documents; and Paint allows you to create and edit graphics that you can then print out or include in your other documents as illustrations.

Because the Windows applications to which you are briefly introduced in this text work much like the more powerful applications programs such as Word, Excel, and Access, the principles and procedures that you learn in this text will work with those application programs. This simplifies your learning these other programs because you will already know many of the basic operations such as starting them, using menus and dialog boxes, managing their windows, and closing them.

PAL—PROGRAM-ASSISTED LEARNING

For students who learn more effectively via non-print tools, an integrated multimedia adaptation of this text is also available. The multimedia tool, called *PAL (Program-Assisted Learning)*, is designed to guide you through learning Windows 95. PAL teaches you how to use Windows features while using the actual program—not simulations of the program. It does this by displaying interactive animations, graphics, and step-by-step instructions on top of the Windows screen display. PAL is an intuitive, easy-to-use system that makes learning Windows not only more efficient, but more enjoyable.

This text is organized into pictorial tutorials, called *PicTorials*.

PicTorial 1 introduces you to the basic operations of Windows 95—how to start Windows; how to open, close, size, and drag windows; and how to get on-line help.

PicTorial 2 briefly introduces the basic procedures you need to know to work with Windows application programs. Using WordPad, Clipboard Viewer, and Character Map, you learn basic procedures such as opening and closing applications, using menus and dialog boxes, managing multiple windows, and cutting and pasting between applications.

PicTorial 3 introduces My Computer and Windows Explorer and shows you how to use them to explore your system.

PicTorials 4 shows how you use My Computer and Windows Explorer to manage disks, folders, and files on your system.

ORGANIZATION OF PICTORIALS

Each PicTorial has the following structure and features:

▶ Each PicTorial begins with objectives that guide you in understanding what you are about to learn.

▶ A brief introduction to the PicTorial follows the objectives.

▶ Following the introduction is a series of sections. Each section covers a single procedure such as selecting documents, or a few closely related topics such as maximizing and minimizing windows. The concept behind each procedure is first discussed and then a *tutorial* guides you in exploring the concept hands-on at the computer.

▶ At the end of each PicTorial is a *visual quiz* that tests your understanding of the elements you have explored in the PicTorial. The visual quiz is followed by a series of true-false, multiple choice, and fill-in-the-blank questions.

▶ The questions are followed by a number of *drills*, one for each section in the PicTorial. Drills are very narrow in focus and drill you on a single procedure using repetitive practice

▶ Drills are followed by a number of *skill-building exercises* that you use to practice the procedures that you have learned at the computer. Exercises are more challenging than drills and usually require an understanding of more than one procedure.

LAB ACTIVITIES—THREE STEPS TO MASTERY

Learning applications programs takes time and practice. There really aren't any shortcuts. This text recognizes that no one masters procedures the first time through. It takes repetition and practice—and, yes, even mistakes. Our approach uses three steps to mastery: tutorials, drills, and exercises.

▶ Tutorials provide you with step-by-step guidance as you explore a procedure for the first time. If you follow the steps, you can't go wrong.

▶ Drills, which you complete after finishing a matching tutorial, provide repetitive practice. For example, you may open and close six or more documents instead of just the one you opened and closed in the tutorial. This repetition is designed to help you master a procedure.

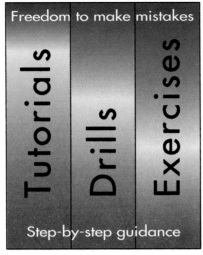

Steps to Mastery
1   2   3
Freedom to make mistakes
Tutorials   Drills   Exercises
Step-by-step guidance

▶ Exercises, which you complete after the drills, are designed to make you think. Procedures are not spelled out for you. You either have to recall them or look them up. These activities are much like the real world, where you are told what to do, but not how to do it.

KEY FEATURES

Windows is a visually oriented program, so this text uses a visual approach. In addition to PicTorials, it contains a number of other features designed to make it a better learning tool.

▶ *QuickSteps boxes* summarize the steps you use for each procedure. These highlighted boxes are easy to find in each concepts section and make the text an ideal reference manual as well as a teaching tool.

▶ *Pausing for Practice boxes* appear periodically in tutorials when essential procedures have been introduced. They encourage you to stop at key points and practice these procedures until they become second nature.

▶ *Common Wrong Turns boxes* alert you to where many people make mistakes and show you how to avoid them.

▶ *Tips boxes* point out shortcuts and other interesting features about many procedures.

▶ *Looking Back boxes* are used whenever a procedure that has been discussed earlier is essential to completing a new task. These summaries are intended to remind you how to perform a task without your having to refer back in the text for the information.

▶ *Looking Ahead boxes* are used whenever a procedure is unavoidably referred to before it has been discussed in detail. Although this text has been written to make that situation occur infrequently, these boxes should help you avoid confusion by providing a brief description and an assurance that a more detailed discussion will follow.

SUPPLEMENTS

The following supplements to this text have been made available by the publisher.

▶ The *Win95 Student Resource Disk* contains all of the files needed to complete the computer activities in this text.

▶ An *Instructor's Manual with Tests* contains suggested course outlines for a variety of course lengths and formats, teaching tips and a list of competencies to be attained for each PicTorial, solutions and answers to Visual Quizzes and all computer activities, and a complete test bank of over 200 questions.

▶ A Windows-based computerized testing program, *Prentice Hall Custom Test*, features user-friendly test creation as well as the ability to administer tests traditionally or on-line, evaluate and track students' results, and analyze the success of each exam—all with a simple click of the mouse.

NOTES TO INSTRUCTORS

▶ This text assumes that certain accessory programs such as Solitaire, WordPad, Quick View, and Windows 95 Tour (CD systems only) are on your system. If they are not, use the Control Panel's Add/Remove Programs command to add them.

▶ Although PAL has been designed for student use, that is not always possible. In these cases, or when you want to demonstrate features even when it is being used, you can use the PAL program in lecture situations. Since its table of contents exactly matches this text's, it's easy to locate the section you want to present.

▶ When working with Windows, you can execute most commands by just pointing and clicking with the mouse. In most cases there are also alternate keyboard commands that you can use. Except where the alternate keyboard commands are obviously superior, this text only discusses mouse commands, and the computer activities assume the computers are equipped with a mouse.

▶ The PicTorials in this text are based on the default Windows screen display that appears when you first install the program. It assumes that your systems are set up so they look like the illustration in PicTorial 1's section "Exploring the Windows Screen."

NOTE TO STUDENTS AND INSTRUCTORS

I am always happy to hear from users or potential users of my textbooks; it's through such exchanges that improvements are made. If you have any comments or questions, send them to me by e-mail on the Internet at Dennis_Curtin@msn.com. (You can use this address when sending e-mail from CompuServe, America Online, or any of the popular commercial services and it will get to me.)

ACKNOWLEDGMENTS

I would like to thank all of those people who have worked hard to make this the best possible text.

On the academic end have been the following reviewers:

- Lisa E. Gueldenzoph, Bowling Green State University
- Rajeev Kaula, Southwest Missouri State University
- William Kornegay, Miami-Dade Community College
- Barbara Hotta, Leeward, Community College
- Randy Stolze, Marist College
- Frederick L. Wells, DeKalb College

At the publisher's end Cecil Yarbrough continued with his efforts to improve the author's texts. His guidance and leadership are always most welcome. Supporting the production at the publisher have been Suzanne Behnke, Warren Fischbach, Joanne Jay, Christy Mahon, John Nestor, Lorraine Patsco, Nicholas Radhuber, Paul Smolenski, and Patricia Wosczyk. And thanks to Cathy Morin, who did the screen illustrations in the book and tested the materials over and over, and then turned a manuscript into the final four-color book.

All of these people, each and every one, took a personal interest in this text, and that interest shows in the work you are now holding. Any shortcomings that remain are my responsibility.

DENNIS P. CURTIN
Marblehead, Massachusetts

DEDICATION

This text is dedicated to Margaret Curtin, without whose support and enthusiasm it, and many other aspects of my life, would not be possible. Thanks again for everything!

About the Author

Dennis Curtin's 25-plus years' business experience in educational publishing provide a rich and unique perspective for his computer applications texts. He has served in executive positions at several companies, including Prentice Hall, where he has been a textbook sales representative, an acquisitions editor, editorial director of the engineering, vocational, and technical division, and editor in chief of the international division. For the past decade he has been primarily a writer of college textbooks on end-user computer applications.

He has been involved with microcomputers since the introduction of the original Apple II and was one of only nine alpha testers of the first version of Lotus 1-2-3, when Lotus Corporation had only a few employees squeezed into a small Kendall Square office. In the years since, he has taught in adult education and corporate training programs, but he readily acknowledges that he has learned most of what he knows about textbooks by working with instructors as an editor and during the writing, reviewing, and revising of his own books.

The primary author of many popular microcomputer texts, he is now spearheading and developing an exciting new multimedia approach to teaching Windows application programs.

PicTorial ONE

A VISUAL INTRODUCTION

After completing this PicTorial, you will be able to:

▶ **Start and exit Windows 95**
▶ **Name and describe the parts of the Windows 95 desktop**
▶ **Point, click, double-click, and drag with the mouse**
▶ **Use on-line Help**

ALTHOUGH most of your computer time will be spent working with word processing, spreadsheet, database, and other types of application programs, these programs can't run by themselves. To work, the computer must be running an *operating system*. This software coordinates all of the computer's functions and makes it possible for application programs to perform all of their functions such as opening, saving, formatting, and printing files.

There are a number of popular operating systems, including DOS, UNIX, and Apple System 7. However, the most widely used operating system is Microsoft Windows. Windows is designed to make it easy to work with application programs.

Windows' *Graphical User Interface* (also called a GUI—pronounced "goo-ey") allows you to execute commands by clicking graphic buttons on the screen or clicking their names on pull-down menus. When you start an application program, it appears on the screen in a boxlike frame called a *window* (hence Windows' name).

This PicTorial introduces you to Windows 95 step by step. All of the procedures you learn here will also apply to Windows application programs. They are fundamental to operating Windows, so take your time. The concepts and procedures that are introduced later will be much easier if you have mastered the procedures presented here. ▶

COMMON WRONG TURNS
Anxiety

If you have never before worked with a computer, now's the time to *relax*. New computer users often have anxieties about things that might go wrong. These fears include the fear they will somehow cause damage to the computer. However, there is nothing you can do to hurt the system, so there is no reason to be anxious. Also, don't be intimidated by others who seem to grasp the procedures more quickly. They may have had previous experience with computers. These differences among users tend to level out after a few weeks when everyone feels comfortable.

1-1 STARTING WINDOWS

To use Windows, you just turn on, or *boot*, the system and Windows appears automatically. (The term *booting* comes from the expression "pulling yourself up by your bootstraps.") Because Windows can be customized, your screen may look different from the one shown here, but you should still be able to find the elements we are about to discuss.

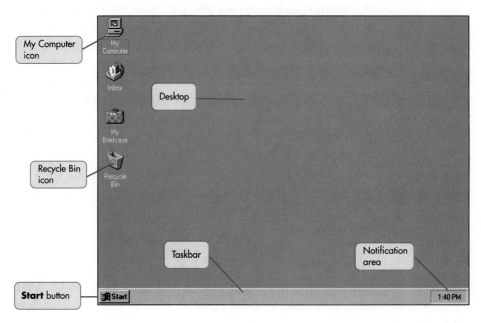

1. The *taskbar* is the strip normally found at the bottom of the screen (it can be dragged to any of the four sides of the screen). It always displays the **Start** button and also displays buttons for all open application programs (some of which may be started automatically when you turn on your system). At the right end of the taskbar is a *notification area*. This area displays the time, but it will also display icons to indicate certain actions being performed. For example, a printer icon is displayed when you are printing documents.

2. Clicking the **Start** button displays the Start menu (clicking is discussed in Section 1-4). This menu lists a number of commands you can use to load programs, open documents, get help, and change the setup of your system.

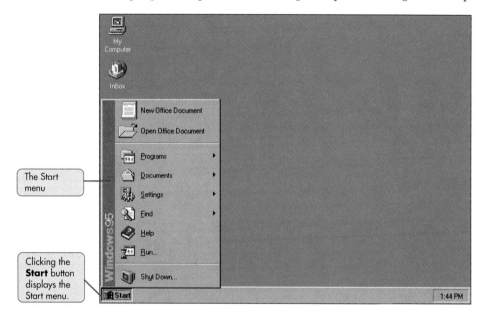

The Start menu

Clicking the **Start** button displays the Start menu.

3. *Icons* on the desktop start application programs and other Windows resources. (An icon is the name for a small graphical image that represents something.) The most common icons include:

   ▶ *My Computer* gives you access to such items on your system as printers and networks.

   ▶ *Recycle Bin* stores any files you delete until you empty it. This allows you to easily recover any files you delete by mistake.

   ▶ *Network Neighborhood* (not on all systems) gives you access to resources on your network such as printers.

4. The *desktop* is the area around and under the icons. This desktop is simply the space on the screen available for the display of Windows' various elements. As you'll see, you can add items to this electronic desktop, move items about on it, or take them away from it just as you can on the top of a real desk.

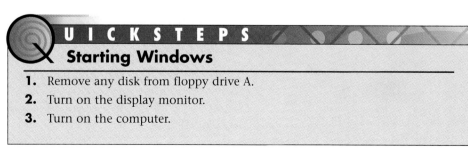

QUICKSTEPS

Starting Windows

1. Remove any disk from floppy drive A.

2. Turn on the display monitor.

3. Turn on the computer.

COMMON WRONG TURNS
Blank Screen

Don't be confused if your screen goes blank or displays a moving pattern. It just means that your monitor has an energy-saving "sleep" mode or Windows' screen saver is on and you haven't pressed any keys for awhile. If this happens to you, just press any key and the Windows screen reappears.

TIP
Your System Hangs

Occasionally your system may *crash* out from under you. The screen goes blank and the system starts over again. This happens with power outages or even power brownouts. At other times, your system may become unresponsive. This is called *hanging* or *freezing*. In some cases you may be able to move the mouse pointer (an arrow on the screen that moves when you move the mouse on the desk), but you can't execute commands. In other cases, some element that should quickly perform an action and then disappear seems to remain on the screen forever. When this happens, you must close the application program. To do so, display the Close Program dialog box by holding down Ctrl and Alt while you press Delete. (This command is usually written out as Ctrl + Alt + Delete.) The Close Program dialog box displays a list of all active programs. If one is indicated as *Not responding*, click it to select it and then click the **End Task** button. This closes the misbehaving application program, but you remain in Windows so you can continue working. If you press Ctrl + Alt + Delete again, you restart your computer and lose unsaved data in all open application programs.

TUTORIAL

In this tutorial you start your system so it loads Windows 95. On some systems additional steps may be required. If this is the case with your system, your instructor will supply you with the information you need.

Getting Ready

1. Open the door to floppy drive A or eject any disk from that drive. When you turn on a computer, it looks for the operating system files that it needs to start up. First it looks in drive A and then in drive C. If there is a disk in drive A that does not contain the startup files, you will see a message telling you the wrong disk is in the drive. Just open the drive's door and press any key to continue.

Booting the System

2. To start Windows, just turn on the computer and the display monitor. If you can't find the on/off switches, ask someone where they are. When you turn on the computer, the computer first runs a diagnostic program to be sure the system is operating correctly. Then the Windows loading sequence begins. At some point in the process, you may be prompted to log onto Windows or a network.

3. When the Windows desktop and taskbar are displayed, you can begin work. If a *Welcome to Windows 95* screen appears on the desktop, point to the **Close** button in the lower-right corner of its window and click the left mouse button. There also may be other windows that appear on your screen automatically.

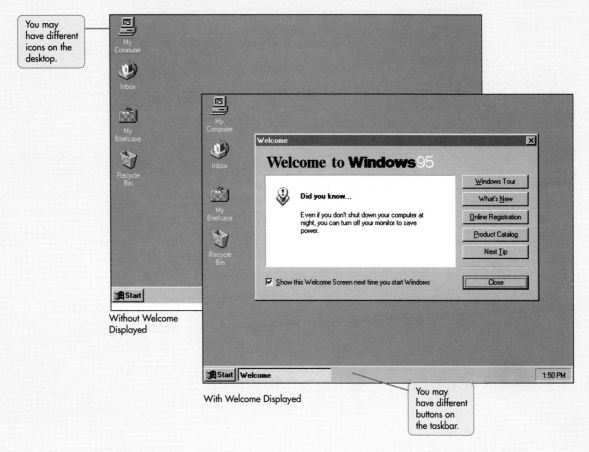

You may have different icons on the desktop.

Without Welcome Displayed

With Welcome Displayed

You may have different buttons on the taskbar.

Finishing Up

4. Continue to the next section to see how you exit Windows.

1-2 EXITING WINDOWS

When you have finished for the day, you should always shut down Windows correctly and then turn off the system. Windows frequently creates temporary files on the disk and when you shut down correctly, these files are closed and all data is stored where it should be. If you just turn off the computer with Windows on the screen, you could corrupt your files.

TIP
QuickSteps Boxes

QuickSteps boxes summarize the steps you follow to complete a procedure. These boxes can be found throughout this text and serve two purposes:

▶ On your first pass through a section, QuickSteps give you an advance look at the steps you must follow to complete the procedure. Don't actually execute the commands this time around. If you do so, you may not know how to recover from any mistakes you might make.

▶ Later on, when you want to refresh your memory about a procedure, QuickSteps make it easy to find and review the steps you must follow. At this stage, you can use them as a quick reference guide.

QUICKSTEPS
Exiting Windows

1. Using the mouse, point to the **Start** button on the taskbar and click the left mouse button to display the Start menu.

2. Using the mouse, point to the **Shut Down** command on the menu and click the left mouse button to display the Shut Down Windows dialog box. The dialog box offers you choices. The first, which is on by default, specifies that you want to shut down your system.

3. Using the mouse, point to the **Yes** button in the dialog box and click the left mouse button. Wait for the screen to display the message *It's now safe to turn off your computer*.

4. Turn off your computer.

5. Remove any disks from the floppy disk drives. This will prevent their loss, increase security, and ensure that no one mistakenly erases them. Make sure you take your own disks with you.

TIP
Exiting When You Haven't Saved Your Work

If you try to shut down Windows without first saving your work in an open application program, a dialog box appears. It has the title of the application program, asks if you want to save changes, and offers three choices.

▶ To save the file, click the **Yes** button.

▶ To abandon the file, click the **No** button.

▶ To cancel the Exit command and return to where you were, click the **Cancel** button.

IN this tutorial you exit Windows and shut down your system following the correct procedure to prevent any loss of data..

Getting Ready

1. Start Windows as described in Section 1-1 if it isn't on the screen.

Exiting Windows

2. Using the mouse, point to the **Start** button on the taskbar and click the left mouse button to display the Start menu.

LOOKING AHEAD
Pointing and Clicking

To execute many commands, you use the mouse to point to a button or menu command and then click. To point to an item, hold the mouse perpendicular to the face of the monitor so moving it sideways moves the mouse pointer sideways on the screen. When the mouse pointer is positioned over the button, click the left mouse button gently so you don't move the mouse at the same time.

3. Using the mouse, point to the **Shut Down** command and click the left mouse button to display the Shut Down Windows dialog box. Notice how the first option, *Shut down the computer?*, has a dot in it, indicating that it is on (◉). This is the option that you use when you are quitting a session.

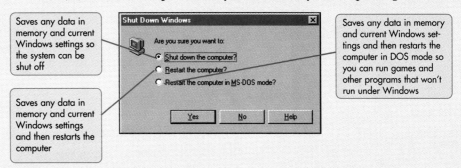

Saves any data in memory and current Windows settings so the system can be shut off

Saves any data in memory and current Windows settings and then restarts the computer

Saves any data in memory and current Windows settings and then restarts the computer in DOS mode so you can run games and other programs that won't run under Windows

4. Using the mouse, point to the **Yes** button and click the left mouse button. Wait for the screen to display the message *It's now safe to turn off your computer.*

Finishing Up

5. Turn off your computer.

1-3 MASTERING MOUSE POINTING

Although Windows can be operated from the keyboard, it is designed to be used with a pointing device. Using a pointing device, you can point to objects to select them, drag objects on the screen, click menu commands, specify options, and indicate where you want to type in data.

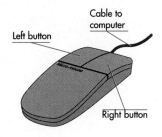

Left button

Cable to computer

Right button

A Typical Mouse

There are different kinds of pointing devices available but most desktop systems use a *mouse*. Mice can vary considerably in design, but the most common mouse has two buttons and is connected to the computer by a thin cable.

Turn your mouse over and you may see part of a ball protruding through the bottom (not all mice use balls). When you move the mouse across the desk's surface, this ball spins and sends electrical signals to the computer through the cable. These signals move the *mouse pointer* (usually just called the *pointer*) on the screen. The mouse pointer is usually a diagonal arrow. However, as you move it around the screen, it can change shape depending on what you are pointing to. It even displays an hourglass shape to tell you to wait because Windows in busy. The many shapes you might see are shown in the table "Mouse Pointer Shapes."

Mouse Pointer Shapes

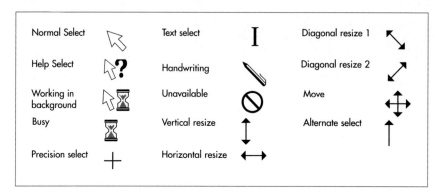

Normal Select	Text select	Diagonal resize 1
Help Select	Handwriting	Diagonal resize 2
Working in background	Unavailable	Move
Busy	Vertical resize	Alternate select
Precision select	Horizontal resize	

TUTORIAL

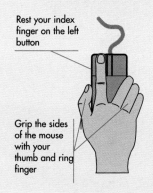

Rest your index finger on the left button

Grip the sides of the mouse with your thumb and ring finger

I N this tutorial you practice using the mouse to point to objects on the screen. If you are a first-time user, keep in mind that this takes practice, so be patient.

Getting Ready

1. Start Windows as described in Section 1-1 if it isn't on the screen.

2. With the mouse cable facing away from you, grip the mouse with your thumb and ring finger so that your index finger rests on the left mouse button.

Locating the Mouse Pointer

3. Jiggle the mouse a few times to make it easier to locate the mouse pointer on the screen.

Aligning the Mouse

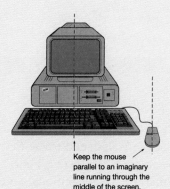

Keep the mouse parallel to an imaginary line running through the middle of the screen.

4. Hold the mouse exactly perpendicular to the front of the screen so that when you move it left or right, the pointer on the screen moves left or right on the screen. When you move the mouse forward or back, the pointer moves up or down on the screen. If you hold the mouse at an angle other than perpendicular to the front of the screen, it's harder to predict the direction in which the pointer will move.

Pointing with the Mouse

5. Move the mouse about the desk and watch the mouse pointer move about the screen. This is called *pointing*. If you haven't used a mouse before, you'll see that you need practice to make the mouse pointer move in a predictable fashion. If you run out of room on the desk or mouse pad when moving the mouse, lift it and place it in a new position and then continue moving it.

6. Point to the **Start** button on the taskbar and pause for a moment to display the message *Click here to begin.*

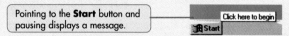

Pointing to the **Start** button and pausing displays a message.

Click here to begin

Start

7. Point to the time displayed in the notification area at the right end of the taskbar, and today's date is displayed.

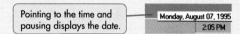

Pointing to the time and pausing displays the date.

Monday, August 07, 1995
2:05 PM

8. Point to the very top border of the taskbar and you'll see the pointer change into a two-headed vertical arrow. This is just one of the many other shapes the mouse pointer can take.

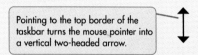

Pointing to the top border of the taskbar turns the mouse pointer into a vertical two-headed arrow.

Finishing Up

9. Continue to the next section, or shut down your system as described in Section 1-2.

PAUSING FOR PRACTICE

Moving the mouse pointer is one of the most fundamental skills you must master. Pause at this point to practice. At first, it seems hard to point to just the right place. Don't be discouraged; it just takes some practice. Pick out an object on the screen, perhaps one of the letters in an icon's title, and then quickly move the mouse pointer to it. Continue practicing until you can move it to any point you want on the first try.

1-4 MASTERING MOUSE CLICKING

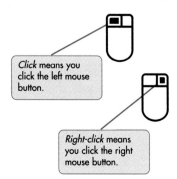

Click means you click the left mouse button.

Right-click means you click the right mouse button.

Moving the mouse pointer around the screen isn't enough to operate Windows. You must also know how and when to click the mouse buttons and which to click.

Depending on the situation, you click once or twice. The first question a new user always asks is "When do I click and when do I double-click?" Generally, you click once to select an item and double-click to execute an action. In other words, clicking an item tells Windows you want to use it. Double-clicking starts an application program or executes a command.

Depending on the situation, you click either the left or right button. You use the left button for most operations—for example, to select menu commands and click buttons. You use the right button mainly to display shortcut menus that allow you to execute commands quickly. The shortcut menu that appears when you click with the right button depends on where you click on the screen. Since the left mouse button is the one you use most frequently, the terms *click* and *double-click* in this text refer to the left button. When you are to click the right button, you will be told to *right-click*.

QUICKSTEPS
Clicking Your Mouse

▶ To *click*, you quickly press and then release the left mouse button. The finger action is similar to typing a character on the keyboard. The mouse should not be moved during the click. (Windows has a command that swaps the functions of the left and right buttons on the mouse. If you are left-handed and having trouble, ask for help.)

▶ To *right-click*, you click the right mouse button rather than the left. (Since the left button is used far more often, it is just called *click* instead of *left-click*.)

▶ To *double-click*, you quickly press the left button twice in succession. Double-clicking takes practice since the mouse should not be moved during the click.

COMMON WRONG TURNS
Pointing and Clicking

▶ Be sure to point to the right place before clicking. The point of the mouse pointer must be over a button, or one of the letters in a command or its icon, when you click. If it is out of position, even by a little bit, you may execute the wrong command or the menu or dialog box may disappear.

▶ When double-clicking, be sure not to move the mouse between clicks. To avoid this, relax. The mouse moves because you are putting too much force into your action. Just grip the mouse lightly and then lightly click with your index finger.

▶ When double-clicking, the second click must closely follow the first. If you pause too long between clicks, the command won't be executed. If this happens, just try again.

TUTORIAL

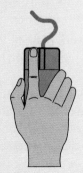

Iɴ this tutorial you practice clicking and double-clicking the mouse. Again, if you are new to mice, keep in mind that this takes practice—especially double-clicking. Take your time and be sure you master this important skill.

Getting Ready

1. Start Windows as described in Section 1-1 if it isn't on the screen.

2. With the mouse cable facing away from you, grip the mouse with your thumb and ring finger so that your index finger rests on the left mouse button.

Clicking the Mouse

3. Point to the **Start** button on the taskbar and click the left mouse button to display the Start menu. (Yours may not look exactly like the one shown here.)

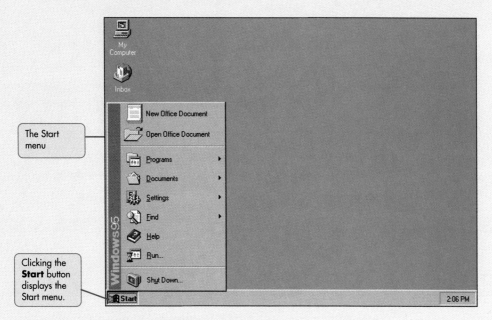

The Start menu

Clicking the **Start** button displays the Start menu.

4. Click anywhere on the desktop outside of the Start menu and the menu closes.

Double-Clicking the Mouse

5. Double-click the time on the taskbar and a dialog box opens that gives the date and time properties.

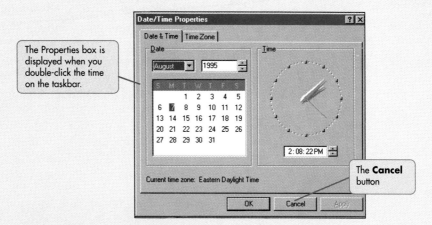

The Properties box is displayed when you double-click the time on the taskbar.

The **Cancel** button

6. Click the **Cancel** button in the dialog box to close it.

Clicking the Right Mouse Button

7. Point to the time on the taskbar and **right-click** to display a shortcut menu.

Right-clicking the time displays a shortcut menu.

8. Click the **Adjust Date/Time** command to display the Date/Time Properties dialog box.
9. Click the **Cancel** button in the dialog box to close it.

PAUSING FOR PRACTICE

Clicking and double-clicking are fundamental skills for using Windows. Pause here and continue practicing these skills by repeating this tutorial until they are second nature.

Finishing Up

10. Continue to the next section, or shut down your system as described in Section 1-2.

1-5 MASTERING MOUSE DRAGGING

Dragging means you hold down the left mouse button and move the mouse. *Right-dragging* means you hold down the right mouse button when you move the mouse.

One of the many time-saving features of Windows is your ability to *drag and drop* items on the screen. For example, you can drag and drop icons, windows, or the taskbar. Later on, you'll see how you can also drag and drop files or sections of documents to copy or move them to new locations. You can even drag a document's icon onto a printer icon to print the document.

Normally you drag an object by pointing to it, holding down the left mouse button, and moving the mouse. However, in some situations if you hold down the right button (called *right-dragging*), a shortcut menu appears when you drop the object that offers options such as moving or copying.

QUICKSTEPS
Dragging and Dropping Objects

1. Click the object to be dragged to select it.

2. Press the left mouse button and hold it down as you move the mouse to drag the object on the screen. (Hold down the right button instead of the left if you want a shortcut menu to appear when you drop the object. This is called right-dragging.)

3. When the object is where you want it, release the left mouse button to drop it.

TUTORIAL

I n this tutorial you practice dragging and dropping icons on the Windows 95 desktop.

Getting Ready

1. Start Windows as described in Section 1-1 if it isn't on the screen.

Dragging and Dropping Icons

2. Point to the *Recycle Bin* icon on the desktop.

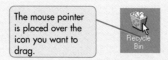

The mouse pointer is placed over the icon you want to drag.

3. Hold down the left mouse button and move the mouse to drag a copy of the icon around on the screen.

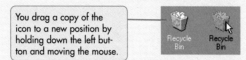

You drag a copy of the icon to a new position by holding down the left button and moving the mouse.

4. When the icon is where you want it, release the left mouse button to drop it. (If it snaps back into a neat alignment, the program's Auto Arrange command is turned on. To turn it off, right-click the desktop to display a short-cut menu, point to the **Arrange Icons** command to cascade the menu, and then click the **Auto Arrange** command to remove the check mark from in front of it.)

Right-Dragging and Dropping Icons

5. Point to the *Recycle Bin* icon on the desktop.

6. Hold down the **right** mouse button, drag a copy of the icon elsewhere on the screen, then release the mouse button to drop it and display a shortcut menu.

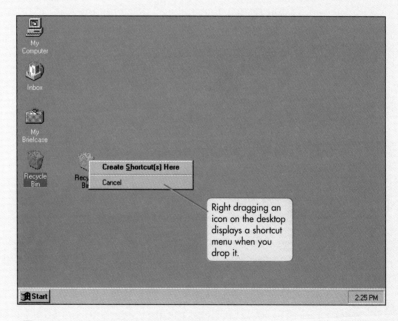

Right dragging an icon on the desktop displays a shortcut menu when you drop it.

7. Click the **Cancel** command.

Dragging and Dropping the Taskbar

8. Point to an open area on the taskbar (not a button), hold down the left mouse button, and drag the mouse pointer to the right edge of the screen. Depending on your system, an outline appears as you drag the taskbar, or the taskbar pops into view in a vertical position as the mouse pointer approaches the edge of the screen.

9. With the taskbar or its outline displayed vertically, release the left mouse button to drop it into position.

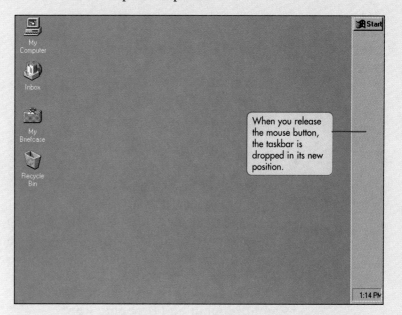

When you release the mouse button, the taskbar is dropped in its new position.

PAUSING FOR PRACTICE

Dragging and dropping is one of the most important skills you can master. Pause here to practice dragging and dropping the taskbar to each of the four sides of the screen. When you have mastered the skill, drag and drop it back along the bottom of the screen.

Finishing Up

10. Continue to the next section, or shut down your system as described in Section 1-2.

1-6 USING ON-LINE HELP

Windows has extensive *on-line Help* available from almost anywhere in any program. Help is organized into topics. You can think of them as sections in a book.

Starting Help

To look up Help, the first step is to start the Help program and display the Help Topics window. You can then use any one of three techniques to locate the information you need.

1. Click the **Start** button to display the Start menu.

2. Click the **Help** command to display the Help Topics window.

3. Locate Help using the tabs *Contents*, *Index*, or *Find* as shown in the accompanying text. You may see *hypertext links* within the Help windows that take you directly to other places. Hypertext links are simply "hot spots" you click to jump to another location. (You know you are pointing to a hypertext link when the mouse pointer turns into a pointing finger.)

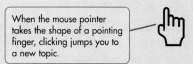

   When the mouse pointer takes the shape of a pointing finger, clicking jumps you to a new topic.

   ▶ *Shortcut buttons* take you directly to the dialog box where you make the changes related to the Help topic.

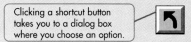

   Clicking a shortcut button takes you to a dialog box where you choose an option.

   ▶ *Pop-ups* are displayed when you click words with green underlines. Click in a pop-up or any area but a button or menu command to close it.

4. After locating and reading Help, do one of the following:

   ▶ Pull down the **Options** menu and click the **Print Topic** command.

   ▶ Click the **Help Topics** button to return to the Help Topics window.

   ▶ Click the Help window's **Minimize** button to display it as a button on the taskbar. Clicking the button on the taskbar reopens the window.

   ▶ Click the Help window's **Close** button to close it.

   Clicking the **Minimize** button displays the window as a button on the taskbar.

   Clicking the **Close** button closes the Help window.

   ▶ Click the shortcut button to perform the procedure. (Only a few Help windows display shortcut buttons.)

Help—The Contents Tab

The *Contents* tab lists topics grouped by subject much as the table of contents in a book.

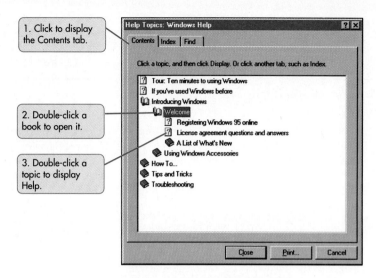

1. Click to display the Contents tab.

2. Double-click a book to open it.

3. Double-click a topic to display Help.

Help—The Index Tab

The *Index* tab lets you look up topics much as you would in the index of a book.

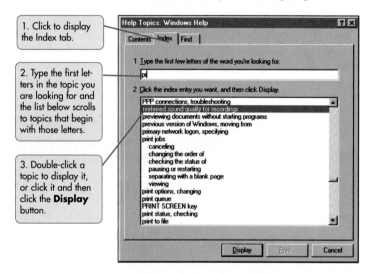

1. Click to display the Index tab.

2. Type the first letters in the topic you are looking for and the list below scrolls to topics that begin with those letters.

3. Double-click a topic to display it, or click it and then click the **Display** button.

Help—The Find Tab

The *Find* tab lets you search for words or phrases that might appear in a Help topic's title.

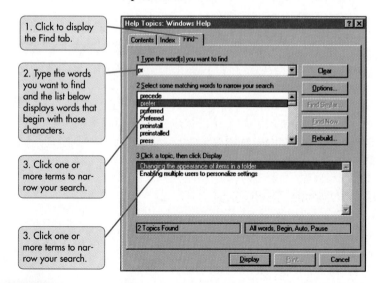

1. Click to display the Find tab.

2. Type the words you want to find and the list below displays words that begin with those characters.

3. Click one or more terms to narrow your search.

3. Click one or more terms to narrow your search.

I N this tutorial you practice using Windows' on-line Help to locate information on some of the topics you have explored in this PicTorial.

Getting Ready

1. Start Windows as described in Section 1-1 if it isn't on the screen.

Displaying Help

2. Click the **Start** button to display the Start menu.

3. Click the **Help** command to display the Help Topics window. It has three tabs from which to choose: *Contents*, *Index*, and *Find*.

Exploring the Question Mark Button

4. Click the *Contents* tab to display it.

5. Click the question mark button at the right end of the blue bar at the top of the window (called the title bar). This adds a question mark to the mouse pointer.

6. Click the lower window listing Help books to display a pop-up describing it.

7. Click anywhere to close the pop-up.

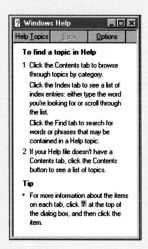

Exploring the Contents Tab

8. Double-click the *How To* book to display a list of its contents.

9. Double-click the *Use Help* book to display a list of its contents. (You may have to click the scroll bar's down scroll arrow (▼) to see the topic.)

10. Click the *Finding a topic in Help* topic and then click the **Display** button to display Help. Read the Help.

11. Click the **Help Topics** button in the Help window to return to the Help Topics window.

Exploring the Index Tab

12. Click the *Index* tab to display it. The insertion point, a flashing vertical line, is in the top text box labeled *1 Type the first few letters of the word you're look-ing for.*

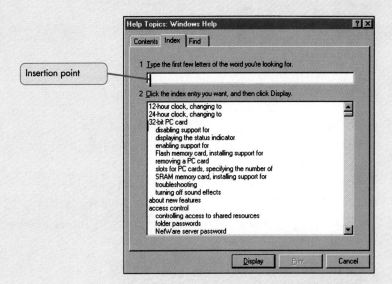

Insertion point

13. Type **m**, then **o**, then **u**, and watch the list scroll closer and closer to words beginning with those letters. You should be able to see the heading *mouse* in the bottom window below the highlighted heading *mouse pointer*.

14. Click *buttons, reversing* under the *mouse* heading and then click the **Display** button to display a Help window. Notice the shortcut button with the curved arrow in the Help window.

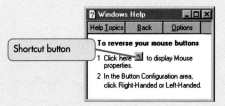

Shortcut button

15. Click the shortcut button (the one with the bent arrow on it) to display the Mouse Properties dialog box. Instead of giving you detailed help, Help sometimes takes you right to the spot where you have to make the settings. In this case, it takes you to the dialog box where you can switch a mouse between right-handed and left-handed.

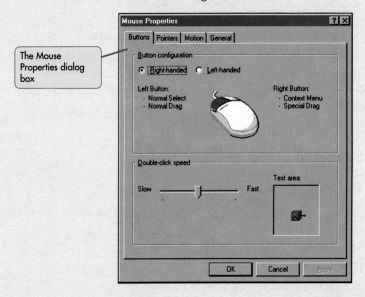

The Mouse Properties dialog box

16. Click the **Cancel** button in the Mouse Properties dialog box to close it.

17. Click the **Help Topics** button to return to the Help Topics window.

Exploring the Find Tab

18. Click the *Find* tab to display it. The insertion point, a flashing vertical line, is in the top text box labeled *1 Type the word(s) you want to find*.

Type the word you are looking for here.

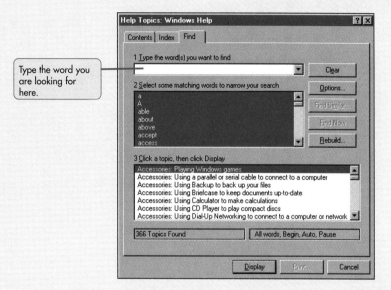

19. Type **find**, and topics that begin with that word appear in the box labeled *2 Select some matching words to narrow your search*.

20. Click *Find* (the one with the first letter capitalized) in the box labeled *2 Select some matching words to narrow your search*. Topics related to that word are listed in the bottom box labeled *3. Click a topic, then click Display*.

21. Click *Finding a topic in Help* (or its check box if it has one) in the box labeled *3. Click a topic, then click Display* (you may have to scroll the list to see it), and then click the **Display** button to display Help on that topic.

Finishing Up

Clicking the **Close** button closes the Help window.

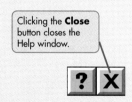

22. Click the Help window's **Close** button to close the Help window. This is the button with the X in it at the far right of the title bar.

![hand icon] **PAUSING FOR PRACTICE**

When working with Windows or any of its application programs, help is always available on line. Knowing how to find the information you need is a very useful skill. Pause here to practice using on-line Help. For example, you might look for help on printing Help topics and navigating Help.

23. Continue to the lab activities, or shut down your system as described in Section 1-2.

A VISUAL INTRODUCTION

VISUAL QUIZ

1. Name and briefly describe each of the Windows 95 elements indicated here.

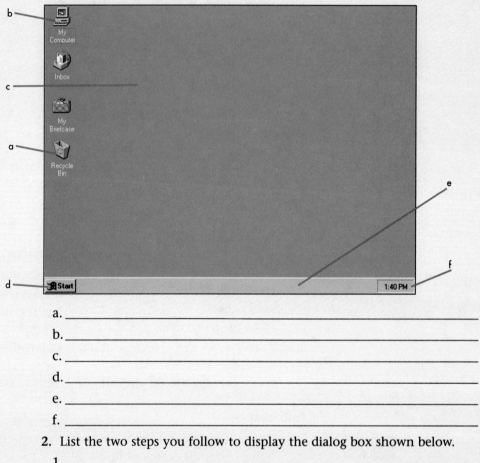

a. _____

b. _____

c. _____

d. _____

e. _____

f. _____

2. List the two steps you follow to display the dialog box shown below.

1. _____

2. _____

Write down what happens when you click the buttons labeled a, b, and c.

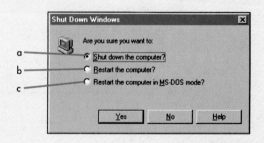

a. _____

b. _____

c. _____

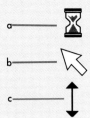

3. Describe the circumstances in which the mouse pointer will take each of the shapes shown here.

   a. _____

   b. _____

   c. _____

4. Label each of these illustrations on clicking the mouse. The dots on the button indicate which is clicked and the dots to the left of the mouse indicate how many times it is clicked—no dots means it's clicked once.

_____   _____   _____

5. Label each of these illustrations on dragging with the mouse. The dots on the button indicate which is held down when the mouse is dragged.

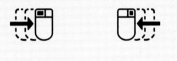

_____   _____

6. Write down a brief description of how you look up Help using each of the labeled tabs.

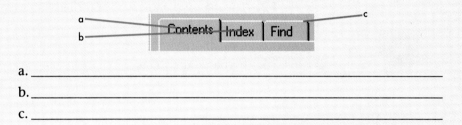

   a. _____

   b. _____

   c. _____

7. What happens when you click a button in a Help window that looks like this?

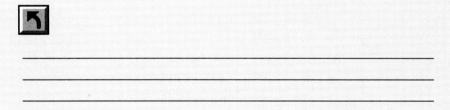

_____

_____

_____

REVIEW QUESTIONS

TRUE-FALSE

T F **1.** A computer's operating system coordinates all of the computer's functions.

T F **2.** Windows is the only operating system currently in use.

T F **3.** To boot a computer, you give it a stiff kick in the side.

T F **4.** The drive the computer looks to first when you turn it on is always drive A.

T F **5.** When you boot a computer, Windows 95 is loaded automatically.

T F **6.** Normally, when you boot a computer, there must not be a disk in drive A.

T F **7.** The taskbar always displays the **Start** button.

T F **8.** The Windows desktop is the screen area where various windows and icons can be displayed.

T F **9.** When you have finished working with Windows for the day, just turn the computer off and everything will automatically take care of itself.

T F **10.** The mouse is the only pointing device you can use with Windows.

T F **11.** When you move the mouse on the desk, its movements are followed by a mouse pointer on the screen.

T F **12.** The mouse pointer is always the same shape, so it is easy to identify.

T F **13.** When you double-click the mouse button, the pause between clicks isn't important.

T F **14.** If you are left handed, you can only use Windows easily by buying a left-handed mouse that has the buttons reversed.

T F **15.** Although mice have more than one button, you only use the left one.

T F **16.** To drag something on the screen, you point to it, hold down one of the mouse buttons, and move the mouse.

T F **17.** When you have dragged an object to where you want it, you double-click to drop it.

T F **18.** You display Windows Help using the **Start** button on the taskbar.

T F **19.** Some words and phrases on Help screens are underlined only to make them stand out so you can read them better.

T F **20.** When the mouse pointer turns into a pointing finger on a Help screen, clicking the mouse takes you to another screen or displays a definition.

T F **21.** To force you to buy books on Windows, Microsoft designed it so you cannot print out Help screens.

MULTIPLE CHOICE

1. When you first turn on your computer, it always looks first to ___ for the operating system files that it needs to run.

a. Drive A   b. Drive B

c. Drive C   d. Drive D

2. If Windows stops working (it "freezes up"), you press __ to open the Close Program dialog box.

    a. ⌜Esc⌝

    b. ⌜Enter ↵⌝

    c. ⌜Ctrl⌝+⌜Alt⌝+⌜Del⌝

    d. ⌜⇧ Shift⌝+⌜Tab⇆⌝

3. When finished for the day or for a session, you should ___.

    a. Click the **Start** button and then the **Sh<u>u</u>t Down** command

    b. Select the way you want to shut down on the Shut Down dialog box

    c. Wait for a message telling you it's safe to turn off your computer

    d. All of the above

4. To point to an object on the screen, you ___.

    a. Use your finger

    b. Move the mouse to position the mouse pointer

    c. Pick up the mouse and point to it on the screen

    d. None of the above

5. To click an object on the screen, you ___.

    a. Quickly press and release the left mouse button

    b. Quickly press and release the right mouse button

    c. Point to it and hold down the left mouse button till the object is highlighted

    d. None of the above

6. To right-click an object on the screen, you ___.

    a. Quickly press and release the left mouse button

    b. Quickly press and release the right mouse button

    c. Point to it and hold down the left mouse button till the object is highlighted

    d. None of the above

7. To drag an object on the screen, you ___.

    a. Double-click the object to select it, then click where you want it moved to

    b. Point to the object, hold down both buttons, and move the mouse

    c. Point to the object, hold down the left button, and move the mouse

    d. Point to the object, hold down the right button, and move the mouse

8. To look up Help, you have to ___.

    a. Look it up as you would in the contents of a book

    b. Look it up as you would in the index of a book

    c. Search for a specific word in a topic title

    d. Any of the above

FILL IN THE BLANK

1. To use a computer for word processing, spreadsheet, or database application programs, the computer must be running a(n) _____.

2. Windows has what is known as a graphical _____.

3. Turning on your computer is referred to as _____ it.

4. The drive the computer looks to when you first turn it on is _____.

5. If your system freezes up when using Windows, you press ____+_____+____ to display the Close Program dialog box.

6. To exit Windows, you click the _____ button and click the _____ command.

7. When you click the right mouse button, it's called _____ .

8. When you click the mouse button once it is called clicking, and when you click it twice it's called _____.

9. To drag an object, you hold down the _____ mouse button and move the mouse.

10.. To right-drag an object, you hold down the _____ mouse button and move the mouse.

11. If you click a word or phrase on a Help screen that is underlined, you _____.

12. If you click a button on a Help screen that has a graphic of a bent arrow, you _____.

13. When the mouse pointer changes to a pointing finger on a Help screen, it indicates that you can _____.

LAB ACTIVITIES

DRILLS

1-1   Starting Windows

When you start Windows 95, some programs may be loaded automatically. These appear on the desktop or taskbar. Here, make a record of these so you can look them up later to see what they do.

1. Write down the name of each of the icons on your desktop when you start your system.

_____   _____

_____   _____

_____   _____

2. Write down the name of any buttons on your taskbar when you first start your system.

_____ _____

_____ _____

_____ _____

1-2   Exiting Windows

You should always shut down Windows correctly so your work isn't damaged. Now you try an alternative method.

1. Start Windows 95 if it isn't already running.
2. Point to the **Start** button and click the left mouse button, then point to the **Sh<u>u</u>t Down** command on the Start menu and click the left mouse button to display the Shut Down Windows dialog box.
3. Point to the round option button (◉) titled *Restart the computer?* and click the left mouse button to move the dot to it and turn it on.
4. Point to the **<u>Y</u>es** button, click the left mouse button, and watch what happens.

1-3   Mastering Mouse Pointing

Pointing is a skill that you master with practice. In this drill you practice this procedure.

1. Practice picking out areas of the screen to see how fast you can point to them. Begin with large items like icons and then do small items such as individual characters in names such as *My Computer*.
2. Point to the **Start** button on the taskbar to display a pop-up message.

1-4   Mastering Mouse Clicking

When clicking, it's important to do so without moving the mouse. This comes with practice. In this drill you practice this procedure.

1. Click the **Start** button on the taskbar to open the Start menu, then click in any open area of the desktop to close the Start menu.
2. Right-click anywhere on the open desktop to display a shortcut menu, then click in any open area of the desktop to close it.
3. Repeat Steps 1 and 2 until you have mastered pointing and clicking.

1-5   Mastering Mouse Dragging

Dragging and dropping speeds up many procedures not only in Windows, but also in word processing and spreadsheet applications, among others. In this drill you practice this procedure.

1. Drag the icons around on the desktop and drop them in new positions. (If an icon snaps back into a neat alignment, the program's Auto Arrange command is turned on. To turn it off, right-click the desktop to display a shortcut menu, click the **Arrange <u>I</u>cons** command, and then click the **<u>A</u>uto Arrange** command to remove the check mark from next to it.)
2. Drag the taskbar to the left, top, right, and then bottom edges of the screen. Drop it in each position before dragging it to the next.
3. If you turned off the program's Auto Arrange command in Step 1, turn it back on. To do so, right-click the desktop to display a shortcut menu, click the **Arrange <u>I</u>cons** command, and then click the **<u>A</u>uto Arrange** command to add a check mark next to it.

1-6 Using On-Line Help

On-line Help is always just a few clicks away, and you may have left the manual at home. It's smart to master the on-line Help system so you can find what you want, when you need it. In this drill you practice those procedures.

1. Click the **Start** button to display the Start menu, then click the **Help** command to display the Help Topics window.

2. Click the *Contents* tab to display it and look up Help on these topics:

Book	Topic	Subtopic
How To...	Use Help	Finding a Topic in Help
How To...	Use Help	Printing a Help Topic
Tips and Tricks	Tips of the Day	Using Help
Tips and Tricks	Tips of the Day	Viewing the Welcome screen
Troubleshooting	If you have trouble starting Windows	

3. Click the *Index* tab to display it and look up Help on these topics:

Topic	Subtopic
exiting	Windows
window	getting Help on parts of a window
Windows 95	license agreement
Welcome screen, viewing	

4. Click the *Find* tab to display it and look up Help on these topics:

Topic	Subtopic
Welcome	Tips: Viewing the Welcome screen again
piracy	Are there different types of software piracy?
Windows keys	General Windows keys

5. Click the Help window's **Close** button to close the Help window.

EXERCISES

Exercise 1. Starting Windows on Your Own System

There are a number of ways a Windows-based system can be set up. On some, you start Windows exactly as described in the text. On others, you may have to enter a password or log onto a network. List the steps here that you use to load Windows 95 so that you have them for future reference.

1. _____

_____

2. _____

_____

3. _____

_____

4. _____
    _____
5. _____
    _____

Exercise 2. Booting Your System with a Disk in Drive A

When you turn on your system, watch the lights on the disk drives. You will see the light on drive A flash momentarily as the computer looks to that drive for the files that it needs to start up. If it can't find them there, it looks to drive C. However, if there is a disk in drive A without the needed files, the computer stops and displays a message telling you to change the disk and press any button.

Insert your *Win95 Student Resource Disk* into drive A and turn on the computer. You will see the error message that your machine gives in this situation. Write down the error message and the instructions it gives to continue.

_____
_____
_____

Follow the instructions that appear on the screen to continue.

Exercise 3. Exploring Windows 95 If You Have Used Previous Versions of Windows

Windows 95 has a built-in introduction to the program for those who are familiar with the previous release 3.1. In this exercise, you run this introduction.

1. Click the **Start** button to display the Start menu and click **Help** to display the Help topics window.
2. Click the *Contents* tab to display it.
3. Click *If you've used Windows before* to select it, and then click the **Display** button.
4. Click any of the square, gray buttons on the left side of the screen to read about various new features.
5. Click the Help window's **Close** button to close the window.

Exercise 4. Exploring the New Features of Windows

Windows has a new look and feel. In this exercise, you'll use Help to explore some of the features it offers.

1. Click the **Start** button to display the Start menu and click **Help** to display the Help topics window.
2. Click the *Find* tab to display it and search for **buttons**. This will display a topic *The new look and feel of Windows* in the lower window.
3. Double-click *The new look and feel of Windows* in the lower window to display a list of features. Explore each of them, then click the Help window's **Close** button to close it.

PicTorial TWO

INTRODUCTION TO APPLICATIONS

After completing this PicTorial, you will be able to:

▶ **Start and close application programs**
▶ **Describe the parts of application program windows**
▶ **Execute commands with pull-down and shortcut menus**
▶ **Change settings in dialog boxes**
▶ **Run multiple applications and switch between them**
▶ **Size and move windows**
▶ **Copy data between application programs**

THE computer is a versatile machine. With it you can calculate a budget for this year's college expenses, plot a graph of the results, and, finding that you won't have enough money, write a letter to your boss asking for a raise. Each of these tasks is an *application*. To perform each task, you load a specific type of *application program*. For example, WordPerfect® and Microsoft® Word are word processing application programs used to enter, edit, and format memos, letters, reports, and other documents. Excel and Lotus 1-2-3® are spreadsheet application programs used to work with numbers and make calculations. ▶

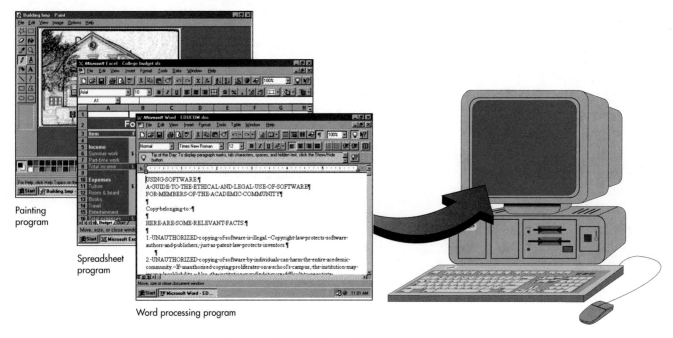

Painting program

Spreadsheet program

Word processing program

Tasks and Application Programs

In one sense, the computer is like an actor, and application programs are like scripts. When the actor changes scripts, he or she can perform a different role. By changing application programs, you can make your computer perform different applications. Being *computer literate* means that you understand how to use application programs to perform useful tasks.

For every type of task there is usually a specific application program that works best. Here are some common tasks and the programs used to perform them.

Tasks	Application Programs	Examples
Write a letter	Word processing program	Word, WordPerfect
Prepare a budget	Spreadsheet program	Excel, 1-2-3
Maintain a mailing list	Database program	Access, Paradox
Create a line drawing	Drawing program	CorelDRAW
Alter a photograph	Painting program	Photoshop
Send e-mail	Communication program	ProComm
Prepare an illustrated talk	Presentation program	PowerPoint
Connect to the Internet	Web browser program	Netscape, Mosaic

TIP
Programs—What's in a Name?

The PC is just over a decade old, and computer language is in flux. New words are added and the meanings of old ones are changed almost daily. This is the reason you frequently hear two or more names for the same thing. For example, the terms *application, program*, and *application program* are commonly used interchangeably—as they are in this text. However, strictly speaking, an application is a task you want to do such as write letters, and a program can be something other than an application program. For example, there are operating system programs, utility programs, and even educational programs.

Windows and Application Programs

Although you do most of your work with application programs, Windows is your gateway to those applications. It has a number of features that make this possible and enhance their performance. For example:

▶ Windows 95 gives a common look to programs that are developed to be used with it. Most include pull-down menus that list commands you can choose and buttons you can click to perform tasks. Standard commands and buttons start programs; call up help; save, open, and print files; enter and edit data; and quit application programs. This makes it easier to learn new programs because many of your existing skills are transferable from one Windows-based application program to another.

▶ Windows 95 allows you to run more than one program at the same time. You can run a spreadsheet in one window and a word processor in another and work on either at any time.

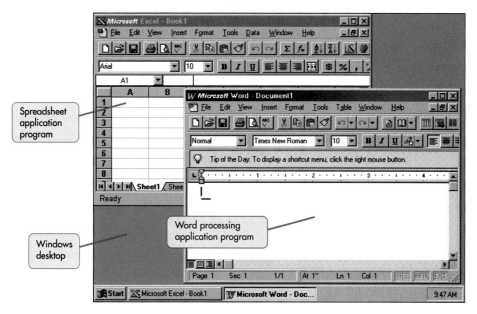

▶ Windows 95 makes it easy to copy or move data from one application to another. You can even create an illustration in one application program and copy it into a document created with another.

Windows 95 Applications

Most applications that you use are purchased separately from Windows. However, Windows does include a number of its own applications, some of which are called *applets* because they are simplified versions of more powerful application programs that you can purchase separately. For example, Windows 95's WordPad program is a very simple word processing program. Windows 95's Paint is a simple version of a painting program used to create and edit illustrations. The main applications included with Windows 95 are briefly described below. You are not taught how to master these programs in this text because its goal is to get you quickly working with major applications. However, some of these built-in applications are used in tutorials, drills, and other lab activities to show you how to start and close applications, manage application windows, and use menus and dialog boxes.

Here are brief descriptions of many of the application programs that come free with Windows 95. Not all of these applications will be on all systems and you may have a number that aren't mentioned here.

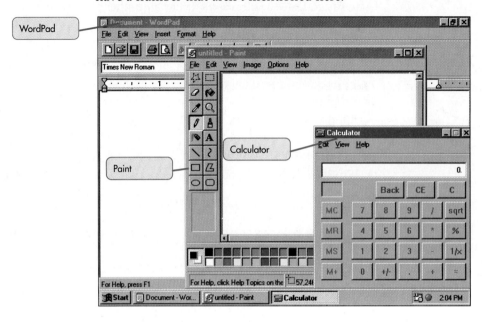

▶ **WordPad** is a mini word processing program. **Notepad** is a similar but simpler application used for very small files.

▶ **Paint** is a mini paint program used to work with bitmap images such as photographs.

▶ **Calculator** is an electronic version of a pocket calculator.

▶ **Character Map** displays special characters such as ®, ™, ¶, ¼, and » that you can copy into a document.

▶ **Clipboard Viewer** stores data you copy or cut in one application so you can paste it elsewhere.

Windows 95 communications application programs allow you to communicate with other computers, fax machines, and phones. To use these your system must be equipped with a modem or fax/modem.

▶ **HyperTerminal** connects you to bulletin-board systems (BBS) running on other computers. It allows the computers to talk to one another.

▶ **Fax** sends and receives faxes and allows you to design a cover sheet.

▶ **Phone Dialer** dials phone numbers for you automatically.

Windows 95 games provide entertainment but have been included mainly for you to practice basic Windows skills, especially pointing, clicking, and dragging with the mouse.

▶ **Solitaire and Hearts** are computerized versions of the card games of the same name.

▶ **Minesweeper** is a game where you try to locate the mines in a minefield without exploding them.

▶ **Free Cell** is a game where you try to move cards to their home cells using free cells as temporary holding places.

Windows 95 multimedia application programs allow you to play, create, and edit sounds, movies, and animations.

▶ **CD Player** plays music CDs that you put in the computer's CD drive.

▶ **Media Player** plays sounds, animations, and movies in a window on the screen.

▶ **Sound Recorder** records, plays back, and edits sounds.

Windows 95 system tools are included so you can perform maintenance tasks on your system's hard disks.

▶ **Backup** allows you to make backup copies of selected documents or folders or whole drives to floppies or a tape drive.

▶ **Disk Defragmenter** moves parts of fragmented files back together so your drive works faster and file parts aren't lost. Files become fragmented when parts of them are scattered all over the disk.

▶ **ScanDisk** checks your hard disk for problems and corrects them.

2-1 STARTING APPLICATION PROGRAMS

Windows' job is to make it easy to operate and use application programs such as word processors, spreadsheets, and databases. To use any Windows application program, you must first start it. This is variously called *starting, opening, running,* or *launching* the application. Starting a program loads it from the disk into the computer's memory and displays it on the screen. When a program is open, it always has a button on the taskbar with its name on it.

The most common way to start Windows 95 application programs is to select them from the Start menu. To display the Start menu, you just click the **Start** button on the taskbar. The Start menu that pops up lists commands you click to run programs, get help, and even change system settings.

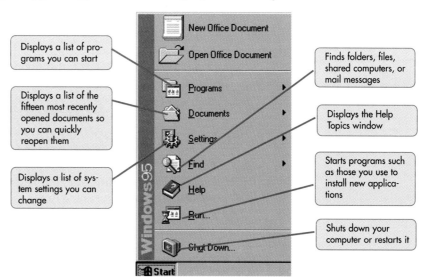

When you click any name on this menu with an arrowhead next to it (▶), or point to it and pause for a moment, a submenu cascades out from the first menu. This submenu is called a *cascading menu* because it "cascades" out of the menu you point to. When you click a name on the cascaded submenu or point to it and pause, another submenu may cascade from it.

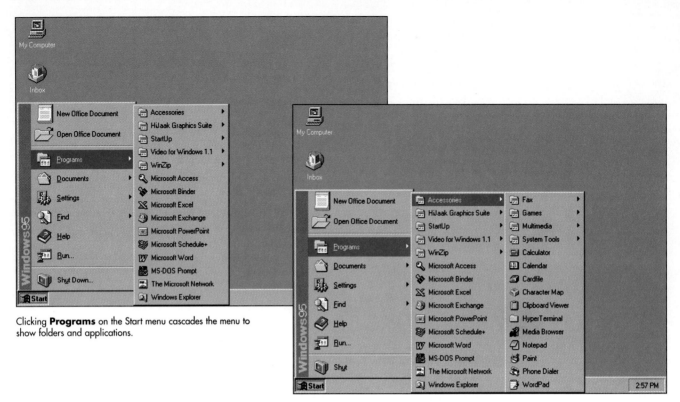

Clicking **Programs** on the Start menu cascades the menu to show folders and applications.

Clicking a folder such as **Accessories** cascades a submenu.

The menus usually list three kinds of objects: *folders, programs,* and *documents.*

▶ Clicking a folder displays another menu listing the folder's contents. (A *folder* is what used to be called a *directory.*) A folder's icon includes an image of a file folder.

▶ Clicking an application program's name or icon starts it. A program's icon includes an image representing the program.

▶ Clicking a document opens it and, if necessary, first starts the program that created it. A document's icon includes an image that looks like a page with a corner turned down or like a spiral notebook.

 U I C K S T E P S

Starting Application Programs

1. Click the **Start** button to display the Start menu.
2. Point to the **Programs** folder or click it to cascade a menu listing the folders and programs on your system.
3. Click the name of an application program to start it, or point to any folder (indicated with ▶ symbols) in which the application program is stored to cascade the menu, and then click the name of the application program listed on the submenu.

ɪɴ this tutorial you explore using the Start menu and the menus that cascade from it. You then use the menu to start an application program.

Getting Ready

1. Start Windows as described in Section 1-1 if it isn't on the screen.

Displaying the Start Menu

2. Click the **Start** button on the taskbar to display the Start menu. If Microsoft Office is installed on your system, the top two commands shown in the accompanying figure, *New Office Document* and *Open Office Document*, are listed. On other systems, these commands do not appear or the menu may have been customized in other ways.

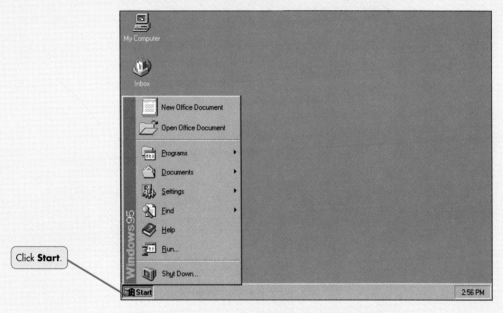

Click **Start**.

3. Point to any place other than the Start menu and click to close the menu without making a selection.

Displaying Cascading Menus

4. Click the **Start** button on the taskbar to display the Start menu again.

5. Point to each of the folders or commands on the menu one at a time. You'll find that if you pause on them for a moment submenus cascade from the **Programs**, **Documents**, **Settings**, and **Find** folders. The arrowhead to the right of these commands (▶) is a visual indicator that they cascade.

6. Point to the **Programs** folder to cascade the menu and display the folders or programs it contains. (Your submenu may look different from the one shown here.)

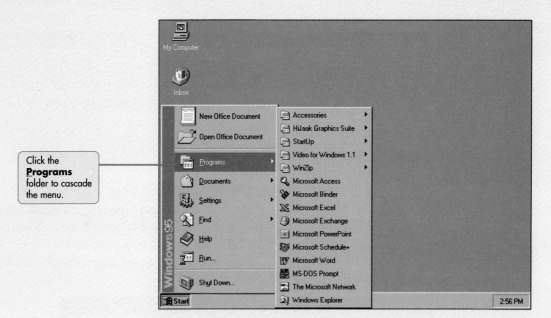

Click the **Programs** folder to cascade the menu.

7. Move the mouse to the right to move the highlight to the cascaded submenu. Don't move it up and down until the highlight moves to the submenu.

8. Point to the **Accessories** folder on the submenu to cascade another submenu listing the folders and programs it contains. Here is where you will find most of the applications that come with Windows 95. Some, such as **Games**, **Multimedia**, and **System Tools**, are folders that cascade when you point to them. Others, such as **WordPad** and **Paint**, are applications that start when you click them.

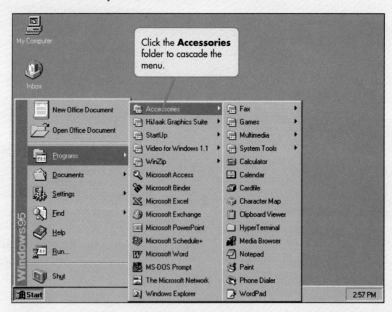

Click the **Accessories** folder to cascade the menu.

COMMON WRONG TURNS
Moving Between Cascaded Menus

When you point to a folder or application's name on the Start menu, a submenu may cascade out from it. To make a selection from this new menu, you need to move the mouse to the right to move the highlight to that submenu. If you move it up or down, you will just cascade out a different submenu. Moving the highlight from one menu to its cascaded submenu takes a little practice.

9. Point to the **System Tools** and then the **Multimedia** folders on the submenu to display the programs stored in those folders.

10. Click anywhere but on one of the menus to close the Start menu and all submenus.

Starting the WordPad Application Program

11. Click the **Start** button on the taskbar to display the Start menu.

12. Point to the <u>P</u>rograms folder to cascade the menu.

13. Point to the **Accessories** folder to cascade a submenu.

14. Click the **WordPad** application program to start it. This application is used to create simple documents such as memos and letters. Notice how a button for WordPad appears on the taskbar.

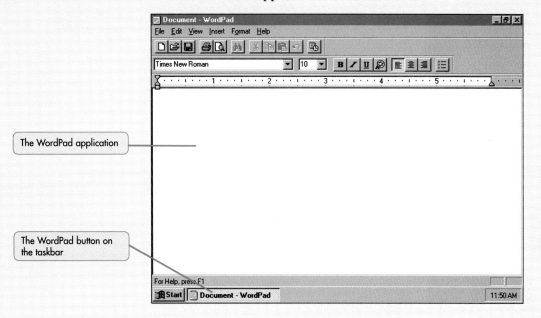

The WordPad application

The WordPad button on the taskbar

Exploring the WordPad Application Program

15. The buttons on the two toolbars execute commands when you click them. Point to each of the buttons that you can see to display their names in little boxes. Also a description of what each button does is displayed on the status bar at the bottom of the window. Some of the buttons may be hidden by the edge of the window or dimmed because they cannot be used until some text has been entered or selected.

Toolbars

16. The window contains a flashing insertion point. Type your name and then click the **Print** button on the toolbar to make a printout.

The **Print** button

Type your name here.

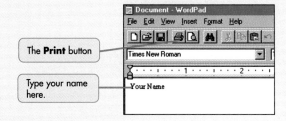

Starting the Clipboard Viewer Application Program

17. Click the **Start** button on the taskbar to display the Start menu.

18. Point to the **Programs** folder to cascade the menu.

19. Point to the **Accessories** folder to cascade a submenu.

20. Click the **Clipboard Viewer** application program to start it. This application is used to store text or graphics that are cut or copied from an application program so they can be pasted elsewhere in the same or even a different document. Notice how a button for Clipboard Viewer also appears on the taskbar.

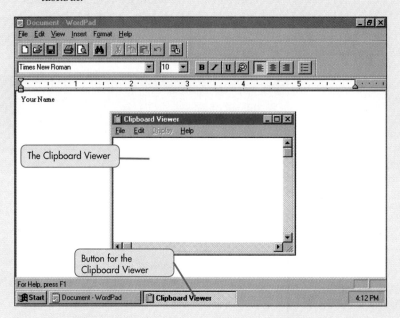

21. Press ⌈PrtScr⌉ on the keyboard and you'll see an image of the screen appear in the Clipboard Viewer's window. You have captured a "snapshot" of the screen and placed it on the Clipboard so it can be pasted elsewhere (you'll see how to do this later).

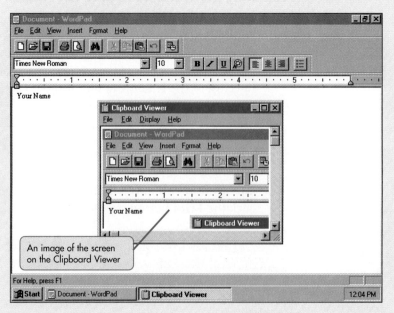

Finishing Up

22. Continue to the next section to see how to close the application windows, or shut down your system as described in Section 1-2. If you want to close the two applications now, refer to the Looking Ahead box "Closing Windows."

LOOKING AHEAD
Closing Windows

There are many ways to close open windows, but the most popular is to just click the **Close** button at the far right of a window's title bar. If prompted to *Save changes to Document?*, click the **No** button. You'll learn about the other ways in the next section.

2-2 CLOSING APPLICATION PROGRAMS

When you are finished with an application program, you close it. This removes it from the computer's memory and removes its window from the desktop and its button from the taskbar. However, the application remains safely stored on the hard disk so you can start it again at any time.

It is important to close application programs using the commands designed for this purpose. They create temporary files on the disk while you are working, and these are deleted only if you exit correctly. If you quit incorrectly, your files may be left damaged.

You can close almost any window simply by clicking the **Close** button at the far right of the title bar. This and other methods are described in the QuickSteps box "Closing an Application Program."

QUICKSTEPS
Closing an Application Program

To close an application program:

▶ Click the **Close** button at the far right of the application's title bar. (If a document is open, there are two **Close** buttons. Clicking the upper one closes the program; clicking the lower one closes the document.)

However, you can also use these procedures:

▶ Pull down the application's **File** menu and click the **Exit** command.

▶ Right-click the application's button on the taskbar to display a shortcut menu, and click the **Close** command.

▶ Double-click the application's icon at the left of the title bar, or click the icon to display a shortcut menu, and then click the **Close** command.

▶ Right-click the application's title bar to display a shortcut menu, and then click the **Close** command.

▶ Hold down [Alt] and press [F4] when the application program is the active window.

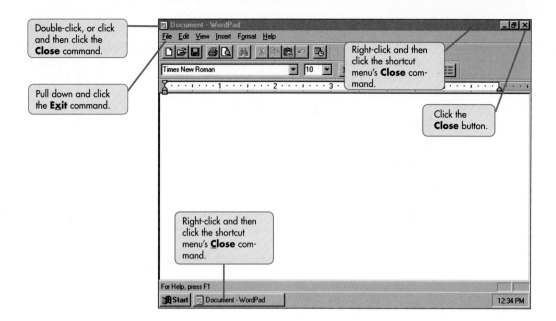

Double-click, or click and then click the **Close** command.

Pull down and click the **Exit** command.

Right-click and then click the shortcut menu's **Close** command.

Click the **Close** button.

Right-click and then click the shortcut menu's **Close** command.

TUTORIAL

I N this tutorial you explore using the Start menu and the menus that cascade from it. You then close the two application programs you left open at the end of the last tutorial.

Getting Ready

1. Start Windows as described in Section 1-1 if it isn't on the screen. If WordPad and Clipboard Viewer are not displayed, repeat Steps 11-14 and 17-20 in the tutorial in Section 2-1. If you open WordPad, type your name in it. (The Clipboard Viewer may still display data from a previous session if you haven't shut down your system.)

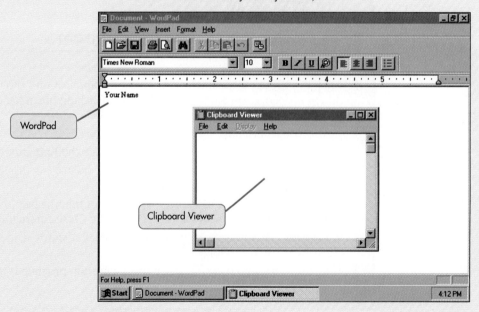

WordPad

Clipboard Viewer

Using the Close Button to Close an Application Program

2. Click the **Close** button at the far right of the Clipboard Viewer window's title bar to close that application program.

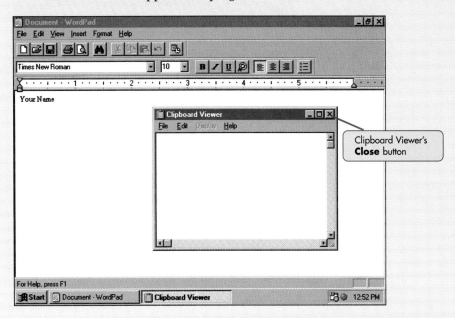

Clipboard Viewer's **Close** button

3. Click the **Close** button at the far right of the WordPad window's title bar. Since you have entered your name into a document and not saved it, a message box asks if you want to *Save changes to Document?*. Click the **N**o button to close that application program without saving the text.

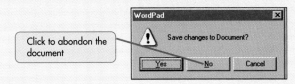

Click to abandon the document

Finishing Up

4. Continue to the next section, or shut down your system as described in Section 1-2.

PAUSING FOR PRACTICE

There is nothing you will use Windows for as much as you'll use it to start application programs. Pause here to open and close any of the applications listed in the Accessories folder. To open that folder, display the Start menu, point to the **Programs** folder, then point to the **Accessories** folder. Click the icon or name of any application to open it.

2-3 EXPLORING APPLICATION PROGRAMS

Application program windows vary from program to program but they generally have a number of identical features. This makes it easy to learn new Windows-based application programs once you know one because much of what you know transfers to the new program.

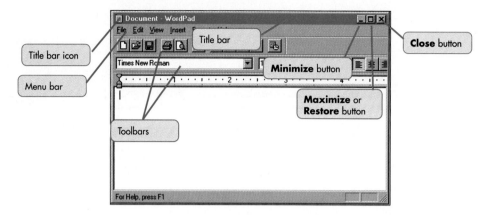

1. At the top of each application program window is a title bar that lists the name of the application program running in the window or otherwise describes the window's contents. You can also right-click this title bar to display a shortcut menu or use it to drag the window to a new position.

2. Every window displays three buttons at the right end of the title bar. A window can be any one of three sizes: maximized so it fills the entire screen, minimized so it appears only as a button on the taskbar, or restored to its original size to occupy only a part of the screen. You use the **Minimize**, **Maximize**, and **Restore** buttons to change among these sizes. To close a window, you click the **Close** button at the right.

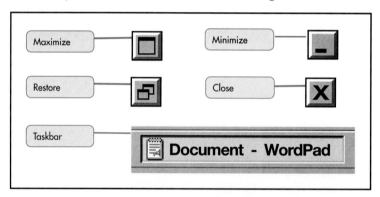

3. The upper left corner of every window displays the application's icon that displays a shortcut menu when you click it (you can also right-click the title bar). You can use commands on this menu to move or size the application program's window. You can also double-click this icon to close the application.

4. A *menu bar* immediately below the title bar displays the names of menus. These menus list commands that you execute to operate your program.

5. The *toolbar* below the menu bar contains buttons you can click to execute commands. The icons on the buttons indicate what they are used for, but you can also point to them to display their names.

QUICKSTEPS

Using Minimize, Maximize, Restore, and Close Buttons

▶ Clicking the **Minimize** button minimizes the window to a button on the taskbar. (Clicking the taskbar button opens the window to the same size it was before it was minimized.)

▶ Clicking the **Maximize** button expands the window to fill the screen. Once you have clicked the **Maximize** button, it is replaced by the **Restore** button.

▶ Clicking the **Restore** button returns a maximized window to its original size. Once you have clicked the **Restore** button it is replaced by the **Maximize** button.

▶ Clicking the **Close** button closes the application and the window.

TUTORIAL

ɪɴ this tutorial you explore changing the size of application program windows by clicking the buttons located at the right end of the title bar.

Getting Ready

1. Start Windows as described in Section 1-1 and start WordPad as described in Section 2-1's tutorial Steps 11-14.

Changing the Size of a Window

2. Click the window's **Minimize** button to reduce the window to a button on the taskbar.

3. Click WordPad's button on the taskbar to reopen the application window.

4. Click either the **Restore** or **Maximize** button (they never appear at the same time, and they replace one another when clicked).

PAUSING FOR PRACTICE

Changing the size of windows with the **Minimize**, **Maximize**, and **Restore** buttons is a basic skill you should master. Pause here to continue practicing until you have mastered each of the buttons.

Finishing Up

5. Continue to the next section, or close WordPad and shut down your system as described in Section 1-2.

2-4 EXPLORING MENUS

To use Windows and all Windows applications, you have to understand menus that list choices available to you. It is with these choices that you execute commands. There are several types of menus, including pull-down menus, shortcut menus, and cascading menus.

Pull-Down Menus

A *menu bar*, one of the most common forms of a menu, is a special area displayed across the top of a window directly below the title bar. A menu bar includes a number of *menu names*. Each menu name provides access to a *pull-down menu* composed of a collection of *menu items* or choices. Horizontal separator bars sometimes separate related commands into groups. Some of the commands may appear dim at times. This tells you that these commands cannot be executed from where you are in the procedure.

QUICKSTEPS

Displaying and Closing Pull-Down Menus

Using a Mouse

▶ To pull down a menu, click its name on the menu bar.

▶ To choose a command from a pulled-down menu, click the command.

▶ To close a menu without choosing a command, point to another menu to pull it down or click anywhere outside of the menu or menu bar.

Using the Keyboard

▶ To pull down a menu, hold down Alt while you press the underlined letter in the menu's name.

▶ To choose a command from a pulled-down menu, press the underlined letter in the command's name.

▶ To close a menu without choosing a command, press Esc once to hide the menu and again to remove the highlight from the menu bar.

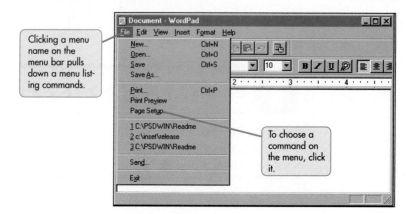

Clicking a menu name on the menu bar pulls down a menu listing commands.

To choose a command on the menu, click it.

Shortcut Menus

Shortcut menus are menus that pop up when you right-click an object such as a selected part of a document. These menus list the commands most frequently used with the object you click.

T U T O R I A L

In this tutorial you explore both shortcut and pull-down menus using Windows' built-in WordPad application.

Getting Ready

1. If WordPad isn't open, start Windows as described in Section 1-1 and start WordPad as described in Section 2-1's tutorial Steps 11-14.

2. Click WordPad's **Maximize** button if the window isn't maximized.

Using a Shortcut Menu

3. Right-click in the blank document area to display a shortcut menu.

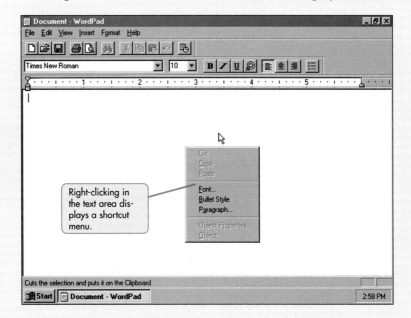

Right-clicking in the text area displays a shortcut menu.

4. Click the **Bullet Style** command to turn it on, and a bullet appears on the top line where the insertion point is positioned.

5. Type your name and press Enter↵ to display a bullet on the next line.

6. Type the name of your course and press Enter↵ to display a bullet on the next line.

7. Click the **Date/Time** button on the toolbar to display a list of date and time formats.

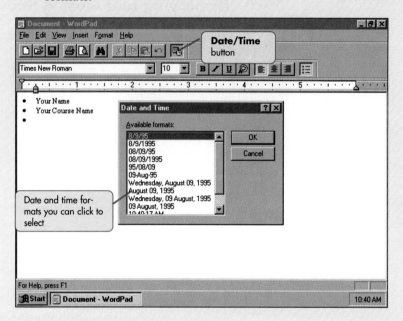

8. Click the date in the format *Month day, year* (it will read today's date—for example, November 10, 1997).

9. Click the **OK** button and then press Enter↵ to move the insertion point to the next line.

10. Right-click in the blank document area to display the shortcut menu again.

11. Click the **Bullet Style** command to turn it off and the bullet on the line where the insertion point is positioned is removed.

Using Pull-Down Menus

12. Click the **View** menu to pull it down, then click the **Toolbar** command to turn it off. The toolbar is no longer displayed.

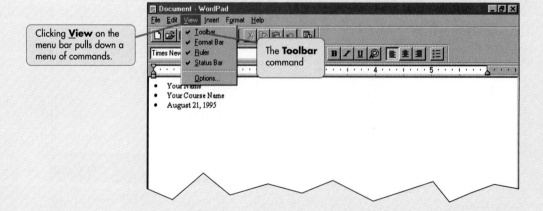

13. Click the **View** menu to pull it down, then click the **Ruler** command to turn it off. The ruler is no longer displayed. The ruler, when displayed, can be used to set tab stops and change paragraph indents.

14. Click the **View** menu to pull it down, then click the **Toolbar** command to turn it back on.

15. Click the **View** menu to pull it down, then click the **Ruler** command to turn it back on.

Finishing Up

16. Click WordPad's **Close** button to close the application. When a message box asks if you want to *Save changes to Document?*, click the **No** button.

17. Continue to the next section, or shut down your system as described in Section 1-2.

2-5 EXPLORING DIALOG BOXES

To use Windows and all Windows applications, you have to understand how to specify options in *dialog boxes* that appear for many commands. Dialog boxes allow you to make choices and provide the information needed to carry out a particular command or task.

There are many different dialog boxes, but each is made up of elements that include boxes into which you enter text, lists from which you can choose items, and check boxes or buttons that you click to turn options on or off. Many of the commands have already been set (although you can change them). These settings are either default settings built into the program or are remembered from a previous session.

Help

When executing commands, dialog boxes often offer many choices. When the dialog box is displayed, there are ways to find out what each of these choices does. This allows you to quickly learn more about the program and make more informed choices.

Q U I C K S T E P S

Dialog Box Help

▶ Click the question mark button (?) on the title bar, then click an object to display a pop-up description of it. To close the pop-up description box, click anywhere.

▶ Right-click the item in question to display a shortcut menu, then click the *What's this* command to display a pop-up description of the object. To close the pop-up description box, click anywhere.

▶ Click a **Help** button to display Help on the currently selected element.

▶ Press F1 to display Help on the currently selected element.

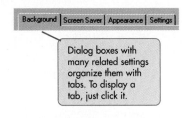

Dialog boxes with many related settings organize them with tabs. To display a tab, just click it.

Tabs

Many dialog boxes contain more than one group of settings. These dialog boxes feature tabs that you click to display the settings you want to check or change.

Buttons and Check Boxes

Dialog boxes contain three types of buttons: command buttons, option buttons, and check boxes.

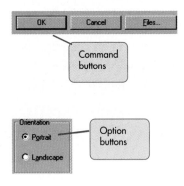

Command buttons

Option buttons

▸ *Command buttons* execute commands when you click them. Dialog boxes normally include **OK** and **Cancel** command buttons. The **OK** button applies the current settings in the dialog box and closes the window. Your latest settings are then preserved for subsequent openings of the dialog box while the application is running. The **Cancel** button ignores changes and closes the box, canceling the operation the you chose.

▸ *Option buttons* offer mutually exclusive choices. They are sometimes called *radio buttons* because, like a car radio where you select stations by pressing one of a series of buttons, only one can be on at a time. The one that is on contains a black dot (◉). If you click a button that is off (○), it is turned on and any other option button in the group that is on is turned off.

Check boxes

▸ *Check boxes* offer nonexclusive options. More than one of them can be on at the same time. To turn them on or off, you click them. Those with a check mark in them are on.

Boxes and Lists

Dialog boxes may contain a number of boxes into which you type text or select items from lists. A few of the more common ones are described and illustrated here but there are many variations of each. However, understanding the ones described here will allow you to figure out any of the variations you encounter.

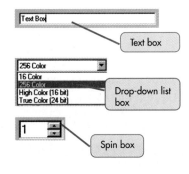

Text box

Drop-down list box

Spin box

▸ *Text boxes* contain space for typing data. When empty, you click in them to move the insertion point into them. When they already contain text, you can edit it, as explained in the Quicksteps box "Editing Text in a Text Box" on page 49. A variation of the text box is the combo box that combines a text box and a list box.

▸ *Drop-down list boxes* display an arrow (▾) that you click to drop-down a list of choices. The currently selected choice is displayed in the box when it is closed.

▸ *Spin boxes* display a value that you can increase or decrease by clicking the spin buttons ◆.

Scroll Bars

Some lists are too long to be displayed in their entirety. When this happens, a scroll bar appears next to the list. A *vertical scroll bar* is located on the right edge of the list, and a *horizontal scroll bar* is located on the bottom edge.

A vertical scroll bar contains three basic elements: the *up scroll arrow* (▲), the *down scroll arrow* (▾), and the *scroll box* (☐). A horizontal scroll bar contains the same three elements, but its scroll arrows are left and right.

You scroll a list by clicking the scroll arrows or by dragging the scroll box. The scroll box (☐) serves three functions:

Editing Text in a Text Box

▶ If the text box already has an entry, the entire entry will be selected when you double-click in the text box. The first character you type deletes this previous entry. To edit the entry instead, click in the box to remove the highlight, and then position the insertion point.

▶ To insert characters in an existing entry, click with the mouse to position the *insertion point* (a flashing vertical bar) where you want to insert text, and type them in. The characters to the right move aside to make room for the new characters as you type them in.

▶ To delete a character to the left of the insertion point, press `←Bksp`. To delete a character to the right of the insertion point, press `Delete` Holding down either of these keys deletes characters one after another.

▶ To delete a word and the space that follows it, double-click the word and then press `Delete`

▶ To delete adjacent characters or words, move the insertion point to the left of a character, hold down the left mouse button, drag the highlight over adjoining text to select it, and then release the mouse button. (Holding down `⇧Shift` while you press an arrow key also extends the selection.) When the text is selected, press `Delete`to delete it.

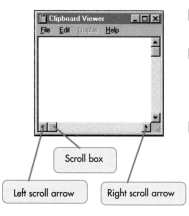

Scroll box

Left scroll arrow   Right scroll arrow

▶ When you drag it up or down the vertical scroll bar with the mouse, you move quickly to any point in a list.

▶ The scroll box also indicates where you are in a list. If it is at the top of the scroll bar, you are at the top of the list. If it is at the bottom of the scroll bar, you are at the bottom of the list. If it is halfway between the top and bottom of the scroll bar, you are at the middle of the list.

▶ The size of the scroll box varies to reflect the difference between what is visible in the window and the entire content of the list. For example, it is small when only a small portion of the list can be displayed at one time, and large when a large portion can be displayed. Basically, the longer the list, the smaller the scroll box.

Scrolling a List with the Scroll Bar

▶ To scroll the contents of the window a line at a time, click one of the scroll arrows.

▶ To continuously scroll the contents of the window, point to one of the scroll arrows and hold down the mouse button.

▶ To scroll one screen at a time, click the scroll bar above or below the scroll box.

▶ To scroll to a specific place in the list, drag the scroll box to where you want to move, and then release it.

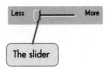

The slider

Slider Bars

Slider bars are like the heater or air conditioning control in many automobiles. As you drag them from one end of the scale to another, you increase or decrease the setting.

IN this tutorial you explore dialog boxes. Not all of the elements discussed in this section appear in any one dialog box but the practice you have here should allow you to use any element when you encounter it.

Getting Ready

1. Start Windows as described in Section 1-1 and start WordPad as described in Section 2-1's tutorial Steps 11-14.

2. Click WordPad's **Maximize** button if the window isn't maximized.

3. Type your name and press [Enter ↵].

Selecting Your Name

4. Pull down WordPad's **Edit** menu and click the **Select All** command to select the characters in the document.

Changing Fonts

5. Pull down the **Format** menu and click the **Font** command to display the Font dialog box.

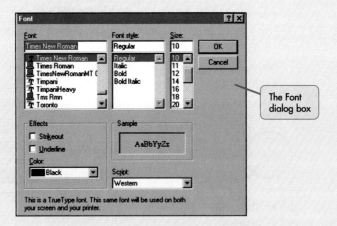

The Font dialog box

6. Use the scroll bar to scroll the **Font** list to find and click the font named *Arial* to select it. (Fonts are listed alphabetically.)

7. Use the scroll bar to scroll the **Size** list to find and select the font size *36*.

8. Click the **Underline** check box to turn it on.

9. Click the **OK** command button to close the dialog box and apply the selected font.

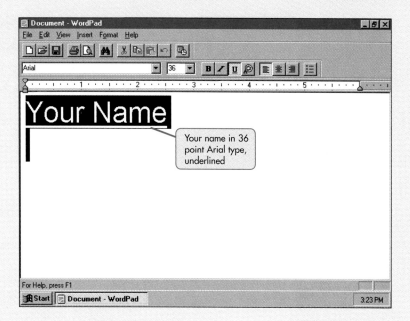

Your name in 36 point Arial type, underlined

Changing Alignment

10. Pull down the **Format** menu and click the **Paragraph** command to display the Paragraph dialog box.

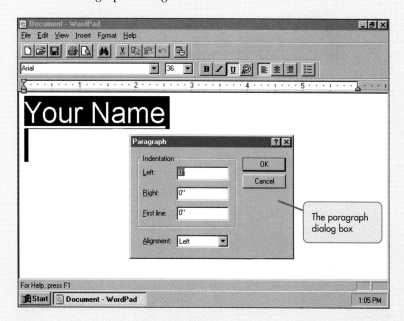

The paragraph dialog box

11. Click the **Alignment** drop-down arrow to display a list and click *Center* to select it.

12. Click the **OK** command button to close the dialog box and apply the selected alignment.

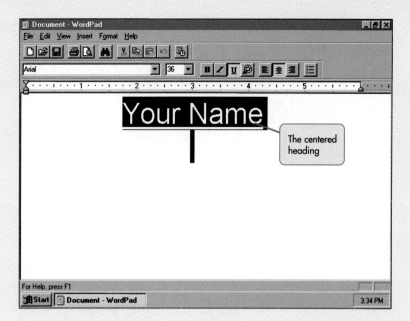

The centered heading

Changing Orientation

13. Pull down the **File** menu and click the **Page Setup** command to display the Page Setup dialog box.

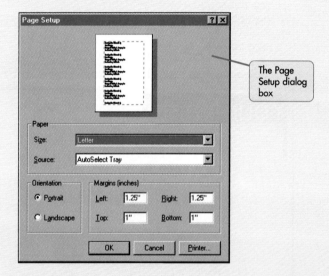

The Page Setup dialog box

14. Click the **Landscape** option button. Notice how when it turns on, the **Portrait** option button turns off—only one can be on at a time. The small graphic at the top of the dialog box illustrates the difference between portrait and landscape modes.

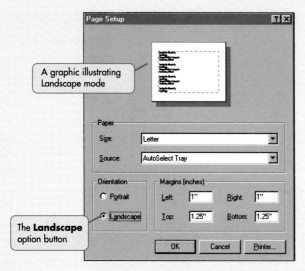

A graphic illustrating Landscape mode

The **Landscape** option button

15. Click the dialog box's **Cancel** button to close it.

Finishing Up

16. Click WordPad's **Close** button to close the application. When a message box asks if you want to *Save changes to Document?*, click the **No** button.

17. Continue to the next section, or shut down your system as described in Section 1-2.

2-6 MANAGING MULTIPLE WINDOWS

Since you can have a number of applications open at the same time, sometimes windows get in the way of each other. The active application always appears on top of the other application windows, partially or entirely covering them. In these cases, there are a number of procedures you can use to organize the windows on the desktop so you can see more than one.

Switching Between Applications

When more than one application program is open at the same time, only one of them can be active at a time. You can tell which is active because its title bar is a different color and its button on the taskbar appears to be depressed. You can quickly switch among open applications just by clicking the button on the taskbar of the one you want to use.

T I P
Buttons on the Taskbar

When a number of windows are open, the taskbar may become filled with buttons. In these cases, the buttons may be reduced in size. If the name of a button is not displayed completely, point to it with the mouse and the name of the application and its document will be displayed in a small box.

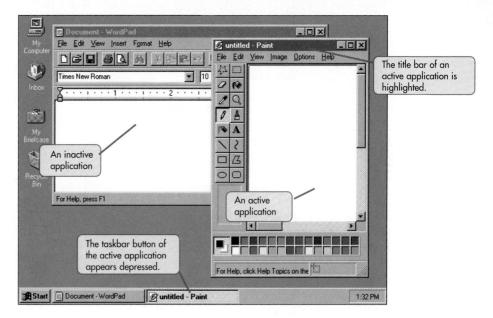

The title bar of an active application is highlighted.

An inactive application

An active application

The taskbar button of the active application appears depressed.

Arranging Windows

When more than one application program is open, you can arrange their windows so they overlap one another or are side by side or above one another. You can even minimize them all with a single command so they appear only as buttons on the taskbar.

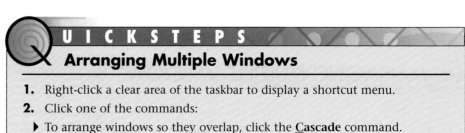

QUICKSTEPS

Arranging Multiple Windows

1. Right-click a clear area of the taskbar to display a shortcut menu.
2. Click one of the commands:
   ▶ To arrange windows so they overlap, click the **Cascade** command.
   ▶ To arrange windows above one another, click the **Tile Horizontally** command.
   ▶ To arrange windows side by side, click the **Tile Vertically** command.
   ▶ To minimize all windows, click the **Minimize All Windows** command.

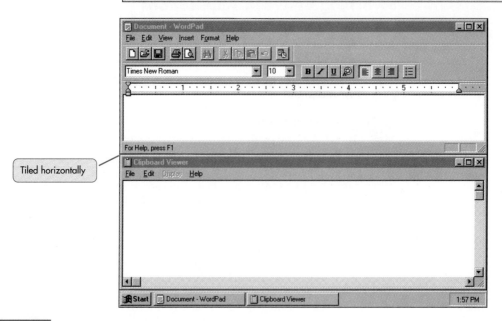

Tiled horizontally

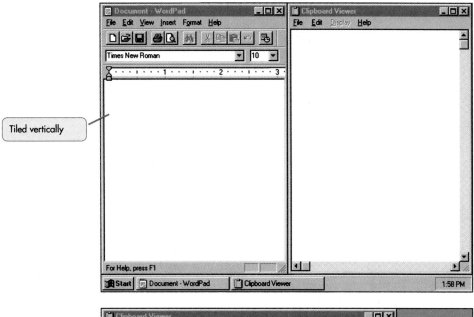

Tiled vertically

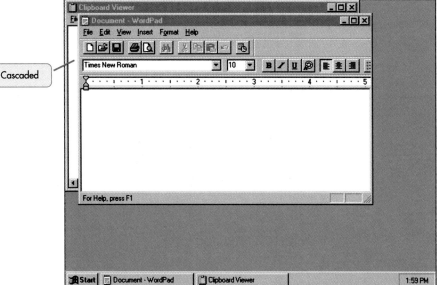

Cascaded

Sizing Windows

When you first open a window or click its **Restore** button, it takes a specific size and shape on the screen. How do you change this original size permanently? You do so by dragging one of the window's borders or corners.

▶ Dragging the top, bottom, or side borders changes the window's size in a single direction.

▶ Dragging one of the corners changes the shape and size in two directions at the same time.

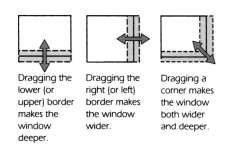

Dragging the lower (or upper) border makes the window deeper.

Dragging the right (or left) border makes the window wider.

Dragging a corner makes the window both wider and deeper.

UICKSTEPS
Sizing Windows

1. Click the window's **Restore** button if it's maximized so you can see the borders.

2. Point with the mouse to a border or corner so that the mouse pointer turns into a two-headed arrow.

3. Hold down the left mouse button and drag the border or corner to make the window larger or smaller. On some systems, the window itself changes size as you drag. On other systems, an outline of the window temporarily indicates its new size.

4. Release the mouse button.

Dragging Windows

In addition to dragging a window's borders, you can also drag the entire window using its title bar and drop it into a new position.

UICKSTEPS
Moving Windows

1. Click the window's **Restore** button if it's maximized so it doesn't fill the screen.

2. Point with the mouse to a window's title bar.

3. Hold down the left mouse button and drag the window to a new position. On some systems, the window itself moves as you drag it. On other systems, an outline of the window temporarily indicates its new position.

4. Release the mouse button to drop the window.

TUTORIAL

IN this tutorial you start two applications and then manage their windows on your desktop. You cascade them, tile them, and practice dragging the borders and corners to change their size and shape. You then drag and drop a window to move it to a new position.

Getting Ready

1. Start Windows as described in Section 1-1 and start WordPad and Clipboard Viewer as described in Section 2-1's tutorial Steps 11-14 and 16-20.

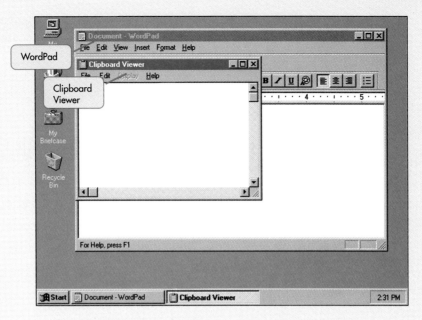

Switching Between Application Programs

2. Click the **WordPad** button on the taskbar to make that the active window.

3. Click the **Clipboard Viewer** button on the taskbar to make that the active window.

Cascading, Tiling, and Minimizing Windows

4. Right-click a clear area of the taskbar, then click the shortcut menu's **Cascade** command.

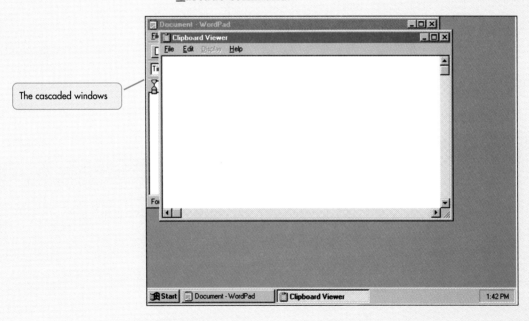

The cascaded windows

5. Right-click a clear area of the taskbar, then click the shortcut menu's **Tile Horizontally** command.

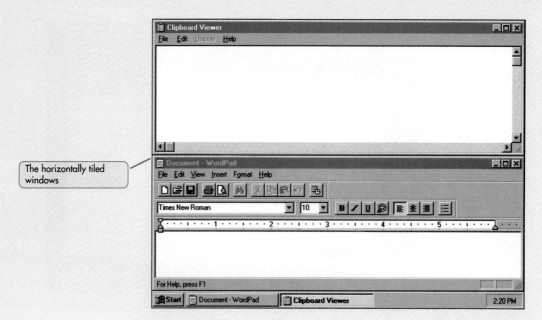

The horizontally tiled windows

6. Right-click a clear area of the taskbar, then click the shortcut menu's **Tile Vertically** command.

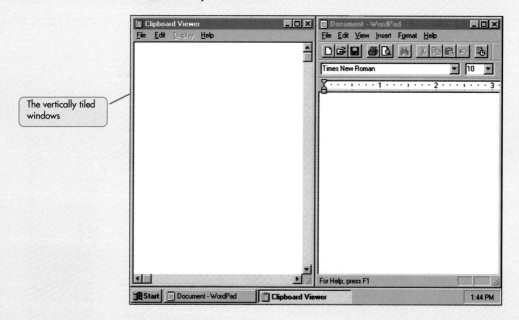

The vertically tiled windows

7. Right-click a clear area of the taskbar, then click the shortcut menu's **Minimize All Windows** command.

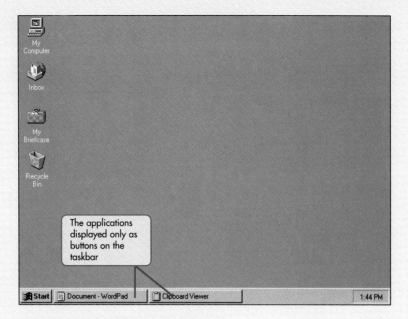

The applications displayed only as buttons on the taskbar

Changing a Window's Width

8. Click the **WordPad** button on the taskbar to make that the active window. (Click its **Restore** button if it has been maximized.)

9. Point to one of the side borders of the WordPad window so the mouse pointer turns into a horizontal two-headed arrow.

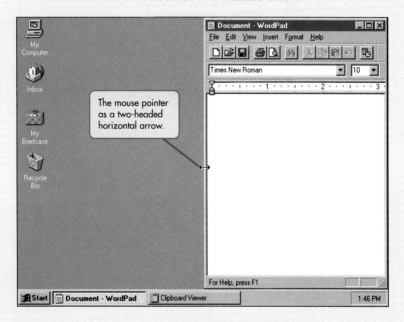

The mouse pointer as a two-headed horizontal arrow.

10. Hold down the left mouse button and drag the window's border wider or narrower. On some systems, the window itself changes size as you drag. On other systems, an outline of the window temporarily indicates its new size.

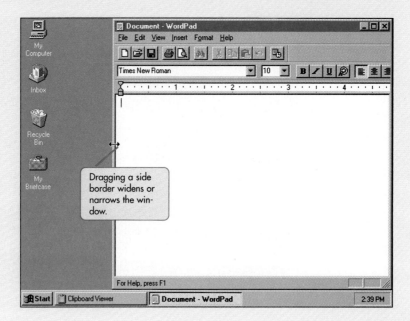

Dragging a side border widens or narrows the window.

11. Release the button and the window takes the new size or fills the outline.

Changing a Window's Height

12. Point to the bottom border of the WordPad window so the mouse pointer turns into a vertical two-headed arrow.

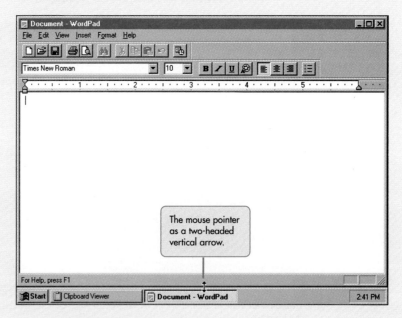

The mouse pointer as a two-headed vertical arrow.

13. Hold down the left mouse button and drag the window's border so it or its outline is shorter. (If you find you are dragging the taskbar wider, press [Esc] before releasing the mouse button, then try again.)

14. Release the button and the window takes the new size or fills the outline.

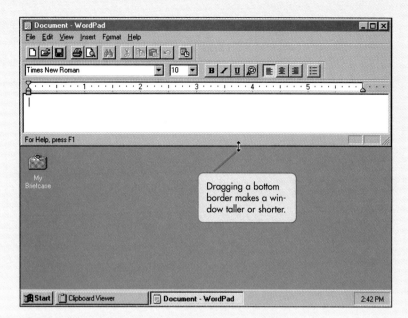

Dragging a bottom border makes a window taller or shorter.

Changing a Window's Width and Height

15. Point to one of the corners of the WordPad window so the mouse pointer turns into a diagonal two-headed arrow.

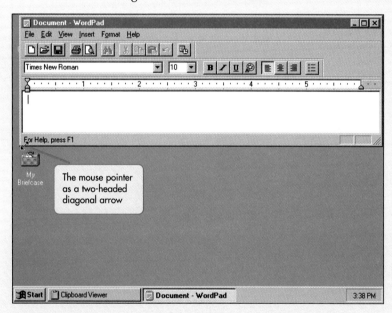

The mouse pointer as a two-headed diagonal arrow

16. Hold down the left mouse button and drag the window so it, or its outline, is narrower and shorter. (Dragging diagonally—toward or away from the center of the window—changes the size in two directions at the same time.)

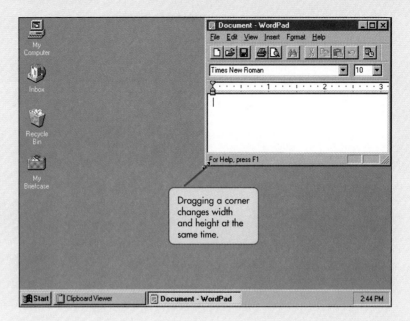

Dragging a corner changes width and height at the same time.

17. Release the button and the window takes the new size or fills the outline.

Dragging and Dropping a Window

18. Point to WordPad's title bar and hold down the left mouse button.

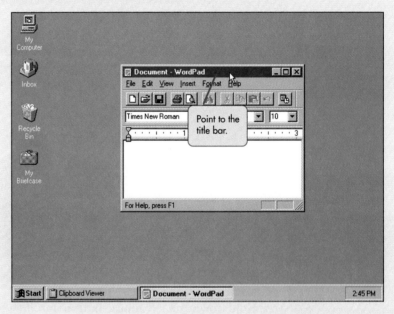

Point to the title bar.

19. Drag the window to a new position and release the mouse button to drop the window into a new position. On some systems, the window itself moves as you drag it. On other systems, an outline of the window temporarily indicates its new position.

PAUSING FOR PRACTICE

Sizing and dragging windows is one of the basic skills you must master to use Windows. Pause here to practice changing the shape, size, and position of the WordPad window until you have mastered these skills.

Finishing Up

20. Continue to the next section, or close WordPad and Clipboard Viewer and shut down your system as described in Section 1-2.

2-7 COPYING DATA BETWEEN APPLICATIONS

What if you wanted to put a table you created with a spreadsheet program into a report you were creating with a word processing program? The easiest way to do it is to copy it.

THE CLIPBOARD VIEWER

To copy data from one application to another, you first copy it to the Clipboard, switch to the other application, and paste it in. The data is pasted into the application in a format that the application recognizes. The data you copied or cut to the Clipboard remains there until you cut or copy other data or shut down Windows. For this reason you can paste it into more than one place.

Normally there is no need to see data on the Clipboard, but a Clipboard Viewer is supplied in case you want to. As you have seen, it is started from the Accessories folder—the same place where WordPad and other applications supplied with Windows 95 are stored.

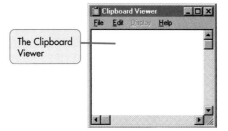

The Clipboard Viewer

Q U I C K S T E P S

Copying Data Between Applications

1. Select the data in one application, and use the **Cut** or **Copy** buttons on the toolbar or the **Cut** or **Copy** commands on the **Edit** menu to move the data to the Clipboard.

2. Click in the other application's document where you want to copy or move the material and click the **Paste** button on the toolbar or the **Paste** command on the **Edit** menu to paste it in.

THE CHARACTER MAP

One application designed specifically to copy from is Character Map. This application displays a grid or palette of characters that you can select and copy. When you copy them, they are stored on the Clipboard so you can paste them into any other application.

The Character Map application is started from the Accessories folder—the same place where Clipboard Viewer, WordPad, and other applications supplied with Windows 95 are stored.

The Character Map application

QUICKSTEPS

Using Character Map

1. Click the **Start** button on the taskbar to display the Start menu, point to the **Programs** folder, then to the **Accessories** folder to cascade a submenu. Click the **Character Map** application program to start it.

2. Use any of the following commands:
   ▶ To display a set of characters from another font, click the **Font** drop-down arrow and select the font from the list of fonts on your system.
   ▶ To enlarge a character so you can see it better, point to it on the grid and hold down the left mouse button.
   ▶ To select a character, double-click it or click it and then click the **Select** button.
   ▶ To copy a selected character to the Clipboard, click the **Copy** button.

TUTORIAL

In this tutorial you open three applications: WordPad, Clipboard Viewer, and Character Map. You then arrange their windows and see how data is copied from one application to another using the Clipboard.

Getting Ready

1. If WordPad and Clipboard Viewer aren't open, start Windows as described in Section 1-1 and start WordPad and Clipboard Viewer as described in Section 2-1's tutorial Steps 11-14 and 16-20.

2. If either WordPad or Clipboard Viewer is minimized, click its button on the toolbar so both are open.

Starting Character Map

3. Click the **Start** button on the taskbar to display the Start menu, then point to the **Programs** folder, then to the **Accessories** folder to cascade a submenu.

4. Click the **Character Map** application program to start it. This application is used to copy special characters into documents of all kinds.

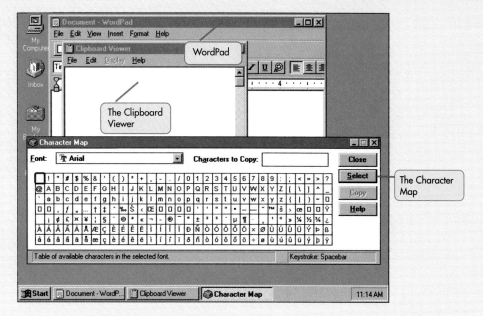

The Clipboard Viewer

WordPad

The Character Map

Arranging Application Windows

5. Right-click a clear area of the taskbar, then click the shortcut menu's **Cascade** command. If the Character Map isn't the top application, click its button on the taskbar.

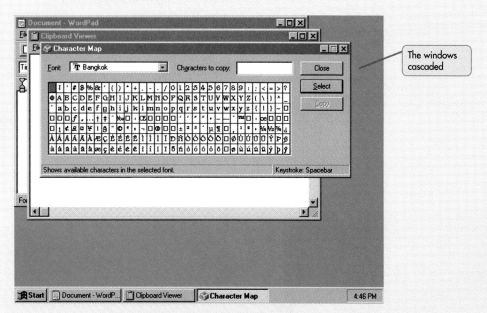

The windows cascaded

Copying Characters Using the Clipboard Viewer

6. Click the Character Map's **Font** drop-down arrow and use the scroll bar to locate and select the font named *Arial*. The grid now displays all of the characters in that font.

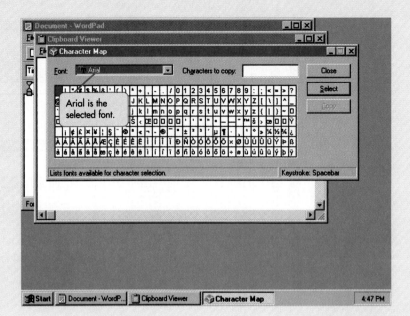

Arial is the selected font.

7. Double-click the copyright symbol (©) on the grid to select it and move it to the box labeled *Characters to copy:*.

8. Click the Character Map's **Copy** button and you see the selected character appear on the Clipboard Viewer. If it's hidden, click the Clipboard Viewer's button on the taskbar.

9. Click WordPad's button on the taskbar to make it the active application.

10. Click in WordPad's window where you enter text and click the **Paste** button on the toolbar. The character is copied from the Clipboard into the document.

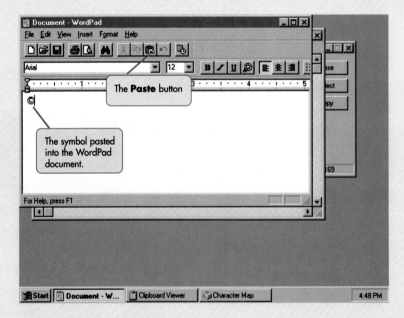

The **Paste** button

The symbol pasted into the WordPad document.

Copying Graphics Using the Clipboard Viewer

11. Press PrtScr on the keyboard and then click Clipboard Viewer's button on the taskbar to see an image of the screen displayed in the Clipboard Viewer's window.

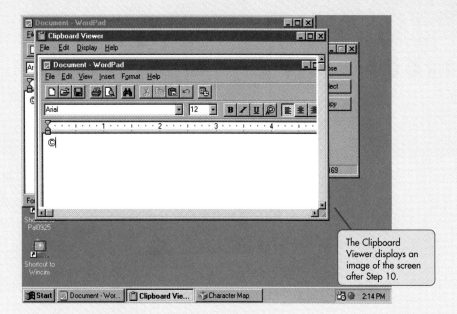

The Clipboard Viewer displays an image of the screen after Step 10.

12. Click WordPad's button on the taskbar, then press ⌷Enter↵⌷ a few times to insert blank lines in the WordPad document.

13. Click WordPad's **Paste** button on the toolbar. The graphic displayed on the Clipboard Viewer is pasted into the document. Maximize WordPad's window and scroll the document to see the copyright symbol and the graphic.

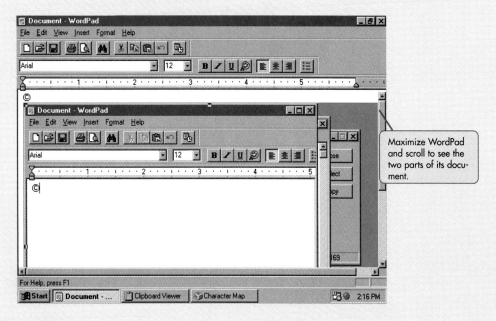

Maximize WordPad and scroll to see the two parts of its document.

Finishing Up

14. Close all open windows. When closing Wordpad, when prompted to *Save changes to Document?*, click the **No** button. Continue to the lab activities, or shut down your system as described in Section 1-2.

INTRODUCTION TO APPLICATIONS

VISUAL QUIZ

1. Here are the menus you would display to start the WordPad application.

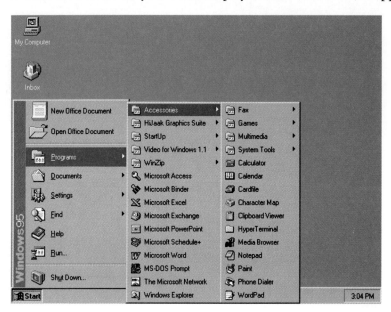

a. List the steps you would follow to get to this point.

_____

_____

_____

_____

_____

b. Write down the names of four applications other than WordPad listed on the Accessories menu.

_____

_____

_____

_____

c. Write down the names of four folders that will cascade when you point to them.

_____

_____

_____

_____

2. There is more than one way to close an application window. Briefly describe ways you can close one using the labeled items in this illustration.

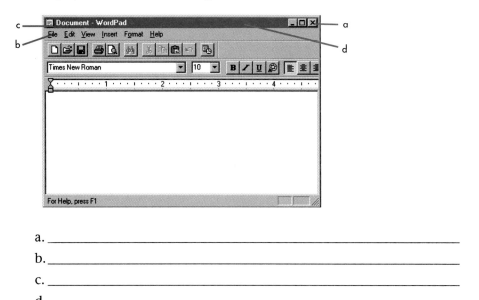

a. _____

b. _____

c. _____

d. _____

3. Name and briefly describe each of the window parts indicated here.

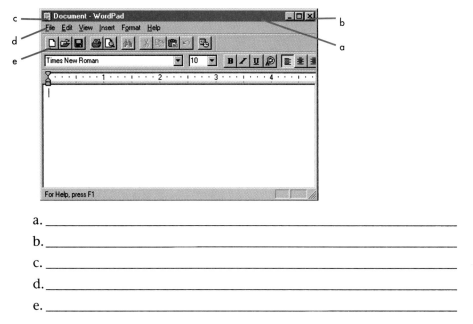

a. _____

b. _____

c. _____

d. _____

e. _____

4. For each of these buttons, write down the name and what happens when you click it.

a. Name: _____ What happens: _____

b. Name: _____ What happens: _____

c. Name: _____ What happens: _____

d. Name: _____ What happens: _____

5. This figure shows a menu. What kind of menu is it?

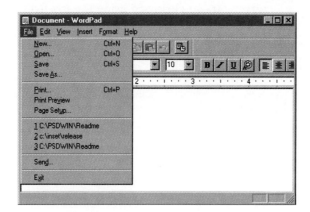

   a. How was it displayed?

   _____

   b. What does the underlined character in the menu's name indicate?

   _____

   c. What do the underlined characters in the menu's commands indicate?

   _____

   d. How would you close it without selecting a command?

   _____

6. This figure shows a menu. What kind of menu is it?

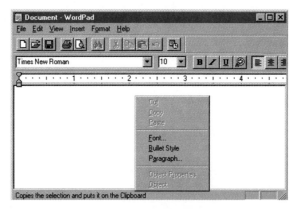

   _____

   a. How was it displayed?

   _____

   b. How would you close it without selecting a command?

   _____

7. For each of these dialog box elements, write down the name and what happens when you click (or drag) it.

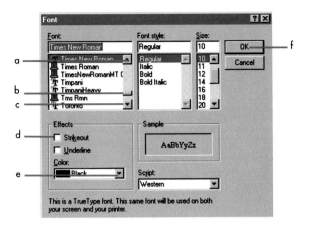

a. Name: _____ What happens: _____

b. Name: _____ What happens: _____

c. Name: _____ What happens: _____

d. Name: _____ What happens: _____

e. Name: _____ What happens: _____

f. Name: _____ What happens: _____

8. Indicate the name of each of these elements of a dialog box.

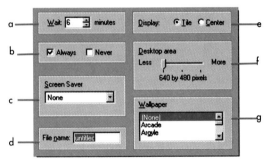

a. _____

b. _____

c. _____

d. _____

e. _____

f. _____

g. _____

9. Here is a screen with two applications open. Describe how you do each of the following procedures.

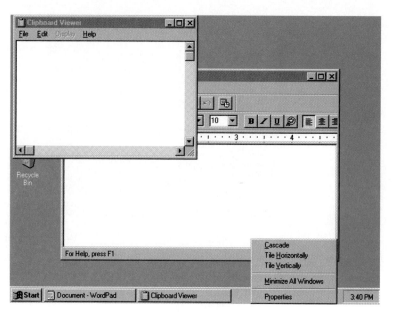

a. How do you display the shortcut menu shown in the lower-right corner of the screen?

_____

b. Which application is the active one?

_____

c. How do you switch between the two applications?

_____

d. How do you minimize both at the same time?

_____

10. Here is an illustration of the Character Map application.

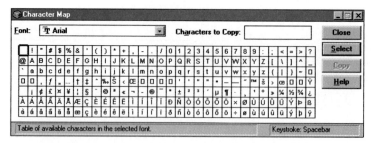

a. How do you enlarge one of the characters so you can see it better?

_____

b. What are two ways you can select a character?

_____

c. How do you copy a selected character to the Clipboard?

_____

d. How could you view the current contents of the Clipboard?

_____

REVIEW QUESTIONS

TRUE-FALSE

T F **1.** To work on a specific type of application, you use an application program.

T F **2.** To be computer literate you must be able to explain in detail how a computer's parts operate.

T F **3.** The terms *application program, program,* and *application* are never used interchangeably.

T F **4.** Windows' sole function is to make the screen pretty.

T F **5.** You can run only one application program at a time with Windows.

T F **6.** Windows includes no application programs so you must buy them all separately.

T F **7.** To start an application, you begin by clicking the **Start** button and then the **Programs** folder.

T F **8.** To start an application once you locate it, you must double-click its name or icon.

T F **9.** Pointing to a folder listed on the Start menu opens it to display its contents.

T F **10.** An arrowhead (▶) on the Start menu indicates that pointing to that item cascades the menu.

T F **11.** A cascaded menu "cascades out" from another menu.

T F **12.** The only way to close an application window is to click the **Close** button on its title bar.

T F **13.** If you close an application without saving text you have entered, a prompt asks if you want to *Save changes to Document?*

T F **14.** The **Maximize** and **Minimize** buttons display the window so it fills the screen or reduce it to a button on the taskbar.

T F **15.** The **Restore** button is displayed only after you have clicked the **Minimize** button.

T F **16.** Application windows almost always display a menu bar and a toolbar.

T F **17.** The only way to pull down a menu from the menu bar is to click it.

T F **18.** To choose a menu command, you double-click it.

T F **19.** To close a menu without making a choice, you click it again.

T F **20.** To display a shortcut menu, you right-click an object on the screen.

T F **21.** To scroll with the scroll bar, you can drag the scroll box to a new position and then release it.

T F **22.** To choose a command button, you just click it.

T F **23.** The flashing vertical line in a text box indicates where the next character that you type will appear.

T F **24.** You turn check boxes and option buttons on and off by clicking them.

T F **25.** Only one option button can be on at a time. When you turn one on, the other automatically turns off.

T F **26.** When you run more than one application, only one of them can be active.

T F **27.** The active window is always the one on top of other windows when they overlap.

T F **28.** To change the size of a window, you drag the borders or corners.

T F **29.** To drag a window to a new position, you point to the **Close** button, hold down the left mouse button, and move the mouse.

T F **30.** If you have more than one window open, you can tile or cascade them.

T F **31.** Tiled windows overlap one another on the screen. Cascaded windows don't.

T F **32.** In order to copy data from one application, you must first start the Clipboard Viewer.

T F **33.** When you copy or cut data to the Clipboard, it remains there even when you copy or cut other data.

T F **34.** The Character Map application program is used to paste special characters into documents.

MULTIPLE CHOICE

1. A typical application program is __.

   a. Windows   **b.** DOS

   c. Microsoft Word   **d.** on-line Help

2. The menu that you first display to start application programs is called ___.

   a. The Start menu   **b.** The cascaded menu

   c. A shortcut menu   **d.** A pop-up menu

3. To open an application program once you have located it on the Start menu, you ___.

   a. Click its name or icon

   b. Click its icon and then pull down the **File** menu and click the **Run** command

   c. Double-click its icon

   d. Click its icon and then pull down the **File** menu and click the **Open** command

4. To close or exit an application properly, you ___.

   a. Click its **Minimize** button   **b.** Click its **Close** button

   c. Turn off the computer   **d.** None of the above

5. When you click a window's **Maximize** button, the window ___.

   a. Fills the screen

   b. Is displayed only as a button on the taskbar

   c. Returns to its original size

   d. None of the above

6. To close a window down to just a button on the taskbar, you click the ___.

   a. Menu bar   **b.** **Minimize** button

   c. **Restore** button   **d.** Icon on the title bar

7. To pull down a menu from a menu bar, you __.

    a. Press [Ctrl] and the underlined letter in the menu's name

    b. Click it with the left mouse button

    c. Double-click it

    d. Press [Tab⇆] to highlight it, and then press [Enter↵]

8. To find out what a part of a dialog box is used for, you click the ___ and then click the item.

    a. The **Help** command button   **b.** The question mark button

    c. The Help menu   **d.** Ask your lab instructor

9. Dialog boxes provide __ so you can supply information on a command.

    a. Text boxes, list boxes, option buttons, and check boxes

    b. Menus and screens of text describing options

    c. Foreign language translations

    d. A **Maximize** and **Minimize** button

10. When windows overlap on the screen, you can __.

    a. Drag them to new positions

    b. Click their buttons on the taskbar to switch between them

    c. Click the one you want to use

    d. All of the above

11. To arrange all open windows quickly, you can __.

    a. Drag and size them one by one

    b. Right-click the taskbar and select one of the commands from the shortcut menu

    c. Exit Windows and start over

    d. None of the above

12. To copy or move data from one application to another, you __.

    a. Select it in one document

    b. Cut or copy it to the Clipboard

    c. Paste it into the other document

    d. All of the above

13. When copying or moving data from one application to another, you needn't __.

    a. Display the Clipboard Viewer

    b. Cut or copy it to the Clipboard

    c. Paste it into the other document

    d. Select it before you cut or copy it

FILL IN THE BLANK

1. To work on a task, you use a(n) _____ program.

2. If you understand how to use a computer and application software to do useful work, you can consider yourself _____.

3. The first step in starting an application is to click the _____ button to display the _____ menu.

4. To start an application, you _____ its name or icon on the Start menu.

5. To quickly close an application, you click its _____.

6. Clicking the _____ button displays a window only as a button on the taskbar.

7. When a window is displayed only as a button on the taskbar, you _____ to open it.

8. To enlarge a window to fill the screen, you click the _____ button.

9. When a window fills the screen, you click the _____ button to keep it open but make it smaller.

10. You can pull down a menu by holding down _____ when you press the underlined character in its name.

11. To close a menu without making a choice, point _____ and click.

12. To scroll a list in a dialog box one line at a time, you click the _____.

13. To scroll continuously, you point to one of the _____ and hold down the left mouse button.

14. If a command button is dimmed, you _____ use it from where you are in the program.

15. To edit the entry in a text box, you move the _____ to indicate where you want to insert or delete characters.

16. When you click an option button that was previously off, any other related option button automatically turns _____.

17. When windows overlap, the one on top is the _____.

18. When you point to one of the borders of a window, the mouse pointer changes shape into _____.

19. To tile or cascade windows, you _____ to display a shortcut menu.

20. If windows are displayed side by side without overlapping, they are _____. If they overlap one another, they are _____.

21. If you want to copy a special character into a document, you start the _____ application.

22. Anything you cut or copy in an application is stored on the _____.

23. To see what is currently on the Clipboard, you start the _____.

LAB ACTIVITIES

DRILLS

2-1 Starting Application Programs

To do any useful work on a computer you have to first start an application program. In this drill you practice that procedure.

1. Click the **Start** button on the taskbar to display the Start menu, then click **Programs**, **Accessories**, **Calculator** to open that application.

2. Click the **Start** button on the taskbar to display the Start menu, then click **Programs**, **Accessories**, **NotePad** to open that application.

3. Click the **Start** button on the taskbar to display the Start menu, then click **Programs**, **Accessories**, **Paint** to open that application.

4. If you have to quit at this point, shut down Windows and all of the applications also shut down. You can also close the applications by clicking the button with an X in it at the right end of each title bar. This is called the **Close** button.

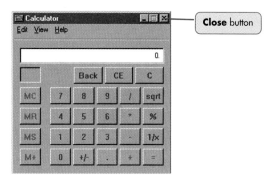

2-2 Closing Application Programs

When finished with an application, you have to know how to close it. In this drill you practice those procedures. This drill assumes that Calculator, NotePad, and Paint are open from the previous drill. If they aren't, open them as described in Drill 2-1, "Opening Application Programs."

1. Click the **Close** button to close the active application. (Its title bar is blue.)

2. Right-click the button of any application on the taskbar, and click the shortcut menu's **Close** command to close the application.

3. Right-click the title bar of the active application, and click the shortcut menu's **Close** command to close the application.

2-3 Exploring Application Programs

Almost all windows have buttons you can click to change their size. In this drill you practice using these buttons.

1. Click the **Start** button on the taskbar to display the Start menu, Then click **Programs**, **Accessories**, **WordPad** to open that application.

2. Click the **Minimize** button and then the WordPad button on the taskbar to minimize and then open the application's window. Do this a few times until you are familiar with the results of clicking each button.

3. Click the **Maximize** and **Restore** buttons to maximize and restore the application's window. Do this a few times until you are familiar with the results of clicking each button.

4. Click the application's **Close** button to close it.

2-4 Exploring Menus

To execute commands, you frequently select commands from pull-down or shortcut menus. In this drill you practice these procedures.

1. Click the **Start** button on the taskbar to display the Start menu, Then click **Programs, Accessories, WordPad** to open that application.

2. Pull-down the **View** menu and click the **Toolbar** command to turn it off. Repeat this to turn off **Format Bar, Ruler,** and **Status Bar**.

3. Use the commands on the **View** to turn back on the **Toolbar, Format Bar, Ruler,** and **Status Bar**.

4. Right-click anywhere in the text area, and click the shortcut menu's **Bullet Style** command to turn it on.

5. Right-click anywhere in the text area, and click the shortcut menu's **Bullet Style** command to turn it off.

6. Click WordPad's **Close** button to close the application. Don't save any changes when asked if you want to.

2-5 Exploring Dialog Boxes

Windows and all of its application programs frequently display dialog boxes when you execute commands. Although the options in each dialog box are unique, the way to specify choices is limited. In this drill you practice the various procedures.

1. Right-click the Windows desktop to display a shortcut menu, then click the **Properties** command to display the Display Properties dialog box.

2. Click the tabs at the top of the screen to see each of them.

3. Click the **Background** tab, then click the scroll arrows to scroll the **Pattern** list up and down.

4. Click first the **Tile**, then the **Center** option buttons to turn them on.

5. Click the **Screen Saver** tab.

6. Click the **Screen Saver** drop-down arrow to see a list of screen savers. If no screen saver is in use, click one to select it.

7. Click the **Wait** spin buttons to spin the time up and down. Leave it set at 5 when finished.

8. Click the Display Properties' **Cancel** button to close the dialog box and cancel any of the changes you made.

2-6 Managing Multiple Windows

At any time, you can drag a restored window to a new position on the desktop. In this drill you practice this procedure.

1. Click the **Start** button on the taskbar to display the Start menu, Then click **Programs, Accessories, WordPad** to open that application.

2. Click WordPad's **Restore** button to restore the application.

3. Practice dragging all four sides of the window.

4. Practice dragging all four corners of the window.

5. Practice using the title bar to move the application window.

6. Click the application's **Close** button to close it.

2-7 Copying Data Between Applications

One of the big advantages of an operating system such as Windows is the ease with which you can copy or move data between applications. Here you practice one way of doing this by copying characters from the Character Map into a WordPad document.

1. Open both the WordPad and Character Map applications.

2. Right-click a clear area on the taskbar, and then click the shortcut menu's **Tile Horizontally** command.

3. Click the Character Map's **Font** drop-down arrow and select a font.

4. Double-click any character in Character Map's grid, and then click the **Copy** button to copy it.

5. Click in WordPad's text area and click the **Paste** button to copy the character. (Depending on the font you selected, it may be the same character you selected in Character Map or another.)

6. Repeat this with other characters. To delete the previous character you copied in Character Map so it isn't copied again, double-click in the *Characters to copy* text box to select it and then press Delete

7. Click both applications' **Close** buttons to close them and don't save any changes when asked if you want to.

E X E R C I S E S

Exercise 1. Taking the Windows Tour

On some systems you can take the Windows tour.

1. Load Windows, then click the **Start** button on the taskbar to display the Start menu. Click the **Help** command to display the Help dialog box, and then click the *Contents* tab if it is not displayed.

2. Double-click *Tour: Ten minutes to using Windows*. If a message appears telling you that Windows cannot find the file or tour, or cannot run it as your system is currently set up, ask the lab instructor how to install the tour. If it is installed on your system, the *Welcome to the Windows Tour* dialog box will appear listing the opening menu.

3. Click the *Starting a Program* icon and follow the instructions that appear on the screen. Use the buttons described in the table "Buttons You'll Encounter on Your Tour." When finished, you'll return to the menu.

4. Click the *Using Help* icon and follow the instructions that appear on the screen. Use the buttons described in the table "Buttons You'll Encounter on Your Tour." When finished, you'll return to the menu to pick another topic.

5. When finished, click the **Exit** button in the upper-right corner of the screen and then click the **Exit Tour** button.

Buttons You'll Encounter on Your Tour

Menu returns you to the opening menu.
Exit ends the tour and returns you to Windows.
Show Me points out an item or demonstrates the procedure you have been asked to perform.
OK closes an open dialog box.

Exercise 2. Exploring the Basics

Windows Help has a section covering the basics of using windows and dialog boxes. In this exercise, you explore that section of Help. (Note: This is a very elusive Help topic. It is available on some systems but not on others, and the author has been unable to determine why this is so. If you have it on your system, enjoy this exercise. If you don't, just continue on to the next exercise.)

1. Display the **Start** menu and click the **Help** command.
2. On the Help dialog box, select the *Index* tab, then look for and display **basic skills**.
3. Explore each of the topics and then close the window.

Exercise 3. Building Your Skills Playing Solitaire

Windows comes with several built-in games. Although they are enjoyable to play, the primary purpose for including these in Windows is to let you practice pointing and clicking.

The game of Solitaire is normally played by one person using a deck of cards. Using Windows, you play the game electronically. As you do so, you are able to build pointing and clicking skills with the mouse, selecting commands from menus, responding to options presented to you in dialog boxes, and using on-line help.

1. To open Solitaire, click the **Start** button on the taskbar to display the Start menu. Then select **Programs**, **Accessories**, **Games**, and finally **Solitaire**.

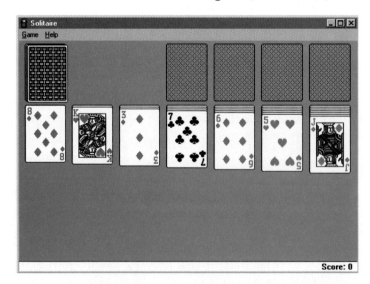

2. To learn the rules of the game, pull down Solitaire's **Help** menu and click the **Help Topics** command. Now click *How to play Solitaire* to select it, then click the **Display** button to display a Help screen listing the rules of Solitaire. Pull down the **Options** button and click the **Print Topic** command to print the rules of the game. Close the Help window.
3. Play the game using what you have learned.
4. Click the Solitaire window's **Close** button to close the window.

PICTORIAL THREE

EXPLORING YOUR SYSTEM

After completing this topic, you will be able to:

▶ **Explore your system with My Computer**
▶ **Explore your system with Windows Explorer**
▶ **Change the way documents, folders, and drives are displayed**
▶ **Change the selected drive and folder**
▶ **Find documents and folders**
▶ **View the contents of documents**
▶ **Display the properties of documents and other files**

A PPLICATION programs are stored on the disk in a digital form called a *file*. All the data you create in your computer is stored in a type of file called a *document*. A disk can easily have hundreds or even thousands of files and documents stored on it—each with a unique name. To make documents and other files easier to find and manage, you divide the disk into *folders* so related files and documents can be stored together. One of the basic skills you need to master is locating folders and documents on your disk drives. To help you do so, Windows provides two applications to explore and manage your system: My Computer and Windows Explorer.

▶ My Computer has been designed specifically for beginners to make it easier for them to explore their systems.

▶ Windows Explorer gives a more traditional and more powerful view of the system.

You'll find that these tools give you two different ways to look at the disks, folders, documents, application programs, and other files—often referred to with the all-encompassing term *objects*. However, once you have located the object that you want to use, the two tools work the same way. As you'll see in this and the next PicTorial, you use identical procedures to manage these objects. ▶

T I P
What's in a Name

If you have any previous experience with computers, you probably already know how fluid the language is. In this opening section alone, a number of new terms, or usages, were introduced.

▶ Until recently the word *data* was used as a plural, so you always said *data are*, not *data is*. The singular form was *datum*. However, recently it has become customary to use the term *data* as both a plural and a singular.

▶ Over the past few years Microsoft, the developer of the Windows program, has worked toward changing the name *file* to *document*. When you create and save a letter, budget, or list of names and addresses, you now call the digital copy saved on the disk a document. Previously you would have called it a file. However, there are still *files*. Application programs, utilities, and other programs are stored in files.

▶ With the introduction of Windows 95, Microsoft has dropped the previously used name *directory* and replaced it with the friendlier *folder*.

▶ You can perform the same procedures on a variety of items such as disks, folders, documents, application programs, or files. For example, you can copy, rename, or delete any of them. Therefore, it's simpler in discussions to use a single generic term to refer to all of them as a class. The term now being used is *object*, which can mean any and all of these items.

During the transition period, as people become comfortable with these new terms, you'll find all in common usage and none is really wrong.

3-1 MY COMPUTER—A FIRST LOOK

Most computer systems you work on will have more than one disk drive. If a system has been used or set up by an experienced person, related documents and other files will be stored together in folders. The amount of information stored on the drives can be enormous. Finding it can also be a challenge—the biggest challenge for many new users.

A new hard disk is like a file drawer. It has lots of room for files but no organization.

You can divide the hard disk into folders, which is like dividing the file drawer with hanging folders.

If you want, you can then subdivide the folders into smaller subfolders, which is like dividing the hanging folders with manila folders.

You can save files in any of these folders or subfolders the same way you would file a document in one of the hanging or manila folders.

Disks, Folders, and Documents

The developers of Windows 95 spent a great deal of effort making it as easy as possible to locate the objects you want to use. The result is a program called *My Computer*. Whenever Windows is on the screen, My Computer's icon is on the desktop. You double-click this icon to open and search through the drives and folders on your system, open the Control Panel to change settings, or open a folder with information about your system's printers. When you open a drive or folder, its contents are displayed in a new window.

The icon on the desktop

Menu bar

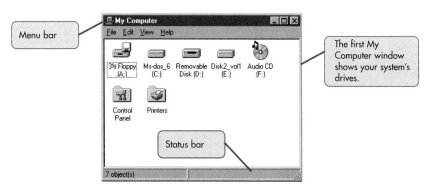

The first My Computer window shows your system's drives.

Status bar

The contents of folders vary. The first window you'll see when you start *My Computer* displays icons for both local and remote drives (remote drives are those located elsewhere on a network). Also listed are the Control Panel folder (used to change system settings) and the Printers folder (used to check and control the status of jobs being printed). When you open a drive, you may see more folders. Those folders may contain application programs, documents, or more folders—folders within folders—or they may be empty.

As you use My Computer to explore a system, you may find you have opened the wrong folder. If this happens, you can easily close the folder's window and "back up" to the window displaying the folder that contained it. From there you can open another folder. It's like taking the wrong fork when driving a car—you can back up to the intersection and take the right fork. Once you have located a folder or document, you can perform a number of procedures including copying, renaming, deleting, or opening it.

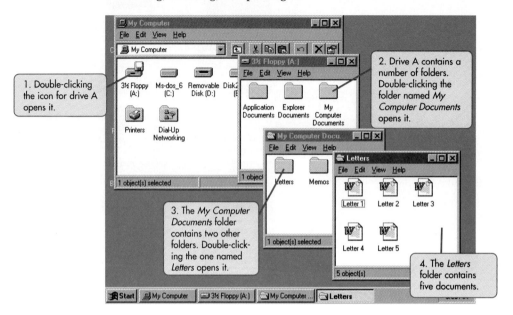

1. Double-clicking the icon for drive A opens it.

2. Drive A contains a number of folders. Double-clicking the folder named *My Computer Documents* opens it.

3. The *My Computer Documents* folder contains two other folders. Double-clicking the one named *Letters* opens it.

4. The *Letters* folder contains five documents.

UNDERSTANDING
Understanding Icons You'll Meet

When using My Computer (or Windows Explorer), you'll encounter a variety of icons that you should learn to recognize and differentiate.

▶ Drive icons have different graphics that represent floppy, hard drive, network, or CD-ROM drives.

Floppy

Hard

CD

▶ Document icons look like pages with the right corner folded down or like a notebook. A small graphic overlaid on this "page" indicates the specific program that created it.

New Text Document

New Microsoft Word Document

▶ Folder icons look like file folders. Some have graphic images on them to identify them further. For example,

the Control Panel and Printers folders are special and contain these graphics.

Printers

Control Panel

▶ Application icons use graphics specific to the application they represent.

Xpress

▶ Shortcut icons (those that perform a function for you) always have bent arrows as part of the graphic.

Microsoft Excel

1. To display the drives on your system, do one of the following:
   ▶ Double-click the *My Computer* icon on the desktop.
   ▶ Right-click the *My Computer* icon on the desktop, then click the shortcut menu's **O**pen command.
2. To open a drive, folder, or document, or start an application, do one of the following:
   ▶ Double-click it.
   ▶ Right-click it, then click the shortcut menu's **O**pen command.
   ▶ Click it to select it, then pull down the File menu and click the **O**pen command.

Managing Windows

Each time you open a folder to see what's inside it, My Computer opens a new window. Soon you may find that you have a number of windows open among which you can easily switch back and forth. This makes it easy to "back up" to a previous folder so you can open other folders within it. There are also a number of commands that allow you to easily close or arrange these windows.

▶ To "back up" to a previous window, click its button on the taskbar, or click any part of the window that you can see.
▶ To close a minimized window, right-click its button on the taskbar, and click the shortcut menu's **C**lose command.
▶ To minimize all windows, right-click a clear area of the taskbar and click the shortcut menu's **M**inimize All Windows command.
▶ To arrange all open windows, right-click a clear area of the taskbar and click the shortcut menu's **C**ascade, Tile **H**orizontally, or Tile **V**ertically command.

T U T O R I A L

Iɴ this tutorial you open My Computer and use it to explore the folders and documents on the *Win95 Student Resource Disk* designed to be used with this text. This disk contains all of the folders and documents on which you work while completing the lab activities in this text. If you do not have a copy of this disk, ask your instructor how you can obtain one.

Getting Ready

1. With Windows running, insert your *Win95 Student Resource Disk* into the drive you use to open and save documents.

Opening My Computer

2. Double-click the *My Computer* icon on the desktop. It contains icons for the drives on your system, plus Control Panel and Printers folders. (The contents of your window may look different from those shown here.)

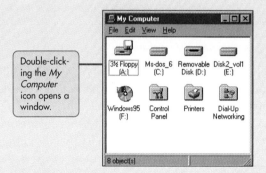

Double-clicking the *My Computer* icon opens a window.

3. Double-click the icon for the drive into which you put the *Win95 Student Resource Disk*. This opens a second window displaying the folders on that disk.

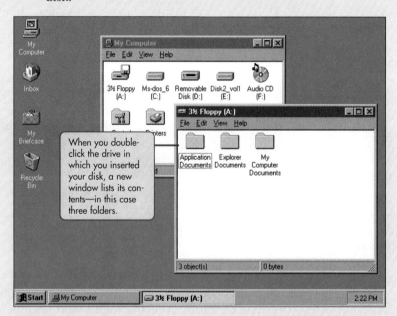

When you double-click the drive in which you inserted your disk, a new window lists its contents—in this case three folders.

4. Double-click the *My Computer Documents* folder to open it and see the two folders it contains.

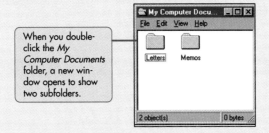

When you double-click the *My Computer Documents* folder, a new window opens to show two subfolders.

5. Double-click the *Letters* folder to open it and see the documents that it contains.

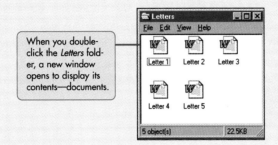

When you double-click the *Letters* folder, a new window opens to display its contents—documents.

Backing Up

6. Click each of the buttons on the taskbar to see the previous windows. Point to each of the buttons on the taskbar and on those with titles ending in 3 periods you will see their entire name displayed in a small box.

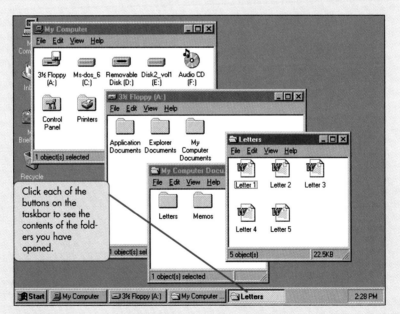

Click each of the buttons on the taskbar to see the contents of the folders you have opened.

 PAUSING FOR PRACTICE

Using My Computer to locate documents and applications is a useful skill. Pause here to practice using this application until you feel comfortable using it to navigate the *Win95 Student Resource Disk*.

7. Click the **Close** button on all open windows.

3-2 WINDOWS EXPLORER—A FIRST LOOK

Windows Explorer is a more powerful tool than My Computer because it shows the relationship between files and folders. It shows the *hierarchy* in which folders are arranged. This is important, because often there are folders within folders, and sometimes folders within those folders. Seeing these relationships displayed graphically gives you a much better understanding of your system's file organization.

TIP
File Manager

Windows 3.1 users will see similarities between Windows Explorer and the Windows 3.1 File Manager. In fact, an updated version of File Manager is stored as *Winfile.exe* in the *Windows* folder.

Starting Explorer

When you start Windows Explorer, its window contains two panes: the Tree pane and the Contents pane.

▶ The *Tree pane* on the left lists the resources on your desktop. The list is arranged in a hierarchical order called a tree.

▶ The *Contents pane* on the right lists the contents of the folder or other object that is currently selected in the Tree pane.

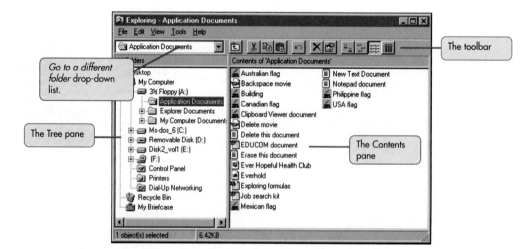

To open Windows Explorer, use this procedure:

▶ Click the **Start** button to display the Start menu, click **Programs** to display a list of programs on your system, then click *Windows Explorer* to open the application.

You can also use these procedures to open Windows Explorer:

▶ Right-click the **Start** button on the toolbar and then click the shortcut menu's **Explore** command.

▶ Right-click the My Computer or Recycle Bin icon on the desktop, then click the shortcut menu's **Explore** command.

▶ When My Computer is open, right-click a disk or folder and click the shortcut menu's **Explore** command. Alternatively, you can click the disk or folder to select it, pull down its File menu, and click the **Explore** command.

TIP
Changing a Pane's Size

To widen either the Tree or Contents pane, drag the split bar that separates the two panes to the right or left. (When you point to the bar, the mouse pointer turns into a double-headed arrow.)

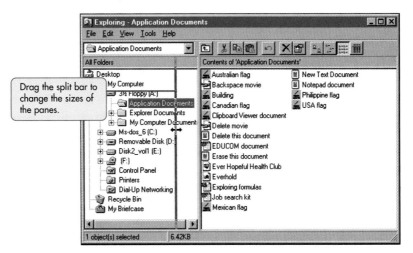

Understanding the Tree Pane

Windows Explorer's Tree pane graphically displays the disks and folders on your system. (Documents or other files are never listed in the Tree pane; they are only seen in the Contents pane.) Your system's disks and folders are displayed as a *tree*. The most important items are listed under the heading *Desktop*. There are a limited number of these items and they vary from system to system, but may include the following:

▶ *My Computer* lists all of the drives on your system, both local and remote (remote drives are those located elsewhere on a network). It also lists the Control Panel (used to change system settings) and the Printers folder (used to check and control the status of jobs being printed).

▶ *Recycle Bin* is the folder where all deleted files are stored until you empty it.

▶ *Network Neighborhood* is included if your system is part of a network.

▶ *My Briefcase* contains documents that are being worked on with both a desktop and a laptop computer.

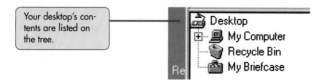

Your desktop's contents are listed on the tree.

Some folders have ⊞ or ⊟ symbols next to them that indicate they contain other folders—called subfolders. The ⊞ symbol means the subfolders are hidden—the folder they are in is collapsed. The ⊟ symbol means they are displayed—the folder they are in is expanded. When subfolders are displayed, they are indented under the folder that contains them. You click the symbols to switch back and forth between hiding (collapsing) and displaying (expanding) the subfolders.

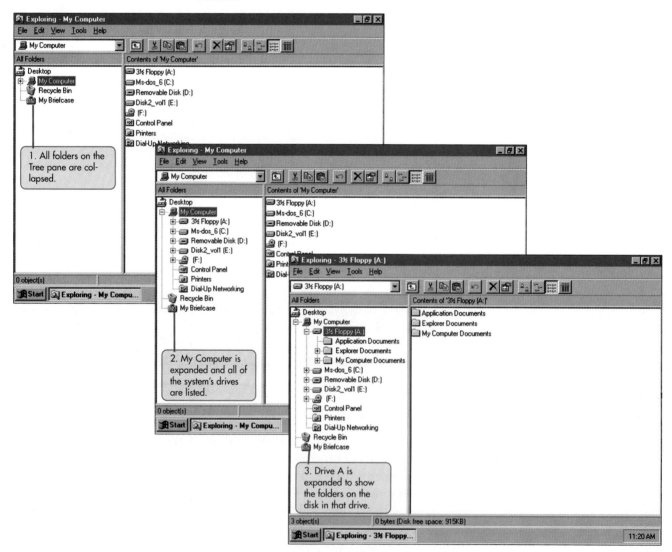

1. All folders on the Tree pane are collapsed.

2. My Computer is expanded and all of the system's drives are listed.

3. Drive A is expanded to show the folders on the disk in that drive.

QUICKSTEPS

Exploring Drives and Folders

▶ To expand a collapsed drive or folder, click the ⊕ in front of it, or double-click its name or icon.

▶ To collapse an expanded drive or folder, click the ⊖ in front of it, or double-click its name or icon.

▶ Click the *Go to a different folder* drop-down arrow to display a list of objects, then click the one you want to open. This is an especially useful way of jumping to a drive or folder that isn't currently displayed on the screen (when not all of the folders will fit in a single screen display).

COMMON WRONG TURNS
No Disk in Drive

If you select a drive that doesn't contain a disk, a dialog box is displayed. Insert a disk and click the **Retry** command button, or click the **Cancel** command button to cancel the command.

Understanding the Contents Pane

Only one folder in the Tree pane may be open at a time. It is highlighted on the tree, its folder icon is shown open, and its contents are displayed in the Contents pane.

The open folder on the tree

The contents of the open folder displayed in the Contents pane

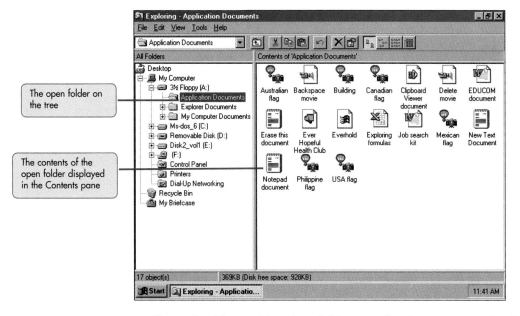

To work with an object in a folder, you first have to open the folder in which it is stored. For example, you can only select an object to be renamed, copied, moved, or deleted in a folder that is open.

QUICKSTEPS

Displaying Drive and Folder Contents

▸ To open a folder or drive and display its contents, click it to select it.

▸ To display the contents of a collapsed drive or folder, click the ⊞ in front of it, then click the object you want to open.

▸ Once you have moved down one or more levels in the Tree pane, you can click the **Up One Level** button on the toolbar to move back up the tree. When this button is dimmed, you are at the top level and can't move up any further.

TUTORIAL

Iɴ this tutorial, you use Windows Explorer to look through the tree and folders on the *Win95 Student Resource Disk*.

Getting Ready

1. Insert the *Win95 Student Resource Disk* into the drive you use to open and save documents.

Starting Windows Explorer

2. Click the **Start** button on the taskbar to display the Start menu.

3. Point to the **Programs** folder to cascade a submenu.

4. Click **Windows Explorer** to start the application and display the Exploring window. Scroll the tree so you can see *My Computer* listed in the Tree pane just below *Desktop*. (The Contents pane on the right may look different from the one shown here. This is because it appears the way it was displayed when last closed. You'll see in the next section how to change the way it looks.)

The My Computer folder in the Tree pane

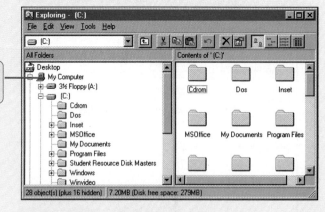

Expanding and Closing My Computer

5. Click the ⊟ or ⊞ box in front of *My Computer* in the Tree pane. It changes from collapsed to expanded and the symbol in the box changes to indicate which. Repeat this clicking a few times to get a feel for the difference. When finished, leave it expanded so it has a ⊟ in front of it.

Opening the Drive with Your Disk in It

6. Under *My Computer* the floppy drives on your system are listed, as *3½ Floppy or 5¼ Floppy* followed by *(A:)* or *(B:)*. Click the icon or name of the drive into which you inserted your disk to display its contents in the Contents pane. The contents are the folders on the disk.

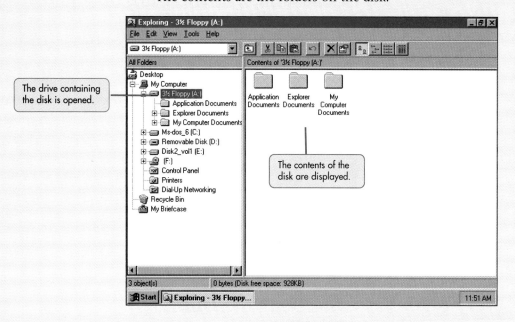

Expanding and Collapsing Folders

7. Click the ⊞ or ⊟ box in front of the drive you opened in the Tree pane. Each time you click it changes from expanded to collapsed or vice versa. Repeat this clicking a few times to get a feel for the differences. When finished leave it expanded so it has a ⊟ in front of it. Notice how expanding and collapsing the folder doesn't change the Contents pane.

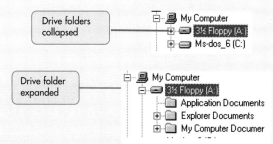

8. Click the ⊞ box in front of *My Computer Documents* in the Tree pane. It expands to show the folders it contains.

Opening and Expanding or Collapsing Folders

9. Double-click the icon or name of any folder marked with a plus sign (⊞) to expand it or minus sign (⊟) to collapse it. When you do so, its folder-shaped icon opens or closes, its symbol changes, and its contents are displayed or hidden. When finished, be sure all folders on the drive are expanded and have a ⊟ in front of them. (Those without a ⊟ or ⊞ contain no folders so they can't be expanded or collapsed.)

Exploring Folder Contents

10. Click each of the folder icons or names listed under the drive you have opened to display their contents in the Contents pane. As you do so, notice the following:

▶ The file-folder-shaped icon of the selected folder is opened and the name of the folder is highlighted.

▶ The folder's name is listed on the title bar and at the top of the Contents pane.

▶ The contents of the folder, if any, are displayed in the Contents pane.

▶ Folders with a ⊞ or ⊟ in front of them contain folders (as well as documents) which are displayed in the Contents pane. Folders without a ⊞ or ⊟ in front of them contain no folders.

▶ The number of objects in the folder, their total size in bytes, and the amount of free space remaining on the disk are listed on the status bar.

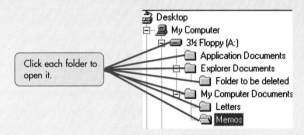

Using the Up One Level Button

11. Click the *Letters* folder to select it.

12. Click the **Up One Level** button on the toolbar and you move up one level to the *My Computer Documents* folder. That folder is outlined in the Tree pane, and its folder icon is open.

Each time you click the **Up One Level** button, the highlight moves to the first item above it that is not as indented. It jumps over items indented as much or more because they are at the same or a lower level.

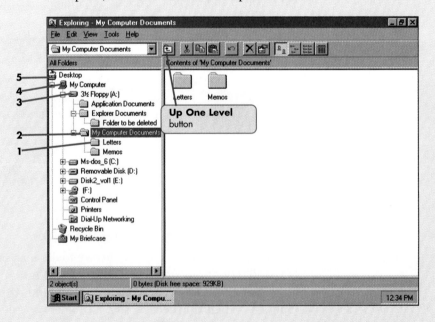

13. Click the **Up One Level** button on the toolbar until it dims and you can move up no further.

PAUSING FOR PRACTICE

Exploring drives and folders is one of the Windows skills that you must master. Pause here to practice changing to each of the drives listed for your system, expanding and collapsing folders, and looking carefully at the listings that result.

Finishing Up

14. Click the **Close** button on any and all open windows.

15. Continue to the next section, or exit Windows.

3-3 CHANGING THE DISPLAY

There are a limited number of options you can use to change the way My Computer or Windows Explorer looks. They include hiding or displaying the toolbar and status bar, and changing the way folders or documents are displayed in Windows Explorer's Contents pane or My Computer's window.

Displaying the Toolbar and Status Bar

The toolbar contains a number of buttons that perform many operations with just a single click. It is displayed by default in Windows Explorer but you have to turn it on in My Computer windows. You may have to maximize a window to see all of the buttons. Point to any button on the toolbar and in a moment the button's name is displayed. Because Windows can be customized, your buttons may not exactly match those shown here.

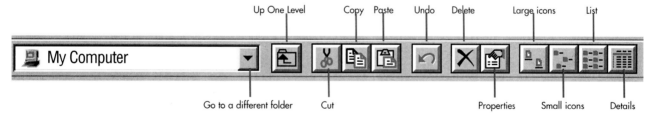

The status bar can display the number of objects in a folder, their total size in bytes, and the amount of free space remaining on a disk. Like the toolbar, it is displayed by default in Windows Explorer but you have to turn it on in My Computer windows. If you find that you aren't using it, you can turn it off to give more room for objects to be displayed in the window.

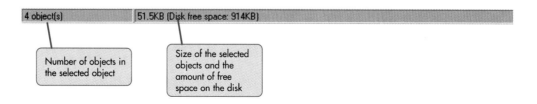

▶ To hide or display the toolbar, pull down the **View** menu and click the **Toolbar** command. (When on, it has a check mark in front of it.)

▶ To hide or display the status bar, pull down the **View** menu and click the **Status Bar** command. (When on, it has a check mark in front of it.)

Displaying Folders and Documents

The way drives, folders, documents, and other files are displayed in the My Computer window or Windows Explorer's Contents pane depends on the view that has been chosen. There are four possible displays:

▶ **Large Icons** displays items as large labeled icons.

▶ **Small Icons** displays items as small labeled icons.

▶ **List** displays icons and filenames under each other in a list.

▶ **Details** displays not only icons and names of objects but also their size, type, and date and time last modified.

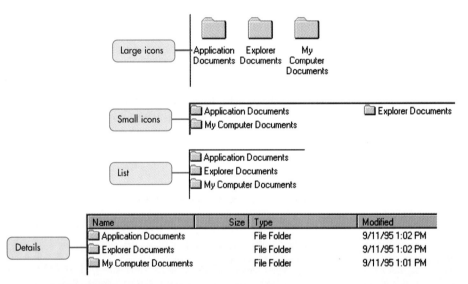

▶ To change the way drives, documents, and folders are displayed in the My Computer window or Windows Explorer's Contents pane, do any of the following:

▶ Click the **Large Icons**, **Small Icons**, **List**, or **Details** buttons on the toolbar.

▶ Pull down the **View** menu, and click the **Large Icons**, **Small Icons**, **List**, or **Details** command.

▶ Right-click in a clear area of the My Computer window or Windows Explorer's Contents pane, click the shortcut menu's **View** command to cascade the menu, and then click one of the menu choices.

Sorting Icons

You can arrange into various orders the icons displayed in a My Computer window, in Windows Explorer's Contents pane, or even on the desktop. For example:

▶ **by Name** (the default) sorts them in ascending alphabetical order (A-Z).

▶ **by Type** sorts them by type. For example, Word, Excel, or Access documents are grouped together, as are application programs.

▶ **by Size** sorts them in ascending order by their size.

▶ **by Date** sorts them by date last modified, the most recent listed first.

If you choose to arrange icons in the first window that appears when you open My Computer, or select *My Computer* on Windows Explorer's Tree pane, you will also see the following choices:

▶ **by Drive Letter** arranges the icons in alphabetical order by drive letter.

▶ **by Free Space** arranges the icons in descending order of free disk space.

U I C K S T E P S
Sorting Icons

1. To sort the icons in the My Computer window, in Windows Explorer's Contents pane, or the desktop, do one of the following:
   ▶ Pull down the **View** menu and click the **Arrange Icons** command to cascade the menu.
   ▶ Right-click in a clear area of the window or desktop, and click the shortcut menu's **Arrange Icons** command to cascade the menu.
2. Click one of the menu choices.

Arranging Icons

In addition to sorting icons you can also arrange them automatically in a My Computer window, in Windows Explorer's Contents pane, or even on the desktop. In a My Computer window or in Windows Explorer's Contents pane, automatically arranging them ensures that as many filenames as possible are displayed even when you change the size or shape of the window. This command works only when icons are displayed large or small, not when displayed as a list or details.

U I C K S T E P S
Arranging Icons

To automatically arrange or line up icons, do one of the following:
▶ To automatically arrange icons, right-click the My Computer window, Windows Explorer's Contents pane, or the desktop, click the shortcut menu's **Arrange Icons** command, then click the **Auto Arrange** command to turn it on or off. (You can also pull down the My Computer or Windows Explorer **View** menu, and click the **Arrange Icons** command.) The **Auto Arrange** command is dimmed when the Contents pane is set to List or Details.
▶ To line up icons, right-click the My Computer window, Windows Explorer's Contents pane, or the desktop, and then click the shortcut menu's **Line Up Icons** command. (You can also pull down the My Computer or Windows Explorer View menu, and click the **Line Up Icons** command.)

I N this tutorial you start Windows Explorer, view the contents of various objects, and change the view of those contents. You also practice hiding and displaying Windows Explorer's toolbar and status bar and practice arranging and aligning icons.

Getting Ready

1. Insert the *Win95 Student Resource Disk* into the drive you use to open and save documents.

Starting Windows Explorer

2. Click the **Start** button on the taskbar to display the Start menu.
3. Click the **Programs** folder to cascade a submenu.
4. Click **Windows Explorer** to start the application and display the Exploring window.

Hiding and Displaying the Toolbar

5. To hide the toolbar, pull down the **View** menu and click the **Toolbar** command to remove the check mark from in front of it.
6. To display the toolbar, pull down the **View** menu and click the **Toolbar** command.

Hiding and Displaying the Status bar

7. To hide the status bar, pull down the **View** menu and click the **Status Bar** command to remove the check mark from in front of it.
8. To display the status bar, pull down the **View** menu and click the **Status Bar** command.

Displaying Information in Different Ways

9. In the Tree pane, click the ⊞ box in front of the drive into which you inserted your disk so you can see the *Application Documents* folder in the Tree pane.
10. Double-click the *Application Documents* folder to open it and list its contents in the Contents pane.
11. Click the **Large Icons, Small Icons, List,** and **Details** buttons on the toolbar one at a time. (Hold the mouse pointer over each for a moment and its name will be displayed.) Notice how the listings change.

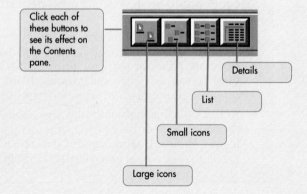

Click each of these buttons to see its effect on the Contents pane.

Details

List

Small icons

Large icons

Arranging Icons by Type

12. Click the **Details** button on the toolbar to display file types.

13. Pull down the **View** menu, and click the **Arrange Icons** command to cascade the menu.

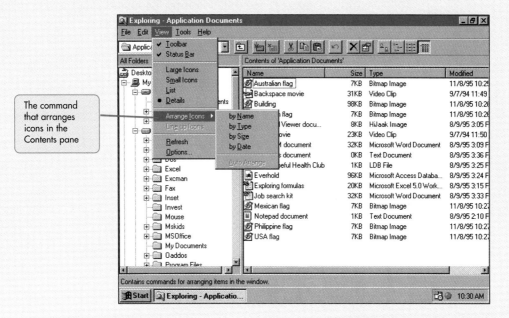

The command that arranges icons in the Contents pane

14. Click the **by Type** command to list the files in ascending order by type. For example, all *Bitmap Image* files (graphic files) are listed together, as are *Microsoft Word* documents and *Video Clips*.

Arranging Icons by Size

15. Right-click in a clear area of the window, then click the shortcut menu's **Arrange Icons** command to cascade the menu.

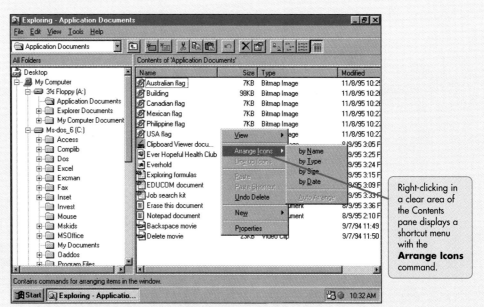

Right-clicking in a clear area of the Contents pane displays a shortcut menu with the **Arrange Icons** command.

16. Click the **by Size** command to arrange files by their size with smaller files listed first.

Arranging Icons by Date

17. Pull down the **View** menu, click the **Arrange Icons** command, then click the **by Date** command to list files in descending order by date in the *Modified* column. (You may have to click the **Maximize** button or scroll the Contents pane to see that column.) Those last modified on the same date are subsorted in descending order by time.

Arranging Icons by Name

18. Right-click in a clear area of the Contents pane, click the shortcut menu's **Arrange Icons** command to cascade the menu, then click the **by Name** command to return the list to its original order.

Turning Auto Arrange Off

19. Click the **Large Icons** button on the toolbar to change the display of files in the Contents pane.

20. Right-click in a clear are of the Contents pane, and click the shortcut menu's **Arrange Icons** command to cascade the menu.

21. If the **Auto Arrange** command has a check mark in front of it, click the command to turn it off. If it doesn't have a check mark, click anywhere but the menu to close the menu.

22. Drag several of the icons in the Contents pane to new positions and drop them randomly.

Turning Auto Arrange Back On

23. Right-click in a clear are of the Contents pane, and click the Shortcut's **Arrange Icons** command to cascade the menu.

24. Click the **Auto Arrange** to turn it back on. All of the dragged icons snap back into a neat arrangement.

Finishing Up

25. Continue to the next section, or exit Windows.

3-4 OPENING DOCUMENTS AND APPLICATIONS

Windows 95 gives you many ways to start applications and open new or existing documents. Some of these procedures can be done from My Computer or Windows Explorer.

Opening Existing Documents

You saw earlier how to start applications using the **Start** button on the taskbar. However, you can also start them from My Computer or Windows Explorer. In addition you can open a document the same way, and if its application isn't already running, it will be started.

UICKSTEPS

Opening Existing Documents and Starting Applications

To start an application or open an existing document, do one of the following:

▶ Double-click the application's or document's icon. (All documents have icons that look like pages with the right corner folded down. The graphic displayed on this "page" indicates the specific program that created it.)

▶ Click the application's or document's icon to select it, then pull down the **File** menu and click the **Open** command.

▶ Right-click the application's or document's icon and click the shortcut menu's **Open** command.

▶ Drag the document's icon onto the desktop and then double-click it. You can start the application by double-clicking the icon. You can also click the icon to select it, then press Del to delete the icon from the desktop without deleting the file on the disk.

Opening New Documents

There are many times when the document you want doesn't exist and you have to create it. At times such as these you open a new document. You can do so from within My Computer or Windows Explorer. When you do so, the application opens with a new document ready for you to use.

Opening New Documents

1. Open the folder you want to save the new document in.
2. Do one of the following:
   ▶ Pull down the **File** menu and click the **New** command to cascade the menu.
   ▶ Right-click in a clear area of the Contents pane, and click the shortcut menu's **New** command.
3. Select the type of file you want to open (all applications are listed). A temporary name for the document is highlighted.
4. Type in the new document's name and press Enter↵. (The first character you type deletes the temporary name).
5. To open the new document's application, do one of the following:
   ▶ Double-click the new document's icon or name.
   ▶ Click new document's icon or name to select it, then pull down the **File** menu and click the **Open** command.
   ▶ Right-click the new document's icon or name and then click the shortcut menu's **Open** command.

TUTORIAL

I N this tutorial you use Windows Explorer to open a document and start an application. The results are not entirely predictable since there is so much variation in systems.

Getting Ready

1. Insert the *Win95 Student Resource Disk* into the drive you use to open and save documents.

Starting Windows Explorer

2. Click the **Start** button on the taskbar to display the Start menu.
3. Click the **Programs** folder to cascade a submenu.
4. Click **Windows Explorer** to start the application and display the Exploring window.
5. Click the **Large Icons** button on the toolbar to change the display of files in the Contents pane.

Opening a New Document

6. In the Tree pane, expand the drive into which you inserted your disk, then in the Tree pane click the *Application Documents* folder to open it and list its contents in the Contents pane.

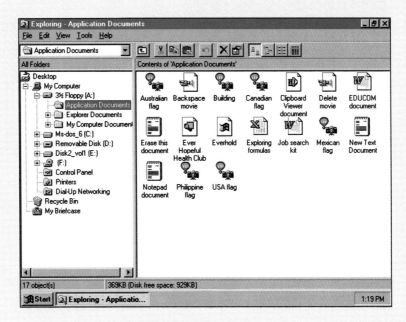

7. Right-click in a clear area of the Contents pane, and click the shortcut menu's **New** command. This displays a list of the types of new files you can create. (Your list may vary from the one shown here.)

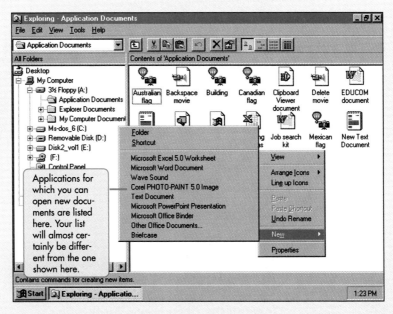

8. Click *Text Document* and an icon for the document appears in the Contents pane. A temporary name for the file, *New Text Document*, is highlighted.

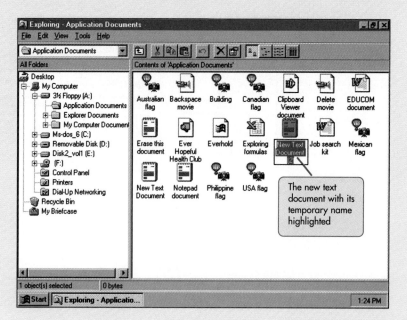

9. Type **Delete this document** as the new document's name and press [Enter⏎]. (The first character you type deletes the temporary name).

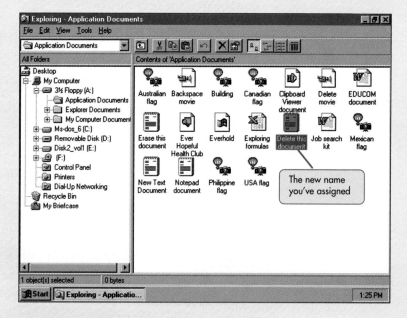

Opening the Document's Application

10. Double-click the new document's icon or name. This opens Windows' built-in Notepad application and the new document.

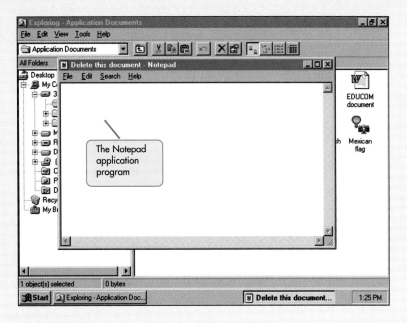

The Notepad application program

11. Click Notepad's **Close** button to close it.

Finishing Up

12. Continue to the next section, or exit Windows.

3-5 FINDING DOCUMENTS AND FOLDERS

Windows 95 makes it easy to locate a specific file without browsing through lots of folders to do so. You do so using the **Find** command, available from the Start menu and Windows Explorer.

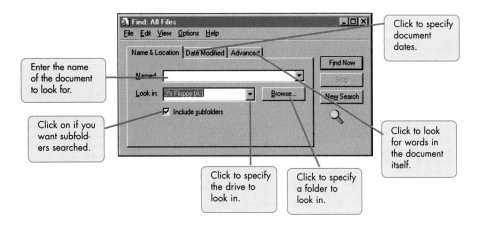

Enter the name of the document to look for.

Click on if you want subfolders searched.

Click to specify document dates.

Click to look for words in the document itself.

Click to specify the drive to look in.

Click to specify a folder to look in.

QUICKSTEPS

Finding Files and Folder

1. To display the Find dialog box, do one of the following:
   ▶ Pull down Windows Explorer's **Tools** menu and click the **Find** command to cascade the menu, then click the **Files or Folders** command.
   ▶ Click the **Start** button on the taskbar, click the **Find** command to cascade the menu, then click the **Files or Folders** command.
   ▶ Right-click the Start button on the taskbar, and then click the shortcut menu's **Find** command.

2. Enter the information you want to search for:
   ▶ On the *Name & Location tab*, enter the folder's or document's name into the *Named* text box and use the **Look In** drop-down arrow to specify the drive or folder to search. You can also click the **Browse** command button to select a specific folder on a drive. You can click on the **Include subfolders** check box if you want to search all subfolders.
   ▶ On the *Date Modified* tab, specify a date or range of dates. Click the **All Files** option button to turn it on if you don't want dates to be a criterion.
   ▶ On the *Advanced* tab, specify the type of files you want to find, text that is within the document, and file size limits.

3. Click the **Find Now** command button. When the search is completed, the files and folders that matched your filename specification are listed.

TUTORIAL

IN this tutorial you use Windows Explorer's **Find** command to locate files on the *Win95 Student Resource Disk*.

Getting Ready

1. Insert the *Win95 Student Resource Disk* into the drive you use to open and save documents.
2. Open Windows Explorer. In the Tree pane, expand the drive into which you inserted the disk to list its folders in the Contents pane.

Finding Files

3. Pull down Windows Explorer's **Tools** menu and click the **Find** command to cascade the menu.
4. Click the **Files or Folders** command to display the Find dialog box. The *Look in* text box should list the drive containing your *Win95 Student Resource Disk*. Make the following settings:
   ▶ Enter **Australian flag** into the *Named* text box.
   ▶ If the **Include subfolders** check box doesn't have a check mark in it, click it to turn it on.

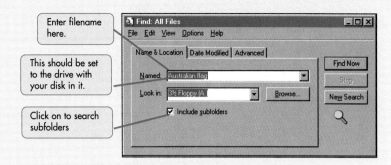

Enter filename here.

This should be set to the drive with your disk in it.

Click on to search subfolders

5. Click the **Find Now** command button. When the search is completed, the file that matches your filename is listed in the lower window. (On early versions of Windows, a bug causes all documents that end with the word *flag* to be displayed. Including in the filename any spaces or wildcard characters such as asterisks or question marks causes unpredictable results.)

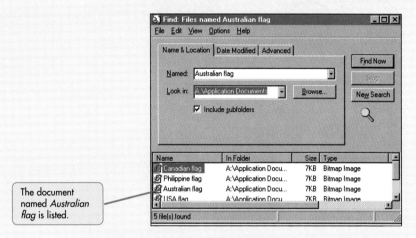

The document named *Australian flag* is listed.

6. Click the **New Search** button to clear the dialog box. When a message box warns you that this will clear your current search, click the **OK** button.

Finding a Group of Files

7. Enter the following new settings:

▶ Enter **Building** into the *Named* text box.

▶ Click the *Look In* drop-down arrow and then click the drive containing your *Win95 Student Resource Disk*.

▶ The **Include subfolders** check box should still be on; if it isn't, click it.

8. Click the **Find Now** command button. When the search is completed, the file that matches your filename is listed in the lower window.

9. Click the **New Search** button to clear the dialog box, then click the **OK** button that appears when you are asked to confirm the command.

Finishing Up

10. Click the Find window's **Close** button to close it.

11. Continue to the next section, or exit Windows.

All of the objects displayed by My Computer and Windows Explorer have characteristic attributes called properties that can be viewed in a dialog box. When you display an object's properties, the information displayed varies depending on what kind of object it is. For example, the properties of a disk include its label (name) and the amount of used and free space. The properties of a folder include its location, size, and the number of files or folders it contains. The properties of a document include its type, size, and dates when it was created or last modified or accessed.

Most properties are just displayed for you, but there are a few you can change. For example, you can label each of your disks so its name appears when you display the disk's properties.

QUICKSTEPS
Displaying Properties

To display an object's properties, do one of the following:

▶ Click a drive, folder, or document icon or name to select it, then click the **Properties** button on the toolbar.

▶ Click an object to select it, then pull down the **File** menu and click the **Properties** command.

▶ Click an object with the right mouse button, then click the shortcut menu's **Properties** command.

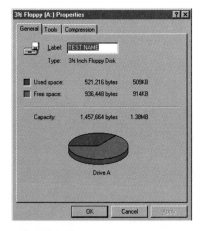

Disk properties

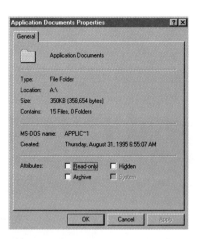

Folder properties

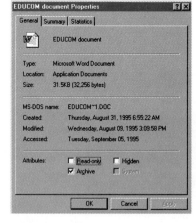

Document properties

TIP
Labeling Disks

When you display the properties of a drive, you can change the label on the disk by typing a new one in the **Label** text box and clicking the **Apply** button.

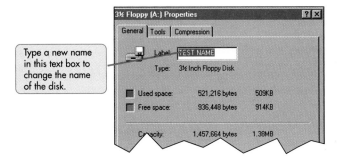

Type a new name in this text box to change the name of the disk.

I N this tutorial you display the properties of folders, files, and disks. When looking at the properties of a disk, you change one of them—its label.

Getting Ready

1. Insert the *Win95 Student Resource Disk* into the drive you use to open and save documents.

2. Open Windows Explorer. In the Tree pane, expand the drive into which you inserted the disk to list its folders in the Contents pane. Click the **Large Icons** button on the toolbar.

Displaying a Drive's Properties

3. In the Tree pane, right-click the icon for the drive into which you inserted the *Win95 Student Resource Disk*, and click the shortcut menu's **Properties** command. The *General tab* should be displayed.

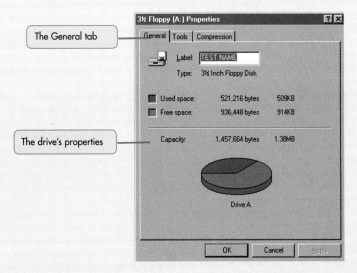

The General tab

The drive's properties

4. With the *General tab* displayed, click in the **Label** text box to move the insertion point there, then type your name (up to 11 letters) and click the **Apply** button. Now you can always see the disk's name by displaying its properties.

5. The dialog box may have other tabs on it depending on how your system has been installed. If it has them, click them to look at their contents. In each tab, click the question mark on the title bar and then click each item for a description.

6. Click the Properties dialog box's **Close** button to close it.

Displaying a Folder's Properties

7. In the Tree pane, right-click the icon for the *Application Documents* folder, and click the shortcut menu's **Properties** command. Read the information displayed on the folder.

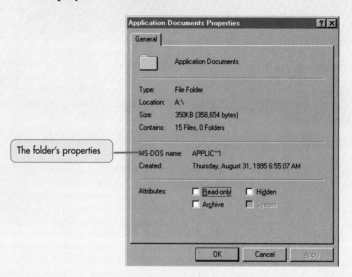

The folder's properties

8. Click the Properties dialog box's **Close** button to close it.

Displaying a File's Properties

9. In the Tree pane, click the *Application Documents* folder to open it and display its contents in the Contents pane.

10. In the Contents pane, right-click the icon for the file named *Backspace Movie*, and click the shortcut menu's **Properties** command.

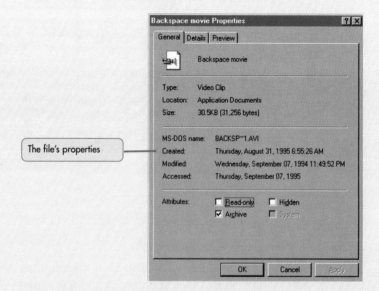

The file's properties

11. Click the *Details* tab to see specific details about the file. In this case it is a series of movie frames.

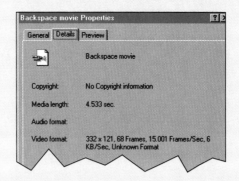

12. Click the *Preview* tab and then click the arrowhead to play the movie. (If your system is equipped for multimedia, you'll see a movie of what happens when you press `←Bksp`.)

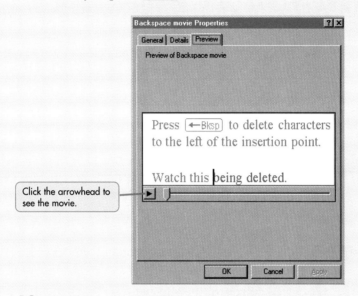

Click the arrowhead to see the movie.

13. Click the Properties dialog box's **Close** button to close it.

Finishing Up

14. Continue to the next section, or exit Windows.

3-7 VIEWING DOCUMENT CONTENTS

Windows Explorer (but not My Computer) gives you the ability to view a document's contents without first opening it. It does this with the **Quick View** command which uses file viewers that recognize a number or popular file types. These viewers are able to display a document's contents without first starting the application that created it. When you use this command, Windows first checks the file's type against the file viewers it has:

▶ If Windows can display the contents of the file, it does so.

▶ If it can't display the file but does recognize it, it displays a description of the document.

▶ If Windows can't recognize the file, **Quick View** isn't even displayed on the menu. (It also isn't displayed on the menu if it hasn't been installed on your system.)

TUTORIAL

IN this tutorial you use the **Quick View** command to view the contents of documents on the *Win95 Student Resource Disk* without opening them.

Getting Ready

1. Insert the *Win95 Student Resource Disk* into the drive you use to open and save documents.
2. Open Windows Explorer. In the Tree pane, expand the drive into which you inserted the disk to list its folders in the Contents pane. Click the **Large Icons** button on the toolbar.

Viewing File Contents

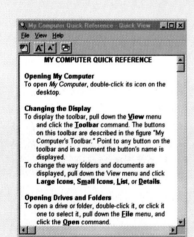

3. Click the Explorer Documents folder in the Tree pane to open it, then click the *My Computer Quick Reference* document to select it in the Contents pane.
4. Pull down the **File** menu and click the **Quick View** command to display the document's contents, as shown at the left.
5. Click the **Close** button on the Quick View window to close it.
6. Click the *Explorer Quick Reference* document to select it.
7. Pull down the **File** menu and click the **Quick View** command to display the document's contents.
8. Click the **Close** button on the Quick View window to close it.

Finishing Up

9. Continue to the lab activities, or exit Windows and shut down your system.

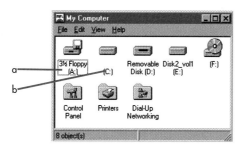
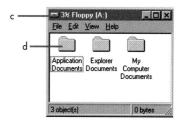

EXPLORING YOUR SYSTEM

VISUAL QUIZ

1. This illustration shows two My Computer Windows.

    a. What does this icon represent?
    b. What does this icon represent?
    c. How was this window opened from the window on the left?
    d. What do icons such as this represent?

2. Here is shown an illustration of Windows Explorer.

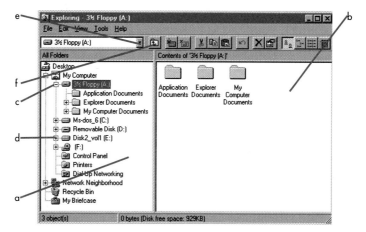

    a. What is the name of this area of the window?

    _____

    b. What is the name of this area of the window?

    _____

    c. What does this symbol mean?

    _____

    d. What does this symbol mean?

    _____

    e. What does clicking this drop-down arrow allow you to do?

    _____

    f. What does clicking this button do?

    _____

3. This illustration shows Windows Explorer's window with parts labeled.

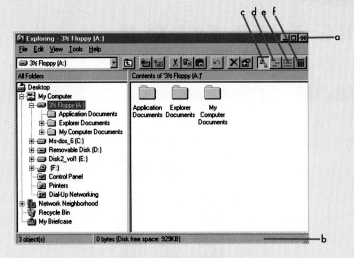

a. What is the name of this element?

_____

b. What is the name of this element?

_____

c. What does clicking this button do?

_____

d. What does clicking this button do?

_____

e. What does clicking this button do?

_____

f. What does clicking this button do?

_____

4. This illustration shows Windows Explorer's Contents pane.

a. Assuming the flags were created by Windows' Paint application, what would happen if you double-clicked one of them?

_____

b. How would you create a new document in this window?

_____

_____

5. This illustration shows the Find dialog box.

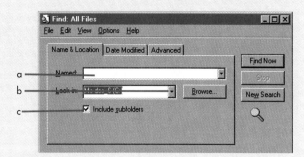

a. What do you enter into this text box?

_____

b. What can you do when you click this drop-down arrow?

_____

c. What happens when this check box is on?

_____

6. This illustration shows a Properties dialog box.

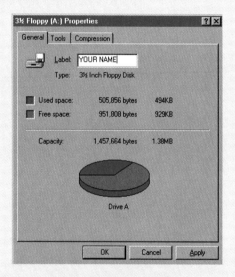

a. What object does it display properties for?

_____

b. How would you add a label to this object?

_____

7. This illustration shows a quick view of a document.

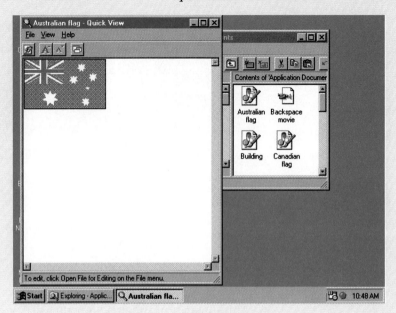

a. How was the quick view displayed?

_____

b. What two things might account for the **Quick View** command not being available?

_____

REVIEW QUESTIONS

T F **1.** When you use a Windows application to create a file containing data, the file is referred to as a *document*.

T F **2.** To keep related documents together and make them easier to find, they are stored in folders.

T F **3.** Disks, folders, and documents are all examples of *objects*.

T F **4.** The first window you see when you start My Computer contains icons for the documents you have created.

T F **5.** To open a folder, you click it.

T F **6.** When you open a folder using My Computer, a new window is opened showing the contents of that folder.

T F **7.** When more than one My Computer window is opened, the only way to switch among them is by clicking the **Close** button on the top window.

T F **8.** When My Computer windows overlap one another, you can cascade or tile them.

T F **9.** The Contents pane displays all of the objects on the selected drive.

T F **10.** To open the folders on another drive on the Tree pane, you double-click its icon or name.

T F **11.** You can drag the split bar that separates the Tree pane from the Contents pane so one or the other has more space.

T F **12.** To select a folder, you just click its name or icon on the Tree pane and this displays the folder's contents in the Contents pane.

T F **13.** To expand a folder, you can double-click its name or icon on the Tree.

T F **14.** To collapse a folder, you can double-click its name or icon on the Tree.

T F **15.** A ⊡ symbol next to a folder on the Tree pane indicates that it has been expanded and a ⊞ indicates it has been collapsed.

T F **16.** When a folder on the Tree pane has neither a ⊡ or ⊞ it means that all of the folders in that folder are empty.

T F **17.** The toolbar is normally displayed in Windows Explorer's window but not in My Computer's.

T F **18.** You can turn the toolbar and status bar off and back on at any time in Windows Explorer's and My Computer's windows.

T F **19.** You can choose from four different ways to display filenames and icons in Windows Explorer and My Computer.

T F **20.** The only way to know the size of a file is to click the **List** button on the toolbar.

T F **21.** You can sort the icons in My Computer's window or Windows Explorer's Contents pane only by name and size.

T F **22.** Double-clicking a document's icon in My Computer's window or Windows Explorer's Contents pane deletes it from the disk.

T F 23. One way to create a new document in My Computer's window or Windows Explorer's Contents pane is to right-click to display a shortcut menu.

T F 24. When you search for a file in a folder, you cannot also search for it in subfolders within the folder.

T F 25. One reason to check a disk's properties is to see how much free space it has for new files.

T F 26. You can display a disk's properties and add or change the label on the disk.

T F 27. You can view the contents of a document provided Windows has a file viewer to display that application's documents.

T F 28. The only reason Quick View won't be on the menu as expected is because it hasn't been installed on your system.

MULTIPLE CHOICE

1. The term *objects* refers to ___.
   a. Disk drives   b. Folders
   c. Documents   d. All of the above

2. My Computer shows you the ___ on your system.
   a. Disk drives   b. Folders
   c. Documents   d. All of the above

3. Explorer's window is divided into two parts so ___ can be displayed at the same time.
   a. Contents of two different drives
   b. Filenames and sizes
   c. The tree and the contents of the open folder
   d. Folders in one and subfolders in the other

4. To expand a folder on the Tree pane, you ___.
   a. Double-click the folder
   b. Click the folder
   c. Drag the folder to the Contents pane
   d. All of the above

5. To list filename sizes in a My Computer window or Explorer's Contents pane, you click the ___ button on the toolbar.
   a. Large Icons   b. Small Icons
   c. List   d. Details

6. To open an existing document whose icon is displayed in a My Computer window or Explorer's Contents pane, you ___.
   a. Click the icon.
   b. Double-click the icon.
   c. Drag the icon onto the desktop.
   d. None of the above.

7. You can display the properties of ___.
   a. Disk drives   b. Folders

c. Documents   **d.** All of the above.

8. Quick View shows you the contents of documents but it may not be on the menu because ___.

    a. It wasn't installed on your system.

    b. It doesn't recognize the file type.

    c. You've displayed the wrong menu.

    d. All of the above.

FILL IN THE BLANK

1. When a folder contains other folders, they are called _____.

2. When you open Explorer, its window is divided into two parts. On the left is the _____ and on the right is the _____.

3. To change the selected drive you _____ one of the _____.

4. To display a document's date in Windows Explorer's Contents pane, you have to first click the _____.

5. To open a document displayed in a My Computer window or Windows Explorer's Contents pane, you can _____.

6. To display properties, you _____ an object to display a shortcut menu.

7. The _____ command allows you to view the contents of documents on your system.

LAB ACTIVITIES

3-1 My Computer—A First Look

With My Computer you can fully explore a disk and have windows for each folder open on the desktop at the same time. In this drill you practice that procedure.

1. Insert your *Win95 Student Resource Disk* into the drive you use to open and save documents.

2. Double-click the *My Computer* icon on the desktop to open it and use it to open (by double-clicking), in this order:
   ▶ The drive you put the disk in.
   ▶ The *My Computer Documents* folder.
   ▶ The *Letters* folder.

3. Return to the window that displays the *My Computer Documents* folder but this time open the folders in this order:
   ▶ The *Explorer Documents* folder.
   ▶The *Folder to be deleted* folder.

4. Return to the window that displays the *My Computer Documents* folder but this time open the *Application Documents* folder.

5. Close all My Computer windows.

3-2 Windows Explorer—A First Look

As you have seen, the big difference between My Computer and Windows Explorer is the latter's tree. In this drill you explore this tree to see how easy it makes it to quickly locate folders and documents.

1. Insert your *Win95 Student Resource Disk* into the drive you use to open and save documents.

2. Open Windows Explorer and use it to open the drive into which you inserted the disk. This displays the disk's contents in the Contents pane.

3. Click the ⊞ and ⊟ symbols in front of the drive to practice expanding and collapsing it. When finished, leave it expanded.

4. Click the ⊞ and ⊟ symbols in front of the folders on that drive to practice expanding and collapsing them. When finished, leave them all expanded.

5. Click each of the folders in the Tree pane to display its contents in the Contents pane.

6. Close Windows Explorer.

3-3 Changing the Display

There are a number of commands and buttons that change the way folders and documents are displayed in My Computer windows and Windows Explorer's Contents pane.

1. Insert your *Win95 Student Resource Disk* into the drive you use to open and save documents.

2. Click the **Start** button, point to **Programs**, and then click **Windows Explorer** to open it. Use it to open the drive into which you inserted the disk.

3. Select the *Applications Documents* folder to display its contents in the Contents pane.

4. Click the **Large Icons**, **Small Icons**, **List**, and **Details** buttons on the toolbar to explore their effects on the display.

5. Use commands on the **View** menu to turn off and then back on the toolbar and status bar.

6. Click the **Large Icons** button on the toolbar, right-click in a clear area of the Contents pane, and use the shortcut's menu to arrange the icons first by name, then by type, size, and date.

7. Close Windows Explorer.

3-4 Opening Documents and Starting Applications

Although you normally open an application and then use it to open a document, Windows 95 provides a number of other ways to open documents. In this drill you practice some of them.

1. Insert your *Win95 Student Resource Disk* into the drive you use to open and save documents.

2. Open Windows Explorer and use it to open the drive into which you inserted the disk.

3. Select the *Applications Documents* folder to display its contents in the Contents pane. (You may have to first expand the tree.)

4. Double-click any of the flag documents to open the application that created them (Paint) and then open the document. Click the application's **Close** button to close it.

5. Double-click the *Backspace movie* or *Delete movie* and it should run and then automatically close.

6. Double-click the *Notepad document* to open the application that created it (Notepad) and then open the document. Click the application's **Close** button to close it.

7. Drag the *Building* document out of the Contents pane and drop it on the desktop. (You may have to click the **Restore** button first if Windows Explorer is maximized.) Double-click the icon on the desktop to open the application and then the document.

8. Click the application's **Close** button to close it. Then with the icon on the desktop selected, press [Del] to delete it. When asked to confirm that you are willing for it to be sent to the Recycle Bin, click the **Yes** button.

9. Close Windows Explorer.

3-5 Finding Documents and Folders

A floppy with a few folders and documents isn't hard to explore, but larger hard disks and networks can have hundreds of folders and thousands of documents. Here you practice using the **Find** command that is so valuable on those kinds of systems.

1. Insert your *Win95 Student Resource Disk* into the drive you use to open and save documents.

2. Use the **Find** command on the Start menu to display the Find dialog box used to find files or folders.

3. Make the following settings, click the **Find Now** button, and on a sheet of paper write down the location of the document:

   ▶ In the **Named** text box, enter **Job search kit**.

   ▶ On the **Look in** drop-down list, select the drive you inserted your disk into.

   ▶ If the **Include subfolders** check box isn't on, click it on.

4. In the **Named** text box, enter **Memo**, then click the **Find Now** button, and write down the location of the documents that are displayed.

5. Close the Find dialog box.

3-6 Displaying Properties

There is a lot of information available about the objects on your system. In this drill you practice displaying some of it.

1. Insert your *Win95 Student Resource Disk* into the drive you use to open and save documents.

2. Open Windows Explorer and use it to open and expand the drive into which you inserted the disk.

3. Select the *Applications Documents* folder to display its contents in the Contents pane.

4. Right-click the icon or name of the drive into which you inserted your disk, and click the shortcut menu's **Properties** command. Click each of the dialog box's tabs, read the information, and then click the dialog box's **Cancel** button.

5. Right-click the icon or name of the *Applications Documents* folder, and click the shortcut menu's **Properties** command. Read the information, and then click the dialog box's **Cancel** button.

6. Right-click the icon or name of the *Backspace movie* document in the *Applications Documents* folder, and click the shortcut menu's **Properties** command. Click each of the dialog box's tabs, read the information, and then click the dialog box's **Cancel** button.

7. Close Windows Explorer.

3-7 Viewing Document Contents

When searching for the right document, it's a big help if you can see its contents before you open it to be sure it's the right one. In this drill you practice this procedure. You can only complete this drill if Quick View has been installed on your system.

1. Insert your *Win95 Student Resource Disk* into the drive you use to open and save documents.

2. Open Windows Explorer and use it to open and expand the drive into which you inserted the disk.

3. Select the *Applications Documents* folder to display its contents in the Contents pane.

4. Right-click the *Australian flag* document and then click the shortcut menu's **Quick View** command. After checking the preview, click the Quick View window's **Close** button.

5. Right-click *Notepad document* and then click the shortcut menu's **Quick View** command. After checking the preview, click the Quick View window's **Close** button.

EXERCISES

Exercise 1. Calculating File Sizes

Managing disk space is one of the most important things you can do on a system. Once space begins to run out, applications begin to misbehave and you may not be able to save new documents.

1. Use Explorer to display the contents of the *Win95 Student Resource Disk*. Can you calculate how much space on the disk is occupied by files?

2. Display the contents of drive C or any other drive on your system that contains a disk. How much space on the disk is occupied by files?

Exercise 2. Exploring the Windows Folder

If you can, use Explorer to explore the tree of the hard disk on your system where Windows is stored. You should be able to locate a tree similar to the one shown here.

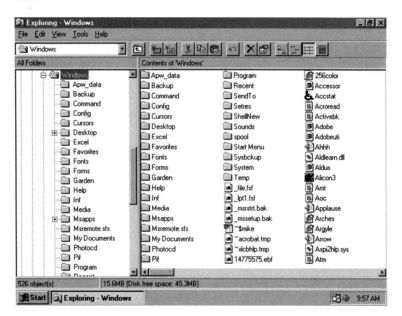

Exercise 3. Identifying File Icons

Display the Contents pane for the *Windows Student Resource Disk*, search the icons for an example of each type listed below, and write in its filename:

File Type	Filename
Folder	_____
Document associated with an application	_____

PICTORIAL FOUR

MANAGING YOUR SYSTEM

After completing this PicTorial, you will be able to:

▶ **Select documents and folders**
▶ **Rename documents and folders**
▶ **Create documents and folders**
▶ **Delete and undelete documents and folders**
▶ **Copy and move documents and folders**
▶ **Format disks**
▶ **Copy disks**

A S you've seen, both My Computer and Windows Explorer are used to explore your system. When you locate the objects such as documents, folders, or disks that you want to manage, the two programs work the same way. For example, the way you rename, copy, move, or delete a document is the same with both programs.

As you explore procedures for managing objects on your system, you'll see there is almost always more than one way to perform a procedure. These generally include clicking buttons on the toolbar, right-clicking to display shortcut menus, using pull-down menus, and even dragging and dropping. There is no single right way to do these procedures. As you gain experience, you'll find that one method appeals to you more than the others. For example, you may find that toolbar buttons are the fastest way to execute a command but menu commands are easier to remember.

4-1 SELECTING OBJECTS

To perform operations on objects such as copying, renaming, or deleting, you must first select the objects. You can select any single document or folder by clicking its name or icon. However, at times you want to select more than one document or folder. Ways you can do so are described in the QuickSteps box "Selecting Objects."

When you select objects, important information is given on the status bar.

▶ When you select documents, the number selected and their total size is indicated.

▶ When you select folders, just the number of selected folders is given. (However, if you select a folder in the Tree pane, the number of objects in it, their combined size, and the amount of free space remaining on the disk is displayed.)

▶ When you select a disk, the number of folders it contains and its free space are given.

UICKSTEPS
Selecting Objects

To select documents or folders in a My Computer window or Windows Explorer's Contents pane, do one of the following:

▶ To select an object, click its name or icon.

▶ To select a group of adjacent objects, click the first object to select it, and then either hold down ⟨⇧ Shift⟩ while you click the last object or hold down ⟨⇧ Shift⟩ and use the arrow keys to extend the highlight over other objects in the list.

▶ To select nonadjacent objects, click the first object to select it, then hold down ⟨Ctrl⟩ while you click each of the next objects. To cancel a selection, hold down ⟨Ctrl⟩ and click the object again.

▶ To select more than one group of adjacent objects, click the first object to select it, and then hold down ⟨⇧ Shift⟩ while you click the last object in the first group. To select the next group, hold down ⟨Ctrl⟩ while you click the first object. Then hold down ⟨Ctrl⟩+⟨⇧ Shift⟩ while you click the last object.

▶ To unselect some selected objects, hold down ⟨Ctrl⟩ and click each of them.

▶ To select all objects, pull down the **Edit** menu and click the **Select All** command.

▶ To select all objects that haven't been selected and unselect those that have been, pull down the **Edit** menu and click the **Invert Selection** command. For example, if you want to select all objects but one, click the one to select it and then use this command to unselect it while selecting all of the others.

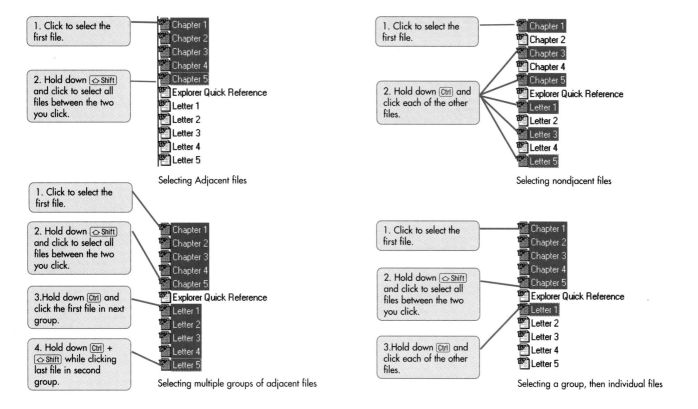

1. Click to select the first file.

Chapter 1
Chapter 2
Chapter 3
Chapter 4
Chapter 5

2. Hold down ⇧ Shift and click to select all files between the two you click.

Explorer Quick Reference
Letter 1
Letter 2
Letter 3
Letter 4
Letter 5

Selecting Adjacent files

1. Click to select the first file.

Chapter 1
Chapter 2
Chapter 3
Chapter 4
Chapter 5

2. Hold down Ctrl and click each of the other files.

Explorer Quick Reference
Letter 1
Letter 2
Letter 3
Letter 4
Letter 5

Selecting nondjacent files

1. Click to select the first file.

Chapter 1
Chapter 2
Chapter 3
Chapter 4
Chapter 5

2. Hold down ⇧ Shift and click to select all files between the two you click.

3.Hold down Ctrl and click the first file in next group.

Explorer Quick Reference
Letter 1
Letter 2
Letter 3
Letter 4
Letter 5

4. Hold down Ctrl + ⇧ Shift while clicking last file in second group.

Selecting multiple groups of adjacent files

1. Click to select the first file.

Chapter 1
Chapter 2
Chapter 3
Chapter 4
Chapter 5

2. Hold down ⇧ Shift and click to select all files between the two you click.

Explorer Quick Reference
Letter 1
Letter 2
Letter 3
Letter 4
Letter 5

3.Hold down Ctrl and click each of the other files.

Selecting a group, then individual files

TUTORIAL

IN this tutorial you explore selecting one or more objects on the *Win95 Student Resource Disk*.

Getting Ready

1. Use Windows Explorer to open the *Explorer Documents* folder on the *Win95 Student Resource Disk* so the contents of the folder are displayed in the Contents pane.

2. Click the **Details** button on the toolbar.

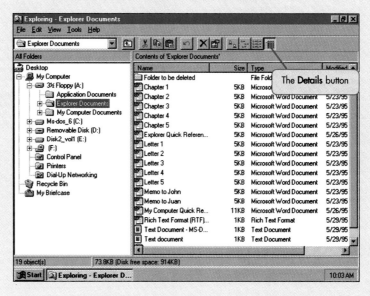

Selecting Objects by Clicking

3. Click the names or icons in the Contents pane to select each document one at a time. When you select a new one, the previous one is automatically unselected.

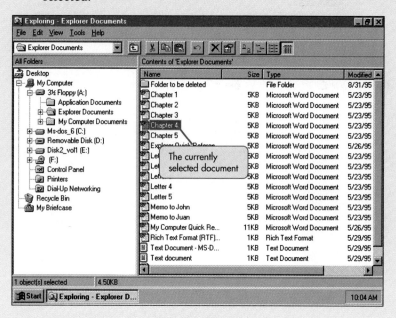

Selecting Adjacent Objects by Clicking

4. Click *Chapter 1* to select it. Then hold down ⟨⇧Shift⟩ and click *Chapter 4* to select all documents between it and the first document you selected.

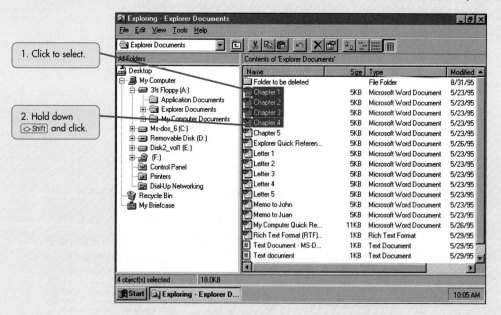

Selecting Nonadjacent Objects by Clicking

5. Click *Chapter 1* to select just it again. Then hold down ⟨Ctrl⟩ while you click *Chapter 3* and *Chapter 5* to select these nonadjacent documents.

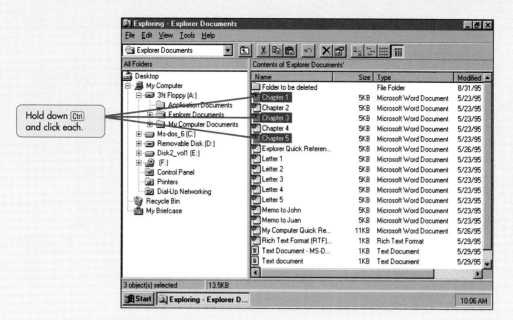

Hold down Ctrl
and click each.

Selecting All Objects

6. Pull down the **Edit** menu and click the **Select All** command to select all documents in the Contents Pane. Click the *Chapter 1* document's icon to unselect all but it.

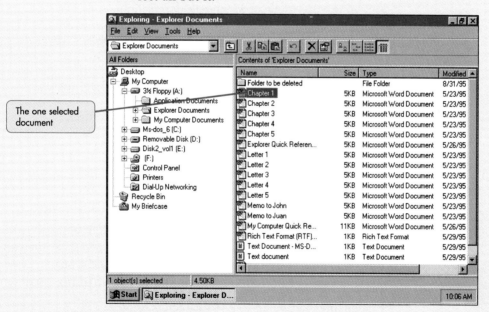

The one selected
document

Inverting a Selection

7. Pull down the **Edit** menu and click the **Invert Selection** command to unselect the previously selected document and select all of the others.

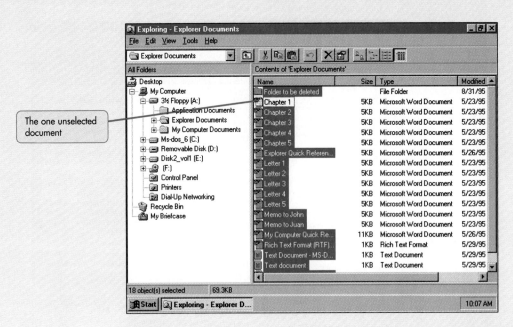

The one unselected document

Selecting objects is one of the most important procedures you need to know. Pause here to practice using all of the selection techniques described in the QuickSteps box "Selecting Objects."

Finishing Up

8. Continue to the next section or shut down your system.

4-2 RENAMING OBJECTS

Occasionally you may want to change the name of a document or folder. For example, you may not have started with a consistent approach and may decide to make things more understandable as you gain experience. You can rename a document or folder any time you can see its name and icon.

There are certain rules to keep in mind when naming documents and folders:

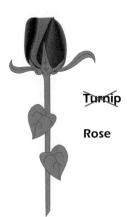

Turnip

Rose

▶ Filenames can be up to 255 characters long.

▶ Filenames can include spaces and as many periods as you want.

▶ Filenames cannot include the characters \ / : * ? " < > or |. If you use any of these characters, a message box appears and lists them for you so you can change the name.

▶ Each filename should be unique. If you assign an object the same name as a file that is already on the disk in the same folder, the new object can overwrite the previous file and erase it.

▶ Not all applications support long filenames. For example, earlier versions of Windows programs were developed for Windows 3.1, a different operating system. This earlier Windows limited filenames to eight characters followed by an optional three-character extension separated from the filename by a period. These are known as the 8.3 filenames. If you rename a document in Windows 95 and then open it with one of those earlier programs, Windows converts the long name to an 8.3 name called an *alias*.

▶ When you name a file of a type that Windows recognizes, Windows assigns a three character extension but does not normally display the extension on the screen. To display filename extensions, pull down Windows Explorer's **View** menu, click the **Options** command, and turn off the check box for *Hide MS-DOS file extensions for file types that are registered*.

T I P
Objects Not to Rename

Don't rename any of the folders or files associated with Windows and its applications. If you do so, the application may not be able to find the files that it needs to run correctly.

U I C K S T E P S
Renaming Documents and Folders

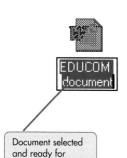

Document selected and ready for renaming

1. To begin renaming a document or folder, do one of the following:

▶ Click the folder's or document's name to select it, pause a moment and click it again. (If you click the second click too fast, you may open the document.)

▶ Right-click the folder's or document's name or icon, then click the short-cut menu's **Rename** command.

▶ Click the folder's or document's name to select it, then pull down the **File** menu and click the **Rename** command.

A box appears around the name, the name is highlighted, and an insertion point is at the end of the filename.

2. Type a new name (the first character you type deletes the highlighted name), or move the insertion point to edit the existing name.

T I P
Contents Pane Isn't Accurate

When you change disks in a drive or when you copy, move, rename, or delete objects, My Computer and Windows Explorer are not always updated. To be sure the current folders and documents are listed, pull down the **View** menu and click the **Refresh** command to update the window's listing.

TUTORIAL

I N this tutorial you rename documents and folders by entering new names and editing existing ones.

Getting Ready

1. Insert the *Win95 Student Resource Disk* into the drive you use to open and save documents and use Windows Explorer to open that drive.

2. Click the **Large Icons** button on the toolbar to display objects in the Contents pane as large icons.

Renaming a Folder

3. Click the *Explorer Documents* folder in the Tree pane to select it, then click it again to outline it. The current name is selected and at the right end is a flashing insertion point.

The highlighted folder name

4. Type **Explorer Folder** and press [Enter ◄┘]. The first character you typed deleted the previous name. The new name is now listed in the Tree pane.

The new folder name

Editing a Folder Name

5. With the *Explorer Folder* still selected in the Tree pane, click its name to outline it again. The current filename is selected and at the right end is a flashing insertion point.

The highlighted folder name

6. Press [→] to remove the highlight from the folder name, then press [← Bksp] to delete the *Folder* part of the name.

7. Press [Spacebar] (if necessary), type **Documents**, and press [Enter ◄┘]. The folder name should now read as it did originally: *Explorer Documents*.

Renaming a Document

8. With the *Explorer Documents* folder still selected in the Tree pane, click the *Memo to John* icon in the Contents pane to select it, then click its name to outline it.

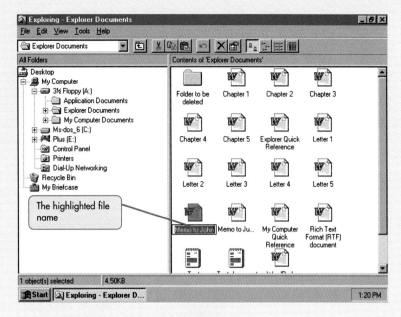

The highlighted file name

9. Press → to remove the highlight from the folder name, press (Spacebar), type **Davis** and press (Enter ←) to rename the document.

Finishing Up

10. Continue to the next section, or shut down your system.

4-3 CREATING FOLDERS

When working on a computer it is essential that your documents be organized. When you first begin using a computer, folders may not seem important. However, after a while you will have so many documents that if they aren't organized into folders, you'll have trouble finding the document you want to use. You organize documents by saving related ones in the same folder. To do so, you create folders. When the folders are no longer needed, you delete them. Folder names follow the same conventions that you use for filenames. When creating folders, you should have some kind of a plan.

▸ Do not store documents in the same folder as the application program files. For example, the Microsoft Word's program files might be in the *MSOffice* folder but you might store its documents in a folder named *Word documents*.

▸ Keep all related documents in their own folders. You might have separate folders for memos, letters, reports, financial documents, and name and address lists. The actual breakdown depends on the kinds of documents you create.

▸ Do not create too many levels of folders within folders. Most disks can be well organized with no more than three levels, including the topmost folder.

QUICKSTEPS

Creating New Folders

1. Open the folder you want the new folder to be in.

2. To create the new folder, do one of the following:

   ▶ Pull down the **File** menu, click the **New** command to cascade the menu, then click the **Folder** command.

   ▶ Right-click in a clear area of the window, click the shortcut menu's **New** command, then click the **Folder** command.

   The new folder appears in the window with its temporary name New *Folder* highlighted.

3. Type the name of the new folder and press Enter ↵ or click elsewhere.

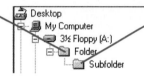

1. To create this folder, select *3 1/2 floppy (A:)*, then use the **File**, **New**, **Folder** command.

2. To create this folder, select *Folder*, then use the **File**, **New**, **Folder** command.

TIP

Creating New Folders on the Desktop

You can create a new folder that is displayed right on Windows' desktop. To do so, right-click a clear area on the desktop, click the shortcut menu's **New** command to cascade the menu, and click the **Folder** command. This folder becomes a folder within the *Windows Desktop* folder. To see it, you'd open the *Windows* folder and then the *Desktop* folder.

TUTORIAL

In this tutorial you create a number of folders and subfolders on the *Win95 Student Resource Disk*.

Getting Ready

1. Insert the *Win95 Student Resource Disk* into the drive you use to open and save documents and use Windows Explorer to open and expand the folders on that drive.

2. Click the **Large Icons** button on the toolbar to display objects in the Contents pane as large icons.

Creating a Folder

3. Click the ⊞ in front of the *Explorer Documents* folder to expand it.

4. Click the *Explorer Documents* folder in the Tree pane to select it.

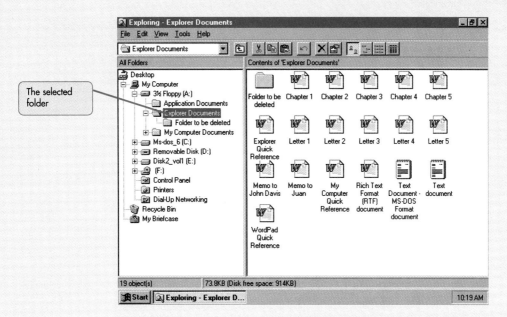

The selected folder

5. Pull down the **File** menu and click the **New** command to cascade the menu.

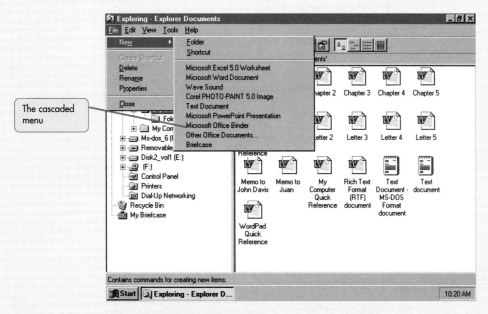

The cascaded menu

6. Click the **Folder** command to display the new folder in the Contents pane. Its temporary name *New Folder* is highlighted.

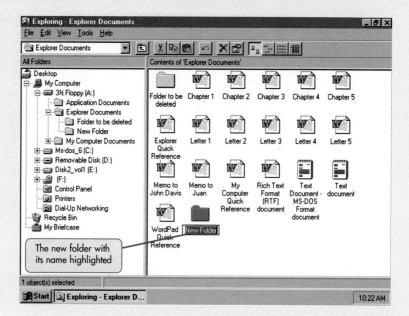

The new folder with its name highlighted

7. Type **Backup Documents** and press [Enter ←]. The new folder is now listed in the Contents pane.

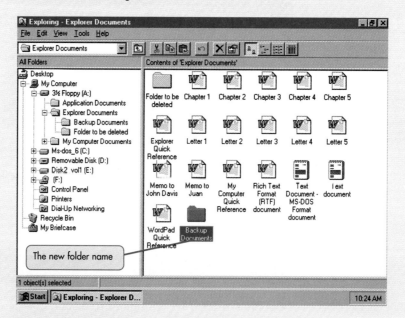

The new folder name

Creating Subfolders

8. Click the *Backup Documents* folder in the Tree pane to select it. It is empty so no documents or folders are listed in the Contents pane.

9. Right-click in the Contents pane, and click the shortcut menu's **New** command to cascade the menu.

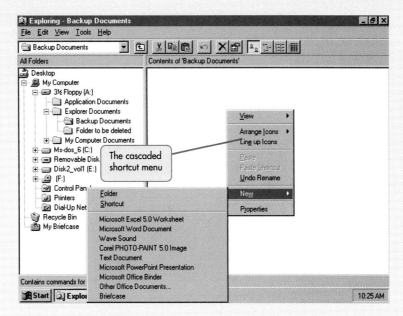

10. Click the **Folder** command to display the new folder in the Contents pane. Its temporary name *New Folder* is highlighted.

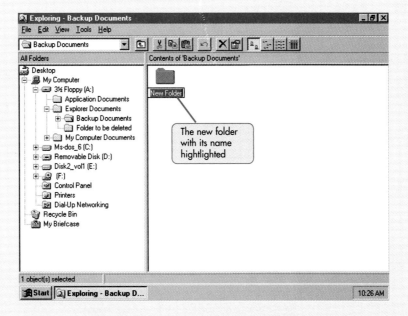

11. Type **Chapter Documents** and press Enter⏎. The new folder is now listed in the Contents pane.

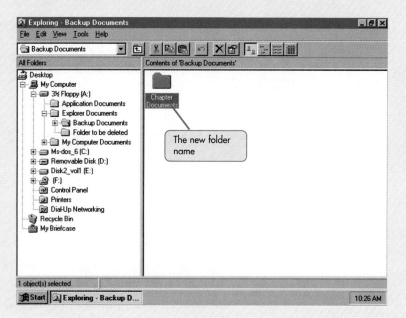

The new folder name

12. Click the [+] in front of the *Backup Documents* folder in the Tree pane to open it and see the new folder under it.

13. Repeat Steps 9 through 11 but name the new folder **Other Documents**.

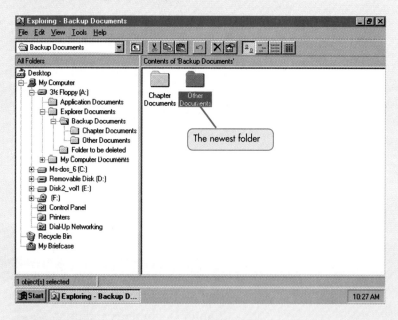

The newest folder

Finishing Up

14. Continue to the next section, or shut down your system.

4-4 DELETING OBJECTS

If you use a system extensively, eventually even the largest hard disk drive will become full of documents or folders. It's good system management to delete objects that are no longer needed so that room is freed up on the disk. If the documents or folders may be used later, they can first be copied to a backup disk or tape and then deleted from the hard drive.

When you delete a document or folder, it usually isn't actually deleted from the disk. Instead it is moved to the Recycle Bin. This way you can restore the object should you discover that you need it. However, the Recycle Bin stores only the objects that fit in the specified disk space. Older documents are deleted to make room for new ones, so you can't wait forever to restore a document. Also, files you delete from floppy disks are not saved in the Recycle Bin.

TIP
Bypassing the Recycle Bin

You can delete objects without saving them in the Recycle Bin. To do so, select them and then press `⇧ Shift`+`Delete` instead of `Delete` If you use this procedure, you cannot then undelete the object.

The **Delete** button

One side affect of moving documents to the Recycle Bin is that deleting them doesn't give you more room on the disk because they are just moved to another folder on the disk. To gain disk space, you have to delete documents from the Recycle Bin, as described in Section 4-5.

TIP
Write-Protecting Your Disks

When you work with documents and folders on floppy disks, you can lose work if you make a mistake. To protect important documents, write-protect the disk. If a disk is write-protected, you can read documents on the disk, but you cannot save documents on it, format it, or erase documents from it. To rename, copy, move, or delete documents or folders on a floppy disk, remove write-protection.

▶ To write-protect a 5¼-inch floppy disk, cover the write-protect notch with a piece of write-protect tape.

▶ To write-protect a 3½-inch floppy disk, open the sliding tab in the write-protect window.

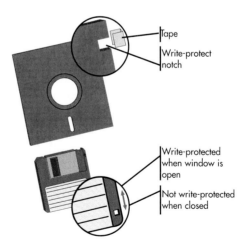

Why do you write-protect one type of disk by *covering* the notch and the other by *uncovering* the window? If you are paranoid and believe in conspiracies, this may be evidence you need to prove that there is a plot to make computers as difficult as possible!

QUICKSTEPS

Deleting Documents and Folders

1. Select the documents or folders to be deleted.
2. To delete selected objects, do one of the following:
   ▸ Press [Delete]
   ▸ Click the **Delete** button on the toolbar.
   ▸ Right-click the object's name or icon, then click the shortcut menu's **Delete** command.
   ▸ Pull down the **File** menu and click the **Delete** command.
3. When a message box asks you if you want to send the document or folder to the Recycle Bin, click the **Yes** button to delete the selected documents or folders or **No** to cancel the command.

TUTORIAL

IN this tutorial you delete documents and folders from the *Win95 Student Resource Disk*.

Getting Ready

1. Insert the *Win95 Student Resource Disk* into the drive you use to open and save documents and use Windows Explorer to open and expand the folders on that drive.
2. Click the **Large Icons** button on the toolbar to display objects in the Contents pane as large icons.

Deleting a Folder

3. If necessary, click the ⊞ in front of the *Explorer Documents* folder in the Tree pane to expand it. Then click the subfolder *Folder to be deleted* to select it. Its contents, five documents named *Book 1* through *Book 5*, are displayed in the Contents pane.
4. Click the **Delete** button on the toolbar and a dialog box asks you to confirm the deletion.

The **Delete** button

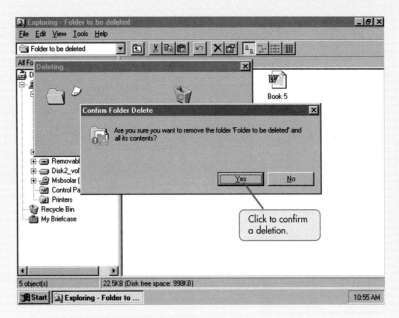

Click to confirm
a deletion.

5. Click the **Yes** button and the Deleting dialog box keeps you posted on the progress. When it disappears, the folder is no longer listed in the Tree pane. (Its contents have not been moved to the Recycle Bin because you deleted it from a floppy disk.)

Deleting a Document

6. Open the *Explorer Documents* folder and click the *Memo to Juan* in the Contents pane to select it.

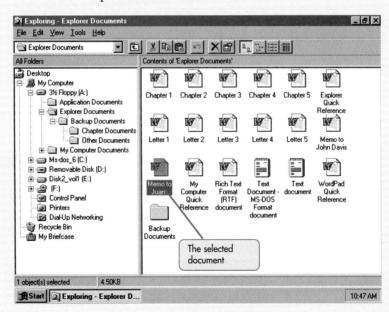

The selected
document

7. Click the **Delete** button on the toolbar and a dialog box asks you to confirm the deletion.

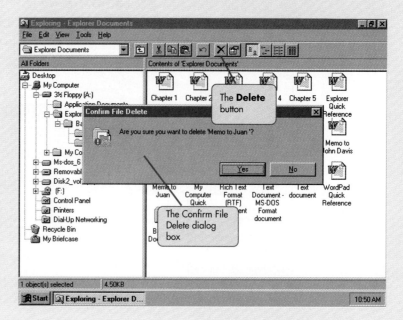

8. Click the **Yes** button to delete the listed document, and the document is no longer listed in the Contents pane.

Finishing Up

9. Continue to the next section or shut down your system.

4-5 UNDELETING OBJECTS

It's easy to delete documents or folders by mistake. For example, you may select a document by mistake, or delete a folder that contains a subfolder you didn't mean to delete. When this happens, if you notice the mistake soon enough, you can recover the deleted document or folder (although objects deleted from a floppy disk are not moved to the Recycle Bin).

T I P

Undoing the Last Act

Windows has a command that quickly undoes many actions you take such as renaming, deleting, moving, or copying an object. To use it, do one of the following:

▶ Right-click in a My Computer window, Windows Explorer's Contents pane, or on the desktop, then click the shortcut menu's **Undo** command.

▶ Pull down My Computer's or Windows Explorer's **Edit** menu, and click the **Undo** command.

If the command is dimmed on the menu, it means the last action cannot be undone.

Undeleting Documents and Folders

To undo some or all document deletions, you open the Recycle Bin. Windows keeps track of where objects were deleted from. If you restore a document, it is restored in its original location. If you delete a folder, only the documents that were stored in that folder are listed in the Recycle Bin, not the folder. If you restore a document that was originally in a deleted folder, the deleted folder is restored with the document in it.

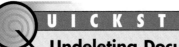

Undeleting Documents and Folders

1. To open the Recycle Bin, double-click the *Recycle Bin* icon on the desktop.
2. To undo a deletion, select any listed object(s), pull down the **File** menu and click the **Restore** command.

TIP
Properties

To see details about a document in the Recycle Bin, right-click it and then click the shortcut menu's **Properties** command.

TIP
Opening the Recycle Bin

In addition to double-clicking the *Recycle Bin* icon on the desktop, Windows gives you many more ways to open the Recycle Bin.

▶ Right-click the *Recycle Bin* icon on the desktop and click the **Open** command.

▶ In Windows Explorer, right-click *Recycle Bin* on the Tree pane and then click the shortcut menu's **Open** command.

▶ Click the *Go to a different folder* drop-down arrow on My Computer's or Windows Explorer's toolbar and click *Recycle Bin*.

Emptying the Recycle Bin

As you delete folders and documents, they are added to the Recycle Bin and not actually deleted from the disk. Instead, they are moved to a separate folder on the disk. As a result, deleting documents does not gain you more free disk space. The only way to do that is to empty the Recycle Bin. When you do so, the documents are permanently deleted.

Emptying the Recycle Bin

To empty the Recycle Bin, do one of the following:

▶ Open the Recycle Bin, pull down the **File** menu, and click the **Empty Recycle Bin** command.

▶ Right-click the *Recycle Bin* icon on the desktop, then click the shortcut menu's **Empty Recycle Bin** command.

IN this tutorial you delete some documents and folders and then restore them. Because Windows doesn't save documents deleted from floppy disks in the Recycle Bin, you will first create some new documents on the desktop.

Getting Ready

1. Right-click the desktop, then click the shortcut menu's **Ne<u>w</u>** command to cascade the menu.

2. Click the **Text Document** command and an icon named *New Text Document* appears on the desktop. Press [Enter ◄┘] to complete the procedure.

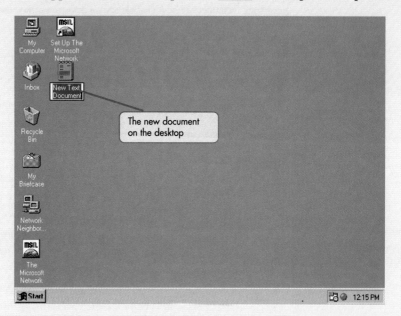

The new document on the desktop

3. Right-click the desktop, then click the shortcut menu's **Ne<u>w</u>** command to cascade the menu.

4. Click the **<u>F</u>older** command and an icon named *New Folder* appears on the desktop. Press [Enter ◄┘] to complete the procedure.

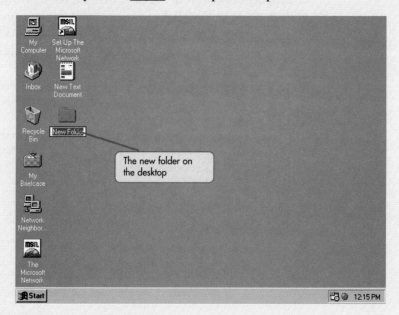

The new folder on the desktop

5. Repeat Steps 1 through 2 to create a second new document on the desktop named *New Text Document (2)*.

Deleting a Document

6. Click the *New Text Document* icon on the desktop to select it, and press `Delete` to delete it.

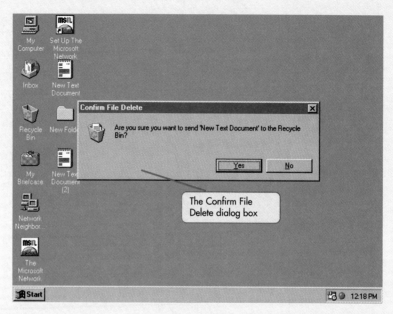

The Confirm File Delete dialog box

7. When asked to confirm the deletion, click the **Yes** button.

Deleting a Folder

8. Click the *New Folder* icon on the desktop to select it, and press `Delete` to delete it.

9. When asked to confirm the deletion, click the **Yes** button.

Restoring Documents

10. Double-click the *Recycle Bin* icon on the desktop to open it. Click its **Maximize** button to display it full screen. Notice how the deleted folder is not listed. The Recycle Bin doesn't save folders, just the documents they contain.

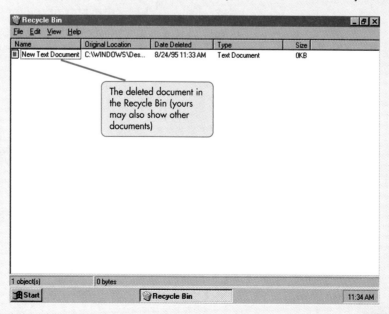

The deleted document in the Recycle Bin (yours may also show other documents)

11. Click the document named *New Text Document* to select it, then pull down the **File** menu and click the **Restore** command.

12. Click the recycle Bin's **Close** button to close the application and return to the desktop.

Emptying the Recycle Bin

13. Click the *New Text Document* icon on the desktop to select it, and press Delete to delete it. When asked to confirm the deletion, click the **Yes** button.

14. Repeat Step 13 to delete *New Text Document (2)*.

15. Double-click the *Recycle Bin* icon on the desktop to open it.

16. Pull down the **File** menu and click the **Empty Recycle Bin** command. A dialog box asks you to confirm the procedure.

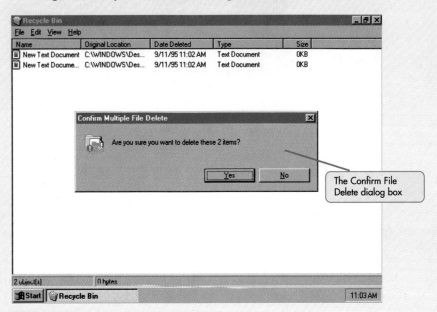

The Confirm File Delete dialog box

17. Click the **Yes** button on the Confirm File Delete dialog box to delete the documents in the Recycle Bin.

Finishing Up

18. Click the Recycle Bin's **Close** button to close the application.

19. Continue to the next section, or shut down your system.

4-6 COPYING AND MOVING OBJECTS

You can copy or move selected documents or folders between drives or between folders. To do so, you first select them, then *cut* or *copy* them from one location and *paste* them into another.

▶ If you cut and paste objects, they are first copied to the new location and then deleted from their original location.

▶ If you copy and paste objects, they are copied to the new location and also remain in the original location.

▶ If you copy and paste a document in the same folder, Windows uses the same filename but automatically adds the phrase *Copy of* in front of it.

QUICKSTEPS

Copying or Moving Objects with Buttons or Menu Commands

1. To copy or cut a document or folder, select the objects to be copied or moved, then do one of the following:
- ▶ Click the **Cut** or **Copy** button on the toolbar.
- ▶ Pull down the **Edit** menu and click the **Cut** or **Copy** command.
- ▶ Right-click the object's name or icon and then click the shortcut menu's **Cut** or **Copy** command.

2. To paste the document into a new folder, select the folder, then do one of the following:
- ▶ Click the **Paste** button on the toolbar.
- ▶ Pull down the **Edit** menu, and click the **Paste** command.
- ▶ Right-click the folder's name or icon and then click the shortcut menu's **Paste** command.

In addition to using Cut, Copy, and Paste buttons and commands, you can also use the **Send To** command to copy folders and documents to a floppy disk drive. This is especially useful when you want to copy some objects to transfer to another system or send to another user.

QUICKSTEPS

Sending Objects to a Floppy Disk

1. To send objects, insert a floppy disk in drive A, then use My Computer or Windows Explorer to select the objects you want to copy.

2. Right-click the selected object's name or icon and then click the shortcut menu's **Send To** command to cascade the menu.

3. Click the *3½ Floppy (A)* choice and the selected objects are copied to the floppy disk.

TUTORIAL

In this tutorial you copy and move documents on the *Win95 Student Resource Disk*.

Getting Ready

1. Insert the *Win95 Student Resource Disk* into the drive you use to open and save documents and use Windows Explorer to open and expand the folders on that drive.

2. Click the **Large Icons** button on the toolbar to display objects in the Contents pane as large icons.

Copying Documents

3. Click the *Explorer Documents* folder in the Tree pane to open it and list its contents in the Contents pane.

4. Hold down Ctrl and click the documents named *Chapter 1, Chapter 2,* and *Chapter 3*. Release Ctrl and all of the documents remain selected.

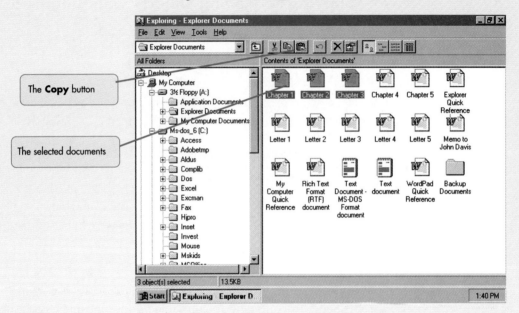

The **Copy** button

The selected documents

5. Click the **Copy** button on the toolbar.

6. Click the *Application Documents* folder in the Tree pane to open it and then click the **Paste** button on the toolbar. The Copying dialog box keeps you posted on the progress. When it disappears, the three documents are listed in the Contents pane showing they have been copied to the *Application Documents* folder. (You may have to scroll to see them.)

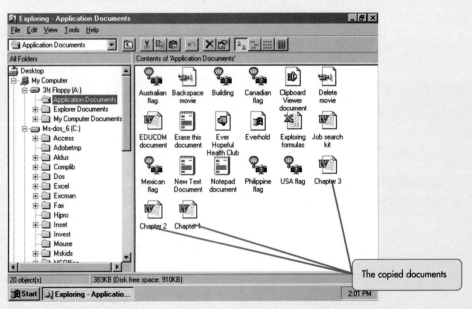

The copied documents

Moving Documents

7. Hold down Ctrl and click the documents named *Chapter 1, Chapter 2,* and *Chapter 3*. Release Ctrl and all of the documents remain selected.

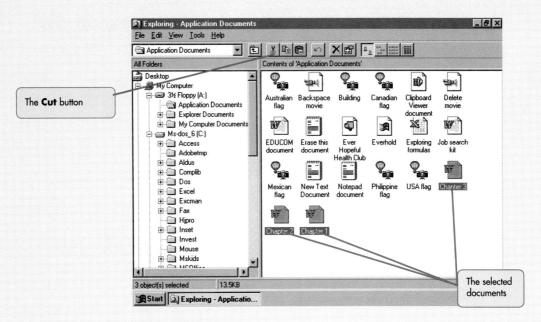

The Cut button

The selected documents

8. Click the **Cut** button on the toolbar.

9. Click the *Explorer Documents* folder to open it and then click the **Paste** button on the toolbar. Since the original copies remain in the *Explorer Documents* folder, the Confirm File Replace dialog box appears. Notice how information is supplied for both documents so you can tell one from the other. In this case they are identical.

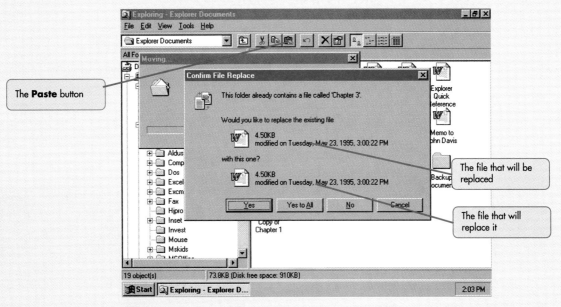

The **Paste** button

The file that will be replaced

The file that will replace it

10. Click the <u>Y</u>es command button to copy the document anyway. After it has been copied, the Confirm File Replace dialog box appears again, listing the next document.

11. Click the **Yes to <u>A</u>ll** command button to move all of the documents into the folder.

12. Click the *Application Documents* folder in the Tree pane to open it and see that the documents are no longer listed in the Contents pane for the folder.

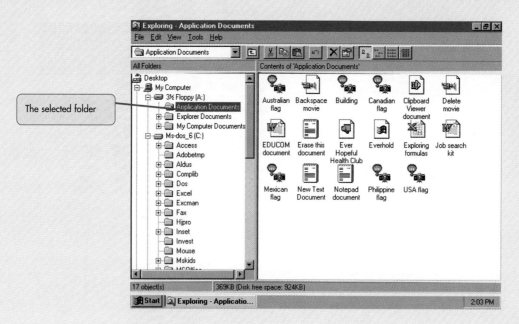

The selected folder

Finishing Up

13. Continue to the next section, or shut down your system.

4-7 DRAGGING AND DROPPING OBJECTS

Instead of using buttons and menu commands to copy or move objects, you can drag them from one place to another with the mouse and then release them. This is called *dragging and dropping*, and it is a quick way to copy or move folders or documents.

As you drag an object, a dimmed copy of the object appears attached to the mouse pointer. It is this dimmed copy of the object that you drop where you want the object copied or moved. Symbols on the mouse pointer alert you to certain conditions:.

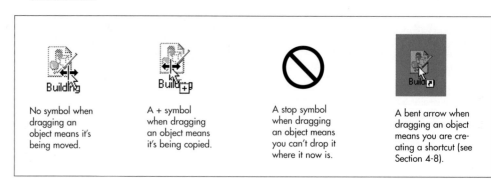

No symbol when dragging an object means it's being moved.

A + symbol when dragging an object means it's being copied.

A stop symbol when dragging an object means you can't drop it where it now is.

A bent arrow when dragging an object means you are creating a shortcut (see Section 4-8).

▶ A mouse pointer with a plus sign means the document or folder will be copied. Without one, it means the object is being moved.

▶ A mouse pointer shaped like a circle with a slash through it means you are pointing to a place on the screen where the object can't be dropped.

If you right-drag an object, a shortcut menu opens when you drop it to let you choose between moving it and copying it. If you do this, you won't make a mistake.

Copying and Moving Objects by Dragging and Dropping

1. In My Computer or Windows Explorer find the object you want to drag.
2. Display the place where you want to drag the object. To do so, open another My Computer window, or scroll Windows Explorer's Tree to see the destination folder.
3. Right-drag the objects and drop them to display a shortcut menu that allows you to choose between **C**opy Here and **M**ove Here.
4. If a confirmation message appears, read it and choose the appropriate option.

TIP

Expanding and Opening Folders

The Tree pane is designed so you can click ⊞ or ⊟ to expand and collapse folders without actually opening them. This means the objects listed in the Contents pane do not change. This is very useful when you want to drag a document from the Contents pane and drop it into a folder that you can't immediately see on the screen. As you drag it, Windows Explorer's Tree pane will scroll if you drag against its borders.

TUTORIAL

In this tutorial you copy and move documents on the *Win95 Student Resource Disk* by dragging and dropping them.

Getting Ready

1. Insert the *Win95 Student Resource Disk* into the drive you use to open and save documents and use Windows Explorer to open and expand the folders on that drive.
2. Click the **Large Icons** button on the toolbar to display objects in the Contents pane as large icons.

Moving Documents

3. Click the ⊞ in front of the *My Computer Documents* folder in the Tree pane to open it.
4. Click the *Memos* folder in the Tree pane to open it and display its contents.
5. Click the filename *Memo 1* to select it in the Contents pane, hold down ⇧Shift, click *Memo 3*, and then release ⇧Shift.
6. Point anywhere in the selected documents, and hold down the left mouse button. Drag the documents to the *Application Documents* folder in the Tree pane. An outline is shown for all three documents so you can position them over the *Application Documents* folder so it is highlighted.

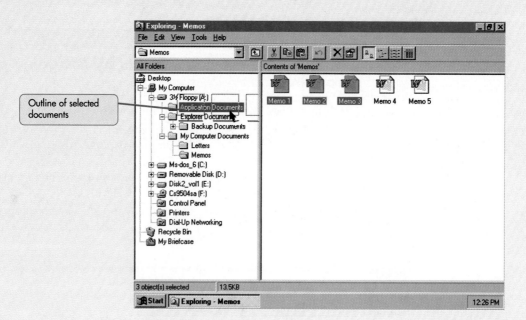

Outline of selected documents

7. Release the mouse button to drop the documents into the *Application Documents* folder. Dragging objects to another folder on the same disk moves them there. The objects are no longer listed in the *My Computer Documents* folder. Click the *Application Documents* folder to see the documents listed in the Contents pane.

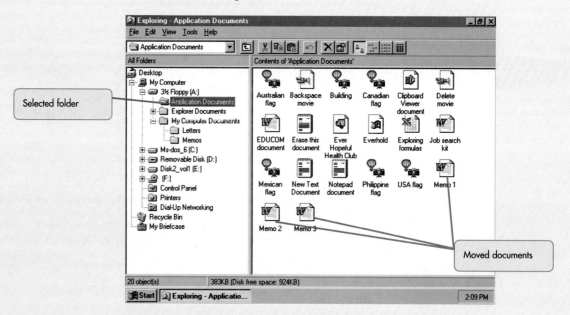

Selected folder

Moved documents

Copying Documents

8. With the *Application Documents* folder still open, click the filename *Memo 1* to select it in the Contents pane. Then hold down ⟨⇧Shift⟩ while you click the filename *Memo 3* and then release ⟨⇧Shift⟩.

9. Point anywhere in the selected documents, and right-drag them to the *Explorer Documents* folder in the Tree pane. An outline is shown for the documents so you can position them over the *Explorer Documents* folder so it is highlighted.

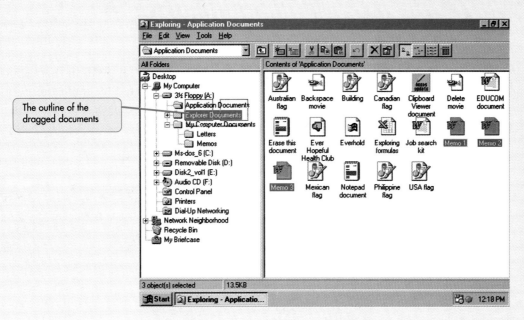

The outline of the dragged documents

10. Release the mouse button and click the shortcut menu's **Copy Here** command.

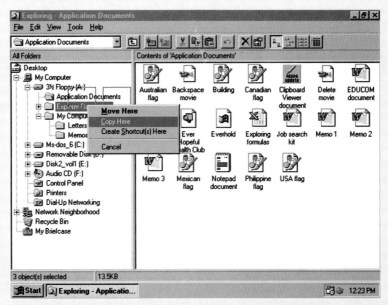

11. Click both the *Application Documents* and *Explorer Documents* folders and you'll see the documents listed in both. Right-dragging allowed you to copy the documents to the same disk instead of moving them.

Finishing Up

12. Continue to the next section, or shut down your system.

4-8 WORKING WITH SHORTCUTS

Sometimes it can seem like a hassle searching through menus to open an application, then searching through folders to open a document. But it needn't be.

When you use a program or document frequently, you can create a shortcut to it from the desktop or a folder. A *shortcut* is simply a link or pointer to an object stored elsewhere. When you double-click the shortcut, it opens the object. If the shortcut points to a document, it also opens the application that created it.

Shortcuts can point to almost any object, including applications, documents, folders, the Control Panel, or a printer; and these objects can be on the local computer or elsewhere on a network. You can have more than one shortcut to the same object. This makes applications or documents available from different places without having to copy them—which would take up additional disk space.

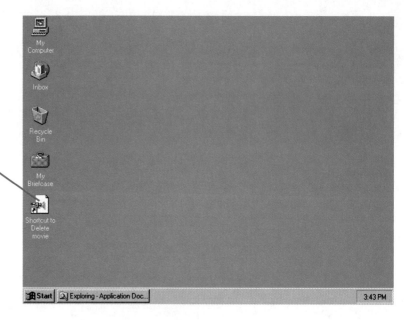

Right-dragging a document onto the desktop, dropping it, and selecting the shortcut menu's **Create Shortcut(s) Here** command creates a shortcut. Double-click the icon and you start the application and open the document.

Windows provides many ways to create shortcuts. The simplest and most frequently used are described in the QuickSteps box "Creating A Shortcut."

QUICKSTEPS

Creating a Shortcut

▶ To create a shortcut in the same location as the object itself, right-click the object to display a shortcut menu, or pull down the **File** menu. Click the menu's **Create Shortcut** command and a new icon for the object appears with a bent arrow. You can drag this shortcut icon to the desktop or to another folder.

▶ To create a shortcut in the same or a new location, right-drag and then drop the object onto the desktop or into the same or a different folder. When the shortcut menu appears, click the **Create Shortcut(s) Here** command. You can do the same thing by holding down Ctrl + ⇧ Shift while dragging and dropping the object.

TUTORIAL

I N this tutorial you create and then delete shortcuts that open documents on the *Win95 Student Resource Disk*.

Getting Ready

1. Insert the *Win95 Student Resource Disk* into the drive you use to open and save documents and open Windows Explorer.

2. Click the **Large Icons** button on the toolbar to display objects in the Contents pane as large icons.

Creating a Shortcut to a Document by Dragging

3. Click the *Application Documents* folder to open it.

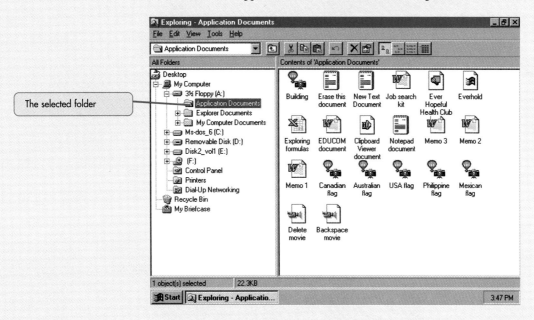

4. Make sure the Exploring window is sized so you can see a part of the desktop where we will place the shortcut. (Click its **Restore** button if necessary.)

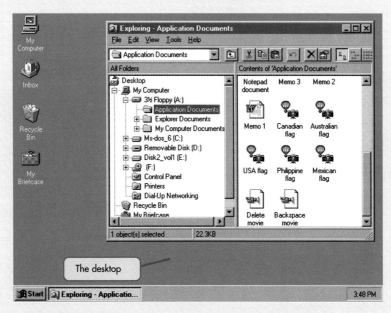

5. Right-drag the *Notepad document* and drop it onto the desktop.

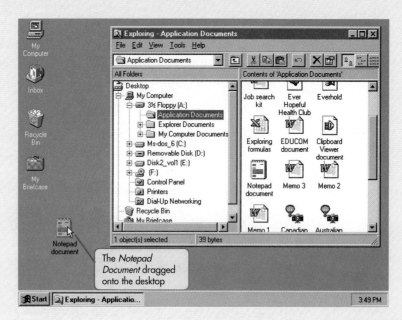

The *Notepad Document* dragged onto the desktop

6. When you drop the document, click the shortcut menu's **Create Shortcut(s) Here** command. A new icon named *Shortcut to Notepad document* is now on the desktop. (You may have to minimize the Exploring window to see it.)

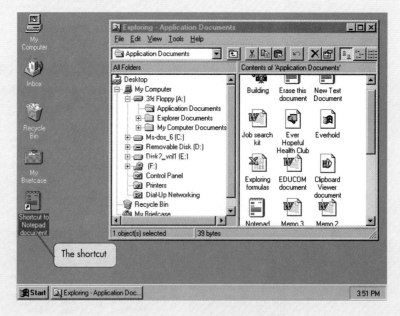

The shortcut

7. Double-click the *Shortcut to Notepad* document icon and it opens Notepad and the document.

8. Click Notepad's **Close** button to close the application.

Deleting the Shortcut

9. Click the *Shortcut to Notepad* document icon on the desktop and press [Delete] Click the **Yes** button when asked to confirm sending it to the Recycle Bin.

Finishing Up

10. Continue to the next section or shut down your system.

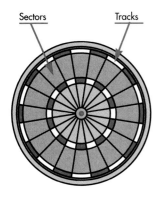

Sectors   Tracks

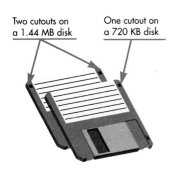

Two cutouts on a 1.44 MB disk   One cutout on a 720 KB disk

A computer cannot store data on a disk until the disk has been formatted for the type of system you are using. Some new disks come already formatted for use with Windows and DOS, but others have to be formatted before you can use them.

Formatting checks the disk surface for unusable spots, divides the disk into tracks and sectors, and creates a folder in which to store a map of the documents on the disk. Tracks and sectors are an invisible magnetic pattern on the disk that looks something like the pattern on a dartboard. On a formatted disk, tracks run in circles around the disk. Because tracks can store a great deal of data, the computer needs to divide them into sectors, which makes it easier to find a location on the disk. These sectors are like pie-shaped wedges that divide each track into the same number of sectors.

To store more data, the tracks on some disks are placed closer together. The spacing of these tracks is measured as *tracks per inch* (TPI). The number of TPI determines the density of the disk and the amount of data that can be stored on it. The commonly used 3½-inch floppy disks store 1.44MB. These disks can store more data than the larger 5¼-inch disks because they have more tracks per inch than the larger disks. (You can tell the newer 3½-inch disk from an older one that stored only 720KB, because the older disk has a single square cutout and a 1.44MB disk has two square cutouts.)

QUICKSTEPS
Formatting Disks

1. Insert the disk you want to format into one of the system's floppy disk drives. Make sure the drive isn't selected in Windows Explorer or My Computer and that it has no open folders.

2. Right-click the drive's icon in My Computer's window or Windows Explorer's Tree pane, and then click **Format** to display the Format dialog box.

3. Make any of the settings described in the table "The Format Dialog Box Choices" and then click the **Start** button.

TIP
Warning

Formatting a disk effectively erases any data that may already have been saved on it. You therefore have to be careful with this command. You should never format a previously used disk unless you are sure you will not need any of the documents on it. Moreover, you should never format a hard disk drive unless you are willing to lose every document on the disk. However, to keep you from making mistakes, Windows won't let you format a disk that has an open file on it, a compressed drive, or a remote network drive.

The Format Dialog Box Choices

▶ **Capacity** drop-down list displays a list of the formats from which you can choose for the selected drive. Unless you specify otherwise, Windows formats a disk to match the drive it is being formatted in.

Quick (erase), when on, erases the files contained on a previously formatted disk but doesn't check the disk for bad sectors and other problems.

Full, when on, completely formats a disk. You must use this option with any disk that has not been previously formatted.

Copy system files only, when on, transfers only the system files needed to boot a system to an already formatted disk.

▶ The **Label** text box is where you enter a label for the disk up to 11 characters long. (You can also add or change a disk's label by right-clicking its icon and then changing the disk's properties.)

▶ **No label**, when on, removes any label from the disk.

▶ **Copy system files**, when on, copies the files needed to boot a system. When you boot the computer with a startup disk such as this in drive A, the operating system is loaded from that disk instead of from drive C.

TUTORIAL

IN this tutorial you format a blank disk. **Be sure the disk does not contain any data that you want to save because formatting it will erase the data!**

Getting Ready

1. Label a blank floppy disk, using as a guide the label shown here, then insert the disk into the drive you use to open and save documents.

Formatting a Disk

2. Double-click the *My Computer* icon on the desktop to open it.

3. Right-click the icon for the drive into which you inserted your new disk, and a shortcut menu is displayed.

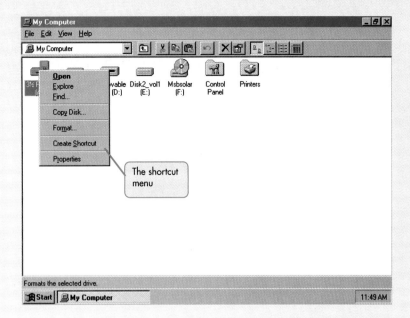

4. Click the **Format** command to display a dialog box. The command automatically lists the drive you right-clicked, but your **Capacity** setting may be different depending on the type of drive that you clicked.

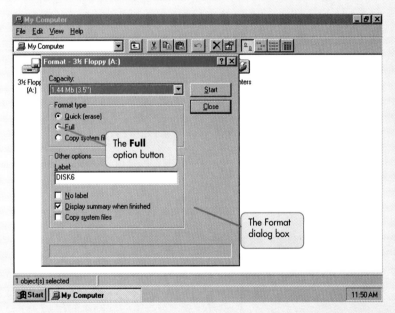

5. Click the **Full** option button in the *Format type* section of the dialog box.

6. Click in the **Label** text box to move the insertion point there, then type your first name (abbreviate to 11 characters if necessary).

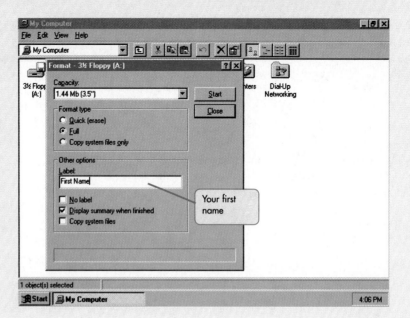

7. Click the **Start** button to format the disk and the drive spins and its light comes on as the disk is formatted. A progress indicator displays the status of the formatting procedure.

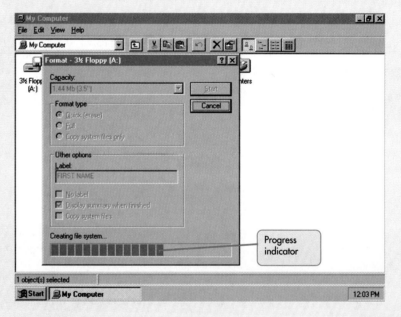

When the disk has been formatted, the Format Results box tells you how much total space is on the disk and how much is available for your documents.

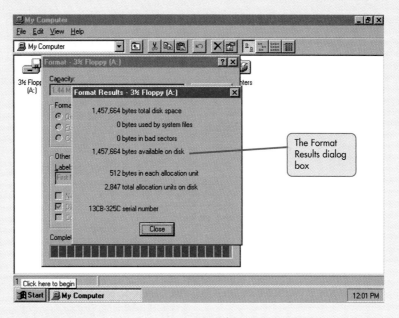

The Format Results dialog box

Finishing Up

8. Click the **Close** button and you return to the Format dialog box. Click its **Close** button and you return to My computer.

9. Continue to the next section or shut down your system.

4-10 COPYING DISKS

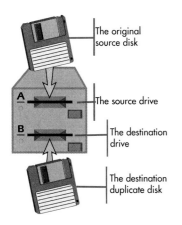

The original source disk

The source drive

The destination drive

The destination duplicate disk

There are times when you want to make an exact duplicate of a disk. For example, you may want to make a backup copy of an application program you bought so you can store the original in a safe place.

▶ The destination disk will be formatted as part of the process, if necessary.

▶ The command copies not only documents but also folders and subfolders.

▶ If you use this command to copy objects to a disk that already contains documents or folders, the existing objects on that disk will be erased.

▶ You can only use the **Copy Disk** command to copy documents and folders between disks with identical storage capacities. For example, you cannot use **Copy Disk** between a high-density 5¼-inch disk and a disk in a 360KB drive. And you cannot use this command between 5¼-inch and 3½-inch drives.

QUICKSTEPS

Duplicating Disks

1. Right-click the icon for the floppy drive containing the disk you want to duplicate to display a shortcut menu.

2. Click the **Copy Disk** command to display the Copy Disk dialog box. The dialog box contains two drop-down list boxes you use to specify the drives you want to **Copy from** and **Copy to**.

3. If the drives are set correctly, click the **Start** button. If you are copying from and to the same drive, you will be prompted to change disks periodically.

ɪɴ this tutorial you copy your *Win95 Student Resource Disk* to the disk you labeled *Backup Resource Disk* and formatted in the previous section.

Getting Ready

1. Insert the *Win95 Student Resource Disk* into the drive you use to open and save documents and use Windows Explorer to open and expand the folders on that drive.

Copying the Disk

2. Right-click the icon for the floppy drive you put the *Win95 Student Resource Disk* into to display a shortcut menu.

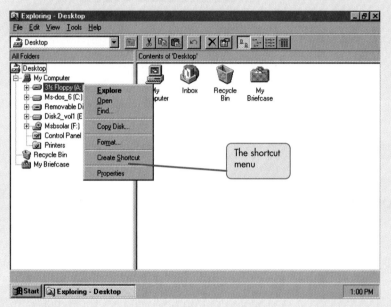

3. Click the **Copy Disk** command to display the Copy Disk dialog box. This box indicates the drives you will **Copy from** and **Copy to**.

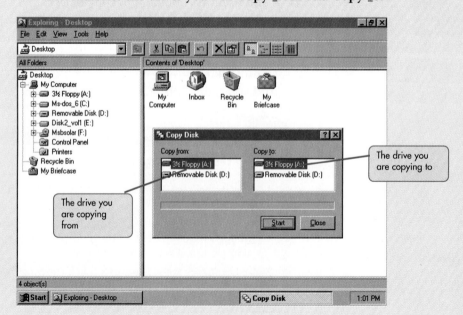

4. Click the **Start** button and what then happens depends on your system:

  ▶ If you are copying from and to the same drive, you will be prompted to change disks periodically. (The *destination disk* is the new disk labeled *Backup Resource Disk*).

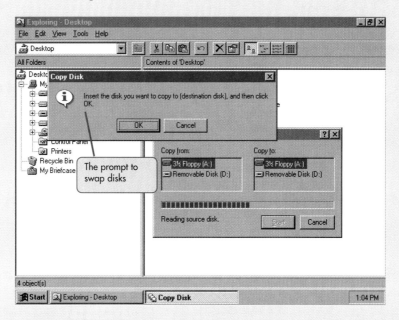

  ▶ If you are copying between two identical drives, the copy is made without any prompting.

5. When copying is completed, click the dialog box's Close button. Save the duplicate disk. If anything happens to your original, you can always make another copy from it.

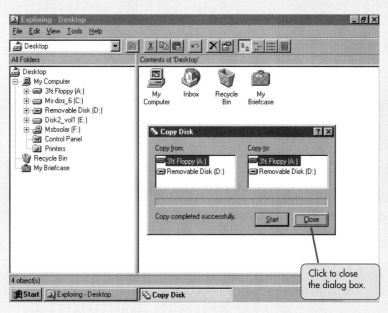

Finishing Up

6. Continue to the lab activities, or shut down your system.

MANAGING YOUR SYSTEM

1. These two illustrations show documents selected in My Computer windows.

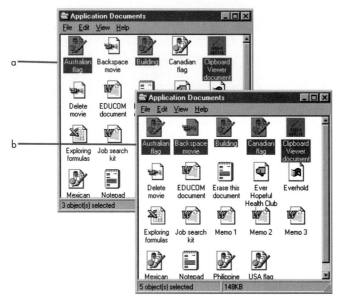

a. Describe how these files were selected.

_____

b. Describe how these files were selected using the fastest possible procedure.

_____

2. The illustration at the left shows an icon in My Computer's window. What has been done to it to make its name look the way it does?

_____

_____

3. The illustration at the left shows a folder on the floppy disk in drive A that contains a subfolder.

a. Briefly describe how you would create the folder.

_____

_____

b. Briefly describe how you would create the subfolder.

_____

_____

4. The following illustration shows the toolbar that you can display in My Computer or Windows Explorer. Which button will delete a selected document?

---

5. This illustration shows the Recycle Bin.

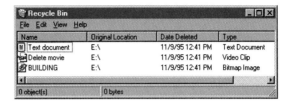

a. Briefly describe one way to open this window.

_____

b. Briefly describe how you would undelete the *Building* document.

_____

6. This illustration shows the toolbar that you can display in My Computer or Windows Explorer.

a. Which button would you click to cut a selected document or folder?

_____

b. Which button would you click to copy a selected document or folder?

_____

c. Which button would you click to paste a selected document or folder?

_____

7. This illustration shows Windows Explorer.

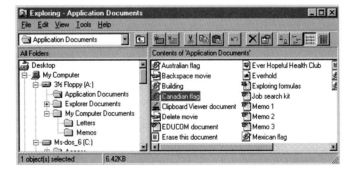

a. Describe how you would use dragging to move the document named *Canadian flag* into the *Letters* folder.

_____

_____

_____

b. Describe how you would use dragging to copy the document named *Canadian flag* into the *Letters* folder.

8. This illustration shows a My Computer window and a shortcut to one of its documents on the desktop. Explain how the shortcut may have been created.

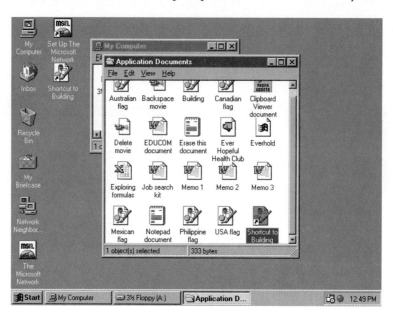

9. The illustration at the left shows a window that appears when you double-click the My Computer icon on the desktop. Describe how you would format a disk in drive A.

10. The illustration at the left shows a window that appears when you double-click the *My Computer* icon on the desktop. Describe how you would copy the disk in drive A.

REVIEW QUESTIONS

TRUE-FALSE

T F 1. Before you can copy, move, or delete a document, you must select it.

T F 2. You can only select documents that are next to each other in the Contents pane.

T F 3. To select all of the documents in the Contents pane, you have to be patient and click them one at a time.

T F 4. To rename a document or folder you double-click it.

T F 5. Sometimes the list of filenames in the Contents pane isn't accurate—it doesn't list all of the documents that it contains.

T F 6. When you create a new folder, you begin by selecting the folder on the Tree in which you want the new folder to appear.

T F 7. Hard disks are so well designed, you never have to worry about where your documents are stored on them.

T F 8. Before you can delete a folder, you must first delete all of the documents that it contains.

T F 9. Deleting documents moves them to a new folder on the disk called the Recycle Bin.

T F 10. Once you have deleted documents of folders, it's impossible to recover them.

T F 11. The Recycle Bin cannot restore deleted directories, just the documents that were in them.

T F 12. When you cut an object and then paste it elsewhere, it's the same as moving it.

T F 13. When you copy an object and then paste it elsewhere, the object is no longer found in its original location.

T F 14. When you drag a file to the same disk, it's copied and not moved.

T F 15. When you drag a file to a different disk, it's copied and not moved.

T F 16. To copy a document to the same disk, you can right-drag it.

T F 17. To move a document to a different disk, you can cut and paste it.

T F 18. A shortcut is a link to an object stored elsewhere.

T F 19. To open a shortcut, you click it.

T F 20. When formatting a data disk, Windows automatically formats the disk to the capacity of the drive it's in unless you specify otherwise.

T F 21. You can tell a 3½-inch floppy disk's capacity by its cutouts. For example, a 1.44MB disk has one cutout.

T F 22. When formatting a disk, you turn on the **Copy system files** check box only if you want to be able to boot the computer from the disk you are formatting.

T F 23. To make a copy of a disk, the first step is to right-click the drive with the disk to display a shortcut menu.

T F 24. When you copy a disk, the disk you are copying to doesn't need to be formatted.

1. To select adjacent files in My Computer or Windows Explorer's Contents pane, you ___.

    a. Click the first filename to select it, and then hold down `⇧ Shift` while you either click the last filename

    b. Hold down `⇧ Shift` and use the arrow keys to extend the highlight

    c. Hold down `Ctrl` while you click each filename

    d. Any of the above

2. To rename an object, you ___.

    a. Click the object, pause a moment and click it again

    b. Right-click the object, then click the shortcut menu's **Rename** command

    c. Click the object, then pull down the **File** menu and click the **Rename** command

    d. Any of the above

3. To create a new subfolder, you begin by selecting the folder on the tree ___ where you want the new one.

    a. Immediately below

    b. Immediately above

    c. On the same level as

    d. None of the above

4. The Recycle Bin is actually a ___.

    a. Large file without a name

    b. Special disk located somewhere in the system

    c. Folder on the disk into which deleted objects are moved

    d. None of the above

5. Once you have deleted objects, you can restore them from the Recycle Bin until ___.

    a. You empty the Recycle Bin

    b. The Recycle Bin first becomes full

    c. You turn the system off

    d. You quit Windows

6. If you copy and paste a document into the same folder as the original copy ___.

    a. The original copy is overwritten by the new copy

    b. A warning message appears

    c. The new copy has *Copy of* added to its filename

    d. None of the above

7. To copy a file to the same disk by dragging and dropping, you must hold down ___ while dragging it.

    a. Right mouse button

    b. Left mouse button

    c. Both mouse buttons

d. None of the above

8. To move a file to another disk by dragging and dropping, you must hold down ___ while dragging it.

   a. Right mouse button

   b. Left mouse button

   c. Both mouse buttons

   d. None of the above

9. You can create shortcuts that ___.

   a. Open documents

   b. Start applications

   c. Open documents and start applications

   d. All of the above

10. Formatting a disk ___.

    a. Prepares it for use on your computer

    b. Erases any data that might be on it

    c. Divides it into tracks and sectors

    d. All of the above

11. When you use the command that copies a disk, ___.

    a. Documents and folders are copied

    b. The duplicate disk is formatted if necessary

    c. Existing files on the duplicate disk are erased

    d. All of the above

FILL IN THE BLANK

1. To select nonadjacent files in the Contents pane, you hold down _____ while you click each file.

2. To select all of the files in the Contents pane, you use the _____ command on the _____.

3. To ensure that the Contents pane lists all of the files that it contains, you should pull down the Window menu can click the _____ command.

4. Windows 95 filenames can be up to _____ characters long.

5. When you delete objects, they are saved in the _____.

6. When you delete a folder containing documents, you restore the folder when you restore the _____.

7. If you use the cut and paste command, the document in the original location is _____.

8. When dragging an object to another location on the same disk, it is normally _____. When dragging it to another disk, it is normally _____.

9. Icons for shortcuts can be identified by the _____ graphic on them.

10. To make a copy of a disk, use the _____ command on the _____ menu.

LAB ACTIVITIES

4-1 Selecting Objects

Before you can copy, move, or delete objects, you must first select them. In this drill you practice various procedures to do so.

1. Insert your *Win95 Student Resource Disk* into the drive you use to open and save documents.

2. Open Windows Explorer and use it to select the drive into which you inserted the disk. This displays the disk's contents in the Contents pane.

3. Expand the tree and select the *Application Documents* folder to display its contents in the Contents pane.

4. Select each of the following combinations of documents, then click anywhere to unselect them before selecting the next batch:

   ▶ All of the flag documents using Ctrl

   ▶ All of the documents using the **Select All** command.

   ▶ The two movie documents using Ctrl

5. Close Windows Explorer.

4-2 Renaming Objects

There are times when you decide to change the name of a document or folder. In this drill you practice this procedure.

1. Insert your *Win95 Student Resource Disk* into the drive you use to open and save documents.

2. Open Windows Explorer and use it to select the drive into which you inserted the disk. Then expand the tree and select the *Application Documents* folder to display its contents in the Contents pane.

3. Change the name of the following documents to the one indicated:

Original Name	New Name
Delete Movie	Movie demonstrating the Del key
Building	Illustration of a building
Everhold	Ever Hopeful Health Club members

4. Close Windows Explorer.

4-3 Creating Folders

Keeping related documents together is the only way to ensure a well-managed system. In this drill you practice creating folders and subfolders that could be used to store related documents.

1. Insert your *Win95 Student Resource Disk* into the drive you use to open and save documents.

2. Open Windows Explorer and use it to select the drive into which you inserted the disk.

3. With the drive name or icon selected, use the **File**, **New**, **Folder** command to create a new folder named **Drill Folder**. Expand the tree to see the new folder in the Tree pane.

4. Click the folder named **Drill Folder** in the Tree pane to select it, then use the **File**, **New**, **Folder** command to create a new folder named **Drill Subfolder**. Expand the tree to see the new folder in the Tree pane.

5. Click the folder named **Drill Subfolder** in the Tree pane to select it, then use the **File**, **New**, **Folder** command to create a new subfolder named **Drill Subfolder within Subfolder**. Expand the tree to see the new folder in the Tree pane.

6. Close Windows Explorer.

4-4 Deleting Objects

When you no longer need an object, it's best to delete it. In this drill you practice this procedure.

1. Insert your *Win95 Student Resource Disk* into the drive you use to open and save documents.

2. Open Windows Explorer and use it to select the drive into which you inserted the disk. With the tree expanded in the Tree pane, select the *Drill Folder* to display its contents in the Contents pane.

3. With the *Drill Folder* selected, click the **Delete** button on the toolbar and a message asks if you are sure you want to delete the folder and its contents. Click the **Yes** button.

4. Select the *Application Documents* folder to display its contents in the Contents pane.

5. Select the document named *Erase this document* and press ⟨Delete⟩ A message asks if you want to delete the document. Click the **Yes** button.

6. Close Windows Explorer.

4-5 Undeleting Objects

It's not hard to delete an object by mistake; everyone does it at some point. Luckily, you can use the Recycle Bin to restore deleted files. In this drill you practice this procedure.

1. Right-click the desktop, then click the shortcut menu's **New** command to cascade the menu. Click the **Text Document** command and an icon named *New Text Document* appears on the desktop.

2. Right-click the desktop, then click the shortcut menu's **New** command to cascade the menu. Click the **Folder** command and an icon named *New Folder* appears on the desktop.

3. Click the *New Text Document* icon on the desktop to select it, and press ⟨Delete⟩ to delete it. When asked to confirm sending it to the Recycle Bin, click the **Yes** button.

4. Click the *New Folder* icon on the desktop to select it, and press ⟨Delete⟩ to delete it. When asked to confirm sending it to the Recycle Bin, click the **Yes** button.

5. Double-click the *Recycle Bin* icon on the desktop to open it. Click its **Maximize** button to display it full screen.

6. Click the *New Text Document* to select it on the list of deleted documents, then pull down the **File** menu and click the **Restore** command.

7. Pull down the **File** menu and if the **Empty Recycle Bin** command isn't dimmed, click it. A dialog box asks you to confirm the procedure. Click the **Yes** button.

8. Click the Recycle Bin's **Close** button to close the application. You'll notice that the *New Text Document* has been restored to the desktop.

9. Select the icon of the restored *New Text Document* on the desktop and press Delete to delete it.

4-6 Copying and Moving Objects

Copying documents is a good way to protect them or distribute them to others. Moving documents is a useful way to reorganize your disk drives. In this drill you practice these procedures.

1. Insert your *Win95 Student Resource Disk* into the drive you use to open and save documents.

2. Open Windows Explorer and use it to select the drive into which you inserted the disk. Then expand the tree and select the *Application Documents* folder to display its contents in the Contents pane.

3. Expand the *My Computer Documents* folder so you can see its subfolders.

4. Use the **Copy** and **Paste** buttons on the toolbar to copy the document named *Job search kit* from the *Application Documents* folder into the *Letters* subfolder under the *My Computer Documents* folder.

5. Use the **Cut** and **Paste** buttons on the toolbar to move the document named *Exploring formulas* from the *Application Documents* folder into the *Letters* subfolder under the *My Computer Documents* folder.

6. Close Windows Explorer.

4-7 Dragging and Dropping Objects

Forget menus and buttons—drag and drop is faster. In this drill you practice this procedure.

1. Insert your *Win95 Student Resource Disk* into the drive you use to open and save documents.

2. Open Windows Explorer and use it to select the drive into which you inserted the disk.

3. Expand the tree and then expand the *My Computer Documents* folder so you can see its subfolders. Select the *Letters* subfolder to display its contents in the Contents pane.

4. Drag the document named *Job search kit* from the *Letters* subfolder and drop it on the *Application Documents* folder on the tree. When a Confirm File Replace dialog box asks whether you want to replace the existing file, click **Yes**.

5. Right-drag the document named *Exploring formulas* from the *Letters* subfolder and drop it on the *Application Documents* folder on the tree. When the shortcut menu appears, click the **Copy Here** command.

6. Close Windows Explorer.

4-8 Creating and Using Shortcuts

If you have a document or application you use all of the time, you can easily create a shortcut to it. In this drill you practice this procedure.

1. Insert your *Win95 Student Resource Disk* into the drive you use to open and save documents.

2. Double-click the *My Computer* icon on the desktop to open it.

3. Double-click the drive into which you inserted the disk.

4. Double-click the *Application Documents* folder to open it.

5. Drag the *EDUCOM document* from the *Application Documents* window and drop it on the desktop.

6. Drag the *Backspace movie* document from the *Application Documents* window and drop it on the desktop.

7. Drag the *Mexican flag* document from the *Application Documents* window and drop it on the desktop.

8. Close all open My Computer windows.

9. Double-click each of the shortcut icons on the desktop to see what happens. If there is an application for them on the system, it will open and display the document. If an application opens, click its **Close** button if necessary to close it.

10. Click each of the shortcut icons on the desktop to select them and press [Delete] to delete them.

4-9 Formatting Disks

There are times when you need to copy or move data to a floppy disk. For example, you may want to send some documents to a friend or coworker. In these cases, you must first format the disk that you are planning to copy them to. In this drill you practice this procedure.

1. Insert the disk you formatted in Section 4-9's tutorial into the drive you use to open and save documents. (The disk is labeled *Backup Resource Disk*.)

2. Double-click the *My Computer* icon on the desktop to open it.

3. Right-click the icon for the floppy drive into which you inserted the disk and then click the **Fo_r_mat** command to display the Format dialog box.

4. Click the **F_u_ll** option button to turn it on, then click the **S_tart** button to format the disk. When the process is finished, click the **Close** button on the Format results dialog box then on the Format dialog box.

4-10 Copying Disks

Duplicating a floppy disk is the quickest way to copy it. In this drill you practice this procedure using the same disks you used in the tutorial.

1. Insert the *Win95 Student Resource Disk* into the drive you use to open and save documents and open My Computer.

2. Right-click the icon for the floppy drive you put the *Win95 Student Resource Disk* into to display a shortcut menu.

3. Click the **Cop_y_ Disk** command to display the Copy Disk dialog box. This box indicates the drives you will **Copy _f_rom** and **Copy _to**.

4. Click the **S_tart** button and swap disks if necessary. (The *destination disk* is the new disk labeled *Backup Resource Disk*.)

5. When copying is completed, click the dialog box's **C_lose** button.

Exercise 1. Creating and Deleting Folders

1. Insert the *Win95 Student Resource Disk* into one of the disk drives.
2. Create a folder named *1996*.
3. Create two subfolders in the *1996* folder named *sales* and *budgets*.
4. Delete the new folders and subfolders from the disk.

Exercise 2. Revising Your Disk

In this exercise, you put to use many of the procedures you have learned in this PicTorial.

1. Insert your *Win95 Student Resource Disk* into the drive you use to open and save documents.
2. Use Windows Explorer to create a new folder on the disk named *Exercise Documents*.
3. Use drag and drop to copy all of the documents in the *Letters* subfolder in the *My Computer Documents* folder into this new folder.
4. Use drag and drop to move all of the documents in the *Memos* subfolder in the *My Computer Documents* folder into this new folder.
5. Delete all of the documents in the new folder.
6. Delete the new folder.

PAGEMAKER 6.5
Design and Applications

L. Louise Van Osdol

EMCParadigm

Cover Image	© Michael Ventura/International Stock
Cover Designer	Jennifer Wreisner
Developmental Editor	Mary Verrill
Copy Editor	Roberta Mantus
Proofreader	Amy Boxrud
Indexer	Nancy Sauro
Art Director	Joan M. D'Onofrio
Desktop Production Specialist	Vern Johnson

A list of registered trademarks appears after the Index. Internet Project Web site reproduced with permission of George A. Baker III, President, National Initiative for Leadership and Institutional Effectiveness (NILIE).

Library of Congress Cataloging-in-Publication Data

Van Osdol, L. Louise
    PageMaker 6.5: design and applications / L. Louise Van Osdol.
        p. cm.
    Includes index.
    ISBN 1-56118-805-0. — ISBN 1-56118-802-6 (text & Windows 3.5
        disk pkg.). – ISBN 1-56118-801-8 (text & Macintosh 3.5 disk pkg.)
    1. Adobe PageMaker.   2. Desktop publishing.   I. Title.
Z253.532.P33V36   1998
686.2'2544536—dc21   97-42025
                                         CIP

Text + Windows 3.5" disk package, ISBN 1-56118-802-6, Order Number 06240
Text + Macintosh 3.5" disk package, ISBN 1-56118-801-8, Order Number 05240
Instructor's Guide + CD-ROM package, ISBN 1-56118-804-2, Order Number 42240

Previously published as *Desktop Publishing: Technology and Design* by Holly Yasui (1989).

Printed in the United States of America

10 9 8 7 6 5 4 3 2

BRIEF CONTENTS

CONTENTS

PREFACE

This book is designed to teach desktop publishing with Adobe PageMaker 6.5 for Windows or Macintosh by focusing on principles of design. Each chapter in the text provides graphic arts and publishing information essential for all students and professional desktop publishers.

The text discusses basic technical and graphic arts concepts, print industry practices, and the typography terminology needed to efficiently use a desktop publishing system. In many programs, students will receive no other instruction in the area of design principles. In the business world, office workers without any graphic arts background are asked to use desktop publishing systems to produce publications, and this often means disappointing and unprofessional results. The text provides the information needed to use desktop publishing programs in order to produce professional-looking publications.

Adobe PageMaker 6.5 is a standard, versatile, and popular desktop publishing software program. Students will become comfortable with using it as they apply the design principles presented and follow the step-by-step tutorials in this book.

ORGANIZATION AND PEDAGOGY

There are 12 chapters in this book designed for use in a semester or quarter course. Chapters 1, 3, 5, 7, 9, and 11 cover principles of desktop publishing, and Chapters 2, 4, 6, 8, 10, and 12 cover desktop publishing applications in the form of hands-on projects that provide PageMaker 6.5 step-by-step directions. Each hands-on chapter uses a color bar on the outside of the page to indicate that those pages are to be followed while at the computer. The chapters are paired as principles and their applications and thus form cohesive parts of the book.

Because projects in each chapter are independent of those in all other chapters, the Parts can be chosen as units or modules in the order preferred by the instructor. However, it is recommended that students cover the introductory material in chapters 1 and 2 before proceeding to the other units.

An integrated project entitled Internet Project: Creating Web Pages with PageMaker 6.5 combines principles presented in several chapters and shows how to use HTML (HyperText Markup Language) in PageMaker 6.5 to create documents to post on the Web. Best of all, the project uses a real Web page found at *http://www2.ncsu.edu/ncsu/cep/acce/nilie* and is used with permission of the National Initiative for Leadership and Institutional Effectiveness (NILIE). Other culminating projects for extra hands-on experience are included in the Instructor's Guide.

FEATURES IN THE TEXT

This book makes extensive use of figures to illustrate the text to accurately convey concepts and step-by-step PageMaker commands. Students should refer to these figures as directed. The figures communicate how the finished projects are achieved, by what principles they are guided, and why certain design decisions are made.

In addition to figures, these pedagogical features expand on text content and help students troubleshoot their computer work:

- **Mac Memos** are short notes in the margin that point out the differences between Macintosh commands and the commands given for Windows in the text.

- **Did You Know...** adds brief commentary and background for the concepts or hands-on work being discussed at that point in the text.

- **Checking Your Understanding** sections at the end of each chapter provide a self-test and review of concepts and the student's cognitive knowledge of main points presented in the chapter.

- **Applying Design Principles** at the ends of all chapters give students extra hands-on exercises to practice applications that they have learned, short projects to do in the lab, or instructions to go outside of the classroom and find examples of the text discussion in the real world.

- A **Glossary** is included at the end of the book for easy reference to new technical terms as needed.

ANCILLARIES

This text is accompanied by:

Student Files

Student files are provided on a 3-1/2" disk. These PageMaker 6.5 and graphics files are available in Macintosh or Windows formats. Completed projects using the student files are also provided on the Instructor's CD-ROM that comes with the Instructor's Guide.

Instructor's Guide with CD-ROM

The dual-read CD-ROM that accompanies the Instructor's Guide contains all Macintosh and Windows completed student files, templates, and instructor's files as well as any files needed to complete the additional projects found in the Instructor's Guide. Additional start-to-finish projects are included in the Instructor's Guide as well as answers to all Checking Your Understanding questions for all chapters. The Instructor's Guide also includes chapter exams to use for the semester or quarter course.

PowerPoint Slides

PowerPoint images are provided on the Instructor's Guide CD-ROM disk. The art is taken from key figures in the text and can be used to illustrate and discuss concepts or applications.

Internet Site

An Internet site is used as an on-line reference in the Internet Project: Creating Web pages with PageMaker 6.5, with permission of the National Initiative for Leadership and Institutional Effectiveness (NILIE).

ACKNOWLEDGMENTS

The author and publisher would like to thank the following reviewers and contributors for their excellent academic and technical assistance: Karen Conners, Adirondack Community College, Glen Falls, NY; Meredith Flynn, Bowling Green State University, Bowling Green, OH; Mary Louise Kelly, Palm Beach Community College, Lake Worth, FL; Elynor Seck, Hutchinson Community College, Hutchinson, KS; John Tuck, Johnson County Community College, Overland Park, KS.

Special thanks to my children, Jimmi Ruth Lossing and Sean R. Lossing, for their encouragement during the writing of this manuscript. I also acknowledge the keen and professional development and production of this text and its ancillaries by the Paradigm team: Mel Hecker, Publisher; Janice Johnson, Instructional Design Manager; Mary Verrill, Developmental Editor; and PJ Andemar, Desktop Production Manager. Special thanks to George A. Baker III, Director, National Initiative for Leadership and Institutional Effectiveness (NILIE), for granting permission to reproduce the NILIE Web site in the Internet Project.

Dedicated with love, respect, honor, and appreciation to my mother, Linnie Williamson Van Osdol, and to the memory of my father, Jack L. Van Osdol (1911-1981)

L. Louise Van Osdol

INTRODUCTION
TO PAGEMAKER

The term *desktop publishing* was first used by Aldus Corporation president Paul Brainard to describe Aldus® PageMaker®, one of the first page-makeup software packages for the personal computer. Desktop publishing came to mean the use of page-makeup software, such as PageMaker, on a desktop computer to produce publication materials—typeset or near-typeset quality text and graphics integrated on a page. These materials include memos, correspondence, notices, fliers, posters, certificates, office forms, brochures, schedules, catalogs, reports, manuals, newsletters, newspapers, magazines, books—anything that is made up of words and pictures.

What makes desktop publishing different from traditional publishing is that equipment small enough to fit on a person's desktop can provide all the resources needed to prepare and assemble pages. Today, routine materials that once were simply typewritten or word-processed with a letter-quality printer are enhanced with custom type and graphics. Previously, many high-quality publications were costly and required the contracted services of many different graphic arts professionals. Now they are produced with desktop publishing at a fraction of the cost and time required by traditional means.

Another important aspect of desktop publishing is that it provides a WYSIWYG (What-You-See-Is-What-You-Get, pronounced "wizzy-wig") environment for graphic design and page assembly of typeset-quality text and graphics. WYSIWYG is an interactive mode of running computer programs, in which you *see* on the display monitor how the type and graphics will appear when you *get* the actual printed output. The type specifications (size and style, for example) and adjustments of type or graphics, are shown on the screen instantaneously as they are made.

Aldus Corporation deserves much credit for beginning the desktop publishing revolution. In July of 1985, Aldus distributed the first version of PageMaker page-makeup software. Since version 1.0, PageMaker has been updated through versions 2.0, 3.0, 4.0, and 5.0. Version 6.0 was released as Adobe PageMaker after Aldus Corporation was absorbed by Adobe Systems, Inc. The latest version, PageMaker 6.5, was distributed in December 1996 for Windows 95 and in February 1997 for Macintosh.

ABOUT ADOBE PAGEMAKER 6.5

Adobe PageMaker 6.5 is a fully functional page assembly program. Accessory programs included with the program are Adobe Table 3.0, Dictionary Editor, QuarkXPress Converter, Adobe Acrobat Distiller, and

Adobe Type Manager. This version of PageMaker provides file compatibility between the Macintosh, Power Macintosh, Windows 95, and Windows 98 versions. In addition to having the ability to create and save publications in PageMaker 6.5 format, you can convert an object to a graphic format and export a publication to a PDF or HTML format.

A few of the outstanding features of Adobe PageMaker 6.5 are its ability to create multiple master pages, ease of cropping graphics, efficiency while importing and exporting text and graphics in a variety of formats, extensive printing features, the Plug-ins and Plug-in palettes in the program, and creation and use of styles. The Help menu in PageMaker 6.5 provides detailed information and instructions on all of these features and more.

This text teaches the features and commands of PageMaker 6.5 within the larger context of design principles and printing standards. Students will grasp the hands-on applications in the text to create attractive documents in the lab or classroom, and throughout their respective careers.

part

1

Basic Design Principles

PRINCIPLES of Design & Production

This chapter introduces basic concepts of desktop publishing and how to set up a publication in PageMaker.

Upon completion of this chapter | you will be able to

- distinguish among: Gestalt, figure and ground, negative space, and graphic effects
- utilize the basic principles of design: focus, balance, visual weight, directional flow, unity, and visual identity
- determine methods for setting up a publication, choosing options for paper orientation, double-sided documents, and columns and alleys
- describe PageMaker's basic design tools: guides, style palette, and master pages
- identify ways a publisher can maintain consistency in style within and among publications

Desktop publishing software such as PageMaker allows the desktop publisher to set up a publication; design the layout; and position text, graphics, or charts on a page—all on a computer. Traditional design methods require the services of graphic designers and costly typesetting and graphics camera work. The advantage of desktop publishing for businesses is that it can save a great deal of money while allowing design experimentation that was previously not feasible.

On the other hand, the relative ease of desktop publishing has resulted in nonprofessionals designing work that is below standard. Some people speak out against this trend and point to the flood of poorly designed publications produced by inexperienced publishers. As one commentator put it, "Desktop publishing enables anyone to make more ugly publications faster." The problem of bad design is that it interferes with effective communication. This chapter provides you with the basic principles of good design and introduces you to PageMaker 6.5.

THE DESKTOP PUBLISHING PROCESS

Desktop designers must be familiar with the two basic components of document design: type and artwork.

Type

Type is the basic component of all designs. Hundreds of type-faces exist; however, you will be limited to those available in your software and printer. It would be worthwhile for you to access each typeface and key the complete alphabet in upper- and lower-case letters as well as all the numbers and symbols. You can then store these for reference, print them out, or both. (See Chapter 4 for more on type and typography.)

Type selection also involves the issue of type size and **copyfitting**, or estimating the amount of space that will be taken up by the copy at a given size. This requires that you determine the average number of words per line and then multiply that figure by the approximate number of lines available.

Continuous-tone art   Line art

FIGURE
1.1

Line art vs.
continuous-tone art

Creation and Preparation

Most text and graphics creation and preparation can be handled on a computer. Because computers are multipurpose, writing and editing of text can be done on the same computer used for the creation of the art and the page assembly.

If original text is prepared on one computer or word processor, it can be accessed by the desktop publisher on a different computer if a filter for the format of the text is available in the desktop publishing program, or if the text is in ASCII format. **ASCII** (American Standard Code for Information Interchange, pronounced "ask-ee") is a word processing text file format that may be imported into PageMaker as well as most other desktop software. It is a text-only format containing no type specifications.

In desktop publishing, graphics files created with drawing, charting, drafting, and image-capture programs are easily accessed. The standard **EPS** (Encapsulated PostScript, a format used for line art) and **TIFF** (Tagged Image File Format, used for photographs) graphics file formats can be used to transport files from one computer to another and from one program to another. Imported into the page assembly program, computer graphics provide great flexibility for resizing and repositioning of artwork within a page layout in both the design and the assembly processes. Page assembly programs have automatic cropping and proportional scaling tools; graphics can be "uncropped" and rescaled on the screen for immediate output of corrected copy.

If original work is provided to the desktop publisher in **hard copy** (on paper), a **scanner** (a piece of equipment that can read the text images and "translate" them so that the computer can understand them) can be used to digitize the pages without retyping or redrawing. Both line art and continuous-tone photographs can be scanned and saved in a graphics file to be used in a page-assembly program.

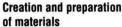

Creation and preparation of materials

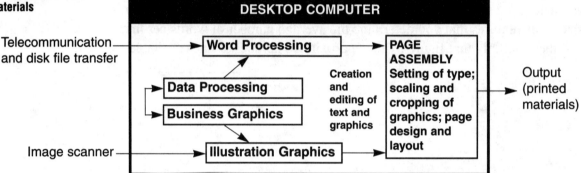

Page Assembly

Desktop publishing software with page assembly capability enables the desktop publisher to design, prepare text and graphics, and assemble work all at once. The desktop publisher can set the type and crop or resize artwork while performing electronic **pasteup** (page assembly). Blocks of type and graphics are cut, positioned, and pasted on the electronic page, and can be "uncut," repositioned, and "unpasted."

DESIGN AND GESTALT CONCEPTS

Assembling pages does not automatically result in good design. Good design is a process that involves an understanding of the purpose of the publication and the character of the source materials. It also involves an understanding of visual principles that can make design an art.

The Gestalt theory of perception provides a conceptual tool that can help designers analyze and solve visual problems. In its most simple form, **gestalt** means that "the parts are greater than the whole." Publications are more than words and pictures. They are structures that communicate not only information but also attitudes, moods, and cultural assumptions.

Gestalt psychology, a school of thought developed in Germany in the 1920s, investigates the way human beings process visual information in order to perceive meaning. The perception of any element, whether type, graphic, or blank space on a page, depends upon the relationship of the other elements around it.

Figure and Ground

The classical gestalt image is the faces/vase image, which shows the interplay of **figure and ground** relationships (see Figure 1.3). Whether you see profiles of human faces or a vase depends on how you look at it. If you perceive the profiles as the figure (foreground), then the vase is their (back)ground; if you look at the vase as the figure, then the profiles are the ground.

Interplay of figure and ground
Figure and ground relationships are affected by how you look at images.

An understanding of figure and ground is basic to graphic design. Any mark made on a page can be seen as either figure or ground. In the most common figure/ground relationship, dark marks on a light background are seen as the figure. Figure 1.4 shows stable figure-ground relationships.

Stable figure and ground
The vase or faces can be made into stable figure/ground compositions by eliminating the background space and adding detail.

Beginning designers often concentrate on the figure and neglect ground, which is the space surrounding the figure called **negative space** or white space. However, the negative space is important to the overall composition. The creative use of figure-ground relationships may make an eye-catching and memorable publication instead of an ordinary, forgettable one.

Perhaps the easiest way to understand negative space is to look at the space where the figure is not. Figure 1.5 shows a composition in which the blank elements, the negative space, represent shadows that define the image.

FIGURE 1.5

Negitive space
Logo by Goldsholl
Associates for gear
manufacturer Perfection
American: negative space
represented as shadows
defines the figure.

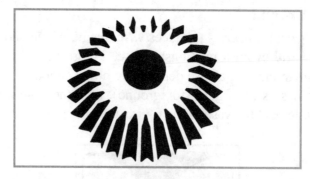

One way to make a figure-ground relationship more interesting, or **dynamic**, is to reverse or make ambiguous the normal figure-ground relationship. Figure 1.6 shows a figure-ground relationship where the figure acts as both figure and ground.

Figure 1.7 shows how reversing black and white, and the use of outlines, gets the eye to group different elements in the perception of figure and ground.

FIGURE 1.6

Dynamic figure and ground
In this composition, the "figure" acts as both figure (black against white) and ground (for the white type).

FIGURE 1.7

Reversing and outlining
A. A white arrow in a black box is seen as a negative image.
B. A small box is seen when it is outlined.
C. A large box with a cutout is seen when it is outlined and the arrow reversed.

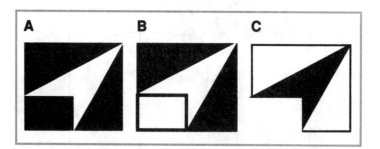

Figure and ground relationships in publications are most visible when the design is simple. A basic rule of good design is: keep it simple and it will be more effective. Many desktop-published pieces look cluttered and uninviting because the designer did not keep in mind that negative space is not empty, but is an active part of good design.

For publications with a lot of printed text, intelligent use of negative space helps to show groupings and to guide the eye through a page that has a lot of type (see Figure 1.8).

FIGURE 1.8

White space in a publication
Publications **A** and **C** do not have enough white space. The reader can be overwhelmed by designs such as these. Publications **B** and **D** use white space to help the reader organize the elements on the page.

Continuity

When people see patterns they are familiar with, they will automatically fill in whatever is missing in order to perceive a whole. The use of **repetition** (exact duplication) and **gradation** (duplication with a fixed and regular change) creates such patterns. Conventional symbols with which we are familiar, such as the shapes of the letters of the alphabet, also have strong gestalt that overcomes discontinuities.

The principle of **continuity** means that the eye, given enough visual information, will see a continuous shape even when it is confronted with a partial, or fragmented, image. Figure 1.9 illustrates the principle of continuity based on gradation, and Figure 1.10 shows continuity based on repetition.

An underlying **grid** design helps to create continuity and order among different kinds of graphics and text materials. The underlying grid (usually geometric), even if it is interrupted by other elements, will be seen as a continuous, unifying form.

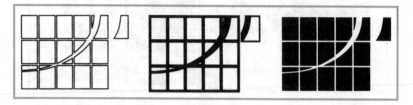

FIGURE 1.9

Continuity based on gradation
The eye sees 15 lines and a curve. In actuality, there are 30 lines, each with one curved end and one straight end.

FIGURE 1.10

Continuity based on repetition
The eye sees the grid and a curve. In actuality, many of the grid boxes are polygons with curved sides.

Closure

The principle of **closure** means that the eye will see a closed shape when confronted with a familiar image that is not closed, as shown in Figure 1.11.

Images based on the principles of continuity and closure make the viewer's eye and brain participate more actively, and so they are more dynamic than complete images. Figure 1.12 shows the principles of continuity and closure in a logotype design.

FIGURE 1.11

Closure
The edges of the oval are not complete, but the eye fills in the missing parts. The black shapes are actually rounded triangles.

FIGURE 1.12

Continuity and closure
Words are seen as a continuous shape and the eye fills in white space between them to see a key-shaped form.

BASIC DESIGN PRINCIPLES

The concept of Gestalt in design provides an overall view and approach that goes beyond the physical elements of the design. However, a solid foundation in the accepted principles of good design is essential in order to create a design that is functional and practical as well as visually interesting and attractive.

Focus

The **focus** is the element to which the eye looks first in a visual composition. A focus is most effective when it is surrounded by enough **white space** (negative space) to contrast with other elements on the page.

On pages made up of all text, focus is usually created by the use of **display type** (large and/or bold type) for titles and headings. Display type should be surrounded by enough white (negative) space to provide noticeable contrast with the main text, or **body type** (also referred to as **text type**). For maximum contrast, two different typefaces are used—one for display and the other for body type.

Graphics also provide focus on a page, and may share the focus with display type. The use of graphics in a publication enhances the look of a composition, and thus heightens readers' interest. All other factors being equal, publications featuring illustrations will generally be noticed first and perused before text-only compositions on a bulletin board or literature rack, in the day's mail, or on a page full of ads. Figure 1.13 shows how display type and graphics can be used to provide focus in a publication.

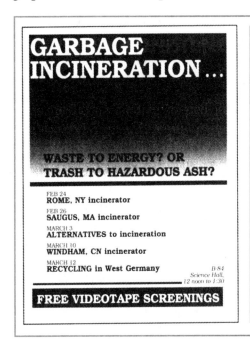
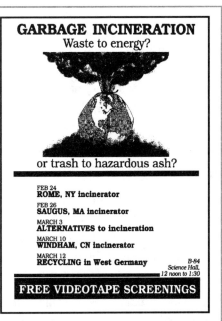

Focus
Large display type and graphics create focus on a page.

Balance

Balance in a composition is achieved by the way elements are distributed on a page. There are two kinds of balance. The first is **symmetrical balance**. Symmetry is the mirroring of elements so that there is an equal distribution of weight on the left and right sides or top and bottom of a central axis (see Figure 1.14). Symmetrical design was popular in the past.

Symmetrical balance
Book cover pages from the 18th century. Notice how the elements are evenly distributed.

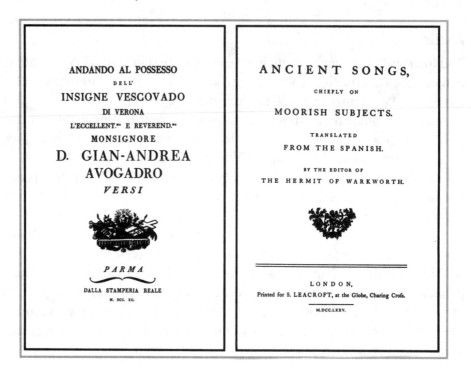

Modern design, however, favors **asymmetrical balance**—which is a counterbalance of contrasting elements that are not fixed around a central axis. Asymmetrical balance is more flexible and visually stimulating. It is created by the contrast of relative weights of elements on the page. In asymmetrical balance, the contrast between elements must be great enough to be immediately noticeable. Small variations that are not perceived as differences may not achieve a balanced effect. Parts (B) and (D) of Figure 1.8 show good asymmetrical balance.

Visual Weight

Visual weight serves to create both focus and balance. **Visual weight** is the impact an element has on the eye. This is in contrast to **intrinsic interest**, which is an element that is interesting to look at on its own merits; that is, for what it is rather than how it looks. Methods used to control the visual weight of elements are: size and number, density, position, and anomaly.

Size and Number The primary factor in the visual weight of an element is its size. All other factors being equal, a large element has more visual weight than a small element. However, a single large element may be balanced by a number of small elements, as shown in Figure 1.15.

Typography and the use of different sizes of graphics enable the designer to create contrast between different sizes of type and graphics. For example, the use of headings can provide contrast on text pages where the body type is small. In addition, illustrations can enhance text pages not only because of their intrinsic interest, but also because they contrast with the small characters of type that make up the text.

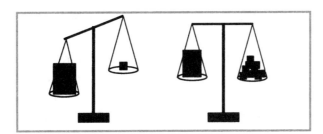

Visual weight—size and number
A large element can be balanced by a number of small elements.

Density Density in design is the relative darkness of an element. A dense element, one with greater **value** (darkness), has more visual weight than a lighter, less dense element. Density may also be measured by the amount of detail in an element. The more detail, the greater the density. Small, detailed images may balance a larger, simpler image; a small solid or dark shape may balance a larger gray or light element (see Figure 1.16).

At first glance, blocks of small type on a page look gray, while blocks of large type are seen as separate characters. Bold type is more dense than normal type, and italic type is usually lighter than normal type. Reversed type or images (white type or images on a dark background) have more density than positive type or images and, therefore, carry greater visual weight.

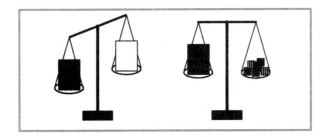

Visual weight—density
Darker elements, those with greater density, carry more visual weight than lighter elements. Also a large element can be balanced by a number of small, dense elements.

Page Position The center and top of a composition should have less visual weight than the sides and bottom. Small or light elements placed at the edges and/or bottom of the composition can balance a large element in the middle or top, as shown in Figure 1.17.

The visual center of a page is slightly above the mathematical center. This is why type on title pages is usually positioned approximately one-quarter to one-third of the page from the top; also, headlines in a newspaper are larger on the top one-third of the page. In text-only publications, it is a good idea to leave extra white space at the bottom of the pages so that the pages do not look too heavy. In display pieces, the heavy bottom edge of the composition is often reserved for the name of the product, service, organization, or other important pieces of information that need to be emphasized.

FIGURE

1.17

Visual weight—page position
The bottom of a page should be heavier than the top of a page.

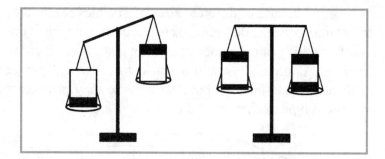

Anomaly In design, a single element that looks different from a group of other elements is an **anomaly**. Because the difference makes it stand out, an anomaly has greater visual weight than a whole group. Anomaly may be a function of position (an isolated element versus a group of elements close together, or one that breaks an established pattern), density and contrast (a dark/detailed element versus a group of light/simple elements or vice versa), or shape (round versus angular, irregular versus geometric). (See Figure 1.18.)

FIGURE

1.18

Visual weight—anomaly
An anomaly has more weight than a group of other elements, because the anomaly draws attention.

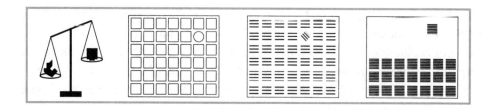

Directional Flow

Directional flow is the direction the eye moves as it perceives a design. It is created by lines in a composition. These may be actual lines, such as those within illustrations, or they may be **rules**, or ruling **lines**, which are geometric lines used as graphic enhancements to type. Lines of type, and paths of visual focuses also create lines that the eye follows.

In symmetrical designs, there is not much directional flow, except down the invisible central axis. This is why symmetrical design is static. The focus tends to be only on the center of the composition. In asymmetrical designs, directional flow is used to lead the eye to particular words or images that the designer wishes to emphasize.

Graphics within Pages For illustrations and graphic elements such as logos, which will be used within text pages, the directional flow should be from left to right and from bottom to top. Images that lead the eye from right to left tend to look like they are facing or moving backwards, and images that lead the eye from top to bottom may appear bottom-heavy. Figure 1.19 shows some logo designs that use left-to-right and bottom-to-top directional flow.

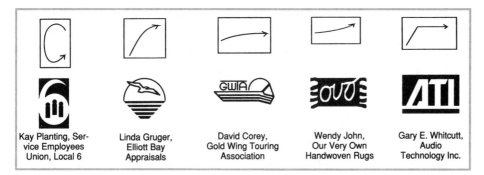

FIGURE 1.19

Directional flow in logo designs
Students designed these logos at Shoreline Community College in Seattle, WA. The arrows above the logos indicate the directional flow.

On text pages, images should face the text on the page. At first glance, the eye is first attracted to the pictures in a publication, but the substance of the message is usually contained in the text. Therefore, the image should direct the eye to the text. In particular, the person's eyes in a photograph or drawing should be looking toward the text, or in the direction that the page should be turned. Figure 1.20 shows the effective use of directional flow in the integration of an illustration and logo in a brochure cover.

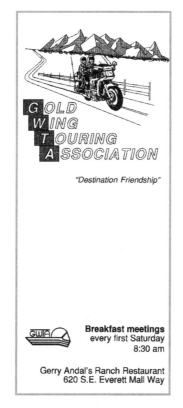

FIGURE 1.20

Directional flow in a brochure cover
Design by David Corey, Shoreline Community College, Seattle, WA.

Text Pages Because we read from top to bottom and from left to right, the eye tends to scan a page in the same way—from the upper-left corner to the upper-right corner, down to the lower-left corner, and then across to the lower-right corner, in a "Z" pattern.

In publications that are mostly text, such as newspapers, magazines, and books, landmarks for the eye should be set in these strategic positions. In a display piece containing a considerable amount of text information (for example, an advertisement or a flier), the lower-right corner is the spot where the eye ends up after a cursory glance. Hence this spot is often used for placement of important information, such as a telephone number, logo, or organization name.

Unity

Unity is the overall look that tends to hold the composition together visually. It is accomplished when the page has a clear focus, is well balanced, has a fluid directional flow, and utilizes appropriate elements, both type and graphics, that are internally consistent on each page and from page to page.

Appropriateness On the most apparent level, graphics and the content of the text communicate characteristics such as humor, elegance, warmth, formality, and so on. Illustrations and color should be chosen for their appropriateness in terms of the content of the publication, as should typefaces.

Different type sends different messages. The type used in a composition should not only work well with the content, but should also be compatible with the graphics.

More subtly, formal characteristics such as angularity or roundedness, overall density, and degree of symmetry or asymmetry are characteristics of all typefaces as well as of graphics; certain typefaces "go" with certain types of graphics. (See Figure 1.21.)

FIGURE 1.21

Type and graphics in a logo
With the delicate curving graphic and romantic message, a heavy typeface is inappropriate. A more refined typeface is appropriate.

Consistency Consistency in the text is accomplished by using the same specifications for some elements in a design such as headings, subheadings, footnotes, captions, and other text elements. For graphics, the consistent use of line thicknesses, fill patterns, and the consistent scaling and cropping of illustrations contribute to the unity of a publication.

A method of ensuring consistency is the use of a **style sheet**, which is a computer file that contains the type specifications for different categories of text; in electronic form, style sheet specifications can be applied automatically to text characters for quick and consistent specification. Style sheets help maintain consistency both *within* and *among* publications. For long documents, PageMaker can set repeating elements on all pages of the publication; for a series of publications, PageMaker can save the style sheet in a **template**, or master form, to be used over and over again.

Visual Identity

A **visual identity** is often a nonverbal image that is closely associated with a company or organization. Two strong, well-known visual identities are CBS's eye and NBC's peacock. In a broader sense, a company's visual identity is the result of the use of a unified set of design elements that are present in the materials that the organization produces, and which convey its image or personality to the public.

Paper-based publications form an important part of a company's communication with the public and are important in establishing the organization's visual identity. Stationery—letterhead, envelopes, and business cards—is a basic carrier of the visual identity. But all publications should bear a family resemblance. (See Figure 1.22.)

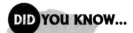

DID YOU KNOW...

You should always be consistent and use a unified set of design elements (colors, typeface, layout, etc.) in all of an organization's publications; it will increase market recognition.

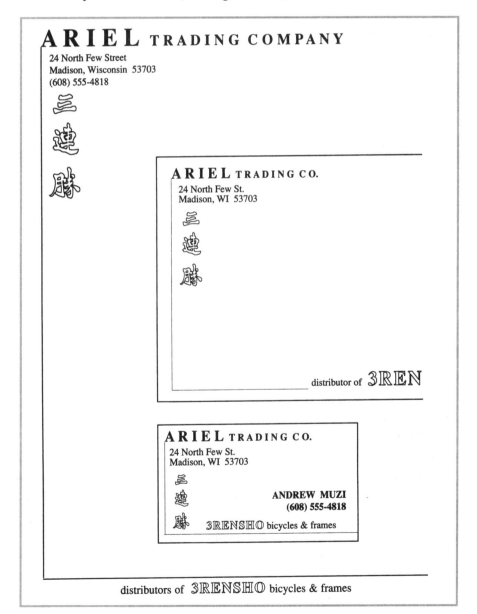

FIGURE 1.22

Visual Identity
Letterhead, envelope, and business card.

Since desktop publishing opens the way for small organizations to produce professional-quality publications, the desktop publisher often has the opportunity and responsibility to help create, develop, and continue a visual identity. A desktop publisher who works for an organization with an established visual identity must be sensitive to the design decisions that have been made in the past and work within the organization's design guidelines.

The single most important element of an organization's visual identity is its logo. The logo is an identifying symbol, a kind of visual shorthand for the organization, and is used on all the organization's materials, whether paper-based or not. The look of the logo is reinforced by other elements, such as color and decorative shapes that can be used in a variety of ways.

In a subtle way, the typeface that an organization uses for its publications usually supports its visual identity. Although most people not trained in graphic design cannot name typefaces, they are aware of and are affected differently by varying typefaces. Since desktop publishing is concerned with the production of paper-based publications, familiarity with typefaces and their family resemblances is an important part of helping an organization create or maintain its visual identity.

SETTING UP A PUBLICATION USING PAGEMAKER

DID YOU KNOW...

PageMaker is a powerful page layout program and the documents you create using this program are called **publications**.

Now that you have been introduced to some basic design principles, you can learn how PageMaker works so that you can begin designing publications. PageMaker, like all page assembly programs, enables the desktop publisher to specify basic page parameters: paper size and orientation, page numbering, margins, columns, and space between columns. Pasteup tools assist in designing layouts and positioning text and graphic elements on the page. Templates can be created using style sheets and master pages to help to maintain consistency of style within and among publications.

Page Parameters

Standard paper sizes are:

- Letter—8½" x 11"
- Legal—8½" x 14"
- Tabloid—11" x 17"
- Baronial—5½" x 8½"

PageMaker's default for baronial-size stationery is called Letter half. Other PageMaker defaults include Magazine broad (10" x 12"), Magazine wide (9" x 10.875"), Magazine narrow (8.125" x 10.875"), and Legal half (7" x 8.5"). There are twenty-two PageMaker 6.5 default paper sizes.

For pages that exceed the size of paper used in most printers, the printout can be **tiled**—a process by which the page is printed in sections with some overlap so that the pieces can be pasted together. The screen representation of the page, however, is shown in full size so that the whole page can be viewed and laid out with all elements in place.

Paper Orientation **Portrait** refers to a page that is longer than it is wide, and **landscape** refers to a page that is wider than it is tall. For this reason, PageMaker's setting for portrait is called tall, and the setting for landscape is called wide. These terms come from the art world. Paintings of people (portraits) are usually taller than they are wide to accommodate the shape of a human being. On the other hand, landscapes are usually wider than they are tall to accommodate the expanse of scenery being painted.

Image Area

The **image area** is the area on the page in which all type and graphics will be positioned. The exceptions are **bleeds**, which are graphics or photos that run directly to the edge of a page. Bleeds actually go beyond the edges of the page. In order to print a bleed, the publication is printed on oversized paper and then trimmed.

Desktop laser printers have a limited imaging area, usually about $3/8''$ from each edge of letter-sized paper. (This varies depending upon the software as well as the physical limitations of the printer.) Legal-sized paper generally requires larger margins. The amount of overlap for tiled tabloid pages is generally user-specifiable. Production laser printers (as opposed to desktop printers) and imagesetters can produce 11" x 17" pages in one piece.

Offset presses (used by professional printing companies) cannot print completely to the edge of the paper because of a device called the gripper, which holds the paper in place as it passes through the press. Therefore, it is best to leave at least one **gripper edge** free of images, or else the paper must be specially trimmed, which costs extra.

Margins and Double-Sided Documents Minimum margins should be determined by the output device, as described above. Publications may be single-sided or double-sided—printed on one side only or on both sides of the paper.

A double-sided publication, when opened, has **facing pages**, one on the left and one on the right. The left page is called a **verso**; the right page is called a **recto**. Usually, verso pages carry even page numbers, and recto pages carry odd page numbers.

The two-page **spread** of the facing pages should be designed as a unit. For publications that will be bound, the **inside margin** (the right margin of a verso and the left margin of a recto) is often set wider than the outside margin. The combination of the inside margins of facing pages creates the **gutter** (see Figure 1.23).

Two-page spread
Publications that are to
be printed on both sides
of the paper should be
designed in spreads.

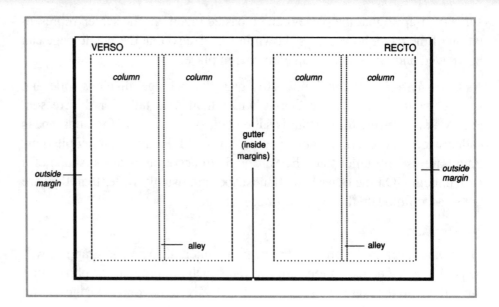

Columns and Alleys **Columns** are vertical divisions within the image area into which text and graphics are placed; **alleys** are the spaces between columns. Many word processors can set text in columns with alleys. If the document will be laid out in PageMaker, the word processing text should be set using the default margins. Then the file should be set up in columns in PageMaker.

The optimum width for columns and alleys depends on the size and set width of the type. Adjustments can be made in PageMaker for narrower and wider column measures, as needed.

Pasteup Tools

PageMaker provides a number of devices that enable you to assemble the pages with precision.

Rulers and Measurement Systems PageMaker has two sets of rulers: one across the top for measuring horizontal positioning, and the other down the left side for measuring vertical positioning.

The rulers and options within menus and dialog boxes can use different measurement systems. Inches are generally used for initially specifying page size; **points** (abbreviated **pts**) and **picas** (abbreviated **px** or **pi**) are used for the actual layout. Twelve points equal one pica, and six picas equal one inch. One point, therefore, is equal to about 1/72 of an inch.

Manipulating What Appears On Screen Because computer screen monitors are fixed in size, PageMaker offers various levels of zooming in for close detail work and zooming out to enable you to see the overall layout (see Figure 1.24).

A

B

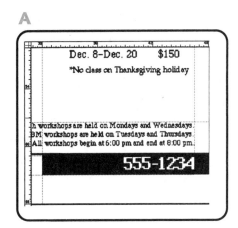
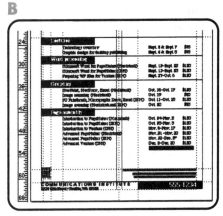

FIGURE
1.24

Zooming
A. Zooming in enlarges a small section of the screen so that you can focus on details.
B. Zooming out reduces the size of the copy on the screen, thus enabling you to see more of a document.

Since PageMaker provides the ability to look at the overall layout of a document and manipulate it onscreen with pasteup tools, the user must expect the onscreen view to be accurate. This is the principle behind **WYSIWYG** (What You See Is What You Get). However, you must understand that What-You-See on the monitor is not always *exactly* What-You-Get in the printout. The differences between WYS and WYG result from limitations and inconsistencies between capabilities of the display monitor and the printer. Printers can produce far more precise and detailed output than can display screens. As you gain more practice with PageMaker, you will become familiar with the quirks of WYSIWYG discrepancy and will learn how to adjust page layouts by eye.

In terms of WYSIWYG, the most accurate way of evaluating what appears on the monitor is seeing the document in its *actual size*. Unfortunately, a document seen in actual size is only partly visible, because most screens measure less than 11 inches deep. Therefore, only about $\frac{1}{4}$ to $\frac{1}{3}$ of a given page can be seen at a time. Full-page display monitors show whole pages—and even spreads—in actual size. However, on a standard display monitor, the image must be scrolled in order to view parts that do not appear on the screen.

In order for the whole page to be displayed on standard-size monitors, the image must be reduced. Full page size, or fit-in-window size, is often used for the initial placement of text and graphics, especially for long word processing files that will fill up page-long columns. Full-page size is also used to look at the overall design—to see how the different parts of the page fit together.

Magnified view can be used to zoom in on a page. When many edits are made quickly in a page layout, errors sometimes occur. Bits and pieces of an image are left on the screen, but these will not print. To make sure that a mark on a screen will not print, the view can be magnified. If the mark disappears, it will not print.

Magnified views also can be used for the fine-tuning of text and graphics. Always keep in mind, however, that a magnified view is not as accurate in terms of WYSIWYG. When a publication is in magnified view and you want to return the view of the page to full page size, you must zoom out on the page.

Magnetic "Snap-to" Guides PageMaker offers guides that help in the positioning of type and graphics. Nonprinting guides appear on the screen as light dotted or dashed lines. These lines can be given magnetlike properties so that when an element containing text or a graphic is positioned very close to a guide, the text or graphic will be drawn to it and align with it exactly. These may be arbitrary guides, or column, gutter, alley, or margin guides, set and positioned like other elements of the layout.

Consistency of Style

Desktop publishing provides automated tools that are especially useful for maintaining consistency of style. All publications should be internally consistent; that is, all parts of each page and multiple pages should look like they belong to the same document. This requires that design elements be repeated within the publication.

Serial publications, such as newsletters and magazines, should look like they are part of the same series; their design elements should be repeated from issue to issue. This is of particular importance in serial publications, but the maintenance of a similar look among all publications produced by a single organization helps to establish and promote a visual identity for the organization.

Standing Elements In multipage documents, **standing elements** are design elements that repeat *exactly* from page to page in terms of style, page position, and content. (See Figure 1.25). Standing elements such as running headers or running footers with automatic page numbering are set on a PageMaker **master page**. Their specifications and position are then copied to all pages associated with that master page. Using PageMaker 6.5, you can create an ulimited number of master pages in each publication.

Standing elements such as the styles of headings, subheadings, and body text are set using PageMaker's **Styles** palette. The styles defined in the **Styles** palette are applied to format the text in the publication. Using styles to format text makes it easy to change the style later if necessary. For example, assume you have designed a 50-page booklet. If you apply a style using the **Styles** palette to all the headings, subheadings, and body text, and later want to change the font used in the headings and subheadings, you just edit the styles for the headings and subheadings you want to change. Once you edit the styles in the **Styles** palette and apply them, the font used in the headings and subheadings will be changed throughout the whole 50-page booklet. It is a lot faster and much more accurate to format the text in a publication or make changes to the format using the **Styles** palette than it is if you format each heading, each subheading, and the body text without using styles.

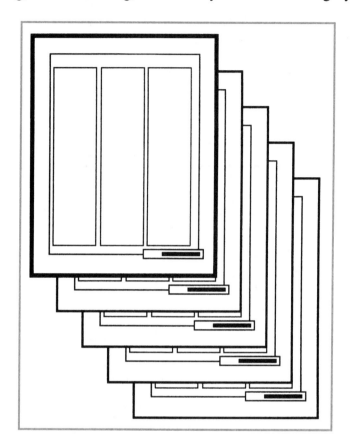

FIGURE

1.25

Standing elements
Elements set on the master or base page are copied to each page of the publication.

Serial Elements A **serial element** is an element that occurs once within a single publication but is repeated in every issue of the publication. The most common serial elements are cover pages for a series of reports or books, and banners and mastheads for newsletters and magazines. Figure 1.27 shows a newsletter banner which appears in every edition of the publication. Other serial elements may include mailers, calendars, and regular features in a newsletter or magazine.

A publication with styles applied using the **Styles** palette and all standing and serial elements in place on master pages can be used as a template for future issues. PageMaker has a special feature for saving templates.

The use of template files is ideal for serial publications such as newsletters or magazines. In PageMaker 6.5, you open the template file as a copy. All master pages and all styles in the **Styles** palette contain the standing elements previously defined and created. Learning to use PageMaker's **Styles** palette and **Master Pages** to create and use templates will save you many, many hours of design and layout work.

Serial elements and templates
A template can be used to create different issues of the same series.

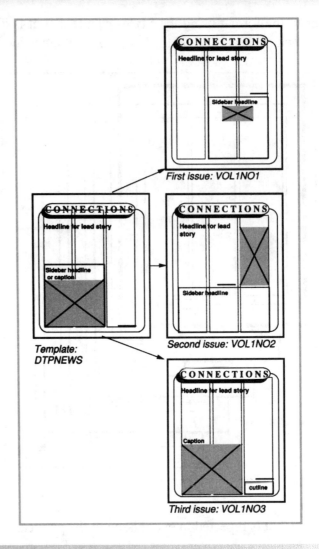

First issue: VOL1NO1

Template: DTPNEWS

Second issue: VOL1NO2

Third issue: VOL1NO3

CHECKING YOUR UNDERSTANDING

Answer true or false for questions 1-5. If false, explain why.

1. The ground of a composition is always the page; the figure is the marks on the page.

2. White space in a publication is negative space.

3. Directional flow can be accomplished through the placement of graphics.

4. The "Z" pattern of eye movement across a composition leaves the eye at the lower left corner of the page.

5. The unity of a publication is determined by the kind of illustrations used.

Give short answers to questions 6-10.

6. Name the two kinds of paper orientation. Describe each.

7. Explain the difference between the inside margin and the gutter in a publication.

8. What happens when you zoom in on a display screen? What happens when you zoom out?

9. What is a style sheet and how does it help you?

10. What are the differences between display type and body type?

APPLYING DESIGN PRINCIPLES

Exercise 1 Examining Layout and Composition

For these exercises, you will need a variety of magazines, reports, or newspapers from which you can clip examples and create new layouts. Keep these examples and start a collection that you will add to during the course of this book. For questions a–c, select examples that you consider to be well-designed.

a) Find a composition in which the primary means of establishing a focus is through the use of element size. This may be in black and white or color. Explain why you think it is effective. Sketch a rough using the same basic design, but with different content.

b) Find a composition in which the primary means of creating directional flow is through the use of color consistency and density. Explain why you think it is effective. Photocopy it in black and white, and describe how you might make it more effective.

c) Find a composition in which balance is established through the contrast of size and/or density and page position. Explain why you think it is effective. Sketch a rough using the same basic design, but with different content.

d) Select six photographs and/or drawings that have a similar "look." Choose one typeface that you feel is appropriate for this look and explain why. Then choose another typeface that is not appropriate, and explain why.

Exercise 2 Evaluating Publication Designs

Refer to the basic design principles covered in this chapter as you proceed with this exercise. The basic principles include: focus, balance, visual weight, directional flow, and unity.

The first step in designing a publication is to analyze the organization, the subject matter of the publication, and the audience for the publication. This means clearly defining the primary products or services provided, the types of people that this organization wishes to reach with its products and/or services, and the "personality" or image that the organization wishes to convey.

On the last pages of this chapter are (A) original documents and (B) remakes. Using the basic principles of design and the descriptions of the organizations, analyze both the originals and the remakes. Were the remakes an improvement? Make suggestions for further improvements. Issues to consider are:

a) What is the primary focus of the publication? What factors (size, density, page position, anomaly, intrinsic interest) make this the primary focus?

b) What is one secondary focus? Why is it important?

c) What direction does this make the eye move, and is this effective?

d) Is the page balanced? What factors are weighed against each other top and bottom, left and right?

e) Is the page unified? Are typefaces and graphic themes utilized in a unified manner?

f) Discuss the use of white space on the page. Is it fragmented or unified?

Organization 1:

THE UNIVERSITY OF WISCONSIN EXTENSION offers continuing education courses for professionals in various fields. The flier is to be distributed at a broadcasting conference. The local Public Broadcasting Service station is programmed and transmitted from the University. The Communications Programs and Telecommunications departments are particularly interested in building an image of being up-to-date and on the "cutting edge" of technology.

Organization 2:

FELDENKRAIS CLASSES are movement-therapy classes for people of all ages, but the instructor would like to appeal particularly to young-at-heart, older women like herself. The courses are held at community centers, schools, and churches. The half-page fliers are to be posted on bulletin boards, and the brochure is to be mailed as an insert in local newsletters. The instructor would like to project an "ageless, lively, and healthy" image with her publicity materials.

FIGURE 1.27

A. Original flier
B. Remade flier

A

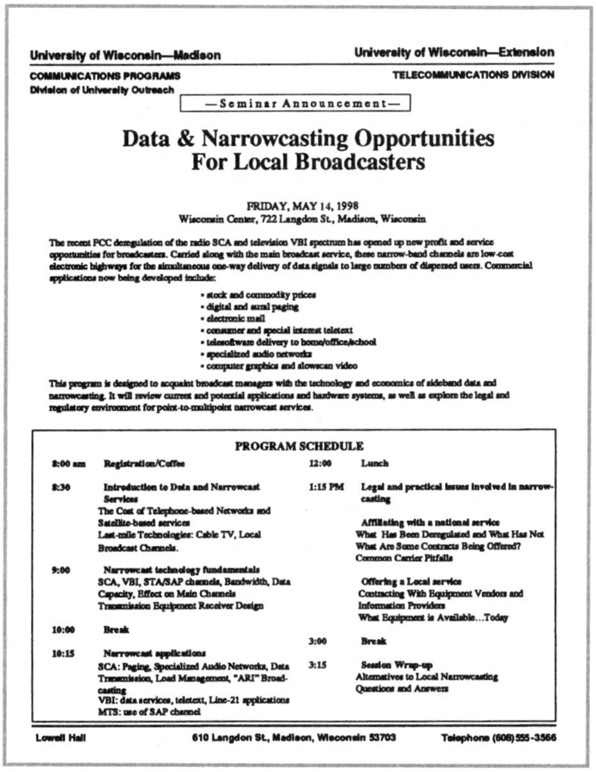

University of Wisconsin—Madison   University of Wisconsin—Extension

COMMUNICATIONS PROGRAMS   TELECOMMUNICATIONS DIVISION
Division of University Outreach

—Seminar Announcement—

Data & Narrowcasting Opportunities For Local Broadcasters

FRIDAY, MAY 14, 1998
Wisconsin Center, 722 Langdon St., Madison, Wisconsin

The recent FCC deregulation of the radio SCA and television VBI spectrum has opened up new profit and service opportunities for broadcasters. Carried along with the main broadcast service, these narrow-band channels are low-cost electronic highways for the simultaneous one-way delivery of data signals to large numbers of dispersed users. Commercial applications now being developed include:

- stock and commodity prices
- digital and aural paging
- electronic mail
- consumer and special interest teletext
- telesoftware delivery to home/office/school
- specialized audio networks
- computer graphics and slowscan video

This program is designed to acquaint broadcast managers with the technology and economics of sideband data and narrowcasting. It will review current and potential applications and hardware systems, as well as explore the legal and regulatory environment for point-to-multipoint narrowcast services.

PROGRAM SCHEDULE

8:00 am Registration/Coffee	12:00 Lunch
8:30 Introduction to Data and Narrowcast Services	1:15 PM Legal and practical issues involved in narrowcasting
The Cost of Telephone-based Networks and Satellite-based services	
Last-mile Technologies: Cable TV, Local Broadcast Channels.	Affiliating with a national service
	What Has Been Deregulated and What Has Not
	What Are Some Contracts Being Offered?
	Common Carrier Pitfalls
9:00 Narrowcast technology fundamentals	
SCA, VBI, STA/SAP channels, Bandwidth, Data Capacity, Effect on Main Channels	Offering a Local service
Transmission Equipment Receiver Design	Contracting With Equipment Vendors and Information Providers
	What Equipment is Available...Today
10:00 Break	
	3:00 Break
10:15 Narrowcast applications	
SCA: Paging, Specialized Audio Networks, Data Transmission, Load Management, "ARI" Broadcasting	3:15 Session Wrap-up
	Alternatives to Local Narrowcasting
VBI: data services, teletext, Line-21 applications	Questions and Answers
MTS: use of SAP channel	

Lowell Hall   610 Langdon St., Madison, Wisconsin 53703   Telephone (608) 555-3566

B

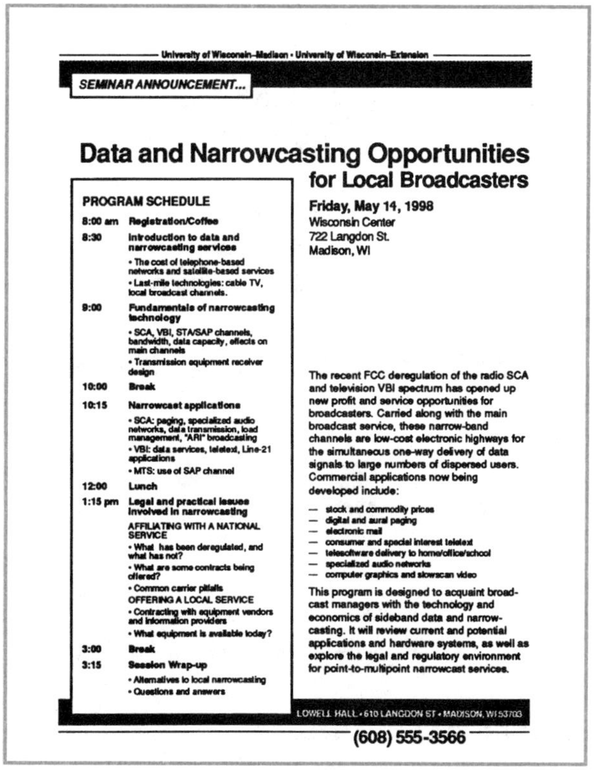

University of Wisconsin–Madison · University of Wisconsin–Extension

SEMINAR ANNOUNCEMENT...

Data and Narrowcasting Opportunities for Local Broadcasters

PROGRAM SCHEDULE

8:00 am Registration/Coffee

8:30 Introduction to data and narrowcasting services
- The cost of telephone-based networks and satellite-based services
- Last-mile technologies: cable TV, local broadcast channels.

9:00 Fundamentals of narrowcasting technology
- SCA, VBI, STA/SAP channels, bandwidth, data capacity, effects on main channels
- Transmission equipment receiver design

10:00 Break

10:15 Narrowcast applications
- SCA: paging, specialized audio networks, data transmission, load management, "ARI" broadcasting
- VBI: data services, teletext, Line-21 applications
- MTS: use of SAP channel

12:00 Lunch

1:15 pm Legal and practical issues involved in narrowcasting
AFFILIATING WITH A NATIONAL SERVICE
- What has been deregulated, and what has not?
- What are some contracts being offered?
- Common carrier pitfalls
OFFERING A LOCAL SERVICE
- Contracting with equipment vendors and information providers
- What equipment is available today?

3:00 Break

3:15 Session Wrap-up
- Alternatives to local narrowcasting
- Questions and answers

Friday, May 14, 1998
Wisconsin Center
722 Langdon St.
Madison, WI

The recent FCC deregulation of the radio SCA and television VBI spectrum has opened up new profit and service opportunities for broadcasters. Carried along with the main broadcast service, these narrow-band channels are low-cost electronic highways for the simultaneous one-way delivery of data signals to large numbers of dispersed users. Commercial applications now being developed include:

- stock and commodity prices
- digital and aural paging
- electronic mail
- consumer and special interest teletext
- telesoftware delivery to home/office/school
- specialized audio networks
- computer graphics and slowscan video

This program is designed to acquaint broadcast managers with the technology and economics of sideband data and narrowcasting. It will review current and potential applications and hardware systems, as well as explore the legal and regulatory environment for point-to-multipoint narrowcast services.

LOWELL HALL · 610 LANGDON ST · MADISON, WI 53703

(608) 555-3566

FIGURE 1.28
A. Original fliers
B. Remade fliers

FELDENKRAIS AND GARDENING

SAVE YOUR BACK
EASE YOUR KNEES
INCREASE YOUR STRENGTH

FOR INFORMATION ABOUT CLASSES,
PLEASE CALL PAT TOMLIN: 555-1212

FELDENKRAIS MOVEMENT CLASSES

MONTLAKE: TUES. EVENING, 7-9
GREENLAKE: WED. MORNING, 10-12

FOR INFORMATION ABOUT CLASSES,
PLEASE CALL PAT TOMLIN: 555-1212

A

**FELDENKRAIS
and gardening**

- SAVE your back
- EASE your knees
- INCREASE your strength

FELDENKRAIS
PAT TOMLIN, Instructor • call for Information about classes In your neighborhood • **555-1212**

**FELDENKRAIS
movement classes**

- MONTLAKE: Tues. evening, 7–9
- GREENLAKE: Wed. morning, 10–12

FELDENKRAIS
PAT TOMLIN, Instructor • call for Information about classes In your neighborhood • **555-1212**

B

CREATING Documents with PAGEMAKER

2

This chapter gives hands-on practice in the basic text and graphics functions necessary to create documents.

Upon completion of this chapter you will be able to

- set up a new document in PageMaker
- use dialog boxes
- activate rules, guides, and scroll bars
- use the **Zoom** feature to magnify or reduce your document on screen
- save a document
- work with text and text blocks
- change type specifications
- draw and edit rules, boxes, and circles using the tools in PageMaker's Toolbox
- import graphics and text files using the **Place** command
- scale graphics
- save a file as a template
- print a document

CREATING A NEW PAGEMAKER FILE

The first step in creating a PageMaker file is to start PageMaker in Windows by selecting **Start**, **Programs**, **Adobe**, **PageMaker 6.5**, then **Adobe PageMaker 6.5**. The PageMaker 6.5 menus appear at the top of the screen.

Document Setup

1. Click the **File** menu and select **New**.

The **Document Setup** dialog box appears. Look at the margin settings. If it shows margins in units other than picas and you desire picas, click the **Cancel** button in the upper-right-hand corner, and change the measurement unit to picas. You can change the measurement system to picas (or other units) by pulling down the **File** menu, selecting **Preferences**, then **General**. The first section of the **Preferences** dialog box has menus for changing both the **Measurement system** used in dialog boxes and the **Vertical ruler** in the PageMaker window. Choose your preferences and click the **OK** button. Once you have changed the measurement system to picas, click the **File** menu again and select **New**.

FIGURE

2.1

Document Setup dialog box

```
Document Setup                              OK
    Page size:  Letter              ▼      Cancel
  Dimensions:  51    x  66    picas
  Orientation:  ⦿ Tall   ⦿ Wide           Numbers...
       Options:  ☐ Double-sided    ☐ Adjust layout
                 ☐ Facing pages     ☐ Restart page numbering
  Number of pages:  1    Start page #:  1
     Margins
        Left:  9     picas      Right:  9     picas
        Top:  12     picas     Bottom:  9     picas

  Target output resolution:  300  ▼  dpi

  Compose to printer:  NEC Silentwriter2 Model 90 on LPT  ▼
```

The information for the document setup for the first project is shown in Figure 2.1. If you need to change any of the page specifications or if you have never used a dialog box before, do the following:

2. For **Page** (size), use **Letter**. To change the kind of page, click the down arrow to the right of the **Page size** box. A drop-down list appears. Select **Letter**. Page dimensions automatically change according to the page size you choose.

3. For **Orientation**, click the button for **Tall**.

4. Under the **Options** list, make sure **Double-sided**, **Facing pages**, and **Restart page numbering** are turned off. A ✔ in the box tells you that the feature is on; to turn it off, click the box—the ✔ will disappear. If the box is blank, clicking it will turn the feature on.

5. For **Number of pages** type **1**, and for **Start page #** type **1**. There are three ways to type into text boxes that are in a dialog box:
   - Click to place the cursor where you want to insert and type the new text, or **Delete** to eliminate text.
   - Click twice on the text box to highlight all the characters and type over the highlighted text.
   - Use the **Tab** key to move from one text box to the next. **Shift + Tab** will bring the cursor back to a previous box.

6. For **Margins,** type in **12p** for the top margin, **9p** for the left, right, and bottom.

7. For **Target output resolution**, your instructor will tell you what number to type or select from the menu. Desktop laser printers print resolution in units of dpi (dots per inch), such as 300 dpi (low resolution), 600 dpi (medium resolution), 1270 dpi (high resolution), or 2540 dpi (very high resolution).

8. When the dialog box is correctly filled in, click the **OK** button in the upper-right corner of the dialog box or press the **Return** key. After you click **OK** on the **Document Setup** dialog box, a blank PageMaker page appears on your screen. The parts of the PageMaker window are labeled in Figure 2.2.

Changing the Ruler Zero Points

Ruler zero points are the locations on the horizontal and vertical rulers labeled zero. If the ruler zero points are not set in the same position shown in Figure 2.2, you must change them. Changing the ruler zero point is just like moving an actual ruler. You want the zero on the horizontal ruler to line up with the left edge of your page so you can easily see how wide it is. Likewise, you want the zero on the vertical ruler to line up with the top of the page so that you can easily see the length of your page.

1. Position the mouse pointer on the zero point cross hairs in the upper-left corner where the two rulers intersect.

2. Drag to the right if you need to change the zero point of the horizontal ruler. The vertical dotted line should line up with the left side of the page size, as shown.

3. Drag downward to change the zero point of the vertical ruler. The horizontal dotted line should line up with the top edge of the paper size, as shown.

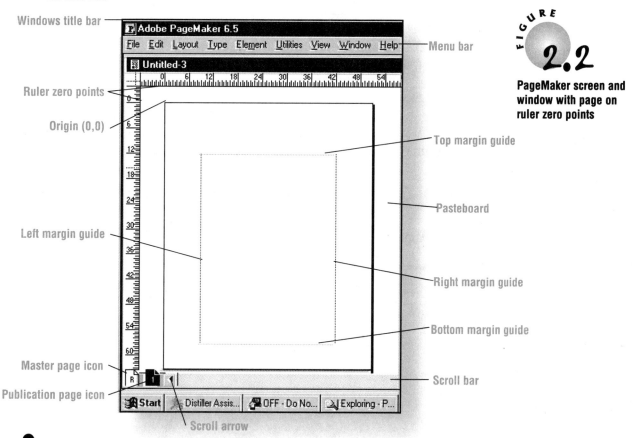

FIGURE 2.2

PageMaker screen and window with page on ruler zero points

The Toolbox

The Toolbox appears on your screen whenever you open a publication, but you can hide it by clicking the **Window** menu and selecting **Hide Tools**. Make the Toolbox appear again anytime by clicking the **Window** menu and selecting **Show Tools**.

The Toolbox contains many tools for working with text and graphics. See the following table for a list of the tools and the functions they perform.

The Toolbox

Tool	Cursor	Used for
Pointer		Selecting/moving and resizing text blocks and graphics
Text		Entering, selecting, and editing text
Rotating		Rotating graphics and text blocks
Cropping		Trimming graphics
Line		Drawing lines in any direction
Constrained-line		Drawing vertical or horizontal lines
Rectangle		Drawing squares and rectangles
Rectangle frame		Creating rectangular placeholders for text and graphics
Ellipse		Drawing circles, ovals, and ellipses
Ellipse frame		Creating circular or oval placeholders for text and graphics
Polygon		Drawing basic polygons
Polygon frame		Creating polygonal placeholders for text and graphics
Hand		Scrolling the page or previewing and testing hyperlinks
Zoom		Magnifying or reducing an area of the page

Rulers, Guides, and Scroll Bars

Margin and ruler guides are nonprinting horizontal and vertical lines that can help you position type and graphics. To activate the ruler and margin guides, or the **scroll bars**, click the **View** menu.

Margin Guides When you specify margin guides in the **Document Setup** dialog box, they are automatically drawn on the page. You can hide the margin guides by clicking **View**, then clicking **Hide Guides**.

Ruler Guides Ruler guides are dragged out of the ruler at the top (for horizontal ruler guides) and the ruler at the left (for vertical ruler guides). For the first letterhead project, start with two ruler guides, at **3p** and **60p** from the top of the page.

1. Point, click, and hold at the top ruler. Your pointer changes to a double-headed arrow. Drag downward (to **drag**, keep the mouse button depressed). Watch the dotted line in the left ruler to see the position of the guide (see Figure 2.3).

2. Release the mouse button when the guide is **3p** from the top of the page. This is the guide for the positioning of the workshop title.

3. Point at the ruler again and drag a guide to **60p** from the top of the page. This will be the position for the company name and address in the letterhead.

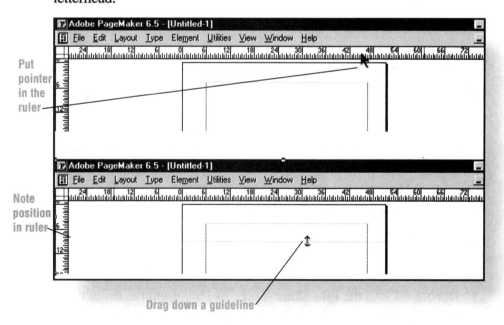

Put pointer in the ruler

Note position in ruler

Drag down a guideline

FIGURE

2.3

Dragging ruler guides

DID YOU KNOW...

If you accidentally release the mouse button in the wrong place, you can simply point at the guide and drag it into position. It is not necessary to drag a new guide out of the ruler. If you end up with too many ruler guides, you can drag the extras back into the ruler.

Zooming In and Out

The default view of the page in a new file is **Fit in Window**, which enables you to see the whole page, reduced, on your screen. This is useful for blocking out a page and to see the overall design of the page. In **Fit in Window** view, the rulers are very small, and the positioning is imprecise.

1. Click the **View** menu.

2. In the **View** menu, select **Actual size**.

Notice that the rulers, as well as the page, have become larger. You can check the accuracy of your guides by scrolling up and down, and left and right on the page. Another way to bring different portions of your document into view is to use the **Hand** tool. Practice using the **Hand** tool:

1. Click on the **Hand** tool in the Toolbox.

2. Your pointer becomes a hand.

3. Hold down the mouse button while you move the hand up and down on the screen.

You can also use the **Hand** to move your page around when your publication is in **Fit in Window** size.

PageMaker 6.5 has a **Zoom** tool in the Toolbox (shown as a magnifying glass) that magnifies or reduces the display of any area in your publication. To magnify or reduce with the **Zoom** tool:

1. Select the **Zoom** tool. The pointer changes to a magnifying glass.

2. Point the magnifying glass on the area you want to magnify and click to **Zoom in**. To **Zoom out**, press the **Ctrl** key while clicking.

3. Choose **Actual size** in the **View** menu to return your document to its previous size.

4. Re-select the **Pointer** tool.

Saving the File

Now save your PageMaker file. Name it **lhead1**.

1. Click the **File** menu and select **Save As**. You will probably want to save the file on your own disk. However, PageMaker operates faster when the file is saved on the hard drive. When you leave the classroom for the day, save the file to your disk. For now, ask the instructor for the name of the folder you can use to save your file temporarily on the hard drive.

2. Access your disk by clicking the drop-down list by the **Save in** list (see Figure 2.4). To save to your disk, select the **a:** drive. Otherwise, select the folder on **drive c:** per your instructor's directions. (*Note:* Your folder names will not be the same as the folder names shown in Figure 2.4.)

3. Double-click in the **File name** text box to highlight the default filename. Then enter the filename **lhead1**, and click **Save**.

Save and **Save As** are two different things:

- Use **Save As** when you are saving your document for the first time and need to give it a name, or when you want to save the document to a new drive or disk or give it a new name.

MAC MEMO

The **Command** key on a Macintosh is equivalent to the **Control** key on an IBM-compatible PC.

- Use **Save** periodically as you work on a document, to save changes as you go along. Always remember to use **Save** when you close a document! If you forget, PageMaker will ask if you want to save the document with any changes. Click **Yes** to save and **No** if you do not want to save the changes.

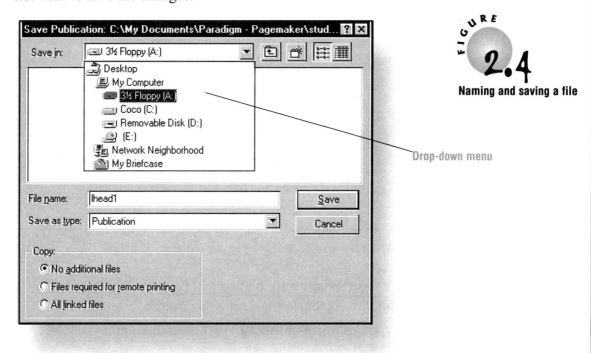

FIGURE

2.4

Naming and saving a file

Drop-down menu

BASIC TEXT FUNCTIONS

Text can be typed directly in PageMaker, or it may be imported from word processing or ASCII files. For small amounts of text, as on letterhead, it is more efficient to type directly in PageMaker. For longer blocks of text, such as the body of the letter, advertisement, flier, or poster you will be working on in this book, text is provided as ASCII files, which you will import.

Text Insertion

When working with text, it is often most convenient to use **Actual size** so that you can easily read the characters on the screen. To type text, you need to use the **Text** tool—the **T** icon.

1. Click the **Text** tool in the toolbox.

2. The cursor changes into an **I-beam** (a vertical line with small curly lines at the top and bottom); see Figure 2.5. Click the I-beam where you want to make an insertion. The **insertion cursor** (flashing vertical bar) indicates where the characters you insert will appear.

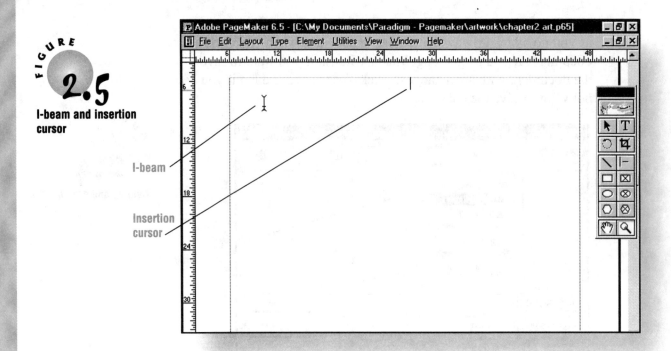

F I G U R E

2.5

I-beam and insertion cursor

3. Click just below the top margin of the page. The insertion cursor will appear at the top left margin of the page.

4. Type **Desktop Publishing Workshop** (use upper- and lowercase letters).

PageMaker Text Modes

There are two basic ways to work with text in PageMaker depending on the function you wish to perform:

- **Character or typographical operations:** To enter and edit text or to apply type specifications, highlight the text characters with the **Text** tool.
- **Block or layout operations:** To position a whole block of type without affecting the individual characters within the block, select the text block with the **Pointer** tool.

Remember that PageMaker is both a typographical and a layout program. These two modes correspond to its typesetting (word processing) functions and its pasteup (graphics) functions. The distinction between these two modes will become more familiar to you as you work with text characters and text blocks in PageMaker.

Highlight Text Characters To enter text, for editing, or for specifying type, use the **Text** tool. For now, just practice **highlighting** the characters.

1. Click the **Text** tool in the toolbox (if it is not already activated) so that your cursor changes into an I-beam.

2. Click to insert the I-beam in front of the "D" in "Desktop."

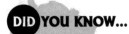

YOU KNOW...

In general, it is best *not* to use the **Caps Lock** key. Text typed erroneously as all caps with the **Caps Lock** key cannot be changed to upper- and lowercase letters without retyping it. If you typed upper- and lowercase to begin with, the text can be changed to all caps with a single command—without having to retype.

3. Holding down the mouse button, drag the I-beam across the characters. This will highlight them.

4. The highlighted characters will appear white on a dark background, as shown in Figure 2.6.

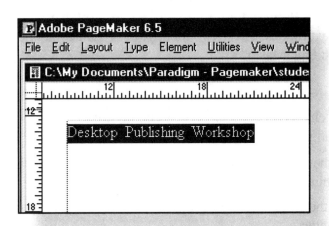

FIGURE **2.6**
Highlighted text

5. While the characters are highlighted, use the shortcut for the *all caps* type specification: press **Shift + Ctrl + K** (Windows) or **Shift + Command + K** (Macintosh).

6. Press **Shift + Ctrl + K** (Windows) or **Shift + Command + K** (Macintosh) again to change back to the original (upper- and lowercase) specification.

Select a Text Block For positioning an existing text block (such as the one you have just typed) on the page, use the **Pointer** tool.

1. Click the pointer in the toolbox so that your cursor changes into a pointer.

2. Click anywhere on the text to select it. **Handles** (small knobs or tabs) appear on the text block, as shown in Figure 2.7.

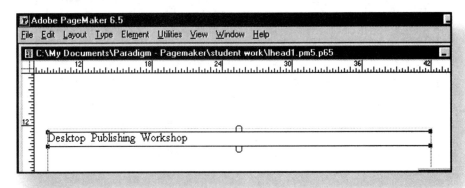

FIGURE **2.7**
A text block with handles

3. Put the pointer on the block (anywhere between the block handles), **Click** (hold), and drag. The pointer turns into a four-directional arrow, indicating that the text block can be moved in any direction.

PageMaker has a convenient **undo** function that enables you to cancel the last operation. This **undo** function works for most simple operations, such as moving text blocks. Use the **Undo** command (under the **Edit** menu) to put the text block back in its original position.

Practice highlighting the text with the **Text** tool and selecting the text block with the **Pointer** tool until you feel comfortable with PageMaker's two basic text modes. These two modes are fundamental to everything that you do with PageMaker.

Type Specifications

In order to change the type specification, highlight the text characters you wish to change with the **Text** tool.

DID YOU KNOW...

You must highlight the text to specify it. If type is not highlighted, the specifications will not be applied, but will become the new default specifications that will appear when you type any new text.

1. Click the **Text** tool in the toolbox, and highlight the words "Desktop Publishing Workshop."

2. While the characters are highlighted, click the **Type** menu and select **Character**.

3. In the **Character Specifications** dialog box, specify the typeface, point size, leading, set width, position, case, and track as shown in Figure 2.8. Then click **OK**.

4. While the characters are still highlighted, click the **Type** menu and select **Paragraph**.

5. In the **Paragraph Specifications** dialog box, use the drop-down list after **Alignment** to specify **Center**, as shown in Figure 2.9. Then click **OK**.

FIGURE

2.8

Character Specifications dialog box

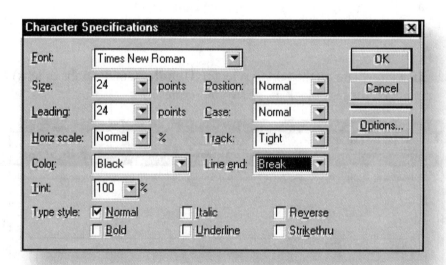

Paragraph Specifications ✕

Indents:

Left [0] picas

First [0] picas

Right [0] picas

Paragraph space:

Before [0] picas

After [0] picas

OK

Cancel

Rules...

Spacing...

Alignment: [Center ▼] Dictionary: [US English ▼]

Left
Center
Right
Justify
Force justify

Options:

☐ Keep
☐ Colum
☐ Page break before
☐ Include in table of contents

☐ Keep with next [0] lines
☐ Widow control [0] lines
☐ Orphan control [0] lines

FIGURE **2.9**

Centering highlighted text

Text Block Positioning

To change the position of the block of text, select the text block with the **Pointer** tool (refer to Figure 2.7).

1. Click the **Pointer** tool (arrow) in the toolbox, and select the "Desktop Publishing Workshop" text block.

2. Drag the block upward so that the top handle aligns with the **3p** guide that you dragged from the ruler. When you release the mouse button, the text block should "snap" to the guide.

3. To save the file with the same filename, click on the **File** menu and select **Save**.

Continue your work on the letterhead by following these steps:

1. Type the organization's name and address. Highlight and apply **Character** and **Paragraph Specifications** as shown in Figure 2.15 at the end of this chapter. Refer to the next "Did You Know..." tip for help with inserting the bullets. (Do not worry about drawing the lines now.)

2. Position the text block at the **60p** guide.

3. Save the **lhead1** file when you have completed these steps.

MAC MEMO

On the Macintosh, you can save a file by going to the **File** menu and selecting **Save** or by using the **Option + S** keys.

DID YOU KNOW...

You can add a bullet by pressing **Alt + 8** (Windows) or **Option + 8** (Macintosh).

BASIC GRAPHICS FUNCTIONS

Like text, graphics can be created directly in PageMaker, or imported. For very simple graphics such as rules, boxes, and circles (typographical enhancements), the PageMaker graphics tools can be used. For more complex graphics such as logos and illustrations, the graphics should be created in a graphics program (or scanned, or purchased as clip art), and then imported into PageMaker.

The Toolbox

The drawing tools in the Toolbox are used to create rules, boxes, and circles (see Figure 2.10). To draw a graphic in PageMaker, select the tool you wish to use by clicking it in the toolbox. The cursor changes to a cross hairs. Position the cross hairs approximately where you wish to start drawing, and drag to make the shape you want. The graphic can be moved and repositioned later.

FIGURE 2.10

The PageMaker Toolbox

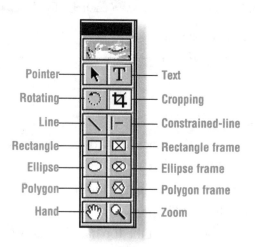

Pointer ——— Text
Rotating ——— Cropping
Line ——— Constrained-line
Rectangle ——— Rectangle frame
Ellipse ——— Ellipse frame
Polygon ——— Polygon frame
Hand ——— Zoom

You can practice using the drawing tools before you create the graphic on the letterhead. PageMaker's **revert** function enables you to discard all changes from the point at which you last saved your publication. If you did not save the **lhead1** file just before starting this section, save it now.

Drawing and Editing Rules In order to draw or edit rules, follow these guidelines.

1. Click the **Constrained-line** tool, position the cross hairs where you want to start the rule, and then drag. Draw the lines shown in Figure 2.15 at the end of this chapter.

2. Edit the lines if necessary. Tips for editing:
   - To select a rule, click it with the pointer. Graphics handles appear at the ends of the rule.
   - To stretch the rule, position the pointer on a handle and drag. The pointer changes into cross hairs.

DID YOU KNOW...

Once a graphic is drawn in PageMaker, use the pointer, not the cross hairs, to select it or edit it (alter its length, direction, weight, style, or color). (See Figure 2.11.) If you use the cross hairs, you will create another rule.

- To reposition the rule (without changing its length or direction), position the pointer on the rule itself, and then click and drag. The pointer turns into a four-directional arrow. Note that this is the same cursor that appears when you reposition a text block.
- To delete a rule, select it and press the **Delete** key on the keyboard.

3. To specify the line rule weights shown in Figure 2.15, select the rule and click the **Element** menu. Then select **Stroke**. 1p is the default.

4. Save under the same filename, **lhead1**.

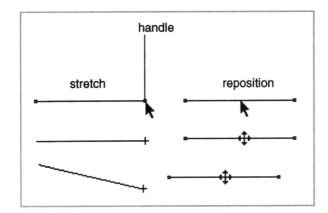

FIGURE **2.11**

Editing rules

Drawing and Editing Boxes and Circles To draw a box or circle, select the **Box** or **Circle** tool in the toolbox, position the cross hairs approximately where you want to start the graphic, and then click and drag.

Remember, once you have drawn a graphic in PageMaker, you must use the *pointer* (not the cross hairs) to select or edit it (alter its length, direction, weight, style, or color). See Figure 2.12. If you use the cross hairs, you will create another graphic.

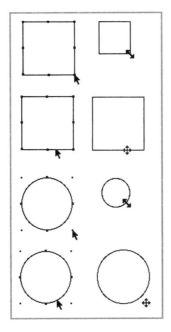

FIGURE **2.12**

Editing boxes and circles

To practice drawing and editing boxes and circles:

1. Select the box or circle with the pointer. Box handles appear on the outer rules of the box; circle handles appear on an imaginary box in which the circle is positioned.

2. To stretch (enlarge or reduce) a box or circle, put the pointer on a corner handle.

3. Click and drag *away* from the opposite corner to enlarge the box or circle.

4. Click and drag *toward* the opposite corner to reduce the box or circle.

The graphic handles on a box or circle have different functions depending on whether they are in the corner or at the midpoint.

- Dragging on a middle handle limits stretching to either *up and down* only or *sideways* only.
- Dragging on a corner handle permits stretching in both *vertical* and *horizontal* directions at the same time.
- Pressing the **Shift** key while dragging limits the box or circle to a *square or circle* (as opposed to a rectangle or an oval).

Moving and applying attributes to boxes or circles is similar to moving and applying attributes to rules.

- To *move* a box or circle, put the pointer on a line of the graphic (not a handle), and then click and drag.
- To *specify* the lines and/or fill of a box or circle, select it and click the **Element** menu. Select **Fill and Stroke...** and in the **Fill and Stroke** dialog box, use the drop-down lists to specify the stroke type and fill percentage. (Stroke means "line.")
- To *delete* a box or circle, select it and press the **Delete** key.

When you have finished practicing, delete the graphics from the page. Select all the graphics (not the type) and press the **Delete** key.

To select multiple elements:

1. Click one element, hold the **Shift** key on the keyboard and click the next object(s) to be selected, *or*

2. Position the pointer in a space where there are no elements. Then click and drag a dotted box to surround the elements to be selected. Release the mouse.

In case you missed deleting a graphic, or accidentally deleted type as you were practicing, you can use PageMaker's *revert* function to go back to the last saved version of the file.

1. Click the **File** menu, and select **Revert**.

2. Click **OK** in the **Revert** alert box.

Importing Files

For the letterhead you are creating, you will import the logo graphic, save the file as a template, and then import a letter. The most common way to import text or graphics to a PageMaker file is by using the **Place** command, which is accessed in the **File** menu.

First, scroll to the top of the page where you will place the logo, and draw some guides to help in the positioning of the logo.

1. Drag horizontal guides for the top and bottom of the logo at **5½p** and **9½p**. You can use the handles of the text block to find the center of the page.

2. To set the vertical guide at the center of the margins, select the **Pointer** tool in the toolbox, and then select the text block. Handles appear at the midpoint of the text block.

3. Drag a guide from the left ruler to the middle of the text block handles.

Importing Graphics   The logo is an encapsulated PostScript file called **logo.eps**, and is located on the student data disk.

1. Click the **File** menu and select **Place**.

2. In the **Place** dialog box, select **logo** and click **Open**. The cursor changes into a PostScript text-place symbol.

3. Position the PostScript text-place symbol anywhere on the **5½p** guide and click. The logo image will appear, selected—with handles around the outside. You will need to reduce (scale it down) it and then position it in the center of the page.

Scaling Graphics   Scaling is the reduction or enlargement of a graphic. **Proportional scaling** maintains the ratio of height and width in a graphic. Most imported graphics should be proportionally scaled in order to avoid distorting the dimensions of the original image. Use the **Shift** key for proportional scaling.

1. Select the graphic if it is not already selected. While holding down the **Shift** key, drag the lower-right-corner handle toward the opposite corner.

2. When the logo fits between the guides that you drew, release the mouse button.

If you scale the logo too large or too small, simply repeat the steps above until it is the proper size.

Positioning Graphics   Once the graphic is properly scaled, use the pointer to position it in the center of the page:

1. Put the pointer on the logo itself (not on a handle) and drag it to the center of the page, remaining within the horizontal guides.

DID YOU KNOW...

If you do not see the **logo** filename and can't find the file, you are probably not accessing your disk. Check to verify that you are logged on to the **a:** drive. If you are not, double-click the **a:** drive to view and then open the contents of your disk.

2. When you release the mouse button, you will see that the center handles align with the vertical guide.

Saving a Template

Now you will save the PageMaker file you have just created as a template. A **template** is a master file that contains standard layout elements that you can use over and over again with different content. Templates are used most commonly for letterheads, serial publications such as newsletters and magazines, and for chapters of a book or report.

1. Click the **File** menu and select **Save As**.
2. Click the **Template** button in the **Save As** menu.
3. Click the **Save** button.

MAC MEMO

In Windows, the extension of the template file will automatically change from .p65 (publication) to .t65 (template). On the Macintosh, you will need to type the new extension.

A template is like an ordinary PageMaker file except that when you open it, it creates an untitled file. Then, when you import text and/or graphics, you can save the file under a different name, leaving the template "empty" for the next time you use it. In order to use the template again, you will need to first close it, then reopen it.

1. Under the **File** menu, choose **Close**.
2. Reopen the template file, again using the **File** menu and the **Open** option. (*Note:* When you click on the filename **lhead1**, the **Open As** selection by default is **Copy**. This means you are opening a copy of the template.)

Note that the new file is untitled.

Importing Text

The letter you are going to import is an ASCII text file named **letter.txt**. It is located on the student data disk.

1. Click the **File** menu, and select **Place**.
2. In the **Place** dialog box, select **letter** and click **Open**.
3. Since this is an unformatted ASCII text file, the **Text-only Import Filter** dialog box appears. Choose **No conversion, import as is** and click **OK**. The cursor changes into a text-place symbol.
4. Position the text-place symbol at the intersection of the **12p** margin guide and the left margin and click.

The text will appear, as a selected text block positioned within the margins. If it does not fit into the margins of your page, you positioned the text-place cursor outside the margins when you clicked. You can "stretch" it or place it again. See the following instructions.

The PageMaker text block has a flexible column width and column length. **Windowshades**, the horizontal lines that stretch across the top and bottom of a selected text block, are used to resize the text block. Notice that each windowshade has a handle. An empty handle at the top indicates the beginning of the text block. An empty handle at the bottom indicates the end of a text block. A down arrow in a windowshade handle indicates there is more text to be placed (see Figure 2.13).

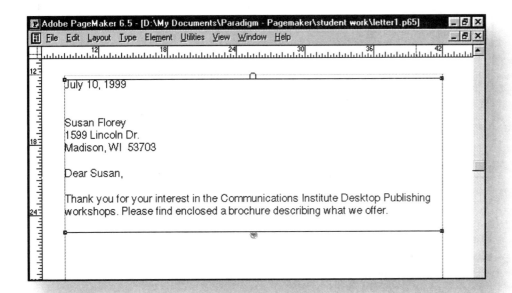

FIGURE 2.13
Increasing text block length

1. Scroll down until you see the bottom handle.

2. Click and drag the bottom handle upwards to reduce the text block length. Note that when there is more text in a block than appears on the page, the bottom handle contains an arrow pointing down.

3. Drag the bottom handle downward to increase the text block length.

4. To reposition the entire text block, drag the bottom handle all the way to the top handle.

5. Click the bottom handle (the one with the down arrow). The cursor will change to a text-place cursor; it has been "loaded" with text.

6. Position the text-place cursor within the margins and click. The text block appears with handles.

You can also stretch the text block; that is, change the column width (line length) by dragging the corners at the ends of the windowshades. Drag the right corner on the bottom of the text block handle to the left (see Figure 2.14).

Because the smaller column width requires more lines to accommodate the text, the bottom of the text block will contain a down arrow, indicating that there is more text to be placed.

FIGURE

2.14

Changing the column width

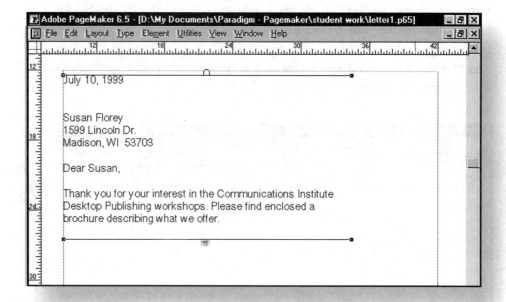

Practice dragging down on the bottom handle to gain lines in the text block. Then drag up on the bottom handle to lose lines in the text block.

For your printout, set the letter within the margins of the letterhead and specify the type.

1. Drag the bottom handle to the top handle, click the bottom handle, and reposition the text block within the margins of the page.

2. Use the **Text** tool and highlight all the text. Click the **Type** menu, then **Character**, and specify the type as 11/13 Helvetica.

3. Save the file as **letter1**.

PRINTING THE FILE

To print a PageMaker file, use the **Print** option under the **File** menu. Click the **File** menu and select **Print**.

Your instructor will tell you if you need to specify any special options in the **Print** dialog box for the printer connected to your computer.

FIGURE 2.15

Printout of letterhead ***(letter1)***

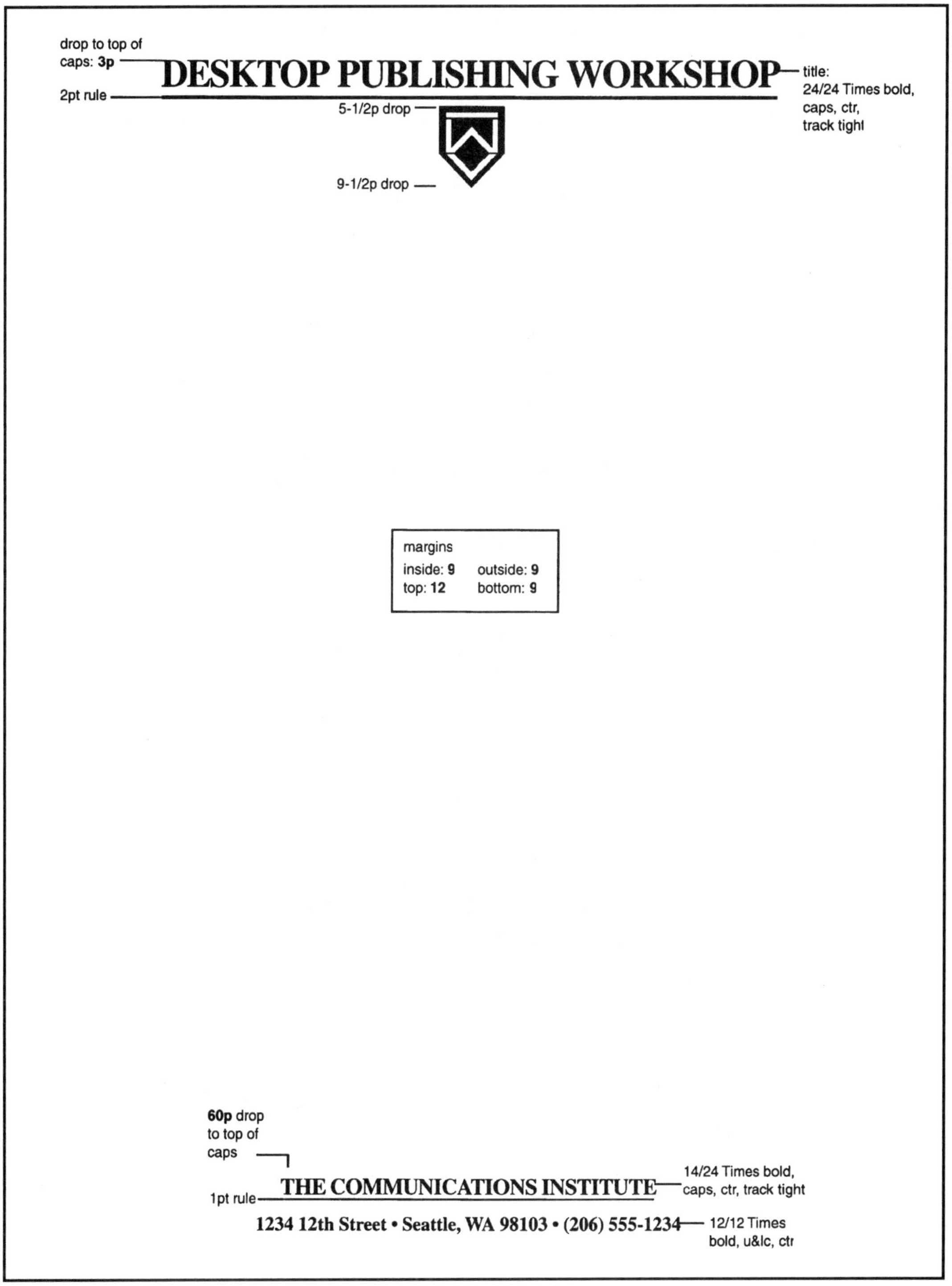
drop to top of caps: **3p**
2pt rule
DESKTOP PUBLISHING WORKSHOP
title: 24/24 Times bold, caps, ctr, track tight
5-1/2p drop
9-1/2p drop
margins
inside: **9** outside: **9**
top: **12** bottom: **9**
60p drop to top of caps
1pt rule
THE COMMUNICATIONS INSTITUTE
14/24 Times bold, caps, ctr, track tight
1234 12th Street • Seattle, WA 98103 • (206) 555-1234
12/12 Times bold, u&lc, ctr

CHECKING YOUR UNDERSTANDING

Answer true or false in questions 1–10, and if false, explain why.

1. Ruler guides are automatically drawn on the page when you specify the margins in the **Document Setup** dialog box.

2. When you click the **Text** tool, the cursor changes into an I-beam.

3. Editing text is a function for which the **Text** tool is used.

4. Imported graphics are scaled using the **Box** tool.

5. Changing the width of a text block is a function for which the **Text** tool is used.

6. Files are imported using the **Place** command.

7. Characters are highlighted with the I-beam.

8. When a text block is selected, it has handles.

9. Line weights are specified under the **Element** menu.

10. The **Ruling** tool is used to lengthen or shorten a rule.

APPLYING DESIGN PRINCIPLES

Exercise 1   Creating an Invitation Flier

Create an invitation flier, inviting your friends to a party, open house, or any event of your choosing. Use the **Line**, **Box**, or **Circle** tool to create a map showing the location of the party. If you have access to clip art files, import a graphic that matches the theme of the party (e.g., a mortarboard for graduation, a cake for a birthday, and so on). Use Figure 2.16 as a guide to give you some ideas.

a) Create a new document with ½-inch margins on all sides. Draw a large box that is 1 inch from each of the four edges of the page.

b) Draw a box for the map. Use the **Box** tool to draw the streets, and use the **Send to back** or **Send to front** commands (under the **Element** menu) to layer.

c) Use the **Text** tool to type the street names; then layer the names on top of the streets.

d) Draw and fill a large box at the top of the page. Layer the word **Party** on top.

e) Save the file as **party** and print.

Party

What: Graduation Party
When: May 21 at 8:30 p.m.
Where: 10423 Amber Lane
Who: Hannah DeMarte

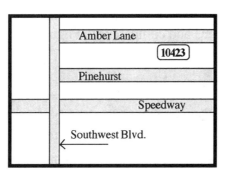

Amber Lane
10423
Pinehurst
Speedway
Southwest Blvd.

Lost?
Call: 555-1234

FIGURE

2.16

**Printout of Invitation
Flier, Exercise 1**

Exercise 2 Creating Letterheads and Importing Text

Create the letterhead samples shown in Figures 2.17 and Figure 2.18. Drag guides onto the page as needed.

a) Create the letterhead shown in Figure 2.17. (*Note:* the screens behind the workshop title and address are boxes with lines specified as **None**.)

- Create the document and save it as a template called **lhead2**.
- Import the **letter.txt** into **lhead2** template.
- Specify the type as Helvetica 11/13.
- Save the file as **letter2**.
- Print out **letter2** and compare it to Figure 2.17.

b) Create the letterhead shown in Figure 2.18.

- Create the document and save it as a template called **lhead3**.
- Import **letter.txt** into the **lhead3** template.
- Specify the type as Helvetica 10/15.
- Save the file as **letter3**.
- Print out **letter3** and compare it to Figure 2.18.

Exercise 3 Creating a Map

Create a map of the classroom or computer lab where this class takes place. If you have access to clip art files, import pictures of desks and computers.

a) Use the **Box**, **Circle**, and **Line** tools to indicate desks, the locations of chalk or whiteboards, windows, the instructor's desk, doors, storage cabinets, and shelves.

b) Add your name, the name of this class, and today's date in the upper right-hand corner.

drop to top of —— box **3p**

drop to top of caps **4-1/2p**

DESKTOP PUBLISHING WORKSHOP

24/24 Helv bold, caps, ctr, track tight

drop to bottom of box **8p**

box to left margin

top of logo: **6-1/2p** drop
bottom of logo: **9-1/2p** drop

box to right margin

margins

inside: **9**   outside: **9**
top: **12**   bottom: **9**

drop to top of box **58-1/2p**

14/18 Helv bold, caps, ctr, track tight

THE COMMUNICATIONS INSTITUTE
1234 12th Street • Seattle, WA 98103 • (206) 555-1234

drop to bottom of box **64p**

12/18 Helv bold, ctr, track tight

FIGURE
2.18

Letterhead
(letter3), Exercise 2b

**Desktop
Publishing
Workshop**

drop to top of caps **2p**

type: 30/28 Helv bold

drop to top of logo **8p**

drop to bottom of logo **12p**

horizontal
position **6p**
from left edge

margins

inside: **9**	outside: **9**
top: **12**	bottom: **9**

drop to top of caps **59p**

**The
Communications
Institute** 1234 12th Street • Seattle, WA 98103 • (206) 555-1234

org name: 18/18 Helv bold

addr: 11/18 Helv

part

2

Typography

PRINCIPLES of Typography

This chapter discusses typography, its terminology, and typesetting.

Upon completion of this chapter | you will be able to

- identify the differences between screen fonts and printer fonts
- identify the parts of a letter form
- distinguish among the three categories of typefaces (sans serif, serif, and decorative)
- utilize the measuring system of typography
- identify type alignment, indentation, and line, letter- and word spacing

An understanding of typography is essential to desktop publishing, because type is the basic element in a design. Even for simple office documents such as correspondence, memos, forms, and informal reports, knowing the right type to use can make your documents stand out. For more complex publications, such as newsletters, magazines, brochures, and formal reports, and for special documents such as posters, ads, and covers, all of which can be processed through PageMaker, you must be familiar with typography in order to specify and select type.

The terms and concepts from the centuries-old publishing and printing traditions are used in PageMaker as well as in modern typesetting systems. The type-handling capabilities of desktop publishing software are improved with each new version. Companies that develop and distribute digital typefaces are making new as well as old typefaces available to desktop publishers at the rate of hundreds each year.

TYPE: BASIC INFORMATION

In typography, a **typeface** is defined as a set of characters created by a type designer, including upper- and lowercase alphabetical characters, numbers, punctuation, special characters (such as a dollar sign), and ligatures (characters that are physically connected to each other, such as fi, fl, œ and æ). A **font** is defined as a set of characters in a specific typeface, at a specific size, and in a specific style.

Desktop publishing has two ways of producing typefaces. The first is with **bitmapped characters**, which are characters created with a group of small dots. Together these dots form the shape of a character (letter, number, and so on). With bitmapped characters, each type size and style must be stored separately.

Desktop publishers sometimes use the term *font* interchangeably with typeface. Although this is technically incorrect, the loose usage has arisen because of **outline fonts**, which are outlines created by a series of lines and arcs. Outline fonts are more efficient than bitmapped characters; they can be scaled to any size and adjusted to different styles.

PostScript is the page-description language (PDL) most often used to provide these outline fonts. PostScript carries instructions to a PostScript-compatible printer or other output device as to how a particular document should be handled. It defines the outlines of characters, so that the printer can fill them in to a given resolution.

A fourth factor, **page orientation**, adds another dimension to the definition of a digital font: a font may be designed for printing on a page that is *portrait* or *landscape*. The following table shows the four factors that define a digital font: typeface, point size, type style, and orientation.

FOUR FACTORS OF DIGITAL FONTS

Typeface	Point Size	Type Style	Orientation
Times, Garamond, Helvetica, Goudy, Optima, Courier,	6, 8, 9, 10, 11, 12, 14, 18, etc.	roman, bold, italic, bold italic, etc.	portrait or landscape

SCREEN FONTS VS. PRINTER FONTS

WYSIWYG desktop publishing systems provide a screen representation of the printed output. Therefore, two sets of fonts are needed: **screen fonts**, to show the positioning and size of characters on the screen (what you see), and **printer fonts**, to actually lay down the characters on a page (what you get). Both screen fonts and printer fonts may be bitmapped, but screen fonts have a much lower resolution than printer fonts. Printer fonts may be fixed bitmaps, or they may be generated from PostScript font outlines that map to the resolution of any output device, including high-resolution image setters.

Screen Fonts

Depending on the system, program, and size used, screen fonts can be:

- Matching (specific fonts, installed in the computer system, that match the printer fonts).

- Extrapolated (specific fonts that are bitmapped enlargements or reductions of installed screen fonts—used in Macintosh systems).

- Generic (nonspecific fonts that come with the drawing or page assembly program—used in IBM/compatible systems).

Matching Screen Fonts   Matching screen fonts are made specifically for either the Macintosh or the IBM/compatible screen; they correspond as well as possible, given their lower resolution, to the printer fonts (see Figure 3.1). Matching screen fonts provide the most accurate page display. However, they take up extra disk space and take longer to redraw on the screen than generic fonts (see below). Most desktop publishers find it most efficient to install a minimum number of screen fonts on their system. The printer fonts are what count, since they determine the final output, no matter what the screen fonts look like.

FIGURE 3.1

Matching screen and printer fonts
The same typeface and size are installed for both screen and printer. A printer font is created from an outline master.

screen font   *printer font*

Extrapolated Screen Fonts   On Macintosh systems, disk space can be conserved by using extrapolated bitmapped screen fonts. The typeface is installed in one point size, and all other sizes can be extrapolated from it, as shown in Figure 3.2. The larger the fonts, the more jagged they appear on the screen. However, this has no effect on the printer fonts if PostScript outlines or 600 **dpi** (dots per inch) printer fonts are installed in the printer.

Extrapolated screen fonts allow you to see how the characters will appear on the page, and they show accurate line breaks.

FIGURE 3.2

Extrapolated screen font
Larger sizes are extrapolated from bitmaps of smaller sizes, so larger characters look jagged on the screen but the printer fonts are not affected.

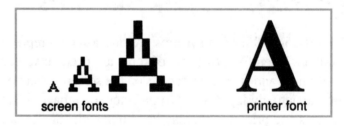

screen fonts   **printer font**

Generic Screen Fonts   On IBM/compatible systems, generic screen fonts may be used instead of extrapolated screen fonts. Like extrapolated fonts, generic fonts conserve disk space.

Generic fonts may be bitmapped or outline masters. The use of outline generic fonts increases the **screen refresh rate**, the speed at which images are drawn on the screen. Generic fonts, however, are less WYSIWYG than extrapolated or matching screen fonts (see Figure 3.3). Generic fonts do not necessarily look like the font that will be printed, but they do show accurate line breaks in text.

screen font   printer fonts

Generic screen font
The same screen font is
used for all printer fonts;
it is not apparent on the
screen what typeface is
used.

Greeked Text Most page assembly programs have a zoom-out feature for a fit-on-screen view of page layouts. When a full page fits on a normal-sized screen, type is reduced and is too small to be represented clearly on most monitors. On both IBM/compatible and Macintosh systems, text is **greeked**—that is, shown on the screen as gray bars rather than as individual characters—when the type is too small to be displayed (see Figure 3.4.)

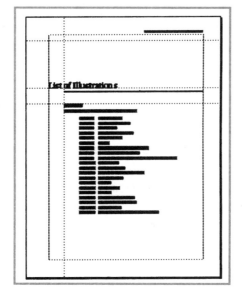

Greeked text
At small sizes, grey bars
appear on the screen
instead of type characters.

The use of greeked text greatly increases the screen refresh rate. Some page assembly programs enable text to be greeked at any size in order to speed up the display while the user experiments with layout variations.

Printer Fonts

Printer fonts may be PostScript or non-PostScript. (Non-PostScript fonts include PCL, which uses bitmapped fonts; and QuickDraw, which uses outlines that are more rudimentary than PostScript outlines.) Printer fonts may be present in the printer's **ROM**, installed on cartridges that are plugged into the printer, or downloaded from the computer to the printer's **RAM**. ROM (read-only memory) is permanent memory that is etched in a chip. RAM (random-access memory) is temporary memory.

The number and type of ROM-resident fonts and cartridge fonts available for laser printers is limited. PostScript printers normally have four to nine typefaces; PCL printers generally have 16 fonts installed (one typeface: the typewriter face Courier), and 16 fonts (one typeface) per cartridge.

Therefore, downloadable fonts, also called **soft fonts**—as opposed to the "hard" fonts in ROM or on cartridges—are used to expand the number and types of fonts available.

Downloadable (Soft) Fonts Soft fonts can be downloaded to the printer's RAM temporarily or "permanently"—that is, for the duration of a work session. When temporary, the fonts are flushed from RAM as soon as they are used; when permanent, they remain in RAM until the printer is turned off.

It takes longer to print pages with a variety of fonts using temporarily downloaded fonts, since the 600 dpi images must be rebuilt (for PostScript fonts) or retransmitted (for non-PostScript fonts) each time a different font is used. Fonts downloaded permanently to the printer's RAM take less time to print because the bitmaps are built or transmitted only once during a work session. But permanent downloading may cause problems for printers with limited RAM. An attempt to print with additional fonts when RAM is already full of fonts results in an error message; some fonts must be removed, or the printer must be restarted with fresh, empty RAM.

PostScript Printer Fonts PostScript printer fonts are created from font outlines. Only the font outlines (one for each style of the typeface), not the individual 600 dpi bitmaps for each font, are installed in or downloaded to the printer, so the RAM limitation problems described above are less frequent. Each font outline takes up about 10K to 30K of RAM. The microprocessor in the PostScript printer itself generates 600 dpi bitmaps from the font outline at varying sizes and at the orientation required.

Because PostScript printer fonts are generated from outlines, they can be scaled and rotated for different sizes, styles, and orientations. Typography programs and PostScript drawing programs can also be used to stretch, compress, variably fill, and stroke PostScript outlines for special graphic effects (see Figure 3.5). In addition, documents made with PostScript printer fonts can be used with higher-resolution PostScript imagesetters as well as with 600 dpi laser printers.

FIGURE 3.5

PostScript printer font
PostScript typefaces can be scaled, rotated, and have other effects applied, without affecting the resolution of the printed output.

Non-PostScript Printer Fonts Non-PostScript printer fonts for PCL and QuickDraw printers are in the form of 600 dpi bitmaps. Because bitmaps are considerably larger than PostScript's font outlines, more time and more RAM are needed for their transmission and storage. Each 600 dpi bitmapped font, depending on its size, may take from 20K to 200K of printer RAM. Therefore, a printer with less than 1 Mb of RAM may not be able to handle even a single page if it contains many large fonts that need to be permanently downloaded.

If a font used in a publication is not installed or downloaded to the printer, the printer will do one of the following:

- Substitute a generic font that is installed.
- Extrapolate a font that is installed.
- Print a screen-resolution bitmap.
- Not print at all.

None of these options is acceptable. The use of non-PostScript printer fonts, therefore, requires some planning. Each separate font—typeface, style, size, and orientation—must be either installed on a cartridge in the printer or downloaded.

Non-PostScript fonts for PCL printers, because they are bitmaps, generally cannot be scaled or rotated, nor may other special effects be applied to them without major distortion and jaggedness (see Figure 3.6). Because bitmaps are by definition resolution-dependent, non-PostScript fonts for 600 dpi laser printers can be used only on 600 dpi printers, not on higher-resolution output devices such as imagesetters.

Non-PostScript printer font
When a bit-mapped font is used for larger sizes, the bitmap itself is enlarged, and the resolution of the printed output is reduced.

INSTALLING FONTS

Digital type manufacturers sell fonts for specific types of printers. Depending on the manufacturer, the fonts come with specific screen fonts or utilities for building the screen fonts.

PostScript fonts come with limited screen fonts (usually in five or six sizes) and outline printer fonts. The lack of screen fonts at particular sizes is not a problem, because printer fonts generated from PostScript font outlines can be scaled to any size. Even if the representation is extrapolated or generic, the specified font will appear at good resolution on the printer.

Non-PostScript fonts must be purchased for the specific orientation and sizes at which they will be used (for example, cartridge-based fonts), since rotating or scaling bitmapped fonts results in distortion or no printout. One digital type company, Bitstream, provides a utility for IBM/compatible computers which generates both screen and printer fonts in 66 sizes; each font must be individually built before it can be used in a document.

DIGITAL TYPE AND TYPOGRAPHY

Professionally designed typefaces, many of them derived from designs created centuries ago, are available today. One mark of professional type design is its certification by the International Typeface Corporation (ITC). An ITC typeface is guaranteed to follow high standards of type design and fidelity to the designer's specifications. Adobe, Bitstream, and other digital typeface companies offer licensed ITC typefaces as well as ITC variations.

Readability and Legibility of Type Fonts

Many typefaces designed for early desktop publishing systems are decorative and whimsical, but not truly professional typefaces. In particular, bitmapped typefaces originally designed for use on dot-matrix printers fall short of professional typographic standards. Typewriter fonts, widely used in word processing, are also less preferable than typographical fonts, which are designed for maximum **readability** (the ease with which words on the page can be read) and **legibility** (distinctiveness and clarity of individual characters).

Monospaced versus Proportionally Spaced Typefaces

The primary distinction between typewriter typefaces and typographical typefaces is that typewriter typefaces are mostly **monospaced**, while most typographical typefaces are **proportionally spaced**. In a monospaced typeface, each character takes up the same amount of horizontal space. This width is referred to as **set width**. In a proportionally spaced typeface, the set width of different characters varies, depending on the shape of the character itself and on the characters surrounding it. For example, a monospaced typeface takes the same amount of space for a "W" and an "I." On the other hand, a proportionally spaced typeface allows more space to the wider character, "W" (see Figure 3.7).

FIGURE 3.7

Monospaced vs. proportionally spaced type
A. Courier (monospaced);
B. Bookman (proportionally spaced;
C. Times (Proportionally spaced)

A. set width: Ml
B. set width: Ml
C. set width: Ml

In a monospaced typeface, the set width of the characters is fixed because most typewriters have a fixed **escapement**—the amount of horizontal space that the carriage or type element can be advanced. Some electronic typewriters and daisy-wheel printers can advance half- and quarter-spaces for narrower letters, thus altering the overall escapement on monospaced type by setting the **pitch**—or characters per inch—of the type. In this case, however, the intervals (usually 10 and 12 pitch) are still fixed.

At the normal set widths of a proportionally spaced typeface, the capital "M" usually is the widest character, and the lowercase "l" is usually the narrowest. Typefaces vary in the *average* set width of their letter forms; this is one of the characteristics that distinguishes one typeface from another—for example, Times has a narrow set width, while Bookman has a wide set width (see Figure 3.7).

DISTINGUISHING CHARACTERISTICS OF TYPE

There are three ways in which typefaces can be distinguished from one another: the design of the letter forms, the weight of the strokes, and the stress of the strokes.

Anatomy of Letter Forms

The parts of **letter forms**, that is, the character shapes themselves, are shown in Figure 3.8. Many of these parts are defined relative to the **baseline** of the type, which is the imaginary horizontal line upon which the letter forms sit. Actually, characters with rounded bases sit slightly below the baseline. This gives the *appearance* of an even horizontal baseline.

- **Cap height** is the distance from the baseline to the top of the capital letters.

- **Counters** are enclosed areas within letter forms.

- **Ascenders** are the parts of letter forms that rise above the x-height; the term is used with lowercase letters only.

- **x-height** is the height of the main body of the lowercase letter forms; it is equivalent to the height of a lowercase character "x."

- **Descenders** are parts of letter forms that extend below the baseline.

- **Serifs** are cross-strokes on letter forms, projecting from the ends of the main strokes. Serif typefaces constitute a category of type distinguished from typefaces with no serifs (called *sans serif*, described later in this chapter).

FIGURE

3.8

Parts of type

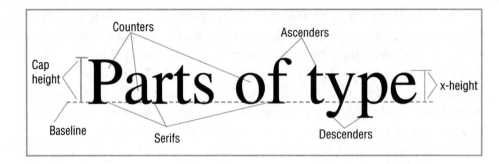

Stroke Weight

Typefaces vary in the amount of contrast between thick and thin strokes that constitute the letter form. **Stroke weight** (the width of the main strokes of characters) may be uniform or variable (including the thickness of serifs and the way they are connected to the main strokes—see below, *Serif Typefaces*). Typefaces with apparent thick-and-thin strokes look more old-fashioned than typefaces with uniform stroke weight, since most typefaces based on pre-nineteenth century designs have variable stroke weight, whereas many contemporary typefaces, including sans serif and monospaced typefaces, have uniform stroke weight (see Figure 3.9).

FIGURE

3.9

Stroke weight
From left to right: Bodoni (very strong contrast); Baskerville (strong contrast); Goudy (moderate contrast); Optima (slight contrast); Futura (uniform)

Stress

Typefaces vary in stroke **stress**, the axis around which thick and thin strokes are drawn. This is not to be confused with the angle of the strokes themselves. Typefaces that have uniform stroke weights have no stress. (See Figure 3.10.) The calligrapher's pen produces characters with a strong left-slanted stress, which old-style typefaces imitate. Modern typefaces tend to have vertical stress, and most sans serif typefaces, since they have no thick and thin strokes, have no stress.

FIGURE

3.10

Stroke stress
From left to right: Garamond (strong slant); Goudy (moderate slant); Optima (slight right slant); Bodoni and Baskerville (vertical)

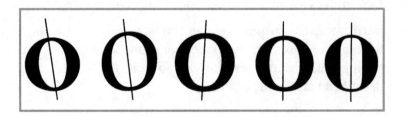

CATEGORIES OF TYPEFACES

In general, typefaces may be categorized by function: *display type* is large type, often 14 points and larger, used in display pieces (posters, announcements, covers, and so on), and for titles, headlines, and headings within documents. *Body type* is smaller type used for large blocks of text, such as stories in a newsletter or magazine, or the chapters of a book. The function of display type is to add emphasis or attract attention, so display typefaces are often unusual and ornamental. The function of body type is to enable the reader to read easily, so body typefaces are usually unobtrusive and unadorned. However, any well-proportioned typeface can be used effectively as both body type and display type.

Typefaces can also be categorized by more formal characteristics that correspond to the historical development of type design. The oldest typefaces are serif typefaces; sans serif and decorative typefaces are more recent designs.

Serif Typefaces

Serif typefaces are derived from ancient Roman letter carving in stone, in which engravers finished each stroke with a serif to correct unevenness in the baseline and cap height. The ancient Romans used all capital letters. Lowercase letters were introduced by Irish scribes in the sixth century, and were developed further by Continental and Gothic scribes in the seventh to ninth centuries. Until the nineteenth century, all typefaces used in printing were serif typefaces. Figure 3.11 shows some samples of the historical stages of serif typeface designs.

Old Style   Old style typefaces, based on design conventions developed in the sixteenth century, are classical text typefaces. The serifs are strongly **bracketed**, that is, connected to the main stroke of the letter form with a tapering curve. The horizontal strokes and serifs are scooped, and the ascender serifs are tapered and slanted downward. Old style typefaces have moderate contrast between thick and thin strokes, and left-slanted stress. (See Goudy in Figure 3.11.)

Modern/Transitional   The term *modern* is relative; it was coined in the late eighteenth century to distinguish a then new style of typography from designs based on original sixteenth-century typefaces. In a modern typeface, serifs are very thin and are not bracketed. Baseline, cap height, and ascender serifs are flat and horizontal. In a prototypical modern typeface, the contrast between thick and thin is extreme, and the stress is vertical.

Typefaces based on designs developed in the seventeenth century are often called *transitional*. In a transitional typeface, the serifs are less heavily bracketed than the serifs of old style faces, but they are not as thin and geometric as the serifs of modern faces. Contrast between thick and thin strokes is more pronounced than in old style typefaces, but is not as pronounced as

DID YOU KNOW...

For the greatest contrast, use sans serif faces for display and serif faces for body type. For less contrast, use the same typeface in different sizes and weights for both display and body type.

in modern typefaces; stress is vertical or nearly vertical. (See Baskerville in Figure 3.11.)

Slab (Square) Serif Slab serif or square serif typefaces are also called Egyptian, after a popular nineteenth century typeface. The serifs are thick and rectangular and are slightly bracketed (more traditional faces) or not bracketed (more contemporary faces, often adapted from sans serif faces). In more traditional slab serif typefaces, there may be moderate to strong contrast between thick and thin strokes; many contemporary slab serif faces have uniform strokes. The stress is vertical or nearly vertical. (See Century and Memphis in Figure 3.11.)

FIGURE 3.11

Serif typefaces

Goudy (old style)

ABCDEFGHIJKLMN
OPQRSTUVWXYZ
abcdefghijklmnopqrst
uvwxyz 1234567890

Baskerville (transitional)

ABCDEFGHIJKLMN
OPQRSTUVWXYZ
abcdefghijklmnopqrst
uvwxyz 1234567890

Bodoni (modern)

ABCDEFGHIJKLM
NOPQRSTUVWXYZ
abcdefghijklmnopqrs
tuvwxyz 1234567890

Century (slab serif)

ABCDEFGHIJKLM
NOPQRSTUVWXYZ
abcdefghijklmnopqrs
tuvwxyz 1234567890

Memphis (slab serif adapted from sans serif)

ABCDEFGHIJKLMN
OPQRSTUVWXYZ
abcdefghijklmnopqr
stuvwxyz 1234567890

Sans Serif Typefaces

Sans serif typefaces were introduced in the early nineteenth century, but were not commonly used in large blocks of type until the twentieth century, when the Bauhaus typography workshop in Germany popularized the use of sans serif typefaces in a variety of display and functional pieces. In marked contrast to the elaborate medieval typefaces then still in use in Germany and in contrast to traditional serif typefaces used for books and display pieces, the use of sans serif typefaces represented a major departure from centuries of typographic tradition.

Sans serif faces are simple, clear, and unadorned. The strokes are generally of uniform thickness, and the stress is most often vertical, but there are exceptions and variations (see Figure 3.12).

Futura
ABCDEFGHIJKLMN
OPQRSTUVWXYZ
abcdefghijklmnopqrst
uvwxyz1234567890

Eras
ABCDEFGHIJKLMN
OPQRSTUVWXYZ
abcdefghijklmnopqrs
tuvwxyz1234567890

Eurostile
ABCDEFGHIJKLMN
OPQRSTUVWXYZ
abcdefghijklmnopqrst
uvwxyz1234567890

FIGURE 3.12
Sans serif typefaces

Decorative Typefaces

A number of decorative and special typefaces are available to desktop publishers for use in display publications such as posters, announcements, and advertisements.

A. Script

B. Novelty

C. Special set: Zapf Dingbats (Macintosh)

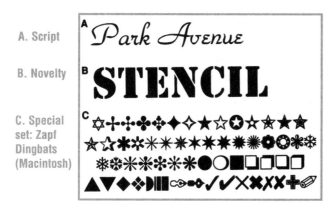

FIGURE 3.13
Decorative and special typefaces

Script Typefaces Scripts, related to italics, imitate calligraphy. The letter forms of script are connected by curved strokes and are slanted to the right. Scripts should never be used in all capital letters, since the connecting strokes will look distractingly unconnected; scripts are designed to be used in upper- and lowercase. Electronic bolding and italicizing of scripts usually produce clumsy results (if any), since these faces are generally designed for one weight and style only (see Figure 3.13).

Miscellaneous Typefaces   There are a number of decorative typefaces that defy categorization and are often simply called novelty or display typefaces.

Such typefaces may imitate various types of writing such as block lettering, stencil lettering, or dot-matrix computer screen lettering. They may be traditional designs with **swashes** (long, curved strokes that extend below the baseline and/or to the right or left of the character), **inlines** (thin lines surrounding the strokes), or **bracelets** (knobby protrusions at the midline of the characters), special fills, or unusual shapes.

The variations are limited only by the imagination of the type designer. Many of these novelty typefaces that are available to desktop publishers are of lower quality than ITC and standard book faces (see Figure 3.13).

Special Set Typefaces   Several typefaces available on desktop publishing systems consist of symbols and images rather than alphabetical characters. These nonalphabetical characters are typed on the keyboard directly. Each symbol replaces the upper- and lowercase letters. Therefore, a keyboard map is needed in order to type the proper characters. For example, in Zapf Dingbats on the Macintosh (see Figure 3.13), the lowercase "a" key corresponds to ❀; the uppercase "A" corresponds to ✿.

Special set typefaces include special symbols such as mathematical, musical, and architectural notations, and a variety of images—arrows, asterisks, boxes, circled numbers, and so on.

Type Families

Popular typefaces have been modified with variations in weight and width, in order to give the typographer more options. Such typefaces may be available in *light* and ultralight faces. Boldface is usually considered one style of the standard face. A ***black*** typeface is heavier than bold.

Typefaces may also be ***condensed*** or ***expanded***, so that the set widths of the characters are narrower or wider than the standard face. Despite these variations, all share the same x-height, cap height, and ascender and descender lengths. For this reason, they can be mixed on pages without causing a cluttered and disorganized look that results from mixing unrelated typefaces.

For example, the Helvetica family of typefaces includes Helvetica, Helvetica Light, Helvetica Black, Helvetica Condensed, and Helvetica Expanded (see Figure 3.14).

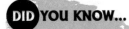

DID YOU KNOW...

Do not use script typefaces in all caps or in large blocks because it is difficult to read.

DID YOU KNOW...

Do not use decorative typefaces as body text; they are display typefaces and should be used only in small blocks.

Helvetica
Helvetica bold
Helvetica black
Helvetica light
Helvetica condensed
Helvetica condensed bold
Helvetica expanded
**Helvetica
expanded bold**

FIGURE 3.14
The Helvetica family

TYPE SPECIFICATIONS

When designers select type for a design, they are said to be *specifying* the type, or creating the specifications (specs) for the design. Type should include specifications of the following:

- Typeface and style.
- Type size.
- Column measure (width, or line length).
- Alignment, indentation, and tabulation.
- Letterspacing and word spacing.
- Paragraph spacing.

The standard measurement system used in typography, and therefore also in desktop publishing, is based on points and picas. As you remember from Chapter 1, twelve points equal one pica, and six picas equal approximately one inch. (See Figure 3.15.) A point is exactly 0.138 of an inch, but most typesetters and desktop publishing systems value it as 1/72 of an inch, which is actually 0.13888888 of an inch.

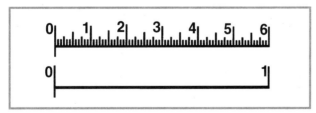

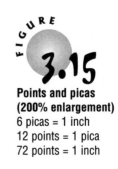

FIGURE 3.15
Points and picas
(200% enlargement)
6 picas = 1 inch
12 points = 1 pica
72 points = 1 inch

Layouts and manuscripts can be marked (spec-ed) in one of the following ways, all of which mean 4 picas and 6 points:

4p6   4p6'   4 pi 6'   4½ px

PageMaker uses the first notation (4p6). Point measurements of less than one pica are usually noted on layouts with the "pt" notation.

Type specifications set up in a word processing program may or may not be imported into a page assembly program. If a type specification cannot be imported, it must be set up in the page assembly program, which has more sophisticated typographical controls. In particular, spacing specifications are generally set in a page assembly program.

Type Size

Type size is measured in points. However, the actual size of a type character is not exactly equal to its point size; for example, the letter "A" in 72-point type is not precisely one inch high. This is because point size is measured from descender to ascender; therefore, a single character must be less than 72 points tall because no single character has both ascenders and descenders. In addition, the point size of type was originally measured not from the strokes of the character itself, but in the old days when type was set by hand, from the block of wood or metal upon which the type character was engraved! Therefore, a precise measurement from the ascenders to descenders of 72-point type will still fall slightly short of an actual inch.

For body type, common type sizes are 9, 10, 11, and 12 points. Reference materials (citations, footnotes, indices, and the like) are often set at smaller sizes: 7, 8, and 9 point. Type smaller than this is difficult to read, but type with tall x-heights and big set widths can be read at 4 points at high resolution (not recommended for 600 dpi desktop laser printing).

For display type, common sizes are 14, 18, 24, 30, 36, 48, 60, and 72 points. In the old days of handset type and separate font cases, typesetters were limited to these sizes, and font cartridges and most non-PostScript soft fonts contain a subset of these sizes. But modern phototypesetting and PostScript fonts enable the designer to specify any size type, and even fractional sizes, such as 17½-point type.

Type Style

In desktop publishing, standard styles include:

- Roman (book, normal, plain).
- Bold (*demibold* is slightly lighter, *black* and *ultra* are darker).
- Italic. Note that in sans serif typefaces, italics are not actually used. *Oblique* is used instead. Whereas italic is a redesigned version of the roman face, oblique is simply a slanted version of the roman. (See Figure 3.16.)

In addition to the standard styles, many publishing programs offer underline, outline, and shadow styles. These should be used with care. In particular, the underline of the underline style is usually rather thick and runs through the

…

Roman	abcdefghijklm nopqrstuvwxyz
Bold	**abcdefghijklm nopqrstuvwxyz**
Italic	*abcdefghijklm nopqrstuvwxyz*
Oblique	*abcdefghijklm nopqrstuvwxyz*

FIGURE 3.16

Type styles
Roman—plain, normal, regular, or book weight;
Bold—can be created electronically from the roman font;
Italic—a separately designed font. In Bookman, the "a" and "g" change shape, serifs become curved strokes, and all characters become more rounded; and
Oblique—in sans serif typefaces, oblique replaces italic characters. Oblique is a slanted version of the roman face.

descenders of lowercase characters; this is far too distracting for most purposes. More appropriate are the page assembly program's ruling lines, which can be set at a specified distance from the baseline of the characters, at a specified thickness and length. The strokes in the outline style are often very thin, and nonstandard. Likewise, the shadow style is nonstandard, and at 600 dpi usually results in a rather coarse image that blurs rather than enhances the characters.

Roman and Bold Normal type is **roman** type, derived from the letter forms in ancient Roman inscriptions, which established the height of the letter at approximately ten times the stroke width. The term "roman" is used in contrast to boldface or italic. Roman is also referred to as book weight, regular, and, in desktop publishing systems, plain or normal. Roman type is usually used for body type.

The **boldface** (or just **bold**) letter form is usually about twice the thickness of the roman style, although different typefaces have different proportions. Bold type is used for emphasis and contrast within a publication. Bold is always darker than roman and lighter than black. True bold letter forms are designed separately from the roman version of the typeface, but acceptable bolds can be created with electronically thickened versions of a roman font outline.

Italic The **italic** letter form was developed for the first pocket book printed in Italy in the fifteenth century. Italic is characterized by light strokes inclined to the right, as in handwriting. True italics are closely related to script; they are a separate font from the roman version of the typeface, and in many typefaces are quite distinctive.

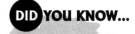

DID YOU KNOW...

Restrict the use of all caps, bolds, and italics caps to small blocks, as they are more difficult to read than roman type.

Italics are used for emphasis, foreign words, book titles, and so on. As mentioned earlier in this chapter, PostScript outlines can be used to approximate italics by simply skewing the outlines to the right. These electronically generated **obliques**, however, are not true italics, and for serif faces are less acceptable than bolds created in this manner. However, since most sans serif faces do not have true italics, electronic obliquing is acceptable and used frequently.

Case and Baseline Variations Case and baseline variations include:

- Upper- and lowercase (also called *u/lc*, or *caps and lowercase*).
- All caps (also called simply *caps*).
- Small caps (often: *caps and small caps* or *c/sc*).
- Superscript and subscript (text entered above and below the baseline, respectively).

Type set in all caps tends to look more formal than type in upper- and lowercase letters. Script and decorative typefaces that do not have squarish capital letters should not be set in all caps. All caps is more difficult to read in blocks because capital letters are less distinct from one another than are upper- and lowercase letters. (See Figure 3.17.)

In the past, newspapers would set each word in a headline in all caps. This has become less popular; in the words of one designer, it can give you "visual hiccups." The more common practice today is capitalizing only the first word in a heading and proper names.

Small caps are capital letters set at the x-height of the font (see Figure 3.17). For visual effect, small caps are used with capitals; **caps and small caps** has an old-fashioned look since this style was popular among early publishers and printers.

FIGURE 3.17

Case variations

Do not set script in all caps.

SCRIPTS AND DECORATIVE TYPEFACES THAT DO NOT HAVE SQUARISH CAPITAL LETTERS SHOULD NOT BE SET IN ALL CAPS.

Caps vs. uppercase and lowercase

ALL CAPS IS MORE DIFFICULT TO READ IN BLOCKS BECAUSE CAPITAL LETTERS ARE LESS DISTINCT FROM EACH OTHER THAN UPPER- AND LOWERCASE LETTERS.

All caps is more difficult to read in blocks because capital letters are less distinct from each other than upper- and lowercase letters.

Caps and small caps combined

SMITH, JONES & COMPANY

Superscripts, or **superiors**, are characters set above the baseline, at a point size slightly smaller than that of the text (see Figure 3.18). Superscripts are commonly used to point out footnoted text. **Subscripts**, or **inferiors**, are characters set below the baseline, at a point size smaller than that of the text. Subscripts are frequently used in mathematical and chemical notations. Superscripts are also used in mathematics. Superscripts and subscripts can be used for visual effect in typographical designs.

Footnote[1]

DESK^{TOP}PUBLISHING

H_2O

MAC_{CONNECT}PC

FIGURE 3.18

Baseline variations
Superscripts are set above the baseline, and subscripts below the baseline.

Choosing and Combining Type Choosing and combining type is an art, not a science, so the rules of thumb below should be viewed as simply starting points or general guidelines. Your own analysis of typefaces can help in your choice of typeface for a publication; for example, if the copy needs to fit into a small space, use a typeface with a small set width; if legibility is important, use one with a tall x-height.

Some rules of thumb in specifying type are:

- Do not use all caps or all italics in large blocks, and do not use script in all caps.
- Be consistent in the use of type style and size for like elements.
- Set more space above than below headings.
- Use bold and italic for emphasis (not too frequently, or they will lose their impact).

Analyze the formal characteristics of different typefaces before you begin combining them. As a rule, you should use no more than two typefaces in the same publication (not including typefaces in ads and identity elements such as logos).

In general, keep the following points in mind:

- *Always safe*: Using only one typeface, with variations in size and style for different elements.
- *Usually safe*: Using sans serif display with a serif body type similar in x-height and shape. Use neutral typefaces such as Times, Trump, or Century for body type, with decorative display type; or Futura, Helvetica, or Univers as display.

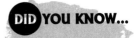

DID YOU KNOW...

Restrict the number of typefaces used in a single publication; one or two is usually enough.

- *Take your chances*: Using nonneutral display and nonneutral body type—the faces should have enough similarities so that they "go together" but enough dissimilarities to provide contrast.
- *Rarely effective*: Using two typefaces that are very similar (such as Univers and Futura or Goudy and Palatino) or two typefaces that are very dissimilar (such as Lubalin Graph and Baskerville or Avant Garde and Bodoni).
- *Never*: Do not use serif display with sans serif body type.

Alignment

Text **alignment** is the manner in which text is lined up. Text may be aligned at the left, aligned at the right, aligned at both right and left (justified), or not aligned at either side but centered. How text is aligned affects not only the textual material but the distribution of white space as well.

Flush Left (Ragged Right) **Flush left** with **ragged right** is the most common alignment; lines of text return to the same position on the left margin, and the extra white space is set at the right (see Figure 3.19). Text set flush left and ragged right is easy to read and maintains the word spacing and letterspacing that was intended by the designer of the typeface (see *Letterspace and Word Space*, later in this chapter).

FIGURE 3.19
Flush left/ragged right

Flush left/ragged right is the most common alignment; the lines of text return to the same position on the left margin, and the extra white space is set at the right. Text set flush left and ragged right is easy to read and maintains the word spacing and letterspacing that was intended by the designer.

Justified (Right Justified) **Justified** text is set so that the text is even at the right margin as well as at the left margin; the extra white space is evenly distributed between words and sometimes between characters on the line. This kind of alignment is seen in professionally produced publications, such as books, newspapers, and magazines.

One of the problems with justified text is that if the column width is too narrow relative to the type size, the words may become unevenly spaced. This creates "rivers" and "lakes" of white space in the block of text, as shown in Figure 3.20. Some solutions are to:

- Increase the line length.
- Decrease the type size.
- Use hyphens to break words. (Note that whenever three or more lines in a row end in hyphenation, the reader's eye may unintentionally return to a line that has been read previously. The term for three or more hyphens in a row is a **block**.)

Adequate line length

Justified text is set so that the text is even at the right margin as well as at the left margin; the extra white space is evenly distributed between words, and sometimes between characters on the line.

Rivers of white space	Hyphen block
One of the problems with justified text is that if the column width is too narrow relative to the type size, the words may become unevenly spaced. This creates "rivers" and "lakes" of white space.	Note that whenever three or more lines in a row end in hyphenation, the reader's eye may unintentionally return to a line that has previously been read.

FIGURE

3.20

Justified

Centered In centered text, extra white space is distributed evenly at the left and right sides of the copy (see Figure 3.21). Centered text should be used only in small blocks, since it is not easy to read; the eye does not have a regular position to which it can return, as it does with flush left or justified text. The shape of centered lines should be contoured, otherwise the centering may simply look like improper indentation. To control the length of each line of text, use returns to force line breaks.

The shape of centered
lines should be
contoured; otherwise
the centering may
simply look like
improper indentation

The shape of centered
lines should be
contoured;
otherwise the
centering may simply
look like improper
indentation

FIGURE

3.21

Centered

Flush Right (Ragged Left) With **flush right** alignment, the text runs ragged left; the extra white space is at the left margin (see Figure 3.22). Flush right text, like centered text, should be used only in small blocks and in a contoured shape. Also, too much punctuation at the ends of lines can cause the right margin to appear uneven. Because of the natural breaks signaled by punctuation, however, these punctuation blocks are sometimes unavoidable. Use returns to control the line breaks—to create a contoured shape and to avoid excessive punctuation and blocks whenever possible.

FIGURE

3.22

Flush right

> Flush right text, like
> centered text, should
> be used only in small
> blocks and in a
> contoured shape.
>
> Flush right
> text, like centered
> text, should be used
> only in small blocks and
> in a contoured shape.

Indentation

Indentation is white space that is set at a fixed interval relative to the margins or column width of the type. Indentation is distinguished from **tabulation** in that tabulation is white space set at fixed intervals within a line.

In typography, indentation is usually measured in em spaces and en spaces. An **em space** is as wide as the point size of the type, and an **en space** is half an em space. For example, in 12-point type, an em space is 12 points wide, and an en space is 6 points wide; however, in 24-point type, an em space is 24 points wide, and an en space is 12 points wide (see Figure 3.23).

In many desktop publishing programs, indentation is specified in points or inches, which can be translated into em and en spaces.

FIGURE

3.23

Em and en spaces

> This is an em in 12 point type: □
> This is an en in 12 point type: ▫
>
> This is an em
> in 24 point type: □
>
> This is an en
> in 24 point type: □

First-Line Indent The most common indentation is a 1-em or 2-em *first-line indent*, used frequently in typewriter style. The first line is set in 1 or 2 ems from the left margin, while subsequent lines run flush left.

As an alternative, or in addition to first-line indents, an extra line space can be used to visually separate paragraphs. When no first-line indents are used, this is called *block paragraph* style. Publications are often set with the first paragraph under headings in block paragraph style and subsequent paragraphs set with first-line indentation, as in this book. (See Figure 3.24.)

FIGURE 3.24

Indentation

First line indent

The most common identation is a 1-em or 2-em *first-line indent,* used frequently in typewriter style. The first line is set in 1 or 2 ems from the left margin while subsequent lines run flush left.

Block paragraph style

As an alternative, or in addition to first-line indents, an extra line space can be used to visually separate paragraphs.

When no first-line indents are used, this is called *block paragraph* style. Publications are often set with the first paragraph under headings in block paragraph style, and subsequent paragraphs with first line indents, as in this book.

Hang Indent and Full Indent A hang indent is the opposite of a first-line indent. In a **hang** (or **hanging**) **indent**, the first line is flush left, and subsequent lines are indented, usually 2 or 3 ems. Hang indents are used in bibliographies, indexes, and paragraphs in which the first word has special significance, or when the first character is set apart from the rest of the text, as in certain kinds of lists. (See Figure 3.25.)

Full indents are paragraphs in which all lines are indented from the left and/or right margin. Left full indents are often set under hang indented lists, with extra line space above and below. Full indents, left and right, are often used for long quotations, called **block quotes** or **extracts**.

FIGURE 3.25

Hang and full indents

THIS is a sample of a hang indent, which is used to emphasize the first word in a paragraph.

1. Hang indents are used with lists to separate the number from the body text.

 Full indents are also sometimes used under hang indents in lists.

This is a sample of some normal body text set flush left and flush right, with a full indent paragraph following it.

> This is a full indent, left and right, used to set apart a passage such as a long quotation from the body text. This is a full indent, left and right, used to set apart a passage such as a long quotation from the body text.

This is a sample of some normal body text set flush left and flush right, with a full indent paragraph preceding it.

Spacing and Line Length

A good desktop publisher is able to adjust spacing and line length to correct bad breaks. Bad breaks occur when a page break separates text in a way that is visually or logically unappealing. Common bad breaks include **widows** (single, incomplete lines at the top of a page or column) and **orphans** (the first line of a paragraph at the bottom of a page or column). Also to be avoided are headings that fall at the bottom of a page and quotes that begin on the last line or end on the first line of a page.

Line Space (Leading) Vertical space or line space is called **leading** (pronounced "led-ding"). The term is derived from the traditional practice, in hand typesetting, of inserting thin strips of lead between the lines of type in order to spread them apart at regular intervals. Leading is measured in points, traditionally from baseline to baseline (see Figure 3.26).

FIGURE 3.26
Leading

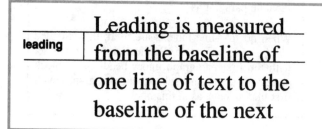

Leading is specified in points. When you are spacing type, the leading goes with the point size of the type: for example, 10/12 (read *ten on twelve*) means that the type is 10 point and the distance from the baseline of one line to the baseline of the next is 12 points (12 points of leading). Type that is set with no leading is called **set solid**—for example, 10/10. In type that is set solid, the descenders of one line nearly touch the ascenders of the line below. Automatic leading in PageMaker is approximately 120% of the type size; for example: 9/11, 10/12, 11/13, etc.

Leading or line space is used within blocks of text and to vary the space above and below display heads in text-intensive publications. Type in all caps is sometimes set with negative leading (for example, 18/16) because caps have no descenders. Adjustment of leading is also used to make text easier to read at less-than-optimal word spacing (see Figure 3.27) and line lengths.

Line Length and Columns The length of a line is called its **measure**. When type is set in columns, the column width is called the **column measure**. Whereas type size is designated in points, line length or measure is designated in picas.

Because the characters in typeset copy are much more closely spaced than they are in typewritten copy, body type should not be set in one column across the full width of a letter-sized page with normal typewriter (1" to 1½") margins. There are simply too many characters per line for the eye to read easily.

Wider margins or multiple columns can be used to reduce the column width. Very narrow columns, however, can cause ragged-right text to be too ragged, and in right-justified text, columns that are too narrow can cause those rivers and lakes of white space and hyphen blocks as shown in Figure 3.20.

For optimum legibility, the maximum column measure at normal leading (120% of the type size) should not be more than 2½ alphabets (65 characters) long or less than one alphabet (26 characters) long.

The optimal column measure varies according to the point size and the set width of the typeface. In general, typefaces with narrow set widths (such as Times) and small point sizes can be set at a relatively narrow column measure, whereas typefaces with wide set widths (such as Bookman) and larger point sizes require wider column measures. (See Figure 3.27.) Type that is set at a longer-than-optimum measure should be set with extra leading. Type that is set solid—with no leading—should be set at a narrower column measure.

Set at maximum optimal column measure (65 characters)
10/12 TIMES X 23
12345678901234567890123456789012345678901234567890123456789012345.

    The recent FCC deregulation of the radio SCA and television VBI spectrum has opened up new income and service opportunities for public broadcasters. The recent FCC deregulation of the radio SCA and

├─────────────── 23 px ───────────────┤

10/12 BOOKMAN X 29
12345678901234567890123456789012345678901234567890123456789012345.

    The recent FCC deregulation of the radio SCA and television VBI spectrum has opened up new income and service opportunities for public broadcasters. The recent FCC deregulation of the radio SCA and television

├─────────────── 29 px ───────────────┤

Longer-than-optimum line set with extra leading
10/14 TIMES X 27
12345678901234567890123456789012345678901234567890123456789012345

The recent FCC deregulation of the radio SCA and television VBI spectrum has

opened up new income and service opportunities for public broadcasters. Carried

along with the main broadcast service, these narrow-band channels are low-cost

├─────────────── 27 px ───────────────┤

Type set solid on narrower column measure
9/9 TIMES X 11
12345678901234567890123456789
The recent FCC deregulation of the radio SCA and television VBI spectrum has opened up new income nad service opportunities for public broadcasters.

├───── 10 px─────┤

FIGURE
3.27
Column measure and leading

The space between columns on a page is called the **alley**. The optimum width of the alley depends upon the point size of the type as well as the set width and the word spacing. (See below for more on word spacing.) In general, the alley should be at least 1½ ems (3 ens) wide but not more than 2 ems (see Figure 3.28). The eye may skip over an alley that is too narrow and misread adjacent columns as one line. Typefaces with wide set widths should have generous alleys; typefaces with narrow set widths can take narrower alleys.

FIGURE

3.28

Alleys

9/10 Times

The recent FCC deregulation of the radio SCA and television VBI spectrum has opened up new profit and service opportunities for broadcasters. Carried along with the main broadcast service, these—the line.

narrow-band channels are low-cost electronic highways for the simultaneous one-way delivery of data signals to large numbers of dispersed users. More text to fill out the line.

9 pt. alley (1 em)

9/10 Times

The recent FCC deregulation of the radio SCA and television VBI spectrum has opened up new profit and service opportunities for broadcasters. Carried along with the main broadcast service, these narrow-band channels are low-cost electronic highways for the simultaneous one-way delivery of data signals to large numbers of dispersed users. More text to fill out the line.

1 pica alley (1-1/2 em)

9/10 Times

The recent FCC deregulation of the radio SCA and television VBI spectrum has opened up new profit and service opportunities for broadcasters. Carried along with the main broadcast service, these narrow-band channels are low-cost electronic highways for the simultaneous one-way delivery of data signals to large numbers of dispersed users. More text to fill out the line.

1p6. alley (2 ems)

Alleys should not exceed 2 ems in width, unless the piece is to be folded, like a brochure; in that case the columns do not function as a page unit, but as panel units. Alleys that are too wide on a page make the columns appear too separate.

In desktop publishing, the columns and alleys are usually not set until word processing files are imported into the page assembly program. Columns set in a word processing program may import as indentation, so it is best to use the default line lengths in the word processor.

Letterspace and Word Space

Letterspacing is the horizontal space between characters. **Word spacing** is the horizontal space between words.

For word spacing and letterspacing, the em space is divided into **units**. Different typesetting systems and desktop publishing programs use different unit divisions; 16, 32, and 64 are common. One unit or fractional unit is a **thin space**, or a **hair space**.

In some desktop publishing systems, word spacing and letterspacing for blocks of text may be specified as fractions of normal. "Normal" is defined by the set-width tables for each font being used by a typesetting machine or typographically sophisticated page assembly program.

Display Type If a program utilizes set-width tables, the default letterspacing and word spacing is generally well-proportioned for body type. However, larger display type almost always needs to be kerned. To **kern** type is to squeeze together individual characters for a better fit of strokes and white space.

Kerning is available in some word processing and graphics programs and in all professional page assembly programs (see Figure 3.29). Some set-width tables may include kerning pairs so that any occurrence of such a pair will automatically be kerned when the type is set; but at large sizes, additional kerning is usually needed.

Display type that is set in all caps can have increased letterspacing for an old-fashioned, formal look (see Figure 3.29). Lowercase letters should *not* be letterspaced because they are designed for a close fit of characters.

Display type may have the word spacing adjusted in order to fill a line with characters. If the characters are well-kerned, word space may be reduced without impeding readability. If the word spacing adjustments are too extreme, however, the words will appear too separate or too close. In this case, it is better to slightly increase or decrease the type size.

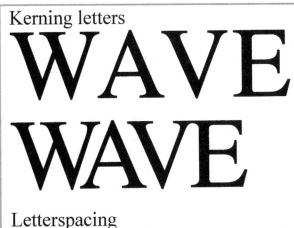

Kerning letters

WAVE

WAVE

Letterspacing

LETTERSPACE

EXTRA SPACE

FIGURE

3.29

Letterspacing adjustments
Kerning and letterspacing.

Body Type Body type is sometimes **tracked**—that is, the space between all characters is uniformly reduced—to make the type more dense or run less long. Control over tracking is available in some word processing and graphics programs and in most page assembly programs. Tracking applies to lines of type, usually whole paragraphs, whereas kerning applies to individual characters.

To make type run *longer*, the word spacing of the body type may be slightly increased. If this is done, the leading should not be increased, because when the line spacing is greater than the word spacing, the eye tends to move up and down a column of text rather than from left to right.

In general, word spacing should not be decreased, because the words tend to run together, making them too dense to read easily. If it is necessary to reduce the word spacing, the type should also be tracked.

Body type should not have the letterspacing increased. Unlike typewriter typefaces, typographical typefaces are designed for a close fit of characters, and when the spacing is increased, the lines appear too loose to read easily (see Figure 3.30).

FIGURE 3.30

Word spacing and letterspacing

10/12, normal letterspacing and word spacing

For word spacing and letterspacing, the em space is divided into units. Different typesetting systems and desktop publishing programs use different unit divisions: 16, 32, and 64 are common.

10/12, tracked, normal word spacing

For word spacing and letterspacing, the em space is divided into units. Different typesetting systems and desktop publishing programs use different unit divisions: 16, 32, and 64 are common.

10/11, increased word spacing, decreased leading

For word spacing and letterspacing, the em space is divided into units. Different typesetting systems and desktop publishing programs use different unit divisions: 16, 32, and 64 are common.

10/11, reduced word spacing with tracking

For word spacing and letterspacing, the em space is divided into units. Different typesetting systems and desktop publishing programs use different unit divisions: 16, 32, and 64 are common.

10/12, increased letterspacing (AVOID)

For word spacing and letterspacing, the em space is divided into units. Different typesetting systems and desktop publishing programs use different unit divisions: 16, 32, and 64 are common.

10/13, increased word spacing and leading (AVOID)

For word spacing and letterspacing, the em space is divided into units. Different typesetting systems and desktop publishing programs use different unit divisions: 16, 32, and 64 are common.

10/11, reduced word spacing, no tracking (AVOID)

For word spacing and letterspacing, the em space is divided into units. Different typesetting systems and desktop publishing programs use different unit divisions: 16, 32, and 64 are common.

CHECKING YOUR UNDERSTANDING

Answer true or false, and if false, explain why.

1. Sans serif typefaces have no serifs.
2. The set width of a typeface is the same for every character.
3. The stroke weight of serif typefaces is usually uniform.
4. A point is approximately 1/6 of an inch.
5. Type size and leading are usually measured in picas.
6. Line length and page positioning are usually measured in picas.
7. An em space is half of an en space.
8. Display type is usually large type.
9. Small caps are set at the height of the ascenders of the base font.
10. Flush right type is set with a ragged left margin.
11. In a hang indent, the first line is indented and the subsequent lines are not.
12. The length of a line is called its measure.
13. Tracking is the same as kerning, except that kerning is used for display type and tracking for body type.
14. A widow is the first line of a paragraph at the bottom of a page.

APPLYING DESIGN PRINCIPLES

For these exercises, you will need a variety of magazines and newspapers or pages from a type sample book from which you can clip or photocopy examples of different typefaces.

Exercise 1 Typefaces

Typefaces can vary widely. Find five typefaces that have:

a) Cap heights that are shorter than the ascenders.
b) Unusually long ascenders or descenders.
c) Unusually short ascenders or descenders.
d) Capital letters that have descenders.
e) Set widths that are wider than the type is tall.

Exercise 2 Headings

Find a sample of a publication that uses one typeface and more than three levels of headings. Describe how different styles and sizes are used for different levels of headings.

Exercise 3 Justification

Find two samples of publications that use justified body text.

Exercise 4 Indentation

Find samples of publications that use the following styles of indentation:
- a) hang indent
- b) full indent
- c) first-line indent

USING Typography FUNCTIONS

The following discussion gives experience with PageMaker's typography features and functions.

Upon completion of this chapter you will be able to

Apply these formats to text:

- tracking
- kerning
- leading
- shift baseline
- drop caps
- hyphenation
- justification
- em and en dashes
- indentation
- bullets
- tabs
- leaders
- superscript
- subscript

USING THE CONTROL PALETTE TO WORK WITH TEXT

PageMaker has a palette that makes working with typographic functions relatively easy. It is called the **Control** palette. This palette can be used with other functions of PageMaker, such as graphics. The **Control** palette enables you to work with graphics and text blocks with precision. You can make changes without switching to the toolbox or choosing commands from the menus.

We use the **Control** palette to make changes to text. The **Control** palette displays options that let you assign specific attributes to text. The contents of the **Control** palette vary, depending on whether you select **Character** or **Paragraph view**. Figure 4.1 displays the two views.

Many of the **Character Specifications** and **Paragraph Specifications** discussed in chapter 2 are also found on the **Control** palette discussed in this

FIGURE 4.1

Views of *Control* palette

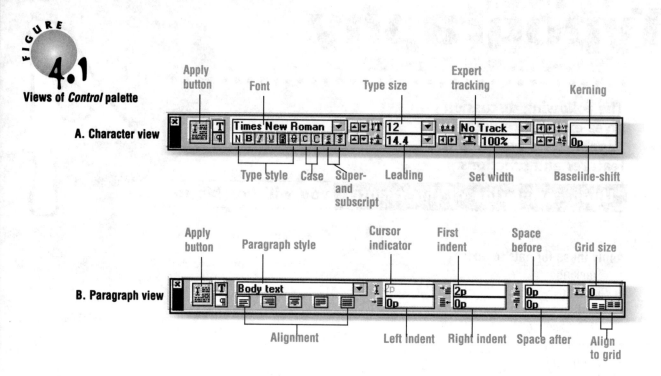

A. Character view

Apply button · Font · Type size · Expert tracking · Kerning

Type style · Case · Super- and subscript · Leading · Set width · Baseline-shift

B. Paragraph view

Apply button · Paragraph style · Cursor indicator · First indent · Space before · Grid size

Alignment · Left indent · Right indent · Space after · Align to grid

chapter. For example, in **Character view**, you can make changes to the font, size, or leading of selected text. In **Paragraph view**, you can apply paragraph styles, select alignment options, and set other paragraph attributes. PageMaker immediately applies a selected option to selected text.

If you type a numeric value in the **Control** palette, for example to change the font size, the new setting can be applied by any of these four methods:

1. Press **Enter** (Windows) or **Return** (Macintosh) to apply the change.

2. Press **Tab** to apply the change and move to the next **Control** palette option.

3. Click the **Apply** button on the left end of the **Control** palette. (See Figure 4.2.)

4. Click any other option on the **Control** palette.

FIGURE 4.2

***Apply* button**

First, prepare a new document using the default **Document Setup**. To open the **Control** palette:

1. Click on the **Window** menu.

2. Select **Show Control** palette.

3. Click on the **Text** tool in the Toolbar.

TRACKING

Tracking is the amount of space between words and characters. You can use tracking to change the visual density of type on the page. PageMaker has six built-in tracks which decrease or increase the space between characters to varying degrees, from **Very loose** to **Very tight**. **No track** removes any tracking, and the letters are displayed as intended by the type's designer. Tracking is font- and point-size dependent; each track is a collection of values that correlates the size of a font with a specific amount of change in letterspacing.

Looser tracking is often used to make a block of text expand to fill a set amount of space, and tighter tracking can reduce the number of lines needed to display the same amount of text. Tracking has an effect on the look of your page—tighter tracking makes a page appear darker, while looser tracking lightens the look of the page. Note the differences among the six built-in sets of tracking values in Table 4.1.

Table 4.1

TRACKING VALUES

No track:
The store, Amicone Sails, is located in Oriental, North Carolina.

Very loose:
The store, Amicone Sails, is located in Oriental, North Carolina.

Loose:
The store, Amicone Sails, is located in Oriental, North Carolina.

Normal:
The store, Amicone Sails, is located in Oriental, North Carolina.

Tight:
The store, Amicone Sails, is located in Oriental, North Carolina.

Very tight:
The store, Amicone Sails, is located in Oriental, North Carolina.

You can apply tracking to any block of text. You can apply one track to a block of text, and then apply a different track to text that is in the same font, even the same size, somewhere else. A track can also be applied as part of a paragraph style. The **Track** command is located in the **Character Specifications** dialog box in the **Type** menu, which is shown in Figure 4.3a.

FIGURE 4.3

Track command

A. Track command in **Character Specifications**

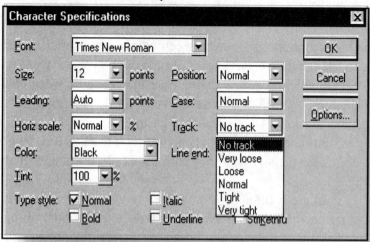

B. Expert Tracking command in **Type** menu

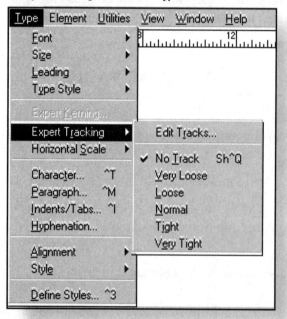

In order to apply the **Track** command to a paragraph, first start PageMaker and create a new file.

1. Click the **File** menu and select **New**. (Make sure that the **Double-sided**, **Facing pages**, and **Restart page numbering** options are turned off.) Set 1-inch margins for this document.

2. Type the following paragraph using PageMaker's text editor, which is called the **Story Editor**, and check your spelling. To access the **Story Editor**, select **Edit Story** from the **Edit** menu. To run spell check in the **Story Editor**, select **Spelling** from the **Utilities** menu. Use 12-point

Times Roman for the paragraph. Press the **Enter** key twice at the end of the paragraph to create an extra blank line.

Crickets make their chirping sound by sliding one wing cover back and forth over the other very rapidly. Naturalists have long been aware that there is a linear relationship between temperature and the frequency of chirping. For example, the warmer it is, the faster the chirping. This suggests that, if we estimated the mathematical equation that describes the chirping-temperature relationship, we could use a cricket as a thermometer.

After typing the text and checking the spelling, click the **Close** button on the **Story Editor's** title bar. When prompted "Story has not been placed," click the **Place** command. Then place text in publication. *Note:* Whenever you type text in PageMaker, it is a good idea to use the **Story Editor**. The only way to use PageMaker's **Spell Checker** is by viewing text in the **Story Editor**.

3. Use the **Text** tool to select the paragraph, including the blank line. Use the **Copy** and **Paste** commands in the **Edit** menu to copy the paragraph five times.

4. Before each copied paragraph, type each of the following headings, one for each paragraph: **No track**, **Very loose**, **Loose**, **Normal**, **Tight**, and **Very tight**. Make sure that there is one blank line between each paragraph and the headings.

5. Use the **Text** tool to select the text in the first paragraph. You will apply the **No track** value to this paragraph. From the **Type** menu, click on **Expert Tracking** (see Figure 4.3b) and choose **No track**. (If you are using the **Control** palette, click on the down arrow by the **Expert Tracking** option and select **No track**.)

6. Use the **Text** tool to select the text in the second paragraph and apply the **Very loose** value of tracking.

7. Continue the above steps to apply the other tracking values of **Loose**, **Normal**, **Tight**, and **Very tight** to the other paragraphs.

8. Print the document. From the **File** menu, select **Print**. Make sure that the correct printer is selected and click **OK**. Save the file and name it **TRACK**.

When you look at the printed paragraphs, do you notice that the type appears to darken as you look toward the bottom of the page? Tracking is particularly useful for darkening or lightening a page and for changing the spacing of selected lines of very large or very small type (headlines and captions). Use tracking to make text fit into a defined space on the page.

KERNING

Kerning is used to adjust the spacing between specific pairs of letters that draw attention to themselves by being too close together or too far apart. When you are working with headlines, titles, or any large or decorative characters, it is often necessary to use kerning to improve the letterspacing. PageMaker provides three different kerning options: automatic pair kerning, manual kerning, and expert kerning.

Automatic Pair Kerning

Automatic pair kerning uses the information built into the font. Most fonts kern the following pairs of characters: LA, P., To, Tr, Ta, Tu, Te, Ty, Wa, WA, We, we, Wo, Ya, Yo, and yo. Kerning is not as discernible in smaller point sizes (usually used for body text). PageMaker lets you set a size threshold above which all kerning pairs are used. Figure 4.4 displays the **Spacing Attributes** dialog box where you can change the point size.

Automatic pair kerning is applied to single paragraphs, to selected paragraphs, or to a whole document. It cannot be applied to specified characters in a paragraph. You can adjust automatic pair kerning at the paragraph level in the **Spacing Attributes** dialog box.

FIGURE 4.4

Spacing Attributes
dialog box

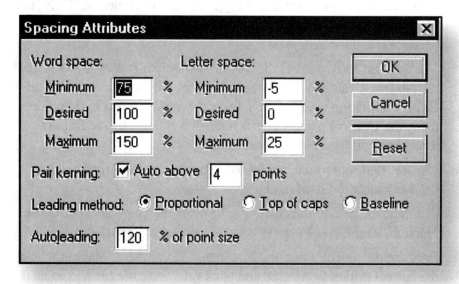

Manual Kerning

Manual kerning allows you to kern any block of text, from one character pair to a selected block. The spacing between characters can be adjusted a bit at a time or by specifying a value to alter the original spacing. PageMaker's finest kerning increment is 0.001 of an em. Table 4.2 lists the keystrokes needed to increase or decrease the space between two characters.

Table 4.2

MANUAL KERNING

To manually...	Press these keys:
Increase spacing 1/25 (.04) em	*Windows*: **Ctrl** + **Alt** + Right arrow or **Ctrl** + Shift + Backspace *Macintosh*: **Command** + Shift + **Delete** or **Command** + Right arrow
Increase spacing 1/100 (.01) em	*Windows*: **Alt** + Right arrow *Macintosh*: **Option** + Shift + **Delete** or **Command** + Shift + Right arrow
Decrease spacing 1/25 (.04) em	*Windows*: **Ctrl** + **Alt** + Left arrow or **Ctrl** + Backspace *Macintosh*: **Command** + **Delete** or **Command** + Left arrow
Decrease spacing 1/100 (.01) em	*Windows*: **Alt** + Left arrow *Macintosh*: **Option** + **Delete** or **Command** + Shift + Left arrow
Clear all manual kerning from selected text	*Windows*: **Ctrl** + **Alt** + **K** *Macintosh*: **Command** + **Option** + **K**

Kerning can be accomplished by using the above keystrokes or by typing a specific value in the **Kerning** option on the **Control** palette. PageMaker accepts kerning values between -1 and 1 (1 equals 1 em space). Negative values move characters closer together, and positive values move them farther apart. For example, to move letters apart half an em, type **0.5** in the text box. Next to the **Kerning** option are two nudge buttons that can be used to manually kern character pairs or selected text. Arrows on the nudge button indicate the direction of the kerning. To remove manual kerning, type **0** in the **Control** palette and then click the **Apply** button.

1. Continue with the **TRACK** document or open it if necessary.

2. Add a new page: Click on the **Layout** menu and select **Insert Pages**. Insert 1 page **After** the current page. Click on **Insert**. (See Figure 4.5.)

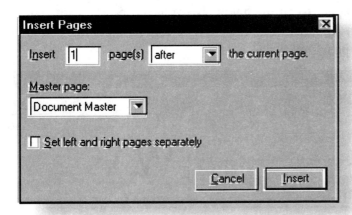

FIGURE

4.5

Dialog box for *Insert Pages*

3. Using the **Story Editor**, type the following state names in 24-point Times Roman.
   Washington
   West Virginia
   Oklahoma
   Florida
   North Carolina

Close the **Story Editor** and place the text on page 2.

4. Switch to **Actual Size**, select the text, and apply manual kerning by using the keystrokes from Table 4.2 or by using the **Control** palette. You can type specific values or use the nudge buttons in the **Control** palette. Practice kerning character pairs such as Fl, Vi, Wa, and We. (See Figure 4.6.)

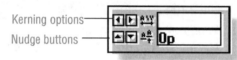

Kerning options
Nudge buttons

Kerning options and nudge buttons

5. Practice kerning a block of text such as the word *Oklahoma*. Select the word and then use the left nudge button on the **Control** palette to decrease the spacing between each of the characters.

6. Print this page and save the file.

Expert Kerning

Expert kerning in PageMaker is recommended for the short blocks of text used in headlines, posters, and other display type at large sizes. Expert kerning allows you to establish fine kerning values even if you have mixed fonts and sizes in the same line. You should turn off PageMaker's automatic pair kerning when using expert kerning. This option estimates every character pair in the selected text, removes all manual kerning, and inserts kern-pair values into the text as manual kerning. You can still manually adjust letterspacing after you have kerned type with expert kerning. Note, however, that this feature requires PostScript Type 1 or Type 2 fonts and the corresponding printer fonts.

In the **Expert Kerning** dialog box, you can specify a kern strength value from 0.00 to 1.00. (See Figure 4.7.) The **Expert Kerning** option is selected from the **Type** menu.

Expert Kerning dialog box

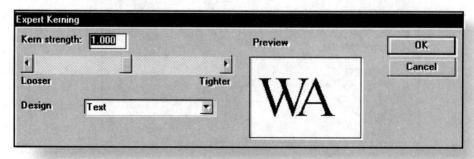

LEADING

As you know, the vertical spacing between lines of text is the leading. The right amount of leading can make text easier to read. There are two parts to the leading setting: leading value, which measures the entire vertical space allotted for a line of text; and the leading method, which defines where the text is positioned in the slug. A **slug** is the horizontal bar you see when text has been highlighted or selected. The height of the slug indicates the amount of leading chosen for the text. (See Figure 4.8.)

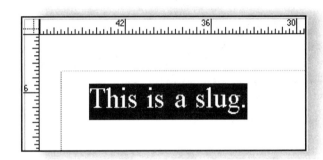

A slug as it appears on a display screen

Leading is measured in points, just as typefaces are. For example, you would say, "Arial ten on twelve," which means ten-point Arial type with twelve points of leading. It is written "Arial 10/12." Generally, leading is 120% of type point size.

The leading method determines the position of the text within the slug. Three positions are available: **Proportional**, **Top of Caps**, and **Baseline**. Proportional leading is the default leading, and the one you will use most often. The leading method is applied uniformly to all characters in a paragraph, even if the leading amounts differ. You can change the leading method in the **Spacing Attributes** dialog box option within the **Paragraph** dialog box as was shown in Figure 4.4.

Leading can be specified in any of the following three ways:

- Choose a leading value from the **Leading** command in the **Type** menu. (See Figure 4.9.)

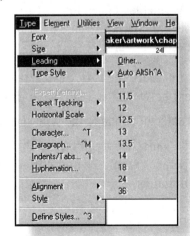

Leading command in **Type** menu

- Type a leading value in the **Character Specifications** dialog box. (See Figure 4.10.)

FIGURE

4.10

Character Specifications dialog box

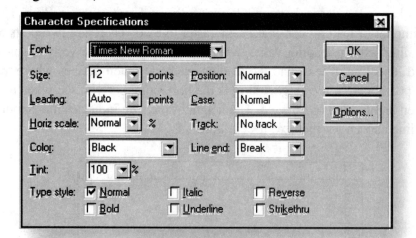

- Type a value in the **Leading** option on the **Control** palette. (See Figure 4.11.)

FIGURE

4.11

Paragraph and *Leading* options on *Control* palette

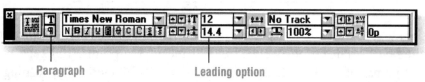

Paragraph   Leading option

To continue the exercise on tracking:

1. Add a page to the **TRACK** document after page 2.

2. Click on the **Layout** menu and select **Insert page**. Type **1** in the **Insert** box and select **After** the current page. Click on **Insert**.

3. Using the **Story Editor**, key the following menu items in Times Roman 10/12, and place on page 3.

    THANKSGIVING DINNER
    Sweet Potato Pie with Country Ham and Corn-Thyme Sauce
    Braised Fennel and Cauliflower Soup with Seared Sea Scallops
    Roasted Turkey with Cornbread and Pecan Stuffing, Pan Gravy
    Gratin Mixed Root Vegetables, Green Beans, Cranberry-Orange Relish
    Cranberry Pecan Pie with Sweet Cream Ice Cream
    or Ginger-Pumpkin Creme Brulee

4. Close the **Story Editor**. Place the text: Select the text with the **Text** tool and center the text between the 1-inch margins.

5. While the text is still selected, change the type size and leading to 14/28.

6. Practice with different fonts, keeping in mind that this is a rather formal menu. Decorative typefaces would be appropriate. You might also want to format the text with italics.

7. Print this page and save the **TRACK** file.

BASELINE SHIFT

The baseline of selected characters can be moved up or down in relation to the rest of a word or line. Text with an unchanged baseline has the value of 0. The **Control** palette has a baseline option that allows you to move the shift up or down in increments as small as a tenth of a point. For example,

the frog ^hopped

You can use baseline shift and manual kerning to create a special effect that embeds text within an enlarged capital letter. For example, look at Figure 4.12. In the company name, Grub Catering, note how the text is embedded within the initial cap letters G and C.

FIGURE 4.12
Baseline shift special effect

1. If you are continuing with the above exercises, return to page 2 of the **TRACK** file to practice using the Baseline shift feature (refer to Figure 4.13).

2. Use the **Text** tool with 10/12 Bookman Old Style and type: Grub Catering

3. Select the first letter in each word and enlarge each to 48-point type.

4. Select the remaining letters in each word and change the type size to 18 points.

5. While the remaining letters are still selected, type a baseline shift value of .21 in the **Control** palette **Baseline shift** option area.

To embed the text within the larger capital letters, follow these directions:

1. Click the cursor between the first and second characters of the word *Grub*.

2. Typing a negative value in the **Kerning** option of the **Control** palette will move the remainder of the word to the left, or within the capital letter. Type **-0.25**.

FIGURE 4.13
Control palette with *Baseline shift* option area

Kerning

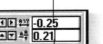

Baseline shift option

3. Practice using different typefaces. As the faces change, the kerning and baseline shift values will have to be changed to accommodate the different sizes of the type.

DROP CAPS

You can quickly add a **drop cap**—a large uppercase character—to one or more paragraphs. The baseline of the uppercase character is dropped one or more lines below the baseline of the first line of a paragraph. You have the option of selecting the number of lines the baseline drops. PageMaker automatically sets tabs and inserts line breaks to adjust the remaining text in the paragraph around the drop cap. See the examples in Figure 4.14.

FIGURE 4.14

Drop caps

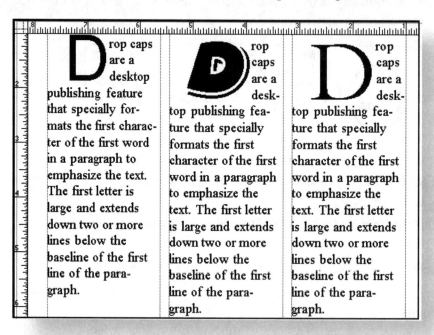

The **Utilities** menu is used to create a drop cap. The **Drop cap** dialog box in Figure 4.15 specifies the number of lines that should wrap around the drop cap, as well as an option to go to the **Next** or **Previous** paragraph to apply another drop cap.

FIGURE 4.15

Drop cap dialog box

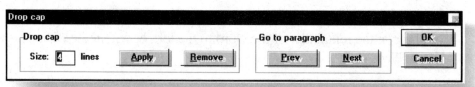

1. If you are continuing with the above exercises, go to page 2 of the **TRACK** file to practice using the drop cap feature.

2. With the **Text** tool, draw a bounding box that is approximately 2 inches wide. Type the paragraph from Figure 4.14. (*Note:* You only need to type it once. Do not use columns as shown.)

3. Click an insertion point anywhere in the paragraph.

4. Select the **Utilities** menu. Click on **Plug-ins** and select **Drop Cap**.

5. Specify 3 lines as the size of the drop cap. Click **Apply** to view the drop cap without leaving the dialog box, and then click **Close** to close the dialog box and return to the paragraph.

6. Print this page and save the **TRACK** file.

HYPHENATION

Hyphenation is used to divide long words at the end of a line rather than wrapping the entire word to the next line. PageMaker has a dictionary that it uses to place the hyphens at appropriate locations within words. The hyphens are added and deleted to text blocks as they are created, formatted, or resized. PageMaker determines where to hyphenate a word based on three methods listed in the **Hyphenation** dialog box in the **Type** menu. (See Figure 4.16.)

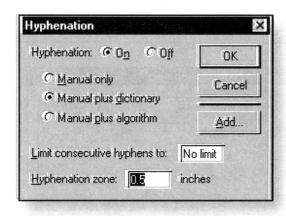

Figure 4.16
Hyphenation dialog box

- Manual only: Only hyphens found in the original text will be used.
- Manual plus dictionary: PageMaker determines where to hyphenate. Any hyphens in the original text will also be used.
- Manual plus algorithm: PageMaker uses certain rules about words (an algorithm) to determine where to place hyphens. Any hyphens in the original text will also be used.

PageMaker's default settings are Hyphenation **On** with **Manual plus dictionary** selected. The other two methods are rarely used. If the Hyphenation option is set to **Off**, no automatic hyphenation will occur.

In order to avoid hyphen blocks, PageMaker can control the number of consecutive lines on which hyphenation occurs. In the **Hyphenation** dialog box under **Limit consecutive hyphens to**, type the maximum number of consecutive lines in a paragraph that can end with hyphens or dashes. A number from 1 to 255 can be typed, or you may type the **No Limit** value, which is PageMaker's default setting.

In ragged right text, a **Hyphenation zone** determines the words eligible for hyphenation. The zone may vary in size but is usually about 1/5 to 1/10 of the length of a line. The larger the zone, the fewer number of words will be hyphenated. Larger hyphenation zones cause the right margin to be more ragged. More hyphens occur in a smaller zone. You can change the length of this zone in the **Hyphenation** dialog box. The zone is measured from the right side of the text.

Some words, phrases, or titles which contain hyphens should not be divided over two lines. For example, a Social Security number should not be divided over two lines. You can avoid this situation by using nonbreaking hyphens (**Ctrl + Alt** + hyphen for Windows or **Command** + hyphen for Macintosh). Simply click an insertion point before the first character of the word and type the above keystrokes.

If you wish to change or eliminate hyphenation for every occurrence of a word, phrase, or title in a long document, use the **Add Word to User Dictionary** dialog box. For example, some product names may not be in PageMaker's dictionary (for example, Ikonometric Productions). Press the **Add** button in the **Hyphenation** dialog box to access this command. (See Figure 4.17.)

FIGURE 4.17

Add Word to User Dictionary dialog box

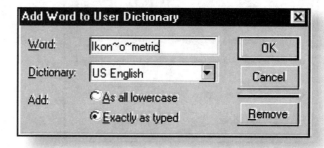

Type the tilde (~) key to indicate the best possible breaking point in a word.

- One tilde indicates the best possible break point in the word.
- Two tildes indicates the next-best choice.
- Three tildes indicates a poor but acceptable break point.
- One tilde at the beginning of the word means you never want the word to be hyphenated.

The following exercise allows you to see the effect of different hyphenation zone lengths. It also provides you with practice at setting the number of lines allowable for consecutive hyphens. You will add another page to the end of the **TRACK** document and import text from your student data disk.

Let's begin by adding a page at the end of the **TRACK** document. An alternative method of adding pages is accomplished through the **File** menu and **Document Setup**. (See Figure 4.18.)

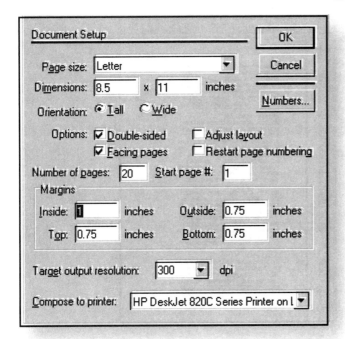

Document Setup dialog box

1. Click on the **File** menu and select **Document Setup**.

2. Click in the **Number of pages** text box and type the number **4**.

3. Click **OK**.

4. Import the **NWSGRFS.TXT** file. Click on the **File** menu and select the **Place** command. Choose this file from the Student Data Disk and click the **Open** button. Since this is an ASCII text file, the **Text-only import filter** dialog box appears.

5. Choose **No conversion, import as is** and click **OK**.

6. Position the text-place icon at the intersection of the top and left margins. Click once, and the text will flow onto the page between the designated 1-inch margins.

Look carefully at the text. It may or may not have hyphens. It may be necessary to change the font and size of the text in order to practice hyphenation.

1. Use the **Text** tool to select all the text. Click an insertion point anywhere in the text and choose **Select All** from the **Edit** menu.

2. From the **Type** menu, select **Character**. Change the typeface to 14 point Times Roman.

3. Click **OK**.

4. Change to the **Fit in Window** view so that you can see the document in full. Use the **Pointer** tool, click on the text, and drag a text block handle so that the width of the text block is only 4 inches. (See Figure 4.19.) After changing the width of the text block, make sure that all the text is placed on the page. You have to drag downward on the bottom handle to allow the unplaced text to flow onto the page.

FIGURE
4.19

Text block of 4-inch width

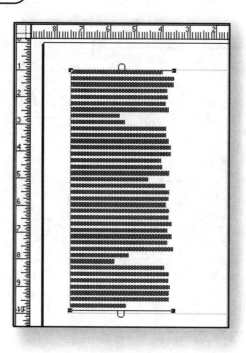

5. Select all the text with the **Text** tool.

6. Click on the **Type** menu and select **Hyphenation**. Change the **Hyphenation zone** to **1** inch and click **OK**. Can you see the difference at the right margin where the lines end? They should be more ragged with the larger hyphenation zone. If you do not notice the difference, follow the above directions and change the **Hyphenation zone** back to .5 inch. For practice, try other settings. (See Figure 4.20.)

7. Try other settings for practice. Type **2** in the **Limit consecutive hyphens to** text box of the **Hyphenation** dialog box.

8. Save and close the **TRACK** file.

FIGURE
4.20

Fit in Window views of hyphen zones

A. 0.5-inch hyphen zone   **B.** 1-inch hyphen zone

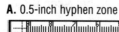
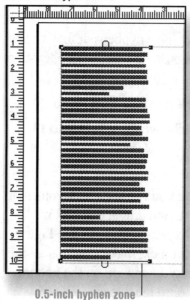
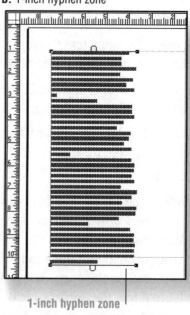

0.5-inch hyphen zone   1-inch hyphen zone

JUSTIFICATION

As you learned in Chapter 3, justified text is text that is aligned with both the left and right edges of a text block. PageMaker sets the justification of text with the **Alignment** command found in the **Type** menu. In Figure 4.21, there are two options for justification. You can **Force-justify** text so that the last line of a paragraph, even if it contains only a few characters, is spaced to fit exactly between the left and right edges of a text block. In addition, alignment, or justification, can be accomplished from the **Control** palette.

A: Alignment menu and submenu

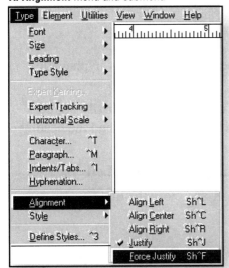

F I G U R E

4.21

Justification

B: Control palette paragraph view

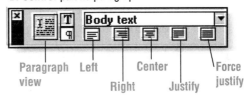

Paragraph view   Left   Center   Force justify

Right   Justify

1. Open the **TRACK** document and go to page 4.

2. With the **Pointer** tool, drag the text handles so that the text block fits between the left and right margins. (See Figure 4.22.)

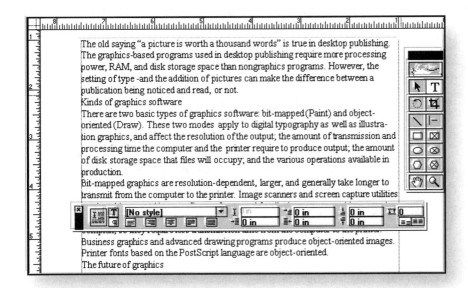

F I G U R E

4.22

Document with text block between the left and right margins

3. Use the **Text** tool to select all the text.

4. Click on the **Window** menu and select the **Control** palette. Click the **Paragraph view** button. (See Figure 4.23.)

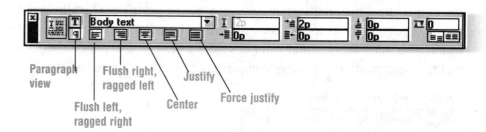

Paragraph view

Flush left, ragged right

Flush right, ragged left

Center

Justify

Force justify

Paragraph view button and *Alignment* buttons

5. Click the **Justify** button. Look to see if you notice any hyphenation changes.

6. With all of the text still selected, click on the **Force justify** button. Note the differences in the last line of the paragraphs and the heading lines between the paragraphs.

7. Before closing the file, change the alignment back to **Left**.

8. Run spell check, save, print the page, and close the file.

EM AND EN DASHES

An **en dash** is used in place of the word *to* or *through* in phrases such as 1-10 or A-Z. En dashes may touch the characters on either side of them, but you can increase the kerning so that the characters do not touch.

An **em dash** is used as punctuation. Use an em dash instead of double hyphens. Just like en dashes, an em dash may touch the characters on either side of it. Use kerning to increase the spacing slightly, if you wish.

1. Open the **TRACK** document and go to page 4.

2. With the **Text** tool, click an insertion point at the left margin below the paragraphs.

3. Practice using en and em dashes by typing these sentences:

   He works 9-5 every day.

   If a typeface or font is missing, PageMaker uses the PANOSE typeface matching system—a numeric classification of typefaces according to visual characteristics—to substitute for typefaces of comparable appearance.

4. Save and Close the **TRACK** file.

DID YOU KNOW...

To type an em dash, press **Alt** + Shift + hyphen (Windows) or **Option** + Shift + hyphen (Macintosh). To type an en dash, press **Alt** + hyphen (Windows) or **Option** + hyphen (Macintosh).

INDENTS

Indents move text inward from the left and right edges of a text block. They are used to set specific text off from the rest of the document or to create visual interest. You can set indents several ways:

- Move indent markers in the **Indents/Tabs** dialog box in layout view only. (See Figure 4.24.)
- Type indent values in the **Paragraph Specifications** dialog box. (See Figure 4.25.)
- Type indent values on the **Control** palette in **Paragraph view**. (See Figure 4.26.)

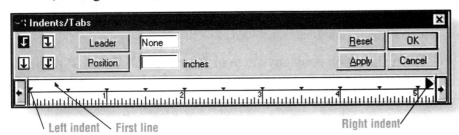

Indents/Tabs dialog box with ruler line

Paragraph Specifications dialog box

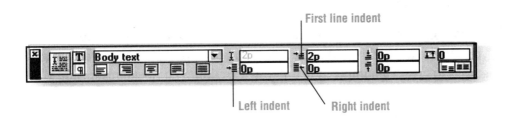

Control palette in **Paragraph view**

The **Indents/Tabs** dialog box provides an easy method for setting indents. Look once again at Figure 4.24. The ruler line has markers that you can click and drag to specified locations on the ruler. The markers represent the left, right, and first-line indents. The following directions create a hanging indent for a paragraph.

1. Open the **TRACK** file and add a page 5.

2. Use the **Text** tool and click an insertion point at the left margin near the top of the page, or use the **Story Editor**, to type the following paragraph.

   Question 2 develops a job description for a new president because the founding president has turned in his resignation. The question also contains a marketing strategy to attract presidential candidates. An advertisement that might appear in a journal is included as well.

3. Click an insertion point anywhere in the paragraph. Select **Type** menu and then **Indent/Tabs**. A ruler line like the one in Figure 4.27 should appear. The ruler line has markers that indicate the left and right edges of the text block, default tab settings, and the first-line indent marker. The zero (0) on the ruler indicates the left edge of the text block.

FIGURE 4.27
Ruler line over "Question 2"

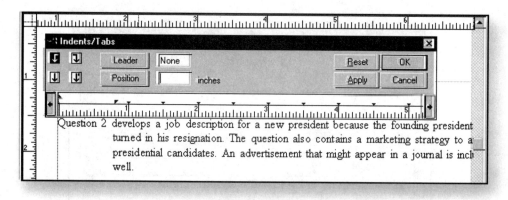

4. Point to the left-indent marker and drag it to 1 inch on the ruler. You must hold down the Shift key as you drag the marker so that the first-line indent marker will not be dragged, too.

5. Click the **Apply** button in the dialog box to see immediately the results of the indentation. Notice that the **Position** edit box displays the numerical position of the indent on the ruler.

6. Click **OK**.

We often use hanging indents with lists. PageMaker has a feature which you can use to quickly add consecutive numbers to a set of consecutive paragraphs to create a numbered list. If you are adding numbers, make sure your numbering scheme is final before using this feature because the numbers are not automatically corrected if you make changes in the text.

Bulleted lists are created in the same way as numbers. A **bulleted list** is a list in which each item is preceded by a symbol, usually a round dot larger than a period. Figure 4.28 shows the dialog box that allows you to select a particular bullet style. You may click the **Edit** button to specify another character of any typeface or size to use as a bullet.

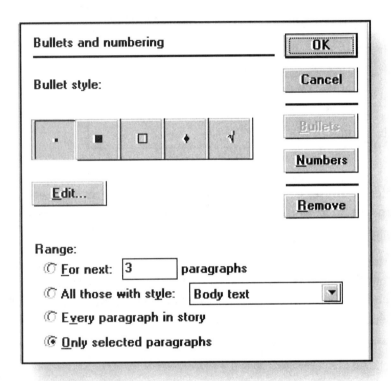

FIGURE 4.28

Bullets and numbering dialog box (bullet styles) The bullets shown are a filled-in circle, a filled-in square, and arrowhead, an open square, and a pointer.

1. Continuing on page 5, click an insertion point at the left margin somewhere below the previous paragraph and type the following recipe directions:

   Mix together flour, baking soda, and cinnamon.
   Beat together butter, brown sugar, and granulated sugar at medium speed until light and fluffy. Beat in egg and vanilla.
   At low speed, beat in flour mixture until blended. Fold in oats and chocolate chips. Cover with plastic wrap; chill for 1 hour.

2. Click an insertion point in the first line of the recipe directions and click on the **Utilities** menu.

3. Select **Plug-ins**.

4. Select **Bullets and numbering**. The dialog box in Figure 4.29 appears.

FIGURE

4.29

Bullets and numbering (numbering styles) dialog box

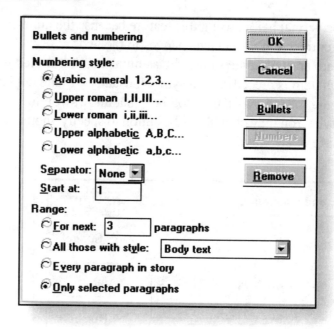

5. Select **Numbers**. Select a **period** from the drop down list as the **Separator**, and type **3** as the **Range: For next 3 paragraphs**.

6. Click **OK**.

The text appears with numbers added to each new paragraph. However, the wraparound portion of the lines are not indented. It is an easy procedure, using the hanging indent directions, to indent the text that wraps around. (See Figure 4.30.)

FIGURE

4.30

Recipe with hanging indents

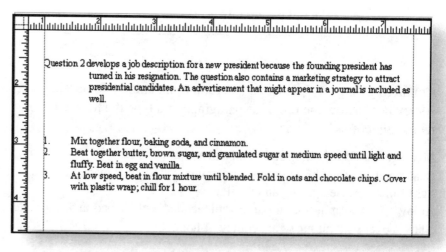

DID YOU KNOW...

Click an insertion point in the first line of the recipe directions and press **Ctrl + A** (Windows) or **Option + A** (Macintosh) to quickly select all of the text.

1. Use the **Text** tool to select all the text.

2. Select the **Type** menu and **Indents/Tabs**.

3. Drag the left-indent marker to the 2-inch (.5) point on the ruler line.

4. Click **OK**.

TABS AND LEADERS

Tabs position text at specific locations in a text block. There are four types of tabs available in PageMaker. They are shown in the **Indents/Tabs** dialog box in Figure 4.31.

- Left-aligned tabs, which indent text from the left edge of the text block.
- Right-aligned tabs, which align text along the right edge of the text block.
- Centered tabs, which center text around the tab.
- Decimal tabs, which align characters at a decimal point.

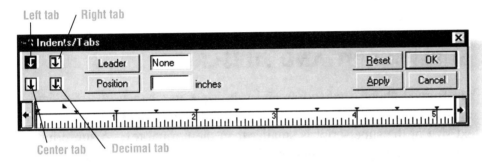

FIGURE 4.31
Indent/Tabs dialog box

Leaders are often used in conjunction with right tabs. **Leaders** are repetitive characters that print before the specific tab setting. You have to select the **Leader** option before you set the tabs. If none of the **Leader** option characters available in the list are what you want, you can select **Custom** to create your own character. You see leaders often in a table of contents. For example,

Chapter 1 3
Chapter 2 19
Chapter 3 28

Let's use the right-aligned tab and leaders to create the above table of contents.

1. On page 5, use the **Text** tool to click an insertion point at the left margin somewhere below the recipe directions.
2. Press **Ctrl + I** (Windows) or **Option + I** (Macintosh) to display the **Indents/Tabs** dialog box.
3. Click the **Leader** button to choose a leader character from the drop-down list in Figure 4.32.

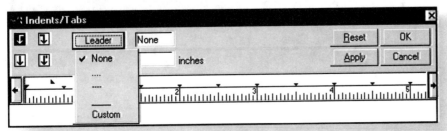

FIGURE 4.32
Leader drop-down list

4. Click on the **Right-tab** button to select the type of tab.

5. Click on the ruler line at the 3.25 inch mark to position the tab. If you do not click the exact position, you may have to drag the tab marker to the correct placement. Click **OK**.

6. Type: **Chapter 1**

7. Press the **Tab** key and type the page number: **3**. The leaders do not yet appear.

8. Press the **Enter** key and the leaders will appear.

9. Continue typing the chapter text, pressing the **Tab** key, typing the page number, and pressing **Enter**.

10. Print page 5 of this document. Save the **TRACK** file.

SUPERSCRIPT AND SUBSCRIPT

You learned about superscripts and subscripts in Chapter 3. To review, a superscript is portion of text that is raised slightly above the current line. The text size of the superscript is smaller than the normal text. A subscript has similar characteristics except that it is printed slightly below the current line.

1. Type the following sentence and the formulas:

   > This is a superscript, and this is a subscript.
   > 28 and H2O

2. Use the **Text** tool to highlight the characters "super".

3. From the **Type** menu, select the **Character** command. Figure 4.33 displays this dialog box.

FIGURE

4.33

Character Specifications dialog box with *Superscript* selected

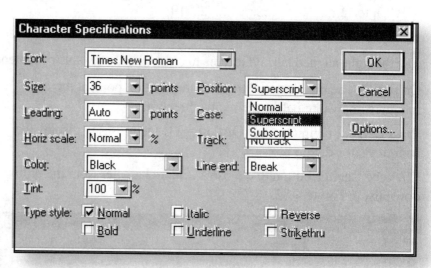

4. Choose the **Position** pulldown list and select **Superscript**.

5. Click **OK**.

6. Use the **Text** tool to highlight the characters "sub".

7. From the **Type** menu, select the **Character** command.

8. Choose the **Position** pulldown list and select **Subscript**.

9. Click **OK**.

10. Follow the above directions to: a) make the character **8** in "28" a superscript; and b) make the **2** in H2O a subscript.

11. Save and print this page. Then close the **TRACK** file.

CHECKING YOUR UNDERSTANDING

1. Explain the difference between tracking and kerning.

2. What is leading?

3. Name the two parts of a leading setting.

4. What is a slug?

5. As a general guideline, what is the percentage larger than the font size that leading should be set?

6. What happens when there is a large hyphenation zone?

7. Explain where an en dash is used; explain where an em dash is used.

8. What is the name applied to the repetitive characters used in a table of contents?

APPLYING DESIGN PRINCIPLES

Exercise 1 Creating a Table of Contents While Following Specifications

Create a table of contents similar to the one in Figure 4.34. Use a numbered list to number the chapters. Use leaders to separate the chapter titles from the page numbers. Follow the specifications on the marked copy.

Exercise 2 Create a Document Using Embedding

Create a document that lists the food items available from Grub Catering. Use kerning to create the special effect of embedding that you practiced earlier in this chapter. Use leading to separate the listed items. Follow the specifications on the marked copy of Figure 4.35.

**Table of Contents,
Exercise 1**

all margins
1 inch

Table of Contents

14/auto Bookman,
bold, italic, 1" drop

left tab: .344"

text: 2" drop

right tab: 6.5"

text:
14/auto Times

FIGURE 4.35
Using embedding,
Exercise 2

Exercise 3 Changing Formats with Track

Create two pages similar to the ones in the marked copy in Figure 4.36. Import the file **NWSTYPE.TXT** and edit it to match the document you see in the marked copy. The title, Text versus type, is in a separate text block from the paragraph text. (*Note:* Always spell check the text.)

Use leading, hanging indents, justified text, hyphenation, and tracking to change the format of the two pages. Follow the specifications on the marked copy. Save as **NEWS**, then apply the drop caps. (*Note:* Always apply drop caps after *all* other formatting.)

F I G U R E

4.36

Changing formats with
***Track*, Exercise 3**

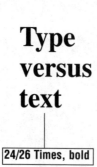

Type versus text

24/26 Times, bold

1 pt. line 2.25 inch from left

2.5 inch from left

1 inch margins

The main distinction between typewriter type and typographical type is that typewriter type is monospaced while most typographical type is proportionally spaced. In monospaced type, the horizontal width of each character is the same. In proportional type, the width of different characters is variable, depending on the shape of the character itself and the characters surrounding it. Each character is drawn on the screen or by the printer as a graphic image.

Desktop publishing programs utilize different typefaces in a variety of sizes and positions on the page. Word processing programs generally have less sophisticated typographic controls than page assembly programs. Page assembly programs can specify fractional type sizes and positions; line spacing, word spacing, and letterspacing; and typographical enhancements such as screens, boxes, and rules of different kinds, in positions specified relative to the type characters.

Page assembly programs cannot match the degree of typographical refinement afforded by dedicated typesetting equipment, nor do desktop publishers have access to the wide variety of typefaces available to typesetters. But the type handling capabilities of desktop publishing software are continuously being improved, and digital type manufacturers are making new as well as old typefaces available to desktop publishers at the rate of hundreds each year.

12/18 Times, left justified, track: tight hanging indent: .5 inch hyphenation, limit 2

part

3

Graphics

PRINCIPLES OF
BITMAPPED
& OBJECT-ORIENTED
Graphics

This chapter discusses bitmapped and object-oriented graphics and how to design and manipulate them.

Upon completion of this chapter — you will be able to

- explain the differences between bitmapped and object-oriented files
- define resolution
- recognize and deal with the discrepancies in WYSIWYG (what you see is what you get)
- create and edit graphics: image plane, duplication and rotation, special effects
- identify and apply the following graphics: originals, ready-made art, scanned images, line art, and continuous-tone art
- identify and apply business graphics (charts) to publications
- design and apply graphics: logos, photographs, charts
- identify and distinguish among graphic functions: internal graphics, imported graphics, and cropping graphics

The old saying "a picture is worth a thousand words" is true in desktop publishing. The addition of visual images can make the difference between a publication being noticed and read or tossed in the recycling bin. The fundamental purpose of publishing is to communicate effectively—to attract and hold the attention of the reader, to emphasize important points, and to make the material informative and interesting. Graphics are essential to this purpose.

BITMAPPED VERSUS OBJECT-ORIENTED GRAPHICS

There are two basic types of graphics software: **bitmapped** (Paint) and **object-oriented** (Draw). These two kinds of software differ in their quality of output, transmission and processing time, the amount of disk storage space required for files, and the various operations available in the programs.

Early graphics programs were all either Paint programs (such as MacPaint™, Windows Paint™, and GEM Paints™) or Draw programs (such as MacDraw™, Windows Draw™, and GEM Draw™). Programs now combine bitmapped and object-oriented modes, as in Adobe Illustrator™.

The Bitmapping Mode

Bitmapping programs produce files and images based on a map of pixels, or picture elements. A **pixel** is the smallest unit that a device can address. This term is used most often in reference to screen monitors, a pixel being the smallest spot that can be lit.

Figure 5.1 shows a laser printout of a typical bitmapped Paint image, alongside the Paint file in which it is stored. The Paint file is the computer's internal representation of the picture. It is a two-dimensional pattern of zeros and ones, arranged to create a sort of analog of the image. Each "1" corresponds to a bit that is turned on; each "0" refers to a bit that is turned off. For the monitor, this translates to a pixel that is on (illuminated) versus a pixel that is off. For the laser printer, each 1 translates into one or more dots of toner (dry ink) on paper, and each 0 to white space.

Bitmapped graphics are also called raster graphics. The term **raster device** means a bitmapping device—such as a display monitor, laser printer, or scanner. A raster device utilizes a scanning mechanism: a television set or computer monitor uses a cathode-ray gun; a laser printer or imagesetter is driven by a **raster-image processor (RIP)**; and an image or text scanner uses an "electric eye" that moves across a page.

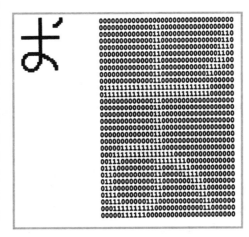

Bitmapped image and file code: A two-dimensional array of zeros and ones

Images created or used by raster devices are bitmapped, but not all raster devices produce the same resolution of output.

The Object-Oriented Mode

Object-oriented programs produce files and images based on a set of **algorithms**, or basic mathematical rules translated into formulas. These formulas describe a graphic form in abstract geometrical terms, as **primitives**, that is, as the most fundamental shapes from which all other shapes are made: straight lines, curves, and solid or patterned areas called **fills**.

Figure 5.2 shows a laser printout of an object-oriented image and the computer's internal representation of that image. This is the same image shown in Figure 5.1, except that it was created with a Draw (object-oriented) program instead of a Paint (bitmapped) program. The Draw file is a series of formulas:

- The first formula specifies the line width (LNWIDTH).
- The second formula describes the stem of the character, giving the coordinates of the beginning and end, and a line between them (LINETO).

- The next several formulas describe the arcs that make up the base of the character (ARC).
- Then there is another formula for a straight line (LINETO), and the formula for the little apostrophe-like arc that makes up the upper-right corner of the character.

FIGURE 5.2

Object-oriented image and file code: A set of algorithms describing graphic primitives

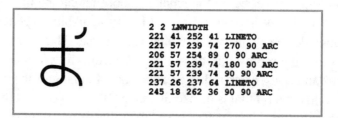

```
2 2 LNWIDTH
221 41 252 41 LINETO
221 57 239 74 270 90 ARC
206 57 254 89 0 90 ARC
221 57 239 74 180 90 ARC
221 57 239 74 90 90 ARC
237 26 237 64 LINETO
245 18 262 36 90 90 ARC
```

Pen-plotters, which are frequently used with computer-aided design (CAD) programs and computer-assisted mapping programs, use the object-oriented graphics mode. Because the formulas they use are made up exclusively of lines, pen-plotters, CAD programs, special CAD screens, and other such object-oriented applications are sometimes called **vector** devices/programs. A vector is the primitive used to create lines: it is a geometrical point with a direction and duration (length).

Bitmapped versus Object-Oriented Files and Output

Two factors that distinguish the bitmapped image and the object-oriented image are important to desktop publishers.

First, the bitmapped file is much larger than the object-oriented file. All the zeros and ones in a bitmap, and especially in a scanned image, take up a lot of storage (disk) space, and therefore take a long time to send to a printer. Object-oriented files take less time to send, but they may take longer to process, since they are encoded in algorithms that must be interpreted by the processor in the computer and/or the printer.

Second, the curved and diagonal lines of a bitmapped image appear jagged in the bitmapped character. This is generally not acceptable in publishing. It is exactly that type of computerized jaggedness, as seen in dot-matrix printer output, that desktop publishing seeks to banish. Jaggedness indicates a resolution problem.

Resolution

Resolution is the crispness of detail or fineness of grain in an image. The resolution of an image depends on two factors: the resolution encoded into the image file, and the resolution of the output device upon which it is displayed or printed.

Image Files Bitmapped files encode a *fixed* resolution—that is, a specific number of zeros and ones per row, and a fixed number of rows. Usually this fixed resolution is optimized for the display screen.

Object-oriented files, on the other hand, encode a *variable* resolution in their formulas for graphic primitives. The algorithms of object-oriented files translate into bitmaps at the resolution of the output device.

Device Resolution The resolution of a device is measured by the number of pixels (or dots, or lines) it can pack into a given amount of space, usually an inch (dpi, dots per inch).

The resolution of display screens used in desktop publishing ranges from 72 to over 150 dpi. The resolution of display screens is generally measured in terms of clarity (pitch). For example, a .25 pitch monitor displays with .25mm distance between dots. The smaller the pitch, the better the quality. The highest resolution today is a 20" (diagonal) with 1800 x 1400 dots.

Desktop laser printers are standardized at 600 dpi to 1200 dpi. Most scanners match that resolution. High-resolution laser printers have a resolution of at least 600 dpi. Imagesetters—professional typesetters that set images as well as type for mass production—have a resolution that falls from 2540 dpi to over 20,000 dpi.

Interplay of Image Files and Device Resolution Figure 5.3 shows that the bitmapped Paint file appears at the *same resolution* on the display screen as it is printed on a laser printer. This is because the resolution encoded in the bitmapped Paint file is fixed at the display-screen resolution. Even though the printer is capable of a higher resolution, the file itself contains information only for the lower display-screen resolution. The printer simply uses groups of its small pixels to map the image to the screen's larger pixels. Thus the curved portions of the image are jagged.

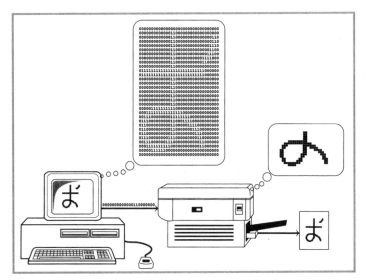

FIGURE 5.3

Bitmapped display and printout

Figure 5.4 shows that the object-oriented Draw file appears at a low resolution on the screen, but is printed at *higher resolution* on the laser printer. This is because the Draw file maps its algorithms to the resolution of the output device. The screen has a relatively low resolution, so the algorithms of the Draw file map the display image to its low resolution. The printer is capable of higher resolution, so the same algorithms map the print image to the higher resolution. The printer uses its smaller pixels individually, to image the objects coded in the file. There are only very slight jags (1/300 inch) on the curved portions of the image.

FIGURE

5.4
Object-oriented display and printout

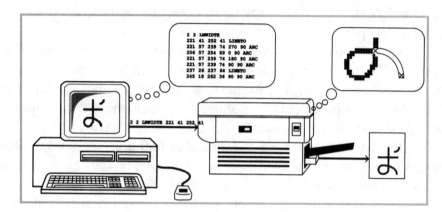

The bitmapped file output produced on a 1270 dpi imagesetter will have exactly the same resolution as it would on a 2540 dpi imagesetter. The object-oriented file output on an imagesetter would have correspondingly higher resolution—the jags would disappear entirely, except under magnification.

In summary, bitmapped images are resolution-dependent while object-oriented files are resolution-independent. In order to improve the resolution of bitmapped images, they must be reduced; this is generally accomplished in a page assembly program. The reduction (and enlargement) of graphic images is discussed later in this chapter.

Special Cases When printing from a 300 dpi bitmapping program on a 300 dpi laser printer, resolution is not a problem. However, the resolution will not be improved when the same files are printed on a 1270 or 2540 dpi imagesetter. Also, 300 dpi Paint files are correspondingly larger than screen-resolution Paint files; and the 1/300-inch pixel editing of these files requires great care.

The PostScript printer language contains sophisticated operators for the definition and manipulation of type and graphics, for scaling, rotating, outlining, filling, page positioning, and so on. It also contains operators for color and the manipulation of bitmaps. Advanced PostScript drawing programs, such as Adobe Illustrator™, Aldus Freehand™, and CorelDRAW!™ can specify lines thinner than 1/300 inch, very precise angles and curves, and increments of less than 1/300 inch. The images produced exhibit correspondingly increased precision as higher-resolution output devices are used.

Resolution and WYSIWYG

The differences in resolution between the display screen and printer in all desktop publishing systems leads to problems in the WYSIWYG interface. The display screen cannot show the fineness of detail or precise spacing that output devices are capable of producing. The mapping to screen of object-oriented images and type will always be approximate. There are simply not enough screen pixels to show the exact shape and placement of each element as it will be produced by the printer.

In the case of object-oriented Draw files, the difference between what-you-see on the display screen and what-you-get in the printout is welcome since what-you-get is better than what-you-see. However, there are other discrepancies that may cause unexpected problems with alignment, such as connecting two lines in a drawing or aligning a rule under a line of type. These problems need to be addressed on a case-by-case basis. Desktop publishing software companies are continuously improving the WYSIWYG correspondence between screen and printer images.

Another problem in the WYSIWYG area arises because of the shape of the pixels used in different monitors. The Macintosh display screen has square pixels, while most IBM/compatible graphics monitors have rectangular pixels. This means that bitmapped images (graphics and type) transferred between the Macintosh and IBM/compatible machines appear elongated or squeezed on the other system, and moiré patterns appear. **Moirés** (pronounced mo-ray) **patterns** are plaidlike patterns that result from the inexact correspondence between pixels in fill patterns (see Figure 5.5).

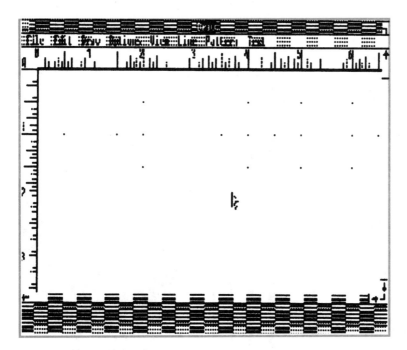

FIGURE 5.5

Bitmapped file transfer
Elongation of shapes and moiré patterns appear in the solid gray areas.

Except in the case of imported bitmaps, PostScript page assembly files created on either IBM/compatibles or Macintosh produce the same printed output, even if the display is slightly different.

Reduction   Figures 5.6 and 5.7 show various reductions of an original bitmapped image, and the same reductions of the same image produced with an object-oriented program.

FIGURE 5.6
Bitmapped reductions

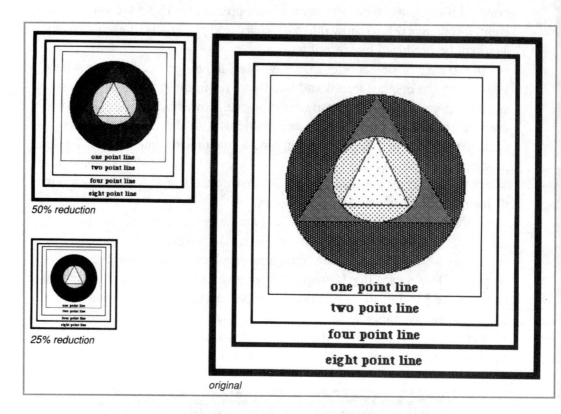

50% reduction

25% reduction

one point line
two point line
four point line
eight point line

original

FIGURE 5.7
Object-oriented reductions

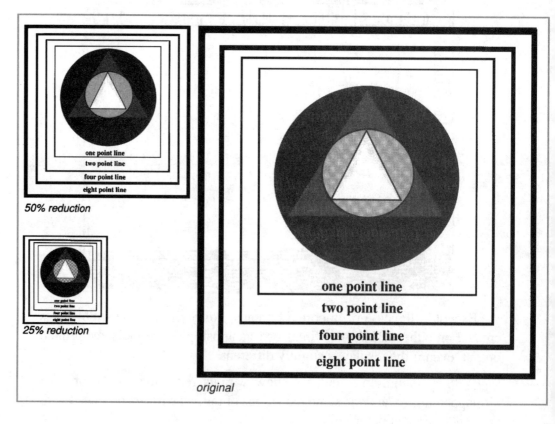

50% reduction

25% reduction

one point line
two point line
four point line
eight point line

original

Two areas that might cause problems in a reduced image are:

1. **Fill patterns**

   - *In bitmapped images*—moiré patterns may appear when pixels are reduced to sizes that do not divide evenly into the number and arrangement of pixels in the original.

   - *In object-oriented images*—fills may look inappropriate (since they are mathematically defined and fixed, they may appear too coarse in small objects).

2. **Thin lines**

   - *In bitmapped images*—thin lines tend to "drop out" of a graphic.

   - *In object-oriented images*—lines may look too thick (some programs have a minimum thickness they can produce).

   - *In all images*—if the publication is to be image set, there may be WYSIWYG discrepancies between the laser proofs and image-set copy (a line within a reduced graphic might appear as a 1/300-inch line on the laser proof, but as a 1/1200-inch line—almost invisible—on the image-set copy).

Note also that the type characters in the bitmapped image are jagged—type entered in Paint programs is usually unacceptable for desktop publishing; it must be cleaned up with pixel-by-pixel editing in the Paint program or reduced in the page assembly program for better resolution. In the object-oriented image, the type is smooth, produced at the resolution of the printer.

Enlargement Figures 5.8 and 5.9 show enlargements of the bitmapped image and the object-oriented image. In the bitmapped image, the irregularity of the type characters and in curved and diagonal lines is worse, and fill patterns may show some moiré patterns. This is not acceptable. The Draw enlargement maintains the smoothness of the type, lines, and fill patterns. However, small errors, such as gaps where lines do not quite meet—perhaps not apparent at the original size—become apparent when images are enlarged.

FIGURE
5.8
Bitmapped enlargement

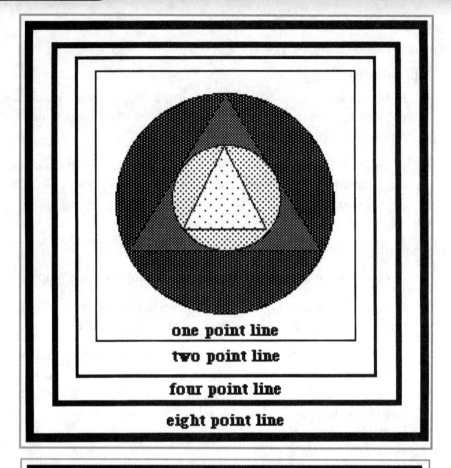

one point line

two point line

four point line

eight point line

FIGURE
5.9
Object-oriented
enlargement

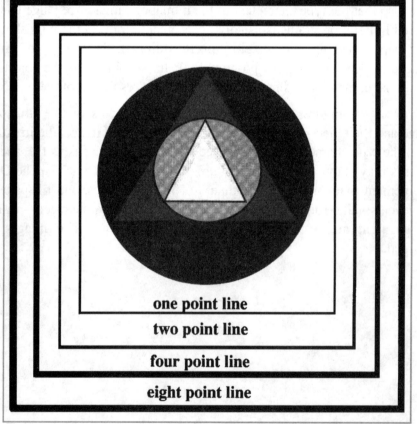

one point line

two point line

four point line

eight point line

The lesson here: do not enlarge bitmapped Paint files. If you need to make an enlargement of an illustration, be sure that it is an object-oriented image, and then be sure that the image is precisely rendered.

Disproportional Scaling Because bitmapped images are encoded with fixed resolution, disproportional scaling creates distortion of the pixels or dots that make up the image. Generally, this is unacceptable, unless the stretched-out pixels are part of the design. Object-oriented images, on the other hand, produce elongated or squeezed images at the resolution of the output device, and so can more frequently be used for high-resolution special effects, as shown in Figure 5.10.

Creating and Editing Graphics

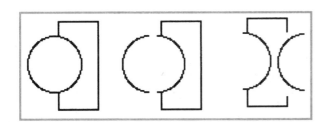

FIGURE

5.10
Disproportional scaling

Bitmapped Paint programs and object-oriented Draw programs differ not only in resolution, but also in the way images are created and edited.

Image Plane Figure 5.11 shows how bitmapped images are created and edited as single-plane images. For instance, if a circle and square overlap, they are "fused" to each other on the single plane of the bitmap. Working with a bitmapped program is like traditional painting; once a mark is set down, it covers up marks that were previously made, and it cannot be removed without affecting the surrounding marks.

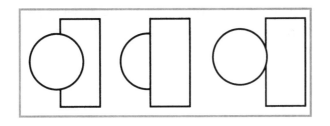

5.11
Single-plane bitmap editing. Areas of the bitmap are selected; these areas may include white space.

Figure 5.12 shows how object-oriented images are edited as multiple-plane images. Graphic primitives and groups of primitives (squares, circles, polygons, etc.) can be addressed separately. Working with an object-oriented program is like creating images on transparent overlays; marks can be set down and repositioned without affecting marks that were previously made.

5.12
Multiple-plane object editing. Discrete objects are selected; each object is separate from the white space that surrounds it.

Duplication and Rotation Both bitmapped and object-oriented programs generally have functions for duplicating and rotating. These functions are useful in making symmetrical shapes.

Figure 5.13 shows how, in Paint programs, *areas of the bitmap are selected* for duplication and rotation. An area includes white space as well as black marks, and thus when repositioned, some parts of the image may be whited out. Some bitmapped programs enable the user to select to the edges of a marked area and thus avoid the white-out problem. However, the internal white space (or pattern) is part of the bitmap and cannot be made transparent.

FIGURE

5.13

Bitmap rotations. White space surrounds shapes and overlaps shapes.

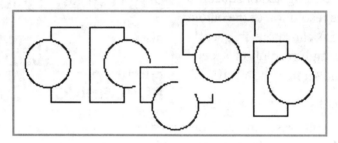

Generally, bitmapped programs allow only 45-degree and 90-degree rotations and reflections, since the bitmap is a two-dimensional array. Rotations and reflections at nonstandard angles create jagged lines that are usually not acceptable for desktop publishing.

Figure 5.14 shows how in Draw programs, *objects are selected* (graphic primitives as well as grouped primitives) for duplication and rotation. Since objects have integrity as objects no matter where in the white space they are positioned, the white-out problem does not occur.

FIGURE

5.14

Object rotations. Each object is separate from the white space that it surrounds, and that surrounds it.

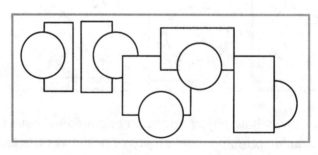

Objects can be grouped—several objects made to act as one—and made transparent or opaque, to give special layering effects. Advanced drawing programs also enable the user to specify fixed layers, so that previously created images can be drawn over without accidentally being altered and rotations and other special transformations can be applied with precise numerical specifications to objects and groups of objects.

Special Effects Because a bitmapped image simply consists of bits that are on or off, Paint programs allow the artist to do pixel-by-pixel editing—that is, turning off and on individual pixels. Different paint programs also have special effects such as speckling (spraying random dots over an area); the creation of custom-made fill patterns and pouring fill patterns into enclosed spaces; bit-wise functions such as inverting areas of an image (turning off bits that were on, and vice versa); and making outlines (turning off bits that were on and turning on adjacent bits). (See Figure 5.15.)

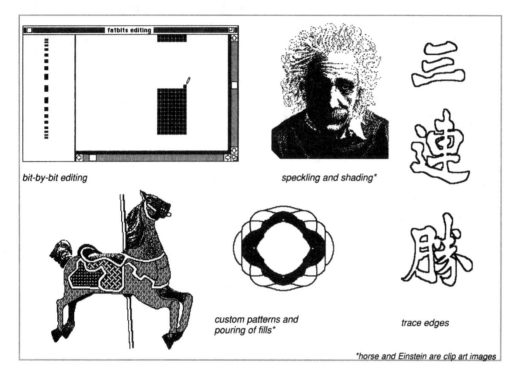

bit-by-bit editing

speckling and shading*

custom patterns and
pouring of fills*

trace edges

*horse and Einstein are clip art images

FIGURE 5.15
Bitmapped special effects

The pixel-by-pixel editing and bit-wise functions described above are not available in object-oriented programs. Instead, the images of object-oriented files are edited in terms of their attributes—the length, thickness, and angle of a line; the sides of a square, rectangle, or polygon; the radius or arcs of a circle or an oval.

In simple WYSIWYG programs, these geometric functions are drawn interactively, freehand; more advanced drawing programs also allow these functions to be precisely specified with numbers. Objects can also be grouped, layered, aligned, and transformed at regular intervals. The advanced PostScript programs described above allow artists to create fluid and flexible curves, called **Bezier curves**, and to create graduated **tints** (a shade of gray or color). (See Figure 5.16.)

FIGURE
5.16
Object-oriented special effects

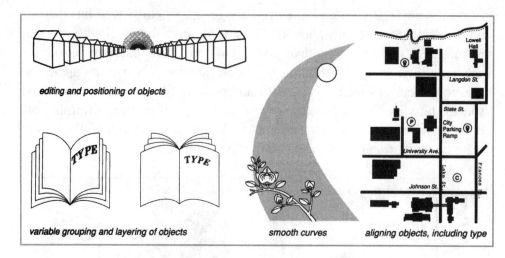

editing and positioning of objects

variable grouping and layering of objects   *smooth curves*   *aligning objects, including type*

SOURCES OF GRAPHICS

Graphics for your publication may be acquired in a number of ways. They may also be created as original artwork. Because so many varieties of graphics are available, it is not necessary that you be a talented artist in order for you to have both functional and attractive graphics in your publications.

Original Illustrations

Object-oriented programs are used more often than bitmapped programs for the production of original illustrations in desktop publishing. This is because object-oriented programs are resolution-independent and generally offer more powerful editing functions.

There are exceptions to this rule, however. Bitmapping special effects make the use of bitmapped programs preferable for certain jobs, such as when the original image is created in a size larger than the final output and then reduced in the page assembly program for improved resolution.

The 300 dpi color bitmapping programs can produce effects unobtainable (or difficult to obtain) with most object-oriented programs. Sometimes logos and illustrations are first designed in easier-to-use bitmapped programs; for final production, reduced bitmaps or bitmaps traced over with a combined Paint-Draw program or a PostScript drawing program may be used.

Depending on the effects you wish to achieve (keeping in mind the limitations of bitmapped resolution), you may choose to work with either a Paint program or a Draw program in producing original illustrations.

Following is a summary of the functional differences between bitmapped and object-oriented programs:

1. Graphics functions available in all graphics programs
   - Rotations and reflections
   - Duplication of areas/objects

2. Bitmapped functions specific to Paint programs
   - Bit-by-bit detail editing
   - Bit-by-bit speckling and shading
   - Creation of custom fill patterns and pouring of fills into selected areas
   - Bit-wise functions: inverting, making outlines, etc.
3. Object-oriented functions specific to Draw programs
   - Positioning of objects and editing of attributes
   - Variable grouping and layering of objects
   - Aligning objects, including type
   - Reshaping and smoothing of objects
   - Drawing of smooth curves

Ready-Made Art

Electronic **clip art** is ready-made line art stored as graphics files on disk. These images can be customized or simply copied and pasted into a page layout. Clip art collections come in many categories, such as people, animals, places, food, sports, holidays, and map outlines. Some clip art comes in graphics database format for easier access.

A great deal of bitmapped clip art is available both for purchase and in the public domain via the Internet and other online services. Much of the commercial clip art currently available is scanned hard-copy clip art or photographs.

Screen Captures

Screen captures, which are pictures of what is on the screen display, are bitmapped since the display screen is a raster device. A screen capture utility is built into the Macintosh operating system; also, there are several screen capture programs available for IBM/compatibles, but they differ in their ability to capture graphics created in various programs.

Image Scanning

Because image scanners are raster devices, they create bitmapped files. Scanned line art, as opposed to scanned continuous-tone art, however, differs greatly because of the mechanics of creating digital halftones.

Line Art When line art is scanned, the scanner simply builds a bitmap by turning on dots where its electric eye sees black, and turning off dots where it sees white (see Figure 5.17). Each dot that the scanner registers is a scan sample. Image scanners are standardized at 600 samples per inch (spi), to match the resolution of standard desktop laser printers. Scanned line art images generally print out well on 300 dpi printers without any special adjustments. However, since scanned images are bitmaps, the resolution of a 300 dpi file does not improve when printed on a higher resolution device.

5.17

Scanned line art

When scanning line art that has vertical and horizontal lines, the artwork must be aligned properly so that the lines are passed through the scanning mechanism as true verticals and horizontals. A slight variance will cause the lines to appear stair-stepped. This is more of a problem with sheet-fed scanners than with flatbed scanners, since on flatbeds the paper itself does not move.

Continuous-tone Scans Scanning continuous-tone images such as photographs is more complex than scanning line art. A scanned image saved as a flat bitmap simply turns dots off or on; all dots are the same size—there are simply more of them in dark areas and less of them in light areas. This method of representing continuous tones is called **dithering**. Figure 5.18 shows a dithered photographic image. Dithered images are generally not acceptable for professional publishing, but may be used simply to show the position of halftones.

A **halftone** is a grid of dots that vary in size so that when they are viewed together, they appear as gray tones. A **gray-scale image**, which is a digital halftone, is a deep bitmap. Each pixel of a gray-scale image has a brightness value ranging from black to white, with different levels of gray in between. In printing, the impression of grayness is a function of the size of the dot; a group of large dots looks dark and a group of small dots looks light. TIFF files encode gray-scale information.

5.18

Continuous-tone scans
Dithered scan (top row); gray-scale scan (bottom row)

In a halftone, two factors determine the clarity of the image: the number of gray-scale levels and the fineness of the screen (the maximum size of each dot). The more gray-scale levels, the smoother the gradations in tone; the finer the screen, the less grainy the image.

For digital imaging devices such as a 600 dpi laser printer, however, this means a trade-off between the number of gray-scale levels and the size of each dot. To create 26 levels of gray (including black and white), a 5 x 5 matrix of dots (25 dots) is needed: when no dots are registered, this represents white; one dot represents a very light gray; two dots, a slightly darker tone; when nearly 25 dots are on, the area is black (see Figure 5.19). The use of a 5 x 5 matrix of dots, however, means that the virtual halftone dot size is no longer 1/300-inch, but is 1/60-inch, since it takes 5 dots per inch to make a halftone dot.

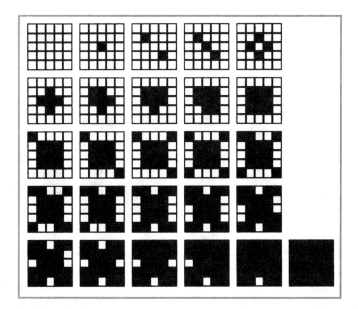

FIGURE
5.19
Digital halftone matrix

A 1/60-inch halftone dot resolution (equivalent to a 60-line photographic halftone) is not a high-quality halftone; most newspapers use between 65 and 85 lines. Most magazines generally use from 120 to 200 lines, and excellent reproductions may run as high as 300 lines. In order to increase the fineness of the screen, the number of gray-scale levels must be reduced. A 4 x 4 matrix of dots (16 dots) creates the equivalent of a 75 line screen, but it can represent only 17 gray-scale levels.

Gray-scale images can be output to higher-resolution devices such as 600 dpi laser printers, or 1270 dpi or 2540 dpi imagesetters, but the problems of storage space as well as transmission and processing time make this option inefficient. An 8½" x 11" gray-scale image may occupy more than a megabyte and can take an hour to print.

To ensure high-quality halftones, it is often more cost- and time-efficient to use the photographic halftones provided by most print shops. However, digital halftone scanning is an area that is currently undergoing rapid development; as new image-editing software and faster image-processing output devices are developed, digital desktop halftones are easily manipulated by desktop publishers.

Business Graphics

Business graphics are data-driven charts that are often included in spreadsheet and/or database programs. Business graphics programs generally produce object-oriented files that may be edited with object-oriented programs.

X–Y Charts An X–Y chart translates numbers entered in a data series into points plotted on intersecting horizontal (X) and vertical (Y) axes. Bar charts and line charts are the most common kinds of X–Y charts.

Bar charts plot vertical or horizontal bars proportional to the values in the data series, as shown in Figure 5.20. They are very versatile, and are the most commonly used business graphics format. They can be used for single or multiple series, and for categorized or time-series data. Negative or positive values may be plotted. In multiple series charts, categories may be plotted side-by-side, or stacked.

5.20

Bar charts

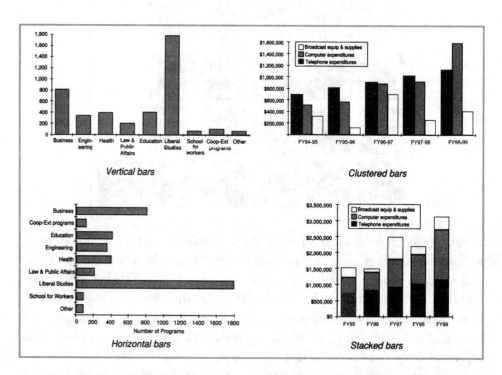

Line charts are generally used for time-series data, that is, values that vary over a period of seconds, minutes, hours, days, weeks, months, or years, as shown in Figure 5.21. The X-axis is used for the time intervals and the Y-axis for values. Line charts can be used for single or multiple series data; negative or positive values may be plotted. For multiple series, lines may be independent, stacked, or area-filled.

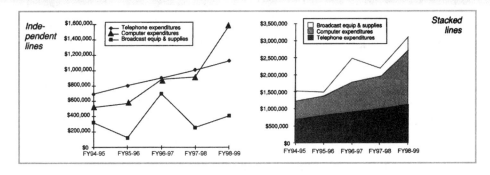

FIGURE 5.21

Line charts

Pie Charts Pie charts are used to show relative parts of a whole, such as how one resource is divided among several categories, as shown in Figure 5.22. Only single-series data can be charted in one pie chart; multiple-series data must be charted as multiple pie charts. Usually it is best if there are not more than five or six categories—otherwise the slices become too thin or too similar in size and the comparison between categories is not apparent.

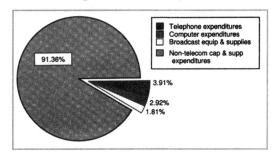

FIGURE 5.22

Pie chart

Other Variations Some business graphics programs offer variations on these standard formats. For example, scatter charts are used to plot data on points relative to variables on both the X-axis and Y-axis (for example, temperature vs. pressure variance). Combination charts may include line charts and bar charts, or charts with two different Y-axes (see Figure 5.23).

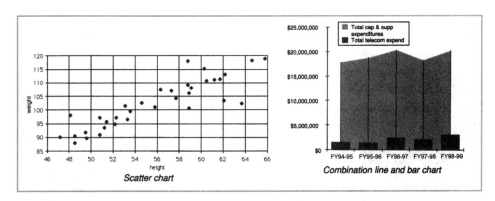

FIGURE 5.23

Chart variations

DESIGN OF GRAPHICS

Approaching the design of graphics requires some planning as well as an understanding of how certain kinds of graphics are traditionally handled.

Logos and Illustrations

A primary consideration in the design of logos and illustrations is the context in which they will be used. Logos must be versatile because, as the primary graphic identifier for an organization, they are used in a wide variety of contexts—including nearly every kind of publication produced, and other materials such as clothing, signs, and vehicles.

Illustrations should be designed, when possible, after their position on the page is determined. (For this purpose, a rough sketch is adequate.) The focus, negative space, balance, and directional flow of the illustrations can be adjusted relative to the text that accompanies them.

Focus A logo should be able to function as a focus, no matter where it is placed, even when it is reduced. It should, therefore, have weight and density—solid black (or colored) and white areas. Delicate fill patterns and fine linear detail should be avoided, because they do not reduce well or read well from a distance (see Figure 5.24). **Reverses** (white images or text on a black background) in particular make eye-catching logos.

For best results, large, heavy reverses should be imageset. The photographic imagesetting process produces very black blacks.

An illustration should have an internal focus—a part of the image to which the viewer's eye will move first. Detail and fill patterns may be used to enhance the informational or representational function of the illustration. Text labels, or **callouts**, are often boxed and/or connected to a graphic with leader lines to draw attention to and identify important parts of an illustration.

Balance Symmetrical balance in logos and illustrations implies stability and solidity—many financial and service institutions use symmetrical logos—but symmetrical balance tends to look static. Asymmetrical balance is more dynamic, but it is difficult to produce effectively. A good way to assess the balance of a logo or illustration is to tack it up on a wall and stand away from it at a distance great enough so that the graphic elements can be seen as abstract rather than as representational forms. In this view, imbalance should be more apparent.

Though a logo should be internally balanced so that it can be used in a variety of publications, a purposely imbalanced display illustration may be used in order to counterbalance text elements. In this case, the page positioning and size of the graphic should be predetermined with a rough sketch (see Figure 5.25).

FIGURE 5.24

Detail vs. weight
A. Fill patterns and detail drop out in images when viewed at a glance, from a distance, or reduced.
B. For logos, solid areas are better for focus.

DID YOU KNOW...

Here is a warning about heavy reverses: large black areas in a negative image often do not print well on laser printers. The toner particles may not distribute evenly; however, this may be overcome by a good photocopier machine.

Directional Flow and Unity In black and white designs, directional flow is accomplished with a primary and secondary focus, and by the use of lines and the edges of large shapes. For logos, the general rule is that designs with left-to-right and bottom-to-top flow are most flexible to work with in a variety of page layouts and other contexts. See examples of logos in Chapter 1, Figure 1.19.

A logo should work as a self-contained unit. It should be designed, however, with other graphic elements in mind. For instance, the use of letter forms in a logo might restrict the appropriate typefaces that will go with it. In general, similarity of line, texture, and shape gives a consistent overall look to a piece, which will include both illustrations and type.

Illustrations also follow this general rule when their final position is undetermined. However, the directional flow of a display illustration can be used to effectively point to important text information.

FIGURE
5.25
Illustration balanced by text

Photographs

The primary consideration in preparing photographic images for publication is cropping for the elimination of unnecessary parts of the image and for making images more dynamic (see Figure 5.26).

When working with scanned images, the desktop publisher should keep in mind the memory requirements for saving and processing gray-scale images. Some foresight will keep scanned image files at minimal size while providing all the information needed for final cropping. Page assembly programs have tools that enable the desktop publisher to fine-tune the cropping of an image.

In shots of people, if the person is not facing straight on, there should be more space on the side of the photo toward which the person is facing. These shots should also be set on the page so that the person is facing the text.

Action shots or static shots can be made to look more dynamic if they are cropped with extra space in the direction of the movement or potential movement. In outdoor shots, the horizon line is created by the intersection of the

FIGURE

5.26

Cropping Head shot (cropped in the direction of the look); outdoor shot (cropped with sky one-third the distance from top); static shot (cropped in the direction of potential movement).

Photo by Dean Wong

Photo by Dean Wong

sky and the ground. All other factors being equal, when action or an object on the ground is the focus, the horizon line should run about one-quarter to one-third from the top of the image; otherwise, there is too much sky and the photograph looks top-heavy.

Charts

In X–Y charts, the categories should be labeled in order of magnitude, alphabetically, or chronologically from the left to the right and from bottom to top (see Figures 5.20 and 5.21). However, when the Y-axis labels are alphabetical, the order is often reversed so that the Y-axis reads from top to bottom (see Figure 5.20). In pie charts, the first slice should be at the 3 o'clock position, and the other slices follow in counter-clockwise order (see Figure 5.22).

With regard to fill patterns, lines, and markers, the main thing is to not overdo it. Generally, all markers in single-series X–Y charts should have the same fill or line pattern. When different fill patterns are used for series in a multiple-series chart the patterns should, as much as possible, be gradations of each other (for example, different color intensity, or thin stripes, medium stripes, thick stripes). (See Figure 5.20 and Figure 5.21.)

When colored markers are next to each other or overlap, their colors should be related: blue next to green or purple, for instance, or red next to purple or orange, or yellow next to orange or green. This is so that if the alignment is not perfect in the final printing, a slight overlapping of colors will not mix into muddy brown.

GRAPHIC FUNCTIONS

As has been mentioned, small amounts of text can be typed directly into PageMaker, and more complex text can be imported as word processing files. Likewise, simple graphics can be created within the page assembly program, and more complex drawings can be imported as separate graphic files.

Internal graphics are those created in the page assembly program, and imported graphics are those created with specialized graphics programs. Both internal and imported graphics can be moved freely on the page, or to another page. Internal graphics can be edited in PageMaker (for example, line thicknesses and fill patterns can be altered), while *imported* graphic files can only be scaled and cropped and not changed in other ways.

Internal Graphics

The drawing tools available in page assembly programs are fairly basic. PageMaker's drawing tools are not made for creating illustrations, but rather for adding simple graphic enhancements to text or imported drawings (see Figure 5.27). Boxed text such as captions and callouts can be tied to graphics.

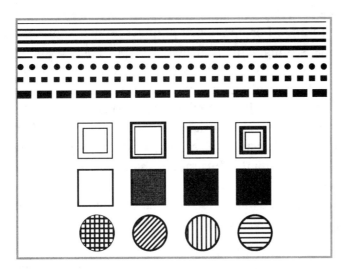

FIGURE

5.27

Internal graphics
Examples of the page assembly program's drawing tools: ruling lines, boxes, circles, and fill patterns.

Internal graphics generally offer a choice of ruling line thicknesses, multiple ruling lines, rounded corners, and fill patterns. These elements are object-oriented, so they can be edited in terms of those attributes, and also in terms of length, width, and direction. In addition, type and images can be layered over them for special effects such as reverses (see Figure 5.28).

FIGURE
5.28
Reverse and surprint
Reverses and surprints
(overprints) are created
with layering within the
page assembly program.

In PageMaker, consistency can be maintained by using manually produced style sheets (separate lists) or by creating graphic elements and placing them outside of the page in an area called the pasteboard. The pasteboard can be accessed from any page of the publication. When a graphic element is needed, it can be copied from the pasteboard and pasted into the page.

Imported Graphics

Page assembly programs automate the sizing and positioning of artwork. Most standard graphics files imported into a page assembly program appear in place on the screen.

All page assembly programs enable the scaling and cropping of images. When using PostScript-based type, characters saved in a graphics program can be disproportionally scaled for stretched type effects. Design-oriented programs such as PageMaker also allow the application of special photographic effects to bitmapped graphics and TIFF files.

Scaling Imported Graphics The scaling of imported graphics in a page layout is similar to the sizing of blocks of text. The block containing the graphic has handles used to reduce or enlarge the image horizontally, vertically, or both.

Electronic scaling offers special features such as automatic proportional scaling; alternatively, an imported graphic may be specified to fit within an established frame. For bitmapped graphics, some page assembly programs have optimal scaling, which calculates the percentages that will avoid moiré patterns on a specified output device. If the original bitmapped graphic, for example, is 72 dpi, for the best reproduction on a 300 dpi printer, the image is reduced 24 percent. In general, bitmaps should not be enlarged, and reducing either bitmaps or object-oriented files may cause problems.

For a series of illustrations, scaling should be as consistent as possible so that the images within the illustrations maintain their proportions. Unrelated illustrations—such as shots of people taken at different times—can be made to seem related if they are scaled so that the human figures within the illustrations are comparable in size.

Cropping Imported Graphics Photographs (halftones) are most frequently cropped for publication. Sometimes screen captures and line drawings are also cropped in order to place the focus on particular details. Photographic images can be precropped during the scanning stage in order keep TIFF files smaller. The final cropping, however, should be determined in the page assembly program where all elements are in place.

Imported graphic files are cropped in a manner similar to traditional cropping: parts of the image are cut away and/or a block is made in the final proportions, which functions as a mask or frame for the image. The image can be moved under the mask until the best cropping is determined.

When possible, cropping should be consistent. However, for overall graphic consistency of a page layout, the final image size, which is determined by scaling, is more important than the actual frame size, which is determined by cropping.

Special Photographic Effects
Advanced illustration and photographic programs open up a number of editing capabilities and special photographic screening effects previously reserved for the darkroom.

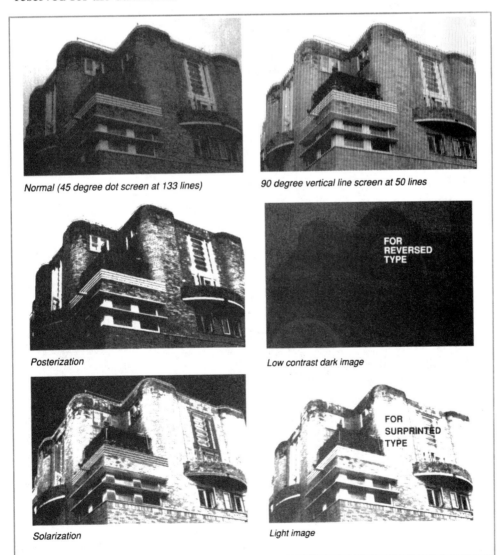

Normal (45 degree dot screen at 133 lines)

90 degree vertical line screen at 50 lines

Posterization

Low contrast dark image

FOR REVERSED TYPE

Solarization

Light image

FOR SURPRINTED TYPE

FIGURE

5.29

Photographic special effects

Images can be cut and pasted, superimposed, and airbrushed (that is, parts of the image selectively erased or filled in). Brightness and contrast can be adjusted and special line screens can be applied to embed linear, circular, or wavy patterns into images. **Posterizing** (reduction of the number of gray-scale levels), **solarizing** (causing both blacks and whites to appear black, while midtone gray-scale levels approach white), and adjustment of specific gray levels to different values are also available with advanced graphics programs (see Figure 5.29).

Positioning Imported Graphics Like blocks of text, imported graphics can be freely positioned on the page and moved from page to page. Consistency should be maintained as much as possible in terms of the relationship of the illustration to the text. The graphics may, for example, be set under major headings, at the top of the page, or at the bottom of the page.

CHECKING YOUR UNDERSTANDING

1. What is resolution?

2. Name two concerns that must be addressed with the reduction of images.

3. Define the term *raster device*.

4. Describe the computer's internal representation of a bitmapped file.

5. Describe the computer's internal representation of an object-oriented file.

6. What is the difference between line art and halftones? How does this difference affect the use of an image scanner?

7. Which file, bitmapped or object-oriented, takes up more storage on a hard disk?

8. Which takes longer to transmit to an imagesetter, a bitmapped file or an object-oriented file?

9. CAD programs utilize which file type: bitmapped or object-oriented?

10. What are moiré patterns?

APPLYING DESIGN PRINCIPLES

Exercise 1 Finding Good Examples of Design Principles

Collect samples of publication designs—posters, fliers, brochures, magazines, booklets—that illustrate very good and very poor use of the basic principles of design: focus, balance, directional flow, unity, and negative space. Share these with your classmates and create a notebook containing the best design examples, which you can use for reference in your own design projects.

Good sources of publication design samples include advertisements in newspapers and magazines; junk mailings; literature racks at public facilities such as libraries, community centers, and colleges; and government offices, especially referral offices.

Exercise 2 Visual Identity

Do some research and analysis for a "visual identity" design project: a series of publications (stationery set, poster, report, brochure, newsletter) for a specific organization. Choose an organization with which you are familiar—a student group, small business, government agency, community group, church group, etc. The background research and analysis should answer these questions:

a) What are the primary products/services provided by this organization? Be specific. Make a list of at least three products or services.

b) Describe the type of people that this organization wishes to reach with its products/services. Is there a specific age group (single or family), income bracket, professional interest, recreational interest, or male/female audience for the organization's products/services? List at least three adjectives or phrases that describe this organization's market.

c) Describe the "personality" that this organization wishes to convey. How is this organization different from others that provide the same products/services? What special qualities will appeal to and interest the group of people you wish to reach? List at least three adjectives or phrases that describe this organization's personality.

d) Other things to note: Is there a slogan or motto associated with the organization? Is there a mascot or symbol? You can create these identity elements if they do not exist.

Exercise 3 Types of Graphic Images

Find samples of the following types of images:

a) Two examples of line art.

b) Two examples of airbrushed images.

c) Two examples of gray-scale images.

d) Examples of business graphics: pie chart, bar chart, X-Y chart.

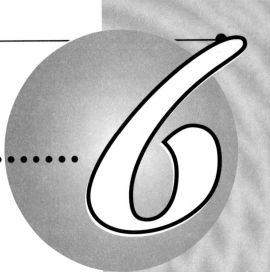

CREATING
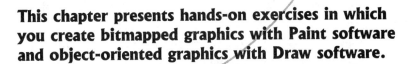
PAINT & DRAW ··················

This chapter presents hands-on exercises in which you create bitmapped graphics with Paint software and object-oriented graphics with Draw software.

Upon completion of this chapter you will be able to

- **Use the commands of Paint software to:**
  create a bitmapped graphic
  use the toolbox
  draw lines and curves
  draw rectangles and ellipses
  correct errors using the **Undo** and **Eraser** tools
  improve resolution through scaling
- **Use the commands of Draw software to:**
  group objects by layering, combining, or aligning
  create circles, arcs, and lines
  create templates
  rotate graphics
  layer text on a graphic

The two basic graphics modes, bitmapped and object-oriented, are fundamental to the understanding of WYSIWYG desktop publishing and the important issue of image resolution. In the production of graphics, the two modes determine the way images are created and edited and the special effects that are available.

When imported into a page assembly program, graphics can be sized and positioned on the page and adjusted in place, surrounded by text. However, the elements within imported illustrations and graphics generally cannot be edited in a page assembly program because scaling and cropping functions treat graphics as a block.

BITMAPPED GRAPHICS PROGRAMS

This section of the chapter deals with general techniques involved in creating images with bitmapped graphics packages for IBM and IBM/compatible computers, such as PC Paintbrush™, Windows Paint™, and GEM Paint™. No attempt is made here to address issues pertaining to one specific program. This section covers only the common functions shared by these programs.

Advantages of Bitmapped Graphics

One area of publishing in which the paint package is crucial is in technical documentation requiring representations of screen images, such as this book. In this case, the coarse nature of the images actually assists the user to identify them as screen representations, rather than as illustrations. The role of the paint package is to occasionally clean up captured screen images, as well as to crop those images prior to importing them into the page assembly program. (Cropping makes the image file smaller, thereby saving disk space and reducing printing time.)

Quick and Easy One of the advantages of bitmapped graphics is the ease with which a new user may get started sketching design ideas for logos and illustrations. Most functions are accomplished easily with the mouse. In addition the tools provided in these programs are simple to understand and use.

Widespread Import Filters Another advantage is that the file formats of bitmapped image programs are easily imported into page assembly programs. They have been available for the PC longer than object-oriented graphics, and as a result, the page assembly programs have been developed to accommodate them.

Disadvantages of Bitmapped Graphics

There are disadvantages to using bitmapped graphics in page assembly programs. The primary problems are resolution and scaling (sizing) of bitmapped images.

Screen-Aspect Ratio Monitors available for PCs seldom use square pixels. A laser printer, on the other hand, uses precisely square pixels. If you draw what appears to be a square or circle on your monitor and then print (or import into a page assembly program and print), you will discover that the shape has been flattened. Therefore, you must draw so that the image appears taller than it really should be. How much taller depends on your monitor. You will need to experiment to find the right proportion. If your paint package supports it, use the function that reports the position of the cursor by pixel count. Then you will be able to draw, say, a square exactly 300 by 300 pixels (1 inch by 1 inch when printed).

Coarse Output/Resolution Problems If the image is used in PageMaker at 100 percent of its original size (shown on the screen in the paint program), diagonal and curved lines (including text characters) will be unacceptably jagged. Certain procedures are necessary to get a better appearance of bitmapped images imported into page assembly programs. For one thing, bitmapped line art should be reduced.

Usually, any text generated by a bitmapped paint package is of inferior quality to text available in the page assembly program. Therefore, such text should be used sparingly, if at all.

File Size Typically, the size of a bitmapped file far exceeds the size of an equivalent file created with an object-oriented drawing program. The image file must explicitly define every pixel that is to be displayed, whereas an object-oriented drawing will simply define points on lines and formulas for curves and fills. Regardless of complexity, the bitmapped file of a given dimension will always be the same size, whereas an object-oriented drawing increases in size with each detail added.

Learning to Use Bitmapped Graphics

This section explores three aspects common to most bitmapped graphics programs. These are drawing functions, coloring (painting) functions, and editing functions (including error correction). Figure 6.1 shows the toolbox in **Microsoft Windows Paint**.

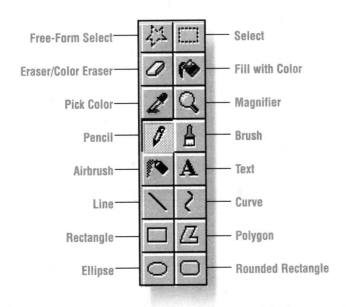

Free-Form Select — Select
Eraser/Color Eraser — Fill with Color
Pick Color — Magnifier
Pencil — Brush
Airbrush — Text
Line — Curve
Rectangle — Polygon
Ellipse — Rounded Rectangle

FIGURE 6.1

Toolbox in *Microsoft Windows Paint*

The Parts of the Window In a Paint package, the **drawing window** is the area in which you create your artwork; the menu bar contains the names of the available menus; and the toolbox or tools palette is the place where you select tools for creating and altering your artwork. The **cursor** is the pointer you use to create objects and select menus, commands, and tools. The cursor will sometimes change appearance when different tools are selected.

Common Basic Drawing Functions Most Paint programs will have all or most of the tools for creating different objects: lines, curves, boxes/rectangles, round-cornered rectangles (round-recs), and circles/ellipses.

Some programs require that you start drawing an object at the top left corner of the area; it will occupy and drag down to the right to complete the object. Others allow you to start at any corner and, in the case of circles/ellipses, in the center.

Some programs require that you hold down a mouse button during the entire creation of the object; others require only a click at the start of an object and a click to end it.

1. Load the Paint program into your computer.

2. Lines and curves are generally drawn by first clicking the beginning point, dragging the mouse cursor to the point where the line is to end, and then releasing. Select the **Line** tool and draw a line anywhere. You may also select a different thickness, or weight, for the line. See Figure 6.2 for examples of line weight selection tools.

FIGURE 6.2

Examples of line weight selection tools

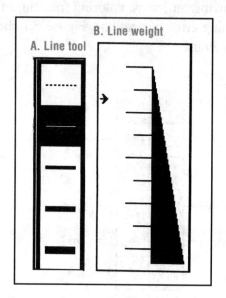

3. Select a different line weight.

4. Now try drawing a perfectly horizontal line; then a perfectly vertical line.

5. Some Paint programs have *constrain* keys that make perfectly horizontal and vertical lines very easily. Try holding down the **Shift** key while drawing a line; also try the **Alt** and **Ctrl** keys. Try combinations of these keys as well.

6. Select the **Curve** tool and draw a line. Pull the cursor around and watch what happens to the line. Click once and move the cursor again, then click again. **Bezier curves** are lines that can be bent after their end points have been established. This is accomplished by manipulating control points relative to the end points. Some programs will not support this function. If yours does not, proceed to the next section.

Now you will begin drawing. This activity involves the use of rectangles (hollow and filled), circles and ellipses (hollow and filled), and lines. You also will use the fill function and some of the editing functions: the eraser and pixel editing. If you make a mistake, read the section below on Correcting Errors before you change tools.

1. First, find the menu option that clears the screen; on some programs, this option is **Clear**; on others, **New**.

2. Select the **Box/Rectangle** tool and a fine line weight. Draw a small hollow rectangle near the upper-right of the screen, as shown in Figure 6.3.

FIGURE

6.3

Box/Rectangle tool

3. In the **Element** menu, select a fill pattern (your choice) to use for drawing a filled rectangle. If you choose **None**, it will be a transparent fill pattern, and any image underneath will show through it.

4. Now draw the filled rectangle, using a black outline, closer to the bottom left of the screen, and a bit larger than the first rectangle (see Figure 6.4), but with the same proportions. Draw this one so that it slightly overlaps the first rectangle.

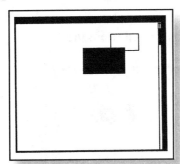

FIGURE

6.4

Clear rectangle and filled rectangle

5. Select the **Line** tool and connect the three exposed corners of the "rear" (first) rectangle with the corresponding three corners of the "front" (second) one (see Figure 6.5).

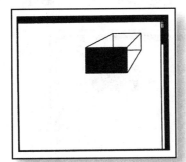

FIGURE

6.5

Clear rectangle and filled rectangle connected by three lines

6. Select the **Eraser** tool and erase most of the left and bottom side of the "rear" rectangle (see Figure 6.6).

FIGURE 6.6

Left and bottom sides of clear rectangle erased

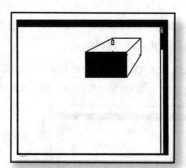

7. To clean up the corners, use the pixel editing function of your program and enlarge each of the corners. Then delete the unwanted pixels (see Figure 6.7).

FIGURE 6.7

Enlarging an image to see pixels that need to be erased

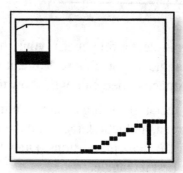

8. Select a new pattern (or color), select the paintbrush (**Fill with Color**) tool, and fill the "top," as shown in Figure 6.8.

FIGURE 6.8

Top filled using *Paintbrush (Fill with Color)* tool

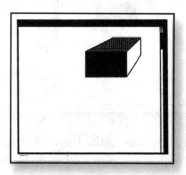

9. Select a different pattern and fill the "side" (see Figure 6.9).

FIGURE 6.9

Sides filled with different color than top, using the *Paintbrush (Fill with Color)* tool

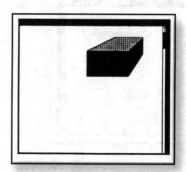

10. Select the **Ellipse** tool and draw three overlapping ellipses with different fill patterns, as shown in Figure 6.10. (*Note:* Some draw programs refer to the **Ellipse** tool as the **Circle/Ellipse** tool.)

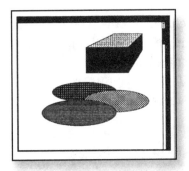

Circles drawn with *Ellipse* tool using different colors (shades)

11. Find the editing tool that allows you to surround an area with an irregularly-shaped line prior to moving or copying that area; with PC Paintbrush, it's the **Scissors**; with Windows Paint, it's the **Free-Form Select**. Surround the block you drew (see Figure 6.11) and move the object on top of the ellipse (opaque).

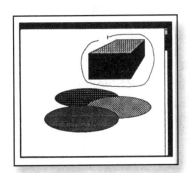

Selecting the rectangular box using the *Free-Form selection* tool

12. Find the **Select** tool (the one that draws a dashed-line rectangle), surround the artwork, and find the menu command that will "flip" the image (change the left side to the right and right to left). See Figure 6.12.

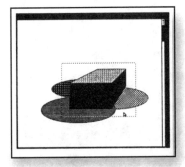

Selecting the rectangular box using the *Select* tool

13. Try the **Flip vertical** function.

14. Saving this image is optional.

Correcting Errors Though the editing functions for your particular bitmapped Paint program may differ slightly from the descriptions below, the primary functions are **Cutting/Copying/Pasting**, **Erasing**, **Undo**, and **Pixel Editing**.

Provided you have not changed tools, you can undo your last action by clicking **Undo** in the **Edit** menu. This will undo *all* actions performed with the current tool since the last tool change.

Selecting the **Eraser** will allow you to "rub out" any image and restore that area to the currently selected background color.

Optimizing Resolution

To achieve the best possible resolution on a laser printer at 300 dpi, you must import the image into an area corresponding to the actual pixel width and height of the file. More specifically, if you have created an image in Paintbrush, the default file size is 720 by 348 pixels. Each of these numbers divided by 300 (300 dpi being the resolution of a laser printer) will yield the recommended size in inches, or 2.4 by 1.16 inches. If you want to produce a larger image, use integer multiples (200 percent, 300 percent, 400 percent). If you want to reduce the image, use a factor of two (½ size, ¼ size, and so on).

If a bitmapped image consists of four dots (2 dots by 2 dots), the image can be scaled down once, at 50 percent of its size, which then resolves the four dots into one (see Figure 6.13). Reducing it by 75 percent does not work because the screen cannot display 1½ pixels; it displays either 1 or 2—nothing in between. If the image consists of a block (8 dots by 8 dots), the image may be scaled down either 50 percent or 25 percent without problems in resolving the pixels (see Figure 6.14).

FIGURE 6.13

Scaled down bitmapped image at 50%, going from 4 dots to 1 dot

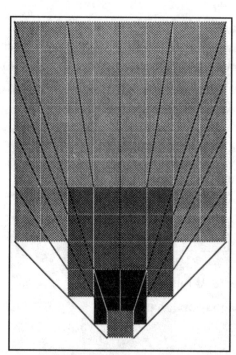

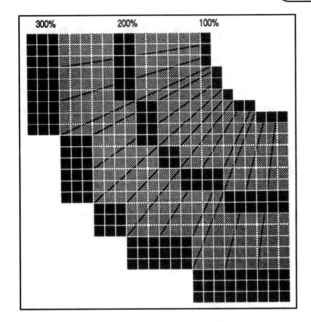

FIGURE 6.14

Scaling down a bitmapped image
The dots at 200% are about one-half the number of dots under 300%. Dots under 100% are about one-fourth the number of dots under 300%.

On the other hand, if you enlarge a bitmapped image, any edges not composed of vertical or horizontal lines appear jagged. Again, the problem of resolving a single pixel into multiple pixels can be accommodated only by enlarging by integer multiples of the original size (i.e., 200 percent, 300 percent, 400 percent). If you use other than integer values for enlargement, the jaggedness of the edges is aggravated to the point of being undesirably irregular (see Figure 6.15).

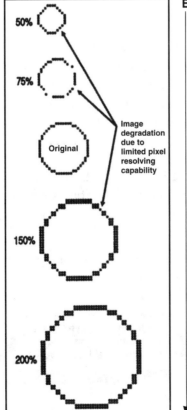

FIGURE 6.15

Enlarging a bitmapped image, making lines appear jagged

OBJECT-ORIENTED DRAWING PROGRAMS

This section of the chapter provides guidelines that can be used with any basic object-oriented drawing program. Since PageMaker utilizes different graphics environments (Windows and Macintosh, respectively) and since these environments import different object-oriented file formats, this section is designed to be *generic* rather than program-specific.

Advantages of Object-Oriented Graphics

The primary advantage of object-oriented graphics over bitmapped graphics is that object-oriented graphics are resolution-independent.

Screen-Aspect Ratio The various pixel shapes and screen resolutions available for IBM/compatible systems do not affect the printed output of object-oriented graphics, whether laser-printed or imageset. In other words, the screen image may be at variance with true WYSIWYG. For example, a circle drawn in an object-oriented program may look slightly elliptical on a screen that does not have square pixels—but it will print as a true circle.

Resolution and File Size Object-oriented graphics can be scaled to any size within a page assembly program, and type used in them is generally acceptable for desktop publishing. Object-oriented files are generally smaller than comparable bitmapped files since the object-oriented files contain formulas for geometric shapes and fill patterns rather than a map of pixels.

Attribute Functions

All object-oriented programs have certain functions in common: the ability to create geometric objects (circles, arcs, rectangles, polygons), to edit them (change their dimensions), and to assign attributes to them (line style and thickness, fill patterns). Unlike bitmapped Paint programs, these attributes are assigned to the object itself and therefore can be altered at any point when the objects are being drawn or edited.

Group Functions

In an object-oriented drawing program, the objects themselves can likewise be addressed separately and given attributes relative to other objects. Three basic object-oriented group functions frequently used to create drawings are *layering*, *combining*, and *aligning*.

Layering When objects are layered, the top object(s) "cover up" the objects beneath them (see Figure 6.16).

FIGURE 6.16

Layering objects

black type layered on a
20% screened box,
layered on a black box.

Combining When objects are combined, they act as a single unit and can be moved and assigned attributes independently of other objects or combined units (see Figure 6.17).

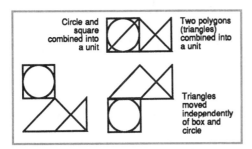

FIGURE
6.17
Combining objects

Aligning Objects may be aligned horizontally at the left, center, or right, and they may be aligned vertically at the top, center, or bottom (see Figure 6.18).

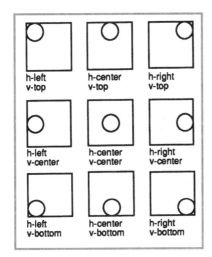

FIGURE
6.18
Aligning objects

Using Object-Oriented Graphics: Drawing a Traffic Light

You will now draw a traffic light by using the **Circle-creation** tool, the **Arc-creation** tool, and the **Rectangle-creation** tool. The group functions include layering of the arcs above the circles, combining the arc and circle into a unit, and aligning the arcs and circles vertically in the center of a rectangle.

Create the Lamp Portion

1. Open your drawing program.
2. Create a circle (see Figure 6.19).

FIGURE
6.19
Drawing a circle

3. Assign a 2-point outline to the circle (see Figure 6.20).

FIGURE

6.20

Assigning a 2-point line to the circle

4. Assign a 40 percent screen fill to the circle (see Figure 6.21).

FIGURE

6.21

Assigning a 40% fill to the circle

Create the Lamp Hood

1. Draw an arc above the circle with a 1-point outline (see Figure 6.22).

FIGURE

6.22

Drawing an arc over the circle

2. Duplicate the arc (see Figure 6.23).

FIGURE

6.23

Duplicating the arc

3. Reflect the arc and move it into position to create a semicircle (see Figure 6.24).

FIGURE

6.24

Reflecting the arc

4. Group the semicircle and fill it with white (see Figure 6.25).

FIGURE 6.25

Grouping the reflected arcs to create a semicircle and filling it with white

5. Draw a line connecting the endpoints of the semicircle. This is your lamp hood (see Figure 6.26).

FIGURE 6.26

Drawing a line to connect endpoints of the semicircle to create a lamphood

Duplicate the Lamps and Hoods

1. Duplicate the lamp and hood, and position the duplicate below the original. Align them vertically at the center (see Figure 6.27).

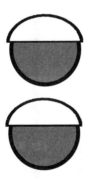

FIGURE 6.27

Duplicating the lamphood

2. Change the fill pattern of the second lamp to an 80 percent screen (see Figure 6.28).

FIGURE 6.28

Changing the lower lamphood's fill pattern

3. Duplicate the second lamp and hood and position the new lamp and hood below the second one (see Figure 6.29).

6.29

Duplicating the lamp-hood and changing the fill, one more time

4. Align them vertically at the center and change the fill pattern of the third lamp to a 20 percent screen.

5. Draw a rectangle with a 4-point outline around the three lamps and hoods and align all vertically at the center (see Figure 6.30).

6.30

Vertically aligning the lamphoods and drawing a rectangle around them

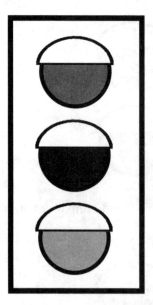

6. Save the file.

Using Object-Oriented Graphics: Drawing a Stop Sign

You will now draw a stop sign by first creating a template to help you draw an octagon with the **Polygon** tool. Then you will type characters that will be reversed and layered over the octagon.

Creating a Template and Tracing

1. Draw a 2" x 2" square with a transparent fill (no fill). (See Figure 6.31).

FIGURE
6.31
Drawing a square

2. If your program is not capable of making 45-degree rotations, skip to item 4. If your program is capable of making 45-degree rotations, duplicate the square and rotate it 45 degrees, lining up the midpoints of the square's sides with the corners of the rotated diamond (see Figure 6.32).

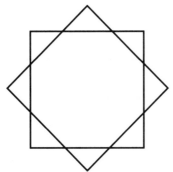

FIGURE
6.32
Drawing and rotating a square at 45°

3. Use the **Polygon** tool with a 2-point outline to trace the octagon shape inscribed in the superimposed square and diamond. Now skip to item 1 in the next section: "Delete the Template and Layer Type."

4. If your program is not capable of 45-degree rotations, draw parallel vertical lines intersecting the top and bottom of the square at 5/8" from the corners (see Figure 6.33).

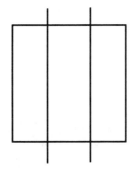

FIGURE
6.33
Drawing parallel vertical lines through a square

5. Draw parallel horizontal lines intersecting the left and right sides of the square at 5/8" from the corners (see Figure 6.34).

FIGURE
6.34
Drawing horizontal lines through a square

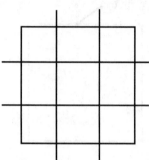

6. Use the **Polygon** tool with a 2-point outline to create an octagon shape, connecting the intersections of the resulting grid (see Figure 6.35).

FIGURE
6.35
Drawing an octagon shape with a polygon tool

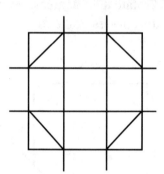

Delete the Template and Layer Type

1. Delete the template—the two squares or the square and grid (see Figure 6.36).

FIGURE
6.36
The stop sign outline

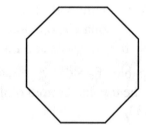

2. Type in the word "stop"—using 36-point Helvetica bold, all caps. Center the word vertically and horizontally in the octagon (see Figure 6.37).

FIGURE
6.37
Typing the word "STOP" in the sign outline

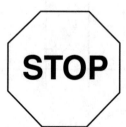

3. Fill the octagon with solid black (see Figure 6.38).

FIGURE **6.38**
Filling the stop sign with black

4. Select the type, specify it as white, and layer it on top of the black octagon (see Figure 6.39). The effect is reversed type, as discussed in chapter 5.

FIGURE **6.39**
White (reversed) text

5. Save the file.

CHECKING YOUR UNDERSTANDING

Paint Questions.

1. List two advantages of using bitmapped graphics in a publication.
2. List two disadvantages of using bitmapped graphics in a publication.
3. List three things common to all bitmapped graphics programs.
4. Explain the term *weight* in relation to a line (rule).
5. How does the **Undo** function work in a Paint program?

Draw Questions.

1. List two advantages of using object-oriented graphics in a publication.
2. Describe a transparent fill pattern.
3. Describe layering.
4. Describe combining.
5. Describe aligning.

APPLYING DESIGN PRINCIPLES

Exercise 1 Using Paint Software to Create Graphics

Create the image shown in Figure 6.40. (*Note:* Instead of drawing each one individually, try creating each element of this figure first as a hollow form, then copy, fill, flip, and rotate it as needed.)

FIGURE

6.40

Exercise 1, Using *Paint*

Exercise 2 Using PageMaker to Create Graphics

Create one or all of the images shown in Figure 6.41. All of them were created using PageMaker's **Circle** or **Box** tools and the **Line** and **Fill** commands from the **Element** menu. Use the **Send to front** and **Send to back** commands to layer the items as they are drawn.

1. Create a new document with 1" margins.

2. The two boxes, A and B, in Figure 6.41 could be used as borders on a page. They are two boxes; one slightly smaller than the other and is filled with paper. The box layered on the bottom has a fill pattern.

FIGURE

6.41

Images created with PageMaker's *Circle* and *Box* tools and *Line* and *Fill* commands

A.
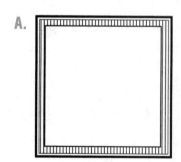

B.
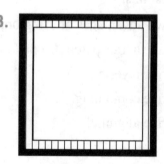

3. Figure 6.41C has a large letter layered on a white (paper-filled) circle. Both are layered on a box with 40% filling.

4. Figures 6.41D and 6.41E are the same, except that the lines around the boxes and circles have been changed to **None** in Figure 6.41E.

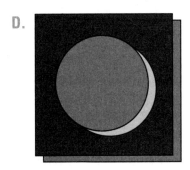 

5. Figure 6.41F contains various combinations of the box, line and fill patterns. There are two dashed lines, 12-point size, and a box filled with a diagonal pattern combined to create the decorative border.

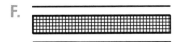

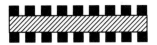

Exercise 3 Analyzing Object-Oriented Graphics

Analyze the examples of object-oriented graphics shown in Figures 6.42, 6.43, and 6.44. Use the following chart to specify how the variations were made from the originals. If you understand how these samples were made, create them yourself using the same principles.

ATTRIBUTE TABLE

Layering: Describe as layer 1 (top), layer 2 (next to top), etc.

Alignment*: h-left v-top   h-center v-top   h-right v-top
             h-left v-center   h-center v-center   h-right v-center
             h-left v-bottom   h-center v-bottom   h-right v-bottom

* h = horizontal; v = vertical

Rotation: Left or right

Scaling: Enlarged or reduced; proportional or disproportional (taller or wider)

a)   Circle and Rectangle Variations

Layering: White circle: _____

           White rectangle: _____

Alignment: White circle and rectangle: _____

Layering: White circle: _____

           Black circle: _____

           Black rectangle: _____

Alignment: White and black circle: _____

           White circle and black rectangle: _____

Layering: White circle: _____

           Black circle: _____

           White rectangle: _____

           Black rounded rectangle: _____

FIGURE 6.42
Circle and rectangle variations

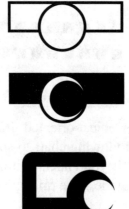

b) Lines and Variation

Layering: Thick grey lines:_____

Thin grey lines:_____

Black lines: _____

Rotation:_____

Scaling: _____

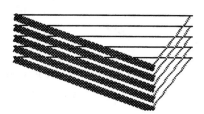

FIGURE 6.43 Line variations

c) Bars and Variation

Layering: Grey bars: _____

White bars: _____

Alignment: Grey bars: _____

White bars: _____

Black bars: _____

Rotation: Grey bars: _____

White bars (made black): _____

Scaling: All bars: _____

FIGURE 6.44 Rectangle variations

Exercise 4 Recreating a Graphic

Use a drawing program or PageMaker's **Circle** and **Box** tools to recreate the finished (third) graphic in Figure 6.42 in Exercise 3.

a) Create a new document with 1" margins.

b) Using the rulers as a guide, draw a rectangle that is 4.5" x 1".

c) If you are drawing in PageMaker, drag the vertical ruler guides onto the page to assist with the placement of the circle. Draw a circle to be layered on top of the rectangle, and fill it with white. Place it as shown in Figure 6.42 (the first graphic).

d) Draw and fill with black a second, smaller circle to be layered on top of the first circle. Go to **Stroke** in the **Element** menu, and select **None**. Align the black and white circles as you see in the second graphic in Figure 6.42.

e) Draw a black rounded rectangle to be layered to the back of all the other objects. What must you do to the initial rectangle in order for this graphic to look like the finished (third) Figure 6.42?

Exercise 5 Creating Your Own Graphic

Design and create a graphic that incorporates the initials of your name. (*Note:* Use layering, alignment, or rotation.)

part

4

Page
Assembly

PRINCIPLES
of Page
Assembly

Typeface

Typeface

This chapter discusses word processing concepts and how to assemble a document.

Upon completion of this chapter | **you will be able to**

- define word processing terminology
- explain the difference between text entry for desktop publishing and text entry for word processing
- format text with indentation commands and tabs
- identify the application of codes in type specifications
- define style sheets
- use ASCII formatted files in word processing, data processing, and PageMaker
- perform text functions with both text characters and text blocks
- fine-tune a page layout by adjusting word spacing, hyphenation, and page and column breaks
- set pointers to source files
- embed copies of word processing and graphics files

Word processing is the most popular computer application in the business world. Many word processing programs can accept imported graphics and permit the user to specify type. These programs can be used for the production of most office documents. For more complex publications that require the more flexible image and typographic controls of a page assembly program, a word processor is still the best tool for the preliminary preparation of text because all word processing programs can do the following:

- Create computer files that can be easily edited by writers and editors and then can be transferred over electronic networks or by disk in the universal ASCII format.

- Automate text entry and editing tasks more efficiently than page assembly programs.

- Automate text formatting tasks—such as the specification of indentations, alignments, and tabulation—for writers and editors who are not familiar with page assembly programs.

Some word processors also:

- Enable the desktop publisher to specify type and to automate this task with style sheets.

- Have features such as glossaries and spell-checkers that facilitate the speed and accuracy of text entry.
- Have authoring tools, such as automatic outlining and table of contents and index generators, that help the writer, editor, and/or desktop publisher to organize text.

WORD PROCESSING FOR THE DESKTOP PUBLISHER

Before using a word processor to prepare text for a page assembly program, the desktop publisher should be aware of which elements can be transferred. A word processing program is said to be *supported* by a page assembly program if all or most of the formatting and type specifications done in the word processor can be imported into the page assembly file.

PageMaker has filters for importing text from specific word processing programs. The filters make it possible to transfer all the formatting from the word processing file; however, they do so with mixed results. For example, PageMaker will strip out indentations and alignments from word processing files. Hence, there is no reason to create these specifications in a word processing file, because they cannot be transferred. Instead, codes must be used to indicate formatting. For the preparation of style sheets for type specifications, the word processing tasks differ from program to program, as explained in a later section of this chapter, under *Specifying, Tagging, and Coding Type.*

If a word processing program is not supported by a page assembly program, text entered and edited in the word processor can be saved in the ASCII format for importation into a page assembly program. When preparing files that will be imported into a page assembly program via ASCII, you should *not* format the text nor specify type in the word processing program, because text formatting and type specification *cannot* be transferred. With ASCII text files, these tasks must be done with the text tools in the page assembly program.

Word Processing Features and Terminology

All word processing programs have common features that automate text entry and text editing. These are the cursor; word wrap; scrolling; selecting, deleting, and duplicating; and search and replace.

The Cursor The **cursor** is a flashing bar or block that marks where the next characters will be inserted during text entry. The user can position the cursor between typed characters for the insertion of text. As the characters are entered, they push forward the characters that follow to make room on the line. The cursor is also used to select characters for deletion or copying, as described below. Depending on the word processing program, cursor keys and/or the mouse are used to move the cursor.

Word Wrapping **Word wrap** means that as text is entered, the characters automatically drop to the next line when the right margin is reached. Because of word wrap, you do not have to press the **Enter** key within a paragraph. It is important to remember that, in general, the **Enter** key should *not* be pressed except at the end of a paragraph or when the text requires a new line, as at the end of a heading.

Several functions affect the word wrap function. These include hard returns, hard spaces, hard hyphens, and discretionary hyphens.

- When you press the **Enter** (or **Return**) key, you create a **hard return**, as opposed to a word wrap, which is sometimes called a **soft return**. As far as the computer is concerned, a hard return is a character. Although this character normally does not appear on the screen, it will cause a new line wherever it is entered. The use of hard returns may cause problems when text is edited. If characters are added or deleted, or if their length or size is changed, the hard returns will remain where they were originally entered and will cause line breaks in inappropriate places. (See Figure 7.1.)

Hard returns must be used, however, at the ends of paragraphs, in specially formatted blocks of text such as lists, tables, titles and subtitles, and for certain special alignments such as centered text or text that is aligned at the right. Hard returns entered in a word processing program are transferred into page assembly programs, whereas soft returns are not.

FIGURE 7.1

Hard returns
A. A paragraph typed with hard returns, not apparent at the type size and line length shown.
B. Decreasing line length results in incorrect line breaks.
C. Increasing type size results in incorrect line breaks.

```
A In this paragraph, hard return
  characters, keyed with the return/
  enter key, have been inserted at
  the end of each line, as in
  typewriting.

B In this paragraph, hard
  return
  characters, keyed with the
  return/
  enter key, have been in-
  serted at

C In this paragraph, hard re-
  turn
  characters, keyed with the
  return/
  enter key, have been inserted
  at
```

- A **hard space** is a space between words on the same line, indicating that a line break cannot occur between these two words. Hard spaces override the word wrap function that will break lines on the normal, or soft, spaces between words. Hard spaces are used when two words should not be separated, as in dates (January 1, 1999) and names (Ms. Smith). Depending on the word processing and page assembly programs, hard spaces may transfer as hard or normal spaces. Therefore, it is best to keep a list of hard spaces used in a document and check them in the final publication after the word processing file is imported into the page assembly program. (See Figure 7.2.)

> A In this sentence, the name Mr.
>   Doe is set with a normal space.
>
> B In this sentence, the name
>   Mr. Doe is set with a hard space.

7.2

Hard space
A. A normal space causes a word-wrapped line break.
B. A hard space will not wrap over a line break.

- A **hard hyphen** is a hyphen that is part of the correct spelling of a word and should not be eliminated by the word wrap function. Word wrap ordinarily breaks hyphenated words on a normal, or soft, hyphen. Hard hyphens are used when the two parts of a hyphenated word should not be separated by a line break. Like hard spaces, hard hyphens can be transferred from a word processing program into a page assembly program as hard or soft hyphens, so they should be checked in the final publication. (See Figure 7.3.)

> A In this sentence, the fraction 8-
>   1/2 is set with a normal hyphen.
>
> B In this sentence, the fraction
>   8-1/2 is set with a hard hyphen.

FIGURE

7.3

Hard hyphen
A. A normal hyphen causes a word-wrapped line break.
B. A hard hyphen will not wrap over a line break.

- A **discretionary hyphen** creates a break within a word *only* when the word is broken at the end of a line, and *not* if the word appears in the middle of a line (see Figure 7.4). Discretionary hyphens are used to even out the right margin of ragged-right text when the text runs too ragged, or to improve excess word spacing in right-justified text. For files to be imported in a page assembly program, it is best to insert discretionary hyphens in the page assembly program. Discretionary hyphens entered in a word processing program may be imported into page assembly programs as normal hyphens and appear within a word in the middle of a line.

PageMaker has a built-in hyphenation dictionary that automatically inserts discretionary hyphens as text is imported. Words not in the hyphenation dictionary can be hyphenated manually; therefore, it is unnecessary to use discretionary hyphens in the word processing program.

> A Discretionary hyphens are used to
>   hyphenate long words that leave a gap at
>   the end of ragged-right lines, or cause
>
> B Discretionary hyphens   C Discretionary hyphens
>   are used to hyphen-ate   are used to hyphenate
>   long words that leave   long words that leave
>   a gap at the end of   a gap at the end of

FIGURE

7.4

Normal vs. discretionary hyphen
A. A long word needs to be hyphenated.
B and C. The line break is changed. A normal hyphen appears within a word in the middle of a line. A discretionary hyphen does not.

Scrolling When a word processor **scrolls** through a file, it shifts the view of the document on which you are working. Autoscrolling means that as text is entered and approaches the bottom of the screen, the previous lines of text automatically move up to accommodate the new lines. A word processing file is simply one long, continuous set of characters, a section of which you are viewing through the window that is defined by the screen or windowing software. (See Figure 7.5.)

Scrolling
A word processing file is a continuous series of characters, a part of which is visible on the screen display.

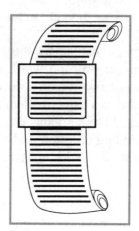

Some word processing programs are page-based, which means that they show a full page on the screen. Most microcomputer-based word processing software, however, simply indicates where page breaks will occur with marks such as dotted lines across the screen. In either case, when characters are entered or removed, the page-break indicator will automatically adjust. Page-based word processors allow scrolling only within a page; with word processors that are not page-based, it is possible to scroll or page to any position in the document.

Selecting, Deleting, and Duplicating Text All word processing programs have some means of **selecting** text, that is, indicating to the program the characters to which the user wishes to apply a function, such as deleting or duplicating. This is accomplished with cursor and function keys, the mouse, or a combination of these.

When text is deleted, it can be saved temporarily in RAM so that it can be inserted elsewhere in the document; in this case, the combination of deletion and insertion functions as a text-move. Text may also be duplicated, left in place, and then inserted elsewhere; in this case, the combination of duplication and insertion functions as a text-copy.

An advantage of electronic insertion and deletion capabilities is that existing documents can be revised easily and quickly, so that whole paragraphs and sections of text can be rearranged. In addition, an entire file or parts of a word processing file can also be inserted into another word processing file, so that a new file can be created by combining two files (see Figure 7.6). Inversely, one file can be split into two or more separate files.

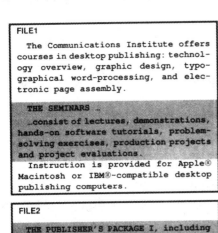
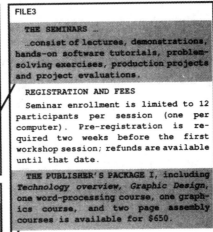

FIGURE

7.6

Combining files
Copy from two different files (FILE1 and FILE2) can be combined to create a new file (FILE3). A single file can also be split into two or more files in this manner.

Search and Replace A **search and replace** function scans the text in a document and finds a string of characters (whether one or two letters, a word, or a phrase) for which the user has instructed it to look. The function then changes the string of characters to another string of characters, word or words if directed to "Replace."

Search and replace functions are useful for writers and publishers. For example, if a standard format has been established for illustrations in a book, all occurrences of the word "Figure" can be searched for and replaced with the characters "Fig." Depending on the word processing program, the search function can be specified as case-sensitive (passing up occurrences of the characters "figure"—all lowercase), font-sensitive (passing up occurrences of the characters *"Figure"*—italic), and sensitive to whole words (passing up, for example, the word "Figures," wherein the six characters being searched do not constitute a whole word). Some word processing programs are also capable of searching for white-space characters such as spaces, tabs, and returns. This is extremely useful for setting up tables.

An automatic search and replace instantly replaces all occurrences of the characters being searched. Often, however, only certain occurrences need to be changed. For example, if all roman numerals are to be changed to Arabic numerals, the program would replace all the "X's" and "I's" in the entire document, without recognizing which are actually independent numeric references and not parts of other words. In this case, the user can specify "whole words" and check each character as it is found in order to apply the replace function only where appropriate.

The search function can also be used without the replace function. This is handy when entering editing changes marked on a hard copy. To move quickly to particular places in the document, such as headings, the user can simply search for specific characters in that heading.

Text Entry for Desktop Publishing

The stylistic rules for text entry in desktop publishing differ slightly from the stylistic rules in typing and nontypographic word processing. In word processing for desktop publishing, typographic considerations play a role in text entry and preparation.

Digits versus Letters People accustomed to typing on a traditional typewriter or with a nontypographic word processing program sometimes make the error of using the lowercase character "l" in place of the "1" (one). In typography, these two characters are different and should be used appropriately. Likewise, the capital letter "O" is distinct from the digit "0" (zero), as shown in Figure 7.7.

FIGURE 7.7
Digits vs. letters

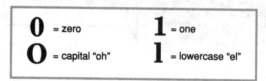

DID YOU KNOW...

Use only one space after end-of-sentence punctuation.

Punctuation In word processing for desktop publishing, as opposed to typing or nontypographic word processing, there should be only one space after end-of-sentence punctuation such as periods, question marks, or exclamation marks. Proportional type is more dense and the characters more closely fitted than in monospaced type, so extra white space at sentence endings is not needed. Two spaces make a block of text appear blotchy since the white space is too large for the type. (See Figure 7.8.)

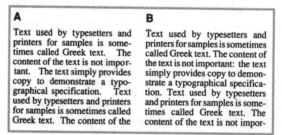

FIGURE 7.8
Spacing after punctuation
A. Extra space after periods
B. Only one space after periods

Typographical Pi Characters **Pi characters** are typographical characters that do not appear on the QWERTY (typewriter) keyboard. They are usually not available on typewriters or in nontypographic word processing programs.

Pi characters that are frequently used in publications include:

" opening quotation mark
" closing quotation mark
— em dash
– en dash
... ellipses
™ trademark symbol
® registered trademark symbol
© copyright symbol
• bullet

A variety of foreign language accent marks (å ç é è Î ñ ø ü), mathematical symbols (× ≥ π ÷), and various other characters are also pi characters.

Some word processing programs enable the operator to enter pi characters directly, either by accessing a dialog box or by using a combination of function keys. In either case, the search and replace function can be used to expedite inserting the pi characters into word processing files to be imported into a page assembly program.

Most pi characters have no ASCII code. If files are to be imported into a page assembly program in ASCII, codes must be used and/or the pi characters must be inserted at the page assembly stage.

Type Styles In typing and nontypographic word processing, underlining is often used to give emphasis to particular words and phrases. In typographic word processing programs and in page assembly programs, however, the availability of italic and bold styles make underlining unnecessary.

In cases when the underline style is desired, it is best formed with set **rules** or **ruling lines**. Rules are geometric lines used as graphic enhancements to type. (The term "rule" is used to distinguish these kinds of lines from lines of type.) Although many desktop publishing programs have an underline style, the use of rules is preferable. Since rules are set separately from the characters, different placements and thicknesses are available. The typewriter underline style generally has just one thickness and runs through the descenders of the characters. (See Figure 7.9.)

> **Underline style**
> A ruling line
>
> **A thicker ruling line**

FIGURE **7.9**
Underline vs. rules

The use of the **Caps Lock** key or **Cap Shift** key in some word processors fixes the characters as capitals, and if the publisher later decides to make them lowercase, they must be deleted and rekeyed. Most word processing and page assembly programs let the user specify all caps as a style. This capability can be applied to any lowercase characters and is used instead of the **Caps Shift** or **Caps Lock** key. This gives the desktop publisher the flexibility to change characters from all caps to lowercase, and vice versa.

Type styles set in word processing supported by a page assembly program are generally transferred intact. The process of saving a file in ASCII, however, strips out all type styles specified in any word processing program. Therefore, if a file is to be imported via ASCII, it is not necessary to specify type styles in the word processing program.

Page Formatting The automatic page formatting features of word processing programs (setting of margins, columns, headers and footers, and page numbers) generally cannot be imported into page assembly programs. It is

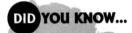
DID YOU KNOW...

When possible, use typographical quotation marks, apostrophes, and dashes instead of their typewriter equivalents. Otherwise, flag them for insertion in the page assembly program.

best to use the default page formats in word processing files that are to be imported into a page assembly program. Word processing files set with wider or narrower margins or columns may have full indents when they are imported into page assembly programs. ASCII does not support page formatting.

The automatic header, footer, and page numbering features of page assembly programs are more appropriate than those used in word processing once the final page layout of the text has been determined. Footnotes may be entered in word processing, but they are usually imported in page assembly programs appended to the end of the file and need to be reformatted.

Formatting Text

The **Tab** key, space bar, and the indentation and alignment commands create white space. On a typewriter, all are equivalent. However, in word processing, the space bar is used only for single spaces between words. In desktop publishing, the formatting of white space follows a hard-and-fast rule:

- Alignments, indentations, and tabs are *always* set with commands and *never* created by pressing the space bar.

In addition:

- For word processing files to be imported via ASCII, it is best if *no* alignments or indentations are set in word processing.

The translation of a word processing file into ASCII changes white-space commands into spaces as if they were entered via the space bar. The white space created by the space bar is not reliable for setting properly formatted type. It is *not* WYSIWYG. Space made with the space bar may appear properly aligned on the screen, but it often will be misaligned in the printout. Moreover, spaces made with the space bar are not fixed. The white space created with alignment commands, indentation commands, and tabs is reliable, more WYSIWYG, and more flexible.

The space bar creates **space characters,** which are characters that appear blank on the screen. Fifteen strikes of the space bar in 12-point type will look like ¾" of white space, but it is actually fifteen characters that take up a specific amount of space. If the type size is decreased from 12 points to 10 points, for example, those fifteen characters take up less space, as shown in Figure 7.10.

Indentation commands and tabs, on the other hand, create white space that can be set at specific sizes. An indentation command or tab at ¾" sets the white space at ¾" regardless of whether the characters are set at 12 points or at 24 points. Thus a rule spanning the white space can be accurately set at any type specification, as shown in Figure 7.11. To increase or decrease the white space, the indentation or tab can be reset.

Formatting with space characters
Spaces are larger in 12-point type than in 10-point type. A 3-pica-long rule spans the space occupied by 15 spaces in 12-point type, but exceeds the space occupied by 15 spaces in 10-point type.

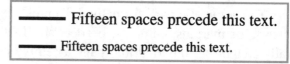

——— Fifteen spaces precede this text.

——— Fifteen spaces precede this text.

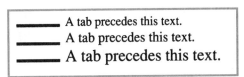

Formatting with tabs
Tabs set a specific amount of space, regardless of the type size.

In addition, all centering should be done through the **Center** command. If space characters are used to center a line, it might appear centered; but should the line length or point size be changed, the line will no longer be correctly centered. (See Figure 7.12.) If the **Center** command is applied to a line of type, that line will remain centered, regardless of any changes made in line length. (See Figure 7.13.)

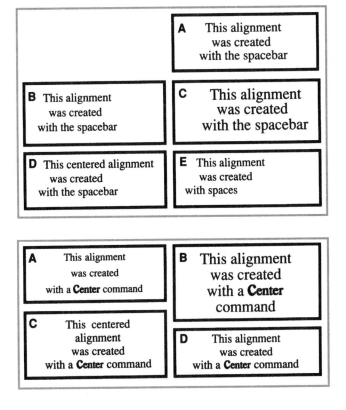

Centering with spaces
A. Center alignment made with spaces.
B and C. Changing type size misaligns the type.
D and E. Insertions or deletions misalign the type.

Center command
A and B. Lines centered with the **Center** command remain centered regardless of type size.
C and D. Lines centered with the **Center** command remain centered regardless of insertions or deletions.

Tabulation Tabular materials are blocks of text set with fixed intervals of white space within lines; tables are rows and columns of text. In a word processing program, the creation of tabular materials entails two steps, as in typewriting: setting of tab stops and entry of tab characters. A **tab stop** is a marker for the position where the tab character will place subsequent type. A **tab character** is a nonprinting character that is entered with the **Tab** key to position the subsequent text at the specified tab stop.

Left tab stops cause the first character of the text following the tab character to align with it; these are the most commonly used tabs. Right tab stops cause the last character of the text following the tab character to align to it; these are often used for page numbers or other elements that need to be aligned at the right. Center tab stops cause the text to be centered under the stop; these are often used to center headings over columns within tables. Decimal tab stops cause the text to be aligned on the decimal point under the tab stop; these are used for aligning columns of numbers. Figure 7.14 shows the use of different tab stops.

Left	Center	Right	Decimal
xx	xx	xx	xx
xxx	xxx	xxx	x.x
xxxx	xxxx	xxxx	xx.x

FIGURE

7.14

Tab stops
Note that the decimal tab stop causes entries with no numbers to align like a right tab.

DID YOU KNOW...

Do *not* use indentation or alignment in files to be imported into a page assembly program via ASCII. Instead, set all text flush left; indentation and alignment must be added in the page assembly program.

As mentioned above the tab character (**Tab** key) causes the text following it to align at a tab stop. Tab characters entered in a word processing program supported by a page assembly program will be imported, and tab stops can be adjusted as needed. Depending on the word processing and page assembly programs, the tab stops may be imported or the page assembly program may set default tab stops. In the latter case and when the line length of the text is changed, the tab stops must be reset in the page assembly program in order to adjust the amount of white space.

ASCII contains a code for the tab character, but some programs do not use it. Because ASCII codes only characters, there is no ASCII code for tab stops. For files to be imported in ASCII, tab stops must be set in the page assembly program, and one should first verify that tab characters transfer. In particular, tab characters are needed for the importation of databases and spreadsheets into word processing and page assembly programs via ASCII.

SPECIFYING, TAGGING, AND CODING TYPE

Typically, final editing changes are entered into the word processing file of a text before page assembly is begun. It is most efficient for editing to be done at this stage because once the text is placed in pages, the insertion or deletion of lines in the copy means difficult page assembly readjustments, especially in long documents.

Since professional word processing programs have sophisticated search and replace functions and keystroke-saving tools, preliminary type specification work can be done in the word processing program. This also gives clients and supervisors a general idea of how the text will look in its final form.

However, specifying type can be done in several ways. It can be done entirely in a word processing program and then imported into PageMaker, or it can be done entirely in PageMaker. The process can also begin in word processing with the insertion of special tags and codes and end in PageMaker with the application of styles to those tags and codes.

Direct Application of Type Specs Since PageMaker has filters for importing word processing files with specifications intact, some of the type specification can be done in a typographical word processor. However, as mentioned earlier, PageMaker tends to strip out indentations and alignments, as well as other kinds of formatting, from word processing files.

Ideally, the actual typeface, font, size, style, and spacing attributes are shown in the word processing printout (see Figure 7.15). However, the word processing printout is only an approximation of how the text will look. Positioning on the page, illustrations, column width, and line breaks are not determined until the word processing file is laid out in PageMaker.

The seminars ...

...consist of lectures, demonstrations, hands-on software tutorials, problem-solving exercises, production projects, and project evaluations.

Instruction is provided for Macintosh or IBM® -compatible desktop publishing computers.

Registration and fees

Seminar enrollment is limited to 12 participants per session (one per computer). Pre-registration is required two weeks before the first workshop session; refunds are available until that date.

A 10% discount is available for registration for three or more workshops, or for three persons from the same company enrolling in the same workshop. Payment must be made in one sum.

The Publisher's Package I, including *Technology Overview, Graphic Design*, one word processing course, one graphics course, and two page assembly courses is available for $650.

The Publisher's Package II, including one word-processing course, one graphics course, and two page assembly courses is available for $500.

Facilities

The Communications Institute computer lab has the following equipment:
- 12 Macintosh
- 12 IBM PC's

FIGURE 7.15

Direct type specification
In the word processing printout, the typefaces, sizes, and styles can be checked.

Even if the word processing file is checked and read as pages with columns and margins equal to the final specifications to be used in the publication, the line breaks and column depths may be slightly different once page assembly is executed. PageMaker has more sophisticated letterspacing and word spacing capabilities than word processing programs. The number of characters per line, and therefore the resulting number of lines, may vary. In general, page assembly programs set characters more tightly than word processors. This may cause some paragraphs to contain fewer lines, and in long documents, whole publications may run to fewer pages. Because of these discrepancies, many desktop publishers find it easier to do all their formatting and type specifying with tags and codes.

Tags and Codes An alternative to the direct application of type specs is to apply external **tags** and **codes** to text in the word processing program, and then import the text into PageMaker. These tags and codes are there to *designate* rather than actually *show* the type specifications. Tags and codes are sets of characters delimited by special characters and embedded in the text itself. (See Figure 7.16.)

FIGURE 7.16

Type specification with tags and codes
In the word processing printout, tags and codes designate the type specifications. In this example, tags are flush left "@xxx=" while codes are set within angle brackets.

```
@heading = The seminars <193>
@body text = <193>consist of lectures, demonstrations,
hands-on software tutorials, problem-solving exercises,
production projects, and project evaluations.
@body text = Instruction is provided for Macintosh
or IBM<190>-compatible desktop publishing computers.
@heading = Registration and fees
@body text = Seminar enrollment is limited to 12 partici-
pants per session (one per computer). Preregistration is
required two weeks before the first workshop session; re-
funds are available until that date.
@body text = A 10% discount is available for registration
for three or more workshops, or for three persons from the
same company enrolling in the same workshop. Payment must be
made in one sum.
@body text = <B>The Publisher<39>s Package I<D>, including
<I>Technology Overview, Graphic Design,<D> one word process-
ing course, one graphics course, and two page assembly
courses is available for $650.
@body text = <B>The Publisher<39>s Package II<D>, including
one word processing course, one graphics course, and two
page assembly courses is available for $500.
@heading = Facilities
@body text = The Communications Institute computer lab has
the following equipment:
@bullet = 12 Macintosh
@bullet = 12 IBM PC's
```

Tags apply to paragraphs—single or multiple lines of text ended with a return character. Because elements such as titles, headlines, and subheads are ended with a return character, they are considered paragraphs. Tags indicate the *function* of paragraphs, not their actual appearance in terms of type specifications. For example, a line of text tagged "@ heading =" indicates that that particular line of text functions as a heading. As such, it may appear in the final publication as 18 point Times bold, or it may appear as 12-point Helvetica bold, depending on what style the publisher has assigned to headings. The style for each tag is stored in a style sheet.

Codes, on the other hand, are applied to single characters or to words within paragraphs. They indicate what the characters *look like*—whether they are bold or italics or underlined—but give no information as to whether those characters are to function as titles or headings or body text, or whatever. Codes are most often used for pi characters and for changing a font in the middle of a paragraph, such as when a word or phrase is italicized or made bold for emphasis. The word processor's search and replace function can be used to insert tags and codes.

Because tags and codes are actual text characters within word processing documents, they may be distracting. Many professional word processing programs have a *hide codes* feature that enables them to display and print out a file with or without the tags and codes appearing, for easier editing and proofing.

In summary:

- Tags indicate function, whereas codes indicate appearance.
- Tags always apply to whole paragraphs of text; codes may apply to single characters or words within paragraphs.

DID YOU KNOW...

In direct application of type specifications (as in PageMaker), codes are attached to characters, but they do not appear on the screen or in a printout since they are not ASCII text characters.

- The type specification of a tag can vary, depending on the style sheet; the type specification of a code is fixed.

Style Sheets

A **style sheet** is computer file that contains the typographic specifications, as defined by the editor or publisher, for different elements of a publication. Once the style of a particular heading, for example, has been decided upon, that style can be recorded in an electronic style sheet and given a name or a **tag**, such as "Heading 1." Style sheet tags can be applied automatically to text characters for quick and consistent specifications.

The use of style sheets is a fast and efficient way to ensure that all related elements, such as titles, headings, and captions, are consistent. All text tagged as "title" in the document will take on the attributes of a chapter title—such as all caps and a larger point size—as stored in the style sheet. This means that each time a title occurs in the document, the desktop publisher does not have to remember or enter the type specifications. It is only necessary to apply the tag "title." (See Figure 7.17.)

Style sheets can be used to set up the attributes of whole blocks of text, such as lists and other special treatments. Style sheets can also contain information about indentation and tabular attributes as well as typeface, font, size, case, alignment, and line spacing.

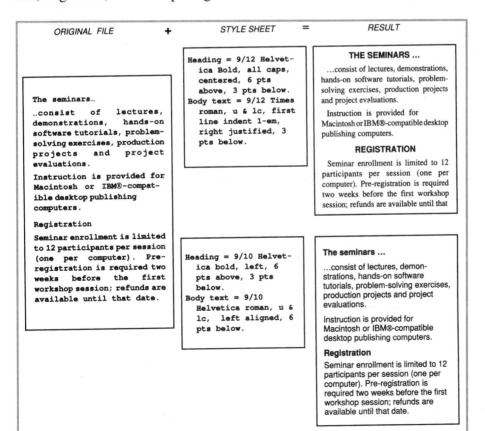

FIGURE 7.17

Style sheets
A word processing file can be associated with different style sheets to produce different specifications and different designs.

Externally Tagged Text The use of style sheets with externally tagged text is a two-stage process. First, tags are embedded in the text; then the file is imported into PageMaker, and the style sheet is applied to the embedded tags. (See Figure 7.18.)

FIGURE 7.18
Externally tagged text

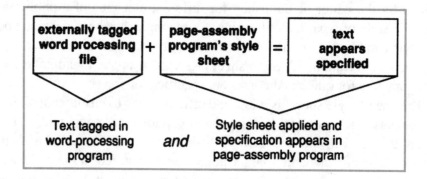

Internally Tagged Text (Direct Type Specs) Tags may also be internally attached to text; that is, not visible as characters on the screen. The use of style sheets in direct type specification is accomplished in one stage: as the characters are tagged, they are immediately associated with style sheet attributes within the word processor or within PageMaker. (See Figure 7.19.) Some desktop publishers prefer to do the specification entirely within a word processing program, such as WordPerfect or Microsoft Word; some prefer to do it entirely within the page assembly program.

FIGURE 7.19
Internally tagged text

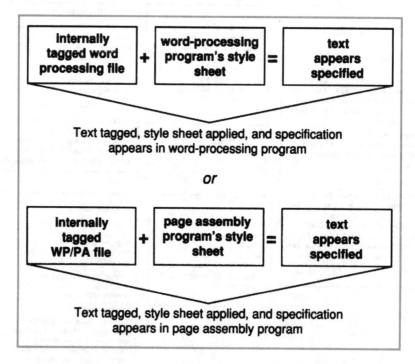

Specifying Type and Inserting Tags and Codes If the desktop publisher is responsible for text entry, the type can be specified or the codes and tags inserted as the text is being entered.

More often, an ASCII file of the manuscript will be provided. The desktop publisher should request that the writer also supply a hard-copy printout in which different levels of heads are apparent or marked. If a hard copy is not supplied, the publisher should make a printout and mark it with the different levels of headings and special treatments. Then the word processor's search function can be used to move quickly to specific words or phrases marked, and the type specifications can be made or the external tags inserted.

Word Processing Tools

Some professional word processing programs have macro and outlining functions that can aid in keystroking, specifying type, and/or the insertion of tags for style sheets.

Macros   A **macro** records and automatically plays back keystrokes and mouse actions. A macro might contain numerous keystrokes that are invoked with one or two special keys, such as **Function** keys or combinations of **Ctrl**, **Alt**, and **Command** keys. A macro that requires simple playback of keystrokes, without mouse movements or special conditions, is sometimes called a **glossary.** In this book, a glossary was used to bring up (invoke) the phrase "desktop publishing" and insert it into the text. Instead of typing 18 characters (d-e-s-k-t-o-p p-u-b-l-i-s-h-i-n-g) at each occurrence of the phrase, two keystrokes were used to invoke the full phrase.

There are usually two steps for setting up a macro: the keystrokes (and mouse actions) to be made into a macro are recorded, and the playback (invoke) keys are designated. The use of a macro entails simply pressing the invoke keys. Macros not only speed up keystroking tasks, but they also ensure accuracy if they are used properly. Macros are very useful for inserting external tags and codes, since the tag and code formats are very specific and if miskeyed will not have the proper effect when associated with a style sheet.

Outline View   Some word processing programs, or utilities that can be used with popular word processors, enable the desktop publisher to view the document in outline form. An outline shows only the different levels of headings and first lines of paragraphs and collapses the body text under them (see Figure 7.20).

```
@heading = The seminars <193>
@body text = <193>consist of lectures…
@body text = Instruction is provided…
@heading = Registration and fees
@body text = Seminar enrollment is…
@body text = A 10% discount is…
@body text = <B>The Publisher<39>s…
@body text = <B>The Publisher<39>s…
@heading = Facilities
@body text = The Communications…
@bullet = 12 Macintosh
@bullet = 12 IBM PC's
@bullet = Four LaserWriter Plus
```

FIGURE 7.20

Outline view
The outline view collapses text under headings and shows the headings and the first lines of paragraphs.

For long documents, this view can make the direct application of style sheets and the tagging of major and minor headings easier, since all the headings can be seen at once. This reduces the need for the search function and for scrolling through the document. Using an outline view is also a good way to check the heading specifications or tags. Codes, however, cannot be inserted reliably or checked in outline view. If they are embedded within a paragraph, they will not appear in the outline view.

DATA PROCESSING AND ASCII

Publications often contain tabular material derived from data processing programs: database and/or spreadsheet files. Databases are used for manipulating large amounts of textual information such as mailing lists, student records, and employee records. Spreadsheets are used for the manipulation and calculation of numerical information for tasks such as budgets, statistical analyses, and financial forecasting.

Printed materials often include summary information from databases or spreadsheets. Word processing, compatible database, and spreadsheet files supplied to the publisher in ASCII format can be prepared for publication with professional data processing compatible word processors. The data provided in spreadsheets can also be plotted as charts for illustrations, as discussed in Chapter 5, under *Business Graphics*.

Data Records and Fields

In databases, information is entered and stored in records which contain a specific number of fields. A **record** is a set of data that contains the same categories as every other record in the database; the categories are the fields (see Figure 7.21). In spreadsheets, records and fields correspond to rows and columns of cells. A **row** is a horizontal collection of cells; a **column** is a vertical collection of cells; and a **cell** is the intersection of a row and column.

FIGURE 7.21
A database

	A	B	C	D	E	F	G
1	Course title	Dept	#	Dates		Days	Units	Fee
2	Technology overview	DTP	1	Sept. 5 & Sept. 7	M,W	2	$75
3	Graphic design for desktop publishing	DTP	2	Sept. 6 & Sept. 8	T,Th	2	$75
4	Microsoft Word for PageMaker (Macintosh)	DTP	10	Sept. 12-Sept. 22	M,W	4	$150
5	Microsoft Word for PageMaker (IBM)	DTP	12	Sept. 13-Sept. 23	T,Th	4	$150
6	Preparing WP files for Ventura (IBM)	DTP	14	Sept. 27-Oct. 6	T, Th	4	$150
7	MacPaint, MacDraw, Excel (Macintosh)	DTP	20	Oct. 10-Oct. 17	M,W	3	$125
8	Image scanning (Macintosh)	DTP	21	Oct. 19	F	1	$50
9	PC Paintbrush, Micrographx Draw, Excel (IBM)	DTP	22	Oct. 11-Oct. 18	T,Th	3	$125
10	Image scanning (Macintosh and IBM)	DTP	23	Oct. 20	Th	1	$50
11	Introduction to PageMaker (Macintosh)	DTP	30	Oct. 24-Nov. 2	M,W	4	$150
12	Introduction to PageMaker (IBM)	DTP	32	Oct. 25-Nov. 3	T,Th	4	$150
13	Introduction to Ventura (IBM)	DTP	34	Nov. 8-Nov. 17	T,Th	4	$150
14	Advanced PageMaker (Macintosh)	DTP	40	Nov. 21 -Nov. 30	M,W	4	$150
15	Advanced PageMaker (IBM)	DTP	42	Nov. 22-Dec. 6*	T,Th	4	$150
16	Advanced Ventura (IBM)	DTP	44	Dec. 8-Dec. 20	T,Th	4	$150

records
(rows 2-16)

Portions of large databases and spreadsheets can be compiled into tables by searching for key fields and then grouping records with those key fields. Generally, the material supplied to the desktop publisher will have been compiled into tabular form, but some additional editing of the table may be needed. Records (rows) and fields (columns) can be inserted, copied, deleted, and sorted alphabetically or numerically in ascending or descending order.

Delimiters **Delimiters** are characters that indicate the end of each field and each record. Most data processing programs set commas, tab characters, or space characters as field delimiters, and returns as record delimiters (see Figure 7.22A). For tables within publications, the return character as a record delimiter is appropriate, but field delimiters should be tab characters (see Figure 7.22B).

Course title,Course#,Dates,Days, Units,Fee¶ A
Technology overview,DTP01,Sept. 5 & Sept. 7,"M,W",2,$75¶
Graphic design for desktop publishing,DTP02,Sept. 6 & Sept. 8,"T,Th",2,$75¶
Typographical word processing¶
Microsoft Word for PageMaker (Macintosh),DTP10,Sept. 12–Sept. 22,"M,W",4,$150¶
Microsoft Word for PageMaker (IBM),DTP12,Sept. 13–Sept. 23,"T,Th",4,$150¶
Preparing WP files for Ventura (IBM),DTP14,Sept. 27–Oct. 6,T, Th,4,$150¶
Computer graphics¶
"MacPaint, MacDraw, Excel (Macintosh)",DTP20,Oct. 10–Oct. 17,"M,W",3,$125¶
Image scanning (Macintosh),DTP21,Oct. 19,F,1,$50¶
"PC Paintbrush, Micrographx Draw, Excel (IBM)",DTP22,Oct. 11–Oct. 18,"T,Th",3,$125¶
Image scanning (Macintosh and IBM),DTP23,Oct. 20,Th,1,$50¶

Course title→	Course#→	Dates→	Days→	Units→	Fee¶	B
Technology overview→	DTP01→	Sept. 5 & Sept. 7→	M,W→	2→	$75¶	
Graphic design for desktop publishing→	DTP02→	Sept. 6 & Sept. 8→	T,Th→	2→	$75¶	
Typographical word processing¶						
Microsoft Word for PageMaker (Macintosh)→	DTP10→	Sept. 12–Sept. 22→	M,W→	4→	$150¶	
Microsoft Word for PageMaker (IBM)→	DTP12→	Sept. 13–Sept. 23→	T,Th→	4→	$150¶	
Preparing WP files for Ventura (IBM)→	DTP14→	Sept. 27–Oct. 6→	T, Th→	4→	$150¶	
Computer graphics¶						
MacPaint, MacDraw, Excel (Macintosh)→	DTP20→	Oct. 10–Oct. 17→	M,W→	3→	$125¶	
Image scanning (Macintosh)→	DTP21→	Oct. 19→	F→	1→	$50¶	
PC Paintbrush, Micrographx Draw, Excel (IBM)→	DTP22→	Oct. 11–Oct. 18→	T,Th→	3→	$125¶	
Image scanning (Macintosh and IBM)→	DTP23→	Oct. 20→	Th→	1→	$50¶	

FIGURE

7.22

Delimiters
A. Commas used as field delimiters. Note typewriter quotation marks around the fields containing commas, as in "M,W."
B. Tab characters used as field delimiters. The → character represents a tab character.

Data processing programs that write ASCII files with spaces as delimiters present special problems for the production of typeset tables. The number of spaces will vary, depending on the character count in each field. It is extremely time-consuming to replace spaces with the proper tab characters in long documents. An automatic search and replace can be used to change multiple spaces into special characters, which are then changed into tab characters. This takes several passes, and when completed, each record must be checked for accuracy.

Punctuation in Delimited Fields When commas, or worse, spaces, are used to delimit fields, it is important to distinguish between commas and spaces within fields and the delimiters themselves. When commas are used to delimit fields, quotation marks are often used to set off an entry that contains a comma, indicating that the comma is a real one, not a delimiter.

When space characters are used as delimiters, the spaces within fields are distinguishable from spaces between fields only by context. Generally, spaces *within* fields are single spaces, whereas spaces *between* fields are multiple. This is why each record must be checked when spaces are stripped out of space-delimited fields.

Preparing Tabular ASCII Files

All database and spreadsheet programs will save files in the universal ASCII format. However, only programs that save field delimiters as tabs (ideally) or as commas (workable, but not ideal)—and *not* those that save field delimiters as spaces—can be easily manipulated by word processing programs.

Three warnings:

1. If the database program delimits with spaces rather than with a special character such as a comma or tab character, the spaces must be stripped out and replaced with a tab.

2. If the database program inserts return characters after every 80 characters, as well as at the end of each record, the 80-character returns must be stripped out.

3. If the word processing program cannot specify the tab character and return character as an automatic replace character, the tabs and returns will have to be manually typed. (Some programs, such as Microsoft Word, can show these characters on the screen and can also search for and replace them.)

In general, the word processor's search and replace function can be used to strip out unwanted characters (quotation marks around internally punctuated records, for example) and to replace nonstandard delimiter characters with tab characters between fields and return characters between records.

Setting Tab Stops Once tab characters are inserted in the proper places, it is the setting of tab stops that makes the database file regain its appearance as a table. It may take several passes to get the positioning of the tab stops right, since each tab stop must clear the longest entry within any column (field) for all records (see Figure 7.23).

The tab stops should be set, as often as possible, to the specifications at which they will be set in the final page assembly program. If they are not, long entries will wrap, causing difficulties in column alignment. If any field is to be type-specified in a larger font (including bold, since bold characters have a wider set width than roman characters), more space will be needed to clear the longest entry. The final tab stops can be adjusted in the page assembly program.

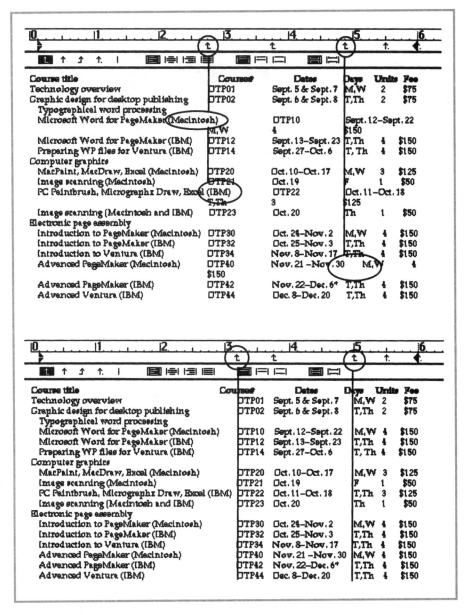

FIGURE

7.23

Setting tab stops
When tab stops do not clear the longest entry, subsequent tab characters on the line are set to incorrect stops and the line wraps inappropriately.

When the tab stops are reset to accommodate the long entries, the tab characters create the proper amount of white space and the lines do not wrap.

Advanced Features Many database and spreadsheet programs have report-writing functions that enable the user to specify punctuation between fields and specify the general format, such as indentations, new lines, and blank lines. For programs that do not have this capability, the well-planned editing of the database file and the use of a word processor's search and replace function can accomplish many of the same basic formatting tasks. The key is *planning ahead.* For example, internal commas and spaces can be inserted as separate fields, and special characters such as the backslash (\) can be inserted as separate fields to indicate the places where return characters are needed in the final copy (see Figure 7.24).

FIGURE

7.24

Inserting format fields
For publication of a database, fields containing format characters can be inserted into the database to facilitate word processing of the file.

	A	B	C	D	E	F	G	H	I	J	K	L	M	N
1	Eastern District	\	i						\		\		,	
2	Franklin School of	\	i	Anderson		Neal	;	Instructor	\	49 Paul Revere	\	Concord	,	MA
3	Boston University	\	i	Beales		Wayne	;	Professor	\	16 Thacher St	\	Boston	,	MA
4	Harvard University	\	i	Bell		Barbara	;	Professor	\	89 Wendell St	\	Cambridge	,	MA
5	Radcliffe College	\	i	Rhiel		James	;	Professor	\	965 Memorial I	\	Cambridge	,	MA
6	Rhode Island Colle	\	i	Deno		Gloria	;	Professor	\	PO Box 6312	\	Providence	,	RI
7	Liberty College	\	i	Fitzgera		James R.	;	Professor	\	288 Brookwood	\	Southington	,	CT
8	University of Conn	\	i	Hamilton		Linda F	;	Associate	\	441 Sullivan I	\	West Reddi	,	CT
9	New School for the	\	i	Hoff		Roger	;	Instructor	\	1775 Sherman &	\	Glen Ridge	,	NJ
10	New Jersey Institu	\	i	Mong		Bill	;	Professor	\	376 Surrey Rd	\	Cherry Hil	,	NJ
11	New Jersey Institu	\	i	Nichols		Judith	;	Professor	\	256 Birdsall I	\	Bridgeton	,	NJ
12	New York Universit	\	i	Parks		David	;	Instructor	\	706 Broadway	\	New York	,	NY

(\) field is for return character	(.i.) field is for index entry	comma field	(;) field is to end index entry

Another feature that enables word processing programs to handle tables well is their capability to copy, move, and specify type in column units as well as line units. Without column-editing features, the table is locked into its current order, and specifying columns of type may entail extensive and repetitive selection of individual words within lines.

Summary of Data Processing and Word Processing Requirements

The database or spreadsheet program must be able to write field delimiters as tabs (ideally) or commas (which can be searched-and-replaced into tabs). An advanced report-writing function can also expedite the preparation of the table for publication. The word processing program must be able to search and replace on tab and return characters. Column-editing functions enable the rearrangement of fields and expedite their type specification within the table.

TEXT FUNCTIONS

Text can be typed directly into the page assembly program and type-specified or tagged immediately. This is appropriate only for short pieces of text within display documents such as letterheads, posters, or announcements.

When dealing with large amounts of text, it is more efficient to import word processing files and, when possible, to do preliminary type specifications or tagging in the word processor. In addition, the word processing file is a better place to do editing. For one thing, professional word processors have spell-checking functions that most page assembly programs lack. And for preliminary type specifications, tagging, and coding of long files, the word processor's sophisticated search and replace functions and advanced tools can automate many repetitive keystroking tasks.

Text as Characters versus Text as Blocks

Whether typed directly or imported, text is handled in one of two general modes within page assembly programs.

- **Text as characters:** for text editing and for type specification. These functions are comparable to word processing functions.

- **Text as blocks:** for the positioning and shaping of blocks of text. These functions are comparable to the functions available for shaping and positioning graphics.

All page assembly programs make the distinction between text as characters and text as blocks. In any page assembly program, the proper mode must be used in order to perform different functions: inserting, deleting, or type specifying text *characters* (or paragraphs), or positioning and shaping *blocks* of text. This is a source of confusion and error for many beginning desktop publishers.

Typing and Editing Text Any typing or editing, including changes to the type specifications or tags and codes in the text, will be stored in the original word processing files if they were imported with pointers (see *Source Files* later in this chapter) or if they are exported from the page assembly program into the original word processing file. The positioning or shaping of the blocks of text, however, does not affect original or exported word processing files.

Positioning and Shaping Blocks of Text Once imported or keystroked into a page assembly program, text becomes a plastic element for layout. Blocks of text can be moved into various positions on the page and from one page to another. Blocks of text can also be shortened or lengthened and made narrower or wider.

In a structured document like a report, newsletter, or magazine, the column measure should not vary for body type. However, the ability to change the line length of titles, headlines, captions, and other flexible elements is a great time-saver. For the design of display documents, the flexibility of the page assembly program in shaping and positioning blocks of text allows for creative experimentation.

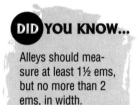

DID YOU KNOW...

Alleys should measure at least 1½ ems, but no more than 2 ems, in width.

Chained Blocks of Text

Text from a word processing file often exceeds the space designated for it on a page. When this happens, the text must be continued in another block, which is "chained" to the first block. When blocks are **chained**, the text automatically flows from one block to the next. Repositioning or changing the *shape* of a block of text does not have any effect upon the sequential flow of the characters themselves as long as the text itself is not edited (see Figure 7.25).

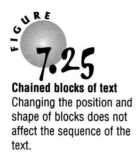

F I G U R E

7.25

Chained blocks of text
Changing the position and
shape of blocks does not
affect the sequence of the
text.

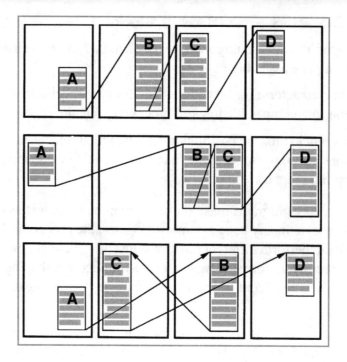

However, if chained text is edited—if blocks of text are moved or new pages are inserted—the entire text may be affected. Whenever a block is lengthened or shortened or when text is inserted or deleted, be sure to check subsequent blocks for appropriate breaks. Also check the last block to make sure that it is long enough to accommodate all the text.

Text can be imported into an auto-extending block. In this case, PageMaker will create new chained blocks until all the text is in place. Text can also be imported into a fixed block, which requires that the user create new chained blocks for the remainder of the text that does not fit in the first block.

Each word processing file imported into PageMaker creates a separate text block. One of the advantages of page assembly programs over word processing programs is their ability to interlace multiple blocks of text on a single page. A newsletter or magazine can run several stories starting on one page, and continue each one on different pages. For this kind of layout, it is best to create separate word processing files for each block of text, since changes made to one continuous file will have the rippling effects described below.

Rippling Effects   When text is chained, changing the shape of a text block and inserting or deleting characters has an impact that ripples through the entire document, as shown in Figure 7.26. This is important to keep in mind when dealing with complex chains of text, especially when the blocks are located on different pages and the rippling effect cannot be seen until other pages are inspected. Intervening blocks keep the same *shape,* even when different characters are pushed in and out of them. The last block is always the one that accommodates text changes in preceding blocks.

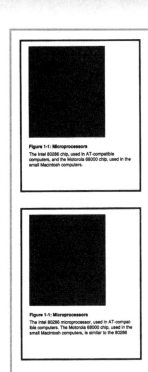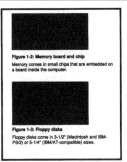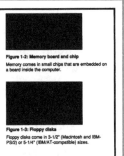

The original file

Inserting text: The characters from the end of the block jump to the next block. This ripples through to the last block.

Deleting text: The characters from the beginning of the next block jump into the first block. This ripples through to the last block.

If several blocks of text are chained and the first block is made shorter, the overflow lines from the first block will be pushed into the second block. This movement will ripple through the chained blocks. The last block will become longer, or, if it is not auto-extending, the last lines of copy may not appear on the page. If characters are inserted into a block of text, the block itself retains its shape and therefore may lose part of a sentence or paragraph. The adjustment of characters into subsequent blocks will ripple through to the last block.

Inversely, if in a chain of text blocks the first block is lengthened, lines from the second block will jump back into it. The movement will ripple through the chain, so that the last block will become shorter. If characters are deleted from a block of text, the block may gain characters from the next one, and so on through to the last block.

All copy in chained text blocks (including text on other pages) must be checked after any reshaping of blocks or text editing that affects the number of characters in a line. Changes made to one block may cause problematic paragraph or line breaks in subsequent blocks.

Tabular Material

Tabular material is among the most complicated forms of text the desktop publisher needs to set. Whether the tabular material is drawn from a database file or originated in a word processing program, most of the preparatory work with tables should be done with the word processor rather than in the page assembly program. Word processors have more sophisticated search and replace capabilities and other column-handling functions.

Simple Tables Most data processing programs produce fields that run on one line only. Tables with short one-line fields are relatively easy to prepare with word processing programs. The word processing file is imported into the page assembly program like any other file, and, if necessary, tab stops are adjusted. Since page assembly programs have more sophisticated letterspacing algorithms for character set widths, the space between fields set in the word processor is sometimes slightly too wide and needs to be reduced.

Complex Tables Complex tables are tables that contain runover (or turnover) lines—fields that must word wrap within columns (see Figure 7.27). These kinds of tables demand special attention. Any adjustment of the column measure will affect the vertical space needed to accommodate the runover lines. The amount of vertical space must clear the entry with the greatest number of lines. Tables with runover lines within columns generally cannot be set reliably with word processing programs and are best composed in the page assembly program.

The internal columns of a complex table can be set in actual columns specified in the page assembly program and/or by specifying varying indentations for the internal columns. In either case, the fields should be delimited not by tabs, but by returns (see Figure 7.28).

FIGURE 7.27

Table with runover lines
Vertical spacing is adjusted to accommodate the longest entries.

Saturday, May 14, 1998¶
11:00 am¶
REGISTRATION¶
1:00 pm¶
WELCOME¶
Roger A. Yockey¶
Executive Director, Pacific Northwest Interfaith Network for Economic Justice¶
Don Comstock¶
President, Washington Association for Community Economic Development¶
1:10¶
OPENING REMARKS: "How do You Give a Cup of Cold Water When the
Waterworks is Busted?"¶
Darel Grothaus¶
Vice President, Seafirst Bank¶
1:30¶
THE NORTHWEST ECONOMY¶
"Overview —Dynamic Changes in our Northwest Economy"¶
Don Hopps¶
Director for Program Planning, Catholic Charities¶

FIGURE 7.28

Fields delimited by returns
For tables with runover lines, returns are used to delimit the fields.

In the page assembly program, the vertical space can be set automatically, or by calculating the number of lines needed for the longest entry. If vertical space must be calculated, it is easiest to use a standard and easily multiplied leading, such as 10, 12, or 15 points.

Using Adobe Table 3.0®

A chart, schedule, list of items, or worksheet to be used in any PageMaker document can be created using Adobe Table 3.0®. It is a separate program that is run outside of PageMaker. A table is created and stored in memory with an extension of **.tbl**. The table is imported into a PageMaker document as a graphic.

Look at Figure 7.29. The table has two major parts: *rows* and *columns*. Rows run horizontally in a table, and columns are vertical. The space created when a column and row intersect is a *cell*. Each cell has an address that gives the location of the column and row designations.

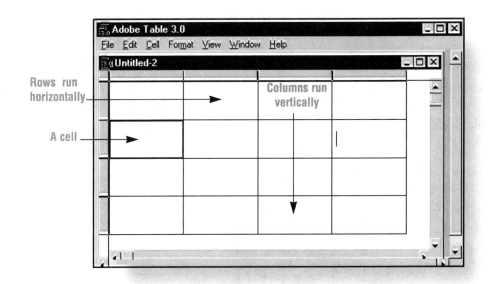

FIGURE 7.29

A typical table

A cell can store text, numbers, or graphics. There is a gutter between the rows and columns in a table that is similar to the gutter between columns of text. You can adjust the gutter width, the number of rows and columns, and the physical size of the table (in inches, picas, and so on).

Adobe Table 3.0 has seven menus, each of which enables you to perform different functions. The menus are similar to those found in PageMaker. The following sections discuss the differences.

File Menu Figure 7.30 shows the **File** menu in Adobe Table 3.0. The major option missing from the **File** menu is the **Print** command. The table must be placed in a PageMaker document before it can be printed. The **Save** and **Save As** options allow a table to be saved as either a file or as a template. The **Export** option sends the table out as a Windows Metafile, which may either be a text or a graphic file. A table can be exported as text, either tab-delimited or comma-delimited text. The **Import** command is similar to the **Place** command in PageMaker.

FIGURE 7.30

File menu in Adobe Table 3.0

Edit Menu The **Edit** menu in Adobe Table 3.0 (shown in Figure 7.31) displays options that are similar to those in PageMaker. The **Copy** command copies a selected group of cells to the clipboard as a Windows Metafile graphic. **Clear** erases information in a cell without copying to the clipboard.

FIGURE 7.31

Edit menu in Adobe Table 3.0

View Menu   The **View** menu in Adobe Table 3.0 is similar to the one in PageMaker. Figure 7.32 illustrates the **View** menu.

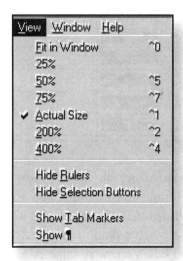

7.32

View menu in Adobe Table 3.0

Cell Menu   In the **Cell** menu shown in Figure 7.33, the **Row/Column Size** command changes the size of the selected column or row. One or more rows or columns can be selected at a time for changing the height or width. You can select an entire row by clicking the shaded row label to the left of the left-most cell in a row. Figure 7.34 shows that the fifth row has been selected. The same procedure works for a column. The second column has been selected in Figure 7.35. When you change a measurement by using the commands from the menus, the size of the whole table is affected.

7.33

Cell menu in Adobe Table 3.0

7.34

Selecting the fifth row

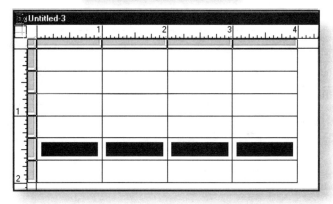

FIGURE

7.35

Selecting the second column

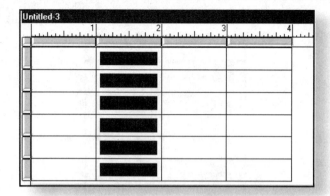

Rows may be inserted using the **Insert Row Above** and **Insert Row Below** commands. Columns may be inserted using the **Insert Column Before** and **Insert Column After** commands. The **Delete Column** command becomes available when a column is selected. The **Delete Row** command becomes available when a row is selected.

The **Group** command connects one or more selected cells and forms them into a single cell. The **Ungroup** command returns the newly formed single cell to the original number of cells.

Format Menu The **Format** menu in Figure 7.36 is similar to the **Type** menu in PageMaker.

FIGURE

7.36

Format menu in Adobe Table 3.0

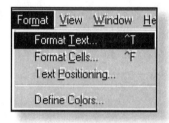

Type specifications are applied to all the text in a cell. You cannot select a single word or phrase and apply a different specification. You can use the **Pointer** tool to select a cell, or you can use the **Text** tool to select the text. The advantage of using the **Pointer** tool is that you can select a group of cells if necessary.

All the text options available in the **Format** menu are also found in the **Text** palette in Figure 7.37.

FIGURE

7.37

Text palette in Adobe Table 3.0

In addition to applying type specifications in the **Format** menu, a variety of different line styles can be chosen for the border. The default is a 1-point border rule around each cell. Figure 7.38 illustrates the border settings in the **Format Cells** dialog box. You see that any of the four perimeters can be chosen. The **Outside** and **Internal** options refer to the lines between each cell within a group. These can be deleted. Figure 7.39 shows two groups of cells. A border has been applied to the perimeter of the first group. The other group of cells has a border applied both around the perimeter *and* to the interior horizontal and vertical lines of the group.

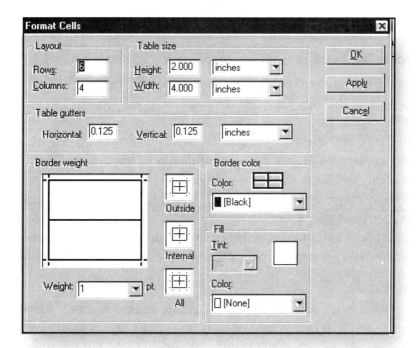

F I G U R E

7.38

Setting borders in *Format Cells* dialog box

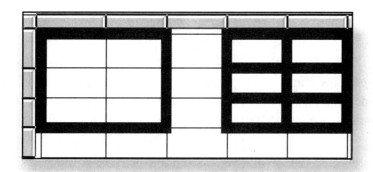

F I G U R E

7.39

Different border styles

The **Color** option under **Border Color** in the **Format** menu refers to different shadings that can be applied to the interior of a single cell or group of cells. Shading can also be applied to alternate rows or alternate columns.

All the border options available in the **Format** menu are also found in the **Table** palette.

FINE-TUNING THE PAGE LAYOUT

Once all the text and graphics are properly blocked out on the page, the pages can be fine-tuned. This includes adjusting the spacing within lines and checking line, paragraph, column, and page breaks.

Since this fine-tuning entails close attention to line and paragraph endings, the copy and layout of the text and graphics should be final at this point. Text editing and the reshaping of blocks of text will change line endings and, therefore, might require that the fine-tuning be redone. These steps should be followed in order, since each step may affect the next:

1. Make letterspacing and word spacing adjustments within lines.
2. Make line break adjustments (hyphenation and justification).
3. Make Paragraph, column, and page break adjustments.

Letterspacing and Word Spacing

The first task in fine-tuning the type is tracking and kerning. Any type that is 14 points or larger (all major headings) should be tracked, and then the individual characters should be kerned as necessary. Printed proofs are needed to check the kerning, since screen previews are not precise enough to show the true proper fit of characters.

If the body text is to be tracked or word spaced, these adjustments should be made as well, since they will affect the line breaks in the publication.

Hyphenation

Most professional page assembly programs have automatic routines that hyphenate text as it is imported or entered. Usually, the hyphenation routines in the page assembly program do an acceptable job, but there are always exceptions. For example, most hyphenation programs will divide *rested* as *re-sted* or, sometimes, *rest-ed*. If the document contains unusual, technical, or foreign words, these words may not be hyphenated correctly.

Ragged-Right Text When long words are not hyphenated in ragged-right text, large gaps sometimes appear in the right margin. The easiest way to determine whether or not a word should be hyphenated is to establish a hyphenation zone about 1/8 to 1/10 the length of the line, as shown in Figure 7.40A.

For lines that fall short of the zone, hyphenation should be used. The long word on the line *following* the too ragged line should be hyphenated. When inserting hyphens in a page assembly program, remember that, at the end of a line, words should be broken with discretionary hyphens (see Figure 7.40B).

If the text is edited, the type respecified, or the shape of the column changed, the line breaks will change. Ordinary hyphenation will cause inappropriate hyphens to appear in the middle of lines but discretionary hyphens will not cause this problem (see Figure 7.40C).

A The recent FCC deregulation of the radio SCA and television VBI spectrum has opened up new profit and service opportunities for broadcasters. | hyphenation zone

B The recent FCC deregulation of the radio SCA and television VBI spectrum has opened up new profit and service opportunities for broadcasters.

C The recent FCC deregulation of the radio SCA and television VBI spectrum has opened up new profit and service opportunities for broadcasters.

FIGURE 7.40

Hyphenation zone
A. The text is too ragged on the right because the word "spectrum" is not hyphenated.
B. A discretionary hyphen is used to break the line.
C. The discretionary hyphen will not appear in the middle of a line.

Right-Justified Text With right-justified or right-aligned text, check for blocks. These result when several consecutive lines end with hyphens. Blocks can sometimes be broken up by tracking and/or word spacing the paragraph (see Figure 7.41). Keep in mind, however, that if hyphens are removed or if the word spacing is increased, lines may become stretched out too much, resulting in rivers and lakes of white space. A block is preferable to that. As an alternative to word spacing, you may kern individual characters within the offending lines. Using prompted rather than automatic hyphenation might also help.

A The recent FCC deregulation of the radio SCA and television VBI spectrum has opened up new profit and service opportunities for broadcasters. Carried along with the main broadcast service, these narrow-band channels are low-cost electronic highways for the simultaneous one-way delivery of data signals to large numbers of dispersed users.

B The recent FCC deregulation of the radio SCA and television VBI spectrum has opened up new profit and service opportunities for broadcasters. Carried along with the main broadcast service, these narrow-band channels are low-cost electronic highways for the simultaneous one-way delivery of data signals to large numbers of dispersed users.

FIGURE 7.41

Block
A. Block (circled)
B. Tracking the type and increasing the word spacing causes the type to be rehyphenated, eliminating the block.

Paragraph Breaks

In page assembly, attention must be paid to how paragraphs are positioned at the top or bottom of a page or column.

Widows As discussed previously, a **widow** is the short last line of a paragraph, left at the top of a page. Widows are usually unacceptable when they are separated from the rest of the paragraph by a column break, and they are always unacceptable when separated by a page break.

The acceptability of widows is often a matter of judgment. One long word on a fairly short measure might or might not be considered a widow. One short word, or worse, part of a hyphenated word on a line by itself, is always a widow. Widows can be eliminated by altering the paragraph with hyphenation, tracking, kerning, or word spacing (see Figure 7.42).

FIGURE

7.42

Widow
A. A widow at the top of a column of text.
B. The widow is eliminated by tracking and reducing the word spacing.

A
What makes desktop publishing different from traditional publishing is that the equipment used is small enough to fit on one person's desktop, and the desktop publishing system provides all the resources needed to prepare and assemble pages on that

desktop.

Hardware and software
Desktop publishing, as defined here, utilizes a microcomputer system that fits on a desk, for WYSIWYG (What-You-See-Is-What-You-Get)

B
What makes desktop publishing different from traditional publishing is that the equipment used is small enough to fit on one person's desktop, and the desktop publishing system provides all the resources needed to prepare and assemble pages on that desktop.

Hardware and software
Desktop publishing, as defined here, utilizes a microcomputer system that fits on a desk, for WYSIWYG (What-You-See-Is-What-You-Get) graphic design and page assembly. WYSIWYG is an interactive mode of computer processing,

Orphans and Feathering First lines of paragraphs that are separated from the rest of the paragraph by a column break or page break are orphans (see Figure 7.43).

FIGURE

7.43

Orphan
A. An orphan at the bottom of the column (circled).
B. The heading set at the top of the column.

A
What makes desktop publishing different from traditional publishing is that the equipment used is small enough to fit on one person's desktop, and the desktop publishing system provides all the resources needed to prepare and assemble pages on that desktop.

Hardware and software
Desktop publishing, as defined

here, utilizes a microcomputer system that fits on a desk, for WYSIWYG (What-You-See-Is-What-You-Get) graphic design and page assembly. WYSIWYG is an interactive mode of computer processing, which requires specialized graphics-oriented software and hardware to process, display and output images and type. Hardware refers to actual physical devices, and

B
What makes desktop publishing different from traditional publishing is that the equipment used is small enough to fit on one person's desktop, and the desktop publishing system provides all the resources needed to prepare and assemble pages on that desktop.

Hardware and software
Desktop publishing, as defined here, utilizes a microcomputer system that fits on a desk, for WYSIWYG (What-You-See-Is-What-You-Get) graphic design and page assembly. WYSIWYG is an

Orphans are usually more acceptable than widows, because they run the full measure of the column (for nonindented paragraphs), or nearly so (for indented paragraphs). Headings without enough body type under them are also considered orphans. There should be as much body type below the heading as the height of the heading itself, including white space. Orphans may be eliminated by reducing the length of the block of text or increasing the length of a previous chained block of text.

Headings that have uneven amounts of space above and below pose problems with baseline alignments of columns. Different numbers of headings in columns will cause the columns to run to different lengths. If the design calls for the text to align at the bottom, short columns can be feathered. **Feathering** is the insertion of small amounts of leading between lines and paragraphs and before and after headings. Alternatively, small amounts of leading may be removed from the long columns (see Figure 7.44).

Feathering
The column baselines can be equalized with feathering—in this case, slightly reducing the leading of the second column. (The same result could be achieved by increasing the leading of the first column.)

What makes desktop publishing different from traditional publishing is that the equipment used is small enough to fit on one person's desktop, and the desktop publishing system provides all the resources needed to prepare and assemble pages on that desktop.

Hardware and software

Desktop publishing, as defined here, utilizes a microcomputer system that fits on a desk, for WYSIWYG (What-You-See-Is-What-You-Get) graphic design and page assembly. WYSIWYG is an interactive mode of computer processing, which requires specialized graphics-oriented software and hardware to process, display and output images and type. Hardware refers to actual physical devices, and software refers to the information (programs) used to control the devices. The combination of hardware and software is called the desktop publishing system.

Like all computer applications, desktop publishing can be seen in terms of three phases: input, processing, and output. These translate roughly to: getting the information into the computer, working on it, and

What makes desktop publishing different from traditional publishing is that the equipment used is small enough to fit on one person's desktop, and the desktop publishing system provides all the resources needed to prepare and assemble pages on that desktop.

Hardware and software

Desktop publishing, as defined here, utilizes a microcomputer system that fits on a desk, for WYSIWYG (What-You-See-Is-What-You-Get) graphic design and page assembly. WYSIWYG is an interactive mode of computer processing, which requires specialized graphics-oriented software and hardware to process, display and output images and type. Hardware refers to actual physical devices, and software refers to the information (programs) used to control the devices. The combination of hardware and software is called the desktop publishing system.

Like all computer applications, desktop publishing can be seen in terms of three phases: input, processing, and output. These translate roughly to: getting the information into the computer, working on it, and

SOURCE FILES

Page assembly programs differ from one another in the way style sheets are implemented and in the way they integrate their **source files**, the word processing and graphics files that are imported into the page assembly program and make up the content of the publication. Two strategies for the importation of these files include:

1. Setting pointers to the source files.

2. Embedding copies of the source files.

In either case, text in imported word processing files can be edited; but some material, depending on its mode of importation, cannot be edited in the page assembly program. Imported graphics, for example, generally cannot be edited. If changes must be made, the original graphics file must be edited either with the original program used to create the graphic or with one that is compatible with the original program.

Page assembly files are frequently transported to other computers or imagesetters. Depending on the mode of importation, different issues arise in transporting the page assembly file, copying the publication onto floppy disks, or transferring it via telephone lines.

Pointers to Source Files

Pointers are either full Windows path names or Macintosh folder names. When files are imported through the use of pointers, the page assembly programs set pointers to the *location* of the original source files. In PageMaker, large TIFF files are imported with pointers. (See Figure 7.45).

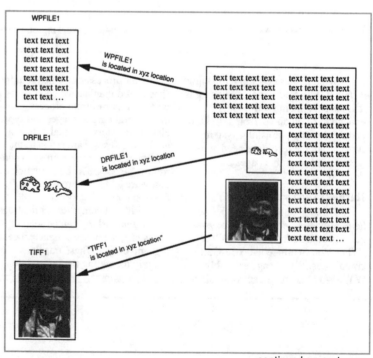

FIGURE

7.45

Import by pointers
In the import process, pointers are set in the page assembly program to all the source files. A representation of the source files is shown in the page assembly file, but the page assembly file actually contains only pointers to the source files.

continued on next page

Figure 7.45, continued

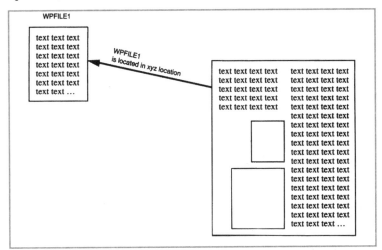

Impact on Origins Because the files imported into the page assembly program are the original files, any text editing, including tagging and coding, alters the original word processing files. Tags and codes do not appear in the screen display of the page assembly program, but if the original word processing file is opened after having been specified in the page assembly program, tags and codes edited or added in the page assembly program will appear in the word processing file. To keep the original word processing files intact, they must be backed up before they are imported into the page assembly program.

Sizing and positioning of graphics, however, do not have an effect upon the original files. As with embedded copies, the elements within imported graphics cannot be edited.

Transporting the Publication When transporting a pointer-based page assembly file, the source files as well as the publication files must be copied onto a floppy disk or transferred along with the page assembly file. This is necessary because:

- The source files cannot be moved from their directories.

- You can't make a straight copy from a hard disk (C: drive) to floppy disks (A: or B: drive), because the pointers in the page assembly file are set to the hard disk (C: drive).

PageMaker will inquire, through a dialog box, about the location of a TIFF file if it cannot find it. When Windows files are transferred via telephone lines, the path names for the source files should be verified on the receiving end.

Embedded Copies of Source Files

In another mode of importation, the page assembly program makes actual duplicates of the source files, which then become part of the page assembly file. This is the importation mode of PageMaker, with the exception of large TIFF files which are imported with pointers, as shown in Figure 7.46.

If text is edited in the page assembly program, the original word processing file is altered. If the original version of the word processing file is needed, it should be backed up and renamed before it is imported into the page assembly program.

DID YOU KNOW...

When working with imported graphics, if possible, keep the image size (through scaling) and frame size (through cropping) of your graphics consistent.

Importation by embedded copies

In the import process, copies are made of the original word processing and graphic files. A pointer is set to large TIFF files. The copies are embedded in the page assembly file. A representation of the TIFF file is shown in the page assembly file, but the page assembly file actually contains only a pointer to the TIFF file.

If text is edited in the page assembly program, it has no effect upon the original word processing file. The edited text can be exported into a word processing file. If the copy is saved under the same name as the original (e.g., WPFILE1), it will write over the original. If the copy is saved under a different name (e.g., WPFILE2), a new word processing file will be created and the original word processing file will be unaffected.

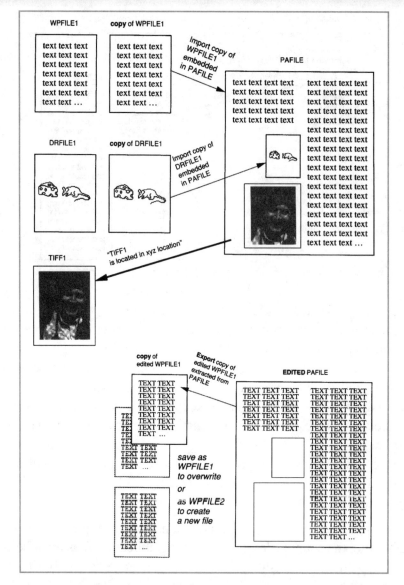

Impact on Origins When duplicates of source files are embedded in the page assembly program file, manipulation of the source files within the page assembly program has no effect upon the originals.

In programs like PageMaker, text editing done in the page assembly file can be reflected in the original word processing file by exporting the text from the page assembly file back into the word processing file. This function extracts another duplicate of the embedded copy from the page assembly file and saves it as a word processing or ASCII file. This function should be used carefully. It is possible to end up with so many different versions of the same word processing file that it is easy to lose track of which is the final version.

Transporting the Publication A page assembly file created with embedded copies of its source files is larger than a pointer-based page assembly file. In fact, it is larger than the sum of its parts. This can cause problems in copying long publications to floppy disks. Compression software such as Adobe Distiller can be used to reduce the file size enough to fit on a floppy disk without changing any contents of the file. In telecommunications or via the Internet, files take a long time to transmit unless they are compressed.

Since the original source files still exist, the total storage capacity needed to store the page assembly and source files can reach the megabyte range, particularly if large TIFF files are used.

CHECKING YOUR UNDERSTANDING

Answer true or false for questions 1-10, and if false, explain why.

1. The **Alt** key creates a hard return in text.
2. Pi characters are typographical characters that appear on a QWERTY keyboard.
3. Decimal tab stops cause the text to be aligned on the decimal point under the tab stop.
4. Tags and codes are the same.
5. A macro records and automatically plays back keystrokes and mouse actions.
6. The symbol ® is a pi character.
7. In databases, fields contain records.
8. A publication can have only one pointer to one source file.
9. A publication can contain an embedded source file.
10. A page assembly file created with embedded source files is larger than a file with pointers to a source file.

APPLYING DESIGN PRINCIPLES

For these exercises, you will need a variety of magazines, reports, newspapers, or pages from a type sample book from which you can clip or photocopy examples. Add the examples to the collection which you started in Chapter 1, Exercise 1.

Exercise 1   Pi Characters

Find a sample of a publication that utilizes pi characters. What are pi characters used to show?

Exercise 2   Tables

Find a sample of a publication that contains text in a table format. Why is a table format appropriate for this information? Is this a simple or complex table? Does the table text have runover lines?

Exercise 3 Typefaces

Find two samples of publications that use two different typefaces for headings and body text. Describe the similarities and differences between the two typefaces.

Exercise 4 Tables of Contents and Indexes

Find a sample of a publication that contains a table of contents and an index. How many levels of headings (indentations) are there in the table of contents? Did the table of contents use leader tabs? Does the index contain single entries, subentries, or cross-references?

Assembling
Documents

In this hands-on chapter, you will apply both PageMaker and word processing software (Microsoft® Word) to create a report.

Upon completion of this chapter you will be able to

- set up a template with PageMaker's **master pages** feature
- create style sheets for consistency in your publications
- edit text with respect to word spaces, special characters, and special character codes
- lay out a report with text autoflow
- scale and position imported graphics with the **Place** command
- fine-tune your text with the **Text Wrap** and **Wrap option** commands
- create special text effects with the **Set Width** command
- use the **Track** command to make spacing adjustments
- add custom paragraph rules to enhance the look of your document
- use **Book** commands to pull your work together
- add finishing touches by including a table of contents, acknowledgments, and an index.

This chapter guides you through the production of the report shown in Figures 8.23 and 8.24 at the end of this chapter. In Chapter 6, you learned about word processing for page assembly. In this chapter, you will use both a page assembly program (PageMaker) and a word processing program (Microsoft® Word) to create a professional looking publication.

PREPARING TO CREATE A REPORT

The cover of the report is a typical *display document*, with variable positioning of elements, including blocks of text, typographical enhancements (shaded boxes and a rule), and an imported graphic (the logo). For the cover, the text will be typed in directly and the boxes and rule drawn in the PageMaker program; the logo—an .eps file provided on the student data disk—will be imported.

The body of the report represents a typical *structured document*, with recurring elements such as the page grid, folios (page numbers), main headings, and subheadings. The graphics will be imported, scaled, and cropped. The graphics are on files provided on the student data disk.

Before going any further, check to make sure that you have and know the locations of all the source files you will need:

- **intro.p65**
- **report1.txt**
- **report2.txt**
- **report3.txt**
- **logo.eps**
- **rfig1-3.tif**

SETTING UP MASTER PAGES

There are several recurring elements in the body of the report which include the page grid, the logo, and a header with page numbers. Each page has two columns with one alley dividing them. The PageMaker **master pages** are templates that contain repeating elements. In publications with printing on only one side of the page, there is only a right master page. However, in publications that have printing on both sides of the page, such as the report, there is a right and a left master page. Whatever is established on a master page is copied to all other pages in the publication.

1. Create a new document with the dimensions and selections shown in Figure 8.1.

FIGURE 8.1

Settings for new document

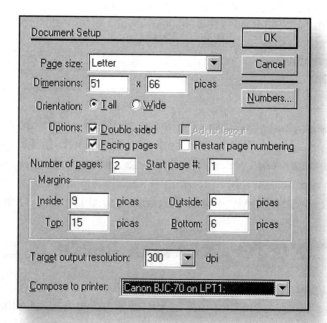

2. Click the master pages icon (the **L** and **R** symbols in the lower left-hand corner).

3. Now establish columns in the publication by clicking the **Layout** menu and selecting **Column guides**.

4. In the **Number of columns** box type **2**.

5. In the **Space between columns** box, type the alley width **1p6** (make sure your measurement system is set to picas).

6. Click **OK**. (See columns in Figure 8.2.)

Master Page Elements

Repeating elements such as the logo and text are established on the master pages so that these elements do not have to be reset or retyped on every page. Likewise, automatic page numbers are established on the master pages. As pages are inserted or deleted from the publication, the page numbers adjust themselves automatically. You can also direct PageMaker to begin numbering the pages with a number other than 1.

Automatic Page Numbers For text entry, it is often best to use **Actual size** so that you can see the characters as they are typed. The page number appears in the header.

1. Drag the **Text** tool to define a bounding box for the automatic page numbers and the header text. The bounding box should be slightly larger than the margins of the page (see Figure 8.2).

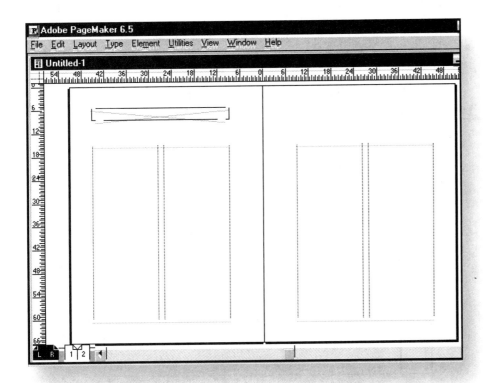

FIGURE 8.2

Master page with text box for header

2. Click an insertion point with the **Text** tool to left align the page number. Alignment of the page number is left by default.

3. Press **Ctrl + Shift + P** (Windows) or **Command + Option + P** (Macintosh).

4. Follow this process to right align the page number on the right master page. (The automatic page number appears as **LM** or **RM** on the master page, but will appear as the appropriate number on publication pages.)

5. Type the header text, **DESKTOP PUBLISHING REPORT**, for each facing page so that it is aligned at the top-right margin on the left page and aligned to the top-left margin on the right page.

6. Specify the type for the header text (**Ctrl + T**) as indicated in Figure 8.3.

Type specifications for header text in report

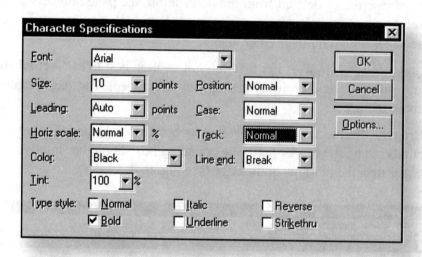

Adding a Graphic Place the **logo.eps** file (used earlier in this book) under each page number. (See Figure 8.4.)

Adding *logo* to the master pages

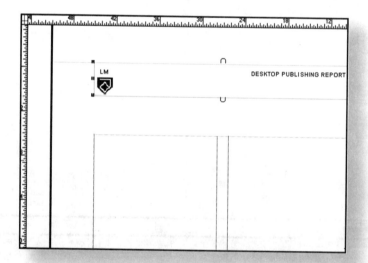

Suppressing Master Page Elements

Click the **page 1** icon to turn to page 1 of the report. The elements set on the master pages have been transferred to this page.

1. In the **View** menu, notice that **Display Master Items** is checked (see Figure 8.5). This choice is made by toggling, like **Options** described earlier. If **Display Master Items** is checked, the elements on the master pages are displayed and choosing this option will hide them, or disable the option. If the option is not checked, choosing this option will display the master page elements, or enable the option.

Display Master Items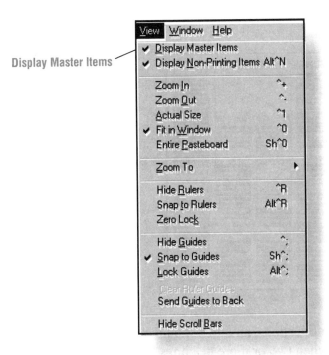

FIGURE

8.5

View menu

2. Select the checked **Display Master Items** to disable it.

3. Save the file as **report**.

CREATING A STYLE SHEET

In any structured publication, certain text elements are standard in design but not in content. These are elements that can be put into the word processing or page assembly program's style sheet: titles, headlines, headings, subheadings, text associated with illustrations, and other elements specific to books, newsletters, and magazines.

Titles (Headlines) and Headings

In books and reports, the publication title and section titles are often given their own separate pages and treated as display pages—that is, set with no headers, footers, or folios. The first page of a chapter is an "opening page;" it has no header, and the folio appears at the bottom of the page.

In magazines and newsletters, headlines should be the largest elements on a page, except for the banner on the front page. (A banner is the title of the publication; it also may include the date, volume, and number.) However, headlines should be kept within a given range (from 18 to 36 points, for example). The largest headlines should be at the top of the page. Headlines should decrease in size as you move down toward the bottom of the page. Magazine and newsletter stories are often in multiple columns at different column depths, or nested. When stories are **nested**, headlines span all columns of a story. They may be one, two, three, four, or five columns, depending on the number of columns in the layout grid, as shown in Figure 8.6.

FIGURE

8.6

Nested stories
With multiple columns,
headlines should span all
columns of the story they
head.

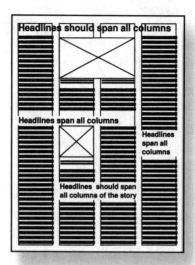

In multicolumned publications, an effort should be made to avoid **tomb-stoning**, which occurs when two or more headings (headlines in periodicals, subheadings in books) run in the same horizontal position on the page. When headings are tombstoned, the reader's eye may skip over the alley and read the two headings as one (see Figure 8.7). If it is impossible to avoid tomb-stoning, a vertical rule can be set between the headings to clearly separate them.

FIGURE

8.7

Tombstoning
Tombstoning can lead to
incorrect readings of
headlines and are less
dynamic than nested
stories.

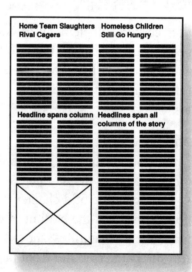

Internal headings within the text can be set on a line by themselves, with more space above than below, or run in on the same line as the text. Different levels of headings should be styled consistently to reflect the outline structure of the document and should be entered in style sheets. In general, head-lines in periodicals and internal headings should not be broken into more than three lines. Separate lines in headings are called **decks.** Headings with more than three decks generally result in too much white in the midst of blocks of body text, as shown in Figure 8.8.

One deck
This is because typography, the foundation of publishing, is a graphics application.

TYPE VS. TEXT

A non-typographical word-processing or data-processing program utilizes characters of one fixed size, positioned within fixed lines on the

Three decks
This is because typography, the foundation of publishing, is a graphics application.

TYPOGRAPICAL FONTS AND NON-TYPOGRAPHICAL TEXT FONTS

A non-typographical word-processing or data-processing program utilizes characters of one fixed size, positioned within fixed lines on the

Run-in
This is because typography, the foundation of publishing, is a graphics application.

TYPE VS. TEXT: A non-typographical word-processing or data-processing program utilizes characters of one fixed size, positioned within

F I G U R E

8.8

Internal headings

Text Associated with Illustrations

Captions are identifications (titles) for illustrations, usually brief phrases. **Cutlines** are full explanatory sentences that describe special points in illustrations. In books and reports, cutlines are sometimes called captions or legends, but these should not be confused with captions as described above, or **key legends**, which are explanatory labels, keyed to colors or fill patterns in an illustration, such as a bar chart in a business graphic. **Callouts** are very brief labels, sometimes boxed, that are attached to illustrations, often with a leader line pointing to a specific part of the illustration (see Figure 8.9).

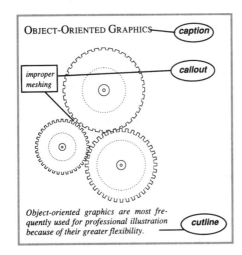

OBJECT-ORIENTED GRAPHICS — caption

improper meshing — callout

Object-oriented graphics are most frequently used for professional illustration because of their greater flexibility. — cutline

F I G U R E

8.9

Text associated with illustrations

Callouts can be created in the drawing program along with the drawing itself, or they may be inserted in the page assembly program. Captions and cutlines are usually set in the page assembly program so that a style sheet can be used. When callouts are created in a drawing program, their final type size should be predetermined so that the size will be appropriate for the document the callouts will appear in.

Captions and cutlines should be set near the illustration. Cutlines should be designed in a manner that distinguishes them from body type. A change of font and a reduction in size are common approaches. In a book or report, captions are used for the list of illustrations.

Tables are often handled in a manner similar to artwork. They are usually imported into the page assembly program as separate word processing files, and, in books and reports, may be listed at the beginning of the publication along with a list of illustrations. The typeface and type size of tabular material can be put into the page assembly program's style sheet.

ADJUSTING THE TEXT

Before the text is imported into a page assembly program, you should review the text in word processing to make final adjustments. This requires careful checking.

Editing the Text

Now you will be using Microsoft Word. The directions are given in MS Word. If you are working in the Windows environment, you can hot key to MS Word and begin preparing the text for the main body of the report.

There are three text files used in the report. They are **report1.txt**, which includes the introductory pages of the report; **report2.txt**, which contains the text that covers basic hardware; and **report3.txt**, which contains the text that covers basic software. The three files will be combined with documents you create: a cover page, a table of contents, and an index.

Text editing includes insertion (entry), deletion, copying, and moving of text characters. First, you must prepare the files so that they can be imported into PageMaker. For this, you will insert certain control codes with a Microsoft Word style sheet. The remaining text for the report has been provided. You will, however, need to make some changes to it.

1. Open **report1.txt**.

2. So that you do not alter the original file, before you do anything else, save the file as **report1.rtf** and in the **Save As** dialog box, select **Rich text format** from the drop down list under **File type**. The **Rich text format** file type will allow the formatting changes to be imported into PageMaker.

You must check the text files for double (or multiple) word spaces, word spaces immediately preceding paragraph returns, and inconsistent em and en dashes.

Multiple Word Spaces Many people are accustomed to putting two word spaces after a period or colon. This is *never done in typesetting*. Extra word spaces in text that is to be imported into page assembly software can create problems. When the page assembly software is determining line endings, it considers the first of a pair of word spaces a valid breaking point when they occur near the end of a line. If the line breaks at that point, the second word space is carried down to the beginning of the next line and causes a visible indent in the left margin.

1. Use **Replace** to change all double word spaces to single word spaces.

2. Repeat this replace procedure until you see a message indicating that Word has finished searching the document.

Word Spaces Preceding Returns   The same sort of line-ending problems can occur if there is a word space before a hard return. If the word space will not fit on the line, it and the return are the only things that are carried down to the next line, usually creating unwanted space below the paragraph. You should then find and replace all space followed by a return with just a hard return.

Em Dashes and En Dashes   When using a word processor, some people use a space, two hyphens, and another space to represent an em dash. These will translate correctly into PageMaker and need no further action on your part.

However, some people use a space, a *single* hyphen, and a space. This combination should be used to indicate an *en* dash rather than an *em* dash, and you should search for these and change them as needed. Sometimes two hyphens with no spaces are used for em dashes. This combination may cause line ending problems unless there is no chance that the em dash will ever occur near the end of a line once the file is imported.

1. *Where appropriate,* replace single hyphens delimited by spaces and double hyphens not delimited by spaces with the correct characters: two hyphens delimited by spaces.

2. Correct any other formatting errors you see, such as improper use of paragraph codes. Do not double space after a paragraph.

3. Save the file.

4. Open **report2.txt** and save as **report2.rtf**. Edit the file as you did for **report1.rtf**. Save the file.

5. Open **report3.txt** and save as **report3.rtf**. Edit the file as you did for **report1.rtf**. Save the file.

Special Codes for Pi Characters   Certain characters that will appear in your final document, such as the trademark symbols ™ and ®, cannot be accessed on the normal keyboard keys. As mentioned earlier, such characters and symbols are called *pi characters*. You could enter these directly in PageMaker, but you may also enter them in your word processing document.

1. Start a **New** document in Microsoft Word, choose **Insert**, then **Symbol**.

2. Click the **Symbols** tab in the **Symbol** dialog box. In the **Font** drop-down box, choose **[normal text]**. If you click twice on a symbol, it is inserted into your document.

DID YOU KNOW...

Watch for incorrectly applied paragraph indents. If tabs or multiple spaces are used to indent paragraphs in the text file, they should be removed. PageMaker uses the **First line indent** formatting function of Microsoft Word.

3. Double-click the ® symbol and see it appear on your blank screen. Practice double-clicking other symbols. (Notice that if you click just once on a symbol, it is enlarged so you can get a better look at it. At the same time, if there is a shortcut key combination for the symbol you clicked, that combination is displayed. Many pi characters can be accessed using these shortcuts.)

4. Click the ® symbol once. Then click once outside the dialog box and enter the shortcut key combination you see displayed in the dialog box: **Alt + Ctrl + R**. The ® is inserted in your document.

Next, you will try inserting symbols through the **Character map** feature of Windows. This feature allows you to copy symbols into any Windows program, including Word. It also provides key combinations for inserting symbols into any Windows program. (If you are working on a Macintosh, the character map is not available, so skip past the following three items.)

1. Close the **Symbol** dialog box. Minimize the Word screen by clicking the "minimize" box on the Microsoft Word title bar. Microsoft Word becomes an icon on the taskbar.

2. Click on **Start**, then **Programs**, and open **Accessories**, then **Character map**. Here, you can select characters to be copied to the clipboard. Double-click the ® symbol, then click the **Copy** button.

3. Close **Character map** and click on the Microsoft Word task button to return to your document. Now, click the **Paste** button on your toolbar. The ® symbol is inserted into your document.

When you are working in Microsoft Word, it is usually easiest to use **Insert**, **Symbol** to access pi characters. However, key combinations come in handy when you need to do a search and replace. Replace the "(TM)" and "(R)" in the **report** files with the necessary codes, using Microsoft Word's replace feature.

1. Replace "(TM)" with the appropriate **Alt** code, **Alt + Ctrl + T**, in all three **report** files.

2. Replace "(R)" with the appropriate **Alt** code, **Alt + Ctrl + R**, in all three **report** files.

3. Save each file after replacing the pi characters.

4. Exit the Word program.

Starting Your Style Sheet

The style sheet can automate the process of applying attributes to the paragraphs and text in a file. Now it is time to work in PageMaker again.

1. Open or hot key in Windows back to the **report** file in PageMaker.

2. Select **Define styles...** from the **Type** menu.

3. Select the style name **Caption**. (See Figure 8.10.)

4. Click **Edit**, and then the **Char** button in the **Style Options** dialog box to specify the following attributes: Helvetica, 8 point; leading: 10; and bold. Then click **OK** to return to the **Style Options** dialog box.

5. Click **OK** to exit the **Style Options** dialog box. (If the dialog box says **Replace existing caption**, click the **OK** button.)

6. Click **OK** to save the new style and exit the **Style Options** dialog box.

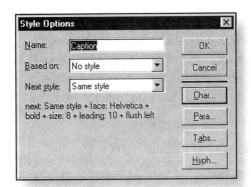

Style Options dialog box

You now need to create more styles. The **Hanging indent** style is used for the numbered and bulleted paragraphs in the report. The paragraphs with numbers (or bullets) are indented, except for the first line. Only the number or bullet hangs, and the text following the number (or bullet) must align with all the lines that follow. This is done by "outdenting" the first line, using a negative number for the first line indent. Then the number on the first line is followed by a tab so that the text following it will align properly.

1. Go to **Type/Define styles...** and define the hanging indent style by selecting the style, then clicking the **Edit**, **Para**, and **Tabs** buttons as follows: based on body text; left indent: 1; first indent: -1; tabs at 1p.

2. Define the following three styles by selecting **[Selection]**, then **New** from the **Style Options** dialog box, typing the name of the style in the **Name** text box, then clicking **Edit**, **Char**, and **Para** buttons.

   - **Name:** based on No style, next style is No style, bold, Helvetica.
   - **Assoc:** based on No style, next style is No style, italic.
   - **Cutline:** based on No style, next style is No style; Helvetica, 8 point; leading: 10; bold.

3. Exit the **Style Options** dialog box.

ASSEMBLING THE COMPLETE PAGES

Most of what you have done so far is preparation for page assembly. It is now time to lay out the pages and add the graphics. These are the final steps in page assembly.

Laying Out the Body of the Report

The report publication is currently only two pages long.

1. Click the **page 2** icon.

2. To add pages to an existing document, under the **Layout** menu choose **Insert pages....** The **Insert pages** dialog box appears. Add three pages after the current page. (Your document should now be five pages long.)

By default, new pages appear in the **Fit in window** size, with the master items in place.

Text Autoflow The text for the main body of the report is stored in the large files **report1.rtf**, **report2.rtf**, and **report3.rtf**. For handling long files, PageMaker has an **Autoflow** feature that will import all the text with one command and create new pages as needed.

1. From the **Layout** menu, select **Autoflow**.

2. From the **File** menu, select **Place** (**Ctrl + D**).

3. In the **Place** dialog box, find the file **report1.rtf** that you edited in MS Word. (The autoflow cursor is slightly different from the regular text-place cursor, as shown in Figure 8.10.)

4. Click the **page 1** icon.

5. Position the cursor at the top of the left column and click.

PageMaker will push the text into the columns and create new pages as needed to accommodate the text to the end of the file. With the **Autoflow** feature, text flows into the columns as defined by the page grid. (See Figure 8.11.)

FIGURE
8.11

Autoflow flows *report1* from column 1 on page 1 to column 2 on page 3

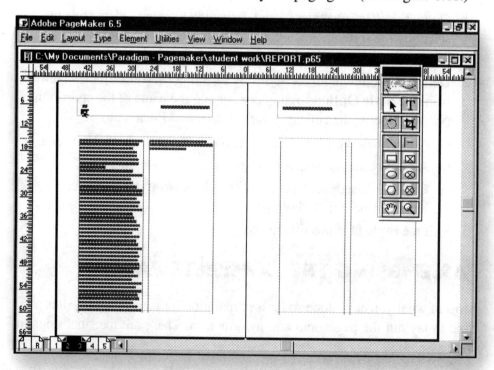

1. Click the page icons to look at the blocks of text.

2. Select a block and note that it has plus handles at the top and bottom, indicating that text precedes and follows the block. (The blocks of text are *chained* together. This means that if text is deleted or inserted, or if any text blocks are extended or shortened, all the blocks will adjust accordingly.)

3. Place the **report2.rtf** file with the beginning of the text at the top left column of the new page. (The **Autoflow** feature will automatically create new pages for the text. The new pages have the same master elements as the previously created pages.)

4. Repeat the previous step to place the **report3.rtf** file. It begins on a new page, too.

5. Save the **report** file.

Creating More Styles in PageMaker   PageMaker offers more capabilities for specifying a particular style. Five more styles must be created for the report: subheads 1, 2, and 3, callout, and body text. Follow these directions to create the first style, subhead 1.

1. Open the **Type/Define styles** menu.

2. Select **Selection**, and click the **New** button.

3. Type **Subhead 1** in the dialog box, and click the **Char** button.

4. Enter the following specifications for the type style: Helvetica, 14 point; leading: 15; set horizontal scale: 150%; case: all caps; bold. Click **OK**.

5. Click the **Para...** button and enter the following specifications for the paragraph style: space after: 0p9; include in table of contents.

6. Click **Rules** and select the **Rule below paragraph**, stroke style **4 pt**. Click **OK** 3 times. Click **OK** again if you see a dialog box that asks **Replace existing Subhead 1?**.

7. Now you will create the remaining four styles:
   - **Subhead 2:** based on subhead 1; Helvetica bold; all caps, font size: 14; leading: Auto; space before: 1 pica; space after: 0p4; horizontal scale: normal; No rule; include in table of contents.
   - **Subhead 3:** based on subhead 2; Helvetica bold; next style: subhead 2; size: 12; leading: Auto; include in table of contents; space before: 0p4; space after: 0p4.
   - **Callout:** based on No style; Helvetica, 9 point; leading: 9; color: red; alignment: flush left; hyphenation off.
   - **Body text:** based on No style; Times New Roman, 12 point; leading: 14; hyphenation on; space after: 0p1; Indent First: 1p.

Cutting and Pasting Text The headings in the **report** file need to be extracted from the text and positioned at the top of a page. The cut-and-paste method can be used to accomplish this. Apply the **Subhead 1** style to the headings. **Save** the file after every successful procedure below.

1. Use the **Text** tool to highlight the heading **Introduction**, and give the **Cut** command, **Ctrl + X**.

2. Make sure the master page items of header and page number are disabled on these pages of the report so that the header will not overlap the headings. (To do this, make sure **Display Master Items** is not selected under the **View** menu.)

3. Use the **Text** tool to create a bounding box into which the text will be pasted.

4. Give the **Paste** command to paste the cut text into the bounding box area. (**Ctrl + V** for Windows, **Command + V** on the Macintosh.) The cut text is pasted in.

5. Highlight the heading and apply the **Subhead 1** style. Expand the text box if needed, using the **Pointer** tool to drag the text box handles.

6. Repeat this procedure to extract the headings **WHAT IS DESKTOP PUBLISHING?**, **HARDWARE BACKGROUND**, and **SOFTWARE BACKGROUND**.

7. Save the file after each procedure.

Subhead 2 or **Subhead 3** styles apply to headings that mark sections within the body of the report. Apply styles to the report as shown in Figure 8.24 by following these steps:

- Insert the **Text** tool anywhere in the line of the heading.
- Select **Show Styles** from the **Window** menu.
- Click either **Subhead 2**, **Subhead 3**, or **Body text** to change the entire text according to the marked copy of the report. Apply the **Hanging indent** style to the numbered paragraphs toward the end of the report.

Adding Graphics to the Report

Look at the marked copy of the report in Figure 8.24. You will notice graphic placeholders and that all the graphics fall at the bottom of the page. The first graphic is placed on page 4 of the main body of the report.

The graphics can be added to the report with the **Place** command. Your current report, however, does not have a location set aside for the graphics, as text is placed in all the columns. The marked copy of the report indicates the location on the page where the graphics should be positioned.

Scaling Images The images should be scaled so that they fit in the column. Remember that to scale an image means to reduce or enlarge it. In general, it is best to scale graphics in page assembly programs rather than in graphics

MAC MEMO

On the Macintosh, use the key combination **Command + X** to cut.

DID YOU KNOW...

The text box is a separate, unchained block; this is indicated by the blank handles on the top and on the bottom. The text has actually been removed from the chain of text blocks that makes up the body of the report.

programs because the final size is determined in the page assembly program, and scaling in the page assembly program gives the desktop publisher greater control over the resolution of the final image. Reducing an image in a bitmapped graphics program, for example, will result in a smaller *low-resolution* image, while reducing it in a page assembly program will result in a smaller *higher-resolution* image.

When working on graphics, the desktop publisher should keep the final destination of the file in mind, and work accordingly. Graphics can be **proportionally scaled** so that the dimensions of the reduction or enlargement are in the same proportions as the original. Graphics can also be **disproportionally scaled** so that the height-to-width ratio of the final artwork is different from that of the original. In most cases, graphics are proportionally scaled, and page assembly programs have automatic features to accomplish this without your having to resort to numerical calculations. However, disproportional scaling can create interesting effects, such as stretched or compressed images or type.

Both bitmapped images and object-oriented images can be scaled proportionally or disproportionally, but the resolution of enlarged bitmapped files is generally unacceptably low.

Adjusting Text Block Length The text blocks in the columns must be shortened to make room for the graphics. The **Pointer** tool is used to extend or shorten a text block. First the text block must be selected with the **Pointer** tool. The windowshade handles will contain plus (+) signs to indicate that text is threaded to an adjoining text block.

1. Position the **Pointer** tool on page 4 of the report and select the text block in the column where the graphic will be placed. Refer to Figure 8.24 if necessary.

2. Use the pointer to shorten the length of the text block. Click the bottom windowshade handle of the text block and drag upward to the position that matches the text in Figure 8.24. Make sure there is enough room for the caption and cutline.

Importing Graphics The first graphic to be imported is a photograph of a microprocessor. For the purposes of this lesson, all you are going to do is draw a placeholder.

1. Draw the placeholder for Figure 1.1 at the bottom of page 4 using the rectangle tool.

2. Enter the caption and outline.

3. Continue using the pointer to shorten text where necessary, drawing placeholders, and entering captions and cutlines for the rest of the figures in the report. Refer to the marked text for positioning of the graphics. Remember to leave additional space for the captions and cutlines.

Scaling and Positioning Imported Graphics and Placeholders

Placeholders can be scaled to the size you want graphics to be when they are imported into the publication. The procedure for scaling an imported graphic and scaling a placeholder is the same.

If you did not scale the placeholders as you drew them, follow the steps below to scale each until they are similar size to those on the marked copy.

1. Put the pointer on a corner handle and drag until it is similar in size to the one on the marked copy. For proportional scaling, hold the **Shift** key as you scale.

2. To position the placeholder, put the pointer on the placeholder itself, within the selection handles. Then click and drag to the desired position.

3. Save the file and close it.

Wrapping Text Around Graphics   Graphics are often adjusted to the same column width as text blocks as is done in the **report** publication. When graphics are wider or narrower than the column measure, though, the text may wrap around the graphic. In some cases, text can also be surprinted over a screened graphic. The spatial relationship between the block of text and the graphic, called the **text wrap**, is specified in the page assembly program.

When text is wrapped around a graphic, space must be maintained between the two. This space is called the **standoff**. The standoff may be rectangular in shape, (available in all page assembly programs and in some word processing programs), an arbitrary shape, or contoured to the shape of the image (see Figure 8.12).

Text wraps
A. Rectangular wrap
B. Arbitrary wrap
C. Irregular contoured wrap

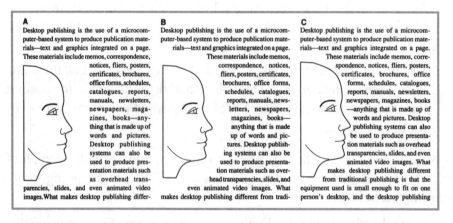

PageMaker's Book Lists

In PageMaker, the **Book** command allows you to link multiple PageMaker files—or publications—to form one large document. The publications may be separate chapters of a book or other sections of a project you are working on. Once linked together, the publications or sections make up a PageMaker **book list**. Then the files in the book list can be printed in sequence to produce a coherent finished project with appropriate page numbers. A table of contents or an index can also be created from the publications in the list.

A book list is created in a document. PageMaker automatically renumbers all the pages in the book list. Look at Figure 8.13. It displays the **Book Publications List** dialog box. The **Auto renumbering** selection is set at **None** so that the **report** file will retain its own page numbering. Create a book list that includes the **intro** and **report** files with the specifications you see in Figure 8.13. It will be used to create the table of contents and the index for the report.

1. Open the **intro** file and select the **Book** command from the **Utilities** menu.

2. Click the **Insert** button to add the **intro.p65** and **report.p65** files.

3. Select the **None** button to specify no page numbering.

4. Make any necessary style changes as noted in Figure 8.24 at the end of this chapter.

5. Click **OK**.

FIGURE
8.13
Book Publication List
dialog box

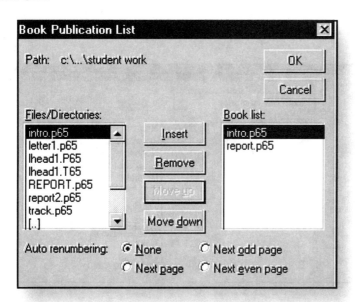

Blank Pages

1. Insert blank pages as you see them in the marked copy. They are needed to create rectos.

2. Suppress the master page items on these pages.

ADDING THE FINAL ELEMENTS

At this point the pages have been made up—the text and graphics have been integrated to form the primary part of the publication. However, longer publications, such as the report you have been working on, have additional elements that must be completed before the publication may be considered finished.

Creating the Cover Page

One of these additional elements is the cover page (also known as the title page if inside of a book), which consists of three shaded boxes, an imported graphic, a pi character, the title of the report, and other text. A cover page containing these elements makes the report look professional.

Set Width and Tracking The **Set width** command in PageMaker, which controls the width of individual characters, can be used to create special effects with text. The width of the text can be changed by from 5% to 250%, in increments of 0.1%.

The **Track** command adjusts kerning, or the space between characters. The default setting for **Track** is **Normal**, but other options include those seen in Figure 8.14. A setting of **Tight** decreases the amount of space in the text.

1. Notice that the **intro** data file has the same margins as the main body of the report and is double-sided.

2. Change the font used in the text on the title page to Helvetica.

3. Resave this file as **intro**.

FIGURE

8.14

The *Track* setting

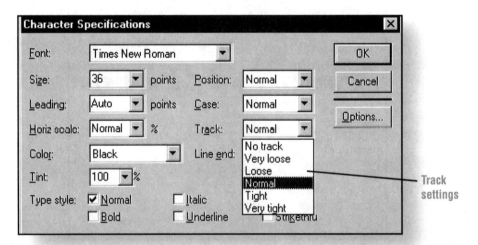

Track
settings

Breaking Blocks of Text At present, the words **FINAL REPORT** are included in a text block that contains the title of the report. The text block will be divided into two blocks so that the last two words may be moved to another position on the cover page.

1. Use the **Pointer** tool to shorten the length of the text block so that the last two words disappear.

2. Notice the small down arrow in the handle at the bottom of the text block in Figure 8.15. To break the text block into two separate blocks, click the bottom handle. This "loads" the cursor with text. The cursor changes into a text-place cursor.

3. Drag the text-place cursor to define a bounding box for the text block that contains the words **FINAL REPORT**.

DID YOU KNOW...

If you accidentally click the bottom handle and load the cursor when you do not want to, reselect the **Pointer** tool to undo your actions.

4. Position the text block at the **12p6** ruler guide and just under the top margin guide.

5. Increase the length of the text block by stretching the right handles out to the right margin guide. Change to Style as indicated in Figure 8.23.

6. Save this file as **intro**.

Down arrow

FIGURE
8.15
Arrow in bottom handle indicating more text in block

Paragraph Rules You can specify the size, color, width, style, and place-ment of horizontal rules above or below a selected paragraph. The rules become a part of the paragraph and cannot be moved independently.

1. Select **Paragraph** from the **Type** menu. Click the **Rules** button to access the **Paragraph Rules** dialog box. Change the specifications to the ones shown in Figure 8.16.

2. Align **FINAL REPORT** as shown in Figure 8.23 at the end of this chapter, if necessary.

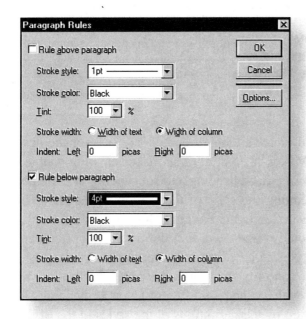

FIGURE
8.16
Paragraph Rules **dialog box**

Finishing the Cover Page

1. Import the **logo.eps** file and replace the logo placeholder to the left of **FINAL REPORT** with the logo graphic.

2. Save the file. Close the **intro** file.

An Acknowledgments page usually follows the cover page. Refer to the specifications in Figure 8.23, page ii, to create an Acknowledgments page.

Creating a Table of Contents

Some desktop publishing programs offer tools that are designed to help the writer and publisher produce internally referenced materials such as a table of contents and an index. These authoring tools may be available in the word processing program and/or in the page assembly program. In either case, the final pagination of the publication as determined by the page assembly program is used to create the index and table of contents.

A table of contents may list different levels of headings: units, chapters, and subsections for books; headlines for newsletters or magazines. A table of contents can be generated from codes inserted in the word processing file.

Tables of contents and other lists (for example, lists of figures and/or tables) are sometimes set up with **leader tabs.** Leader tabs are tabs in which marks such as dots fill the space preceding the tab character (see Figure 8.17).

FIGURE 8.17

Table of Contents
This sample shows tab leaders to the page numbers.

Now you will create a table of contents (TOC) for the desktop publishing report. PageMaker has a utility that makes creating a table of contents a fairly simple process. Each heading and subheading in the report is included in the TOC by editing the style of the particular heading. The **Include in table of contents** option in the **Paragraph specifications** dialog box should be checked. Whenever a style is first defined, this option can be checked. Otherwise, the style can be edited at a later time.

The **Table of contents** utility lists the particular heading along with the page number on which it starts. Different levels of headings in the table of contents are created by the definitions of the styles in the **Style** palette.

1. Open the **Type** menu and choose **Define Styles...**.

2. Scroll through the list of styles and select **TOC Subhead 1**. Click the **Edit** button.

3. Make sure the **Based on** style is **Headline**. If the paragraph heading of subhead 1 is based on **Headline,** then it will appear as a level under the **Headline** style in the table of contents.

4. Click the **Para...** button. Change **paragraph space after** to 1 pica. Click **OK** three times to finish the editing of the style.

5. Make the changes on the styles below:

   - **TOC Subhead 2**: Left indent: 1p6; first indent: 0; paragraph space after: 2 p.

   - **TOC Subhead 3**: Left indent: 2p6; first indent: 0; paragraph space after: 2 p.

The table of contents is on the page just after the cover page of the report. If necessary, insert a page for this now.

6. To generate the contents, select the **Utilities** menu and click the **Create TOC** option. The **Create Table of Contents** dialog box in Figure 8.18 appears.

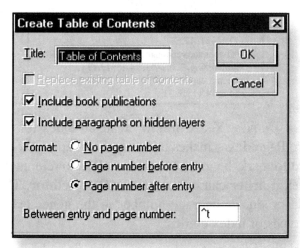

Create Table of Contents dialog box

7. At the top of this dialog box is an option that allows you to type a name for the table of contents page. Type **Table of Contents** in the name text box.

8. Click the **Page number after entry** button.

9. The default setting for **Between entry and page number** is ^t. This setting generates a leader tab (......) between each entry and page number like the ones in Figure 8.23.

10. Click the **OK** button. After a few seconds, a loaded **Text** tool appears.

11. Place the table of contents as you would place any text. PageMaker creates a default style for the table of contents entries.

12. Edit the Table of Contents if necessary. (See Figure 8.23.)

13. Save the file. Then close it.

Creating an Index

An index is generated from nonprinting codes embedded in the text. The codes are best inserted during the word processing stage, since the word processor has more sophisticated searching and keystroking tools. In page assembly programs that use copies of source files rather than pointers, the original word processing file must be repaginated to match the pagination of the laid-out page assembly file.

An index can contain single entries, subentries, and cross-references. Entries can be styled as run in (all subentries run on the same line) or nested (each subentry begins on a new line). The standard style for an index is to have hanging indents in a type size smaller than that of the body text. Subentries are often set with full indents. Indexes are usually set in two or more columns. (See Figure 8.19.)

FIGURE

8.19

Index
This sample shows entries and subentries, both of which have hanging indents.

> Abbreviations, 14.1–56. *See also* Acronyms
>   with addresses, 14.17, 14.21–22
>   of agencies and organizations, 14.15, 18.87
>   alphabetizing, 18.97, 18.103, 18.125
>   in author-date citations, 15.21–23
>   of bibliographic terms, 10.59–60, 14.34, 17.16–21, 17.58
>   of books and versions of Bible, 14.34–35, 17.63
>   capitalizing, 7.152–53, 14.15, 17.17 …
> Academic degrees and honors, 1.11, 7.26, 14.3, 14.8, 14.11, 18.81

Making Index Entries You will now create an index for the desktop publishing report. PageMaker makes this easy. First, an **index entry** is made in the report text to mark the index word, as well as to reference the page number. The **index marker** can be seen in the **Story editor**. The marker is the reference that produces the page number in the generated index. You can define three types of index entries:

- Simple index entries
- Multiple-level entries
- Cross-references

Let's define a simple index entry by first selecting text with the **Text** tool and then adding an index marker. It is a good idea to add index entries when your document is completed or nearly completed.

1. In the **report** file, open the **Story Editor**.

2. From the **Utilities** menu, select **Find**.

3. In the **Find What** text box, type **database**, click **All Stories**, and check **whole word**. Then click **Find**. If asked **Continue from beginning?**, click **Yes**.

4. When "database" is found, press **Ctrl + Shift + Y** in Windows or **Command + Shift + ;** on a Macintosh, to mark for inclusion in the Index.

Set levels of indexing as follows:

1. Use **Find** again to find the words "operating system" and select the two words. (Do not close **Find**.)

2. Select **Index Entry** from the **Utilities** menu (key **Ctrl + Y**). Look at the **Add index entry** dialog box in Figure 8.20. Three levels of topics can be typed. Notice the options for the page range and the formats that can be applied to the page number: bold, italic, and underline.

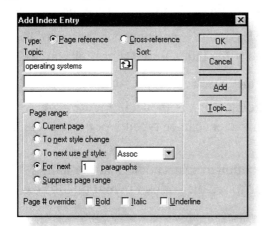

FIGURE 8.20

Add Index Entry dialog box

3. Click the button to select **For next paragraphs**. Type the number **6**.

4. Click **OK**.

To add a second level to the operating system index entry, follow these steps:

1. Find "MS-DOS."

2. Press **Ctrl + Y**.

3. Click the **Topic** button.

4. Type the selections shown in Figure 8.21. The MS-DOS reference will become a second-level index entry under "operating system."

FIGURE 8.21

"MS-DOS" is a second-level index entry under **operating system***.*

Cross-references can be added anywhere in the text because they do not refer to a specific page number.

1. Press **Ctrl + Y** and click the **Cross-reference** button.

2. Click **Topic**.

3. Type **text files** in the level 1 box.

4. Click the **X-ref** button, then **next section** to see entries you have already entered.

5. Type **ASCII** in the level 1 box.

6. Double click **OK**.

Use the report's index in Figure 8.24 to create other entries for the index.

Generating the Index The index is positioned at the end of the report. There should be a blank page for the index. Insert a page if you need to.

1. From the **Utilities** menu, select **Create index**.

2. The **Create index** dialog box is shown in Figure 8.24. A title with a maximum of 30 characters can be typed. For now, delete the word **Index**.

3. Click the **Format** button to select additional formatting specifications. Look at Figure 8.22 to see the **Index Format** dialog box.

FIGURE
8.22

Index Format **dialog box**

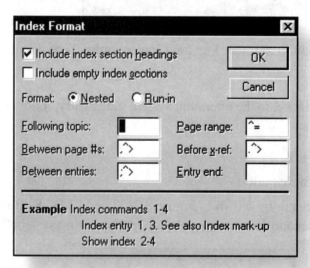

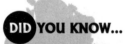

DID YOU KNOW...

PageMaker's default is to add the index section headings of A, B, C, and so on. An example of the **Nested** format is shown at the bottom of the dialog box. The characters that follow the various index entries are represented by their keyboard equivalents. For example, "^=" (the key combination for an en dash) might be listed under the entry **en dash**.

4. Click **OK** to return to the **Create index** dialog box.

5. Click **OK**. After a few seconds, a loaded **Text** tool appears.

6. Place the index text as you would place any text, at the end of the **report** file. (You will notice that the index must be edited.)

7. Save the file. Print, then close it.

PageMaker creates its own paragraph styles for the index. To update the index later on, simply select **Replace existing index** in the **Create index** dialog box.

FIGURE

8.23

Title page acknowledgments and table of contents in *intro* file

Desktop Publishing Workshop

6p drop to top of caps
Helvetica 30/30
bold, track tight

15p drop to top of caps
Helvetica 36/36, all caps,
bold, 150% horizontal
scale, track tight

FINAL REPORT

logo.eps
9p from left

top 20p drop
bottom 32p drop
12p6 from left
21p from right

30% fill
no lines

top 34p drop

top 48p drop

Helv 14/16

Helv 18/16, bold

©1999 The
Communications
Institute

Continued on next page

Figure 8.23, continued

SPECIAL THANKS TO

Style: Subhead 1
3p drop to top of caps
9p from left

Style: Name

Maria Lee
Head Instructor, Communications Institute,
Desktop Publishing Workshop

Style: Assoc

Linda Brown
President, National Association of Desktop Publishing Professionals

Kathleen Moreno
CEO, Office Solutions, Inc.

Chuck Miller
Associate Professor, Shoreline Community College

Michael Brooks
DataPro Statistical Services

Donna Long
Art Director, Center for Peace and Justice

Sara Kashiwa
Director, Impage Perfect Lab

Alvaro Colegio
Professor, Bellevue Community College

Nikolas Sandris
Sole Proprietor, Prospect Printing

ii

Helv 10/16, bold
150% set width

Figure 8.23, continued

CONTENTS

> 18/18 Helvetica, bold
> 150% set width, all caps
> 3p drop to top of caps
> 9p from left

> 15p drop

> 36p from left

iii

Continued on next page

Figure 8.23, continued

This page is left blank in the publication so
that the text can begin on a recto.

F I G U R E

8.24

Report and Index

Helvetica 18/19 200% Horiz.

INTRODUCTION

Style:
Subhead1

Style:
Bodytext

Times New Roman 12/14

Desktop publishing is the use of a microcomputer-based system to produce publication materials with typeset or near-typeset quality text and graphics integrated on a page. These materials include notices, fliers, posters, certificates, brochures, forms, schedules, catalogues, reports, manuals, newsletters, newspapers, magazines, and books — anything made up of words and pictures.

What makes desktop publishing different from traditional publishing is that equipment small enough to fit on a person's desktop provides the resources needed to prepare and assemble pages. In the graphic arts world, desktop publishing is considered a prepress technology; that is, the desktop publishing system itself is generally not used to produce the final multiple copies of a publication, but rather to produce masters for reproduction.

The appearance of microcomputers on the desks of both office workers and graphic artists as well as other professionals indicates an interesting intersection of technology and art. Desktop publishing is an extension of office computing, as well as an extension of graphic arts.

Today, routine materials that in the past were simply typewritten or word processed with a letter quality printer are enhanced with typeset or near-typeset quality type and graphics. Many high-quality publications that in the past were costly and required the contracted services of many different graphic arts professionals are now produced in-house with desktop publishing, at a fraction of the cost and time required by traditional means.

Desktop publishing, because it is relatively inexpensive and user-friendly, has put the power of professional-quality publishing in the hands of many who are not publishing professionals. Some speak out against this trend and point to the flood of poorly designed publications produced by inexperienced publishers. As one commentator put it, "Desktop publishing enables anyone to make more ugly publications faster." While that is sometimes true, the equalizing force of desktop publishing is not a bad thing; it rightly moves us toward the goal of freedom of the press for all who have a message to communicate.

The problem of bad design is not so much that it gives the profession a bad name but that it interferes with effective communication. That is why this report covers not only basic computer literacy and techniques of desktop publishing, but also basic principles of design.

Continued on next page

Figure 8.24, continued

WHAT IS DESKTOP PUBLISHING?

Style:
Subhead1

Style:
Bodytext

Desktop publishing, as defined in this report, utilizes a microcomputer that fits on a desk, for WYSIWYG (what-you-see-is-what-you-get, pronounced "wizzy-wig") graphic design and page assembly of typeset-quality text and graphics. WYSIWYG is an interactive mode of running computer programs in which you see, on the display monitor, how the type and graphics will appear when you get the actual printed output. The type specifications (size and style, for example) and adjustments of the type and graphics, are shown on the screen instantaneously as they are made.

Some word processing and page assembly programs are not WYSIWYG; the user runs them in a mode called "batch processing." This involves embedding codes within the text and then sending the file (text and code information) to the printer, in a batch. Batch processing programs generally cannot handle graphics, and the results of coding cannot be seen until you get the printed output. Batch processing is not interactive, because type specifications are not shown on the screen; just the codes appear. The specified type appears only on the printout.

WYSIWYG has gained great popularity because it is easy to learn and provides greater flexibility in the editing and design process. . . but there is a price to pay. Typographical characters (different type-faces, sizes, styles, and positions on the page) as opposed to typewriter or dot-matrix characters, must be created on the display monitor and printed in a graphics mode. Even for text-intensive publications or publications without pictures, WYSIWYG desktop publishing requires graphics capability — graphics-oriented software and hardware to process, display (WYS), and print (WYG) images and typeset-quality text. Hardware refers to actual physical devices, and software refers to the information (programs) used to control the devices.

Figure 8.24, continued

HARDWARE BACKGROUND

Style:
Subhead1

Style:
Bodytext

Every microcomputer has three main components: a main system unit for processing, an input system, and an output system.

The main system unit is the box that contains the CPU (central processing unit) — the "brain" of the microcomputer that does all the computing work; memory, used to store information temporarily on which the CPU works while the computer is running; disk drive(s), used to store information permanently on disks, for both input and output; (expansion) boards inside the system unit, used for a variety of special functions and ports, which provide data pathways from the CPU to the outside world. Ports are used for both input and output.

For basic input, a desktop publishing microcomputer has a keyboard, the primary input device for text; and a mouse, a pointing device that is well-suited to and required for graphics applications, including page assembly.

For basic output, the desktop publishing system includes a display monitor, providing the WYS part of WYSIWYG, and a laser printer, which provides WYG. (A dot-matrix printer may be used for text proofing, but for final near-typeset quality type, a laser printer is a requirement.)

In specifying a microcomputer system, the first step is to determine what kind of software will be used, and then what hardware is required to run that software. For WYSIWYG desktop publishing, the most demanding software is the page assembly program. Hardware options for running page assembly programs such as Aldus® PageMaker® (Macintosh and IBM/compatibles) are discussed in this report. Other page assembly, graphics, and word processing software will run on systems that can handle PageMaker.

THE SYSTEM UNIT

Style:
Subhead2

One of the main differences between IBM/compatibles and Macintosh microcomputers is that IBM/compatibles have always been open-architecture machines; that is, the system unit can be opened up and the user can separately purchase and install different components. The first Macintosh computers were closed-architecture machines.

Because of IBM's open architecture, a great diversity of components are available for IBM/compatibles from third-party vendors, that is, non-IBM manufacturers. The early Macintosh computers, on the other hand, came with most of their components built into the system unit, and opening the system unit case voided the warranty. In 1987, however, Apple introduced the Macintosh SE® and Macintosh II®, which are open-architecture machines. There are now a growing number of third-party vendors offering a variety of Macintosh components and add-on options.

THE CENTRAL PROCESSING UNIT

Style:
Subhead2

The central processing unit of every microcomputer is a tiny chip inside the

Continued on next page

Figure 8.24, continued

> Style:
> Bodytext

system unit, usually mounted on the main circuit board called the "motherboard." Because a microcomputer's CPU is etched onto a single integrated circuit chip, it is also sometimes called a microprocessor. See Figure 1-1.

Graphics and page assembly require more complex processing than straight word/data processing, and so a powerful and fast CPU is required. The CPU of a microcomputer is identified by the manufacturer's number, and its clock speed — the cycles per second that it processes, measured in megahertz (Mhz).

> Style:
> Subhead3

IBM/compatible and Macintosh CPUs

The first IBM PC, introduced in 1981, was based on the Intel® 8088 CPU running at 4.6 MHz. In 1983, IBM introduced the XT™; based on the same CPU, it came with a hard disk drive. Currently, some XT compatibles can be switched to 8 MHz. In 1984, IBM introduced the AT™ model, based on the Intel 80286 CPU, running at 6 or 8 MHz. Today, AT compatibles may run as fast as 10, 12, 16, or 20 MHz. Some desktop publishing software runs on XT-compatibles, but an AT-compatible is preferable and required for some programs.

IBM has discontinued its line of PCs, XTs, and ATs, but third-party vendors continue to manufacture compatibles, which are widely available, In 1987, IBM introduced a new line of Personal System 2® (PS/2) microcomputers, including a very fast and powerful machine (Model

80) with an Intel 80386 CPU, running at a clock speed of 16-20 Mhz.

The first Macintosh, introduced in 1984, was based on a Motorola® 68000 CPU, running at 7.8 MHz. This processor is comparable to the AT 286 CPU, and is used in the small (13.5" x 10" x 11") Macintosh computers, the original Macintosh, Macintosh 512K, Macintosh 512KE, Macintosh Plus, and Macintosh SE. The main distinction among the small Macintosh computers is the amount of memory installed.

The original Macintosh, the 512K, and the 512KE have been discontinued, but since these machines have a fast CPU, used machines can be upgraded to Macintosh Plus capabilities. Professional desktop publishing software runs on the Macintosh Plus and Macintosh SE. In 1987, Apple introduced the Macintosh II,

Figure 1.1
Microprocessor
The Intel 80286 chip. Photo by Don Metke.

> Style:
> Cutline

> Style:
> Caption

Figure 8.24, continued

> **Style:**
> **Bodytext**

a bigger and more powerful modular machine with advanced color and graphics capability. The Macintosh II is based on a Motorola 68020 CPU, running at 15.66 MHz, which is comparable to an IBM/compatible 386 machine.

> **Style:**
> **Subhead2**

COMPUTER MEMORY

Two types of memory are used in microcomputers: Read Only Memory (ROM) and Random Access Memory (RAM).

ROM is permanently etched in a chip and cannot be altered; it contains routines such as automatic programs that start up the computer when it is powered on. In the Macintosh, ROM also contains graphics routines (for example, how to draw a line or character on the screen), so that the

CPU can quickly execute those instructions without have to access a program on a disk.

RAM is dynamic and temporary; when one is running the computer, instructions are swapped in and out of RAM from a disk as needed. Changes made while working on documents are also saved in RAM until the information is saved as a file on a disk. The information in RAM is lost when the microcomputer is restarted or powered off.

For the most part, RAM is of greater interest to the desktop publisher because ROM is built into the machine and is generally not expandable, while RAM can be added to a microcomputer to improve its performance, RAM can be purchased as chips that are installed directly on the motherboard, or mounted on separate boards attached to the motherboard. See Figure 1-2. Motherboard RAM is faster than RAM on separate boards.

> **Style:**
> **Subhead3**

Bits and Bytes

Both ROM and RAM capacities are measured in bytes. All information is processed by the CPU and stored in bits and bytes. A bit is the computer's smallest unit of measurement; its values is either 0 or 1. A byte is 8 bits, and can represent a number, a part of a graphic's description, or a single character of text. Bits and bytes are such small measurements that a set of larger units is used to describe processing and storage.

1,000 bytes=1 kilobyte(K)

1,000 K=1 megabyte (mb): 1,000,000 bytes

> **Style:**
> **Bodytext, 10pt, italic**

> **Style:**
> **Cutline**

Figure 1.2
Memory board and chip
Memory comes in small chips embedded on a board inside the computer.

> **Style:**
> **Caption**

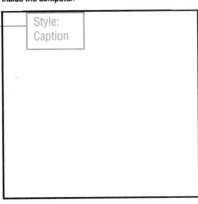

Continued on next page

Figure 8.24, continued

6

A typical page of double-spaced typewritten text contains about 2,000 characters. A byte is approximately equal to a single character of text, so a page of text is equivalent to about 2K. But text is only raw material for desktop publishing. Depending on the program used, a single page of type (including different typefaces, sizes, and styles in different positions on the page) may require as much as 20K. Graphics require even more: a full-page graphic image (such as a digitized photo) may require more than 1Mb! Most graphics require less, but a page of combined type and graphics usually runs in the range of 5K to 50K.

IBM and Macintosh RAM

> Style: Subhead3

Since IBM/compatibles have always been open-architecture machines, the memory configuration on base machines is variable. The first IBM-PCs were able to hold only 64K on the motherboard, but it soon became apparent that more memory was needed. In 1983, IBM switched to higher-capacity memory chips, which enabled PCs and XTs to hold a total of 640K on the motherboard; typical lower configurations are 512K. The Pentium machines now available hold more than 8Mb on the motherboard.

The early Macintosh computers were classified by the amount of memory installed on the motherboard: the original Macintosh was a 128K machine, the 512K and 512KE had 51K (of course!), the Machintosh Plus has 1Mb. The Macintosh machines now available hold up to 8Mb on the motherboard.

Most page assembly programs require a minimum of 640K of RAM, but more memory improves the performance of the computer — the speed at which images appear on the screen, and the response to the keyboard and mouse. When large and complex programs are run on a minimum of memory, the performance level decreases.

> Style: Bodytext

Figure 8.24, continued

SOFTWARE BACKGROUND

Style:
Subhead1

The most important software running on a computer is the operating system, which provides the top level of the user interface — what you see on the screen of the computer when not running any program. The operating system handles file management functions and coordinates the activities of peripheral devices, including, most significantly, the disk drive system. The basic application programs used in desktop publishing are word processing, graphics, and page assembly programs. Data processing programs are often used in conjunction with word processing and graphics programs, and there are a number of special-purpose programs that are useful in desktop publishing.

Software products, including operating systems, are frequently updated by the manufacturers. The version number of the software is changed for each update (for example, in 1994, PageMaker 4.0 was updated to 5.0, then later updated to version 6.0, then 6.5). Like disks, software is usually downward compatible (files created with PageMaker 5.0 for example, can be opened with PageMaker 6.5) but not upward compatible (files created by PageMaker 6.5 cannot be opened with PageMaker 5.0).

Style: Subhead2

THE OPERATING SYSTEM

The most widely used IBM/compatible operating system is MS-DOS®, which stands for Microsoft Disk Operating System. The Macintosh operating system is called System 7. Other operating systems include UNIX®, a multi-user operating system used in many colleges and universities, and OS/2®, a new operating system jointly developed by Microsoft and IBM.

All file operations such as opening, closing, creating, and storing files are accomplished through the operating system, either directly (from the top level of the operating system) or indirectly (while running an application program). MS-DOS and UNIX are command based — the user types in commands from the keyboard. The Macintosh System 7 is icon-based, consisting of pictures at which the user points and clicks.

MS-DOS desktop publishing programs usually run under a graphics environment. These are interfaces that are icon-based like the Macintosh OS. The most popular IBM/compatible graphics environments are Microsoft Windows® and Digital Research's GEM® (Graphics Environment Manager); there are also nonstandard environments built into graphics and page

Style:
Cutline

Figure 1.10
Operating System (Macintosh)

Style:
Caption

Continued on next page

Figure 8.24, continued

DESKTOP PUBLISHING REPORT

Style: Bodytext

assembly programs. The OS/2 icon-based interface, called Presentation Manager, is a version similar to Microsoft Windows.

UNIX and OS/2 are also multitasking operating system; more than one program can be run simultaneously. Version 5.0 and above of the Macintosh OS, and the Windows and GEM environments on IBM/compatibles enable more than one application program to run at a time. Multitasking requires a substantial amount of RAM.

Style: Subhead2

DATA AND WORD PROCESSING

Style: Subhead3

Data processing

Number crunching and database filing were the first applications developed for computers (at first, mainframes and minicomputers). On microcomputers, "number crunching" usually takes the form of spreadsheet calculations and statistics calculating programs. Microcomputer database programs are limited by the memory and disk capacity of the system, so large databases (over 5,000) records are usually kept on minicomputers or mainframes because of the huge number of records and intensive processing required to access and sort them.

There are numerous applications for spreadsheets and databases in desktop publishing. Business graphics are often bundled with spreadsheets so that information typed into calculations can be

quickly charted; the numerical information can also be used for tables. Small-scale database publishing applications include production of mailing lists, identification tags, price lists, schedules, catalogs, and any kind of tabular material within other publications.

Word processing

Style: Subhead3

Word processing has become the most widely used microcomputer application in the business world. Desktop publishing is an outgrowth of this application. It enables writers to produce more attractive materials.

Graphic designers are usually not responsible for typing text in a word processing program. However, designers and publication production assistants need to be familiar with word processing basics in order to edit files in preparation for page assembly. A working knowledge of advanced word processing features can also help the publisher to save time in preparing text.

Figure 1.11
Spreadsheet and chart (Microsoft Excel)

Style: Cutline

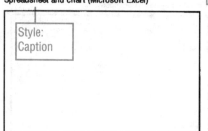

Style: Caption

Figure 8.24, continued

Style:
Subhead3

Word processing and text file standards

Style:
Bodytext

The American Standard Code for Information Interchange, better known as ASCII, is a widely used computer file format for text-only information. All programs create files in their own native format (for example, Microsoft Word® saves Microsoft Word files, WordPerfect® saves WordPerfect files), but professional word processing and data processing programs can also read and write files in ASCII. ASCII files are sometimes called text files, text-only files, or print files. Word processing files can be saved in ASCII format in order to convert text from one program's format into another. ASCII files can also be exchanged among computers, by disk, or via serial ports or telephone lines.

Some programs can read the native formats of other popular programs (for example, Microsoft Word on the Macintosh reads MacWrite files) and

some programs are implemented on both IBM/compatibles and the Macintosh (for example, Microsoft Word and Excel®, WordPerfect, dBASE®). The different machines can transfer compatible files via serial ports or telephone lines.

GRAPHICS SOFTWARE

Style:
Subhead2

Though word processing provides most of the content for publications, graphics are fundamental to desktop publishing. High-quality typography and page assembly are graphics applications, since they require graphics processing beyond the realm of most word processors.

Graphics software usually refers to painting and drawing software used to create and edit pictures. Basic software for desktop publishing enables the artist to create original illustrations; advanced drawing programs, based on PostScript, enable the artist to create originals, trace over existing images, and combine special effects. The software used to create business graphics from spreadsheets and to run scanners and to enhance scanned images can also be considered graphics software. Ready-made electronic clip art and page assembly templates, though not application programs, can also be purchased from retailers for use with graphics software.

Graphics files standards

Style:
Subhead3

Graphics files are less standardized than word processing or data processing files, but this is an area of interest to desktop publishers, since the ability to incorporate

Style:
Cutline

Figure 1.12
Word processing (Microsoft Word)

Style:
Caption

Continued on next page

Figure 8.24, continued

10

DESKTOP PUBLISHING REPORT

> Style:
> Bodytext

graphics is one of the main reasons desktop publishing has become so popular.

The most widely used standards, EPS (Encapsulated PostScript, for line drawings) and TIFF (tagged image file format, for photographic images), are supported on both Macintosh computers and on IBM/compatibles. EPS files are PostScript files with headers and translation routines. Advanced drawing programs can write EPS, and most scanner software can save files in the TIFF format. Professional page assembly programs can import EPS and TIFF files; depending on the program, a variety of native formats may also be imported.

On the Macintosh, .PICT is a graphics file format that any Macintosh program can read, and on IBM/compatibles, .PCX and .PIC files are commonly used in graphics and page assembly programs. There are programs on the Macintosh that can translate .PCX and .PIC files into .PICT files, and program on the IBM/compatible that can read and translate .PICT files into .PCX or .PIC files.

> Style:
> Subhead2

PAGE ASSEMBLY SOFTWARE

The page assembly program is the heart of the desktop publishing software. This is where all other materials — word processing, data processing, and graphics files — are put together for final output. This process is called layout design, page makeup, or page composition.

Page assembly programs enable the desktop publisher to electronically lay out

and design publications, which provides the primary advantages of greater flexibility and automation of tasks, that, in the traditional process, are very time consuming.

1) Text can be edited in the publication in typeset form.

2) Type can be reset (size, style, line length, and column depth) on the page, and space above and below can be adjusted.

3) Graphic elements such as rules, boxes, and tints can be drawn and edited on the page.

4) Pictures can be scaled or cropped on the page, to fit an established area on the page.

5) Repeated elements such as the layout grid, standard artwork, headers, and footers can be assigned to every page of a layout without having to reset and position them.

> Style:
> Hanging
> indent

Figure 1.13
Graphics (MacPaint)

> Style:
> Cutline

> Style:
> Caption

Figure 8.24, continued

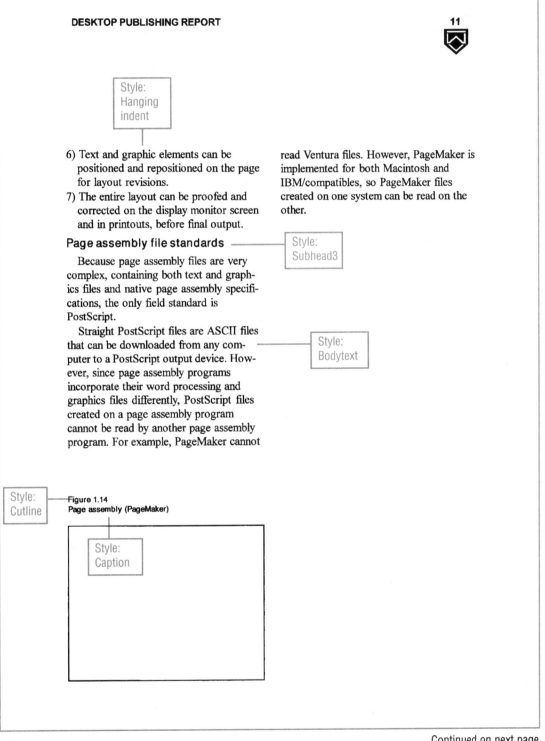

DESKTOP PUBLISHING REPORT 11

Style: Hanging indent

6) Text and graphic elements can be positioned and repositioned on the page for layout revisions.
7) The entire layout can be proofed and corrected on the display monitor screen and in printouts, before final output.

read Ventura files. However, PageMaker is implemented for both Macintosh and IBM/compatibles, so PageMaker files created on one system can be read on the other.

Page assembly file standards ── Style: Subhead3

Because page assembly files are very complex, containing both text and graphics files and native page assembly specifications, the only field standard is PostScript.

Straight PostScript files are ASCII files that can be downloaded from any computer to a PostScript output device. However, since page assembly programs incorporate their word processing and graphics files differently, PostScript files created on a page assembly program cannot be read by another page assembly program. For example, PageMaker cannot

Style: Bodytext

Style: Cutline

Figure 1.14
Page assembly (PageMaker)

Style: Caption

Continued on next page

Figure 8.24, continued

INDEX

Style:
Subhead1

Remember that the index
now needs to be edited.

A

Aldus 3
ASCII 9, 11

B

batch processing 2
bits 5
business graphics 8
bytes 5

C

Central Processing Unit 3
computer 1, 2, 3, 4, 5, 6, 7, 8
computer literacy 1
CPU 3, 4

D

Data processing 8
database 8
desktop publisher 5
desktop publishing 1, 7
disk drive 3

E

EPS 10

F

footers 10

G

graphic arts 1
graphic designers 8
graphics 4, 6, 7

H

hardware 2
headers 10

I

IBM/compatibles 3, 6
information 2, 3, 5

K

keyboard 6

M

Macintosh 3, 6
memory 3, 5, 6
memory board 5
microcomputer 1, 5
monitor 2
motherboard 5
mouse 6
MS-DOS 7
multi-user operating system 7
multitasking 8

N

near-typeset quality 3

O

operating system 7
  MS-DOS 7

P

page assembly programs 2, 6, 8. 10
PageMaker 3, 7
PCX 10
Pentium 6
PICT 10
PostScript 11
Presentation Manager 8
processor 4
programs 2, 6
publication 1

Figure 8.24, continued

INDEX CONTINUED

Style:
Subhead1

R

RAM 5
ROM 5

S

software 7
special-purpose programs 7
spreadsheets 8
storage 5

T

text files 7. *See also* text files: ASCII
TIFF 10
typeset-quality 2
Typographical 2

U

UNIX 7, 8

W

word processing 2, 7, 8, 11
WYSIWYG 2

CHECKING YOUR UNDERSTANDING

1. List items that might be placed on a master page.
2. What does the **Book** command in PageMaker enable you to do?
3. What characters denote automatic page numbers in PageMaker?
4. Why should tombstoning be avoided?
5. Why should you avoid two word spaces at the end of a sentence?
6. How do you find and replace pi characters?
7. Explain the steps one would take to shorten a text block.
8. What does a plus sign in a windowshade handle indicate?
9. Define the term *standoff*.
10. What does the **Track** command of PageMaker accomplish?

APPLYING DESIGN PRINCIPLES

Creating Your Own Report

Create a report similar to the one you created in this chapter. This report can be about the hardware (**report2**) <u>or</u> the software (**report3**).

a) Create a master page with 2 columns, and a page number centered at the bottom.
b) Import either of the above text files to flow the text into the columns.
c) Import one or more graphics from the student data diskette to match the report text.
d) Add a caption to the illustration.
e) Create a table of contents.
f) Add a cover page with your name on it.

part

DESKTOP PUBLISHING

5

Publications and Templates.

PRINCIPLES of PREPARING PUBLICATIONS & TEMPLATES

This chapter delves deeper into display publications and structured publications, and how to create templates.

Upon completion of this chapter **you will be able to**

- identify and distinguish among different kinds of display publications: cover pages, stationery, ads, posters, fliers, and brochures
- identify and determine elements that comprise structured publications
- identify the elements of a template: grids, running headers/footers, page numbers, banners, mastheads, bylines, and continuation lines
- determine traditional copyfitting techniques: line gauge, castoff, and galleys
- identify and distinguish among kickers, pull quotes, and sidebars

This chapter will teach you about creating and designing display publications such as promotional and marketing materials. You will learn about designing stationery, ads, posters, fliers, brochures, forms, and coupons. You will also learn about creating and designing a structured publication—a newsletter. PageMaker offers features that make it ideal for the design and production of newsletters. This chapter explains the elements—such as banners, mastheads, bylines, continuation lines, kickers, and so on—used in a newsletter.

DISPLAY PUBLICATIONS

The term *display publication* is used in this textbook to describe publications that are graphics-intensive and generally single-paged with variable layout elements. Most promotional and marketing materials, such as announcements, advertisements, posters, brochures, fliers, and handouts, are display publications.

Letterheads, envelopes, and business cards (a stationery set) can be considered display publications, since they display the company's logo, name, and contact information. Covers for books, reports, directories, catalogs, magazines, and other long documents also follow the basic principles of display design although the documents themselves are structured.

Covers and Cover Pages

The outside cover of a publication and the cover page set the stage for the content of the publication. For informal publications, the cover page may double as the outside cover. This is called a **self-cover**. A standard cover (external cover) consists of the front, the back, and possibly a spine. A **spine** is created by folds perpendicular to the front and back cover (see Chapter 11 for information on binding processes that create flat spines).

A spine carries the publication title, running vertically from top to bottom (see Figure 9.1). External covers are generally printed as one piece, on paper stock that is heavier than the paper used for printing the publication.

An external cover is equal in width or wider than the two-page spread of the pages. The amount of extra width depends on the spine, which is determined by the thickness (number of pages and bulk of paper) of the publication. When bound, the cover is trimmed to the page size.

Covers and cover pages can include as little as just the title, or as much as the title, author, publication sponsor, table of contents, copyright information, and other bits of information such as organization mottos, notes, and graphics. There are no firm rules, except that the design should be appropriate to the content of the publication.

Generally, if a publication contains an external cover and a cover page, the cover contains minimal information; more information is on the cover page. For long, formal publications, the table of contents and other materials are set up on separate pages.

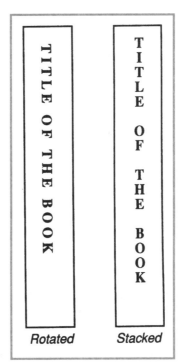

Rotated   Stacked

FIGURE 9.1
Title on cover spine
Rotated type is easier to read.

Stationery Set

Stationery is one of the primary carriers of an organization's visual identity, and so the design is very important. The typeface and graphics will be used in nearly all publications produced by the organization. They must be versatile and, most importantly, they must be choices that the organization can utilize in many ways and for a long time.

Letterhead   Letterheads showcase the organization's logo and name, and contain other pertinent contact information such as address, telephone number, and other numbers (such as telex, fax, and electronic mail addresses). A motto is sometimes included, and for corporate letterheads, the names of board members and company officers are also sometimes listed. The primary consideration in designing a letterhead is to make sure that the letterhead is distinct from the writing area in the middle of the page (see Figure 9.2).

FIGURE

9.2

Stationery set

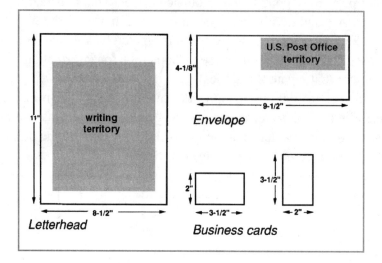

Letterheads are often set in sans serif typefaces. Serif typefaces 10 to 12 points in size may resemble typewriter copy and therefore are not often used in stationery. If a serif typeface is used, rules, boxes, or tints can be added to separate the letterhead from the actual letter. Color can also increase the distinction. Even if the letterhead will be printed in color, it should be designed in black and white. (Letters are frequently photocopied, and a good design will work well in black and white and in color.)

Standard letterhead size is 8½" x 11", which is available in all page assembly programs. For image-set copy, the white space in the center of the page containing the letterhead can be used for setting the business cards, which can then be cut and pasted on a separate board.

Envelopes The envelope contains the organization's logo, name, and return address, and sometimes a motto, but rarely other information such as a phone number. The envelope should match the letterhead design and not interfere with U.S. Post Office territory, which is the upper one-third and right half of the envelope. (See Figure 9.2.)

The standard business envelope size is 9½" x 4 1/8". In page assembly program, you must specify a wide (landscape) page for printing.

Business Cards Business cards contain the same kind of information as the letterhead, plus a person's name. The business card should match the design of the letterhead and envelope. For many businesses, another design consideration is the ease with which names of different lengths can be added to the card. For example, do not set the person's name in a restricted space, or as a wrap around a curve.

Standard business card size is 2" x 3½" and may be tall or wide. Because business cards are small, they are printed in batches of three or four at a time. Because business cards are cut, there is no extra cost for full bleeds. For cost savings, the desktop publisher can duplicate the business cards in the page assembly program (as opposed to having the printer make photostats) and have the cards image-set on the same sheet as the letterhead.

Ads, Posters, and Fliers

Advertisements, posters, and fliers should be designed for an audience that leafs through a newspaper or magazine, passes by a bulletin board, or goes quickly through the day's mail. These messages compete with hundreds of others that bombard us daily. The most effective message is one with a strong and immediate visual impact.

In order to emphasize the primary message, the size of type should be varied dramatically within the piece. Small type is readily distinguishable in increments of 4 points. For instance, 12-point type is noticeably larger than 8-point type. However, in the mid and large type sizes, the size should be varied in increments of at least 12 points. The difference between 24- and 20-point type is not very noticeable. For contrast, the type needs to be enlarged to 30- or 36-point type. The difference between 72- and 76-point type is almost indistinguishable, as shown in Figure 9.3.

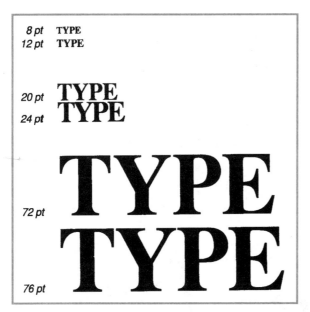

Type size
Differences in small sizes are readily noticeable. However, at larger sizes, differences must be greater to be effective.

Ads A display advertisement should be designed to work effectively within an unknown context on a text-intensive page. The directional flow of the ad should therefore be self-contained and not be dependent upon white space on any particular side. The product or service, the name of the organization offering the product or service, and contact information constitute the primary focuses of an ad.

DID YOU KNOW...

Do not try to fill every inch of space on the page; this results in a crowded, messy look. Give your graphics and type breathing room.

Posters A poster should be designed to be viewed from a distance of at least 10 feet, since it will be hanging on a wall or bulletin board. Large illustrations, or text characters designed graphically, are often used as the main focus. The primary message, graphic or verbal, should be immediately apparent. The poster should impart the maximum amount of information with the minimum number of words. The use of body text sizes (less than 14-point type) and fine or detailed line art should be restricted because they do not read well from a distance.

Fliers A flier is designed to be read while it is held in the reader's hands. It is usually distributed by hand, by mail, or from literature racks or counters. Fliers generally contain more text information than posters do. In some cases, fliers can double as posters and vice versa if the type size is large enough to be read from a distance (14-point type or larger). Blocks of text in a flier should be grouped in a manner that makes their relationship clear. Typographical consistency is a visual cue for this grouping.

Designing with Focus To get and hold the viewer's attention, an ad, poster, or flier should have a strong primary focus and interesting secondary focuses.

Illustrations are good eye-catchers, especially if they are large. Rules and boxes help to lead the eye, to emphasize and/or separate elements. Reverses are also eye-catching. When using screens for reverse type or as a background for surprinted type, large, bold characters (larger than 12-point type) should be used to ensure that the individual letters stand out and that counters do not fill in. (A **counter** is an enclosed area within a letter in capital, lowercase, and numeric letter forms.) The standard outline style in most page assembly programs tends to be light. It should be avoided on posters unless set in very large sizes and bold.

The amount of white space between groups of elements should be varied in order to prevent fragmentation of the negative space. Negative space helps to create focus and logical groupings of elements. Directional flow of graphic elements can be enhanced with the positioning and alignment of type (see Figure 9.4).

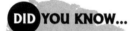

DID YOU KNOW...

In designing display publications, create a single primary focus and various secondary focuses; use illustrations, reverses, large type, and so on.

FIGURE 9.4

White space and directional flow
Equalized spacing (A) is less dynamic than variations of spacing (B and C).

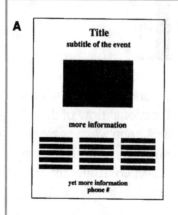

In Western cultures, the movement of the eye over a page is from top to bottom and left to right, because that is the way we read. The lower-right corner of a display piece is where the eye rests after looking at type and graphics above. This spot is frequently used for important information, like the organization's name, phone number, or logo.

Production of Display Pieces An underlying grid can be useful in mapping out the preliminary arrangement of elements of a display piece.

Thumbnails (small sketches used as a first draft of a design) can be used to block out areas where graphics and type will be placed according to a division of the page into equal parts. All elements do not have to be aligned with this invisible grid. The grid is simply used as a guide for positioning elements and for deciding how much space to leave around graphics and type, as shown in Figure 9.5.

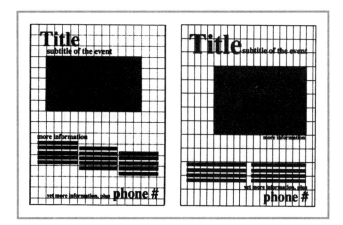

FIGURE
9.5
Use of a grid in display of documents

Brochures

A brochure differs from a flier in that it is printed on both sides of the paper and designed to be folded into panels. Brochures usually need to be printed professionally on a special press because of the quantity, the two-sided printing, and the folding. This means that the desktop published material is used as the master.

Because brochures are folded into panels, the relationship of the height and width dimensions of the page are altered. For this reason, it is useful to refer to tall pages as portrait layouts, and wide pages as landscape layouts. Most brochures are prepared on landscape layouts.

Folds and Panels The most common folds used in brochures are parallel folds. The least expensive and therefore most common type of brochure is a double-sided 8½" x 11" piece that is folded into six panels, as shown in Figure 9.6A. In this format, the printer's folding machine can be set at the same standard settings as for a letter fold. Other common types of brochure folds are also shown in Figure 9.6.

Common brochure folds

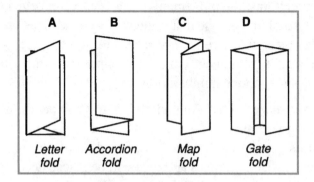

A three-panel letter-fold brochure is opened in a distinct way, and this has an effect on the design of the piece (see Figure 9.7). The page and panel numbers in the paragraphs that follow refer to this illustration.

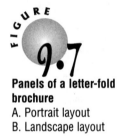

Panels of a letter-fold brochure
A. Portrait layout
B. Landscape layout

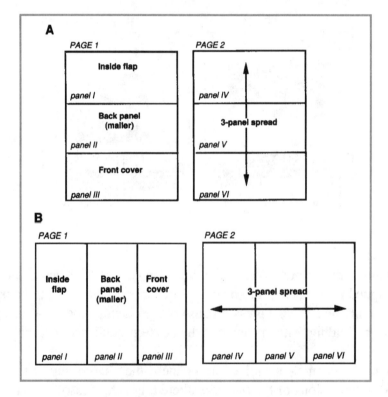

The cover is the *front panel*, which opens from right to left (landscape page layout) or from bottom to top (portrait page layout). The front panel is panel III on page 1. For landscape layout, this is the right panel; for portrait layout, it is the bottom panel.

The *inside flap* appears when the brochure is opened; it opens from left to right (landscape) or top to bottom (portrait). The inside flap panel is on the same page as the cover. It is panel I on page 1. In a landscape, this is the left panel; in a portrait, it is the top panel.

The *back panel* is opposite the front cover in the folded brochure. It is panel II on page 1, in the middle of the same page as the cover panel and the inside panel. If the back panel is used as a mailer, type must be rotated. For a landscape layout, it must be rotated 90 degrees; for a portrait layout, 180 degrees.

In a page assembly program, the *3-panel spread* is the full length or width of page 2. It is the 8½" x 11" page that appears when the brochure is completely opened. The 3-panel spread is printed on the back of the page containing the front panel, the inside flap, and the mailer. For a landscape, the 3-panel spread is printed head-to-head; for a portrait page layout, head-to-tail. This means that in a portrait, panel IV is on the back of panel I. In a landscape, panel IV is on the back of panel III.

Panel Design   The best way to visualize and design a brochure is to create a dummy. A **dummy** is a mock-up of the final planned publication. In this case, it is a piece of paper the size of your final product, with thumbnails of the design sketched on each panel.

The cover of a brochure is a typical display piece. Because it is the first thing the recipient sees, it should have a directional flow that urges the reader to open the brochure. For a landscape layout, the directional flow is from left to right; and for a portrait layout, from top to bottom. The 3-panel spread is viewed next, as whole, and should be designed accordingly. It usually contains the major portion of the text information. The inside flap (panel I of page 1) is often used for information that stands separately from the 3-panel spread.

Forms

As we all know, there are many different kinds of forms we encounter in our everyday lives. The forms discussed here are only those that are a part of the documents being discussed.

Brochures are often designed with tear-out forms to be returned by the recipient. When designing forms, the most important thing to remember is the backup. The **backup** is the material printed on the other side of the paper. It is a major design error to create a publication in which a panel that is to be torn off and returned contains information on the reverse side that the reader should be able to keep, such as the address or phone number of the organization, or the date, time, location, or schedule of an event.

Tear-out forms are most easily detached when at least two adjacent sides are at the edge of the paper. The left or right column (in a landscape layout) or the top or bottom column (in a portrait layout) of the 3-panel spread or the inside flap are good locations for a tear-out form. Boxes and rules can be used to separate the form from the brochure copy. Most page assembly programs have dashed lines that are used to indicate where to cut.

Extra line space (at least 12 points) should be provided for handwriting, and adequate space for long lines like addresses should be allowed. Check boxes and write-in lines, like any elements in a list, should be hang-indented. Extra line space helps to separate entries (see Figure 9.8).

DID YOU KNOW...

If the copy in a brochure runs to more than three panels, begin the copy in the 3-panel spread and continue it on the inside flap and, if necessary, on the back panel.

Form design
Allow at least 12 points of
space for handwriting,
and style checkbox lists
as hang indents.

Name: _____

Company: _____

Address: _____

_____

Telephone: _____

☐ Entry one here; it is styled as a hang indented list with
extra space between entries.

☐ Entry two here; it is styled as a hang indented list
with extra space between entries.

☐ Entry three here; it is styled as a hang indented list
with extra space between entries.

Advertisements often include a coupon on which the consumer can write information and then cut it out and send in or redeem it. Make sure there is enough room to write in the designated area. Remember, the easier the coupon is to use, the more likely the consumer is to use it. Place the coupon in the lower right corner of an advertisement. The ad itself should be located in the lower right corner of a page where it is easier to cut. Dashed lines or rectangles around the coupon often signify the area that is to be cut.

Order forms contain columns of information that are usually divided by vertical and horizontal lines, or rules. A person uses an order form to indicate quantity of products to be ordered, prices, and so on. Make sure there is enough room to write amounts, addresses, and so on. Check boxes are often used so the buyer can check, rather than write, additional ordering information.

An easy method of creating the horizontal rules in an order form is to use the paragraph specification in PageMaker that allows rules below the paragraph. Figure 9.9 shows the dialog box for **Paragraph Specifications**. Figure 9.10 shows the **Paragraph Rules** dialog box.

**Paragraph Specifications
dialog box**

Paragraph Specifications   ☒

Indents: Paragraph space: OK

Left   [0]   picas   Before [0]   picas   Cancel

First   [0]   picas   After   [0]   picas
                                                          Rules...
Right   [0]   picas
                                                          Spacing...

Alignment: [Left ▼]   Dictionary: [US English ▼]

Options:

☐ Keep lines together   ☐ Keep with next [0] lines

☐ Column break before   ☐ Widow control   [0] lines

☐ Page break before   ☐ Orphan control [0] lines

☐ Include in table of contents

FIGURE 9.10

Paragraph Rules dialog box

Rules can be placed above or below a paragraph. Remember, a paragraph in PageMaker is text followed by a carriage return.

STRUCTURED PUBLICATIONS

Structured publications are text-intensive and multipaged with standard repeating layout elements. Books and booklets—including manuals, directories, catalogs, and reports—are clearly structured documents. They contain information structured into sections, chapters, headings, and subheadings. Books and booklets are designed to efficiently and effectively communicate large amounts of information. In them, the logical organization of the material is of primary importance. Magazines and newsletters are also structured. Because they are serial publications filled with highly variable content from issue to issue, the job of design is quite complex. In particular, **copyfitting** (the art of making a variable amount of text fit into a fixed amount of space) becomes a primary consideration in the production of magazines and newsletters.

Books, newsletters, and magazines are professionally printed because of the volume and the double-sided printing. The printing is actually done on large sheets of paper, so that a number of pages are printed at a time. When these large sheets are folded and cut, they create **signatures**, or groups of pages in multiples of 8. Finished newsletters are often folded again, for distribution; these folds should be taken into account when designing pages. It is best if graphics do not fall on distribution fold lines. Letter-sized newsletters (8½" x 11") are usually folded in half or in thirds, and tabloid-sized newsletters (11" x 17") are usually folded in half.

Book, newsletter, and magazine pages should be designed in spreads—as facing pages. Because of the press paper grippers, however, pages cannot bleed between facing pages. Consult with your print shop about how much white space to leave in full page bleeds across a spread gutter; the white space is needed for binding purposes and varies according to trim size.

Template Elements

As noted in Chapter 8, in any structured publication, the column grid, standing elements, and, for serial publications, serial elements, can be placed in a template file. This helps to ensure consistency from page to page, and avoids having to reset these elements for every page and/or issue of the series.

Column Grid The template for a structured document should contain the primary column grid, which is the underlying form into which all the copy is placed. The grid is determined by the number of columns, the alleys, and, when appropriate, by distribution folds.

Pages can have a combination of column grids. The more columns, the greater the design flexibility, but also the greater the complexity in copyfitting. For multicolumn publications, a drawing of the column grid is sometimes made in a graphics program and printed for estimating and sketching the placement of different stories and illustrations. This process is called **blocking** (see Figure 9.11). Sometimes the standard column grid is not used for special layouts; but the grid should generally be consistent, as it establishes the primary structure of the publication.

FIGURE

9.11

Column grid
A multicolumn grid adds flexibility for blocking of text and graphics.

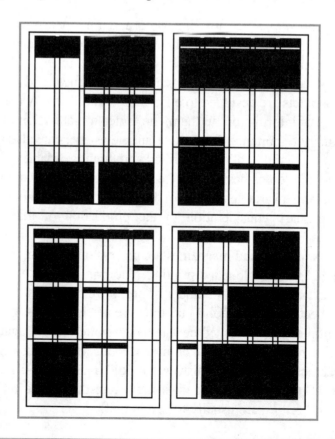

Standing Elements As discussed earlier, standing elements repeat from page to page within a publication. Most page assembly programs have a function for turning off standing elements on pages that do not require them.

Headers (also called *running heads*) are titles set at the top of each *text* page of a multipaged document. **Footers** (also called *running feet*) are set at the bottom of the page. Other design elements such as ruling lines, boxes, and screens may be associated with the header/footer. Headers and footers are generally not set on *display* pages (such as title pages and half-title pages) or on *opening* pages (such as the first page of a chapter or section).

On text pages, *folios* are usually set on the same line as the header or footer. Page numbers can be omitted from display pages and from pages containing full-page advertisements. On chapter or section opening pages, the page number is usually set at the bottom of the page.

In double-sided documents, page numbers should be set toward the outside margin—on the right side of rectos and on left side of versos, as shown in Figure 9.12. This is so a reader can thumb through the publication and see the page number easily, without having to turn each page separately.

4	*Title*	*Title*	5
Some text for this book. Some text for this book. Some text for this book. Some text for this book. Some text for this book. Some text for this book. Some text for this book. Some text for this book. Some text for this book. Some text for this book. Some text for this book. Some text for this book. Some text for this book. Some text for this book. Some		text for this book. Some text for this book. Some text for this book. Some text for this book. Some text for this book. Some text for this book. Some text for this book. Some text for this book. Some text for this book. Some text for this book. Some text for this book. Some text for Some text for this book. Some text for this book. Some text for this book.	

FIGURE 9.12
Running heads and folios
Running heads are set at the top of pages, and folios are set at the outside margin.

As mentioned in Chapter 8, page assembly programs have automatic page numbering features that will adjust the numbering when pages are inserted or deleted. In some page assembly programs, numbering style can also be designated. For frequently updated books, each section is sometimes numbered separately, for example, pages 1-1 through 1-20, pages 2-1 through 2-25. This makes it easier to insert materials at the end of sections; when new pages are added to Section 1, the pagination of Section 2 is not affected.

In books, **front matter** (title page, copyright page, tables of contents, lists of figures and tables, and so on) is often numbered with small roman numerals. **Back matter** (appendixes, end notes, references, bibliographies, glossaries, indexes, and so on) is usually numbered in the same manner as the body of the book, with Arabic numbers that continue the numbering in the body of the text.

Serial Elements Newsletters and magazines usually have at least two serial elements that are always consistent from one issue to the next: the banner and the masthead. Covers and cover pages for series of books or reports often contain similar serial elements.

The **banner** is the title of a periodical and appears on the cover of a magazine and the first page of a newsletter. It contains the name of the publication and serial information—date, volume, number. Volumes generally designate publication years, and numbers designate the series within the year, whether weekly, biweekly, monthly, bimonthly, or quarterly. Other information is sometimes included in the banner, such as the name of the sponsoring organization, its logo, address, and motto. Graphics are often used in a banner to make it more eye-catching and memorable (see Figure 9.13).

FIGURE 9.13
Banners

The **masthead** of a periodical is the credit box that gives information about the publication. It begins with the publication title, and it lists sponsors, editors, writers, illustrators, and photographers, among others. The masthead also includes the publication's office address, subscription and advertising information, and copyright notices. The masthead is usually placed on an inside page and should echo the banner in terms of the design of graphics, fonts, and colors (see Figure 9.14).

FIGURE 9.14
Mastheads

Other Template Elements   For newsletters and magazines, template elements may include a table of contents, a mailer, and headings within the publication for recurring features such as letters to the editor, regular columns, and calendars. In books, credit information and regular introductory elements are usually set on separate pages at the beginning of the publication.

Newsletter and Magazine Elements   Newsletters and magazines generally consist of a number of articles written by different authors, and these articles often begin on one page and continue to another, nonconsecutive page. The typographic style for the authors' credits and continuation elements can be put into the publication's style sheet. Some multi-authored books and reports may also contain these elements.

Bylines give credit to the author of an article and can be placed under the headline, or at the end of the article. In multi-authored books, the byline usually appears at the beginning of each article. Biographical information about the author can be set as a footnote or sidebar on the same page as the beginning of each article.

Bylines should be smaller than headlines. They may be set on a line by themselves or run in, and in any size or style, but they should be consistent throughout the publication (see Figure 9.15).

FIGURE 9.15
Byline

> # Computer graphics for desktop publishing
>
> *by JANE DOE* ——————————— (byline)
>
> The old saying "a picture is worth a thousand words" is true in desktop publishing, both denotatively and technically—graphics require much more processing

Continuation-out lines refer the reader to the page on which the story is continued; **continuation-in lines** refer the reader to the page from where the story started. Continuation lines are often set smaller than body type, in a distinctive style such as italic, on a new line, or run in with delimiters (parentheses, brackets, dashes, and so on).

Continuation lines are not needed for stories that continue from one column to another. Non-nested stories are assumed to continue in the next column, and for nested stories, a spanning headline implies continuation. A single story should not be broken up and set on different parts of the same page. Continuation heads are set above the continued part of the story, and are usually an abbreviated version of the full headline. They can be the same size or smaller than the full headline, and set in the same typeface (see Figure 9.16).

FIGURE
9.16
Continuation elements
A. The bottom of the last column on the first page of the story
B. The top of the first column on the page where the story is continued

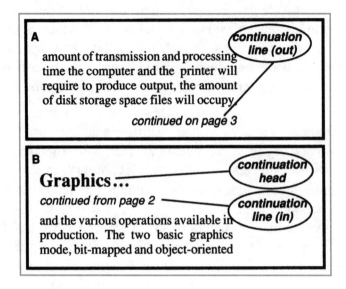

Copyfitting Techniques

In traditional graphic arts, copyfitting entails mathematical calculations for making sure that text will run the proper length (measured in column inches) at a given width (the column measure, specified in picas).

A **line gauge** is used to estimate the number of inches or picas that a piece of copy will run at a particular type specification and measure. The final calculation comes from actually counting the number of characters, or consulting tables that contain this information. A **castoff** is used to estimate how many pages of typeset material will result from a given number of pages of typescript (pages of monospaced type from a typewriter, daisy-wheel printer, or dot-matrix printer).

Galley Samples and Pages In desktop publishing, some copyfitting and a castoff may be needed for gross estimates, especially if outside writers are preparing text. But in most cases, since the desktop publisher is the typesetter, he or she can merely run the text or part of the text in the type specification and measure desired, and thus estimate from this galley sample how long the text will run. A **galley** is a proof of text-only material set at the proper specifications but not yet laid out as a page.

For magazines and newsletters, temporary galleys can be added to the template to make copyfitting easier. These pages will not be printed, but they do contain the column grid of the publication. They are used to place copy in order to determine how many column inches different blocks of text will occupy. Once the length of the text is determined, the word processing files can then be reassigned to an appropriate place in the publication.

Designing Space There are a number of other design elements that can be used to add emphasis and variety to gray text-intensive pages and to assist in copyfitting in newsletters and magazines. These design elements are used when the copy runs *short*. When copy runs *long* in newsletters and magazines, the content is usually edited to make it shorter.

A **kicker** is a brief phrase or sentence lead-in to a story or chapter. It is usually set smaller than the headline or chapter title, but can be larger than the body type. Story kickers can be placed above or below the headline or title (see Figure 9.17). In newsletters and magazines, publication kickers can be set above the banner—as a kind of preview of stories within the publication.

A **pull quote** is a brief phrase (not necessarily an actual quotation) from the body text, enlarged and set off from the text with rules, a box, and/or a screen. The phrase should be from a part of the text set previously, and should be set in the middle of a paragraph, not between paragraphs. Pull quotes should be placed in the middle of the text in a column, not at the bottom or top of a column (see Figure 9.17).

A pull quote is not the same as a block quote. A pull quote is brief (usually less than six lines), often set in type larger than the body text, and repeats a phrase from the body text. It is used often in magazines, to catch the reader's eye and pull the reader into the article. A **block quote** is long (more than four lines), often set in type smaller than the body text, and is attributable to someone other than the author of the body text. It is used often in books and scholarly articles, when the author wants to set off a quote.

TYPOGRAPHY FOR DESKTOP PUBLISHING

BY MARY HARRIS

In most publications, type bears the greatest weight of communication, because type bears the message of the written word. — *kicker*

Even if one expects to work primarily or even exclusively with text, the principles of computer graphics are an integral part of desktop publishing. This is because typography is a graphics application.

A non-typographical word-processing or data-processing program utilizes characters of one fixed size, positioned within fixed lines on the screen and on the printed page. These programs may offer methods for making bolds and underlines, but not larger or smaller characters. Most non-typographical programs produce only single- or multiple line-

spacing, and sometimes half-linespacing (for superscripts and subscripts).

Typographical word processors and page assembly programs, on the other hand, utilize different typefaces in differ-

> *... typography is a graphics application ...* — *pull quote*

ent sizes and positions on the page. In desktop publishing, size and position of text characters are variable, not fixed. Page assembly programs also offer typographical enhancements such as rules,

---

FIGURE 9.17

Kicker and pull quote
Kickers and pull quotes can be used to fill space in a story that runs short.

DID YOU KNOW...

Use kickers, pull quotes, and sidebars to add graphic interest and variety to gray all-text pages.

A **sidebar** is a related story or block of information that is set apart from the main body text, usually boxed and/or screened. Sometimes sidebars are actually topbars or bottombars. They may be set in any position relative to the main body text. In magazines and newsletters, a sidebar is usually set under the span of the main story headline (see Figure 9.18).

FIGURE 9.18

Sidebar
A sidebar can be set on the side, bottom, or top of the main story.

Sidebar

NEW TECHNOLOGY BRINGS PUBLISHING TO THE DESKTOP

BY JANE DOE

Desktop publishing is the use of a microcomputer-based system to produce publication materials—typeset or near-typeset quality text and graphics integrated on a page. These materials include notices, posters, certificates, fliers, brochures, forms, schedules, catalogues, reports, manuals, newsletters, newspapers, magazines, books—anything made up of words and pictures.

JANE DOE is the director of the desktop publishing program at the Communications Institute. She teaches the introductory technology overview course.

Desktop publishing can also be used to produce presentation materials such as overhead transparencies, slides, and even animated video images.

What makes desktop publishing different from traditional publishing is that the equipment used is small enough to fit on one person's desktop, and the desktop publishing system provides all the resources needed to prepare and assemble pages on that desktop.

Hardware & software: Desktop publishing, as defined here, utilizes a microcomputer system for WYSIWYG (What-You-See-Is-What-You-Get) graphic design and page assembly.

continued on page 2

COMMUNICATIONS INSTITUTE
Desktop publishing courses

The Communications Institute is offering courses on desktop publishing: technology overview, graphic design, typographical word processing, computer graphics, and electronic page assembly.

The seminars consist of lectures, demonstrations, hands-on software tutorials, problem-solving exercises, production projects, and project evaluations. Instruction is provided on either Apple® Macintosh or IBM® Model 50 computers.

CHECKING YOUR UNDERSTANDING

1. What kind of information is usually included on external covers? On cover pages?

2. What items are part of a stationery set? What are their standard dimensions?

3. List design considerations for the production of ads, posters, and fliers relative to their use.

4. List three ways to create focus on a page.

5. How is a grid used in designing a display document?

6. Describe the content and position in the page layout for the panels of a 6-panel portrait brochure and of a 6-panel landscape brochure.

7. List three functional considerations in the design of tear-out forms.

8. What kinds of pages do not carry headers or footers?

9. Identify and describe two standing elements frequently used in multipaged documents.

10. What is copyfitting? What is a galley?

APPLYING DESIGN PRINCIPLES

Exercise 1   Newsletter Design

Collect samples of newsletters that exemplify very good and very poor use of the basic principles of design: focus, balance, directional flow, unity, and negative space. Share these with the other students in your class and add the best design examples to the notebook you started in Chapter 1.

Good sources of newsletters are home associations, apartment complexes, museums (history, art, natural science), clubs, computer user groups, churches or temples, companies and corporations, departments, and mutual fund companies or stock brokerages.

Exercise 2 Elements of a Newsletter

Choose one newsletter from the above group and identify and circle the following elements:

a) banner

b) masthead

c) folio

d) byline

e) continuation line

f) kicker

g) pull quote

h) sidebar

Exercise 3 A Newsletter Template

Use the **New File** command to open one of PageMaker's newsletter templates. Print the template and analyze it for focus, balance, directional flow, unity, and negative space.

Exercise 4 Evaluating Display Documents

For these exercises, you will need a variety of magazines, newspapers, journals, and so on from which you can clip samples. Share these with the other students in your class. Add the samples that show good design elements to your notebook.

a) Look for samples of advertisements or announcements of a seminar, workshop, or conference. Find an example that meets each of the following criteria:

• An example with a strong visual impact.

• Uses a variety of type sizes (varied in increments of 12 points).

• Movement of the eye is from top to bottom and left to right. Is there a graphic in the bottom right corner?

b) Collect samples of brochures that meet the following criteria:
- Brochures that are folded with a letter fold, accordion fold, map fold, and gate fold.
- A brochure with a tear-out form.

c) Collect five different business cards. Find samples that
- are printed on colored paper
- have colored ink
- use a serif font
- use a sans serif font
- are printed on tall cards

d) Collect five samples of order forms and coupons. Discuss with other classmates the following elements and determine whether the design is good or bad.
- Use of check boxes.
- Enough room to write names, addresses, amounts, and so on.
- Location of coupon on page so that it is easy to cut or tear out.

CREATING
Portfolio

10

This chapter gives hands-on practice while you create a portfolio for the Desktop Publishing Workshop: a brochure, an order form, a schedule, a program, and name tags.

Upon completion of this chapter you will be able to

For the brochure:
- create a page grid using the **Column Guides** command
- use the **Library** palette to copy design elements into your publication
- use the **Rotation** tool to rotate text and graphics
- copy from PageMaker's clipboard
- rotate a block of text

For the order form:
- use the **Indents/Tabs** command to format first-line indents, left indents, and tabs with leaders
- incorporate rules and tabs with leaders into text

For the schedule:
- format text into tables using the **Row height**, **Define flow**, and **Sum function** commands of **Adobe Table 3.0**
- import and link a table

For the program:
- set up text in multiple columns

For the name tags:
- reset zero points
- paste design elements with the **Paste Multiple** command
- group objects together with the **Group** feature

Many of the documents you have worked on thus far have been for a desktop publishing workshop. The date for the workshop is approaching, and, as one of its organizers, your job is to create a portfolio of documents you need to promote the workshop and keep it running smoothly. The documents you must prepare are a brochure, an order form, a schedule, a program, and name tags for the participants. Better get to the studio!

CREATING A BROCHURE

New techniques you will use to create the brochure include the editing style sheets that are imported from Microsoft Word; setting up a landscape page with multiple columns; chaining text from column to column and page to page; and editing tabular material.

The source files you will need to create the brochure are: **brochtxt.txt**, **broreg**, **horizon.eps**, and **logo.eps**, all supplied on the student data disk.

Before starting this exercise, check your **Preferences** (in the **Edit** menu, select **Preferences**), making sure the measurement system is set in picas. Also check your page layout, **Target output resolution**, ruler zero points, and printer designation.

Creating the Page Grid

The brochure is set up as a two-page landscape. Do not use the facing pages option (the two pages will be printed back to back, not as facing pages).

1. Refer to the marked copy of the brochure (Figure 10.11), which you will find at the end of this section.

2. Create a new file (**Ctrl + N**), and in the **Document Setup** dialog box, select **Wide** for the orientation. (See Figure 10.1.)

FIGURE 10.1

Document Setup dialog box

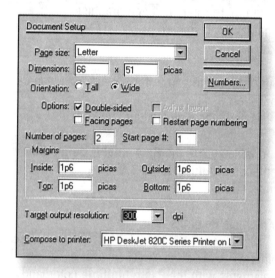

3. Set your measurement system to picas.

4. Set the Left, Right, Top, and Bottom margins as 1p6.

5. Click the **Master Page** icon to set up the columns. For a six-panel brochure, use **Column Guides** in the **Layout** menu to create three panels on each page. Since the outside margins are 1p6, the alleys for the columns should be twice as wide—3 picas—for proper alignment of the panels when the paper is folded. (See Figure 10.2.)

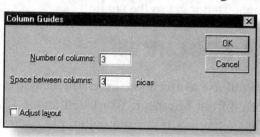

FIGURE 10.2

Column Guides dialog box

6. Click to page 1. Drag a horizontal ruler guide out of the ruler to 3p as shown in Figure 10.3. Drag a vertical guide to 58p6.

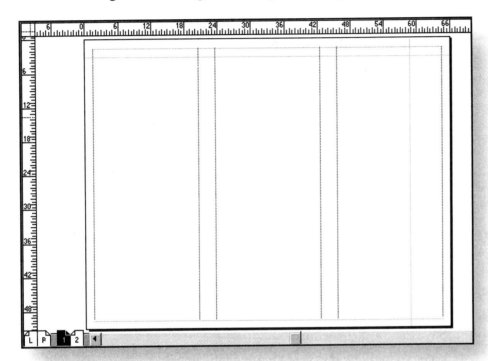

Setting ruler guides

7. On page 2, drag horizontal guides to 9p, 12p, and 47p. Drag a vertical guide from the ruler to the center of the page at 33p.

8. The **Lock Guides** command is useful because it prevents the column guides from being moved by accident when you are manipulating text and/or graphics on a page. **Lock Guides** is a toggle feature; it can be turned on or off. To lock the guides, click the **View** menu and select **Lock Guides**. Now if you try clicking and moving the guides, you will see that they will not move.

Creating the Cover Panel

The cover panel is the right column of the first page. You are familiar with all the elements on the cover since they are the same as the elements in the report you created in Chapter 8: workshop title, logo, tinted boxes, etc. Set up these elements as you see them on the marked copy of the brochure in Figure 10.11A on page 271.

There are two text blocks at the bottom of the front panel. One block contains the name of the association sponsoring the workshop, and the other block contains the association's address and phone number. They are layered on top of each other.

1. Click the **page 1** icon.

2. Key and position the text blocks; make sure the last line of text from each block is aligned on the bottom margin guide. Refer to Figure 10.11A.

3. "The Communications Institute" should be set in Helvetica, bold, 20/20, track tight. The address of the institute should be in Helvetica 9/10.

Importing a Graphic Image

DID YOU KNOW...

To view the screen better when you position the text blocks, click the **Magnifier** tool, then click **Ctrl + 2** for a 200% zoom, and click **Ctrl + 1** when you are finished.

On page 1, the **horizon.eps** image stretches across the bottom of the three panels. The image is enlarged to the point that it bleeds off the page. The distance the image extends off the page is the size of the bleed. PageMaker does not place a limit on the size of the bleed; however, bleeds larger than ¼ inch may interfere with crop marks and other printer's marks. Common sizes of bleeds are 1/16 inch to 1/4 inch.

1. Import the **horizon.eps** image file and position it so that it proportionately stretches across all three panels and extends just beyond the edges of the page.

2. If you have already placed the other elements on the cover panel, select the horizon image with the **Pointer** tool, and use the **Send to back** (**Shift + Ctrl + [**) command to layer the **horizon.eps** image behind, or in back of, all the other elements.

3. Save the file as **brochure**.

4. Later you will be instructed to rotate the image.

Using a Library Palette

PageMaker has a useful tool called the **Library** palette which can help you quickly access text and graphic files. The **Library** palette "floats" on the publication page and contains items that you import frequently. The palette is used to store, organize, view, search for, and retrieve text blocks and graphics. Use the **Library** palette instead of the **Place** command to search for a file to import. Figure 10.4 contains frequently used text blocks and graphics from the publications created in this chapter. Note that you can create several libraries, but only one can be open at a time.

FIGURE

10.4

Library palette with frequently-used text blocks and graphics

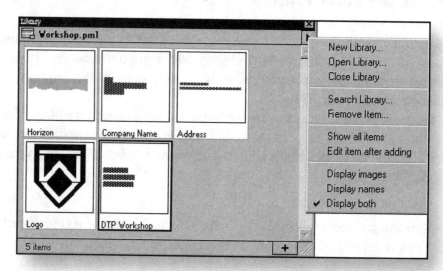

Let's create a library to store the horizon and logo graphic files for this brochure since each file is used more than once. Select **Show Library** from the **Plug-in** palette in the **Window** menu. The **Show Library** option appears. Click on the pointer under the **Close** button, then click on **New**. Because a library has not been created, the **New Library** dialog box appears. Key the name **Workshop** in the **File name** text box, and then click **Save**. (See Figure 10.5.)

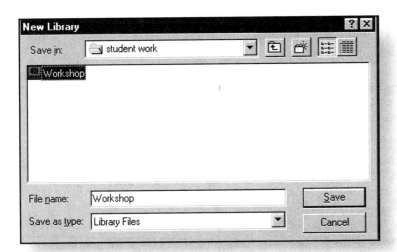

FIGURE

10.5

New Library dialog box

The **New Library** palette is created. Now it's time to add a graphic file to the library. One or more objects can be added to the library at one time.

1. To add the **horizon.eps** graphic to the library, select the horizon graphic with the **Pointer** tool.

2. Click the **Add** button (the plus sign) on the **Library** palette (see Figure 10.6).

FIGURE

10.6

The *Add* button on the *Library* palette

3. Click twice on the image in the library, and the **Item information** box will appear. (See Figure 10.7.)

4. Type **Horizon** in the title area. Click **OK**.

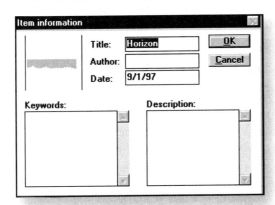

FIGURE

10.7

Item information dialog box

5. Drag the **Library** window to the side of the screen, visible but out of the way.

Creating the Three-Panel Spread

The text for this part of the brochure is in the text file named **brochtxt.txt** on your data disk. The text is placed and chained within the three columns as you see on the marked copy of the brochure.

Create the following PageMaker styles:

Head—based on No style, next style is No style; bold; all caps; Helvetica, 12-point type; leading: 14; horizontal scale: 150%.

Body2 Text—based on No style, next style is same style; Times New Roman, 10-point type; leading: 15; flush left; hyphenation; first-line indent is 2. (*Reminder*: no bold, normal horizontal scale, not all caps.)

Working with Chained Text

1. Click page 2.

2. Place the text from the **brochtxt.txt** file so that it begins in the leftmost column of the page. With **Autoflow** set to "on," position the loaded **Text** tool just under the ruler guide at 12p and click. The text will continue to flow until it is all placed.

3. Assign the **Body2 Text** style to the paragraphs in the text. Assign the **Head** style to the headings on the page. Look at the marked copy to notice where the text begins and ends in each column.

4. Add bullets to the list of topics to be covered.

5. Click and drag the bottom windowshades to adjust the length of the text blocks in the columns so that they match the marked copy. You can tell that the text is chained by the plus signs in the windowshades.

Rotating a Graphic   The **horizon.eps** graphic is to be positioned at the top of page 2 in the brochure. This is the same graphic you positioned on the bottom of page 1. The **Library** palette contains this graphic. You can simply drag the graphic off the **Library** palette to page 2. When you drag the graphic from the library, you are actually dragging a *copy* of the graphic file. The **horizon.eps** file remains on the **Library** palette.

1. Click the **horizon.eps** file in the **Library** palette and drag it to page 2 of the brochure.

2. Resize the image proportionately so that it spans the three columns and bleeds off the top of the page by approximately 2 inches. Remember to send the image to the back.

On page 1, the image should be rotated 180 degrees to change the effect of the reflection of the "horizon." PageMaker has the ability to rotate an image 360 degrees at .01-degree increments. The **Rotation** tool is in the toolbox. First you must select the image with the **Pointer** tool. Then choose the **Rotation** tool. The pointer changes to a starburst shape. The starburst is placed on the image at the point where the rotation will occur. Click and drag the starburst away from the center point. A rotation lever appears that connects the starburst with the center of rotation. Drag the lever in the direction the image should rotate. The farther away you drag the starburst, the more control you have when you rotate the image.

1. On page 1, select the **horizon.eps** image with the **Pointer** tool.

2. Click the **Rotation** tool in the toolbox.

3. Click in the exact center of the image and rotate 180 degrees. Hold down the **Shift** key while rotating.

4. Position the image so that only part of it is showing, as you see in Figure 10.8. The image will bleed off the bottom.

Rotating *horizon.eps* on page 1

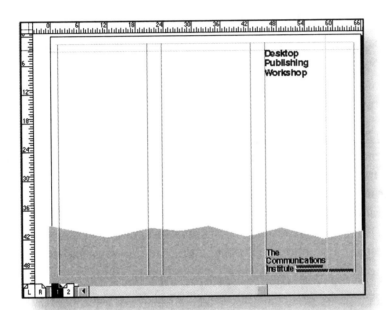

5. Type **EXPAND YOUR HORIZONS** on the top of page 2 as shown in Figure 10.11B. With the **Horizontal Scale** command, extend from margin to margin.

6. Save the file.

Creating the Inside Flap Panel

The inside flap panel is the left column of page 1 of the brochure. It contains a registration form for the workshop. The text block containing the registration form is rotated. The process used to rotate text is similar to that for rotating a graphic. The form also contains check boxes that the registrant checks to provide information.

Copying from the Clipboard It is possible to copy text blocks from other PageMaker files into the current document. The text must first be copied to the clipboard of PageMaker. The **clipboard** is a special area of memory that can store one block of text or one graphic at a time. The registration form is located in the PageMaker file called **broreg**. Another file can be opened in PageMaker while the **brochure** file is open.

1. Click page 1.
2. Click the **File** menu and select the **Open** option.
3. Select the **broreg** filename. It is a one-page document containing the registration form.
4. Select the text block with the **Pointer** tool.
5. Select and copy the text block (**Ctrl + C**) to the clipboard.
6. Close the **broreg** file. The **brochure** file is still open and appears on the screen.
7. Scroll to the pasteboard at the left of the page. Paste the text block containing the registration form to the pasteboard (**Ctrl + V**).

Rotating a Text Block A text block can be rotated by any number of degrees in .01-degree increments. To rotate a text block, first select the block with the **Pointer** tool. Then select the **Rotation** tool in the toolbox. Click and hold the point around which you want the text block to rotate. A rotation lever appears as you click and drag the starburst out from the rotation point. If you drag the lever immediately after clicking, a frame, indicating the text block, spins around the rotation point. If you drag a little more slowly, you can see the text rotating as you turn the lever (see Figure 10.9).

FIGURE
10.9
Rotating a text block

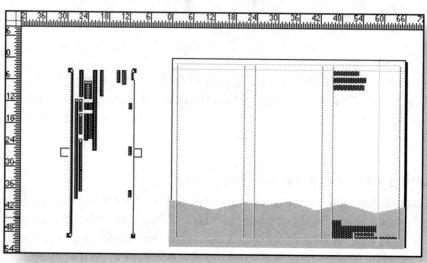

You do not have to click the **Rotation** tool directly on the text block. You can position the **Rotation** tool anywhere on the screen. Just make sure that the text block is selected with the **Pointer** tool before doing this.

1. Change to **25% View** to work with the text block.

2. Select the text block with the **Pointer** tool.

3. Click the **Rotation** tool in the toolbox.

4. Hold down the **Shift** key to limit the rotation to 45 degrees.

5. Position the starburst on the text block and rotate it clockwise by 90 degrees so that the text "reads" in the same direction as is shown on the marked copy.

6. Save the file (**Ctrl + S**).

7. Change to **50% View** and position the text block on the inside flap panel of the brochure.

Drawing a Rule Because the registration form must be detached from the brochure, a dotted line is needed to show the person registering where to cut the form.

1. Use the **Constrained line** tool to draw a vertical rule in the exact center of the alley between the two columns (or panels). The **Constrained line** tool is used to draw lines that are limited to 45 degree angles.

2. Select the line with the **Pointer** tool. From the **Element/Stroke** menu, select a 3-point dashed line format (see Figure 10.10).

3. Save the file.

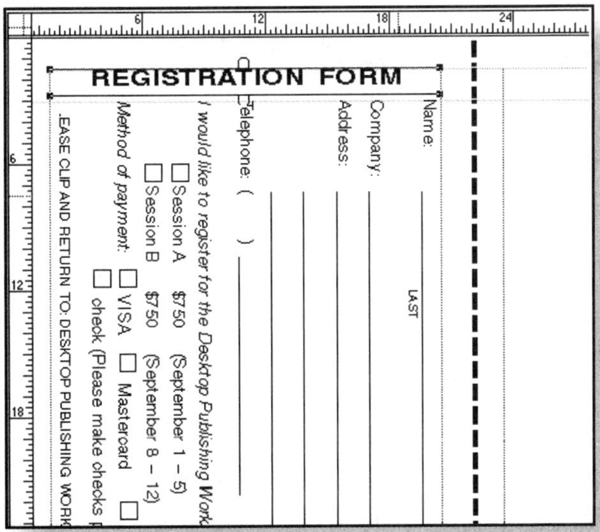

FIGURE 10.10

A 3-point dashed line from the *Element* menu

Finishing the Inside Flap Panel One more line of text must be added to finish this panel.

1. Draw a bounding box with the **Text** tool.

2. Key the text, **REGISTRATION FORM**, and apply these specs: Helvetica, 12-point type; leading 15; bold; set width 150%; all caps; center.

3. Position the text at the top margin of the column (see Figure 10.10).

Creating the Back Panel (Mailer)

The back panel, which is actually the middle column of page 1, is used as a mailer. Follow these steps to rotate and position the address of the Communications Institute in the upper-right corner of the panel. You will also rotate and position another block of text and then add the logo.

1. Key the information for the return address as shown in Figure 10.11A. Format the text and position it as shown. See if you can recognize the font, size, and type style.

2. Import the **logo.eps** image and position it to the left of the return address and on the front of the brochure as shown in Figure 10.11A.

3. Add the **logo.eps** file to the **Workshop library** palette.

4. Key the phrase **EXPAND YOUR HORIZONS** as shown in Figure 10.11A with one blank space between each letter and two blank spaces between words. Format the text with 12-point Helvetica type; auto leading; bold; all caps; horizontal scale 250%, and position it above the dotted line on page 1.

5. Finish page 2 by keying **DESKTOP PUBLISHING WORKSHOP** and placing the logo in column 2 as shown in Figure 10.11B.

6. Save the file.

7. Note that this is a large file and it may take a long time to print.

CREATING AN ORDER FORM

People attending the Desktop Publishing Workshop can order books or disks by using an order form. The instructions in this section explain how to create the order form. See the marked copy of the form (Figure 10.16) at the end of this section. Refer to it while you are working on creating the form.

When you look at the form, you will see that it has 5 columns. Columnar information is easy to create with the use of tabs. Decimal tabs are used with currency, so that the numbers line up on the decimal point. PageMaker allows you to create a style sheet that incorporates rules, tabs, type, and so on.

1. Create a **New** document with top and bottom margins at 3p and left and right margins at **6p**. This order form is one page, so make sure that **Double-sided** is *not* checked.

2. Drag a horizontal ruler guide down 17p from the top of the page.

3. With the **Text** tool, click an insertion point at the left margin just below the 17p ruler guide.

4. For the headings, use 8-point Helvetica; bold. Leave three blank spaces and then key the first heading: **QTY**.

FIGURE

10.11A

Page 1 of the brochure

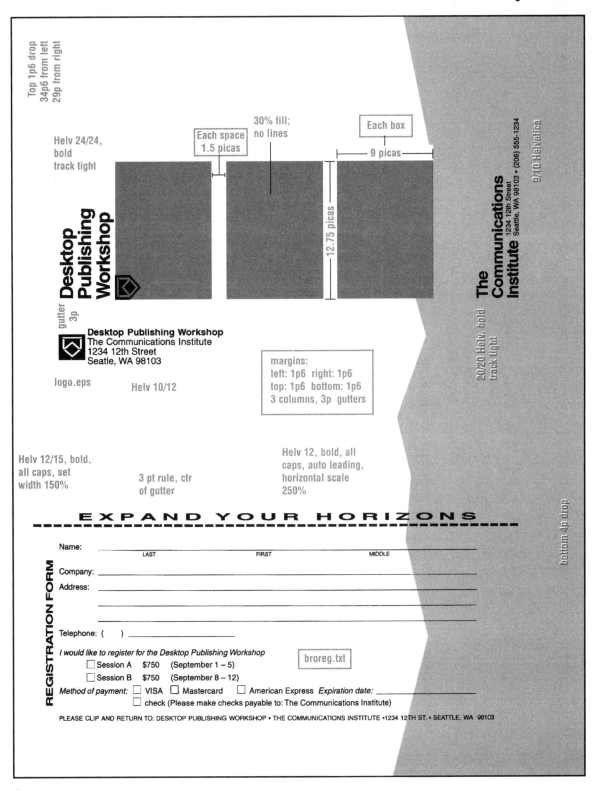

Top 1p6 drop
34p6 from left
29p from right

Helv 24/24,
bold
track tight

Each space
1.5 picas

30% fill;
no lines

Each box

9 picas

12.75 picas

Desktop
Publishing
Workshop

The
Communications
Institute
1234 12th Street
Seatle, WA 98103 • (206) 555-1234

9/10 Helvetica

gutter 3p

20/20 Helv. bold
track tight

Desktop Publishing Workshop
The Communications Institute
1234 12th Street
Seatle, WA 98103

logo.eps

Helv 10/12

margins:
left: 1p6 right: 1p6
top: 1p6 bottom: 1p6
3 columns, 3p gutters

bottom 4p drop

Helv 12/15, bold,
all caps, set
width 150%

3 pt rule, ctr
of gutter

Helv 12, bold, all
caps, auto leading,
horizontal scale
250%

EXPAND YOUR HORIZONS

Name: _____
LAST   FIRST   MIDDLE

Company: _____

Address: _____

_____

_____

Telephone: (   ) _____

I would like to register for the Desktop Publishing Workshop

☐ Session A $750   (September 1 – 5)

☐ Session B $750   (September 8 – 12)

broreg.txt

Method of payment: ☐ VISA ☐ Mastercard   ☐ American Express *Expiration date:* _____

☐ check (Please make checks payable to: The Communications Institute)

PLEASE CLIP AND RETURN TO: DESKTOP PUBLISHING WORKSHOP • THE COMMUNICATIONS INSTITUTE •1234 12TH ST. • SEATTLE. WA 98103

REGISTRATION FORM

FIGURE
10.11B
Page 2 of the brochure

EXPAND YOUR HORIZONS

Helv 36, bold, all caps, auto leading, set width 175%

Top of caps at top margin

Helv 12/15, hold, all caps, set width 150%

THE WORKSHOPS

The Communications Institute Desktop Publishing Workshop is designed to expand the horizons of office professionals. Participants will learn basic principles of typography and design, and create over a dozen different types of publications using the sophisticated and popular program, Adobe PageMaker. No previous experience in graphic design or PageMaker is required, but familiarity with the Macintosh or Microsoft Windows environment is recommended.

Topics covered include:

- text entry and manipulation
- typographic specifications
- graphics enhancements
- importation of text and graphics
- cropping and scaling graphics
- scanning and color printing basics
- column specifications
- production of tabular materials
- use of master pages
- multipaged publications
- authoring tools
- creation and use of templates
- copyfitting

REGISTRATION AND SCHEDULE

Tuition of $750 includes hands-on classes, instruction materials, and luncheon on each day of class. Workshop registration is limited to twenty participants per session so that each participant has exclusive use of his or her own computer. Because space is limited, preregistration is recommended two weeks before the workshop session. Full refunds are available until that date.

Two sessions are available: Workshop A will be held September 1-5, and Workshop B will be held September 8-12. The workshops will be held from 8:00 a.m. to 5:00 p.m. in The Communications Institute's computer lab. Coffee and rolls in the morning and a buffet-style luncheon will be served in the Institute's dining room.

FACILITIES

Each participant will have exclusive use of a 68020 Macintosh or Pentium IBM-compatible system, and have access to a color scanner, and a 600 dpi laser printer. In addition to the PageMaker program, The Communications Institute has several graphics, word processing, database, and spreadsheet programs that are available to participants. No instruction will be provided for programs other than PageMaker, but documentation for all programs is available in the computer lab.

Students may also use and/or order reference books and periodicals distributed by the Institute and available in the Institute's library.

The Communications Institute is located near Seattle's Capitol Hill neighborhood, which boasts of having a lively variety of restaurants and shops, as well as accommodations for out-of-town participants.

THE INSTRUCTOR

The instructor, Ms. Maria Lee, is a certified Adobe trainer with a professional background in teaching, graphic arts, and business. Ms. Lee worked with the beta version of Adobe PageMaker at the University of Wisconsin in 1985, and has owned her own freelance business since 1989.

Helv 10/10, bold, ctr

Desktop Publishing Workshop

logo: Bottom 44p2 drop

*margins:
left: 1p6 right: 1p6
top: 1p6 bottom: 1p6
3 columns, 3p gutters*

Setting Tabs

PageMaker's **Indents/Tabs** dialog box (Figure 10.12) is accessible from the **Type** menu. There are four icons in the dialog box that represent four different kinds of tabs: left (default), right, centered, and decimal. It is important to remember that indents and tabs are measured from the left edge of the selected text block. Do not confuse tab measurements with measurements from the left edge of the page. Always make sure the left margin or left edge of the text block is showing on the screen before you activate the **Indents/Tabs** dialog box. The ruler in the dialog box will be aligned with the left margin or the left edge of the selected text block.

The two small triangles at the left edge of the ruler control the *first-line indent* and *left paragraph indent*. The larger triangle at the right edge of the ruler controls the *right paragraph indent*. The top triangle at the left represents the first-line indent, and the bottom triangle is used for the left paragraph indent. You must drag the indent triangles on the ruler to the desired position. When you release the triangle, the position value is noted in the **Position** edit box.

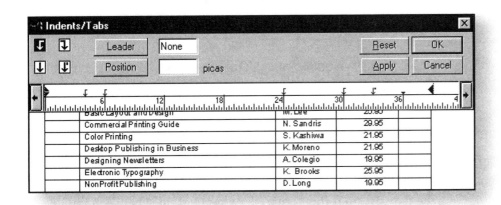

Indents/Tabs dialog box

To set a tab, select the text, click the desired tab icon, and then click at a location on the ruler. An existing tab can be dragged to a new location along the ruler. The exact location is noted in the **Position** edit box.

1. With the text selected, open the **Indents/Tabs** dialog box from the **Type** menu. Set left tabs at 4, 6, 24, 30, and 36.

2. Set a decimal tab at 33. Click **OK** (see Figure 10.12).

3. Select **Paragraph** from the **Type** menu. Click the **Rules** button. Set the specifications for a .5 line style below the paragraph. Click **OK** twice.

4. Save the file as **orderfrm**.

5. Place the cursor after **QTY**.

6. Press **Tab** and finish keying the line. After keying the last word, press the **Enter** key. You should see a rule below the first typed line.

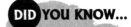

DID YOU KNOW...

To move the left-indent triangle without moving the first-line indent triangle, hold down the **Shift** key as you drag the left indent.

7. Before you key the second line of the order form, create a new style called "Rules" with these specifications: Helvetica, 10/14, .5 point rule below paragraph, left tabs at 4, 6, and 24 and a decimal tab at 33.

8. Continue keying the information on the order form until you finish the **TOTAL # disks** line near the bottom. Tag all with the **Rules** style.

9. Press **Enter** to move the cursor to the next line.

10. Save the file.

Setting Up Left Indents with Ruled Paragraphs

The next three lines of the form shown in Figure 10.13 are indented from the left margin. You can set this indentation in the **Indents/Tabs** dialog box or in the **Paragraph Specifications** dialog box as shown in Figure 10.14. The text is indented to 24p. The paragraph rule under the lines is extended to the right margin. You should change the length so that the rule extends the length of the text and not the column width. This is accomplished by using a right tab marker. Follow these directions:

1. Click the **Type** menu and select **Indents/Tabs**.

2. Drag the first-line indent and left paragraph indent triangles to 24p on the ruler.

3. Set a right tab at 39p on the ruler. (This should be the right paragraph marker).

4. Click **OK**.

5. Key the three lines for the subtotal, tax, and merchandise total.

6. Key the final lines of the order form as they are specified on the marked copy.

7. Use the **Constrained line** tool to draw vertical rules between the columns.

8. Draw a box around this part of the form. Make sure that the lines of the box touch the ends of the ruled paragraphs.

9. Save the file.

FIGURE 10.13

Three indented lines

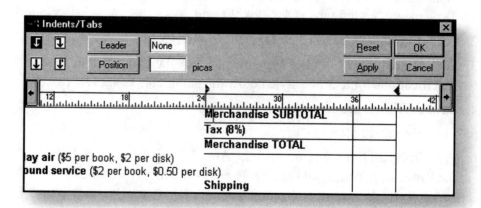

Paragraph Specifications
dialog box

Using a Tab with Leaders

The order form has a section with shipping information, which is in a separate text block. It is the part of the form where a name, address, and phone number are written by the buyer. The lines are created by using a right tab with leaders rather than using the **Line** tool. Leaders can be dots, dashes, lines, or a customized pattern you create. Leaders are specified in the **Indents/Tabs** dialog box. In Figure 10.15 a right tab is set at the 20p location, and the underline character is set as the leader. It is difficult to see the

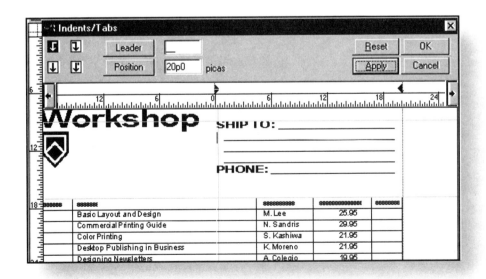

The under character is set as the leader

right tab marker because it is at the same location as the right paragraph triangle. However, notice the setting in the **Position** edit box.

1. Clear all other tab settings and drag a vertical ruler guide to 25p on the page. Drag a horizontal ruler guide to 9p. With the **Text** tool, draw a bounding box that begins in the upper-left corner of these ruler guides and extends over to the right margin guide.

2. Access the **Indents/Tabs** dialog box and set a right tab with an underline leader at 20p. Click **OK**.

3. Key the words **SHIP TO:** and then press **Enter**.

4. Notice that when you press the **Enter** key, the leader appears and the insertion point is on the next line. Press **Enter** for each line of leaders.

5. Finish this section by keying the rest of the text according to the marked copy.

6. Save the file.

7. Finish the order form by dragging the other elements from the **Workshop library** palette and positioning them in the correct locations.

8. Bullets at the bottom of the form can be created, then copied, by using the **Bullets and numbering** dialog box.

9. Save the file.

F I G U R E
10.16
Order form

Desktop Publishing Workshop

Helv 30/28, bold track tight, set width 150%
Top of cap at top margin

Helv 12/14, bold, all caps, set width150%

top of logo: **10p**
bottom of logo: **13p7**

Helv 7/12, bold, all caps, set width 150%

tab: **4p**

Helv 10/14

BOOK / DISK ORDER FORM

Helv 12, bold, all caps, auto leading, set width 150%

SHIP TO: _____

PHONE:

tab: **24p**   tab: **30p**   dec. tab: **33p**   tab: **36p**

QTY	TITLE	AUTHOR	PRICE/UNIT	TOTAL
	Basic Layout and Design	M. Lee	25.95	
	Commercial Printing Guide	N. Sandris	29.95	
	Color Printing	S. Kashiwa	21.95	
	Desktop Publishing in Business	K. Moreno	21.95	
	Designing Newsletters	A. Colegio	19.95	
	Electronic Typography	K. Brooks	25.95	
	Nonprofit Publishing	D. Long	19.95	
	TOTAL # books			
	PageMaker Templates			
	Newsletters		19.95	
	Brochures		19.95	
	Reports		19.94	
	Miscellaneous (posters, fliers, etc.)		19.95	
	Clip Art (.eps format)			
	Animals		9.95	
	Electronics		9.95	
	Food		9.95	
	House & furniture		9.95	
	People		9.95	
	Plants		9.95	
	Religious & seasonal		9.95	
	TOTAL # disks			

margins:
left: **6p** right: **6p**
top: **3p** bottom: **3p**

tab: **6p**

Helv 10/12, bold, all caps, set width 150%

Helv 10/14, bold left indent **24p**

Merchandise SUBTOTAL
Tax (8%)
Merchandise TOTAL

SHIP BY: ☐ **2-day air** ($7 per book, $5 per disk)
☐ **Ground service** ($5 per book, $2 per disk)

Shipping
TOTAL ENCLOSED

☐ **VISA**   ☐ **Mastercard**   ☐ **American Express**
☐ Check – Please make checks payable to: **The Communications Institute**

Helv 9/11, bold set width 150%

Helv 18/18, bold track tight

The Communications Institute

Helv 11/18, bold track tight

1234 12th Street • Seattle WA 98103 • 206.555.1234

CREATING A SCHEDULE

You will now create a speaker's schedule for the Desktop Publishing Workshop, using PageMaker's table editor utility called Adobe Table 3.0. You will need the following source file: **spkr.txt**. Refer to Figure 10.28 as you work on the schedule.

Working with Adobe Table 3.0

The schedule lists the speakers for the workshop, the topics they will be discussing, the time they are scheduled to speak, and the fee they will be paid. When you look at the schedule, you will see at the bottom of the Fee column a total for all the fees.

FIGURE

10.17

Opening *Adobe Table 3.0*

1. Select **Adobe Table 3.0**. (See Figure 10.17.)

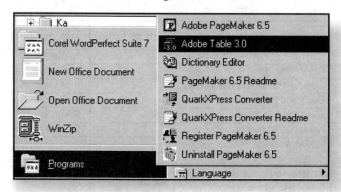

2. When the **Document Setup** dialog box appears, choose ½-inch margins on all sides.

3. Figure 10.18 contains the **New Table** dialog box. Make the choices shown in the figure and click **OK**.

FIGURE

10.18

New Table dialog box

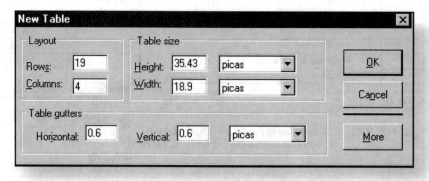

4. Select the **File** menu and save the file as **spkr**.

Column Width

You can adjust the column width manually by placing the cursor on the vertical line between two column labels. The cursor changes to the double-headed horizontal arrow you see in Figure 10.19. Then click and drag the arrow to the new measurement. You may also adjust the row height with this method. However, the overall size of the table does not change. The row or column next to the one being adjusted increases or decreases in size when you use this method. The one exception to this is if you adjust the rightmost column or bottom row of a table. To decrease the size of column A, follow these directions:

FIGURE
10.19
Changing column width in table

1. Place the cursor between the column labels of columns A and B.

2. Click and drag to the 8-pica measurement in the ruler. Notice that column A increases in size.

3. Now make the other column width changes shown in Figure 10.28 by clicking and dragging between the column labels of B and C, then C and D.

The initial row height of a table is calculated from the data specified for the page length in the **New Table** dialog box. A row height will change if the text in any cell wraps around to the next line. Currently, the row height in the table is 3p. Try changing every row so that the height is decreased to 1.6p. To change the height for every row, you select the entire table and then specify the new row height.

1. To select the entire table, click the small label without a header identification that is just to the left of column A and just above row 1. It is shown in Figure 10.20.

Click here ──▶

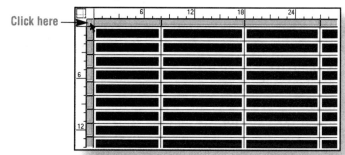

FIGURE
10.20

To select the entire table, click the small label where the black arrow is pointing.

2. Select the **Cell** menu and click **Row/Column size**.

3. Figure 10.21 shows the **Row height** dialog box with the new measurement keyed in the edit box. Type **1.6p** for the new height and click **OK**.

4. Save the file.

FIGURE

10.21

Row/Column Size dialog box

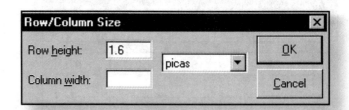

In Figure 10.22, notice that the three lines that make up the table title are centered across all columns. You can accomplish this by using the **Group** command.

1. Use the **Pointer** tool to select the four cells in row 1. Select the **Cell** menu and click the **Group** option.

FIGURE

10.22

Centered table title

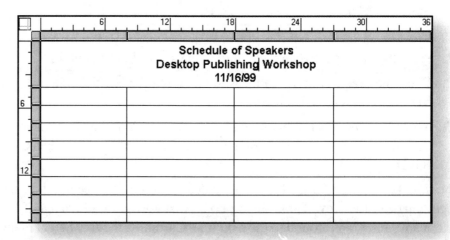

2. Key the three lines of the title and format them as Helvetica 12 point, bold, and centered. Select **Show text palette** from the **Window** menu. Use this palette to format the text.

3. Key the column titles in row 2. Use Helvetica 12-point, bold.

4. Save the file.

Text within a cell can be aligned both vertically and horizontally. You are already familiar with horizontal alignments. Vertically, the text can be placed at the top, middle, or bottom of the cell.

Now align the title so that the three lines are centered horizontally if they are not already centered.

You will now import the **spkr.txt** file into the table. To use the **Import Text** command from the **File** menu, you must select the group of cells where the text will be placed. The text, which has been created in Microsoft® Word, has been aligned in columns with the use of tabs.

1. Place the cursor in the first cell under the heading **Speaker**. (Do not select the cell.)

2. Select the **File** menu and click **Import Text**. The **Import Text file** dialog box is shown in Figure 10.23.

3. Select the file **spkr**.

4. Click **IMPORT**.

5. Save the file.

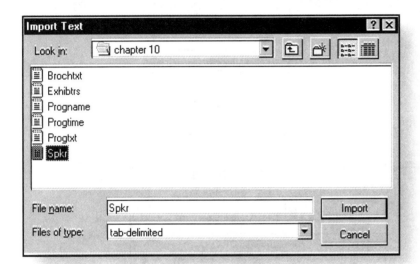

Import Text dialog box

6. Select the whole table. Select **Format Cells** from the **Format** menu and apply a 4-point outside border.

7. Select row 2. Select **Format Cells** from the **Format** menu and apply a fill of 30%.

Finishing the Table   You can now finish the table by making these additional formatting changes:

1. Select the word "Topic" in row 2 and center it horizontally in the cell.

2. Select row 2 and create a top and bottom border using a 1-point line.

3. Select rows 3–19 and change the interior lines so that they are not displayed. With these rows selected, the **Table Attributes** dialog box should look like the one in Figure 10.24. It is accessed through the **Windows** menu.

4. All the text in columns 3 and 4 should be horizontally aligned to the right. You can select both columns and align them at the same time.

FIGURE

10.24

Table Attributes dialog box

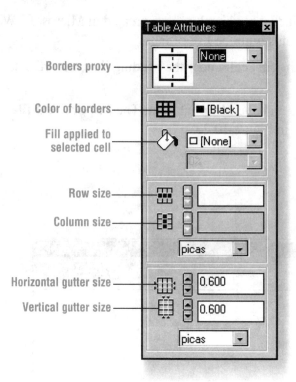

Borders proxy

Color of borders

Fill applied to selected cell

Row size

Column size

Horizontal gutter size

Vertical gutter size

FIGURE

10.25

Changing column width in table

5. Change column widths to those shown in Figure 10.25.

6. Bold **Total** and **$1,825** at the bottom of columns 3 and 4.

7. Save the file.

Importing the Table into PageMaker

Before you can import a table into PageMaker, you must export it as a graphic file. You then use the **Place** command to import the table. Therefore, you cannot make any changes to the table in PageMaker. If you need to update or change the text, this must be done in Adobe Table 3.0.

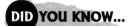

1. Select **Export**, then **Graphic** from the **File** menu. In Windows, save the file **spkr** as file type **.emf**.

2. Create a new document in PageMaker with all margins at 5p5.

3. With the **Pointer** tool, select **Place** from the **File** menu. Double-click the filename **spkr**.

4. Position the loaded graphic icon on the page where you want to place the top of the table.

5. Click the mouse once, and the table flows onto the page.

6. You can enlarge the table by dragging one of the corner handles of the table. The table will enlarge proportionally as long as you hold down the **Shift** key and drag a corner handle.

7. Position the table so that it is centered between the margin guides and begins at the top margin.

8. Save the PageMaker file as **spkrschd**.

Linking a Table to PageMaker

The imported table in PageMaker can be linked to Adobe Table 3.0 with the **Links** command in the **File** menu. The advantage of linking is that the table will automatically update itself in a PageMaker document if the **Update automatically** option is selected.

1. Select the table graphic with the **Pointer** tool.

2. Select **Links Manager** from the **File** menu. The **Links Manager** dialog box is shown in Figure 10.26.

3. Click the **Options** button.

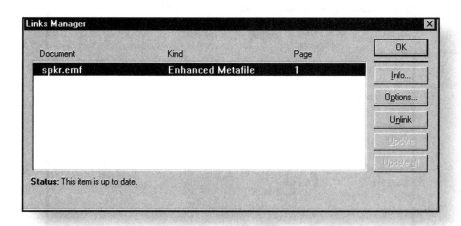

FIGURE 10.26

Links Manager dialog box

4. Click the **Store copy in publication** and **Update automatically** buttons as shown in Figure 10.27.

FIGURE

10.27

Link Options **dialog box**

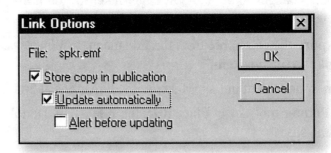

5. Click **OK** and **OK** again.

6. Save the file.

7. Print the file.

FIGURE

10.28

Speaker schedule

Set column headings in Row 2 in Helvetica 12-point, bold, with a 30% fill; top and bottom border use a 1-point line.

The four column widths are A: 8; B: 25; C: 6; and D: 6.

Set text in 10/12 Times Roman.

Use the Group command to center these three lines [top heading].

½-inch margins, all sides.

Schedule of Speakers
Desktop Publishing Workshop
11/16/99

Speaker	Topic	Time	Fee
Maria Lee	Keynote	8:45	$100
Kathleen Moreno	Integration of desktop publishing in the office work flow	9:30	75
Chuck Miller	Form creation for business applications	9:30	75
Michael Brooks	Preparation of files for desktop publishing	9:30	75
Donna Long	Layout and design standardization	9:30	75
Michael Brooks	Converting databases into publications	11:00	75
Sara Kashiwa	Photographic image scanning technologies	11:00	75
Alvaro Colegio	Authoring tools for desktop publishing	11:00	75
Kathleen Moreno	Document management and archiving	11:00	75
Chuck Miller	The editing and proofing cycle in a network environment	2:00	75
Linda Goodman	Graphics programs for desktop publishing	2:00	75
Sara Kashiwa	Alternative output devices	2:00	75
Nicolas Sandris	Commercial printing: paper and ink	2:00	75
All Leaders	Panel Discussion	3:45	750
Maria Lee	Closing Remarks	4:30	75
		Total	**$1,825**

CREATING A PROGRAM

The next document needed for the Desktop Publishing Workshop is a workshop program. You will create it as a landscaped publication that contains columns, a map of meeting room locations, a schedule for the workshop, the logo, and a list of exhibitors. The program is two pages, printed on both sides, and then folded in half. Most of the graphics for the program are already on the **Library** palette. However, one graphic, the **map.eps** file, is new. By now, you should be able to place graphics on the page easily. The text for the inside panels of the program is placed in six columns across a landscaped page. Refer to Figures 10.34A and B, the marked copy of the program, as you work on it.

Creating the Front Panel

Start the program by creating a new publication that is two pages long, landscaped, with these margin settings: left/right: 3p, bottom/top: 2p.

1. Click the **Master Page** icon (bottom right-hand side of the page) and create two columns with a gutter of 6 picas. Page 1 of the publication contains the front and back panels of the program.
2. Create the front panel of the program by copying graphics from the **Library** palette. Refer to the marked copy in Figures 10.34A and B for the exact position of the items.
3. Save the file as **prog**.

Creating the Back Panel

The back panel of the program contains a two-column list of exhibitors. It is created by two text blocks of threaded text. Look at Figure 10.34A. Notice the alignment of each text block. The text block on the left is right aligned, and the text block on the right aligns the exhibitors' names at the left.

1. Place the text file, **exhibtrs.txt**, out on the pasteboard to the left of page 1 as shown in Figure 10.29.

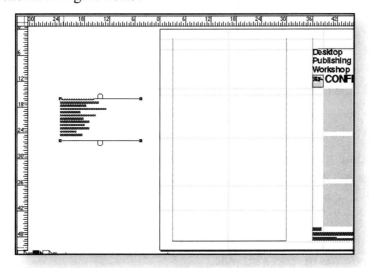

FIGURE

10.29

Place the text on the pasteboard.

2. Click with the **Text** tool anywhere in the text block and press **Ctrl + A**. (On the Macintosh, press **Command + A**.) This selects all the text.

3. Change the type specifications to the ones shown on the marked copy.

4. With the **Pointer** tool, click the bottom windowshade and drag up so that there are only six names showing in the list. Notice the down arrow in the windowshade handle that indicates there is more text in the block.

5. Click the down arrow to load the rest of the text. To the side of the text block, draw a bounding box with the loaded **Text** tool so that two text blocks appear, as in Figure 10.30.

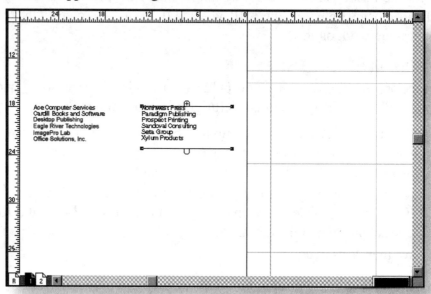

FIGURE 10.30

Two text blocks appear when a bounding box is drawn.

6. With the **Text** tool, select the section of the text block that will appear on the left. Select **Alignment** from the **Type** menu. Click **Align right**.

7. Position the two text blocks as they appear in Figure 10.34A. You may want to drag a vertical ruler guide to the center of this panel to help you position the two text blocks. The edges of the text blocks should be of equal distance from this vertical ruler guide.

8. Draw a horizontal .5-point line at the 13.5p position on the page below the list of exhibitors. It should be the length of the distance between the margins of the column on this panel.

9. Add the heading **EXHIBITORS** in Helvetia 12/12, all caps, set width 150%.

10. Save the file.

In addition to the list of exhibitors, the back panel also contains a map—the **map.eps** graphic file—of the rooms where each workshop session will be held. Use horizontal ruler guides to help place the graphic on the page.

1. Drag two horizontal rulers to the 15p and 42p positions on the page. With the **Pointer** tool, select the **Place** command in the **File** menu to import the **map.eps** graphic.

2. To resize the graphic so that it is in proportion, click a corner handle while holding down the **Shift** key. The graphic will "snap" to a proportional size, but it will not be the correct size for the panel.

3. Resize the graphic again so that it fits between the two horizontal rulers. Hold down the **Shift** key while you do this to keep the proportional size intact.

4. Position the graphic on the panel so that it is horizontally centered and between the two horizontal ruler guides. Use the vertical ruler guide to center the graphic on the panel.

5. Save the file.

6. Drag the logo containing the institute name and address from the **Library** palette and center it at the bottom of the panel.

7. Next, the logo will be edited for alignment. Draw a 1-point line underneath the logo and position it at the bottom margin guide and between the column guides.

8. Draw a .5-point line between the map and list of exhibitors. See the marked copy for positioning.

9. Save the file.

Creating the Inside Panels

Figure 10.34B shows the placement of six columns of text that make up the inside panels of the program. There are three text files that contain the text for this program: the **progname.txt** file contains the speakers' names and affiliations; the **progtime.txt** file contains only the times of the workshops; and the **progtxt.txt** file contains a description of each workshop.

The files are placed in the appropriate column at the left side of the page, and then threaded to a different column on the right side of the page. You create the vertical spacing between the times, workshop descriptions, and speakers' names by pressing the **Enter** key to add blank lines (hard returns).

1. Move to page 2 of the publication.

2. Drag a vertical ruler guide to 33p, which is the center of the page. Drag two more vertical ruler guides to 30p and 36p. This area of the program is reserved for the fold.

3. Create six columns with 1 pica space between columns.

4. Key the headings at the top of the page with the specifications you see in Figure 10.34B. Center the headings in the text block, and then position the text block so that the center windowshade is on the 33p vertical ruler guide.

5. Place the **logo.eps** graphic. Draw a horizontal 1-point line from margin to margin. Drag it to 5p from the top.

6. Save the file.

Moving Column Guides The column guides are placed an equal distance apart when they are defined. The program, however, requires columns of different widths. The column guides can be dragged to new positions to accommodate the various widths. (See Figure 10.31.)

1. Click and drag the column guides so that the left side of the guides are at these locations on the ruler: 5p9, 17p9, 32p6, 38p6, 51p.

2. Save the file.

FIGURE 10.31

Column guides are repositioned to accommodate different text.

Placing Text in Multiple Columns The text must now be positioned in the correct columns. First make sure that the **Autoflow** is turned off before placing any of the text files. The text should not continue to flow from one column to the next.

1. Place the first text file, **progtime.txt**, in the leftmost column. Align the text at the right and change the type specs according to the marked copy.

2. Place the **progtxt.txt** file in the second column from the left. Specify the type according to the marked copy.

3. Place the **progname.txt** in the third column from the left. Specify the type according to the marked copy.

4. Save the file.

In Figure 10.32, the bottom windowshade of the text block indicates that there is text that is not placed. You need to click those bottom windowshade handles and load the **Text** tool to place the unplaced text in the appropriate column on the right side of the page.

FIGURE

10.32

The bottom windowshade indicates that there is more text to be placed.

The marked copy of the program shows the positions at the bottom of the columns where the text stops.

1. Click and drag the bottom windowshade up to the positions where the text stops. You can add the blank lines between the different sections of the text.

2. Click the **Pointer** tool on the bottom windowshade of the column that contains the program text to load the **Text** tool. Place the text in the appropriate column on the right side of the page.

3. Click the **Pointer** tool on the bottom windowshade of the column that contains the speakers' names to load the **Text** tool.

4. Place the text in the appropriate column on the right side of the page. Begin placing the text at the top of the column to align as shown in Figure 10.34B.

The focus is moved to the next text block that continues the story. You can see how this would be convenient in a multipage publication.

As previously mentioned, the vertical spacing between the times, workshop descriptions, and speakers' names is created by pressing the **Enter** key to create blank lines between the entries. As you press the **Enter** key, the text is moved down in the column. It is necessary to extend the length of the columns on the right side of the page to allow for the extra blank lines being inserted.

In the columns containing the workshop titles and descriptions, create the necessary blank lines:

1. Use the **Text** tool to click an insertion point, and then press the **Enter** key. Use Figure 10.34B as a guide.

2. Use the **Text** tool in the same manner as above to enter blank lines in the other columns.

3. Examine the bottom windowshade handles of each column to see if there is unplaced text. If necessary, click and drag the windowshade to lengthen the column. Add blank lines as needed.

4. Save the file.

Finishing the Program

You must now put the finishing touches on the program. At the bottom, there are two notes to the workshop participants. The notes are separated by a line drawn on each half of the page. Notice that the notes are in italics (see Figure 10.33).

1. Draw two rules on each half of the page.

2. Use the **Text** tool to draw a bounding box the width of the rule. Key the text for the note that appears on the left side of the page. Format the type as shown on the marked copy. Be careful. Do not place the text in an area not available to your printer.

3. Repeat the above step for the note on the right side of the page.

4. Save the file.

5. Print the file.

FIGURE

10.33

Lines and notes added to the program, page 2, left side and right side

Left side

Right side

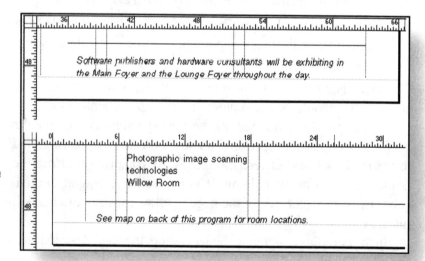

FIGURE

10.34A

Program, page 1

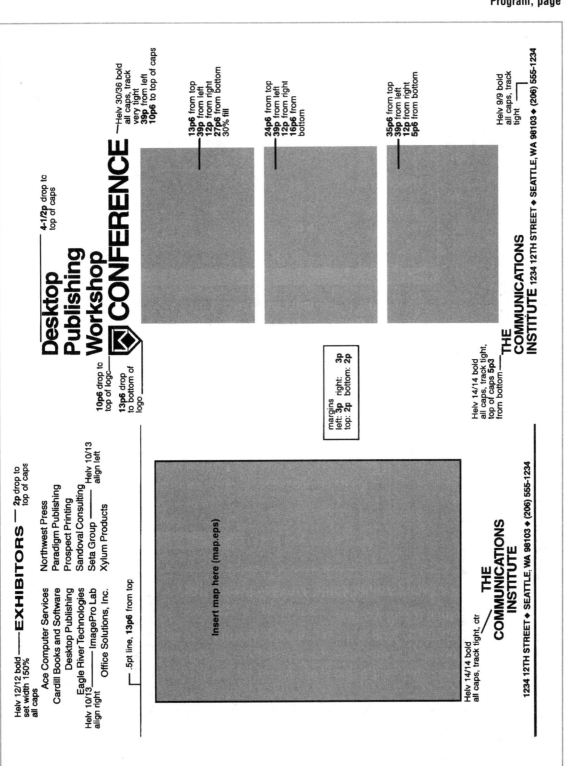

Helv 30/36 bold
all caps, track
very tight
39p from left
10p6 to top of caps

4-1/2p drop to
top of caps

Desktop
Publishing
Workshop
CONFERENCE

10p6 drop to
top of logc

13p6 drop
to bottom of
logo

13p6 from top
39p from left
12p from right
27p6 from bottom
30% fill

24p6 from top
39p from left
12p from right
16p6 from
bottom

35p6 from top
39p from left
12p from right
5p6 from bottom

Helv 9/9 bold
all caps, track
tight

THE
COMMUNICATIONS
INSTITUTE 1234 12TH STREET ◆ SEATTLE, WA 98103 ◆ (206) 555-1234

margins
left: **3p** right: **3p**
top: **2p** bottom: **2p**

Helv 14/14 bold
all caps, track tight,
top of caps **5p3**
from bottom

Helv 12/12 bold
set width 150%
all caps

2p drop to
top of caps

EXHIBITORS

Ace Computer Services
Cardill Books and Software
Desktop Publishing
Eagle River Technologies
ImagePro Lab
Office Solutions, Inc.

Northwest Press
Paradigm Publishing
Prospect Printing
Sandoval Consulting
Seta Group
Xylum Products

Helv 10/13
align left

Helv 10/13
align right

.5pt line, **13p6** from top

Insert map here (map.eps)

Helv 14/14 bold
all caps, track tight, ctr

THE
COMMUNICATIONS
INSTITUTE
1234 12TH STREET ◆ SEATTLE, WA 98103 ◆ (206) 555-1234

FIGURE

10.34B

Program, page 2

18/18 Helv., bold, ctr, 150% set width, no track

DESKTOP PUBLISHING WORKSHOP CONFERENCE

12/12 Helv. — Saturday, November 16, 1999

drop to top of caps 2p

.5 pt rule, 5-1/2p drop

top of logo 6p drop

bottom of logo 9p drop

ctr logo 33p from left

column measure 2-3/4p

Helv 10/13, bold, align right

column measure 11p

column measure 11-1/2p

column measure 13-3/4p

8:00 REGISTRATION
Main Foyer

1p gutter

column measure 11p

8:30 WELCOMING REMARKS
North Auditorium

Helv 10/13

column measure 2-3/4p

Maria Lee
Head Instructor,
Communications Institute,
Desktop Publishing Workshop

8:45 KEYNOTE ADDRESS
North Auditorium

Linda Brown
President, National Association
of Desktop Publishing Professionals

9:30 SESSION A WORKSHOPS

Integration of desktop
publishing in the office
work flow
Cedar Room

Kathleen Moreno
CEO, Office Solutions, Inc.

Forms creation for business
applications
Willow Room

Chuck Miller
Associate Professor, Shoreline
Community College

Preparation of files for
desktop publishing
Oak Room

Michael Brooks
DataPro Statistical Services

Layout and design standard-
ization
Waterfall Room

Donna Long
Art Director, Center for Peace
and Justice

11:00 SESSION B WORKSHOPS

Converting databases into
publications
Cedar Room

Michael Brooks

Photographic image scanning
technologies
Willow Room

Sara Kashiwa
Director, ImagePerfect Lab

margins
left: **3p**   right: **3p**
top: **2p**   bottom: **2p**

.5 pt rule
4p from bottom

See map on back of this program for room locations.

Authoring tools for desktop
publishing
Oak Room

Document management and
archiving
Waterfall Room

Álvaro Colegio
Professor, Bellevue
Community College

Kathleen Moreno

12:30 LUNCHEON
Northstar Dining Room

2:00 SESSION C WORKSHOPS

The editing and proofing cycle
in a network environment
Cedar Room

Chuck Miller

Graphics programs for desktop
publishing
Willow Room

Maria Lee

Alternative output devices
Oak room

Sara Kashiwa

Commercial printing:
paper and ink
Waterfall Room

Nikolas Sandris
Sole proprietor, Prospect
Printing

3:45 PANEL DISCUSSION
North Auditorium

Workshop Leaders

4:30 CLOSING REMARKS
North Auditorium

Maria Lee

.5 pt rule
5p from bottom

Software publishers and hardware consultants will be exhibiting in
the Main Foyer and the Lounge Foyer throughout the day.

CREATING NAME TAGS

The speakers for the workshop will wear name tags, which you will create. You will learn how to group objects using the **Group** command from the **Element** menu, and practice using the **Paste Multiple** command.

The adhesive name tags are printed on mailing label sheets, which are available from stores that sell office supplies. The labels are 4 inches long and 2 inches tall. Ten labels fit on one sheet. Refer to Figure 10.42 as you work through this section.

Before the name tags can be printed, a master page should be created. It contains the **horizon.eps** and **logo.eps** graphics, as well as text. Because the master page is a template, it does not contain the names. For the name tags, you will change the measurement system to inches with the **Preferences** selection in the **File** menu. Figure 10.35 displays the **Preferences** dialog box.

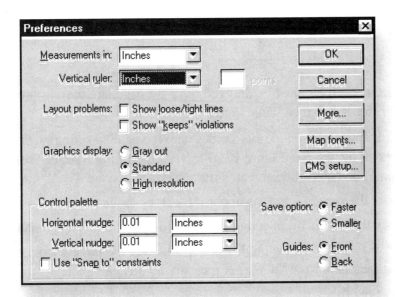

FIGURE **10.35**
Preferences dialog box

1. To change the ruler measurements, click the **File** menu. Select **Preferences General,** and then click **Inches** in both the **Horizontal** and **Vertical** boxes. Click **OK**.

2. Create a new file with margins of .5 inch at the top and bottom and .3 inch on each side. Deactivate the double-sided box.

3. Click the **Master Page** icon in the lower-left corner of the screen.

4. Drag a vertical ruler guide to the exact center of the page, at 4.25 inches.

5. Save the file as **nametags**.

Resetting the Zero Point

A single-sided publication contains a zero point in the top-left corner of the horizontal and vertical rulers, where the two rulers intersect. A publication with facing pages has the zero point positioned at the intersection of the top, inside edges of the facing pages (see Figure 10.36). The zero point can be dragged to a new location on the page to be used for measuring. As it is dragged, cross hairs follow the mouse cursor. When the mouse is released, a new zero point is established.

FIGURE

10.36

Setting zero point at top-left of horizontal and vertical rulers

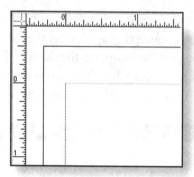

Ruler guides, which must be dragged onto the page, are used as a measurement for the 4- x 2-inch name tags.

1. Drag down horizontal ruler guides onto the page, positioning them every 2 inches. See Figure 10.37 to view the finished page. There should be 10 positions created for name tags that are 4" x 2" each.

2. Reset the zero point to the upper-left corner of the page.

3. Lock the guides by selecting **Lock Guides** from the **View** menu.

4. Move to page 1 of the publication by clicking the **page 1** icon. Notice that the rulers from the master page are on this page, too.

5. Save the file.

FIGURE

10.37

Placing guides 2" apart

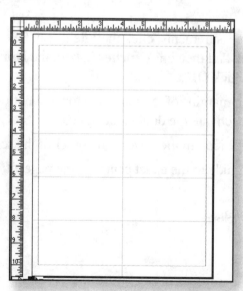

The **Workshop Library** palette contains the files for the graphics that appear on each name tag, namely, **horizon.eps** and **logo.eps**.

Copy these items to the first name tag in the upper-left corner. See the marked copy for exact positions and type formatting. Do not forget the small circle with 10% fill and no line.

Grouping Objects

The objects that make up this particular name tag must be copied to other positions on the page. To copy each object separately is a long, burdensome task. The **Group** command in the **Elements** menu allows you to group objects together so that you can manipulate the objects as one unit.

1. All the objects must be selected with the **Pointer** tool before they can be grouped. Click on each object while holding down the **Shift** key. (See Figure 10.38.)

2. Click the **Element** menu and select **Group**.

3. Save the file.

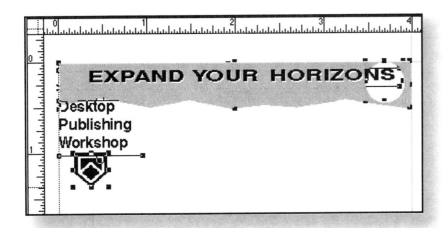

FIGURE
10.38
Selecting all objects

Pasting Multiple Objects

Use the **Paste Multiple** command to paste a copied or cut object a specified number of times onto a page. The name tag needs to be copied to the right side of the page and then copied down several times onto the page. The **Paste Multiple** command is located in the **Edit** menu. The dialog box shown in Figure 10.39 provides options for you to specify the horizontal and vertical offset spacing when the object is pasted, as well as the number of copies.

1. Select the name tag with the **Pointer** tool. Click the **Edit** menu and select **Copy**.

2. Select the name tag with the **Pointer** tool. Click the **Edit** menu and select **Paste Multiple**.

MAC MEMO

On the Macintosh, use the key combination **Command + C** to copy.

3. Make the entries in the **Paste Multiple** dialog box so they match the ones in Figure 10.39. Click **OK**.

FIGURE

10.39

Using the *Paste Multiple* dialog box to copy one name tag design four times

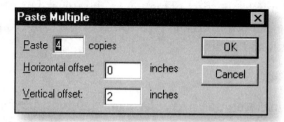

Now group the five name tags on the left into one group. The new object can be copied down the page to the other name tag positions.

1. Press and hold down the **Shift** and **Ctrl** keys while you click the five name tags. (See Figure 10.40.)

2. Select **Group** from the **Elements** menu.

3. Select the new object that contains both name tags. Copy the object, pasting the new copy in on the right side of the page.

4. Save the file.

FIGURE

10.40

Copying the grouped name tag objects

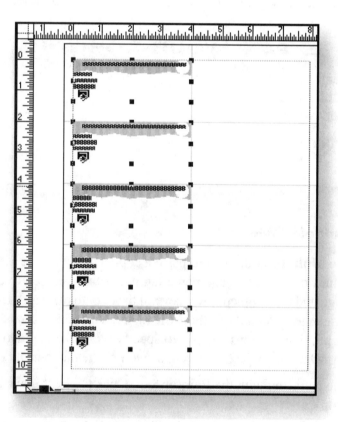

Move the name tags to the master pages. You can insert additional pages to the publication and accommodate any number of participants in the workshop who need name tags.

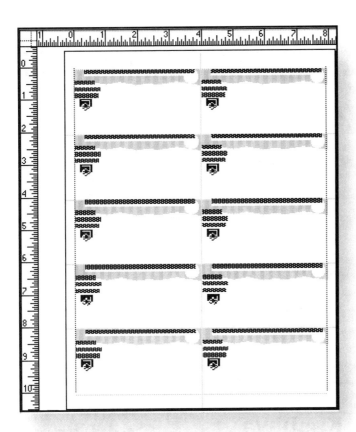

FIGURE

10.41

Placement of name tags
on the page

1. Select all the name tags and select the **Cut** command.

2. Move to the **Master page** and paste the name tags. If necessary, adjust the position of the name tags to align them with the horizontal and vertical rulers. (See Figure 10.41.)

3. Save the file.

4. Move to page 1 of the document. If the name tags do not appear on page 1, click the **Layout** menu and select **Display master items**.

MAC MEMO

On the Macintosh, use **Command + A** for Select All and **Command + X** to cut.

The speakers' names can be added to the name tags at this point. An easy method for doing this is to create a style sheet that assigns the typeface, size, vertical spacing, and so on to the text with the names.

1. Go to **Define styles…** in the **Type** menu. Create a PageMaker style sheet called **tag names**, and add the following attributes:

Helvetica 36/38	Bold
Set width: 100%	Alignment: Center
Track: Very tight	Paragraph, Space after: 1.5 inches

2. Type the name tags as shown in Figure 10.42. Note placement of names on the tags varies with length of names.

3. Save the file.

4. Print the file.

FIGURE

10.42

Finished name tags

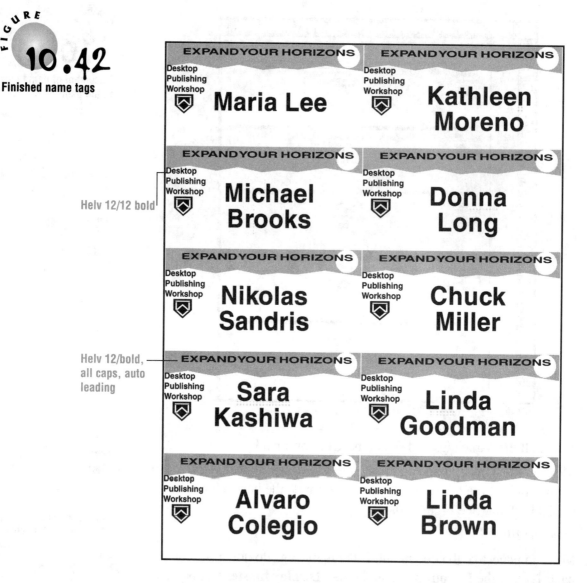

Helv 12/12 bold

Helv 12/bold, all caps, auto leading

CHECKING YOUR UNDERSTANDING

1. What are the major parts of a table?
2. How do you access PageMaker's utility Adobe Table 3.0?
3. Name an export option in Adobe Table 3.0.
4. What are column guides?
5. What is the difference between using the **Paste Multiple** command and the **Paste** command?
6. What capabilities exist with the **Border** option in Adobe Table 3.0?

7. In what format must a table be exported for importing into PageMaker?

8. What happens when a table is linked to a PageMaker file?

9. Explain how graphic files are linked to a PageMaker document.

10. Explain how objects are grouped.

APPLYING DESIGN PRINCIPLES

Exercise 1 Creating a Flier

The Communications Institute offers a number of different desktop publishing workshops for professionals. Create a flier describing one of these workshops. Use the **Workshop Library** palette to access the common elements. Refer to the marked copy in Figure 10.43 for positioning of the text and graphics.

Exercise 2 Creating a Magazine or Newspaper Ad

Create one or both of the advertisements that the Communications Institute might use in a magazine, newspaper, or newsletter. Use the **Workshop Library** palette to access the common elements. Refer to the marked copy in Figure 10.44 for positioning of the text and graphics.

Exercise 3 Creating a Menu

Create the luncheon menu for the Desktop Publishing Workshop. Create at least two choices for each of the following categories: salads, entrees, desserts, drinks and include ratings for hot spices (e.g. a scale from 1 to 5). Use leader tabs to designate the "Hot" rating.

Exercise 4 Creating a Schedule

Create the hourly schedule for the Desktop Publishing Workshop. Follow the specifications on the marked copy in Figure 10.45.

FIGURE
10.43
A flier for Exercise 1

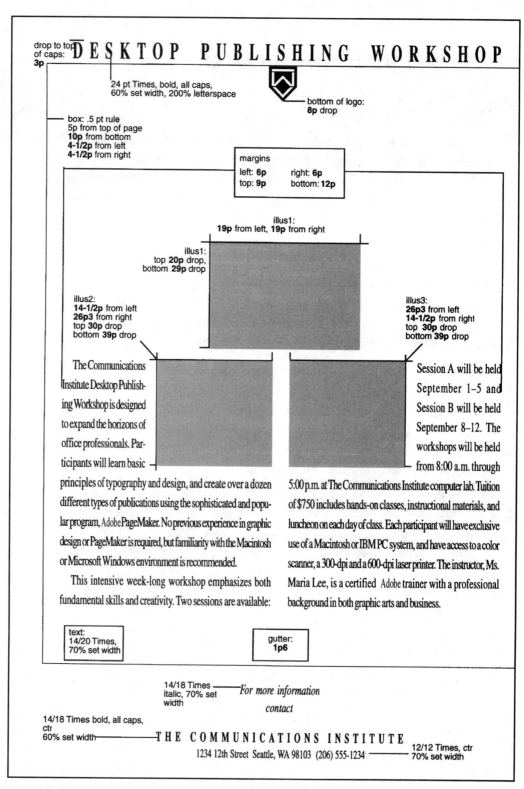

drop to top
of caps:
3p

DESKTOP PUBLISHING WORKSHOP

24 pt Times, bold, all caps,
60% set width, 200% letterspace

bottom of logo:
8p drop

box: .5 pt rule
5p from top of page
10p from bottom
4-1/2p from left
4-1/2p from right

margins

left: **6p**   right: **6p**
top: **9p**   bottom: **12p**

illus1:
19p from left, **19p** from right

illus1:
top **20p** drop,
bottom **29p** drop

illus2:
14-1/2p from left
26p3 from right
top **30p** drop
bottom **39p** drop

illus3:
26p3 from left
14-1/2p from right
top **30p** drop
bottom **39p** drop

The Communications Institute Desktop Publishing Workshop is designed to expand the horizons of office professionals. Participants will learn basic principles of typography and design, and create over a dozen different types of publications using the sophisticated and popular program, Adobe PageMaker. No previous experience in graphic design or PageMaker is required, but familiarity with the Macintosh or Microsoft Windows environment is recommended.

This intensive week-long workshop emphasizes both fundamental skills and creativity. Two sessions are available:

Session A will be held September 1–5 and Session B will be held September 8–12. The workshops will be held from 8:00 a.m. through 5:00 p.m. at The Communications Institute computer lab. Tuition of $750 includes hands-on classes, instructional materials, and luncheon on each day of class. Each participant will have exclusive use of a Macintosh or IBM PC system, and have access to a color scanner, a 300-dpi and a 600-dpi laser printer. The instructor, Ms. Maria Lee, is a certified Adobe trainer with a professional background in both graphic arts and business.

text:
14/20 Times,
70% set width

gutter:
1p6

14/18 Times
italic, 70% set
width

For more information

contact

14/18 Times bold, all caps,
ctr
60% set width

THE COMMUNICATIONS INSTITUTE

1234 12th Street Seattle, WA 98103 (206) 555-1234

12/12 Times, ctr
70% set width

FIGURE

10.44

An ad for Exercise 2

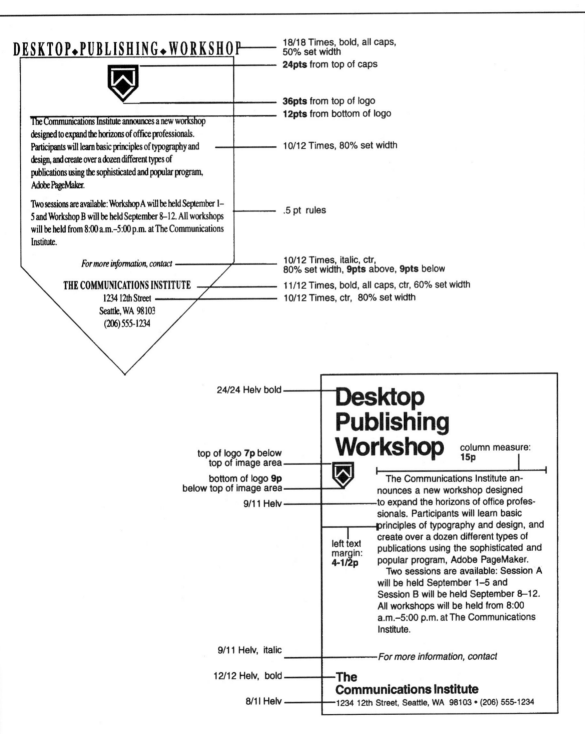

DESKTOP◆PUBLISHING◆WORKSHOP — 18/18 Times, bold, all caps, 50% set width

24pts from top of caps

36pts from top of logo
12pts from bottom of logo

The Communications Institute announces a new workshop designed to expand the horizons of office professionals. Participants will learn basic principles of typography and design, and create over a dozen different types of publications using the sophisticated and popular program, Adobe PageMaker. — 10/12 Times, 80% set width

Two sessions are available: Workshop A will be held September 1–5 and Workshop B will be held September 8–12. All workshops will be held from 8:00 a.m.–5:00 p.m. at The Communications Institute. — .5 pt rules

For more information, contact — 10/12 Times, italic, ctr, 80% set width, **9pts** above, **9pts** below

THE COMMUNICATIONS INSTITUTE — 11/12 Times, bold, all caps, ctr, 60% set width
1234 12th Street — 10/12 Times, ctr, 80% set width
Seattle, WA 98103
(206) 555-1234

24/24 Helv bold — **Desktop Publishing Workshop**

column measure: **15p**

top of logo **7p** below top of image area

bottom of logo **9p** below top of image area

9/11 Helv —

The Communications Institute announces a new workshop designed to expand the horizons of office professionals. Participants will learn basic principles of typography and design, and create over a dozen different types of publications using the sophisticated and popular program, Adobe PageMaker.

Two sessions are available: Session A will be held September 1–5 and Session B will be held September 8–12. All workshops will be held from 8:00 a.m.–5:00 p.m. at The Communications Institute.

left text margin: **4-1/2p**

9/11 Helv, italic — *For more information, contact*

12/12 Helv, bold — **The Communications Institute**

8/11 Helv — 1234 12th Street, Seattle, WA 98103 • (206) 555-1234

FIGURE

10.45

A schedule for Exercise 4

.3 inch margins, all sides

Six columns

14 pt. Arial, bold, all caps, centered

Text: 10 pt. Arial

20% fill

DESKTOP PUBLISHING WORKSHOP

Tuesday 11/16/99	North Auditorium	Cedar Room	Willow Room	Oak Room	Waterfall Room
8:00	8:30 Welcoming remarks 8:45 Keynote address: Maria Lee				
9:00					
		9:30 Integration of desktop publishing in the office workflow: Kathleen Moreno	9:30 Forms creation for business applications: Chuck Miller	9:30 Preparation of files for desktop publishing: Michael Brooks	9:30 Layout and design standardization: Donna Long
10:00					
11:00		11:00 Converting data bases into publications: Michael Brooks	11:00 Photographic image scanning technologies: Sara Kashiwa	11:00 Authoring tools for desktop publishing: Alvaro Colegio	11:00 Document management and archiving: Kathleen Moreno
Noon					
1:00					
2:00		2:00 The editing and proofing cycle a network environment: Chuck Miller	2:00 Graphics programs for desktop publishing: Maria Lee	2:00 Alternative output devices: Sara Kashiwa	2:00 Commercial printing: paper and ink: Nikolas Sandris
3:00	3:45 Panel Discussion Workshop Leaders				
4:00	4:30 Closing Remarks Maria Lee				
5:00					

part **6**

DESKTOP PUBLISHING

Production & Printing

PRINCIPLES
of Printing

This chapter is an overview of printing options, paper quality, and photocopiers, and different types of binding.

Upon completion of this chapter | **you will be able to**

- describe how laser printers work and determine when they are appropriate to use
- apply the special features of photocopiers for publishing needs
- determine when it is appropriate to use quick-copy offset printing
- compare metal-plate offset printing and imagesetting
- distinguish among different paper, ink, and binding options

Advances in desktop publishing technology enable the desktop publisher to produce medium-quality finished or nearly finished products. For high-quality publications, however, paper, ink, and binding will probably remain with professional printing and binding operations for some time to come, since fast, large-scale reproduction of publications requires big, expensive mechanical equipment that simply will not fit on desktops.

LASER PRINTING

Laser printing is based on the same technology as photocopying. An imaging surface is electrically charged, and the charge is transferred to a blank page. Fine particles of dry ink, called **toner**, adhere to the charged areas on the page. They are then fixed onto the paper with a heating mechanism. In a laser printer, the mechanism that charges the imaging surface and transfers the image to the paper is called the **print engine**. (See Figure 11.1.)

FIGURE 11.1

Laser printer print engine

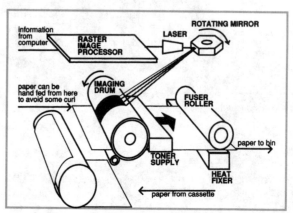

In laser printers, the print engine uses a high-speed laser beam that flashes off and on as it moves across the page from top to bottom. The beam electrostatically charges a rotating imaging drum, which is pressed against the paper. The movement of the laser beam is controlled by a **raster image processor** (RIP), which is a computer chip that interprets the information sent to it by the computer. The paper feeding path for desktop laser printers is short and tightly curved. The paper starts in a tray (or it can be hand-fed), wraps around the imaging drum, and is deposited in a tray or bin.

Time and Cost Considerations

The laser-printed page is sometimes the final copy that is distributed. In small office environments, one-page short-run publications such as correspondence, memos, and announcements are often produced on the desktop publishing laser printer itself. The operator simply specifies the number of copies of the file to be printed in the print command.

Throughput The number of copies per minute, called **throughput**, of desktop laser printers is low compared to that of photocopiers and offset presses. Desktop laser printers average eight pages per minute after the first copy is processed. Depending on the complexity of the page, the first copy may take several minutes. The materials cost (paper and toner) per copy is between 3¢ and 20¢, plus overhead (electricity, wear and tear on the machine, and so on). Therefore, producing more than a few copies of a publication on a desktop laser printer is not efficient in terms of time or money.

Paper Handling The most popular desktop laser printers accommodate only letter-size or legal-size paper. They hold approximately 100 sheets, and they print in order, on one side of the page, and in one stack.

Some programs can control the printing order of pages, and there are devices for stacking collated pages, but the physical size limitations of an 8½" width cannot be altered. Pages can be printed on both sides which can be accomplished by sending paper through the printer twice. The most popular standard laser printers today are capable of **duplex printing**. The paper is fed in, printed and sent to a holding area within the printer (usually directly under the feed path). From there it is automatically brought back in through the feed path where the second side is printed.

High-speed production laser printers are not desktop-sized (or desktop-priced) devices, but they have faster print engines and greater flexibility in terms of paper handling. They are often used for 1-color publications and provide printing and binding in one pass.

Reproduction Quality

When desktop laser printers were first introduced, their 300 dpi resolution was a great leap forward from dot-matrix printers. However, compared to imageset copy, the jags in laser-printed copy are apparent in large type and images, and detail is lost in small type and images.

Higher-resolution laser printers (600 dpi or above) are desktop-sized devices and are more expensive, but they use the same basic imaging mechanism of 300 dpi printers. For increased resolution, they use a finer toner made of smaller particles.

A laser printout is not as stable as imageset or offset printed copy. The toner particles of a laser printout sometimes chip off if the paper is handled extensively or folded. The image will smudge if it is exposed to solvents, including the thinner in rubber cement and typewriter correction fluid.

High-end laser printers that print in color are available to desktop publishers. T-shirt transfers are one favorite application for these printers.

Print Engines In a **write-black** print engine, the black toner particles adhere to areas of the page that are positively charged. This method of imaging results in very fine detail, but the printing of large black areas may fade out, leaving streaks instead of solid toner. The toner density can be adjusted to print blacker, but when this is done, shadow images from previously printed pages sometimes appear on subsequent pages. This is because a strongly charged image is left on the rotating imaging drum when a new piece of paper is fed through the printer.

In a **write-white** print engine, the black toner particles are repelled from areas of the page that are negatively charged. This method of imaging renders very solid blacks. However, the detail of images and type is sometimes imprecise, blurring serifs and filling in counters of very small characters.

Color Desktop publishing software enables the user to print an image or document as a composite or as color overlays (separations). One color can be printed with each pass, but the registration (alignment) of the page in the printer is not precise. This process is also very time-consuming. High-volume color printing is more appropriate with imageset masters and offset printing. More information on color overlays and registration is discussed later in this chapter.

Spot color can be applied to a laser printout (or any toner-based black and white image) with coloring devices such as KroyKolor®. Patches of color-coated sheets are cut and applied on parts of the black and white image. The sheets are then put through a heat-fixing device that melts the color onto the black parts of the image. Both this method of color application and multiple-pass laser printing, however, are extremely labor-intensive and therefore appropriate for only a few special jobs.

As an alternative to laser printing, raster color thermal transfer and ink-jet printers can be used to provide color proofs. There are color printers with and without PostScript controllers; both produce halftone-like screens from primary colors. Purple, for example, is created with a screen of red over a screen of blue. At 600 dpi or higher, primary colors come out with good saturation. At lower dpi, dot patterns are visible in mixed colors, so the output is generally not of final publication quality. The throughput is also low, from about a minute per page to several minutes per page.

Paper Quality Different stocks of paper affect the quality of desktop laser printouts. In general, a lightweight, smooth, but nonglossy surface is best for accurate and precise printing. Heavy paper often jams in the tightly curved feeding mechanism of laser printers. If the paper is not too thick, this can be avoided by using the printer's manual feed rather than the paper tray. On highly textured and coated papers, toner particles might not be fixed properly and can flake off. There are several companies that manufacture very smooth, heat- and curl-resistant papers specifically for laser printers.

Paper designed for photocopiers works well in desktop laser printers, since the imaging process is similar. Heat-resistant clear film sheets made for photocopiers also can be used for making transparencies with a laser printer.

PHOTOCOPYING

Announcements, handouts, posters, and fliers are among the most common publications produced with desktop publishing. Laser-printed masters can be reproduced efficiently and without loss of quality on photocopy machines. In some cases, print quality can be improved by photocopying, and photocopiers are faster and offer more paper-handling flexibility.

Photocopier Print Quality

Good photocopiers are both forgiving and enhancing. They can cover up the edges of white paper pasted on white paper when hand cut-and-paste methods are employed. Photocopiers can also add density to originals containing fade-outs in black areas. (See Figure 11.2.)

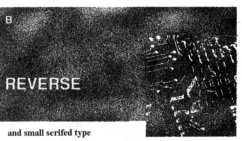

FIGURE

11.2

Photocopy reproduction
A. Original laser-printed copy
B. Photocopy

Halftone images, however, do not always reproduce well on photocopiers. Because photocopiers use the same toner technology as laser printers, photocopies, like laser printouts, are subject to the same chipping and smudging problems.

Photocopier Paper Handling

Production photocopiers have an average throughput of over 100 pages per minute. Standard features include collating slots and paper bins for large amounts of and different standard sizes of paper. Many photocopy machines also provide automatic stapling. Thus photocopiers are a very attractive alternative to tying up a shared laser printer for production of multipage publications.

Since photocopiers utilize a flat imaging surface rather than a rotating drum such as those in laser printers, passing the paper through a photocopier more than once is an effective way to print two-sided pages. Photocopiers can also reduce and enlarge images. In combination with their ability to reproduce on 11" x 17" sheets (two facing 8½" x 11" pages), these features make photocopiers excellent for proofing, and even feasible for final production of short-run brochures, newsletters, and booklets.

QUICK-COPY OFFSET PRINTING

Quick-copy offset printing is a fast-growing printing service offered by many small print shops. Quick-copy printing is a cost-effective alternative to photocopying laser-printed masters for medium-sized runs (over 100 reproductions). These shops often offer not only a lower cost per page but also fast and low-cost folding and binding.

A typical offset press utilizes three rotating drums: a plate cylinder, a blanket cylinder, and an impression cylinder. The printing plate is wrapped around the plate cylinder, dampened, and inked. The plate image is transferred, or offset, to the blanket cylinder. Paper is passed between the blanket cylinder and the impression cylinder, and the image is transferred onto it. (See Figure 11.3.)

FIGURE 11.3

Offset press
Adapted from Adams and Faux, *Printing Technology*, Albany, NY: Delmar Publishers, 1988.

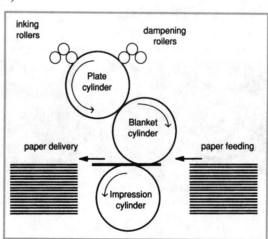

Quick-copy print shops, unlike commercial printers, generally set their presses for one standard sheet size and use paper rather than metal plates. **Commercial printers** can handle nearly any sheet size at any volume. They use metal plates on large production presses. The quick-copy printer's speedy turnaround is often accomplished with the use of an integrated system: automatic plate-making, press, collating, and binding devices in one setup. For quick-copy printing, the desktop publisher can supply a laser-printed master on 8½" x 11" paper, and the finished publications can often be produced in a matter of minutes.

Offset Print Quality

The quality of quick-printed jobs depends on the quality of the laser-printed master and the plate that is made from it. Halftones must be supplied as positives, which limits them to approximately 65 lines for laser-printed files or 100 lines for veloxes. (**Veloxes** are positive halftone paper prints, up to approximately 100 lines per inch, produced with a graphic arts camera.) In either case, the reproduction quality is less crisp than in metal-plate printing. Of two platemaking methods commonly used, electrostatic and photo-direct, the latter is more expensive and of higher quality in rendering of detail and uniform ink distribution. (See Figure 11.4.) Electrostatic plates are produced in a manner similar to laser printing and photocopying; photo-direct plates are produced in a manner similar to the diffusion-transfer technology of producing photostats.

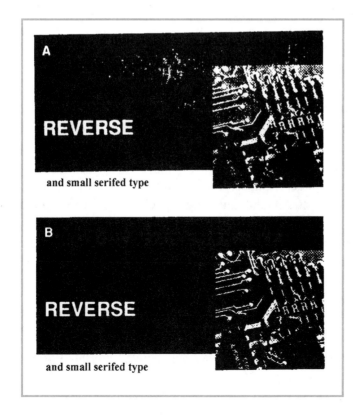

FIGURE

11.4

Electrostatic and photo-direct plates
A. Reproduction from electrostatic plate
B. Reproduction from photo-direct plate
(Both from original shown in Figure 11.2)

In quick-copy printing, generally only one color on standard-sized paper can be reproduced because the plate is made directly from the original and because the press is preset for specific paper sizes. Paper plates can be run for about 5,000 impressions and cannot be reused.

Offset Paper Handling

The throughput of quick-copy offset presses can be as high as 10,000— 12,000 copies per hour, and collating and binding are standard services. Most quick-copy print shops offer a variety of paper stocks, but usually cannot handle sheets larger than 11" x 17". Double-sided printing, trimming (for bleeds and smaller-than-standard sized publications), and folding services are usually available.

METAL-PLATE OFFSET PRINTING AND IMAGESETTING

Metal-plate offset printing is needed if the publication job calls for:

- High-quality reproduction (especially of halftones)
- Over 5,000 copies
- Large, nonstandard paper size
- Multiple colors

If a publication warrants the higher cost of metal plates, the use of 1200— 2500 dpi typeset (imageset) masters rather than 600 dpi laser-printed masters is appropriate. This high-resolution output requires PostScript or PostScript-comparable files.

Imagesetting

An **imagesetter** is a typesetter capable of setting images as well as type. An imagesetter is equipped with a PostScript or comparable RIP (raster image processor). The standard resolution of imagesetters is 1270 dpi or 2540 dpi. In response to the growing popularity of desktop publishing, there are numerous imagesetting service bureaus available to desktop publishers, and several typesetter manufacturers are developing PostScript-compatible RIPs for their equipment.

Obtaining imageset output is usually as easy as supplying page-assembly files to the service bureau, either on disk or by transferring the files via telephone lines. The service bureau, using a microcomputer as front end, prints the file on the imagesetter.

WYSIWYG

WYSIWYG discrepancies occur between laser-printed proofs and imageset copy. The appearance of type is usually fairly accurate, but drawn elements may differ. In particular, thin rules (hairlines) and tints are much finer on an imagesetter. Ten percent at 1270 dpi is a very light gray while 10 percent at 300 dpi appears darker. (See Figure 11.5.)

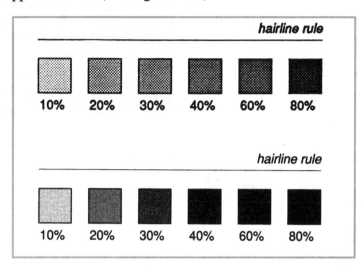

FIGURE

11.5

Hairline rules and screens
A. 300 dpi (laser printed)
B. 1270 dpi (imageset)

The microcomputer running the imagesetter may handle fonts differently from the way the desktop publishing microcomputer on which the publication was made handles them. When you are using several fonts, consult with the imagesetting shop before running your copy.

Output Options Because an imagesetter is a computerized phototypesetting machine, it can output either positive or negative images on resin-coated (rc) paper, or on film. Positive paper output is used to make mechanicals for offset printing. The negative film option may result in faster turnaround and cost savings in the preparation of metal plates for offset printing.

Platemaking

The process of making metal plates is more complicated and exacting than it is for making paper plates. For multicolor work, one plate is made for each color. The plates must be made with very precise registration so that all the images align properly. In addition, metal plates are often made of composite images including halftones and special effects such as reverses and surprints. Each plate carries more than one page so that the publication can be more efficiently printed on large sheets of paper that will be folded and trimmed into individual pages.

Metal plates are made from film negatives, which are traditionally reproduced from positive black and white masters, called **mechanicals**. The mechanicals, provided by the desktop publisher, contain all the elements needed to make film negatives including text and graphics. Negatives are then assembled into **flats** in a labor-intensive process called **stripping**. The flats are used to create the images on the printing plates. (See Figure 11.6.)

11.6

Offset platemaking

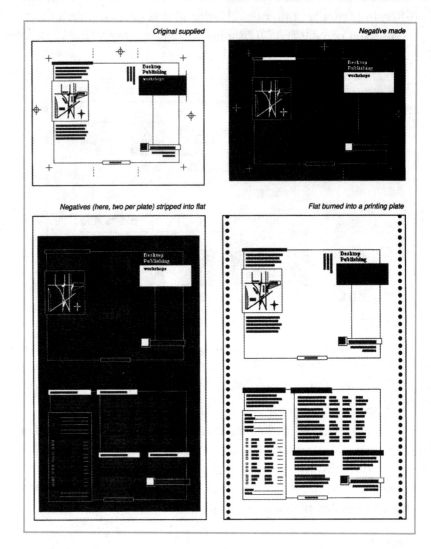

Original supplied   Negative made

Negatives (here, two per plate) stripped into flat   Flat burned into a printing plate

The plates must be custom-made to the exact specifications of the printing press. These specifications include the **press sheet** size (the actual paper that goes through the printing press), the **image area** (the area where ink will be laid down), and the **imposition** (the order and direction in which multiple pages will be printed on the press sheet).

Film imagesetters now impose and output plating film electronically into sheets of four or eight pages. However, the same principles and needs for registration marks apply, whether or not the film is hand-stripped or output electronically.

Preparing Mechanicals

Mechanicals require special preparation. The nature of the material to be printed determines how the mechanicals should be handled.

Boards or Base Sheets   In desktop publishing, the text and graphics are already positioned on the page, thus eliminating the most time-consuming aspect of preparing mechanicals—that is, laying out the pages. For one-color jobs, the originals can be supplied directly to the print shop. They should, however, be pasted on boards, which are convenient and easy to handle. The boards also supply information needed for the final production. Crop marks, bleed and fold lines, and registration marks for multicolor work appear outside the page margins on each board. For short publications, material specifications for the paper and ink can also be written on the board. (See Figure 11.7.)

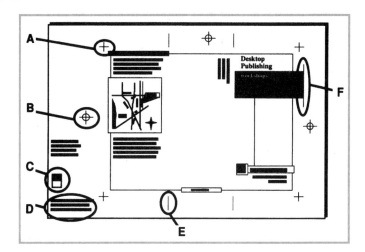

FIGURE 11.7

Baseboard marks
A. Crop mark
B. Registration mark
C. Color sample
D. Instructions
E. Fold line
F. Bleed line

Crop marks are black horizontal and vertical lines that cross each other. They indicate the edge of the printed piece. The person preparing the plates uses these marks to align the pages in the flat and then opaques them out when the plate is made. Most page assembly programs can automatically print crop marks. If they are not created automatically, they can be created with ruling tools. Since imageset output is run on large sheets, the crop marks will appear at the edges of 8½" x 11" pages. Red pencil is used to mark bleeds outside the image area on the board. For pieces that are to be folded, such as brochures, black dashed lines are made outside the image area.

For multicolor work, registration marks are needed to properly align the flats for color separation and for composite elements on overlays. **Registration marks** are made up of circles with cross hairs. Registration marks are not needed for one-color publications. When they are used, at least three registration marks should be placed on the board, outside the image area. Tapes of stick-on registration marks can be purchased at any art supply store.

Pasteup The imageset copy should be pasted on boards to be shot by a camera, if not outputting directly to plating film. If cutting and pasting by hand is needed, prelined pasteup boards can be purchased to help with the precise positioning of the imageset copy on the board. Lines are printed on the boards with a nonreproducible blue ink. The lines match the trim size and page margins. This enables you to use the boards for precision in pasteup without being concerned that the lines will show up in printing.

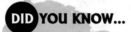

If a job has bleeds or if there will be more than one page per mechanical, consult with the print shop before pasteup. Different methods can save time and costs in stripping and imposition.

Overlay and tissue cover
A. For elements to be printed in the second color, an overlay is hinged over the baseboard.
B. The baseboard contains the elements to be printed in the first color.
C. A tissue cover is hinged over the overlay, to protect the mechanical.

Hot wax can be used to paste the imageset copy on the board. Hot wax provides a good bond yet allows pieces of copy to be lifted and repositioned easily. A burnishing stick or roller is used to press the waxed copy firmly on the board.

Overlays and Tissue Cover An **overlay** is a transparent acetate sheet that is taped and hinged at the top of the board. Overlays are used for designation of colors. Each overlay contains the elements that will be made into separate negatives and plates (ink colors). A tissue cover is then taped and folded over the top of the overlays. (See Figure 11.8.) The tissue protects the camera-ready part of the mechanical and can be used to write on, giving instructions to the print shop regarding elements on the board and overlays.

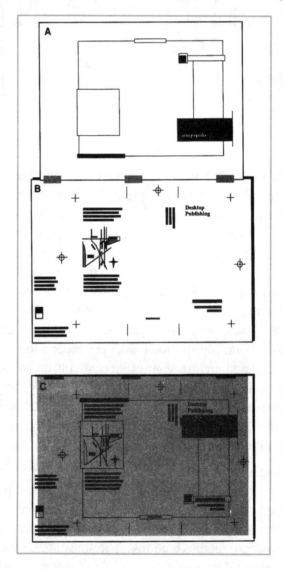

Photographs

Most print shops have cameras for producing halftones from positive photographic prints. In many cases, it is more cost-efficient to simply provide the print shop with photographic prints and mechanicals containing windows for the halftones. A **window** is a solid black area on the mechanical where a photographic negative halftone will be stripped in at the print shop. In this case, the photographic prints should be mounted on boards and marked for cropping, scaling, and screens, when appropriate.

Tagged Image File Format (TIFF) Files For desktop publishers, Tagged Image File Format (TIFF) files, which can be printed on PostScript devices, offer one efficient electronic alternative for the creation and manipulation of gray-scale halftone images. The major drawback to the output of TIFF files is the greater the resolution of the output and the more complex the file, the greater the processing time required. Some imagesetting service bureaus charge according to the time it takes for processing large TIFF files. TIFF files always have the filename extension .tif.

Duotones A **duotone** is a halftone image printed in two colors. The same photograph is halftoned twice, using the same screen at different angles. When the two images are combined, detail and contrast are improved. Duotones are usually produced with one dark and one light color, for sharp detail in the highlights and dark areas of the photograph. Black is best for reproduction of one- and two-color halftones; other colors tend to look washed out without the density of the black ink.

Before they can be printed, the two colors must be separated. Separations for duotones can be created with advanced TIFF/PostScript language-based programs for imageset output. In this case, the two negatives are provided to the print shop for stripping.

Color Separation

For multicolor publications, **color separation** is the process of creating separate negatives and plates for each color of ink. Three kinds of color separation require different treatments: spot color separation, multicolor surprints and knockouts, and process color separation.

Spot Color Separation **Spot color separation** is used for solid colors, specified by a premixed ink (green, light blue, brown, etc.) if the area to be colored is not adjacent to any other color. For example, a publication may be printed with headlines in blue and the body text in black.

Simple spot color separations can be indicated on the tissue cover; in the example just cited, the headlines can be circled on the tissue and the blue ink color noted. (See Figure 11.9.) When the negative for the black ink is shot, the headlines will be masked out. When the negative for the blue ink is made, the body copy will be masked out.

Alternatively, the elements to be printed in different colors can be pre-separated on overlays. For the first color, the overlay is folded back, and the negative for the baseboard images is shot. For the second color, the overlay is folded over the board and the baseboard image area (with the exception of the crop marks and registration marks) is masked out. Then the overlay image is shot. The registration marks on the baseboard, which show through the transparent overlay, are used to line up the negatives properly when the flats are assembled. (See Figure 11.9 for an example of an overlay for spot color separation.) Professional page assembly programs provide the option of printing overlays on PostScript devices when the publication is to have color.

FIGURE 11.9

Spot color separation
A simple spot color separation can be marked on the tissue cover.

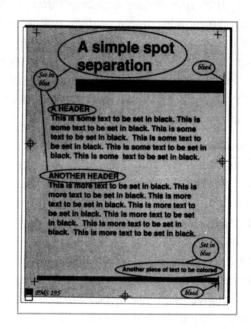

Color Surprints (Overprints) and Knockouts A darker image printed over a lighter one is a **surprint** or **overprint**. In one-color jobs, the lighter image is screened. A one-color surprint on a screen, like a one-color reverse, can be made in place with the page assembly program and pasted on a board in one piece. Multicolor surprints, however, require an overlay.

Black is most commonly used for surprinting over a color because the mixing of different colored inks can be unpredictable. The overlay contains the image to be printed in one of the colors. The elements to be printed in the other color (usually black) are pasted on the board, as shown in Figure 11.10.

For multicolor surprints, a separate plate is made for each color. Do not place the images to be printed in different colors on the imageset copy; they must be separated into overlays.

A **knockout** or **cutout** is one color printed immediately adjacent to another color—for example, yellow type on a blue background. The blue ink cannot be surprinted on the yellow ink because the combination of the two would result in green. Therefore, the plate for the blue ink must be made with blank spaces left for the yellow lettering.

The mechanical for a knockout is made with overlays. The copy for one ink is placed on the base sheet, with the knockout areas in reverse. The copy for the other ink is placed on the overlay (in positive), as shown in Figure 11.10. The two images, on the baseboard and the overlay, are sized and placed so that they slightly overlap. This is called **lap registration** and is used to avoid the appearance of a white line between the two colors of inks.

Process Color   **Process color separation** utilizes not premixed inks but surprinting of the three process colors: cyan (a greenish blue), magenta (a purplish red), and yellow, plus black, to create various hues. Process color is required for reproduction of color photographs. The three process colors and black are separated from the color image. Four separate halftone screens are slightly rotated at a different angle for each color so that the dots form rosettes of color. Black is usually angled at 45 degrees, cyan at 75 degrees, magenta at 15 degrees, and yellow at 0 degrees.

Process color separation is generally contracted out to specialty service bureaus since the scanning devices used are very expensive. Process color separations can be made from photographic prints or transparencies. For a group of color halftones, if there is not too much color variation among them, transparencies and other elements can be set on one clear sheet in position. In this way, all the halftones can be separated at once. This greatly simplifies the stripping job, since the four negatives will have the halftones in place.

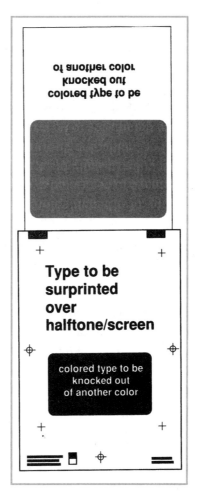

FIGURE 11.10

Surprint (overprint) and knockout
Two-color surprints and knockouts must be separated with overlays or electronically set up to separate.

Film Positives and Negatives

There is generally no extra charge for imageset output of film positives or film negatives. Film positives can be used for transparent overlays. This eliminates one pasteup step.

For one-color and spot-color jobs, the use of imageset film negatives eliminates one step and one generation of duplicating in the print shop's production process. This can result in substantial cost savings and improved quality for simple one-color publications. The major disadvantage of using imageset film negatives is that one full step in the production process for proofing is eliminated. Because of WYSIWYG problems, imageset output cannot be guaranteed to match laser-printed proofs exactly, and so proofing of imageset output is essential.

It is more difficult to proof negative than positive images. Pages that require overlays cannot be proofed until the pages are actually run on the inked printing press. Errors not caught in proofing may require resetting of type, restripping of flats, and/or remaking of plates. This is usually more expensive and time-consuming than simply proofing from imageset positives in the first place.

PAPER, INK, AND BINDING OPTIONS

When you are at the point of printing a publication, a number of key decisions must be made about the paper and ink to be used and how the publication will be bound.

Choosing the Paper

The paper upon which a publication is printed usually represents 30 to 50 percent of the final cost of a printed job and has a major effect upon the look of the final piece. Generally, the best way to choose paper is to look through the printer's paper catalogs—paper distributors supply large books of actual paper samples. For low-budget jobs, choosing paper stock that is on hand, or part of a broken carton (a carton used in one of the printer's previous jobs) can mean great cost savings.

There are thousands of types of paper, so the publisher should have in mind some preliminary requirements. For a final decision, the print shop is usually the best source of advice and information about the paper that is best suited for the job.

General Characteristics   The color of the paper is a primary concern. Most inks are somewhat translucent, so they take on slightly different tones when printed on colored paper. Large amounts of text are most legible on a soft (yellowish) off-white paper, but process colors print most accurately on neutral white.

The finish of the paper may be smooth or textured, uncoated or coated. Papers can be two-sided—one color on one side and another color on the other, or smooth on one side and textured on the other.

The **opacity** of paper refers to the amount of show-through that will occur when a page is printed on both sides. The opacity is affected not only by thickness but also by the paper manufacturing process itself. A lightweight paper with a high mineral content may be more opaque than a heavier paper with low mineral content.

Other characteristics that affect the appearance of type and graphics are reflectance (the shininess of the paper) and ink absorption. Halftones and screen tints reproduce best on smooth, coated papers. Very fine type and graphics can be difficult to read on textured papers—or on high-gloss stocks because of the high reflectance and low ink absorption.

Grades of Paper   There are no standardized ways of classifying the many kinds of paper available, but they can be generally categorized by grade, that is, by their most common usage.

Book papers are most commonly used in the printing industry. They are available in a wide range of weights, but mostly in whites and off-white colors, and they are used for books, of course, and for reports, newsletters, brochures, and magazines. Book papers may be smooth or toothy (vellum), coated or uncoated, but they are generally not textured.

Writing papers are specialty stocks that come in a wide range of colors and textures, but in a small range of weights. They are generally used for stationery, résumés, and higher-quality publications. Some popular writing paper textures are linen (a cross-weave that imitates the cloth fabric), laid (a horizontal texture), and parchment (imitating the variable opacity of animal-skin parchment).

Cover papers are a heavier stock frequently used for greeting cards, business cards, announcements and the outside covers of booklets or brochures. Cover papers are often manufactured to match writing papers in color and texture.

Bristol papers are stiff, heavy stocks that can be used for less-expensive covers, business cards, postcards, menus, tickets, and file folders. Bristols generally come in a variety of colors, smooth or vellum, but they are usually not textured.

Basis Size and Weight   Print shops order paper from distributors in large sheets, which can be cut to nearly any size. Different grades of paper come in different sizes, called **basis size**. The paper is then cut to press sheet sizes.

The thickness of paper is defined in terms of its **basis weight**, which is the weight in pounds of one ream of paper (500 sheets) in its basis size. Paper is specified in terms of this weight—for example, 20-pound bond. Within a grade, the greater the basis weight, the thicker the paper. But because different grades of paper have different basis sizes, the basis weight for another grade of paper is not comparable. A 20-pound writing paper, for example, is about equivalent to a 50-pound book paper.

PAPER TYPE, SIZE, AND WEIGHT

PAPER TYPE	BASIS SIZE (in inches)	BASIS WEIGHT (in pounds)
Book paper	25" x 38"	30, 40, 45, 50, 55, 60, 65, 70, 75, 80, 90, 100, 120 lb
Writing paper	17" x 22"	13, 16, 20, 24, 28, 32, 36, 40 lb
Cover paper	20" x 26"	50, 60, 65, 80, 90, 100 lb
Bristol paper	22½" x 28½"	67, 80, 100, 120, 140, 160 lb

Envelopes Many jobs require printing or ordering envelopes as well as base paper. Many but not all book papers and writing papers come with matching envelopes. Most standard-sized envelopes can be run through commercial presses set for extra thickness and image size. For certain special effect processes, envelopes can be printed flat and then converted—folded and glued. Figure 11.11 shows some standard envelope styles and sizes.

FIGURE 11.11

Envelope styles
A. Letter: 3-⅞" x 8-⅞"
4-⅛" x 9-½"

B. Booklet: 6" x 9"
7" x 10"
9" x 12"

C. String and button
(clasp): 9" x 12"
9" x 14½"

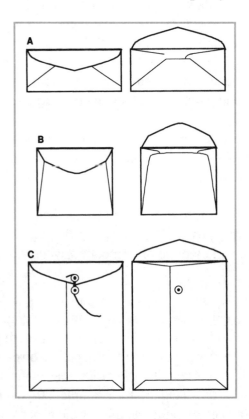

Choosing the Ink (Color)

Choosing ink for spot color, like choosing paper, is generally a matter of looking through catalogs at the printer's shop, or using one of the color-swatch sample books such as the **Pantone matching system (PMS)**, which identifies and matches colors that are standardized by the percentage mixtures of different primary color inks. For low-budget spot-color jobs, the print shop may have samples of premixed colored inks that will cost less than specially mixed inks. In these cases, print shops often have samples of the ink printed on different colored paper so that the combination of colors can be seen.

For process color jobs, different combinations of the three process colors can be specified as percentages. A color wheel made up of layers of transparencies of the process colors at different percentages can be used to view various combinations when the process inks are surprinted.

Advanced desktop publishing programs have functions that allow certain PMS colors and process color combinations to be specified. The accuracy of color proofing from the display screen or a desktop color printer, however, is subject to problems. The lack of technical standards for microcomputer color displays and for thermal printers and ink-jet printers means that even specific PMS colors will vary from device to device.

Even the ink in catalogs and process color combinations will not always match 100 percent in the final printing of a publication. Different combinations of ink and colored paper, and different batches of ink from the manufacturer will be slightly different. The precision of the press operator in mixing the ink and adjusting the press for the ink density also affects the color. For important jobs, the publisher and/or client should request a proof check at the beginning of the press run in order to ensure that the colors are acceptable.

Specialty Inks   High-gloss inks contain an extra amount of varnish, which gives them a very shiny appearance when dry. Paper that is specially coated for gloss ink should be used. The less absorbent the paper, the glossier the ink will appear. Metallic inks are made with aluminum, copper, bronze, or gold-alloy powder, which gives them a sparkling luster because the reflective particles are actually suspended in the ink. As with high-gloss inks, specially coated papers work best for metallic inks. Fluorescent inks contain light-emitting minerals for extra brilliance, and are most effective when printed on a white surface, surrounded by dark, flat colors.

Special Effects   **Thermography** is a printing process that creates a thick, raised surface with highly saturated color. A clear, slow-drying rubber-based or oil-based ink is printed on the paper, and while it is still wet, a colored powder is dusted over it. The excess powder is then removed and the paper is sent through a heating fixer which melts the powder and fuses it with the ink. Fine and dense detail is not appropriate for thermography because of the thick ink used. Thermography is most often used on business cards and other stationery items. (See Figure 11.12.)

FIGURE

11.12

Thermography

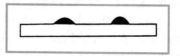

Engraving is produced by etching a design into a die. In printing, the etchings are filled with ink, and paper is pushed against the die, lifting the ink up and creating a raised image on the paper. (See Figure 11.13.) Engraving can reproduce halftones and extremely fine, delicate lines, but large solid areas will sometimes fade out. The inks used in engraving are very opaque and so are not affected by colored paper; however, neither can they be surprinted for color combinations. Engraving is costly, used most frequently for stationery items, formal announcements, and high-quality covers.

FIGURE

11.13

Engraving

Foil **leaf stamping** is not an actual inking process, but the effect is similar. A metal die is made to carry the design, and in printing the die is heated. It transfers a foil coating from a roll of film to the paper. Foils are available in flat and glossy textures, in metallic, and in other special colors and finishes. Leaf stamping is sometimes combined with embossing, so that the design is set in relief from the surface of the paper. This is accomplished by using two dies, one with the areas to be raised from the surface and the other with the areas to be pushed in from the surface. (See Figure 11.14.) For leaf stamping, well-spaced designs are best, since foils can span narrow spaces. Like engraving, foil stamping and embossing are costly, and are used only for special jobs.

FIGURE

11.14

Leaf stamping and engraving

Thermography, engraving, and leaf stamping are usually done at specialty shops. Commercial print shops often have standard subcontractors. For best results, high-quality cotton-fiber papers are used.

Special effects are generally added last in the printing job. Therefore, if a page contains preprinted images, the publisher should be sure that the inks used in primary printing will not be affected by the special effect process.

Choosing the Binding

Binding is the final finishing process for a publication. For laser printouts or photocopies, binding can be as simple as stapling the publication in the corner, or three-hole punching the paper for insertion into a ring notebook or report cover.

For publications that are offset printed, however, more sophisticated options are available from the printer's bindery department or from a subcontractor. The choice of binding will determine whether or not

- Extra space is needed in the gutter margin of the pages.
- The pages of the publication will lie open flat when bound.
- The cover will have a flat spine.

Commonly used binding methods include saddle stitching, side stitching, mechanical binding, perfect binding, and case binding.

Saddle and Side Stitching In **saddle-stitching**, the pages are placed on a device shaped like a saddle and are stapled down the middle. (See Figure 11.15.) Most magazines and many booklets are bound with saddle stitching. This is a simple and inexpensive type of binding. Saddle-stitched publications do not require extra gutter space. They will open flat, but they have no flat spine.

Side stitching is used when the bulk of the publication is too great for saddle stitching and cost considerations make other, more expensive forms of binding not feasible. For side stitching, the pages are placed flat under a stapling head, and thick staples are inserted parallel to the page edge. (See Figure 11.16.) The pages in publications to be side-stitched should have extra gutter space, since they will not open flat. An open spine is trimmed so that the pages create a flat edge, but an open spine cannot carry printing. For a more finished look, printed covers must be glued onto the spine.

Mechanical Binding **Mechanical binding** is used for bulky publications that need to open flat. The pages are punched with a series of holes at the binding edge. A wire or plastic spiral coil is then inserted through the holes. Sometimes a less expensive but also less permanent comb can be used. For publications with frequent updates, ring-binders are often used so that pages can be added and removed. (See Figure 11.17.) Mechanically bound publications require extra gutter space and have no flat spine for printing.

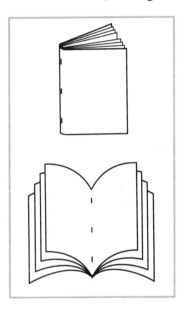

FIGURE 11.15
Saddle stitching

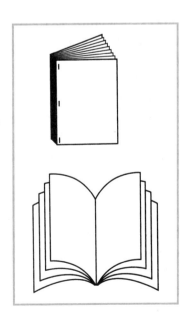

FIGURE 11.16
Side stitching

FIGURE

11.17

Mechanical binding

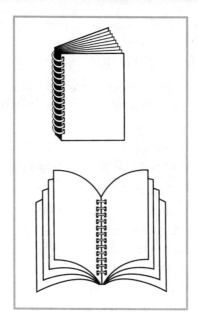

Book Binding **Perfect binding** is a process that uses an adhesive to attach the pages to a glued-on cover. The pages are trimmed and roughened, glue is applied to the spine, the cover is placed over the glue. Then the whole publication is pressed together so that the glue squeezes through the paper. Sometimes a gauze cloth fabric is embedded in the spine to provide additional strength. The page configuration for perfect binding is similar to side stitching, as shown in Figure 11.16. Perfect binding is used widely for paperback books. Perfect-bound books require extra gutter space, and should not be opened flat; depending on the type and age of the glue, the pages may come out. A cover spine is available for printing.

Case binding (also called **edition binding**) is a high-quality binding process that utilizes a rigid cover extending over the body of the book to protect the pages. The pages are gathered into signatures, which are groups of pages, usually 8, 16, or 32, depending on how the pages were imposed on the press sheet. The signatures are trimmed on three sides, with the back side remaining folded. They are then sewn together and passed through a rounding machine which rolls the backbone to give the book the correct shape to open properly. Cloth fabric and backing paper are glued to the rounded edge of the pages, and sometimes a decorative headband is attached to the top and bottom.

The case itself, made from a thick fiberboard glued to leather or cloth, is attached to the pages with end sheets made from durable paper stock that forms the inside covers. (See Figure 11.18.) Case binding is used for hardbound books. Extra gutter space is usually set, even though a properly manufactured case binding allows the pages to open nearly flat. A spine on the cover is available for printing.

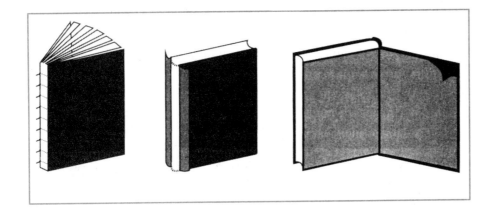

Case binding
Adapted from *Pocket Pal*,
New York, NY:
International Paper
Company.

Burst binding is also used for hardcover books. It is the same as case binding except that the gathered and stitched side of the signatures is sheared off or "burst" and then glued to the case.

CHECKING YOUR UNDERSTANDING

1. Why does the image rub off when there is a paper jam in a laser printer and the page is removed from within the printer?

2. Give four reasons why it is more efficient to make 25 photocopies of a 5-page report containing many bitmaps than it is to print them out directly on a desktop laser printer.

3. Why do dark areas sometimes fade out when printed on a desktop laser printer?

4. How can color be added to laser printouts? What are the drawbacks?

5. Why are some kinds of paper better than others for desktop laser printing?

6. Why is offset printing thus called?

7. What are the advantages of quick-copy printing over photocopying? What are the limitations of quick-copy printing?

8. What factors affect print quality in quick-copy printing?

9. What are the differences between imageset copy and desktop laser printer proofs? Name two specific elements that will vary.

10. Why does an imagesetter take longer than a desktop laser printer to process and output a TIFF file?

11. What are the steps involved in the creation of metal plates from mechanicals supplied to the print shop?

12. What is the purpose of crop marks, registration marks, and bleed lines on a mechanical?

13. What is the purpose of an overlay?

14. What is the difference between spot color separation and process color separation?

15. What are the advantages and disadvantages of using film negative output from an imagesetter?

16. Describe four grades of paper and their common uses.

17. Why does one grade of paper at a particular weight not correspond in thickness to another grade of paper at the same weight?

18. Is premixed ink used for spot color or process color? How is premixed ink color chosen?

19. Describe three specialty inks and three special effects available for finishing publications.

20. Describe five binding processes and the most common types of publications that use each process.

APPLYING DESIGN PRINCIPLES

Exercise 1 Designing a Bid Sheet

Design a bid sheet to use for obtaining prices on copy jobs submitted for offset printing to printshops.

Exercise 2 Communicating Specifications

Assume you have a book prepared for offset printing. It will be submitted in camera-ready format to a printshop for offset reproduction. Using the bid sheet designed in Exercise #1 above, obtain bids from at least two local printers. What are the specifications you need to provide so that the printshops can bid?

Exercise 3 Gathering Printing Information

Contact two or three local printshops and find out their rates for reproducing a 50-page book with 8–1/2" x 11" trim size, using

   a)   black ink only;
   b)   two ink colors (PMS colors);
   c)   four ink colors (process color).

Get the rates for 100, 500, and 2,000 copies. Prepare a report citing your findings.

PRODUCING A *Newsletter*

In this chapter, you will create a four-page newsletter.

12

- create a template for a serial publication, using a PageMaker style sheet
- import ASCII text into PageMaker
- apply styles to imported text
- use copyfitting techniques, including text wrapping around graphics

First you will create a template, import text into PageMaker, and apply styles. The source files you will need for this project are supplied on the student data disk. They include:

nwsintr.txt	**banner.tif**
dtp.tif	**bitmap.pcx**
nwswp.txt	**typebook.eps**
map.eps	**nwstype.txt**
nwsgrfx.txt	**nwsednt.txt**

Because the text files are in ASCII, you can use files prepared by any word processor as long as they have been saved in the ASCII format. Before starting this project, check your **Preferences**, **Options**, **Target output resolution**, printer designation, and ruler zero points.

CREATING A TEMPLATE

A template is a file that contains the standing elements for a serial publication. Standing elements are elements that recur in every issue of the publication. The banner, masthead, and master page (folios and repeating design motifs) of a newsletter, newspaper, or magazine are standing elements; calendars, headings for regular columns, mailers, and cover pages for books or booklets can also be set as standing elements. In desktop publishing, a style sheet can be made part of a template. For the newsletter, you will create a 4-page template with master pages, the banner and masthead, a mailer, and a style sheet.

1. Refer to the finished newsletter as you go (see Figures 12.49 through 12.52).

2. Open a new document. In the **Document Setup** dialog box, specify 4 pages and set all margins to 2 picas.

3. Immediately save the document as a template: in the **Save Publication** dialog box, name the file **nwstmplt** and click **Template**. (See Figure 12.1.)

FIGURE
12.1
Template file type in
Save Publication dialog
box

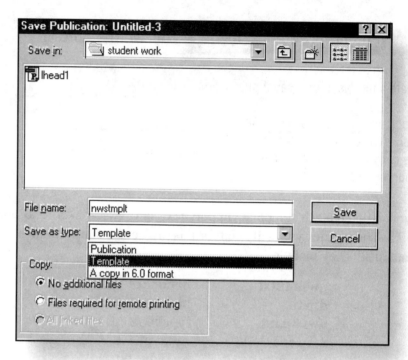

Opening a template creates an untitled copy. Thus the template will not be overwritten, but left blank for future use.

4. On page 1 of the newsletter, set up three columns with 1-pica alleys. (To do this, select **Column guides** from the **Layout** menu.)

5. Turn to the master pages and set up two columns with 1p6 alleys and the page numbers as shown in Figure 12.2.

FIGURE
12.2
Creating automatic page
numbers on the master
page

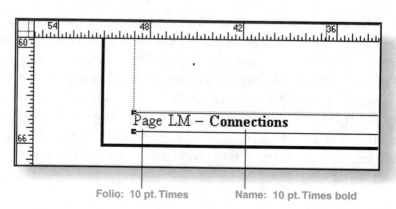

Page LM – Connections

Folio: 10 pt. Times   Name: 10 pt. Times bold

Creating the Banner

The banner is created with two rounded-corner boxes and type that has been saved in draw-graphic form. The graphic elements that make up the banner are used in the masthead on page 2 of the newsletter.

1. Turn to page 1 of the newsletter, and drag guidelines for the positioning of elements in the banner as shown in Figure 12.3.

MAC MEMO

On the Macintosh, the code for automatic page numbers is **Shift + Ctrl + 3** (or **Command + Option + P**).

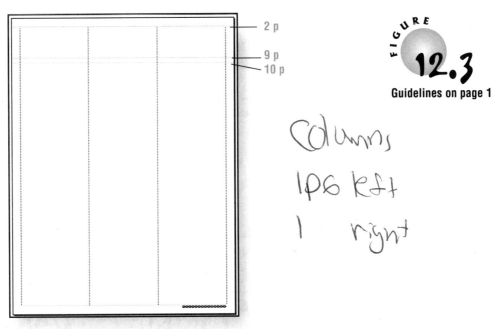

— 2 p
— 9 p
— 10 p

F I G U R E

12.3

Guidelines on page 1

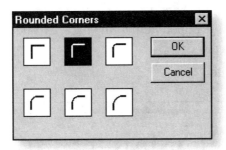

Columns
1p6 left
1 right

2. Use the **Box** tool to draw the drop shadow. While the **Box** tool is selected, choose **Rounded Corners** from the **Element** menu.

3. In the **Rounded Corners** dialog box, select the least-rounded square corner (see Figure 12.4).

F I G U R E

12.4

Rounded Corners dialog box

4. Fill the drop shadow (fill = **Solid**). Copy and paste it to make the opaque box (fill = **Paper**).

5. Adjust the length of the opaque box to 1 pica smaller on the left and right edges.

6. Position the boxes as shown in Figure 12.5.

FIGURE 12.5

Creating opaque over-layed box for banner

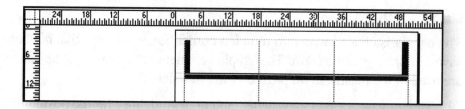

The file **banner.tif** is a graphic file that contains the title of the newsletter.

1. Place **banner.tif** in the publication banner. (See Figure 12.6.)

2. After placing **CONNECTIONS**, resize to the length and width shown in Figure 12.6.

FIGURE 12.6

Placing the newsletter title from the *banner.tif* file

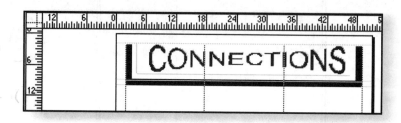

3. Key the organization name, volume, and number using Arial 12-point type. Place as shown in Figure 12.7.

FIGURE 12.7

Creating and placing organization and volume data in banner

4. Select and group all elements of the banner except the text containing the organization name and volume number (see Figure 12.8). You may need to send this grouped item to the back by selecting **Arrange** from the **Element** menu.

5. Save the template.

FIGURE 12.8

Selecting elements of banner to group

Creating the Masthead

The masthead is made with the same graphic elements as the banner. Instead of re-importing the type and graphics, you can simply copy them from page 1 and paste them onto page 2, then scale them and reposition them for a single-column layout.

1. Select the banner as grouped in step 4 above (Figure 12.8).

2. Give the **Copy** command (**Ctrl + Ins**, or **Command + C** on the Mac).

3. Turn to page 2, and give the **Paste** command (**Shift + Ins**, or **Command + V** on a Mac).

4. Scale to fit in the top of the right column on page 2 as shown in Figure 12.9. To scale a graphic by 50% without using arithmetic, you can use guidelines and the graphic's handles, which indicate the top/bottom and left/right midpoints of the graphic.

FIGURE 12.9

Placing organization name in masthead on page 2, column 2

5. Copy and paste the organization name from page 1, placing it on the masthead as shown in Figure 12.9. The text size must be changed to 9 point.

6. To finish the masthead, key the credit information. Specify italics as shown. Figure 12.10 shows how you can use the ruler to align the positions and names. Put a ½-point box on the sides and bottom.

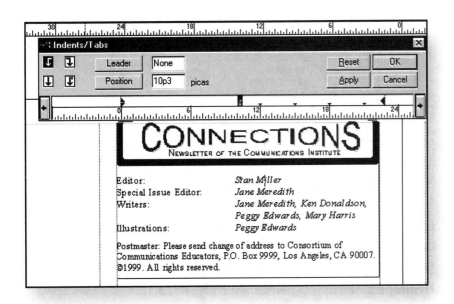

FIGURE 12.10

Finishing the masthead and aligning names using the *Indents/Tabs* dialog box

7. Save the template.

Creating the Mailer Panel

Creating the mailer panel on page 4 requires no new techniques.

1. Key the return address and specify it. Then draw a text box and key the postage permit. Specify bold as shown.

2. Save the template.

Creating a Style Sheet

In order to create a style sheet in PageMaker, you must first identify the style sheet elements. The newsletter style sheet elements are: body text, headline, byline, continuation line, caption, cutline, and pull quote.

1. In the **Styles** palette, key the above list of style sheet elements, and position the cursor after the first one, "Body text."

2. From the **Window** menu, select the **Styles** palette (**Ctrl + B**). (See Figure 12.11.)

3. Hold the **Ctrl** key and click **Body text** in the **Styles** palette to access the **Style Options** dialog box. (See Figure 12.12.)

FIGURE 12.11

Styles palette

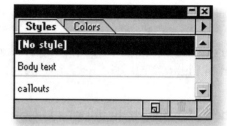

FIGURE 12.12

Style Options dialog box

4. In the **Style Options** dialog box, specify the type and tabs (that is, the indentations) as indicated in Figure 12.12. Then click **OK**.

5. Move the cursor to the end of the word "Headline" and click on **Headline** in the **Styles** palette. (See Figure 12.13.)

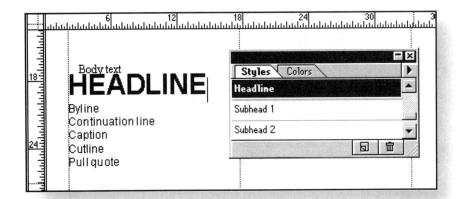

FIGURE

12.13

Headline style

6. Access the **Style Options** dialog box for the headline by holding the **Ctrl** key and clicking **Headline** in the **Styles** palette. Specify the type as you see it in Figure 12.14 and click **OK**.

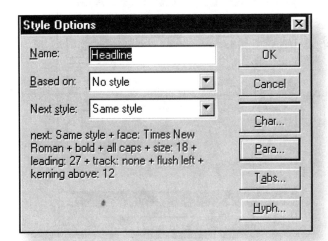

FIGURE

12.14

Type specs for *Headline*

For the byline, the procedure is slightly different since PageMaker has no default byline style.

1. Highlight the paragraph containing the word "byline." To create a new style, hold the **Ctrl** key and click **No style** in the **Styles** palette. (See Figure 12.15.)

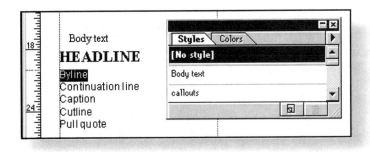

FIGURE

12.15

No style in the *Styles* palette

2. In the **Style Options** dialog box, key the style name, **Byline**, and specify the type as shown in Figure 12.16.

FIGURE

12.16

Type specs for *Byline*

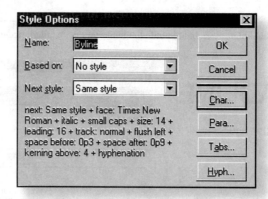

3. Create styles for the caption, continuation line, cutline, and pull quote. You will need to create new styles for all but the caption style, which can be edited. (See Figures 12.17 to 12.20.)

FIGURE

12.17

Type specs for
Continuation line

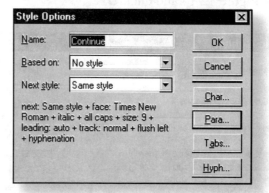

FIGURE

12.18

Type specs for *Caption*

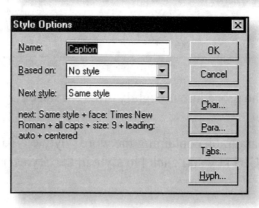

FIGURE

12.19

Type specs for *Cutline*

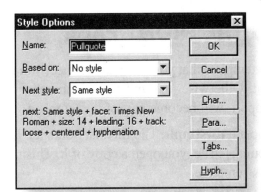

12.20
Type specs for *Pullquote*

4. Create another style called **Kicker** using the type specs shown in Figure 12.21.

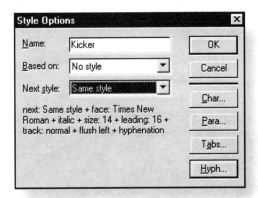

12.21
Type specs for *Kicker*

5. When you have finished creating and editing the style sheet, remove the default styles not used, **Subhead1** and **Subhead2**. From the **Type** menu, select **Define styles**. (See Figure 12.22.)

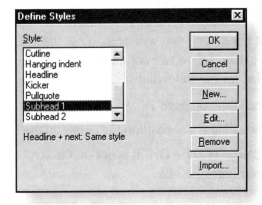

12.22
Removing *Subhead1* and *Subhead2*

In the **Define Styles** dialog box, select the style you wish to delete, and click **Remove**.

6. This completes the preparation of the template. Delete the text "Body text, Headline..." on template.

7. Save the template and close it.

CREATING THE FRONT PAGE

In order to use the template that you have just created, you must close the file and then reopen it. Otherwise, the text and graphics for the current issue, which you will import, will become part of the template.

1. Open the template **nwstmplt**. The file that you open is untitled. When you open a template file, you open a copy of it. This reminds you to not overwrite your template.

2. Save the file as **vol5no1**. (See Figure 12.23.)

F I G U R E 12.23

Saving a copy of the template file

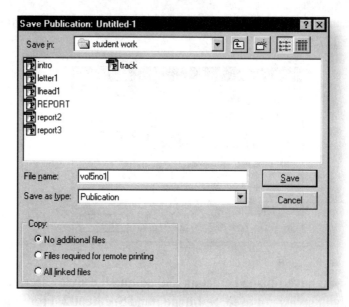

Headlines and Bylines

The headlines and bylines for the newsletter stories are best keyed as separate text blocks, since the leading and space below have been specified in the style sheet. For the front page story, you will need to use the text-drag technique to make the headline extend across two columns. Refer to Figure 12.49, the final document, as needed for the following steps within this section.

1. Key the first headline on page 1.

2. To apply the headline style, position the cursor in the headline.

3. In the **Styles** palette (**Ctrl + B**, if it is not on the screen), select **Headline**. (See Figure 12.24.)

F I G U R E 12.24

Select *Headline* from the *Styles* palette

4. Key the byline in the second line and apply the byline style. The byline style was specified with the proper leading and space below to the next line—the first line of text in the story. (See Figure 12.25.)

FIGURE

12.25

Select *Byline* from the *Styles* palette

5. To determine the proper positioning of the story text block, select the headline/byline block with the **Pointer** tool.

6. Drag a guideline to the bottom handle as shown in Figure 12.26.

FIGURE

12.26

Drag a guideline to the bottom handle

Importing ASCII Text Files

You should be familiar by now with the procedure for importing files. When importing ASCII files, text takes on the style that is selected in the **Styles** palette. Since you have just finished using the byline style, you should change to the **Body text** style before you import the story file, which is in ASCII format.

Below you are given directions for placing text files. Refer to Figures 12-49 through 12-52, the finished product, at the end of this chapter to guide you in placing the text. Upon completion of this chapter, your newsletter pages should look similar to the pages in those figures.

1. Click **Body text** in the **Styles** palette.

2. Import the story (**Ctrl + D**). The name of the file containing the first story is **nwswhat.txt**.

3. Position the text-place cursor at the intersection of the left margin and the guideline you drew below the byline and click to flow the story into the column.

It is usually easiest to use the **Fit in window** size for the overall layout of long text files in PageMaker. Now you will block out the text for the first page.

1. Continue the story from the left column to the middle column.

2. Shorten the text in the middle column to approximately halfway down the page. In a newsletter or newspaper layout, the length of one column is often dependent upon the length of an adjacent column. This is the case with the middle column on the front page of the newsletter. The right column contains a sidebar, and its length will determine the length of the middle column.

3. For now, estimate the column length, and click the bottom windowshade of the middle column to continue the text to the last page.

4. Turn to page 4 of the newsletter, and continue the text in the upper left corner, leaving space for a continuation head and continuation line. The text will flow out to the bottom of the page.

5. Create a second column by dragging upward on the bottom windowshade, and then clicking the resulting small triangle.

6. Position the text-place cursor in the right column and click to flow the last block of text. (See Figure 12.52.)

7. Save the file.

Later you can adjust the columns on page 4 after the length of the previously chained blocks on page 1 is determined.

Creating the Sidebar

The text for the sidebar on page 1 is the file **nwsednt.txt**. Import it into the third column using the **Place** command (**Ctrl + D**). Because it is a text file, you will need to specify it in PageMaker.

1. Place the **nwsednt.txt** file on page 1.

2. To highlight the entire file, even if the whole file does not appear within the text block on the screen, put the insertion cursor anywhere in the text. Choose **Select all** (**Ctrl + A**) from the **Edit** menu. (See Figure 12.27.)

F I G U R E

12.27

Selecting the Editor's note text

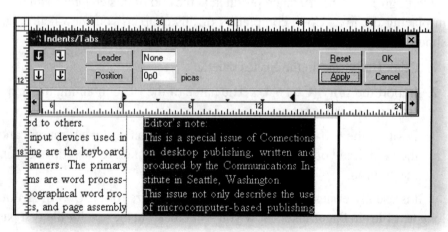

3. Verify the type as Arial, 10 point, 0p2 spacing after paragraphs. To specify the space between paragraphs, use the **Paragraph** dialog box from the **Type** menu (**Ctrl + M**). (See Figure 12.28.)

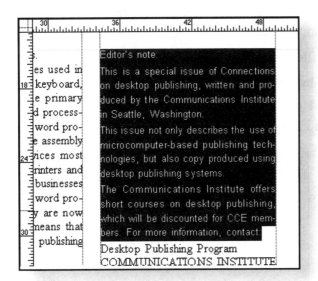

Specifying 0p2 spacing after paragraphs

4. Verify the address is Arial, 10 ~~point~~. Point bold

5. If necessary, lengthen the text block to place all the text. The Editor's note is surprinted over a 10% screen.

6. Draw the box around the type, specify it at 10% shading. This box has no outline. (See Figure 12.29.)

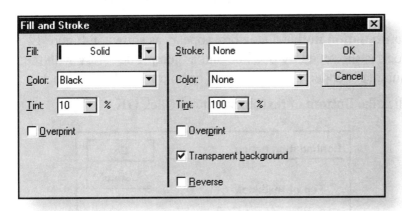

Specifying 10% fill (shading)

7. **Send to back** by selecting **Arrange** from the **Element** menu.

On screen, a surprint breaks up the type very noticeably. On a 300 dpi laser printer, the type is rather rough (for that reason, sans serif typefaces work best at low dpi or else serifs can become obliterated). For best results, serif or sans serif surprinted type is output on an imagesetter at 600 dpi, 1270 dpi or 2540 dpi.

Adding a Continuation Notice

Since the front page story jumps to the back page, you should set a continuation notice on the front page at the end of the last column in which the story runs, and another notice on page 4 where the text continues. Use the **Utilities** menu to accomplish this.

1. Save the file.
2. Click the text block in the middle column.
3. Click the **Utilities** menu, select **Plug-ins**, and then select **Add cont'd line**. (See Figure 12.30.)

FIGURE 12.30

Highlight *Add cont'd line...*

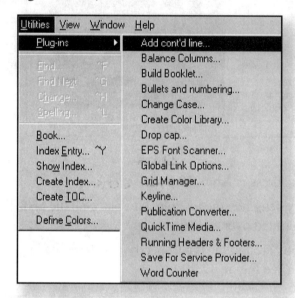

The **Continuation notice** dialog box appears as shown in Figure 12.31. The text block is shortened by one line and a "jump-line" story with the correct page number is added either at the top or bottom of the text block.

4. Click the **Bottom of textblock** button. Click **OK**.

FIGURE 12.31

***Continuation notice* dialog box**

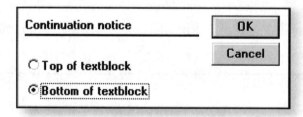

Notice that **Add cont'd line** automatically inserts the correct page number of the page on which the text block continues. The style for the jump-line story can be created and formatted as you wish. The *Continued on page xx* jump line is right-justified, while the *Continued from page xx* jump line is left-justified. You have already created the **Continue from** style and named it **Continue**. Follow these directions to create the **Continue on** style.

1. Press the **Ctrl** key and click **[No style]** in the **Styles** palette.

2. Key **Cont on** as the name of this new style, and change the formatting as is shown in Figure 12.32.

3. Click **OK**.

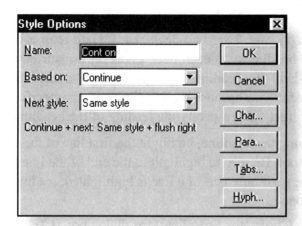

Type specs for *Cont on*

4. On page 1, place the **Text** tool in the line of text that contains the continuation notice.

5. Click the **Cont on** style in the **Styles** palette.

The next jump-line story appears on page 4 at the beginning of the text block.

1. Move to page 4 and select the text in the left column with the **Pointer** tool.

2. Click **Plug-ins** from the **Utilities** menu, then click **Add cont'd line**.

3. Select **Top of textblock** and click **OK**.

4. Now change the style of the jump line to **Continue**.

5. Position the text blocks so that the windowshades are aligned, as shown in Figure 12.52.

6. Save the file.

Note that the page numbers in jump-line stories are not automatically updated if you change the position of the text blocks. You must manually revise the page numbers. This can be accomplished in one of two ways:

• Delete the jump-line stories and run the **Add cont'd line** utility again.

• Search in the **Story Editor** (**Utilities** menu, **Find...**) for the jump-line styles (**Cont on** or **Continue** style) and manually revise the page numbers.

Adding a Graphic

1. Move to page 1.

2. Create a box in the two-column space below the sidebar and import the graphic **dtp.tif** in the box.

3. Proportionally adjust the graphic so that it is positioned across the two columns.

4. Save the file.

CREATING THE INSIDE SPREAD

The inside spread consists of pages 2 and 3 of the newsletter.

Creating a Two-Deck Headline

The headlines on page 2 are two-deck heads. Hard returns are used to force a new line in headlines, so each deck takes on the attributes of a separate paragraph. When the headline style is applied to the lines, extra space appears between them because the headline style is specified with 24-point leading. To correct this, respecify the leading of the headline.

1. After keying the headline, highlight the first line of the headline with the **Text** tool. Be sure to highlight to the end of the line (click 3 times on the line)—if only part of a line is highlighted, leading specifications are not applied.

2. Select the **Character Specifications** dialog box (**Ctrl + T**) and specify the leading as 18 points since there are no descenders in the headline caps. (See Figure 12.33.)

FIGURE

12.33

Specifying leading

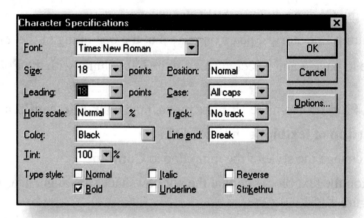

3. Import the file **nwswp.txt** and place it on page 2 as shown in Figure 12.50.

Copyfitting

Electronic copyfitting can be accomplished on screen with PageMaker. When you import the story about word processing (**nwswp.txt**), for example, you can see that it runs too short. There are a number of techniques that you can use to fill space: in this case, a pull quote will be set in the middle of the story.

Creating a Pull Quote The pull quote will need to take up a specific amount of space so that the word processing story will fit the amount of space left at the bottom of the column.

1. Draw a box the size of the white space at the bottom of the column.

2. Move the box from the bottom of the column to the middle—slightly below where the headline for the adjacent story will go to avoid a tombstoned layout.

3. Select the box and open the **Text Wrap** dialog box from the **Element** menu.

4. In the **Text Wrap** dialog box, click the **Wrap even** icon, and specify 0 standoff all around. (See Figure 12.34.)

FIGURE
12.34
Text Wrap dialog box

Because the box is specified for a text wrap, the story will flow around the box, to the length of the column.

5. Select the **Pullquote** style in the **Styles** palette.

6. Use **View/Actual size** to key the pull quote. (See Figure 12.35.)

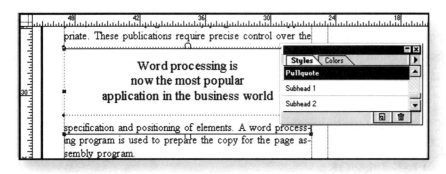

FIGURE
12.35
Using *Pullquote*

7. Make the line around the box invisible by selecting **None** for the **Stroke** style from the **Element** menu.

8. Draw the rules above and below the pull quote.

9. Save the file.

Blocking Out the Pages   There are many strategies for laying out pages. Most production artists block out the text and graphics on the page in an order based on flexibility. The inflexible elements will determine the position and size of the flexible elements. For example, in a newsletter, this means that you should first block out stories that cannot be edited and advertisements that have been sold by size. Then the stories that can be edited or reset in a different typeface, and the graphics that can be scaled and/or cropped to fit, can be copyfitted around the stories and ads.

For this newsletter spread, the graphics story is the most flexible since it contains two graphics that can be cropped or disproportionally scaled to fit. The graphics story will start in the second column of page 2 and jump to the bottom of page 3. The position of the jump will be determined by the length of the type story, which will be set at the top of page 3. Therefore, lay out the **nwstype.txt** story first, to see how much space is left for the graphics story. The finished page 3 is shown in Figure 12.51 and can be used for reference during the following steps:

1. On page 3, leave space for a headline and kicker at the top. Drag a guide from the ruler line to 11p6 from the top of the page.

2. Import the type story (**nwstype.txt**) and place it at the ruler guide in the left column. Be sure that **Body text** is selected in the **Styles** palette before you import the text.

Next, you will use the **Balance columns** command from the PageMaker **Plug-ins** menu to evenly position the text in the two columns. Part of the text must be flowed into the right column before this command can be initiated.

1. Click the bottom windowshade and drag up to shorten this text block.

2. Click the small triangle in the windowshade and load the **Text** tool. Flow the text into the column on the right.

You must select both columns before you activate the **Balance columns** command. This command allows you to align the tops of columns with the topmost text block or the bottoms of the columns with the bottommost text block. Another option in **Balance columns** tells PageMaker where to add remaining lines.

1. Use the **Shift** key to select the two columns of text.

2. Click the **Utilities** menu and select **Plug-ins**.

3. Select **Balance columns** and make the selections you see in Figure 12.36. Click **OK**.

FIGURE

12.36

Balance columns
dialog box

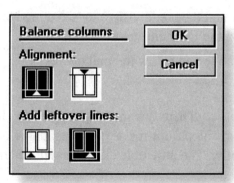

It may be necessary to reposition the two text blocks on the guide. Block out the graphics story (page 2 as shown in Figure 12.50):

1. Enter the headline and byline for the graphics story on page 2. Change the leading of the first line to 17 point.

2. Import the graphics story (**nwsgrfx.txt**) and flow it into the second column of page 3.

Block out the illustrations for the graphics story on page 2:

1. Import the file **bitmap.pcx** (or one of your Paint files that can be disproportionally scaled to fit).

2. Scale the illustration to 8 picas wide. As an alternative to moving the zero point of the ruler, you can move the graphic to the zero point and use the ruler as shown in Figure 12.37.

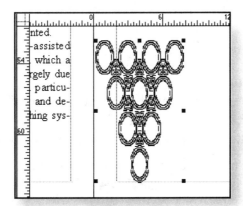

FIGURE

12.37

Scaling the graphic by using the zero point on the ruler

3. Move the illustration into the story. Position it so that you will not cause a bad page break such as an *orphan* (the first line of a paragraph, left at the bottom of a page) or a *widow* (a single line at the end of a paragraph, left at the top of a page). (See Figure 12.38.)

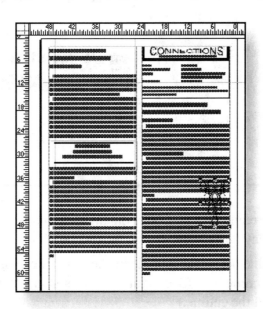

FIGURE

12.38

Positioning the graphic in the story

4. Create the wraparound by calling up the **Text Wrap** dialog box (from the **Element** menu), and entering the values shown (the right value is irrelevant since it is on the margin; the bottom value is large so that a cutline can be fit within the wrap). (See Figure 12.39.)

FIGURE 12.39

Setting standoff in the *Text Wrap* dialog box

Adjusting Standoff You may need to adjust the standoff in order to enter a caption and cutline. If there is not enough room for text within the text wrap border, the text will jump out of the standoff bounding box.

1. Use a text box to key a caption over the illustration. Make sure that the **Caption** style is selected in the **Styles** palette. (See Figure 12.40.)

FIGURE 12.40

Using the *Caption* style

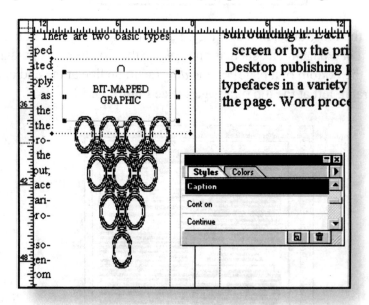

2. If necessary, realign the text box containing the caption and the graphic. It may be necessary to set the text box for text wrap.

3. Key the cutline below the graphic in a text box, keeping within the standoff bounding box. (See Figure 12.39 for standoff and Figure 12.50 for the text of the cutline.)

4. Select text (as in Figure 12.41) and load the **Pointer** tool with text not showing on the screen, then place on the bottom of page 3.

5. Add a continuation notice at the bottom of the column on page 2.

6. Save the file.

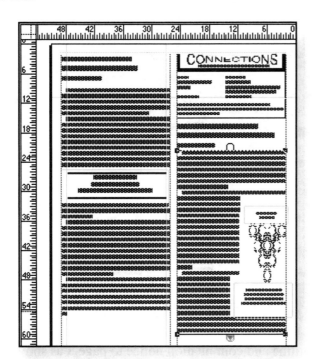

FIGURE

12.41

Selecting text to move to page 4

Mixing Column Grids on a Page

PageMaker can set different column grids on a single page. For the newsletter layout, column grids can be used to set up the graphics story jump on page 3. An illustration can be set in the first of three columns, and then the story can be continued in the middle and outside columns.

1. Access the **Column Guides** dialog box (from the **Layout** menu). The box in the lower-left corner of the dialog box lets you set the facing pages separately.

2. Click the **Set left and right pages separately** box. Then specify the **Right** page (page 3) with 3 columns with a 1p6 pica alley (see Figure 12.42).

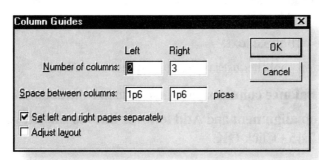

FIGURE

12.42

Specifying page 3 with 3 columns

3. Drag the side knobs on the text block handles to change the line length of the graphics story jump to the three-column measure. (See Figure 12.43.)

FIGURE

12.43

Changing the width of the text block

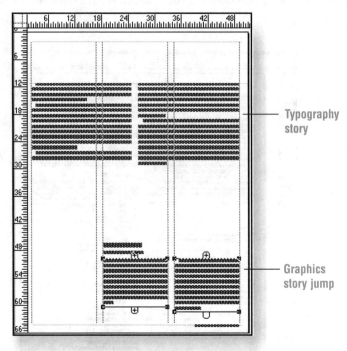

Typography story

Graphics story jump

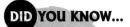

DID YOU KNOW...

When the underlying grid has been changed, the type story (previously set at the top of the page) retains its two-column measure.

4. Add a headline and continuation notice to page 3 as shown in Figure 12.51.

5. Balance the columns in the graphics story on page 3.

Applying More Copyfitting Techniques

The type story is still running short, and its two columns are uneven. PageMaker can create irregular wraps around graphics, which can help in fitting text in columns.

1. Draw a box in the center column of the underlying grid to block out space for an illustration for the pull quote on page 3, as shown in Figure 12.51.

2. Select the **Text Wrap** dialog box from the **Element** menu and specify **Wraparound**. Use default standoffs since you will delete them later. (See Figure 12.44.)

3. Type the pullquote text:

   The desktop publisher uses type as an expressive medium

4. Use the **Balance columns** plug-in to equalize the columns.

5. Select **Top alignment** and **Add leftover lines to the left column**. (See Figure 12.45.) Click **OK**.

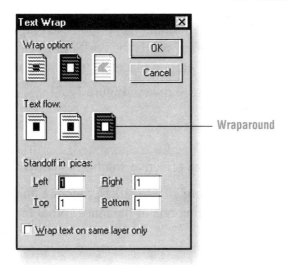

FIGURE

12.44

Text Wrap dialog box
with default standoffs

Wraparound

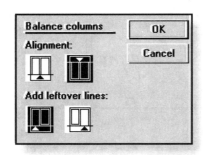

FIGURE

12.45

Balance columns dialog
box with top alignment
and leftover lines added
to left column

Creating a Kicker   Even with the wraparound, the type story is running
short. Another copyfitting device can be used to fill the page: a kicker. The
kicker will be placed at the top of page 3 as shown in Figure 12.51.

1. Key a one-deck headline and byline above the type story so that you
   can estimate the amount of space that the kicker will have to fill. (See
   Figure 12.46.)

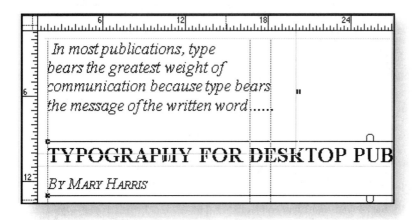

FIGURE

12.46

Keying the kicker above
the headline and byline

2. Select all the type story elements by surrounding them with the pointer,
   and move them down the page.

3. Key the kicker (using returns to force new lines as needed), and specify
   them with the kicker style as shown in Figure 12.46.

4. Create a box for positioning and import the graphic file **typebook.eps** into it. (The **PS** cursor stands for PostScript.) Using Figure 12.51 as a reference, use text wrap to place the graphic appropriately.

5. Realign columns, as shown in Figure 12.51.

6. Save the file.

Creating an Irregular Wrap Around a Graphic Irregular text wraps, if not overused, can provide an effective solution to copyfitting problems.

1. Proportionally enlarge the PostScript picture on page 3 by selecting the picture, then dragging one of the inner corner handles. (See Figure 12.47.)

FIGURE 12.47

Proportionally enlarging a picture by dragging on inner corner handles

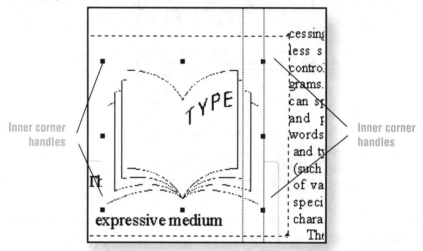

2. Move the picture to the center of the column that you have marked (align its middle selection handle on the guideline). (See Figure 12.48.)

FIGURE 12.48

Moving the graphic to the center of the column

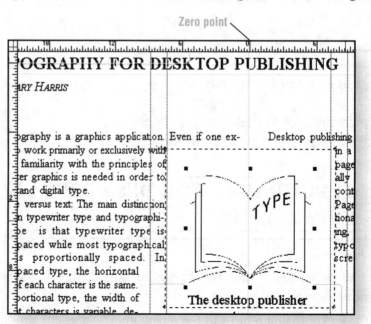

3. Select the **Text Wrap** dialog box from the **Element** menu and specify a 1-pica standoff all around.

4. Reset the zero point to the center of the middle column so that you can make a symmetrical standoff bounding box. (*Note:* This may already be set.)

5. Drag the lower-right standoff bounding box handle (it is diamond shaped) 12 picas to the right of the center point and 18 picas from the top of the page (see Figure 12.49).

6. Drag the lower-left standoff bounding box handle to the lower-left corner of the box 12 picas to the left of center and 18 picas from the top of the page, as shown in Figure 12.49.

7. Select the box and change the **Line** style to **None**. As a result, the PostScript graphic's standoff bounding box will cause the text to wrap in a triangular shape.

If the story is still too short, you may need to further adjust the standoff bounding box handles in order to even out the columns and make the story run longer. Use the distance from the ruler zero point to make the standoff bounding box even.

Fine-Tuned Copyfitting Irregular wraparound creates a very short line length at the base of the triangle shape. You should check for widows, orphans, blocks, and rivers and lakes of white space whenever you make wraparounds that might cause these problems.

Also, type specification can make a difference in line count when bold-face and italics are used at narrow column measures. To ensure that the type story fits on the page properly, you should make bold the internal headings in all the stories before making your final adjustments on the pages.

1. Use the PageMaker bold shortcut, function key **F6**, to make the subheadings bold in the type story (see Figures 12-49 through 12-52):

   Bold = **F6** (On the Mac, use **Shift + Command + B**)

   Italic = **F7** (On the Mac, use **Shift + Command + I**)

2. Enter and specify other pull quotes, and draw the rules above and below them.

3. Save the file.

FINISHING THE NEWSLETTER

The final tasks in the production of the newsletter entail techniques you have used previously in this and other chapters. The order in which you do these finishing tasks is not important; as you design and produce publications with PageMaker, you will develop ways of keeping track of the different tasks involved that work best for you.

1. Specify the subheads in all the stories.

2. Key and specify continuation headlines and continuation lines in the graphics story jump (on page 3 of the newsletter) and the intro page story jump (on page 4 of the newsletter).

3. Adjust the intro story jump columns on page 4.

4. Import the object-oriented graphic named **map.eps** into page 3 and scale it to fit.

5. Key and specify the caption and cutline for the object-oriented graphic on page 3.

6. Save the file.

7. Print.

CHECKING YOUR UNDERSTANDING

1. Why is it improtant to get a good idea of the elements that will go into a style sheet before you begin implementing a design?

2. What can you do to adjust page layout when text on a page is too short?

3. Why does text retain its two-column measure if the grid below it is changed to three columns?

4. What are three copyfitting techniques using text or graphics? Which do you believe are the easiest to achicvc?

APPLYING DESIGN PRINCIPLES

Exercise 1 Flexible vs. Inflexible Items

Look at several pages from a few different sections of a Sunday newspaper. Identify text and/or graphic items on each page that are flexible or inflexible in terms of page layout and mark them accordingly. Those pages can go into the portfolio of examples that you began in chapter 1.

Exercise 2 Designing with Individual Style

What would you do differently with the design of the 4-page newsletter presented in this chapter? How would you make it fit your individual design preferences?

Using the files for the finished pages, copy them and then experiment with making design changes to see how those changes would work or not work with the other elements. How do those changes affect page layout?

FIGURE

12.49

Page 1 of newsletter

Newswhat txt

CONNECTIONS

NEWSLETTER OF THE COMMUNICATIONS INSTITUTE —Arial 12 pt.,
VOL. 5, NO. 1   caps/small caps

WHAT IS DESKTOP PUBLISHING?—18/18 Times, caps, bold, left align

BY JANE MEREDITH —14/16 Times, italics, caps/small caps, left align

Arial 10 pt., surprint on 10% screen

12/14 Times, 1 em first line indent

Desktop publishing is the use of a microcomputer-based system to produce publication materials with typeset or near-typeset quality text and graphics integrated on a page. What makes desktop publishing different from traditional publishing is that equipment small enough to fit on a person's desktop provides the resources needed to prepare and assemble pages.

Hardware and software: Desktop publishing, as defined here, utilizes a microcomputer for WYSIWYG (what-you-see-is-what-you-get) graphic design and page assembly. Desktop publishing can also be used to make presentation materials such as transparencies, slides, and even animated video images.

WYSIWYG is an interactive mode of running computer programs, in which you see, on the display monitor, how the type and graphics will appear when you get the actual printed output. WYSIWYG requires graphics-oriented software and hardware to process, display, and output images and type. Hardware refers to actual physical devices, and software refers to the information (software programs) used to control the devices.

Like all computer applications, desktop publishing can be seen in terms of three phases: Input, processing, and output. Input means getting the information into the computer; processing means working on it; and output means getting the information out of the computer in a form that can be communicated to others.

The primary input devices used in desktop publishing are the keyboard, mouse, and scanners. The primary software programs are word processing (including typographical word processors), graphics, and page assembly programs. The output devices most commonly used are laser printers and imagesetters. Today, most businesses

CONTINUED ON PAGE 4

Times ital caps, right align

Editor's note:

This is a special issue of Connections on desktop publishing, written and produced by the communication Institute in Seattle, Washington.

This issue not only describes the use of microcomputer-based publishing technologies, but also copy produced using desktop publishing systems.

The Communications Institute offers short coursed on desktop publishing, which will be discounted for CCE members. For more information, contact:

COMMUNICATIONS INSTITUTE

1234 12th Street

Seattle WA 98103

(206) 555-1234

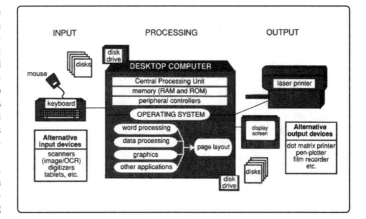

Folio: 10 pt. Times

Connections – Page 1

Name: 10 pt. Times bold

FIGURE

12.50

Page 2 of newsletter

7/7 Times caps/small caps, centered; 14 pt. line space below

8/9 Times

12/12 Times italic names; 1 pt. box on sides and bottom

Headline style

WORD PROCESSING FOR PAGE ASSEMBLY

By Ken Donaldson ——— Byline style

A basic understanding of word processing is important for professional desktop publishing, since word processing files are the primary source materials used in most publications. Word processing is now the most popular microcomputer application in the business world.

Office documents: For many office documents, such as correspondence, memos, forms, and informal reports, a word processor that can specify type is adequate. The operator needs to learn the basics of typography and the stylistic rules for typographical word processing, which differ slightly from typewriting style. For more complex publications such as brochures, fliers, newsletters, and formal reports, the use of a page assembly program is more appropriate. These publications require precise control over the

14/16 Times, center, 9 pt. above to 2 pt. rule; 12 pt. to bottom rule

Word processing is now the most popular application in the business world

specification and positioning of elements. A word processing program is used to prepare the copy for the page assembly program.

Preparation of copy for page assembly: The copy that a desktop publisher receives from a client or writer will usually be in word processing form. For copy that does not already exist in a computer file, text can be directly keystroked, edited, and formatted in a page assembly program. However, if the desktop publisher needs to input or edit more than a page of copy, it is usually most efficient to use a word processor. Word processors have more sophisticated editing features and faster keyboard response rates than page assembly editors.

Preparation of word processing files for page assembly includes preliminary type specification tasks, such as insertion of typographic characters and/or codes for special typographic treatment of words. Today's word processing programs offer time-saving features that help in the preparation of long and/or complex files for page assembly.•

CONNECTIONS
NEWSLETTER OF THE COMMUNICATIONS INSTITUTE

Editor:	*Stan Miller*
Special Issue Editor:	*Jane Meredith*
Writers:	*Jane Meredith, Ken Donaldson, Peggy Edwards, Mary Harris*
Illustrations:	*Peggy Edwards*

Postmaster: Please send change of address to Consortium of Communications Educators, P.O. Box 9999, Los Angeles, CA 90007. ©1999. All rights reserved.

COMPUTER GRAPHICS FOR DESKTOP PUBLISHING

By Peggy Edwards

The old saying "a picture is worth a thousand words" is true in desktop publishing. The graphics-based programs used in desktop publishing require more processing power, RAM, and disk storage space than nongraphics programs. However, the setting of type and the addition of pictures can make the difference between a publication being noticed and read, or not read.

Kinds of graphics software: There are two basic types of graphics software, Bitmapped (Paint) and Object-oriented (Draw). These two modes apply to digital typography as well as illustration graphics, and affect the resolution of the output; the amount of transmission and processing time the computer and the printer require to produce output; the amount of disk storage space that files will occupy; and the various operations available in production.

BITMAPPED GRAPHIC

Bitmapped graphics are resolution-dependent; thus jagged edges are apparent when images are not reduced.

Bitmapped graphics are resolution-dependent, larger, and generally take longer to transmit from the computer to the printer. Image scanners and screen capture utilities produce bitmapped images. Screen fonts used for display

CONTINUED ON PAGE 3

9/10 Times italic, centered

Caption style

Alt 0150

FIGURE

12.51

Page 3 of newsletter

In most publications, type bears the greatest weight of communication because —— 14/16 Times italic *type bears the message of the written word......*

TYPOGRAPHY FOR DESKTOP PUBLISHING — Headline style

By Mary Harris — Byline style

Typography is a graphics application. Even if one expects to work primarily or exclusively with text, a familiarity with the principles of computer graphics is needed in order to understand digital type.

Type versus text: The main distinction between typewriter type and typographical type is that typewriter type is monospaced while most typographical type is proportionally spaced. In monospaced type, the horizontal width of each character is the same. In proportional type, the width of different characters is variable, depending on the shape of the character itself and the characters surrounding it. Each character is drawn on the screen or by the printer as a graphic image.

Desktop publishing programs utilize different typefaces in a variety of sizes and positions on the page. Word processing programs generally have less sophisticated typo-

Pullquote style

The desktop publisher uses type as an expressive medium

graphic controls than page assembly programs. Page assembly programs can specify fractional typesizes and positions; line spacing, wordspacing, and letterspacing; and typographical enhancements (such as screens, boxes, and rules of varying kinds) in positions specified relative to the type characters.

The future of digital typography: Page assembly programs cannot match the degree of typographical refinement afforded by dedicated typesetting equipment, nor do desktop publishers have access to the wide variety of typefaces available to typesetters. But the type-handling capabilities of desktop publishing software are continuously being improved, and digital type foundries are making typefaces available to desktop publishers at the rate of hundreds each year.•

Caption style

OBJECT-ORIENTED GRAPHIC

Object-oriented graphics are resolution-independent

Cutline style

GRAPHICS... — Continuation head: 14/14 Times bold

CONTINUED FROM PAGE 2 — cont. from style

screens are bit-mapped. Object-oriented graphics are resolution-independent. They are smaller but more complex, so they require less transmission time from the computer to the printer. Business graphics and advanced drawing programs produce object-oriented images. Printer fonts based on the PostScript language are object-oriented.

The future of computer graphics: Computer-assisted graphics is a relatively new area. It is an area in which a great deal of development is now taking place largely due to the growing interest in desktop publishing. In particular, advanced color and image scanning programs and devices are becoming available for desktop publishing systems.•

FIGURE

12.52

Page 4 of newsletter

DESKTOP PUBLISHING... ——Continuation head style

CONTINUED FROM PAGE 1

and organizations are using word processing software and many are now using laser printers. This means that in many cases, the desktop publishing system is already partially in place.

Design and production work: With desktop publishing, several separate design and production processes can be accomplished with the page assembly program supplemented by graphics and word processing files. A page assembly program is the software heart of the desktop publishing system, the "gathering place" where artwork and type are integrated into the final product.

One of the most important aspects of desktop publishing is that it joins graphic design and production. Publication production can be begun in earnest on a project during the design stage. The actual illustrations can be put in place and the actual text set in type. Final production is primarily a matter of fine-tuning the publication created

with the page assembly program. With WYSIWYG desktop publishing systems, final copy or camera-ready mechanicals can be previewed, edited, and reviewed on the screen (WYS) before proofing or sending final output to a laser printer. Additional fine-tuning can be done before sending out the publication to be photocopied, printed, or for imageset (WYG).

Desktop publishing, because it is relatively inexpensive and "user-friendly," has put the power of professional-quality publishing in the hands of many who are not publishing professionals. Some speak out against this trend and point to the flood of poorly designed publications produced by inexperienced publishers. As one commentator put it, "Desktop publishing enables anyone to make more ugly publications faster." While that is sometimes true, the equalizing force of desktop publishing rightly moves us toward the goal of freedom of the press for all who have a message to communicate.•

Balance columns

Add box

Connections
1234 12th Street ——12/12 Times
Seatle, WA 98103

10/12 Arial,
centered ——

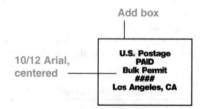

U.S. Postage
PAID
Bulk Permit
####
Los Angeles, CA

INTERNET PROJECT

he documents and publications you have created to this point were intended to print as hard copy. Therefore, you were concerned with formatting documents for the printed page. With the increased popularity of the Internet has come an increased interest in publishing documents electronically (see Figure IP.1). In this project you will learn about the Internet's World Wide Web and about how to create a document for publication on the Web. You will also use PageMaker 6.5 to create some pages suitable for publishing on the Web.

This project has re-created parts of the National Initiative for Leadership and Institutional Effectiveness (NILIE) home page. NILIE manages a consortium of 160 community colleges and universities across the United States and Canada. It is located at North Carolina State University and performs the functions discussed in this project. Dr. George A. Baker, NILIE founder, has granted permission to use the home page for this textbook. As such, please do not post this project to your own server for display on the World Wide Web. You may access the actual NILIE home page at http://www2.ncsu.edu/ncsu/cep/acce/nilie.

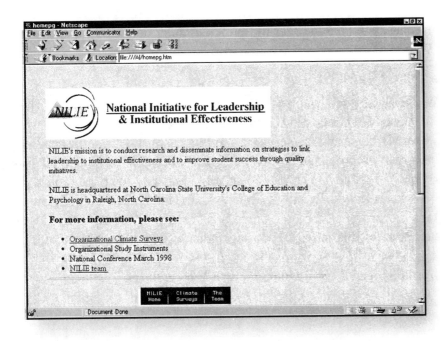

An example of a document published electronically on the World Wide Web

THE INTERNET AND THE WORLD WIDE WEB

The Internet is an enormous network of smaller networks that connect computers all around the world. One of the most popular services provided on the Internet is the World Wide Web. The World Wide Web is a collection of documents found on the millions of Web servers on the Internet. A **Web server** is a computer system on the Internet that contains World Wide Web documents.

Web documents are connected to one another using **hypertext links** or **hyperlinks**. A hyperlink is a specific location in a document that can be selected by clicking. A hyperlink may appear highlighted, in a different color, and/or underlined on the computer screen. When you click a hyperlink, the Web site is changed either to another location in the same document or to a completely different Internet resource. Say, for example, that you want to know about Celtic dancing and you know of a Web document saved on a Web server in New York City that contains all kinds of information about folk dances from around the world. Included in that document might be a hyperlink that, when clicked, takes you immediately to a Web document that contains information on Celtic dancing that is stored on a Web server in Dublin, Ireland. From that second site, you might find other hyperlinks that tell you what you want to know in regard to Celtic dancing.

In order to access the documents found on the World Wide Web, you need software called a **Web browser**. The Web browser allows you to access a Web server, display Web documents, and follow the hyperlinks throughout the Internet. Web browsers can find where Web documents are located because each Web document has what is called a Universal Resource Locator (URL). The URL acts like an address that defines the route that the computer needs to take in order to find a particular document on the World Wide Web.

HyperText Markup Language (HTML)

The World Wide Web displays information in units called pages. These pages, designed for publication on the World Wide Web, are created by using HyperText Markup Language (HTML). HTML uses style tags for headings, body text, paragraphs, indented paragraphs, bulleted lists, numbered lists, and so on. These style tags are conceptually similar to the paragraph styles of PageMaker. Figure IP.2 shows examples of HTML code. Notice how the style tabs are surrounded by the angle bracket symbols. The <HEAD> tag indicates headers, the <CENTER> tag indicates text that is centered, the <LI> tag indicates text that is in a list, and so on. Figure IP.3 shows what the code from Figure IP.2 would look like in a Web browser.

```
Source of: file:///D|/meredith/Internet Project/test.html - Netscape

<HTML>
<!--This line is a comment-->

<HEAD>
  <TITLE>Example HTML page</TITLE>
</HEAD>

<BODY>
  <CENTER><H1>Example HTML page</H1></CENTER>

  <HR> <!--This tag is the horizontal rule-->

  <P>This example page shows several HTML code tag examples.  As can be seen here the HTML tags sur

  <P>The tags surrounding this text is the paragraph tag.  </P>

  <OL><!--This group of tags is a numbered list-->
    <LI>List item #1
    <LI>List item #2
    <LI>List item #3
  </OL>

</BODY>
</HTML>
```

FIGURE IP.2

HTML code

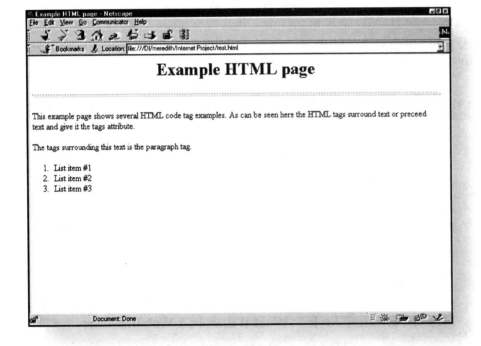

FIGURE IP.3

The HTML code in Figure IP.2, as displayed in a Web browser

Different Web browsers each interpret HTML documents differently. This means that some typographical attributes which you specify in your document, especially the length of a line, the spacing within a line, and the spacing between lines may not be displayed as such in a different Web browser. The following type attributes are controlled by the Web browser:

- typeface, type size, and leading
- type width
- tracking
- strikethrough, outline, shadow, reverse, superscript, and subscript
- color
- paragraph alignment
- indent and tab positions

Basically, an HTML document is a plain text file to which HTML style tags have been added. The text files can be created using a text editor such as Emacs or vi on UNIX computers, Simple Text on Macintosh, or Notepad on Windows. You can use word processing software if you save your document as "Text only." You can also use an HTML editor, such as FrontPage (Windows) or Adobe PageMill (Macintosh), which has the advantage of WYSIWYG capabilities. These methods of creating HTML documents assume that you understand the HTML style tabs. The following table displays basic HTML style names and their meanings. There are other HTML style tags available in this language, but the ones listed here are most commonly used.

BASIC HTML STYLE NAMES AND MEANINGS

Basic Format Tags	What it does in a Web browser:
<HTML>	Begin HTML.
</HTML>	End HTML. Adding a backslash after the first angle bracket of any tag terminates the formatting that comes before that point in the document.
<P>	Paragraph break.
 	Line break.

HTML Heading Style	What it does in a Web browser:
TITLE	Creates the title that appears in the Web browser window's title bar.
H1, H2, H3, H4, H5, H6	Six levels of subheads. H1 is the highest level. Similar to PageMaker's Heading 1, Heading 2, and so on.

HTML Functional Style	What it does in a browser:
ADDRESS	Sets an address (e.g., email address) or other short text apart from the body text.
BLOCKQUOTE	Sets one or more paragraphs of text apart from the body text.
MENU list	Similar to an ordered list, but more compact.
OL list	Ordered list. Use for a numbered list. Usually the browser adds the correct number before each item.
PREFORMATTED	Prevents text from being reformatted when changes are made to a browser's style definitions. Allows you to preserve white space and line breaks that have been formatted into the document.
UL list	Unordered bulleted list. Usually the browser adds a bullet before each item.

HTML Emphasis Style	What it does in a browser:
CITE	Denotes a citation, usually with italics.
CODE	Quotes a computer code, usually with a monospaced font.
DEFINITION	Quotes a definition, usually denoted by quotation marks.
EMPHASIS	Emphasized text, usually with italics.
SAMPLE	Quotes computer status messages.
STRONG	Emphasizes text, usually making the text bold.

Web Page Design Considerations

All of the principles of a good design which you have learned so far in this book also apply to documents published on the Web. Just because the final document is meant to be viewed on a monitor rather than to be printed on paper does not mean that design principles for traditionally published documents are ignored. In addition to these principles, however, there are specific design principles that apply only to publications on the Web which should be considered.

In addition to displaying graphics, publications on the Web can display animation. For example, fonts can blink on and off in electronic publications. A good design for electronic publication does not have too much movement on the page. More than one thing moving at a time on the page is disconcerting to the viewer.

When designing publications for the Web, it is very important to keep track of the size of the graphic images being used. If there are a lot of images or if the images are quite large, it will take a long time for that document to display on a viewer's screen. Try to keep the size of the images down to 20KB to 30KB per image. Another good rule of thumb is to have at least one or two images, but no more than four images, per page.

When designing, keep in mind that the width of many monitors is 17 inches. You should never have the text in a Web document extend the full width of the monitor. Text that is 17 inches wide in one row is very difficult for the eye to follow. Use narrower margins to cut down on the viewing width or break the text up into magazine-width columns.

When preparing graphics to be used in a Web document, it is important to keep in mind the graphic format of the image. HTML only recognizes JPEG (.jpg) and GIF (.gif) file formats. The JPEG file format is best used for full color photographs or images because of its ability to depict millions of colors. In addition, the JPEG file format is able to handle millions of colors without the size of the file becoming huge. If you have created your own graphics using a paint or draw package or if you are using screen captures, those images are best saved using the GIF format. Images created with paint or draw packages and screen captures typically have only 16 to 256 colors. The GIF file format is well-suited to handling these files that have far fewer colors than photographs. The JPEG file format uses an internal compression algorithm to allow it to store the complex color information compactly. The GIF file format does not have this internal compression capability.

If there are several pages in the Web document, there should be a cohesive design in all the pages. For example, the pages should all have the same background, repeat the same graphic image at the top of the page, or use the same fonts and type style. There should be a sense that the pages are all a part of the same document.

Once you have designed a Web page, view the final results from a variety of different monitors using different Web browsers to see if it looks okay on all of them. How your page is displayed on a Macintosh using the Web browser Netscape Navigator will not necessarily be the same as how it is displayed on an IBM/PC using the Web browser Internet Explorer 4.0.

There are a lot of examples of bad Web page designs on the World Wide Web. To see some examples of good designs, however, you might want to look at the Web sites of large corporations. These companies have spent a lot of money to have their Web pages designed professionally and they usually offer examples of good Web page design.

Web Page Templates and Source Files

Some Web browsers provide information about creating HTML pages and even contain templates. For example, the Web browser Netscape Navigator, offers a variety of templates that may help you create pages for personal or family information, company or small business use, product or service advertising, special interest group promotion, or just interesting and fun pages. Netscape also provides information about creating HTML pages in its **Help** menu, but refer to Netscape's documentation for details on where to find help for your specific application. Other Web browsers provide similar kinds of information.

In addition to providing templates, Web browsers allow you to see the HTML code that is used to generate a page. Select **Document Source** from Netscape's **View** menu to see the file contents. The HTML tags are displayed in a new window. This is an excellent method to see how HTML is used, to get tips, and to learn how HTML is constructed. You can copy and save this source code to use as a template for one of your own Web pages. Just modify it to meet your needs.

Posting Your Files on a Server

You must have access to a Web server to display HTML documents on the World Wide Web. Contact your Web master (the individual who maintains Web documents on the server) to see how you can get your files on the Web. If you do not have access to a server at school or work, check to see if your community operates a FreeNet, a community-based network that provides free access to the Internet. You may need to contact a local Internet service provider (ISP) that will post your files on a server for a fee. Check the local newspaper for advertisements of Internet service providers in your area.

PREPARING A PAGEMAKER DOCUMENT TO EXPORT TO HTML

Creating Web pages using PageMaker 6.5 is relatively easy. The HTML Export feature in PageMaker 6.5 allows you to create HTML pages that you can publish on the Web. Most of the procedures for preparing a document to be exported to HTML, such as placing text and graphics, are carried out the same way as when creating a document to be printed. But one of the main differences in preparing a document to be exported to HTML is the need to create hyperlinks.

Hyperlinks and Anchors

Each hyperlink consists of a source and a destination. The source is the text or graphic you want the viewer to be able to click. The destination is the object, page, or document you want to appear once the viewer clicks the source. PageMaker supports two kinds of hyperlink destinations. A destination can be a document on the Web that is a URL destination, or it can be any text or graphic within the same document. When the destination is within the same document, it is called an **anchor** destination.

To create either an anchor destination or a URL destination in PageMaker, begin by clicking on the **Window** menu and select **Show Hyperlinks**. To create an anchor destination, select the range of text, or the graphic you want to be the anchor graphic, by choosing **New Anchor** from the **Hyperlinks** palette menu. Then type a name for the anchor and click **OK**. To create a URL destination, you choose **New URL** from the **Hyperlinks** palette menu, enter the URL in the dialog box that appears, and click **OK**. After they have been created, anchor and URL destinations appear in the **Hyperlinks** palette.

Once destinations have been defined and appear in the **Hyperlinks** palette, you can associate source text or graphics with those destinations. To do so, select the text or graphic that is to be the source. In the **Hyperlinks** palette, click the destination you want to associate with the source you selected and choose **New Source** from the **Hyperlinks** palette menu. Name the new source and click **OK.**

Once the connection between the source and the destination is established, you have a hyperlink. A source can only jump to one destination. A destination, however, can have any number of sources that jump to it. You can preview your hyperlinks by clicking the **Hand** tool in the Toolbox to enter Preview mode. Hyperlinked text is outlined in a blue box while hyperlinked graphics are framed with a blue line.

Using HTML Tags in PageMaker 6.5

When preparing your first PageMaker 6.5 documents to be exported to HTML, it is easiest to use the PageMaker paragraph styles that correspond to the HTML markup tags that you want to use. That way, you will be sure that you are using styles supported by PageMaker's HTML export feature. There are two ways you can do this. You can either add the styles directly to your **Styles** palette or you can import them along with the contents of an HTML file. Once the styles are in the **Styles** palette, you apply them to the text the same way as in a document to be printed.

To add styles directly to the **Styles** palette, click the **Window** menu and select **Show Styles**. Select **Add HTML Styles** from the **Styles** palette menu. To import an HTML file, click the **File** menu and select **Place**. Read the notice that appears and click **OK**. Click the **Place URL** button and enter the URL of the HTML file you want to import in the **Place** dialog box. Click **OK.**

CREATING A HOME PAGE USING PAGEMAKER 6.5

The Web page created in this project contains three sections: the Home page, the Climate Surveys page, and the Team page. The Home page was shown in Figure IP.1. Figures IP.4 and IP.5 show what the Climate Surveys page and the Team page will look like when you are finished.

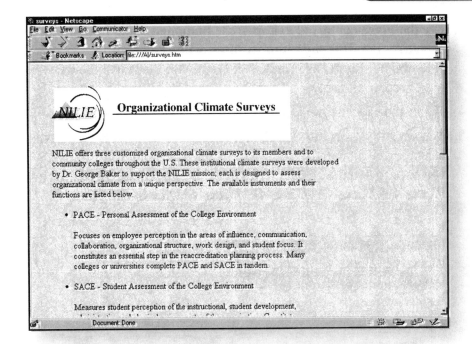

FIGURE IP.4
The Climate Surveys page

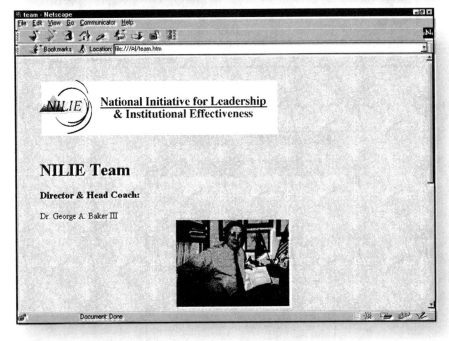

FIGURE IP.5
The Team page

As you create the Home page and Climate Surveys page, use the files called **homepg.txt** and **surveys.txt** on the student data disk which contain the text for the first two pages. You will enter the text needed for the Team page later.

1. Start the **PageMaker 6.5** program. Click the **File** menu and select **New**. Set all the margins to half an inch. Make sure that **Double-sided** is not checked.

2. Make sure that **Autoflow** is on in the **Layout** menu.

3. Use the **Place** command to import the **homepg.txt** file from the student data disk. The **Text-only import filter** dialog box appears. Choose **No conversion, import as is** and click **OK**. Place the text at the left margin approximately 2" down from the top edge of the page.

4. Name and save the file as **homepg.p65**.

5. You want to work with HTML styles. If necessary, display the **Styles** palette by clicking the **Window** menu and selecting **Show Styles**. Next, you need to add the HTML styles to the **Styles** palette. As shown in Figure IP.6, choose **Add HTML Styles** from the **Styles** palette.

FIGURE

IP.6

Adding HTML styles to the *Styles* palette

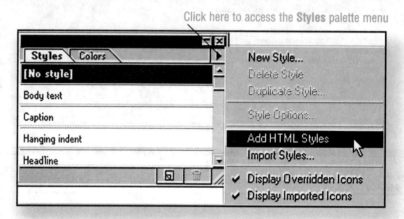

Click here to access the **Styles** palette menu

When you have finished, the **Styles** palette should look like Figure IP.7.

FIGURE

IP.7

The *Styles* palette with HTML styles displayed

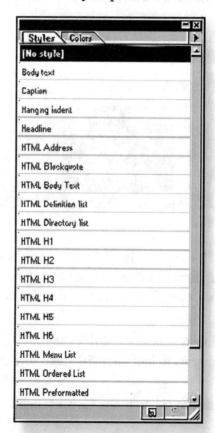

6. Zoom in so that you can read the text by using the **Zoom** tool in the Toolbox.

7. Apply the **HTML Body Text** style to the first two paragraphs. Apply the **HTML H3** style to the third paragraph. Apply the **HTML Unordered List** style to the remaining four lines. When you have finished, your screen should look similar to Figure IP.8.

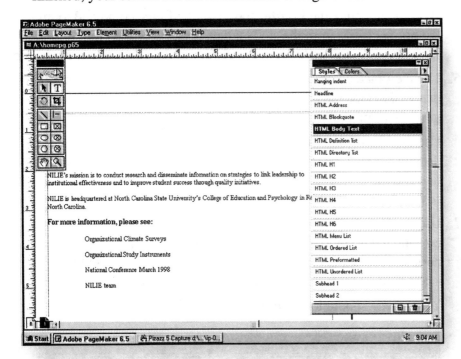

FIGURE IP.8

Applying HTML styles

8. Save the file as **homepg.p65**.

Inserting a Graphic

As mentioned above, Web browsers currently support two types of graphic files: JPEG (.jpg) and GIF (.gif) files. JPEG is a good format for photographs because it can represent millions of colors and the full raster of tones and blends. The GIF file format is used mostly with graphics which were created by using a paint or draw program or for screen captures.

In this project, you will start working with graphics by placing a GIF graphic at the top of the Home page.

1. Click the **Pointer** tool to place the graphic at the top of the page. Use the **Place** command in the **File** menu to import the **nilie_title.gif** file from the student data disk.

2. Place the graphic at the intersection of the top and left margins.

3. Next, you are going to place three small graphics at the bottom of the page. Place a horizontal ruler guide line at approximately 5.5" down from the top of the page. Place three vertical ruler guide lines. The first one should be 3" from the left edge of the page, the second one should be 3.75" from the left edge of the page, and the third one should be 4.75" from the left edge of the page.

4. If necessary, click the **Pointer** tool. Use the **Place** command to import the **home.gif** file from the student data disk. Place the graphic at the intersection of the first vertical guide line and the horizontal guide line.

5. Use the **Place** command to import the **surveys.gif** file from the student data disk. Place the graphic at the intersection of the second vertical guide line and the horizontal guide line.

6. Use the **Place** command to import the **team.gif** file from the student data disk. Place the graphic at the intersection of the third vertical guide line and the horizontal guide line. If necessary, reposition the graphics so that there is no extra space between them.

7. Use the **Constrained-line** tool to draw a horizontal rule between the text and the graphic images at the bottom of the page. Draw a horizontal rule that extends from the left margin to the right margin and is approximately 5.25" down from the top of the page.

8. Your screen should look similar to Figure IP.9.

FIGURE

IP.9

Adding graphics to the page

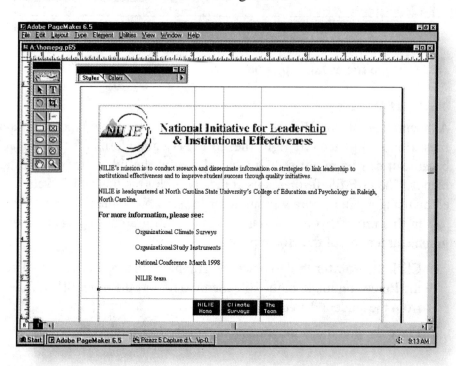

9. Save the file as **homepg.p65**.

Creating Hyperlinks

Now you will create hyperlinks to other Web pages. Two of the items in the unordered list and two of the graphics at the bottom of the Home page will be linked to the other pages you are going to create.

1. Name the two new pages to which you will be linking. That is, you have to define the destination. If necessary, click the **Window** menu and select **Show Hyperlinks**. Click the **Hyperlinks** palette and select **New URL** (see Figure IP.10).

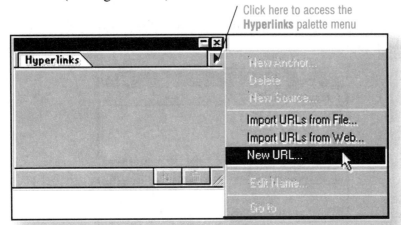

FIGURE

IP.10

Opening the *Hyperlinks* palette

As shown in Figure IP.11, the **New URL** dialog box appears.

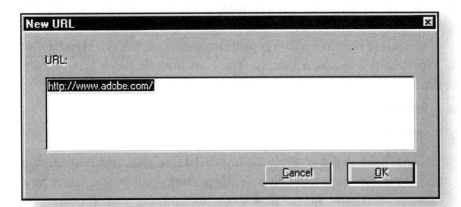

FIGURE

IP.11

The *New URL* dialog box

Enter the following:

surveys.htm

Click **OK**.

If you make a mistake, you can remove a source from the **Hyperlinks** palette by selecting the item you want to remove, clicking the **Trash** button at the bottom of the palette, and clicking **OK** (or click **Delete** on the Macintosh) when the **Trash** confirmation dialog box appears.

2. Repeat step 1: Click the **Hyperlinks** palette and select **New URL**. When the **New URL** dialog box appears, enter the following:

    team.htm

Click **OK**.

3. Again, click the **Hyperlinks** palette and select **New URL**. When the **New URL** dialog box appears, enter the following:

    homepg.htm

Click **OK**. When you are finished, your **Hyperlinks** palette should look like Figure IP.12.

The *Hyperlinks* palette

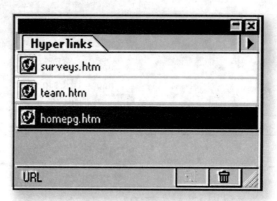

4. You have to select the text you want to be the hyperlink's source. Use the **Text** tool and select the line **Organizational Climate Surveys**. Click **surveys.htm** on the **Hyperlinks** palette. Click the **Hyperlinks** palette and select **New Source**. The **New Source** dialog box appears. Enter the following:

    surveys_list

Click **OK.**

5. Use the **Text** tool and select the line **NILIE team**. Click **team.htm** on the **Hyperlinks** palette. Click the **Hyperlinks** palette and select **New Source**. The **New Source** dialog box appears. Enter the following:

    team_list

Click **OK.**

6. Next, you are going to associate the graphics at the bottom of the page with a URL destination. Use the **Pointer** tool and select the first graphic, NILIE Home. Click **homepg.htm** on the **Hyperlinks** palette. Click the **Hyperlinks** palette and select **New Source**. The **New Source** dialog box appears. Enter the following:

    home_button

Click **OK**.

7. Use the **Pointer** tool to select the second graphic, Climate Surveys. Click **surveys.htm** on the **Hyperlinks** palette. Click the **Hyperlinks** palette and select **New Source**. The **New Source** dialog box appears. Enter the following:

> surveys_button

Click **OK**.

8. Use the **Pointer** tool and select the third graphic, The Team. Click **team.htm** on the Hyperlinks palette. Click the **Hyperlinks** palette and select **New Source**. The **New Source** dialog box appears. Enter the following:

> team_button

Click **OK**.

9. Save the document as **homepg.p65**.

Creating HTML Code

After you have created a PageMaker document that closely approximates what you want the Web page to look like, you export it to HTML pages. When exporting to HTML you have to define which pages or stories will be exported as the HTML document, the document title, and the location to which you want them exported. In addition, you can set many other options, such as defining the background image for the document.

1. Click the **File** menu and select **Export**. From the Export menu, select **HTML**. The **Export HTML** dialog box appears as shown in Figure IP.13.

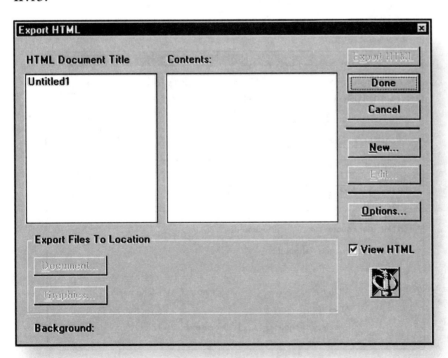

The *Export HTML* dialog box

2. Select **Untitled1** in the **HTML Document Title** box. Click **Edit**.

3. The **Edit Contents** dialog box appears. Enter the following as the document title:

homepg

4. Click the **Background** button at the bottom of the dialog box. On your student file disk is a file called **back1.jpg**. Select the **back1.jpg** file and click **OK** (or click **Select** on the Macintosh). This file will provide the background or what is sometimes called the "wallpaper" to your Web page. Your **Edit Contents** dialog box should look similar to Figure IP.14 when you have finished. Click **Done**.

FIGURE

IP.14

The *Edit Contents*
dialog box

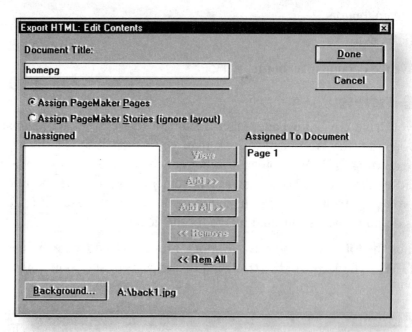

FIGURE

IP.15

The *Options* dialog box

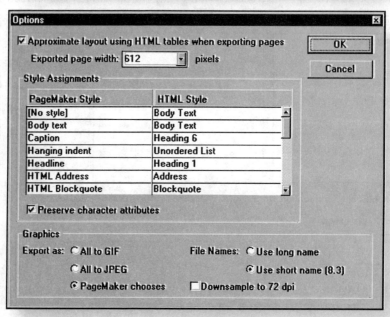

5. The **Export HTML** dialog box returns. There are many options available for how to export text or handle graphics. To make sure the options are set correctly for this project, click **Options**. The **Options** dialog box appears as shown in Figure IP.15.

Check the first option, **Approximate layout using HTML tables when exporting pages**. With this option checked, the layout of the text on the Web page will be as close as possible to the layout in PageMaker. When using the **Approximate layout using HTML tables when exporting** option, the **Exported page width** option should not be set any higher than 612 pixels. If this value is set higher, the viewer will have to scroll right and left to read the document on smaller monitors.

The **Style Assignments** box contains settings associating PageMaker styles with HTML styles. The default settings are fine for most applications. The **Preserve Character Attributes** option should be selected if you want the color and type style of the paragraph style definitions to be applied in your HTML document.

In the **Graphics** box, the **Downsample to 72 dpi** box should be checked if the graphics have not already been prepared for viewing on the World Wide Web. A monitor cannot display a graphic at a resolution higher than 72 dpi. Allowing PageMaker to downsample images to 72 dpi will keep the size of your images at optimal sizes. All of the graphics used in this project were prepared for viewing on the Web, so this option should not be selected for any of the pages you are now creating.

PageMaker will make intelligent choices based on color depth and the number of colors in an image if the **PageMaker chooses** option is selected under **Export as**. The file name option should be set to **Use long name** unless your Web server runs on a Novel network which requires the shorter naming convention. When you have finished making your selections, the settings in your **Options** dialog box should match those in Figure IP.15. Click **OK**.

6. The **Export HTML** dialog box returns. Click the **Document** button at the bottom of the dialog box.

7. The **Location for Saving** dialog box appears. Enter **homepg.htm** as the file name and select a location for the file. Click **OK.**

8. The **Export HTML** dialog box reappears. The HTML document is not actually saved until you click the **Export HTML** button. Click that button now. It will take a few moments for PageMaker to generate the HTML document.

The first time you save a document as HTML, PageMaker checks it for HTML compatibility. If the document contains an element or layout attribute that is not supported by HTML, PageMaker presents a dialog box informing you of the parts of the publication that need to be changed. If this occurs, correct the errors and then export the pages again.

Viewing the HTML Document

Once a document has been exported to HTML, it can be viewed by using a Web browser. In order to view the document in the Web browser, the Web browser software must be installed on your computer. You can indicate to the PageMaker program where the Web browser software is located on your hard drive. If you make that indication, then whenever you export a document to HTML, it is automatically displayed in the Web browser.

If a Web browser is installed on your computer, you can set up the **Export HTML** dialog box so that the document is displayed in the browser as soon as you export it to HTML. Check with your instructor to make sure the **Export HTML** dialog box has been set up to recognize the Web browser installed on the computer. If it already has been set up, skip to step 4.

1. If the **Export HTML** dialog box has not been set up to recognize the Web browser, click the **File** menu and select **Export**. From the **Export** menu, select **HTML**. The **Export HTML** dialog box appears. Click **homepg** in the **HTML Document Title** box (see Figure IP.16).

FIGURE IP.16

Viewing an HTML document

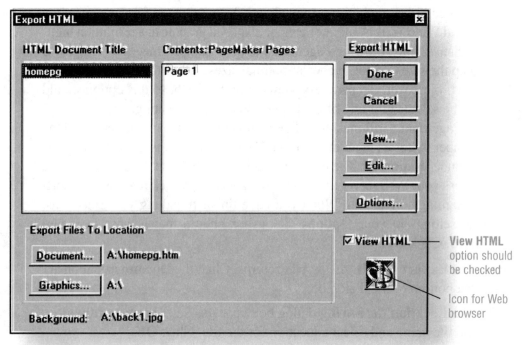

2. In the lower-right corner of the **Export HTML** dialog box is the selection for **View HTML**. Click this box. There should be a check mark in the box if/when the browser is recognized.

3. Under the **View HTML** option there is an icon. Click this icon. The **Choose a WWW Browser** dialog box appears. You need to select the appropriate program for the Web browser on your computer. You might have to ask your instructor for help in identifying where this file is located. Once the appropriate program has been selected, click **Open** (click **OK** on the Macintosh).

4. Your screen should look similar to Figure IP.16. The **View HTML** box has a checkmark in it and the icon for your Web browser appears under the **View HTML** option. Click the **Export HTML** button. When the warning box appears, click **Yes**. Your document is displayed in the Web browser. When you have finished looking at it, exit/quit the browser.

> **MAC MEMO**
>
> In step 4, the "warning box" on the Macintosh will say **Replace File.** Click **Yes.**

CREATING MORE WEB PAGES USING PAGEMAKER 6.5

You now have had practice preparing a document to be published on the World Wide Web. Let's use what you have practiced to create two more pages: the Climate Surveys page and the Team page.

Creating the Climate Surveys Page

As the first step in creating the Climate Surveys page:

1. Close the **homepg.p65** file. Open a new document. Set the margins to 0.5" and make sure that **Double-sided** is not checked.

2. Make sure that **Autoflow** is on.

3. Use the **Place** command to import the **surveys.txt** file from the student data disk. The **Text-only import filter** dialog box appears. Choose **No conversion, import as is** and click **OK**. Place the text at the left margin approximately 2" down from the top edge of the page.

4. Name and save the file as **surveys.p65**.

5. If necessary, display the **Styles** palette (on Macintosh, use **Show Styles** from the **Window** menu).

6. Zoom in so that you can read the text.

7. Apply the **HTML Body Text** style to the first paragraph.

8. Apply the **HTML Unordered List** style to the three paragraphs that begin PACE, SACE, and CESTA.

9. Under each of the paragraphs you just formatted, there is another paragraph. The first one begins "Focuses on employee...," the second one begins "Measures student perception ....," and the third one begins, "Obtains perceptions...." Apply the **HTML Blockquote** style to each of these three paragraphs.

10. Apply the **HTML H3** style to the line "The Survey Process."

11. Under the line "The Survey Process" there are five paragraphs. The first one starts with the words, "The survey process begins...." and the fifth one starts with the words "The result is a bound report...." Apply the **HTML Unordered List** style to all five of these paragraphs.

12. Apply the **HTML Blockquote** style to the paragraph that begins, "NILIE maintains a national...."

13. Apply the **HTML H3** style to the line "Survey Fees."

14. Apply the **HTML Blockquote** style to the last paragraph.

15. Save the file as **surveys.p65**.

16. To place a graphic at the top of the page, click the **Pointer** tool. Use the **Place** command to import the **nbanner3.gif** file at the intersection of the top and left margins.

17. Next, you are going to place three small graphics below the text. Place a horizontal ruler guide line at approximately 9.5" down from the top of the page. Place three vertical ruler guide lines at 3" from the left edge of the page, 3.75" from the left edge of the page, and 4.75" from the left edge of the page.

18. If necessary, click the **Pointer** tool. Use the **Place** command to import the **home.gif** file. Place the graphic at the intersection of the first vertical guide line and the horizontal guide line. Import the **surveys.gif** file. Place the graphic at the intersection of the second vertical guide line and the horizontal guide line. Import the **team.gif** file. Place the graphic at the intersection of the third vertical guide line and the horizontal guide line. If necessary, adjust the graphics so that there is no extra space between them.

19. Use the **Constrained-line** tool to draw a horizontal rule between the text and the graphic images at the bottom of the page. Draw a horizontal rule that extends from the left margin to the right margin and is approximately 9" down from the top of the page.

20. Save the file as **surveys.p65**.

21. The next step is to create the hyperlinks. First you have to name the pages to which you will be linking (define the destination). Click the **Window** menu and select **Show Hyperlinks**. Click the **Hyperlinks** palette and select **New URL**. The **New URL** dialog box appears. Enter the following:

    homepg.htm

    Click **OK**. Click the **Hyperlinks** palette and select **New URL**. Enter the following:

    surveys.htm

    Click **OK**. Click the **Hyperlinks** palette and select **New URL**. Enter the following:

    team.htm

    Click **OK**.

22. Select the text you want to be the hyperlink's source. The very last sentence reads, "See the NILIE Team page for the researcher for your area." Use the **Text** tool and select the words "NILIE Team page" from that sentence. Click **team.htm** on the **Hyperlinks** palette. Click the **Hyperlinks** palette and select **New Source**. The **New Source** dialog box appears. Enter the following:

    team_text

    Click **OK**.

23. Associate the graphics at the bottom of the page with a URL destination. Use the **Pointer** tool and select the first graphic, NILIE Home. Click **homepg.htm** on the **Hyperlinks** palette. Click the **Hyperlinks** palette and select **New Source**. The **New Source** dialog box appears. Enter the following:

    home_button

    Click **OK**. Select the second graphic, Climate Surveys. Click **surveys.htm** on the **Hyperlinks** palette. Click the **Hyperlinks** palette and select **New Source**. The **New Source** dialog box appears. Enter the following:

    surveys_button

    Click **OK**. Select the third graphic, The Team. Click **team.htm** on the **Hyperlinks** palette. Click the **Hyperlinks** palette and select **New Source**. The **New Source** dialog box appears. Enter the following:

    team_button

    Click **OK**.

24. You are ready to export this document to HTML. Click the **File** menu and select **Export**. From the **Export** menu, select **HTML**. The **Export HTML** dialog box appears. Select **Untitled1**. Click **Edit**.

25. The **Edit Contents** dialog box reappears. Enter **surveys** as the **Document Title**. Click the **Background** button. Select the **back1.jpg** file and click **OK** (click **Select** on the Macintosh). Click **Done**.

26. The **Export HTML** dialog box appears. Click **Document**. Enter **surveys.htm** as the file name and click **OK**.

27. If you want to see the document in the Web browser, make sure the **View HTML** option is checked. Click **Export HTML**. After a few moments the document will appear in the Web browser. Scroll through the page to see how it looks. Test out some of your hyperlinks. Click the NILIE Home button at the bottom of the page. The Home page should appear. On the Home page, click the underlined words "Organizational Climate Surveys." The Climate Surveys page should appear.

Creating the Team Page

Now you are ready to create the last page, the Team page. Close the file in your Web browser before you begin building the next page:

1. Save the **surveys.p65** file and close it. Open a new file. Set all the margins to half an inch (0.5"). Make sure that **Double-sided** is not checked.

2. Place a graphic at the top of the page. Using the **Pointer** tool and the **Place** command, place the **nilie_title.gif** file at the intersection of the top and left margins. Name and save the file as **team.p65**.

3. Using the **Text** tool, place the insertion point about 2.5" down from the top edge of the page at the left margin. Type the following:

    NILIE team

    Press **Enter**.

    Type the following:

    Director & Head Coach

    Press **Enter**.

    Type the following:

    Dr. George A. Baker III

4. Place a horizontal ruler guide 2.75" down from the top edge of the page. Place a vertical ruler guide 4" from the left edge of the page. Using the **Pointer** tool and the **Place** command, place the file **george.jpg** where the two ruler guides intersect. Hold down the **Shift** key, click the lower right handle of the graphic and drag to enlarge the graphic proportionately until it is about 3" wide. If necessary, reposition the image so that the upper left corner of the image is where the two ruler guides intersect.

5. Place a horizontal ruler guide 5.75" down from the top edge of the page. Using the **Text** tool, place the insertion point at the intersection of the left margin and the ruler guide. Type the following:

    Assistant Director, NILIE

    Press **Enter**.

    Type the following:

    Judy Dudziak

6. Using the **Pointer** tool and the **Place** command, place the file **judyd.jpg** at the intersection of the 5.75-inch horizontal ruler guide and the 4-inch vertical ruler guide. Hold down the **Shift** key, click the lower right handle of the graphic and drag to enlarge the graphic proportionately until it is about 2.25" wide. Your screen should look similar to Figure IP.17.

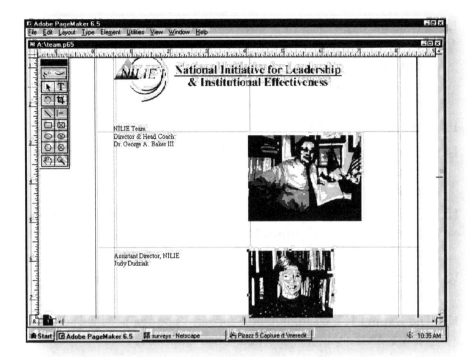

Creating the Team page

7. Save the **team.p65** file.

8. If necessary, display the **Styles** palette and select **Add HTML Styles**. Apply the **HTML H1** style to the line "NILIE Team." Apply the **HTML H3** style to the line "Director & Head Coach." Apply the **HTML H4** style to the line "Assistant Director, NILIE." Apply the **HTML Body Text** style to the names Dr. George A. Baker and Judy Dudziak.

9. Place the three small graphics at the bottom of the page. Place a horizontal ruler guide line at approximately 8.5" down from the top of the page. Place three vertical ruler guide lines at 3" from the left edge of the page, 3.75" from the left edge of the page, and 4.75" from the left edge of the page.

10. Use the **Pointer** tool and the **Place** command to import the **home.gif** file. Place the graphic at the intersection of the first 3-inch vertical guide line and the 8.5-inch horizontal guide line. Place the **surveys.gif** file at the intersection of the 3.75-inch vertical guide line and the 8.5-inch horizontal guide line. Place the **team.gif** file at the intersection of the 4.75-inch vertical guide line and the 8.5-inch horizontal guide line. If necessary, adjust the positions of the graphics so that there is no extra space between them.

11. Draw a horizontal rule between the text and the graphic images at the bottom of the page. Using the **Constrained-line** tool, draw a horizontal rule that extends from the left margin to the right margin and is approximately 8.25" down from the top of the page.

12. Create the hyperlinks from each of the three graphics at the bottom of the page to the appropriate page. Remember there are two steps involved in this process. First, enter the new URLs (homepg.htm, surveys.htm, and team.htm). Second, establish each of the buttons as a new source for each of the three destination URLs.

13. Save the **team.p65** file.

14. Export the file to HTML. Choose **Export** from the **File** menu and select **HTML**. When the **Export HTML** dialog box appears, select **Untitled1**. Click **Edit**.

15. The **Edit Contents** dialog box reappears. Enter **team** as the **Document Title**. Click the **Background** button. Select the **back1.jpg** file and click **OK** (click **Select** on the Macintosh). Click **Done**.

16. Click **Document**. Enter **team.htm** as the file name, select a location, and click **OK**.

17. The **Export HTML** dialog box appears once again. Make sure the **View HTML** option is checked. Click **Export HTML**.

18. Try out all of your hyperlinks. At the bottom of the page, click the **Climate Surveys** button. This should take you to the Climate Surveys page. In the section on Survey Fees in the Team page, click the underlined text NILIE Team page. This should take you to the Team page. At the bottom of the Climate Surveys page, click the **NILIE Home** button. This should take you to the Home page. Try out all the hyperlinks on the Home page.

19. When you have finished trying all the hyperlinks, you can exit (quit) the Web browser and exit (quit) PageMaker.

In this project, you have built a home page with two hyperlinked pages. Tour the real NILIE home page at http://www2.ncsu.edu/ncsu/cep/acce/nilie and compare the site with the one you created. You will notice that the design and the hyperlinks of the real site are very similar to your site.

GLOSSARY

algorithm: in object-oriented (Draw) graphics, a formula that describes graphic forms in abstract geometrical terms.

alignment: the manner in which text is lined up; e.g., flush left, centered, flush right, or justified.

alley: the space between columns of type.

anchor: an object, page, or document destination within the same Web document.

anomaly: a single element that looks different from a group of other elements.

ascenders: the parts of lowercase characters that rise above the x-height (this term is used with lowercase characters only).

ASCII (American Standard Code for Information Interchange): a file format for text-only information, which includes no formatting or typographical information, just characters. ASCII is frequently used for transfer of text files between different computers and between different application programs.

asymmetrical balance: a counterbalancing of contrasting elements not arranged around a fixed axis.

autoflow: a PageMaker command that places text on a page automatically. If a lot of text is placed, additional pages are added automatically.

back matter: in a book, the appendixes, end notes, references, bibliography, glossary, indexes, and so on.

backup: in printing, the copy on the reverse side of a double-sided document. Backup is an important consideration when designing tear-out forms. *Also used as a verb*: in books, headers or footers should backup baseline to baseline.

banner: the title of a periodical, which appears on the cover of a magazine and on the first page of a newsletter. It contains the name of the publication and serial information, such as date, volume, number.

baseline: an imaginary horizontal line upon which type characters sit.

basis size: the size of the paper as it is sold by a paper company. The paper is cut into press sheets for offset printing.

basis weight: the weight in pounds of one ream (500 sheets) of paper in its basis size.

Bezier curves: lines that can be bent after their end points have been established.

bit: the computer's smallest unit of measurement for memory capacity; has a value of either 0 or 1. *See also* **byte**.

bitmapped (mode): the Paint graphics mode. A series of zeros and ones, arranged two-dimensionally, describes an image made up of pixels. Each "0" corresponds to a bit that is off (not in use); each "1" refers to a bit that is on. *See also* **pixel**.

bitmapped character: a character created by a group of dots that together form the shape of a letter, number, etc.

black: (as describing a typeface) a bold slightly darker than the standard bold.

bleed: an element that extends outside the normal margins directly to the edge of the page. To print a bleed, the publication is printed on oversized paper which is then trimmed.

block: occurs in justified text when several consecutive lines end in hyphens.

block quote: a long quotation (four or more lines) within body text, which is set apart in order to clearly distinguish it from the author's own words; *also called* **extract**.

body type: roman (normal, plain, or book weight) type used for long passages of text, such as stories in a newsletter or magazine, or chapters in a book; *also called* **text type**. *See also* **display type**.

boldface type: a type that is blacker than roman type.

book list: in PageMaker, a list of publications or sections of the same publication that make up a larger document. PageMaker repaginates the publications in the list at the time of printing.

bracelet: in a typeface, a knobby protrusion at the midline of a character.

bracketed serif: in a typeface, a serif connected to the main stroke of a letter form with a tapering curve.

Bristol paper: a stiff heavy paper stock that can be used for inexpensive covers, business cards, postcards, menus, tickets, and file folders.

browser: on the Internet, software that looks at various Internet resources; a browser can search for documents and obtain them from other sources.

burst binding: like case binding, pages are gathered into signatures and trimmed on three sides. The remaining side is sown and then sheared ("burst") before gluing to the book's case.

byline: in newsletter or magazine, a credit line for the writer of an article.

byte: a unit of measurement for a computer's memory. One byte is equal to 8 bits. *See also* **bit**.

callouts: an explanatory label for an illustration, often drawn with a leader line pointing to a part of the illustration.

cap height: the distance from the baseline to the top of the capital characters.

caption: an identification (title) for an illustration, usually a brief phrase.

case binding: hardback binding, for which the pages are trimmed on three sides, with signatures sewn together and rounded to give the book the correct shape to open properly. The binding is attached to the pages with end sheets that form the inside covers. *Also called* **edition binding**.

castoff: estimate of how many pages of typeset material will result from a given number of pages of a typescript (monospaced type from a typewriter, daisy-wheel printer, or dot-matrix printer).

cell: in tables and spreadsheets, the intersection of a row and column.

central processing unit: *see* **CPU**.

chained text: in a page assembly program, when text is continued from one block to another in a different column or on a different page.

clip art: ready-made artwork sold or distributed for clipping and pasting into publications; available in hard-copy books and in electronic form as files on disk.

clipboard: a special area of memory that stores items which are to be copied or cut.

clock speed: the cycles per second that a CPU processes, measured in megahertz (MHz).

codes: in typesetting, delimited sets of characters embedded in the text which indicate type specifications. *See also* **tags**, **style sheet**.

color separation: the process of creating separate negatives and plates for each color of ink that will be used in a publication. *See also* **process color separation**, **spot color separation**.

column: in text, the vertical division within the image area into which text and graphics are placed; in a table or spreadsheet, a vertical collection of cells in which each one is under the other.

column measure: the width of a column; the line length. *See also* **measure**.

commercial printers: print shops that can handle nearly any sheet size and volume, using metal plates on production presses.

continuity: in Gestalt psychology, the optical process of seeing a continuous shape even when confronted with a partial, or fragmented, image.

continuous tone: artwork that contains gradations of gray, as opposed to black and white line art. Photographs and some drawings, such as charcoals or watercolors, require treatment as continuous-tone art. *See also* **line art**.

copyfitting: the fitting of an amount of copy within a specific and fixed amount of space.

counter: in typography, an enclosed area within a letter, in capital, lowercase, and numeric letter forms.

CPU (central processing unit): the hardware "brain" of the microcomputer that does all the processing—arithmetic, logic, and data manipulation.

crop marks: on a mechanical, horizontal and vertical crossed lines that indicate the edge of the printed pieces.

cropping: for artwork, cutting out the extraneous parts of an image, usually a photograph.

cursor: a marker on the screen which indicates where the next action will take place. In desktop publishing programs, the cursor changes shape when it changes function—for example, an arrow for graphic functions or a bar for text-entry functions.

cutlines: explanatory text, usually in full sentences, that provides information about illustrations. Cutlines are sometimes called *captions* or *legends*; not to be confused with title-captions, which are headings for the illustrations, or key-legends, which are part of the artwork.

cutout: *see* **knockout**.

decks: the separate lines into which a heading or title is broken.

delimiters: in a database, characters that indicate the end of each field and each record. Most data processing programs set commas, tab characters, or space characters as field delimiters, and returns as record delimiters.

demi: a bold slightly less dark than the standard bold.

density: the relative darkness of a design element, measured in dots per inch.

descenders: the parts of characters that drop below the baseline (in some typefaces, certain capital letters and numbers have descenders).

directional flow: the direction the eye moves as it perceives a composition.

discretionary hyphen: a syllable-breaking hyphen that will occur only when a word is broken at the end of a line, not if the word appears in the middle of a line.

disk drive: the computer's mechanism for reading and writing information, in files, to and from disks. *See also* **floppy disk**, **hard disk**.

display publication: a graphics-intensive, single-paged publication that is designed for visual interest as much or more so than content, such as advertisements, fliers, notices, and covers for text-intensive publications.

display type: type 14 points and larger, used for titles and headings and as graphic elements in display pieces.

disproportionally scaled graphic: a reduction or enlargement of an illustration in which the height-to-width ratio is different from that of the original. *See also* **proportionally scaled graphic**.

dithering: for digital halftones, the creation of a flat bitmap by simply turning dots on or off. Flat bitmaps differ from deep bitmaps in gray-scale images in that all dots are the same size; there are simply more of them in dark areas and fewer of them in light areas. *See also* **gray-scale image**, **halftone**.

double-sided: an option on **Page Setup** that creates inside and outside margins on pages that will be printed on two sides.

download: to transmit and remotely store information, usually from one computer to another (in telecommunications), or from a computer to a printer. In desktop publishing, typefaces may be downloaded from the computer to the printer.

downsample: reducing the file size of a graphic image by reducing its resolution to a lower dpi, as is done in preparing graphics for Web documents.

dpi (dots per inch): the unit of measure used to describe the resolution of printed output. The most common desktop laser printers output at 300 dpi; medium-resolution printers output at 600 dpi; imagesetters output at 1270-2540 dpi.

drawing window: in a Paint package, the area in which you create your artwork.

drop cap: an uppercase letter larger than the body type.

drop-down list: a menu that pops up when you press a particular place in a dialog box or main menu. Usually marked with a downward-pointing or sideways-pointing triangle.

drop folio: a page number that appears at the bottom of the page, usually on the page baseline. Can be centered, flush right (on recto pages), or flush left (on verso pages).

dummy: a mock-up of a planned publication showing where type and graphics will be placed.

duotone: a halftone image printed in two colors, one dark and the other light.

duplex printing: printing on both sides of a sheet of paper.

elements (master page elements): repeating items in a publication, such as page numbers, logos, or text, that appear on every page. PageMaker has an option that will suppress elements on a particular page or pages.

em space/dash: a space equal to the square of the type size; a dash of that length.

en space/dash: a space equal to the square of half the type size; a dash of that length.

engraving: in printing, the process of etching a design into a die, filling the etching with ink, and pushing paper against the die. This lifts the ink and creates a raised image.

EPS (Encapsulated PostScript): a program-independent form of PostScript, written with a special heading that enables files to be transferred among programs and machines. *See also* **PostScript**.

escapement: the amount of space by which a printing element (carriage of a typewriter, type element of a typewriter or daisy-wheel printer, laser controlled by the RIP of a laser printer or imagesetter) is advanced.

facing pages: in a double-sided document, the two pages that appear as a spread when the publication is opened. *See also* **recto**, **spread**, **verso**.

feathering: the insertion of small amounts of additional leading between lines and paragraphs and before and after headings to equalize the baselines of columns on a page.

field: in a database program, the categories, or entries within a record. For example, within a membership record, the fields might be name, address, dues paid, and office held. *See also* **record**.

fills: solid or patterned graphic areas.

flats: in commercial printing, a large frame that contains the images, in negative, that will be carried on a metal printing plate. *See also* **stripping**.

floppy disk: removable disk, commonly 3½", made of Mylar and encased in plastic.

flush left: even with the left edge or margin.

flush right: even with the right edge or margin.

focus: the element in a composition at which the eye looks first.

folio: page number.

font: a set of characters in a particular typeface that are the same size and style.

font outline masters: the outline of a character created by a series of lines and arcs.

footer: title, usually including the folio, that runs at the bottom of the page in multipage documents. *Also called* **running foot**.

front matter: in a book, the title page, copyright page, table of contents, lists of figures and tables, and so on.

full indent: a paragraph in which all lines are indented from the left and/or right margin.

galley: in desktop publishing, a typeset proof in which the type is set but not laid out in a printed page, for copyfitting and proofreading purposes.

gestalt: a set of elements that creates a compositional whole that is greater than the sum of its parts.

GIF (.gif): a graphics file format that can be compressed. Used for images created with a paint or draw program or for screen captures.

glossary: (publishing) a set of definitions for specialized items.

gradation: regular and fixed changes of the same image.

gray-scale image: a "deep" bitmap that records with each dot its level of brightness or gray-scale level. The impression of grayness is a function of the size of the dot; a group of large dots looks dark and a group of small dots looks light. TIFF files encode gray-scale, as opposed to dithered bitmaps. *See also* **dithering**.

greek: in page assembly programs, to replace actual characters with gray bars that show position, length, height, number of lines, etc., of the type. *See also* **screen refresh rate**.

grid: a geometric framework that underlies a composition.

gripper edge: an image-free edge of a paper used by the gripper device to hold the paper in place as it passes through the printing mechanism.

guides: nonprinting horizontal and vertical lines that you can use to help in the positioning of graphics. *See also* **margin guides, ruler guides**.

gutter: in double-sided bound documents, the combination of the inside margins of facing pages; the gutter should be wide enough to accommodate the binding.

halftone: digital halftones are produced by sampling a continuous-tone image and assigning different numbers of dots, which simulate different sized dots, for the same effect. *See also* **TIFF**.

halftone screen: in traditional publishing, the screen through which a continuous-tone image is photographed, measured in lines per inch. Although digital halftones are not actually photographed through a screen, the term is still used to describe the size of the dots; the larger the dots (fewer lines per inch), the more grainy the image. Special screens can be used for special effects.

handles: knobs or tabs at the periphery of text blocks or graphics that indicate that the object is selected; used to resize objects.

hang indent: type set so that the first line is flush left, and subsequent lines are indented.

hard copy: materials printed on paper.

hard disk: nonremovable mass-storage disks made of solid metal-oxide, with built-in drives. Because hard disks come with drives, the terms hard disk and hard drive are often used interchangeably.

hard hyphen: a hyphen that is part of the correct spelling of a word, as opposed to a soft (or discretionary) hyphen, on which the text wrap function of a program will break a line.

hard return: a return created by the **Return** or **Enter** key, as opposed to a word wrap, or soft return, which will adjust according to the character count and column width.

hard space: space between two words on the same line, indicating that a line break cannot occur between these two words. It is used when the two should not be separated. The word wrap function of a program will break a line on a soft (or normal) space.

hardware: the actual physical devices of a computer, including the CPU, disk drives, memory, expansion boards, a keyboard, and a mouse.

header: title, usually including the folio, that runs at the top of pages in multipage documents. *Also called* **running head**.

highlighting: using the I-beam to select text; highlighted text appears white with a dark background.

hypertext link (hyperlink): a specific location in a Web document that can be selected by clicking on it.

I-beam: a vertical line with small, curled lines on top and bottom, used for positioning the insertion cursor. *See also* **insertion cursor**.

image area: the area on a page, determined by the margins, within which copy and graphics are positioned; in printing, the area where ink will be laid down.

image scanner: a device used to digitize existing hard copy artwork, either line art or photographs. Image scanners create bitmapped illustrations or electronic halftones.

imagesetter: a typesetting machine that is capable of setting images as well as type. In order to set images, the imagesetter must be equipped with a PostScript or comparable raster image processor.

importing: placing files into a publication or into another file.

imposition: in printing, the order and direction in which multiple pages will be printed on the press sheet. *See also* **flats**, **stripping**.

indentation: space set at the left or right of a column of type.

inline: in a typeface, a thin line surrounding a stroke.

insertion cursor: a flashing vertical bar that indicates where text characters will appear when inserted.

inside margin: for bound documents, the margin on the side of the page that will be bound—the right margin of a verso and the left margin of a recto.

intrinsic interest: a quality that causes something to attract the eye because of what it is, not because of its size, density, or position.

italic: type that slants upward and to the right.

JPEG (.jpg): a graphics file format that self-compresses file size. Used for color photographs and halftones.

jump text: text that continues to another page.

K (kilobyte): a unit of measurement equal to 1000 bytes (actually 1024 = 210 bytes). File size is usually measured in kilobytes. A page of double-spaced text in a word processing file occupies approximately 2K on a disk. *See also* **byte**, **megabyte**.

kerning: the reduction of horizontal space between two specific characters for a better fit.

key legend: explanatory labels keyed to colors or fill patterns in illustrations, usually business graphics.

keyboard: primary input device of a microcomputer, set up like a typewriter keyboard.

kicker: a brief phrase or sentence lead-in to a story or chapter; usually set smaller than the headline or chapter title, but larger than text type.

kilobyte: *see* **K**.

knockout: in printing, when one color is to be printed immediately adjacent to another color; actually, they are printed with a slight overlap. *See also* **lap register**.

landscape (orientation): a page or layout that is wider than it is tall.

lap register: used with knockouts; images of different colors are slightly overlapped to avoid the appearance of a white line between the two inks.

leader tabs: area preceding tab characters; can be filled in with special characters such as a row of periods.

leading: the vertical space between lines of type.

leaf stamping: in printing, the process of transfering a foil coating to paper; a metal die is prepared with the design, which when heated makes the transfer.

letter form: in typography, the shapes of the characters.

letterspacing: the horizontal space between characters.

Library palette: a palette that "floats" on the publication page; it contains text and graphics that are frequently imported.

ligature: characters in a typeface that are physically connected, such as fi, fl, œ, or æ.

line art: black and white artwork with no gray areas, such as pen and ink drawings. Most graphic images produced with desktop publishing graphics programs can be treated as line art. For printing purposes, positive halftones (electronic halftones made with a desktop publishing system) can be handled as line art.

line gauge: used to estimate the number of inches or picas that a piece of copy will run at a particular type specification and measure.

Links command: reports the status of any text or graphic file that is imported into PageMaker document with the **Place** command. Options with this command allow automatic updating of a linked file, unlinking a file, or storing a copy of the file in the PageMaker document.

M, Mb (megabyte): a unit of measurement equal to 1000 kilobytes (actually 1024 = 210 kilobytes). Hard disk capacity is usually measured in megabytes. Hard disks used for desktop publishing generally store 20–100Mb.

macro: a routine that can record and automatically play back keystrokes and mouse actions. Setting up a macro involves recording the actions or writing code in the macro language and then designating the playback (invoke) keys.

mailer: a panel from a brochure or flier used for addresses.

margin guides: nonprinting horizontal and vertical lines that indicate the top, bottom, left, and right margins.

master page: a template that contains common basic design elements, such as headers, footers, and page numbers, that are common to most or all pages in a publication.

masthead: the credit box, headed by the publication name, that lists sponsors, editors, writers, designers, illustrators, photographers, and other contributors, along with the publication office address, subscription and advertising information, and so on.

measure *(noun)*: in typography, the length of a line, even if the line is not filled with characters (such as a centered or partial line), designated in picas. When the text is set in columns the line length is called the **column measure**.

mechanical: camera-ready copy (text and art) prepared by the desktop publisher for off-set printing; this includes all copy pasted on boards, with overlays when needed, and a tissue cover.

mechanical binding: spiral binding; the pages are punched with a series of holes at the binding edge, and a wire or plastic spiral coil or comb is inserted through the holes.

megabyte: *see* **M**.

megahertz (Mhz): in reference to a CPU, the number of cycles per second that the CPU processes. *See also* **clock speed**.

memory: usually refers to the computer system's capacity for storing information in terms of RAM, but also sometimes refers to the ROM and disk storage capacity. *See also* **floppy disk**, **hard disk**, **RAM**, **ROM**.

microprocessor: a computer processor that fits on a single integrated chip. The CPU of a microcomputer and the processor in a laser printer with a PostScript controller are microprocessors.

moiré patterns (pronounced "mo-ray"): irregular plaidlike patterns that occur when a bitmapped image is reduced, enlarged, displayed, or printed at a resolution different from the resolution of the original.

monospaced type: a typeface in which each character takes up the same amount of horizontal space.

motherboard: the main printed circuit board in a microcomputer upon which the CPU is mounted.

mouse: a pointer that functions as an input device for a microcomputer.

multiple paste command: allows you to specify the number of times an object can be copied as well as the horizontal and vertical offset spacing of the copied objects.

negative space: the space around an element, which contrasts with that element.

nested stories: in newsletter and magazine layout, stories that run in multiple columns at different column depths with the headline spanning all the columns.

object-oriented (mode): the Draw graphics mode. A set of algorithms describes graphic forms in abstract geometrical terms—as object primitives, the most fundamental shapes from which all other shapes (lines, curves, and solid or patterned areas) are made.

oblique type: characters that are slanted to the right; sans serif typefaces often use oblique characters instead of true italics, which are a separate font.

opacity: a characteristic of paper; the amount of show-through that will occur when the paper is printed on both sides.

operating system: computer software that is the top level of the user interface—what you see when you first turn on the computer. All file operations (creating, opening, closing, copying, deleting, viewing a list of directories/folders and files, etc.) are accomplished through the operating system, either directly (from the top level of the operating system) or indirectly (through an application).

optical character reader (OCR): a text scanner, used to transform hard-copy text into computer-readable files.

orphan: the first line of a paragraph at the bottom of a page.

outline fonts: *see* **font outline masters**.

overlay: on a mechanical, a transparent acetate sheet that is taped and folded over at the top of the board, used for designation of colors. Each overlay contains the elements that will be made into separate negatives and plates (colors).

overprint: *see* **surprint**.

page assembly program: software that enables the user to lay out pages containing text and graphics.

Paint package: software application that allows you to create bitmapped graphics.

Pantone matching system (PMS): a standard color-matching system used by printers and graphic designers for inks, papers, and other materials. A PMS color is a standard color defined by percentage mixtures of different primary color inks.

pasteup: the process of assembling pages.

PCL (Printer Control Language): a rudimentary printer language used in Hewlett-Packard/compatible laser printers; it is less capable than PostScript in the definition and manipulation of type and graphics, that is, in terms of type rotations, fineness of lines, surprinting, and reverses.

perfect binding: paperback binding; the pages are trimmed and roughened, glue is applied to the spine, and the cover is placed over the glue. Then the whole publication is pressed together so that the glue squeezes through the back edges of the pages and attaches to the cover.

pi characters (*also called* **special sorts**): typographical characters that do not appear on the standard QWERTY (typewriter) keyboard. Common examples include opening and closing quotation marks, ellipses, and em and en dashes.

pica: a unit of measurement used in typography, equal to 12 points and approximately 1/6 of an inch.

pitch: a unit of type width, based on the number of characters per inch.

pixel: on a display monitor, the smallest spot that can be lit up on the screen.

point: a unit of measurement used in typography, equal to 1/12 of a pica and approximately 1/72 of an inch.

point size: the size of the type.

portrait (orientation): a page that is longer than it is wide.

posterization: for a halftone, the reduction of the number of gray scales to produce a high-contrast image. *See also* **gray-scale image**.

PostScript: a page-description (printer) language developed by Adobe Systems, Inc., the standard used in desktop publishing. It carries instructions to a PostScript-compatible output device as to how a document should be handled in terms of typeface, size, style, and orientation. It contains sophisticated operators for the definition and manipulation of type and graphics, for scaling, rotating, outlining, filling, page positioning, etc. It also contains operators for color and the manipulation of bitmaps. *See also* EPS.

press sheet: in offset printing, the paper used on the printing press. For metal-plate printing, several pages are often printed on a single press sheet that is folded and cut into signatures.

primitives: the most fundamental shapes from which all other shapes are made; these include straight lines, curves, and solid or patterned areas.

print engine: the physical mechanism in a laser printer that charges the imaging surface and transfers the image to the paper; it consists of laser source, mirrors, and an imaging drum, and is controlled by the printer's raster image processor.

printer driver: system software that translates files into a form that can be understood by the printer (or other hard-copy output device such as an imagesetter or a plotter). Different printer drivers are used for the creation of PostScript, PCL, or QuickDraw, for printers with those different capabilities.

printer font: high-resolution bitmaps or outline fonts used for the actual laying down of characters on the printed page. *See also* **screen font**.

process color separation: in commercial printing, used for reproduction of color photographs. The various hues are created by the superimposing of halftone dots of the process colors: cyan (a greenish blue), magenta (a purplish red), yellow, and black. *See also* **color separation**.

proportionally scaled graphic: a reduction or enlargement of an illustration that retains the proportions of the original. *See also* **disproportionally scaled graphic**.

proportionally spaced type: a typeface in which the width of each character varies, depending on the shape of the character itself and the characters surrounding it. *See also* **monospaced type**.

publication: a document created in desktop publishing.

pull quote: a brief phrase (not necessarily an actual quotation) from the body text, enlarged and set off from the text with rules, a box, and/or a screen. It is from a part of the text set previously, and is set in the middle of a paragraph, to add emphasis and interest.

quick-copy offset printer: small, commercial shops that offer fast, inexpensive offset printing. Quick-copy printers generally use paper plates rather than metal plates and set their presses for one standard sheet size.

QuickDraw: a rudimentary graphics language used for Macintosh screen displays, and also for some laser printers; it is less capable than PostScript in the definition and manipulation of type and graphics, in terms of type rotations, fineness of lines, surprinting, and reverses.

ragged alignment: type set so that the extra white space is at the right *(ragged right)* or left *(ragged left)*.

RAM (random access memory): temporary memory—program instructions are swapped in and out of RAM when software is running. The information in RAM is lost when the microcomputer is restarted or powered off.

raster device: a device that utilizes a scanning mechanism that sweeps horizontally making dots, like the cathode-ray gun in a video display monitor, the electric eye that moves across a page in an image or text scanner, or the raster image processor (RIP) that drives a laser printer or imagesetter.

raster image processor (RIP): in a laser printer or imagesetter, the chip that interprets the information sent to it by the computer (printer driver); it controls the movement of the laser beam across the imaging surface. The RIP utilizes a printer or page description language and has different capabilities, depending on the printer type. *See also* **printer driver**.

record: in a database program, information that contains the same categories or entries (fields) as every other record in the database; for example, a payroll database might contain employee records. *See also* **field**.

recto: in a double-sided document, the page that appears on the right side of the spread; an even-numbered page.

registration mark: for commercial offset printing, a cross inside a circle placed outside the image area on a mechanical with overlays. It is used to align the flats properly for color separation on overlays.

repetition: exact duplication of an image.

resolution: the crispness of detail or fineness of grain in an image. Screen resolution is measured in dots by line (for example, 640 x 350); printer resolution is measured in dots per inch (for example, 600 dpi).

reverses: white images or text on a black background.

ROM (read-only memory): permanent memory, etched in a chip, for certain frequently used instructions such as startup routines. ROM remains when the computer is turned off.

roman type: book weight, regular, or in desktop publishing systems, called plain or normal type—used for body type.

row: in a table or spreadsheet, the horizontal collection of cells next to one another.

rule (ruling line): a geometric line used as a graphic enhancement to type.

ruler guides: nonprinting horizontal and vertical lines that are dragged out of the top and left rulers, respectively.

ruler zero points: the locations on PageMaker's horizontal and vertical rulers labeled zero.

run-in heading: a heading set on the same line as the text, usually in bold or italic type.

running head/foot: title (often accompanied by page numbers) set at the top/bottom of text pages of a multipaged publication. *Also called* **header/footer**.

saddle-stitching: a form of binding in which the pages are placed on a saddle-shaped device and stitched through the gutter.

scale: to reduce or enlarge a graphic. Proportional scaling maintains the ratio of height and width.

scanner: *see* **image scanner**, **optical character reader**.

screen font: low-resolution bitmaps of type characters that show the positioning and size of characters on the screen. *See also* **printer font**.

screen refresh rate: the speed at which images are drawn on the screen. Screen refresh errors may leave bits and pieces of images on the screen when images are revised quickly; these do not affect the printout and can be eliminated by zooming or scrolling.

script: a typeface designed to resemble handwritten calligraphy.

scroll: to move through a document, changing the onscreen view of it. Autoscrolling means that as the typed characters or drawn images approach the bottom or side of the screen, the window will automatically move up or to the side to accommodate them.

search and replace: the specification of a string of characters that should be found and automatically changed to another string of characters.

selecting: in computing, to indicate to the program material upon which a function is to be performed. In Paint programs, areas of a bitmap may be selected; in Draw programs, objects may be selected; in word processing programs, text is selected; and in page assembly programs, text and graphics are selected with different tools for different functions. *Also*, using the **Pointer** tool to select text as a block, or graphics.

self-cover: a publication cover that serves as a cover and cover page; printed on the same paper as the publication.

serial element: in page design, elements in periodicals that occur in every issue of a publication, but only once in a given issue. The most common serial elements are banners and mastheads.

serifs: short cross-strokes projecting from the ends of the main strokes of many of the characters.

server: on the Internet, a computer system that manages and delivers information to users.

set solid: blocks of type that are set with no leading, so that the descenders of one line nearly touch the ascenders of the line below.

set width: in typography, the horizontal width of characters. Typefaces vary in the average horizontal set width of each character (Times, for example, has a narrow set width), and set widths of individual characters vary in typeset copy depending on the shape of the character and surrounding characters.

side stitching: a form of binding in which the pages are placed flat under a stitching head and staples are inserted parallel to the paper edge.

sidebar: a related story or block of information that is set apart from the main body text, usually boxed and/or screened. It may be set in any position relative to the main body text.

signature: in printing, a group of pages created by folding and cutting large press sheets on which several pages at a time are printed; there are usually 8, 16, or 32 pages per signature.

slug: horizontal bar that appears on the display screen when text has been highlighted or selected.

small caps: caps set at the x-height of the lowercase letters.

soft fonts: fonts that are downloadable.

software: computer programs—the set of instructions, stored on disk, that is used to create files and control the hardware. Types of software commonly used for desktop publishing include word processing and page assembly programs.

source files: for a page assembly program, word processing and graphics files that are imported for page assembly.

space character: an actual ASCII character created by the spacebar, which happens to be a blank. Such characters take up a specific amount of space, which is increased or decreased as the type size is increased or decreased.

spine: on an external publication cover, a spine is created by folds perpendicular to the front and back covers; it carries the book title, running vertically from top to bottom.

spot color separation: for offset printing, separation of solid premixed ink colors (for example, green, brown, light blue, and so on); used when the areas to be colored are not adjacent. Spot color separations can be indicated on the tissue cover of the mechanical, or made with overlays.

spread: in a double-sided document, the combination of two facing pages, which should be designed as a unit. *Also* the adjacent inside panels of a brochure when opened.

standing element: in page design, elements that repeat exactly from page to page, not only in terms of style, but also in terms of page position and content. The most commonly used standing elements are page headers or footers, with automatic page numbering.

standoff: the amount of space between a block of text and a graphic or between two blocks of text that wrap.

story: a group of related text. A story may consist of one text block or several linked text blocks.

stress: in a typeface, the axis around which the strokes are drawn.

stripping: in commercial printing, the process of assembling flats from negatives; all images must be correctly imposed and registered, and the flats must be custom-made to the specifications of the printing press to be used. *See also* **flats**, **imposition**, **registration mark**.

stroke weight: the width of the main strokes of characters.

style sheet: in a desktop publishing program, style sheets contain the typographic specifications that are associated with tagged text. They can be used to set up titles, headings, and the attributes of blocks of text, such as lists, tables, and text associated with illustrations. The use of style sheets is a fast and efficient way to ensure that all comparable elements are consistent. *See also* **codes**, **tags**.

subscripts: characters set below the baseline of the type, at a point size slightly smaller than that of the text; *also called* **inferiors**.

Sum command: a command in the **Cell** menu of the Table Editor. It will add the numbers in a row or column of a table.

superscripts: characters set above the baseline, at a point size slightly smaller than that of the text; *also called* **superiors**.

surprint (overprint): "printing on top"; dark type or images printed on a screened or lighter-colored background.

swash: in a typeface, a long, curved stroke that extends below the baseline and/or to the right or left of the character.

symmetrical balance: the equal distribution of visual weight on the left and right sides or top and bottom of a central axis.

tab character: a nonprinting character that is typed on the keyboard to position the subsequent text at the specified tab stop.

tab stop: a marker for the position where the tab character will place the subsequent type.

tabulation: white space set at fixed intervals within a line.

tags: for style sheets, delimited sets of characters embedded in the text or internally coded. Tags apply to paragraphs (text terminated with a hard return—this includes titles and headings) and indicate the function of paragraphs. The actual type specification depends on the style sheet that is associated with the tag. *See also* **codes, style sheet.**

template: a master file containing elements that are used in many publications. It is saved as a .pt5 file and opens as an empty, untitled file.

text block: a set of typed characters that acts as a single object, much like a graphic, that can be positioned and "stretched" (column measure and column length altered).

Text tool: the *A* icon in the toolbox, used to enter and edit text characters.

text type: *see* **body type.**

text wrap: the spatial relationship between blocks of text and graphics or between two blocks of text.

thermography: a printing process that creates a thick, raised surface with highly saturated color.

throughput: in printing, the number of copies printed per minute.

thumbnails: small sketches used as first design drafts.

TIFF (Tagged Image File Format): for digital gray-scale halftones, a device-independent graphics file format. TIFF files can be used on IBM-compatible or Macintosh computers, and they may be output to PostScript printers. *See also* **halftone.**

tiling (tile): printing a page layout in sections with overlapping edges so that the pieces can then be pasted together. This is done when a layout to be printed is too large to fit on a standard printer page.

tint: a shade of gray or color—usually accomplished by applying a screen, which breaks up the color into small dots. A 10 percent screen creates a light tint, while a 90 percent screen creates a darker tint.

tombstoning: in multicolumned publications, when two or more headings run in the same horizontal position on the page.

toner: fine particles of dry ink, used in desktop laser printers and photocopy machines.

toolbox: a small window containing the pointer, Text tool, and graphics tools.

tools palette: place from which you select tools for creating artwork.

tracking: in typography, the uniform reduction of space between all characters on a line. This is different from *kerning*, which is the variable reduction of space between specific characters.

typeface: a set of characters created by a type designer, including upper- and lowercase alphabetical letters, numbers, punctuation, special characters, and ligatures. *See also* **ligature.**

unit: in typography, divisions of an em space used for fine-tuning the letterspacing of text type.

unity: the overall look that tends to hold a composition together visually.

value *(in reference to color)*: darkness of a color.

vector: the primitive used to create lines; it is a geometrical point with a direction and duration (length).

velox: a positive halftone paper print, up to approximately 100 lines per inch, produced with a graphic arts camera.

verso: in a double-sided document, the page that appears on the left side of the spread; an odd-numbered page.

visual identity: nonverbal image closely associated with a company or organization.

visual weight: the impact that a compositional element has upon the eye.

wallpaper: the background in a Web document.

Web server: a computer system on the Internet that contains World Wide Web documents.

white space: in designing publications, the areas where there is no text or graphics—essentially, the negative space of the page design.

widow: a single, incomplete line at the top of a page or column.

window: in commercial printing, the working area for a program on the display screen; windows can be opened, closed, and sized. When referring to photographs, a solid black area on a mechanical where a photographic signature would be stripped in.

window shades: the horizontal lines that stretch across a selected text block; used to resize text block.

word spacing: the horizontal space between words.

word wrap: in word processing, the automatic dropping of characters to the next line when the right margin is reached.

write-black: black toner particles adhere to areas of the page that are positively charged in a write-black print engine.

write-white: black toner particles are repelled from areas of the page that are negatively charged in a write-white print engine.

WYSIWYG (what you see is what you get): a term used to describe desktop publishing systems that provide a screen representation of the printed output. WYSIWYG is never entirely accurate because of the difference in resolution between display screens and printers.

x-height: the height of the main body of the lowercase characters (the character "x" is the standard).

zero point: the position at which the zeros on the vertical and horizontal rulers intersect.

zoom: viewing the page in different magnifications—the most commonly used in PageMaker are **Fit in window** and **Actual size.**

INDEX

Photographic images
design, 129–130
imagesetting, 314–315
special effects, 133–134
Picas, 18, 65
Pi characters, 166–167, 207–208
Pi (picas), 18
Pitch, 59
Pixel, 111
Pixel-by-pixel editing, 121
Place command, 41, 212
Placeholders for graphics, 213, 214
Platemaking, metal, 311–312
Plug-ins submenu, 340
PMS (Pantone matching system), 320–321
Pointer, four-directional arrow, 39
Pointers to source files, 194–195
Pointer tool, 34, 35, 213
Points, 18, 65
Portrait orientation, 17
Posterizing, 134
Posters, design, 246
PostScript printer fonts, 56
Preferences dialog box, 293
Press sheet, 312
Primitives, 111, 119
Print engine, laser printer, 304–305, 306
Printer fonts, 53, 55–57
Printing
duplex, 305
files, 44
laser, 304–307
offset. *See* Offset printing
photocopying, 307–308
special effects, 321–322
Print quality. *See* Reproduction quality
Process color separation, 317
Program, creating
back panel, 285–287
example, 291–292
front panel, 285
inside panels, 287–290
Proportional leading, 89
Proportionally spaced typefaces, 58
Proportional scaling, 41, 213
Pts (points), 18
Publication page icon, 29
Pull quote, 257, 342–343

Punctuation
delimited fields, 177
spacing after, 166, 206–207
Px (picas), 18

Quick-copy offset printing, 308–310

Ragged right alignment, 70
RAM (random-access memory), 55
Raster color thermal transfer, 307
Raster device, 111
Raster graphics. *See* Bitmapped graphics
Raster-image processor (RIP), 111
Readability of type fonts, 58
Record, 176
Recto pages, 17, 18
Reduction. *See* Scaling
Registration, lap, 317
Registration marks, 313
Repetition, design, 7
Replacing text, 165
Report
body, 210–215
cover page, 216–218
editing, 206–208
example, 223–239
index, 220–222
master pages, 200–203
style sheet, 203–206, 208–209
table of contents, 218–220
Reproduction quality
laser printing, 305–306
offset printing, 309–310
photocopying, 307–308
Resolution, 112
bitmapped graphics, 138, 144–145, 213
device, 113–114
document setup, 28
enlargement, 117–119
image files, 112–114
object-oriented graphics, 113, 146
reduction, 115–117
WYSIWYG, 114–119
Reverses, 11, 128, 132
Revert function, 38, 40
Rippling effects, 182–183

Trademarks

Adobe Table 3.0, Distiller, Illustrator, PageMaker, PageMill, and PostScript are registered trademarks of Adobe Systems, Inc.; QuickDraw is a registered trademark of Apple Computer, Inc.; MacDraw and MacPaint are registered trademarks of Claris Corporation; CorelDraw! is a registered trademark of Corel Corporation; GEM is a registered trademark of Digital Research, Inc.; PCL is a registered trademark of Hewlett-Packard Company; Microsoft and Windows are registered trademarks of Microsoft Corporation; PANTONE is a registered trademark of Pantone, Inc.; PC Paintbrush is a registered trademark of Wordstar Atlanta Technology Center.